BECOMING A CRITICAL THINKER

A User Friendly Manual

Sherry Diestler
Contra Costa College

PEARSON
Prentice Hall

UPPER SADDLE RIVER, NEW JERSEY 07458

Library of Congress Cataloging-in-Publication Data

Diestler, Sherry.
  Becoming a critical thinker : a user friendly manual / Sherry Diestler.
      p. cm.
  Includes index.
  ISBN–13: 978–0–13–241313–8
  ISBN–10: 0–13–241313–2
  1. Critical thinking—Study and teaching (Higher) 2. Critical thinking—Problems, exercises,
etc. 1. Title.
  LB2395.35.D54 2009
  370.15'2—dc22

                                                          2007036477

Senior Acquisitions Editor: Dave Repetto
Editor-in-Chief: Sarah Touberg
Editorial Assistant: Carla Worner
Marketing Manager: Sasha Anderson-Smith
Senior Managing Editor: Mary Rottino
Production Liaison: Fran Russello
Permissions Specialist: Lisa Black
Operations Specialist: Cathy Petersen
Cover Director: Jayne Conte
Cover Photo: Image Source Pink/Getty Images
Director, Image Resource Center: Melinda Patelli
Manager, Rights and Permissions: Zina Arabia
Manager, Visual Research: Beth Brenzel
Manager, Cover Visual Research & Permissions: Karen Sanatar
Image Permission Coordinator: Craig A. Jones
Photo Researcher: Beth Brenzel
Composition/Full-Service Project Management: Laserwords/Bruce Hobart
Printer/Binder: R.R. Donnelley and Sons Company

Credits and acknowledgments borrowed from other sources and reproduced, with permission, in
this textbook appear on appropriate page within text.

Pearson Education LTD., London
Pearson Education Singapore, Pte. Ltd
Pearson Education, Canada, Ltd
Pearson Education-Japan
Pearson Education Australia PTY, Limited

Pearson Education North Asia Ltd
Pearson Educacion de Mexico, S.A. de C.V
Pearson Educatión Malaysia, Pte. Ltd
Pearson Education, Upper Saddle River,
  New Jersey

10 9 8 7 6 5 4 3 2 1
ISBN-13: 978-0-13-241313-8
ISBN-10: 0-13-241313-2

In loving memory of Anne and Al Goldstein.

And for John, Zachary, Nicole, Jenna, Laura, and Amy,

may we continue their legacy of discernment and compassion.

Contents

3 REALITY ASSUMPTIONS 67

It's Eleven O'Clock. Do You Know Where Your Assumptions Are?

4 INDUCTIVE ARGUMENTS: STATISTICAL AND CAUSAL GENERALIZATIONS 112

Prove It to me: What Are the Statistics?

6 REASONING ERRORS 215

I Know What I Think—Don't Confuse Me with Facts

7 THE POWER OF LANGUAGE 269

What's in a Name?

9 FAIR-MINDEDNESS 379

It's You and Me, Kid, and I'm Not So Sure About You

10 PERSUASIVE SPEAKING 425

What's Your Point? How Do You Sharpen It?

Preface

Everyone thinks. If you ask people where they stand on a particular issue, they will usually tell you what they believe and give reasons to support their beliefs. Many people, however, find it difficult to evaluate a written or spoken commentary on a controversial issue because both sides of the controversy seem to have good arguments. The *critical* thinker is able to distinguish high-quality, well-supported arguments from arguments with little or no evidence to back them. This text trains students to evaluate the many claims facing them as citizens, learners, consumers, and human beings; it also helps students become more effective advocates for their beliefs and work collaboratively with others on creative problem solving.

Becoming a Critical Thinker is designed to be interdisciplinary and to be useful in courses in critical thinking, informal logic, rhetoric, English, speech, journalism, humanities, and the social sciences. It has also been used as either a required text or a supplement in nursing programs and in workshops on staff development and business management. There are important skills that distinguish critical thinkers across various disciplines; the goal of this text is to present and teach these skills in a clear and comprehensible manner.

UNIQUE FEATURES

The process of becoming a critical thinker takes place when critical thinking concepts and skills are clearly understood and put into practice. For this reason, many aspects of the text have been chosen because of their practical application for the student:

1. Each concept is explained with examples, and the examples often proceed from the personal to the social or political. In this way, students can see that the same skills used in understanding arguments in daily life are used in analyzing political and commercial rhetoric.
2. Graphic illustrations and cartoons help students visualize important concepts.
3. Exercises of varying levels of difficulty are given throughout the chapters to help students practice critical thinking skills.

4. Emphasis is placed on understanding and analyzing the vital impact of print and electronic media on arguments. Ideas for film analysis are included at the end of each chapter.
5. Students are taught to construct and present arguments so that they can gain skill and confidence as advocates for their beliefs; they are also given tools for effective problem solving and decision making.
6. There is an early and primary emphasis on understanding conflicting value systems and on ethics in argumentation and decision making.
7. The articles and essays selected for use in the text are contemporary and express a variety of social and political viewpoints and ethical concerns.
8. Multicultural perspectives are presented throughout the examples and articles. Many exercises and assignments encourage students to understand the perspectives of others and to broaden their own perspectives.
9. A variety of writing and speaking assignments are included at the end of each chapter as well as a "Chapter Checkup" that tests students' knowledge of the information covered and provides a guideline for reviewing important concepts.
10. The text is supplemented with an instructor's manual and test bank filled with suggestions and activities for enhancing experiential learning.

SPECIFIC CHANGES IN THE FIFTH EDITION

As with previous editions, the fifth edition of *Becoming a Critical Thinker* has been updated with two priorities in mind: First, we wanted to retain and improve the user friendly format of the first four editions. Also, we wanted to update readings and concepts so that readers will enjoy the application of critical thinking principles to current issues.

New features in the fifth edition include

1. An expanded and updated instructor's manual with revised tests and answer keys for each chapter, discussions of chapter exercises, and suggestions for teaching critical thinking concepts.
2. New articles and essays. These writings cover current topics such as value conflicts in college admissions policies and in coaching; deductive reasoning used by the Supreme Court to rule state determinate-sentencing laws unconstitutional; the redefining of Pluto as a dwarf planet; new research on gender differences; current trends related to female college students' career goals; the growing concern over eco-hypocrisy; the increasing amount of direct and indirect marketing to young children; the use of statistics to advise college students about identity theft, alcoholism, and STDs; an excerpt from Dr. Jerome Groopman's insightful book *How Doctor's Think*; a sheriff-coroner's report on the growing epidemic of methamphetamine addiction; the controversy over a new pill

used to treat post-traumatic stress; an excerpt from Doris Kearns Goodwin's book *Team of Rivals* about Abraham Lincoln's decisions to work collaboratively with his enemies; and article excerpts on how the explosion of new technologies affects critical thinking in today's world.

3. Expanded concepts, explanations, and applications of critical thinking elements and skills. The fifth edition includes a number of new features, such as key terms at the end of each chapter, ideas for life application, and suggested films to use in conjunction with the chapter concepts.

4. A revised chapter design. In response to reviewers, the format has been changed so that most of the chapter exercises are placed at the end of the chapter rather than interspersed with chapter content. Reference is made in each section to the exercises that are most relevant to the material covered in that section.

5. New material includes a section on creative problem solving, an expanded coverage of advertising and marketing techniques, and a discussion of the difficulties with and cures for emotional reasoning.

ACKNOWLEDGEMENTS

My husband, John Diestler, remains an invaluable support. He provided expertise on the "user-friendly" format; he worked out preliminary designs for the original text and created the logos, figures, and photography in the text; in addition, he made useful suggestions on the manuscript throughout the revision process. I thank my editors, Mical Moser and Sarah Touborg, for their patience and guidance and Carla Worner for her continued expertise and help with every detail of the text and its production; thanks also to my former editors for their dedicated work on previous editions, especially Maggie Barbieri who was instrumental in producing the first edition.

Bruce Hobart deserves special thanks for his excellent professional work in supervising the text's production. Sarah Holle worked diligently on the instructor's manual and the copyeditor, Linda Benson, should also receive special mention for her careful and much-appreciated work.

I am grateful to students who used the text and made helpful suggestions for additions and changes; special appreciation is due to those who contributed some of their own writings for exercise examples: Kris Anne Bordalo Nuguid, Susan Bain, Warda Javed, Phil McAlpin, Sonya Shaukat, Janet Fesperman, and Carlota Morales. Professors William Dorman, Connie Anderson, Rafaella Del Bourgo, Lee Loots, and Rachel Dwiggins-Beeler passed along student feedback as well as additional suggestions for exercises and articles. Debra Eberhart suggested excellent materials on critical thinking and resiliency. Suzanne Barton continued to provide new ideas and constant encouragement during the revision process. ZH Diestler researched and reviewed numerous films to discover a variety of storylines related to critical thinking concepts.

I also wish to thank the following reviewers for their invaluable advice and encouragement: Andrea Goldstein, Kaiser College; Iris M. Jerke, San Jose State University; Scott Potter, Marion Technical Community College; Glenda Jackson, Gaston College; and Kevin P. Shannon, Stony Brook (SUNY).

For their practical support and love that allowed me the time and energy to write the text, I thank my father, Al Goldstein; my husband, John; and my precious children, Zachary, Nicole, Jenna, Laura, and Amy Diestler.

Above all, I am grateful to the Creator of the human mind.

Sherry Diestler
Contra Costa College

1

Foundations of Arguments

What Is a Critical Thinker and When Do You Need to Be One?

A critical thinker understands the structure of an argument, whether that argument is presented by a politician, a salesperson, a talk-show host, a friend, or a child.

A critical thinker recognizes the issue under discussion and the varying conclusions about the issue.

A critical thinker examines the reasons given to support conclusions.

This chapter will cover

- The structure of an argument

- The three parts of an argument: issues, conclusions, and reasons

- An approach to making decisions

Ẇe live in what has been called the Information Age because of the many messages that we receive daily from television, radio, newspapers, magazines, books, and the hundreds of millions of sites on the World Wide Web.

Sometimes we turn to this information for its entertainment value, such as when we watch a situation comedy, listen to music, scan the sports page, or read an online movie review. But in a democratic society, in which the people are asked to vote on candidates and political propositions, we also need to use print and electronic sources to help us make decisions about the direction our community, state, and nation will take.

We need to know how to understand and evaluate the information that comes our way. This book will give you tools for coming to rational conclusions and making responsible choices.

> *A critical thinker is someone who uses specific criteria to evaluate reasoning, form positions, and make decisions.*

You can strengthen your critical thinking by becoming aware of and practicing certain skills. The skills will be covered in this text and include an understanding of

- The structure of arguments
- Value assumptions and reality assumptions that are foundational to arguments
- The quality of evidence used to support reasoning
- Common errors in reasoning
- The effect of language on perception, and
- The ways in which media frames issues

In addition, **critical thinkers** develop and exhibit personal traits, such as fair-mindedness and empathy. We will discuss how these qualities strengthen critical thinking and decision making. Finally, critical thinkers use their skills to solve problems and to advocate for causes in which they believe. This chapter covers the first skill: understanding the structure of arguments.

STOP AND THINK   *having good judment*

When people hear the word *critical*, they sometimes associate it with faultfinding. The field of critical thinking, however, uses the word *critical* to mean "discerning." A film, art, dance, or music critic forms and expresses opinions on the basis of standards. The skills you will learn in this text will give you a set of standards with which to evaluate messages. Then, the decisions you make will be thoughtful ones.

When you learn to communicate well in a formal situation, your skill usually transfers to informal situations as well. For example, if you learn to make an effective informative speech in the classroom, you will also feel better about introducing yourself at parties or making a spontaneous toast at your brother's wedding. This same principle applies to critical thinking skills.

When you can listen to a presidential debate and make good judgments about what each candidate has to offer, you may also be more thoughtful about less formal arguments that are presented, such as which breakfast cereal is best for you or which car you should buy. You will be better prepared to deal with sales pitches, whether written, televised, or presented in person.

The methods of discernment and decision making that you will learn apply to choosing a viewpoint on a political issue or to choosing a career, a place to live, or a mate.

In short, critical thinkers do not just drift through life subject to every message that they hear; they think through their choices and make conscious decisions. They also understand the basics of both creating and presenting credible arguments.

THE STRUCTURE OF ARGUMENT

> *The aim of argument, or of discussion, should not be victory, but progress.*
> Joseph Joubert, *Pensees* (1842)

When most people hear the word *argument,* they think of a disagreement between two or more people that may escalate into name calling, angry words, or even physical violence. In their book *Metaphors We Live By,* George Lakoff and Mark Johnson discuss how our metaphors for argument often affect our perception and our behavior. They claim that the metaphor *Argument Is War* "is reflected in our everyday language by a wide variety of expressions":

> *Argument Is War*
> Your claims are indefensible.
> He attacked every weak point in my argument.
> His criticisms were right on target.
> I demolished his argument.
> I've never won an argument with him.
> You disagree? Okay, shoot!
> If you use that strategy, he'll wipe you out.
> He shot down all of my arguments.[1]

Similarly, Deborah Tannen, in her book *The Argument Culture,* notes that as a society, we frame our social issues in warlike terms:

> The war on drugs, the war on cancer, the battle of the sexes, politicians' turf battles—in the argument culture, war metaphors pervade our talk

[1]George Lakoff and Mark Johnson, *Metaphors We Live By* (Chicago: University of Chicago Press, 1980), p. 4.

and shape our thinking. Nearly everything is framed as a battle or game in which winning or losing is the main concern. These all have their uses and their place, but they are not the only way—and often not the best way—to understand and approach our world.[2]

Our definition of **argument** is different. When, as critical thinkers, we speak about arguments, we are referring to a **conclusion** (often called a claim or position) that someone has about a particular **issue**. This conclusion is supported with **reasons** (often called *premises*). If an individual has a conclusion but offers no reasons supporting that conclusion, then he or she has made only a statement, not an argument.

Political slogans, often found on billboards or in television advertisements, are good examples of conclusions (opinions) that should not be relied upon because supporting reasons are not offered. If you see a billboard that proclaims "A vote for Johnson is a vote for the right choice," or if you hear a politician proclaiming "Education has always been a priority for me," you are encountering conclusions with no evidence; that does not constitute an argument.

Critical thinkers withhold judgment on such a claim until they have looked at evidence both for and against Johnson as a candidate.

STOP AND THINK

Can you think of a slogan, perhaps from an advertisement or a bumper sticker, that is a statement without supporting reasons?

An argument has three parts: the *issue,* the *conclusion,* and the *reasons.*

The Issue

The *issue* is what we are arguing about; it is the question that is being addressed. It is easiest to put the issue in question form so that you know what is being discussed. When you listen to a discussion of a political or social issue, think of the question being addressed.

Examples of Issues

- Should North, Central, and South Americans work together to combat acid rain?
- Should air traffic controllers be given periodic drug tests?
- Should the minimum wage be raised?
- Are the salaries paid to professional athletes too high?

[2]Deborah Tannen, *The Argument Culture* (New York: Ballantine Publishing Group, 1999), p. 4.

The same method of "issue detection" will be useful in understanding commercial appeals (ads) and personal requests.

More Examples of Issues
- Is Alpo the best food for your dog?
- Should you marry Leslie?
- Should you subscribe to the *Wall Street Journal*?

Another way to isolate the issue is to state, "The issue is whether _____."

- The issue is whether aspirin can prevent heart disease.
- The issue is whether reproductive cloning should be banned.
- The issue is whether our community should create 200 new homes.

It is important to distinguish issues from topics. Topics are ideas or subjects. Topics become issues when a question or controversy is introduced. In the previous examples, the topics would include Alpo, Leslie, the *Wall Street Journal*, aspirin, and cloning. The issues are questions about the topics.

Issues can be about facts, values, or policies. *Factual issues,* sometimes called *descriptive issues,* concern whether something is true or false, as in the following examples:

- Does zinc prevent common colds?
- Are smog control devices effective in preventing pollution?
- Do we have enough money to buy a new car?

Factual issues can also involve definitions, whether something or someone fits into a certain category:

- Is digital photography a fine art?
- Is drug addiction a disease?
- Is a platypus a mammal?

Issues about *values,* sometimes called *prescriptive issues,* deal with what is considered good or bad or right or wrong, as, for example:

- Is there too much violence on television?
- Is marriage better than living together?
- Are salaries of executives of major corporations too high?

Policy issues involve taking action; often, these issues emerge from discussions of facts and values. If we find that, in fact, smog-control devices are effective in preventing pollution and if we value clean air, then we will probably continue to support policies to enforce the use of these devices. If aspirin prevents heart disease and we value a longer life, then we might ask a doctor whether we should take aspirin. If we do have enough money for a new car and we value a car more than other items at this time, then we should buy the new car.

As we have seen, all issues involve decisions about how to think about a topic or what action to take. We deliberate about issues from our earliest years. For example, children think about how to spend allowance money, what games to play, and what books to choose from the library. Teenagers consider what to wear, how much to study, what sports, musical instruments, and hobbies to pursue and/or languages to learn, and how best to spend the time and money they have. Adults make life choices concerning careers, spouses, children, friends, and homes; they also decide how to think about social and political issues and which causes, organizations, and candidates they will support.

STOP AND THINK

We make large and small decisions every day. List your decisions for a day, from deciding when to wake up through your evening hours. Also, look at your calendar and checkbook and note the decisions about the use of time and money that they reveal.

decisions will be easier if one is clear about issue

Every decision that we need to make, whether it involves public or private matters, will be made easier if we can define exactly what it is that we are being asked to believe or do. Discourse often breaks down when two or more parties get into a heated discussion over different issues. This phenomenon occurs regularly on talk shows.

For example, a television talk show featured the general topic of spousal support, and the issue was "Should the salary of a second wife be used in figuring alimony for the first wife?" The lawyer who was being interviewed kept reminding the guests of this issue as they proceeded to argue instead about whether child support should be figured from the second wife's salary, whether the first wife should hold a job, and even whether one of the wives was a good person.

A general rule is that the more emotional the reactions to the issue, the more likely the issue will become lost. The real problem here is that the basic issue can become fragmented into different subissues so that people are no longer discussing the same question.

SKILL

Understand the issue, make sure everyone is discussing the same issue, and bring the discussion back on target when necessary.

When you listen to televised debates or interviews, note how often a good speaker or interviewer will remind the audience of the issue. Also notice how experienced spokespersons or politicians will often respond to a direct, clearly defined issue with a preprogrammed answer that addresses a different issue, one they can discuss more easily.

If a presidential candidate is asked how he is going to balance our federal budget, he might declare passionately that he will never raise taxes. He has thus skillfully accomplished two things: He has avoided the difficult issue and he has taken a popular, vote-enhancing stand on a separate issue. (See Exercise 1.1 on p. 16.)

REMINDER

Whenever you are confronted with an argument, try to define the issue and put the issue in question form.

The Conclusion

Once an issue has been defined, we can state our *conclusion* about the issue. Using some examples previously mentioned, *we can say yes or no to the issues presented:* Yes, I believe air traffic controllers should be tested for drug usage; yes, I want to subscribe to the *Wall Street Journal;* no, I will not marry Leslie at this time; and so on. We take a stand on the issues given.

The conclusion can also be defined as the position taken about an issue. It is a claim supported by evidence statements. These evidence statements are called *reasons* or *premises*.

We often hear the cliché that "Everyone has a right to his or her opinion." This is true, in the legal sense. North Americans do not have "thought police" who decide what can and cannot be discussed. When you are a critically thinking person, however, your opinion has *substance*. That substance consists of the reasons you give to support your opinion. Conclusions with substance are more valuable and credible than are conclusions offering no supporting evidence.

Critical thinkers who strive to have opinions with substance exhibit two important qualities as they try to understand the truth of a matter:

1. They realize their own personal limitations. They know that they have a lot to learn about different areas and that they may need to revise their thoughts on issues as new information comes to light. This trait is also called *intellectual humility.*
2. They strive to be discerning about what they read and hear; they look for good evidence and are open to hearing all sides of an issue. When they make up their minds about something, they have solid reasons for their decisions.

The term *conclusion* is used differently in different fields of study. The definition given here applies most correctly to the study of argumentation. In an argumentative essay, the thesis statement will express the conclusion of the writer. In Chapters 3 and 4, you will note a related definition of conclusion used by philosophers in the study of deductive and inductive reasoning. In addition, the term *conclusion* is used to describe the final part of an essay or speech.

REMINDER

Conclusions are the positions people take on issues. Other words used to mean conclusions are *claims, viewpoints, positions, opinions,* and *stands.* We use the term *conclusion* because most people who teach argumentation use the term. The other words listed can mean the same thing.

How can we locate the conclusion of an argument? Try the following methods when you are having trouble finding the conclusion:

1. Find the issue and ask what position the writer or speaker is taking on the issue.
2. Look at the beginning or ending of a paragraph or an essay; the conclusion is often found in either of these places.
3. Look for conclusion indicator words: *therefore, so, thus, hence.* Also, look for indicator phrases: *My point is, What I am saying is, What I believe is.* Some indicator words and phrases are selected to imply that the conclusion drawn is the right one. These include *obviously, it is evident that, there is no doubt* (or *question*) *that, certainly,* and *of course.*
4. Ask yourself, "What is being claimed by this writer or speaker?"
5. Look at the title of an essay; sometimes the conclusion is contained within the title. For example, an essay might be titled "Why I Believe Vitamins Are Essential to Health."

SKILL

Find the conclusion or conclusions to an argument. Ask yourself what position the writer or speaker is taking on the issue.

You may hear people discussing an issue and someone says, "I don't know anything about this, but…" and proceeds to state an opinion about the issue. This comment is sometimes made as a means of continuing a conversation. Critical thinkers take a stand only when they know something about the issue; they give reasons why they have come to a certain conclusion. Of course, a critical thinker is open to hearing new evidence and may change his or her opinion on issues, as new information becomes available. (See Exercise 1.2 on p. 16.)

STOP AND THINK

As humans, we have limitations in our perception and knowledge. At the same time, we have wonderful tools for discovering new truths in every area of life. What personal qualities does a person need in order to give a fair hearing to new information?

willinen to leam , humility

The Reasons

> *Everything reasonable may be supported.*
>
> Epictetus, *Discourses* (Second century)

#1

Reasons are the statements that provide support for conclusions. Without reasons, you have no argument; you simply have an assertion, a statement of someone's opinion, as evidenced in the following limerick:

> I do not like thee, Doctor Fell
> The reason why I cannot tell
> But this I know, I know full well
> I do not like thee, Doctor Fell.

cases

(Reasons are also called *evidence, premises, support,* or *justification.* You will spend most of your time and energy as a critical thinker and responsible writer and speaker looking at the quality of the reasons used to support a conclusion. Here are some ways to locate the reasons in an argument:

1. Find the conclusion and then apply the "because trick." The writer or speaker believes _____ (conclusion) because _____. The reasons will naturally follow the word *because.*
2. Look for other indicator words that are similar to *because: since, for, first, second, third, as evidenced by, also, furthermore, in addition.*
3. Look for evidence supporting the conclusion. This support can be in the form of examples, statistics, analogies, reports of studies, and expert testimony.

STOP AND THINK

What was your most recent "argument"? What reasons were given to you, and what reasons did you give to support your conclusion?

There is a world of difference between supporting a political candidate because his or her policies make sense to you and supporting the same candidate because he or she seems like a charismatic person. Information in the

The Born Loser Reprinted by permission of Newspaper Enterprise Association, Inc.

following chapters of this book will give you the skills to help you decide whether a reason supports a conclusion.

Critical thinkers focus their attention on the issue being discussed, the conclusions taken, and the reasons given to support or justify the conclusions. (See Exercise 1.3 on p. 16.)

SKILL

Find the reasons that support the conclusion.

> As a listener: Be able to hear the issue, conclusion, and reasons given for an argument.
> As a speaker: Be able to clearly articulate your own conclusion and the reasons you have come to that conclusion on an issue.

Nothing is more difficult, and therefore more precious, than to be able to decide.
Napoleon, *Maxims* (1804)

Using Reasons to Make Decisions. When people engage in arguments, they usually present their conclusions about issues first and then give reasons to support their conclusions. In decision making, however, people often struggle with reasons on both sides of an issue in order to reach a conclusion (decision). For example, consider the following online dialogue between two friends, jointly deciding on the issue of whether to go to a water park. Note that the conclusion (the decision to go or not to go) does not become clear until they go over the reasons on both sides.

GenPeach: Hey Claire!
ClaireDies: hi Gen!
GenPeach: How are you Sweetie?

ClaireDies:	I'm okay I think. kind of tired.
ClaireDies:	am I going to see you today?
GenPeach:	I think so, . . . Waterworld?
ClaireDies:	yeah. should I go or not?
GenPeach:	If you want, I dunno if I will or not. I'm so tired.
ClaireDies:	Me too, and I have to pack. if you go, I will, but I don't want to come if I'm going to be the only one there
ClaireDies:	my age
GenPeach:	Ditto.
ClaireDies:	so
GenPeach:	The ? is, do we really want to go, or not?
ClaireDies:	well, what's the advantage of going?
GenPeach:	I was just thinking that. Um . . . water and slides and stuff, and we get to see each other
ClaireDies:	and I'm leaving soon . . . but if we stay, well, I'll get to do laundry and sleep
ClaireDies:	and pack and do the dishes
ClaireDies:	I'm leaning towards going now
GenPeach:	Negatives—small children screaming, sun, noise, more energy required than I have
ClaireDies:	very true.
GenPeach:	Not necessarily better than packing and cleaning
ClaireDies:	we wouldn't actually have to get up. We could grab a small section of grass and sleep, sunbathe
ClaireDies:	relax, read
GenPeach:	Yay
ClaireDies:	so . . . sounds like we should go.
ClaireDies:	should we just go?
GenPeach:	OK

STOP AND THINK

Try to list the reasons to go and the reasons not to go that the friends came up with before making their decision. Note that even routine daily decisions involve the process of weighing pros and cons (reasons) in order to come to a conclusion.

A Decision-Making Method

> *If you don't know where you're going, you might wind up somewhere else.*
> —Yogi Berra

A decision involves a dilemma between two or more alternative actions. We face these dilemmas daily in small and big ways. Decisions need to be made about serious matters such as whom to support in an election, which career to pursue, which school to attend, whether to marry, whether to have children, where to live, and how to budget time and money. Virtually every aspect of our lives involves decisions, especially since we live in a "free" society in which most decisions are not made by authorities but are left to individual citizens.

Many methods exist to help people make life decisions. Usually, there are different ways to evaluate reasons on both sides of a difficult decision. The decision to be made can be seen as the issue—Should I vote for Candidate A, Candidate B, or Candidate C? Should I spend money on a car or save the money for future needs? Should I go to graduate school or take a job offer now? The dilemma for the decision maker is that the future consequences of choosing one path over another are not known in the present time; the person making the decision has to choose without knowing the full implications of the choice. He or she must do what seems best with the information available in the present.

To come to a reasoned conclusion about a decision, it helps to weigh the reasons on both sides. Often, however, people can see many reasons to support two or more choices, and they feel paralyzed by indecision as a result.

One method that can be useful in making decisions that should also help you clarify your reasoning involves listing and giving weights to various reasons and then weighing each of your choices against those reasons.

Let's look at one decision-making method, using the example of the decision of whether to attend School X or School Y.

1. The first step in decision making is to define the dilemma in the form of an issue.

Example

Should I attend School X or School Y?

2. The second step in decision making involves looking at your long-term objective. It answers the question: What do I want this choice to accomplish in my life?

Example

I want to get a good education in my field without going into debt for more than two years.

Note that in this step, if either alternative does not meet your objective, the decision is already made. If you find that School X does not have the major that you want or that it would be too expensive to go to School X, then it no longer is an alternative to consider.

3. In the third step, you determine which factors are most important to you in a school. You list the factors and give an importance to each one (on a scale of 1–10, with 10 being the highest).

Example

Strong department in my major	10 points
Affordable (low cost or scholarship)	10 points
Close to friends and family	6 points
Near a large city	5 points
Gives internship option	8 points
Campus is attractive	4 points
Good arts community nearby	7 points
Climate is mild	5 points
Feels like a good fit when I visit	9 points
Professors are accessible	8 points

Note that the criteria in this example would be different for different people. That is why it is hard to receive advice about your decision or to give advice to others—other people may not weigh the factors the way you do. To one person, being in a large urban area is a major plus—to another it would be seen as a disadvantage. One person may value a close relationship with professors, while another prefers more formality and distance. One person may want to take advantage of cultural attractions nearby, while another is more interested in the sports scene on campus.

4. The fourth step gets to the heart of the reasons for and against each choice and gives you clear criteria for your decision. In this step, you take each factor and weigh it against your choices. The choice with the highest score is tentatively chosen.

Factor	Weight	School X Score	School Y Score
Example			
Strong department in my major	10 points ×	8	10
Affordable (low cost or scholarship)	10 points ×	9	5
Close to friends and family	6 points ×	8	6
Near a large city	5 points ×	5	9
Gives internship option	8 points ×	7	9
Campus is attractive	4 points ×	8	8
Good arts community nearby	7 points ×	7	10
Climate is mild	5 points ×	5	7
Feels like a good fit when I visit	9 points ×	8	10
Professors are accessible	8 points ×	9	7
Total: Weight of factor times score of choice		549	521

[Handwritten margin notes: "very important", "people are different, reason why it is difficult to advice others"]

5. The fifth step involves tentatively choosing the highest scoring alternative. Doing this kind of decision analysis may confirm that the individual choice is the right one or that either choice would be acceptable.

   If School X is chosen, the individual has resolved his or her own issue. The "argument" for School X could be stated as follows:

Issue: Should I choose School X or School Y?

Conclusion: I should choose School X.

Reasons: School X is affordable, has a good department in my major with professors that I can talk to, is fairly close to my friends and family, and might offer internship possibilities. School Y is good, too, and has an even better reputation but costs significantly more than School X.

Often, this kind of critical analysis can clarify choices for an individual. If, on the other hand, the alternative chosen does not "feel right," he or she may look at the criteria to determine why. It may be that the strength of the department and the location actually do factor higher for the individual and that the main reason for the low score for the option of School Y is the affordability. If that is the case, the individual making the decision could do more research about scholarships or about the option of getting a job to pay for School Y.

Going through this logical process and seeing which alternative "scores" higher will help you clarify your choice: If you feel satisfied with the choice, the factors listed were the important factors; if you are disappointed or uncomfortable with the choice, there may be some other, perhaps more emotionally based, factors that need to be entered into the equation.

INDIVIDUAL OR CLASS EXERCISE: MAKING A DECISION

Purpose: To use reasoning to make a decision.

By yourself, with a partner, or with a class group, choose a current decision that you are facing, and take it through the steps listed in the decision-making model. You can use the model for two or more alternative choices. After you have listed your criteria and the importance (weight) of each factor, rate each of your alternatives.

After weighing the alternatives, use the one with the higher score as your conclusion. Then state the issue (the decision that needed to be made), your conclusion (the alternative with the higher score), and the reasons (all of the factors that led to the high score). Whether this exercise is done individually or in groups, it would be helpful to share the results with the class as a further review of issues, conclusions, and reasons.

Ideas for the decision: A voting choice, school choice, career choice, relationship choice, or consumer choice.

Humor as Argument

Humor can also be viewed as argument—humorists often make an argument in a disarming way, using irony and exaggeration. If you listen closely to what comedians say, you can isolate issues, conclusions, and reasons in their monologues. Read the following transcript from a Jackie Mason monologue to understand his position on Starbuck's coffee. See if you can identify issues, conclusions, and reasons in his commentary.

reasons

If I said to you, "I have a great idea for a business. I'll open a whole new type of coffee shop. Instead of charging 60 cents for coffee I'll charge $2.50, $3.50, $4.50, and $5.50. Not only that, I'll have no tables, no chairs, no water, no free refills, no waiters, no busboys, serve it in cardboard cups, and have the customer clean it up for 20 minutes after they're finished."

issue

Would you say to me, "That's the greatest idea for a business I ever heard! We can open a chain of these all over the world!" No, you would put me right into a sanitarium. *conclusion*

reasons

And it's burnt coffee! It's burnt coffee at Starbuck's, be honest about it. If you get burnt coffee in a coffee shop, you call a cop. You say, "It's the bottom of the pot. I don't drink from the bottom of the pot."

But when it's burnt at Starbuck's, they say, "Oh, it's a special roast. It's a special bean from Argentina. . . ." The bean is in your head!!! I know burnt!!!

conclusion

. . . And I say this with the highest respect, because I don't like to talk about people. (See Exercise 1.4 on p. 20.)

LIFE APPLICATION: TIPS FOR COLLEGE AND CAREER

When you are listening to a discussion in class or at a meeting, consider the issue being considered, the claims being made, and the reasons given for the claims. If you have an opinion to share, frame it in terms of your position and your reasons.

When writing an essay or report, clarify your conclusion about the issue and support it with several reasons.

If you are called upon to make a speech without much time to prepare, use the same format of taking a stand on an issue and supporting it with reasons. For example, if you are asked to make a speech at your grandparent's retirement, you might say something like, "My grandmother has been wonderful to me [conclusion]. She has always encouraged my dreams, she has been there for all of my important events, and she has been a great role model [reasons]." You can then elaborate on each reason with examples.

If you are trying to get a group to come to consensus about a decision, try using the method outlined in this chapter. Help the group members define the issue that needs to be resolved and the desired outcome and have them weigh each possibility against specific criteria.

CHAPTER EXERCISES

Exercise 1.1 *Purpose:* To be able to identify issues.

1. Read an essay or an editorial, study an advertisement, listen to a radio talk show, or watch a television program about a controversial issue. Decide whether the issue is primarily one of fact, value, or policy. Define the issue and see if the speakers or writers stay with the issue.

2. By yourself or as a class, come up with as many current issues as you can. Think of both light and serious issues; consider campus, community, social, national, and international concerns.

   Now, look at your list of issues and choose three that really concern you. Then, try to choose three about which you are neutral. Finally, answer these questions:

   a. What is it about the first three issues that concern you?

   b. Why are you neutral about some issues?

   c. Do you believe there are issues on the list that should be more important to you? If so, why are they not more important to you?

Exercise 1.2 *Purpose:* To be able to isolate conclusions.
Take your list of issues from Question 2 in the previous exercise. Choose four issues and, in a simple declarative sentence, write your conclusion for each one.

Example

Issue: Should air traffic controllers be given periodic drug tests?

Conclusion: Yes, air traffic controllers should be given periodic drug tests.

REMINDER

Since the reasons answer the question "Why do you believe what you believe?" a good trick in isolating the reasons is to write the conclusion and then add the word *because.*

Example

I believe student athletes should be paid (conclusion) *because*

• They commit to certain hours and demands on their time.
• They make money for their schools.

Exercise 1.3 *Purposes:* To be able to use reasons to support a conclusion. To use knowledge gained in this chapter to both analyze and construct basic arguments.

1. Write a short rebuttal to the previous example about student athletes, using reasons to support your conclusion.

2. Take your conclusions from Exercise 1.2 and support each conclusion with at least three reasons. This exercise can be done alone or in classroom groups, in writing, or as a short speech. One group might present the "pro" side of an issue and another group the "con."

3. Get the editorial page of your favorite newspaper (including your campus paper), and list the issue, conclusion, and reasons given for each editorial. Use this format:

   The issue (question) is:
   The conclusion of this writer is:
   The reasons he or she gives are:

   Then evaluate the editorial by answering the following questions:

   a. Was the writer clear about the reasons given for the conclusion?

   b. Were there other reasons that could have been included in the argument?

   c. Did the writer express any understanding for an opposing viewpoint? If so, how? If not, can you articulate an opposing viewpoint for the editorial?

   d. Were you convinced by the editorial? Why or why not?

4. Read the following editorials, essays, and ad. Then, isolate the issues discussed, the conclusions of the writers, and the reasons given for the conclusions. Answer the following questions:

   a. Are the reasons given adequate to support the conclusions? If not, what other reasons could have been given?

   b. Do you agree or disagree with the conclusions? If you disagree, what are your reasons for disagreeing?

EDUCATIONAL TICKET

Dr. Y. Huda

Some bicycle riders complain about getting tickets for running stop signs, especially when they are "just kids." Those kids who get tickets should be grateful for the important lesson to not run stop signs. If they learn from the tickets, they will live longer.

Running stop signs and red lights hurts the bicycle riders and it also hurts other people. It scares motorists, and if a motorist accidentally hit and hurt a cyclist, the motorist would feel terrible. It also hurts bicycle activists who don't want to anger motorists—if motorists are angry, they won't support measures to improve cycling, such as getting wider roads so motorists and cyclists can share the road more safely.

reasons are ok

Reprinted with permission of the author.

WAR ON DRUGS FAILS: WE NEED NEW APPROACH

Issue

Daryl A. Bergman

Conclusion is ok

The war on drugs is an abysmal failure. A fresh and bold approach is needed—beginning with the legalization of marijuana and the registration of drug addicts. It's also necessary to look to other countries that have been successful. The legalization of pot would:

- Eliminate the stepping-stone to harder drugs.
- Eliminate the crime associated with large dollar street transactions.
- Provide taxes to step up law enforcement efforts (meth labs, heroin smuggling)—and rehab programs.
- Free space in jails housing non-violent criminals, saving incarceration costs.

The registration of addicts would:

reasons are ok

- Eliminate the use of dirty needles, decreasing victims of AIDS and associated health care costs.
- End warehouse rehabilitation programs.

Let's move forward to save our children.

Reprinted with permission of the author.

DRUGGED DRIVING

Lavelle Washington

Like alcohol, marijuana and other drugs can impair many of those skills that are imperative to good driving, such as alertness, the ability to concentrate and to read signs, coordination and reaction time. These effects can last up to 24 hours after smoking marijuana. If you combine drug use with teens' inexperience on the road and risk-taking behavior, we have a recipe for disaster. The National Highway Traffic Safety Administration (NHTSA) estimates that 10 to 22 percent of drivers involved in all vehicle crashes had recently used an illegal drug, often in combination with alcohol.

- The Department of Transportation has published two studies examining the impact of marijuana on driving performance. Marijuana—the most widely abused illegal drug—slows a driver's perception of time, space, and distance, and it leads to drowsiness and distraction.
- Research indicates that cocaine causes drivers to speed and change lanes without signaling and puts other innocent people at risk of a deadly accident.
- While it is illegal in all states to drive a motor vehicle while under the influence of alcohol, drugs other than alcohol, or a combination of alcohol and other drugs, there is no consistent method across states for identifying drug impairment. As a result, we do not know the full impact of illegal drug use on public safety.
- According to the National Commission Against Drunk Driving, impaired driving is the most frequently committed violent crime in America and every 30 minutes, someone in this country dies in an alcohol-related crash, equating to approximately 17,000 deaths per year.

Reprinted with permission of the author.

SAVE FAMILY BUSINESSES

z. haakon

There is a need to voice the concerns about our unsung family businesses. Over the last few years, they have endured the monopoly of "Big Businesses" like Starbucks and Blockbuster. These animal industries have bulldozed their way into our streets and taken over "Mom and Pop Video" and "Joe Schmoe's Java Hut" to make way for their chain mega-stores. And people flock to them. This is how our family businesses, our unsung little people, get their face pushed in the mud until they give up and declare bankruptcy. We cannot allow this to happen. I witnessed the closure of my favorite video store that I had spent hours in since I was a little boy. It had the new releases for the brainwashed general public; but for me, it was a haven for independent and classic greats. I don't think I ever spent so much time in such a little store, but you couldn't drag me away from the hundreds of forgotten classics without my renting at least two of the four tapes I had picked up—choosing which two became one of the most excruciating dilemmas of my life. My video store closed after continuing sales drops from trying to hold its own against the competition, Blockbuster. People from all over the county came in on its closing day to tell stories of how it was their favorite family video store, and how much they looked forward to seeing what new releases they'd pick up, and how much their kids loved the children's section. And yet, the place still went under! It's too late for my favorite video store, but something should be done about the other suffering "little stores"—whether they are video or coffee or local grocery stores.

Used by permission of the author.

Advertisers can make arguments using both words and visual images. As with the preceding essays and editorials, see if you can identify the issue, conclusion, and reasons given in the following ad from Chevron.

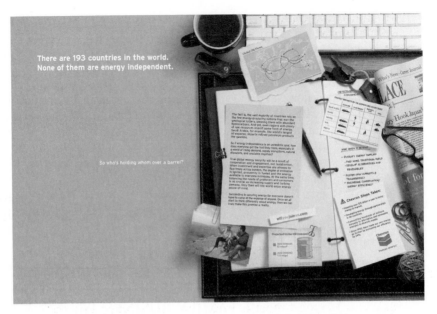

There are 193 countries in the world.
None of them are energy independent.

So who's holding whom over a barrel?

Exercise 1.4   *Purpose:* To practice finding issues, conclusions, and reasons in humor.

Find an excerpt from a book of humor, a list of humorous quotations, or a stand-up comedy routine. You might also look at articles or Web sites that feature humorous political commentary. Isolate the issue, conclusion, and reasons that the comedian covers. Share your findings with the class.

CHAPTER HIGHLIGHTS

1. Critical thinking about information is necessary in order for us to make clear decisions as citizens, consumers, and human beings.
2. An argument consists of issues, conclusions, and reasons.
3. The issue is the question that is raised; our decisions are made easier if we can define the issues on which we are asked to comment or act.
4. The conclusion is the position a person takes on an issue.
5. Reasons, often called premises, provide support for conclusions; reasons are acceptable or unacceptable on the basis of their relevance and quality.
6. Critical thinkers carefully consider their objectives and the reasons on all sides of an issue when they make important decisions.

KEY TERMS

Critical thinker (p. 2)   Issue (p. 4)

Argument (p. 4)   Reasons (p. 4)

Conclusion (p. 4)

CHAPTER CHECKUP

Short Answer

1. What is the difference between a topic and an issue?
2. What are some indictor words for a conclusion?
3. Cite three ways to discover the reasons used to support a conclusion.

True-False

F 4. Everyone's opinion about an issue, though different, has equal substance.

T 5. Traits such as fair-mindedness and empathy are helpful to critical thinkers.

T 6. A critical thinker is someone who uses specific criteria to evaluate reasoning, form opinions, and make decisions.

Sentence Completion

7. The question that is being addressed is called the *issue*

8. You will spend most of your time and energy as a critical thinker and responsible speaker looking at the quality of the *reasons* used to support a conclusion.

9. Since the reasons answer the question "Why do you believe what you believe?" a good trick in isolating the reasons is to write the conclusion and then add the word *because*

10. When we say yes or no to the issues presented, we are stating our *opinion*

ARTICLES FOR DISCUSSION

The following articles give differing viewpoints on the same issue. Read both and then consider the questions that follow.

TALK-SHOW HOST ANGERS DISABLED COMMUNITY

Hand Deformity Inherited from Mom Sparks L.A. Dispute

Michael Fleeman

LOS ANGELES—Aaron James Lampley, all 7 pounds, $14^1/_2$ ounces of him, was only a few hours old when a local radio station dedicated a show for the second time to the circumstances and controversy surrounding his birth.

In addressing the matter again, KFI-AM last week refueled a dispute that pitted the station against activists for the disabled and raised questions about freedom of speech and society's treatment of the disabled.

Aaron Lampley was born Wednesday morning, with ectodactyly, which leaves the bones in the feet and hands fused. His mother, local TV anchorwoman

Bree Walker Lampley, also has the condition and knew the child had a 50 percent chance of inheriting it.

Her other child, a daughter, has the condition as well.

Before the boy's birth, KFI outraged the KCBS-TV anchorwoman and advocates for people with disabilities with a July 22 call-in show in which host Jane Norris asked whether it was fair for Walker Lampley to give birth when the child had a "very good chance of having a disfiguring disease."

Critics of the show said it smacked of bigotry and illustrated societal prejudice and lack of understanding toward the disabled. KFI said the matter was handled properly and that radio talk shows are appropriate forums for controversial issues.

In KFI's second visit to the subject, this time with Norris acting as guest on Tom Leykis' afternoon show, Norris accused Walker Lampley of orchestrating a campaign to discredit her and contended she had a First Amendment right to discuss the matter.

"I was supportive of Bree's decision," Norris said on the show. "All I did, and have done, is voice my opinion of what would be right for me. I thought I handled the topic sensitively, but all [Walker Lampley has] seen fit to do is slander me."

Norris' statements did nothing to cool the situation.

"They came on the air supposedly to set the record straight. In our view, she set the record even more crooked," said Lillabeth Navarro of *American Disabled for Access Power Today.*

"This is like a bunch of thugs ganging up on the disability community. It just rained forth what caused us to be outraged to begin with."

Navarro said activists planned a protest at KFI studios.

The demonstration is part of a grassroots campaign organized in part by a media consulting firm hired by Walker Lampley and her husband, KCBS anchorman Jim Lampley.

The company, EIN SOF Communications, gives the disability rights community a public voice. The firm has sent tapes of the Norris show to disability rights groups and is helping to file a complaint with the Federal Communications Commission.

In the original show, Norris said she wasn't intending to dictate what Walker Lampley should have done. But she said she couldn't have made the same decision if she were in Walker Lampley's position.

Norris said there were "so many other options available," including adoption and surrogate parenting, and "it would be difficult to bring myself to morally cast my child forever to disfigured hands."

Throughout the show, Norris seemed to take issue with people who disagreed with her.

After a caller named Jennifer from Los Angeles said, "I don't really see why it's your business," Norris responded, "Well, I think it's everybody's business. This is life. These things happen in life. What's your problem? Do you have a problem talking about deformities?"

Norris also repeatedly referred to Walker Lampley's condition, ectodactyly, as a disease, even though it is a genetically caused disability.

Walker Lampley and her husband, in interviews before their child was born, said Norris' first program was an attack on the handicapped and Walker Lampley personally, and was full of errors and poorly chosen remarks.

"I felt assaulted and terrorized," Walker Lampley said. "I felt like my pregnancy had been robbed of some of its joy."

She added, "I felt disappointed that someone would be so insensitive."

RADIO SHOW ON RIGHTS OF DISABLED DEFENDED

Crippled Woman's Pregnancy Debated

Associated Press

LOS ANGELES—The chairman of the Equal Employment Opportunity Commission said a local radio station shouldn't be disciplined for a talk show that debated whether a disabled TV anchorwoman should give birth.

Chairman Evan J. Kemp, who is disabled and confined to a wheelchair, said he was "appalled and sickened" by the majority of callers to the KFI program who said KCBS anchor Bree Walker Lampley had no right to become pregnant and should abort if she did.

However, Kemp said the right of free speech should protect KFI from any Federal Communications Commission action.

Kemp's statements were published in the *Los Angeles Times*.

Lampley, who was pregnant at the time of the July, 1991, broadcast, lodged a complaint to the FCC and asked for an investigation. The newswoman, her husband, co-anchor Jim Lampley, and more than 20 organizations for the disabled asked the agency to examine whether the station and its owner, Cox Broadcasting Corp., should lose their license, be fined or reprimanded.

The couple charged the broadcast was not a thorough discussion, but rather an attack on Lampley's integrity without inviting them to appear and harassed callers who attempted to express contrary views.

Lampley gave birth five weeks after the broadcast to a boy who had the same genetic condition as his mother—ectrodactylism, in which the bones of the hands and feet are fused. There was a 50 percent chance that the baby would have the condition.

Kemp said he was not speaking out as chairman of the Washington, D.C.–based EEOC, but as a "severely disabled person" with a rare polio-like disease—Kugelberg-Welander—that may be inherited.

He said he plans to write to the FCC to defend grassroots discussions and radio talk shows such as the KFI program as necessary forums.

QUESTIONS FOR DISCUSSION

1. The author of the first article states that this controversy "raised questions about freedom of speech and society's treatment of the disabled." What were the questions—that is, issues—that were raised?

2. Take one of the issues raised by the talk-show controversy, and discuss how well those mentioned in the articles defended it.

3. Comment on the following excerpt from the first article: What is your opinion of the host's response to the caller?

   After a caller named Jennifer from Los Angeles said, "I don't really see why it's your business," Norris responded, "Well, I think it's everybody's business. This is life. These things happen in life. What's your problem? Do you have a problem talking about deformities?"

4. Are there any issues discussed by radio and television talk shows that you consider inappropriate? Are certain groups targeted for criticism and others left alone, or is every topic fair game? Give examples to support your answer.

5. Each article used a different subheading to explain the controversy. The first article's subheading reads: "Hand Deformity Inherited from Mom Sparks L.A. Dispute." The second article's subheading says: "Crippled Woman's Pregnancy Debated." How do these different subheadings frame the issue? To what extent do you think they are fair and accurate statements about the controversy?

IDEAS FOR WRITING OR SPEAKING

1. Consider the following quote from the first article: "Critics of the show said it smacked of bigotry and illustrated societal prejudice and lack of understanding toward the disabled. KFI said the matter was handled properly and that radio talk shows are appropriate forums for controversial issues."

   The framers of our Bill of Rights did not anticipate the phenomenon of broadcast media. Based on your understanding of the freedom of speech, are there any issues that should not be discussed in a public forum? Does sensitivity to the feelings of a particular group make some topics less desirable for public discussion? State your conclusion and support it with reasons.

2. Take a stand on one of the issues involved in these articles. Write an essay or give a short speech expressing your viewpoint and supporting it with reasons.

3. Imagine that you are a program director for a radio talk show. What guidelines would you give your talk-show hosts? Give reasons for each guideline. Share your guidelines in a group, or write them in essay form.

4. Write or speak on the following: Given the power of talk-show hosts to influence large numbers of people, do you believe there should be stricter licensing requirements for this profession, as there are for doctors, lawyers, and accountants, in order to ensure a uniform code of journalistic conduct? If so, why? If not, why not?

More Ideas for Writing or Speaking

1. Think about an issue that really interests you; it might be an issue currently being debated on your campus, or a community or national problem. The editorial pages of campus, community, or national newspapers may give you more ideas to help you choose your issue.

   In the form of an essay or a brief speech, state the issue and your conclusion and give at least three reasons to support your conclusion.

   In the classroom, take a few minutes for each person to share his or her essay or speech, and see if the rest of the class understands the issue, conclusion, and reasons of the speaker. Don't use this exercise to debate issues (that will come later). At this point, strive only to make yourself clear and to understand the basic arguments of others.

2. Letter or speech of complaint: Practice using your knowledge about the structure of argument by writing a letter of complaint or doing a classroom "complaint speech," using the guidelines devised by Professor Lee Loots:

   Constructive complaining is an important life skill. Use this letter or speech to express your dissatisfaction. Choose the most relevant aspects of the problem to discuss. A clear statement of the issue, your conclusion, and reasons distinguishes complaining from "whining." Whereas whining could be characterized as a long string of feelings expressed vehemently about random aspects of a problem, a true complaint describes the nature of the problem in an organized fashion. Sincerely expressed feelings then add richness to the clear and organized content.

   To make the complaint clear, be sure to support your ideas with examples, illustrations, instances, statistics, testimony, or visual aids. To make your feelings clear, you can use vivid language, humor, sarcasm, understatement, exaggeration, irony, and dramatic emphasis.

   Examples of topics for the complaint letter or speech: a letter or speech to a city planning commission about excessive airport noise, a letter to a supervisor about a change in salary or working conditions, a complaint to neighbors about reckless driving in the neighborhood, a complaint to housemates about sharing the workload, or a letter or speech to insurance agents about rates for college students.

3. Read the classic poem *The Road Not Taken* by Robert Frost. How does Frost use the image of two roads to illustrate the dilemma facing people who have to make a decision with unknown consequences? Write about a difficult decision you had to make or a dilemma that you are currently facing. Give some background to the dilemma and the pros and cons of making a choice as you see them at the present time.

   You might also consider a social or national decision that needs to be made, such as implementing a new policy or choosing a candidate for an election. What consequences might be the result of different policies or candidates? Given the present facts and projected consequences, what choice would you advise?

The Road Not Taken

Two roads diverged in a yellow wood,
And sorry I could not travel both
And be one traveler, long I stood
And looked down one as far as I could
To where it bent in the undergrowth;

Then took the other, as just as fair,
And having perhaps the better claim,
Because it was grassy and wanted wear;
Though as for that the passing there
Had worn them really about the same,

And both that morning equally lay
In leaves no step had trodden black.
Oh, I kept the first for another day!
Yet knowing how way leads on to way,
I doubted if I should ever come back.

I shall be telling this with a sigh
Somewhere ages and ages hence:
Two roads diverged in a wood, and I—
I took the one less traveled by,
And that has made all the difference.

From *Mountain Interval* by Robert Frost. Originally published in 1920 by Hentry Holt and Company, Inc.

FILMS FOR ANALYSIS AND DISCUSSION

Films, plays, and television programs are all rich sources of illustrating the concepts in this text. For Chapter 1, you might view and write about issues, conclusions, and reasons found in any of the story lines. In addition, characters often face and struggle with decision making.

Following are some suggestions for films that illustrate some of the points in Chapter 1. Several deal with important issues and life-changing decisions that are made by the characters.

North Country (2005, R).

Sexual harassment might be the legal name for the struggle Charlize Theron's character, Josey, goes through in *North Country,* but her fight is about the human right to be treated with respect. After a string of low-paying jobs and abusive relationships, Josey, a single-mother of two, finds work in the male-dominated iron mines. At first, the job is seen as a golden ticket to independence and solid provision for her children, but, as time passes, the mines become a cruel and dangerous place for Josey and her female co-workers. Instead of taking the easy way out and quitting, Josey sets out for the fight of her life, turning many of her friends and family against her in the process. Much like Jonathan Demme's *Philadelphia,* this film is an uncompromising look at what can happen when you take a stand for what is right, regardless of the personal cost and obstacles in the way.

Similar Films and Classics

Akeelah and the Bee (2006, PG).

Eleven year old Akeelah is just discovering her gifts and talents and deciding on the identity she wishes to portray to her middle school classmates. She needs to decide whether to take the hard road of spelling bee competition and whether to agree to the demands of her new mentor. Her mother also has to make decisions about whether to let Akeelah spend time on her spelling that takes her away from obligations at home and at school.

Pursuit of Happyness (2006, PG 13).

This film is based on the story of Chris Gardner, a salesman struggling to make a living, while his wife works double shifts and his son stays in extended day care. Chris needs to make decisions about whether to take an internship as a stockbroker, despite his time-consuming sales job. His wife has to decide whether to remain in the marriage, and both need to make decisions concerning the well being of their son.

Good Night and Good Luck (2005, R).

In this film about the McCarthy era of the 1950s, CBS journalist Edward R. Murrow uses his talk show to make arguments against Senator McCarthy and his controversial approach to the threat of communism.

Baby Boom (1987, PG).

In this film, a successful businesswoman has to decide whether to accept responsibility for a baby left in her care, whether to continue working and living in New York City, and eventually, whether to sell her own business for a very large profit. Each decision she makes leads to new choices and dilemmas.

2

Values and Ethics

What Price Ethics and Can You Afford Not to Pay?

A critical thinker understands the value assumptions underlying many arguments and recognizes that conflicts are often based on differing values.

A critical thinker is familiar with ethical standards and tests of ethical decision making.

A critical thinker can compare and contrast ideals with actual practice.

This chapter will cover

- Value assumptions

- Conflicts between value assumptions

- Value priorities

- Ideal values versus real values

- Ethics in argumentation

- Ethical decision making

In the first chapter, we discussed the structure of argument, including issues, conclusions about issues, and reasons used to support conclusions. Chapters 4, 5, and 6 will examine the quality of evidence given to support conclusions. This chapter and Chapter 3 will cover the assumptions underlying arguments that influence all of us as we consider claims and take positions on issues.

<u>**Assumptions**</u> <u>are ideas we take for granted;</u> as such, they are often left out of a written or spoken argument. Just as we can look at the structure of a house without seeing the foundation, we can look at the structure of an argument without examining the foundational elements. To truly understand the quality of a house or an argument, however, we need to understand the foundation upon which it is built.

Assumptions made by speakers and writers come in two forms: value assumptions and reality assumptions. <u>*Value assumptions* are beliefs about how</u> <u>the world should be;</u> they reflect an individual's viewpoint on which values <u>are most important to consider in relation to a particular issue.</u> *Reality assumptions* are beliefs about how the world is; they reflect what an individual takes for granted as factual information. We will look in depth at reality assumptions in Chapter 3. In this chapter, we will focus on value assumptions, which form the foundations of arguments; we will also examine ethical considerations in argumentation and decision making.

TOULMIN'S MODEL: A METHOD FOR DISCOVERING ASSUMPTIONS

<u>British philosopher Stephen Toulmin</u> has developed a method of analyzing arguments that helps us isolate our assumptions. His method identifies **claims,** statements of an individual's belief or stand upon an issue (which are the same as conclusions); **reasons,** direct statements that provide evidence to support a claim; and **warrants,** those unstated but necessary links between reasons and claims, the glue that attaches the reasons to the claims. Warrants are the assumptions made by the speaker or writer that connect claims and reasons.

Example

We'll have to leave at 5 a.m. to make our flight because we'll be driving in rush hour traffic.

Claim (conclusion): We'll have to leave by 5 a.m. to make our flight.
Reason: We'll be driving in rush-hour traffic.
Warrant: Rush-hour traffic moves more slowly than other traffic.

In the preceding example, the reason and claim of the speaker are clear, but the warrant (in this case a reality or factual assumption) that shows the movement from the reason to the conclusion—why the reason is relevant support for the conclusion—is unstated. These assumptions are usually unstated because they are unnecessary in a particular context; for example, most people in a culture that deals with traffic understand the demands of rush-hour traffic.

Similarly, value assumptions often remain as unstated warrants for an argument if most people hearing the argument accept these assumptions without question. For example, if someone cuts in line in front of others who have been waiting, he or she will be told "You need to move back, because the line starts back there."

> *Claim* (conclusion): You need to move back.
> *Reason:* The line starts back there.
> *Warrant* (this is the value assumption): The acceptable action is to take your turn in line, which reflects the value of fairness to everyone.

Sometimes, warrants contain both reality and value assumptions in the same argument. For example, someone might say "Be careful on that floor—it was just washed."

The argument in this case could be analyzed as

> *Claim:* Be careful walking on that floor.
> *Reason:* It was just washed.
> *Warrant:* Floors that have been newly washed are slippery (reality assumption).
> *Warrant:* I don't want you to slip and fall because I value your health and safety (value assumption).

Understanding reality assumptions and value assumptions as foundational, but unstated, parts of an argument becomes important when we discover that other people may hold very different assumptions and thus do not believe that our reasons are warranted. Let's say that someone argues as follows: "There should be no restrictions on public library access to the Internet for children because children need to be able to do research on library computers." The claim (conclusion) is that there should be no restrictions on library access to the Internet for children. The reason given is that children need to be able to do research on the computers. The warrant, in this case a value assumption, is that equal access to information is important for young students.

Someone with a different take on this issue may argue that there should be restrictions on public library access to the Internet because of the easy availability to minors of pornographic material if such a policy were in place. The warrant in this case would reflect a different value assumption—that protection of minor children from inappropriate material is more important than unlimited access.

When you argue that your value assumption is the *best* one for the situation, you often have to persuade others. Your warrant will require what Toulmin calls **backing**, evidence used to support a warrant. You will need to explain why your value assumption is the most important one. In the case of library access, you might state the following as backing for the warrant: "Protection of minor children from inappropriate material is important."

- Parents trust children's sections of public libraries to be free from adult content.
- Libraries create special children's sections, in part, to isolate children from accessing and borrowing inappropriate material.
- If children need to access research material from the Internet, a librarian is available to help them.

When people *agree* about underlying assumptions, they do not need to be made explicit. However, when assumptions are controversial, they need to be acknowledged and defended. Assumptions (warrants) that are controversial need support (backing). We will look more closely at backing, the evidence for warrants, in Chapters 3, 4, and 5. As illustrated in the previous examples, when individuals have differing assumptions (warrants) about an issue, they often reflect a difference in value priorities. When forming opinions and making decisions, critical thinkers need to understand and examine their own value priorities. People may agree that the values of others are also valid but believe that their own values are the most important determining factors for a particular issue.

Consider the values expressed in the following newspaper column. Compare the answers given to the question "Which fictional character do you admire most?" What are the different values represented by the choices? Do you think the careers chosen by the respondents reflect their values?

QUESTION MAN: FICTIONAL CHARACTER YOU ADMIRE MOST?

Kris Conti

Female, 23, curatorial assistant:

Howard Roark of *The Fountainhead* for never compromising his standards. His self-centeredness and arrogance [were] a problem, but I admired the fact that he had standards and lived by them. It seems that standards are fairly loose, sort of ad hoc. People go by the situation they're in rather than a set of standards that they follow. I admire someone who has ideals.

Female, 31, bank teller:

Scrooge. He was a cad but when he had a chance to turn his life around he did. I admire his ability to turn his life around, because it's hard to change. He finally found that being rich is not what makes you happy. That being a true giver and a caring person are very rich qualities, and you can be happy in spite of poverty and adversity.

Male, 28, office manager:

Bugs Bunny. I admire the way he outsmarts his rivals and talks his way out of adverse situations. He always gets the best of any situation. Of course, in the cartoon universe, it doesn't matter how, so it's not applicable in the nonanimated universe. Who's going to discuss morals once you throw the [laws] of physics and gravity out the window?

Male, 38, nuclear industry engineer:

Mr. Spock. He always has the answer. Whatever the problem is, he's always got the solution. He's witty. He's got a great sense of humor. It's just a subtle-type humor. I love that his character is very intelligent. Everything to him has a logic. It has to be logical. It has to click for him in a logical, rational way or it isn't happening.

Female, 25, Salvation Army program assistant:

Cinderella. She overcame . . . all the hardships she had to face and kept that spirit of endurance and forgiveness. She just kept plugging away and was humble. She served her stepsisters and stepmother and didn't gripe. We could all be a little more serving. Not to the point of being oppressed, but be more serving like she was.

The *San Francisco Chronicle,* January 28, 1990. Copyright © 1990 by The San Francisco Chronicle. Reprinted by permission of the publisher.

STOP AND THINK

Which fictional character do you admire most? What does your answer reveal about your values?

Since fictional characters are usually superhuman in some way, think also of real people you most admire—what do your choices reflect about your values?

VALUE ASSUMPTIONS AND CONFLICTS

Have you ever noticed how some issues are really interesting to you while others are not? Your interest in a particular question and your opinion about the question are often influenced by your **values**—those ideals, standards, and principles you believe are important and consider worthy.

Value assumptions are beliefs about what is good and important that form the basis of opinions on issues.

These assumptions are important for the critical thinker because

1. Many arguments between individuals and groups are primarily based on strongly held values that need to be understood and, if possible, respected.
2. An issue that continues to be unresolved or bitterly contested often involves cherished values on both sides. **Value conflicts** are disagreements about the most important value to be considered on an issue. These conflicting value assumptions can occur *between* groups or individuals or *within* an individual.

[handwritten margin note: arguments are strongly related to one's values]

Almost everyone in a civilized society believes that its members, especially those who are young and defenseless, should be protected. That's why we never hear a debate on the pros and cons of child abuse—most of us agree that there are no "pros" to this issue. Similarly, we don't hear people arguing about the virtues of mass murder, rape, or burglary.

Our values, however, do come into the discussion when we are asked to decide how to treat the people who engage in these acts. Some issues having a value component include:

Should we have and enforce the death penalty?
Should rapists receive the same penalties as murderers?
Should we allow lighter sentences for plea bargaining?

Although most of us value order and justice, we often disagree about how justice is best administered and about what should be done to those who break the law.

STOP AND THINK

When you read or hear the words *should* or *ought to,* you are probably being addressed on a question of value.

You can see that the question of the death penalty centers on a conflict about the priorities of justice and mercy, two values cherished by many. Of course, a good debate on this issue will also address factual (not value-based) issues, such as whether the death penalty is a deterrent to crimes and whether the penalty is fairly administered throughout the country.

Keep in mind, however, that most people who argue passionately about this issue are motivated by their values and beliefs concerning justice and mercy. These values are often shaped by significant personal experiences. In fact, we generally hear arguments involving values from persons who are deeply concerned about an issue. Both sides of arguments involving values are likely to be persuasive because of the convictions of their advocates.

In coming to thoughtful conclusions on value-based arguments, the critical thinker needs to decide which of two or more values is best. In other words, the thinker must give one value or set of values a higher priority than the other. The process of choosing the most important values in an issue has been called **value prioritization.** We need to order our values when a personal, social, national, or international issue involving values is at stake.

Examples

We often hear arguments about the legalization of drugs, gambling, or prostitution. People may claim that legalizing these activities would lessen crime, free up prison space for more violent offenses, and direct

[handwritten margin note: people are motivated by their values]

large sums of money to the government and out of the hands of dealers, bookies, and pimps.

Those who oppose legalization of these activities may have equally impressive arguments about the problems communities would face if these activities were legalized. We need to understand the root of this argument as a disagreement about which is more important:

1. Cleaning up the crime problems caused by underground activities linked to illegal vices—that is, the value of taking care of the immediate problem, or
2. Maintaining our standards of healthy living by discouraging and making it a crime to engage in activities that we as a culture deem inappropriate and harmful—that is, the value of honoring cultural standards and long-term societal goals.

If people believe that taking drugs, gambling, and prostitution are morally wrong, then no list of advantages of legalizing them would be persuasive to them. Thus, the argument starts with understanding whether the conclusion is based upon values; relative societal benefits have a much lower priority for those who believe we cannot condone harmful activities.

SKILL

Understand that different values form the basis of many arguments and that conflicts are often based on differing value priorities.

Think of a decision you might be facing now or in the future, such as whether you should work (or continue working) while attending school, which career you should choose, or which person you should marry. An internal conflict about a decision often involves an impasse between two or more values.

Let's say you are undecided about continuing to work. You want to devote yourself to school because in the long run you can get a better job (long-term goal). On the other hand, you'd really like the money for an upgraded lifestyle—a car or a better car, money to eat out, and nicer clothes (short-term goals).

Your career decision may involve a conflict between the value of serving others in a field such as nursing or teaching and the value of a secure and substantial salary (such as you might find in a business career) that would help you better provide for your future family.

You might think of getting serious with one person because he or she has good prospects for the future and is ambitious, but another person is more honest and has cared for you in both good and bad times. In this case, the conflict is between security (or materialism) and proven loyalty.

Whether we are considering personal issues or issues facing our community, nation, or world, we need to understand our values and decide which values are most important to us.

CLASS EXERCISE

Purpose: To isolate value conflicts and to understand how different conclusions can be based on conflicting values.

Try to isolate the various value conflicts in these personal and social issues. Some of the issues may involve more than one set of conflicting values.

Note especially how both values can be important, and we as persons or as citizens need to make tough decisions. Creating policies for difficult problems means giving one value a higher priority than another.

[handwritten: prioritizing]

The first one is done for you as an example.

1. Should teenagers be required to obtain the approval of their parents before they receive birth control pills or other forms of contraception?

    > The conflict in this issue is between the value of individual freedom and privacy on one side and parental responsibility and guidance on the other.

2. Should birth parents be allowed to take their child back from adoptive parents after they have signed a paper relinquishing rights?

3. Should you give a substantial part of your paycheck to a charity that feeds famine-stricken families or use it for some new jeans you need?

4. Should air traffic controllers be given tests for drug usage?

5. Should persons be hired for jobs without regard to maintaining an ethnic mix?

6. Should prisoners on death row be allowed conjugal visits?

7. Should superior athletes receive admission to colleges regardless of their grades or SAT scores?

8. Should criminals be allowed to accept royalties on books they've written about the crimes they committed?

9. Should big-box stores be able to choose to sell only family-friendly CDs?

10. Should children of alumni donors be allowed an advantage in admissions to private schools?

[handwritten: ethics? between individual responsibility & self-fulfillment]

ETHICS—AN IMPORTANT DIMENSION OF VALUES

Without civic morality, communities perish; without personal morality, their survival has no value.

Bertrand Russell, "Individual and Social Ethics,"
Authority and the Individual (1949)

For our purposes, we will examine ethics as one dimension of values. **Ethics,** sometimes called **morals,** refers to standards of conduct that reflect what we consider to be right or wrong behavior. Many conflicts about values involve an ethical dimension; that is, we are asked to choose whether one action or policy is more ethical than another.

ethics morals

Look at the difference in the following value conflicts:

> Should you take a job that pays more but has evening hours, which you value for studying, or should you take a job that pays less but gives you the hours that you want?
>
> If you arrive home and notice that a cashier at a store gave you too much change, should you go back to the store and return the money?

Note that in the first example, you need to decide what you value more—the extra money or the working hours you want. There is no ethical (good-bad) dimension to this decision; you can still study even if you take the job with the less desirable hours.

The second dilemma is about your personal standards of right and wrong, or good and evil. Do you inconvenience yourself by making a trip to the store or sending the money back because you believe it is wrong to take what does not belong to you? Or do you believe that if you didn't intend to take the money, you are not responsible? What are your standards of right and wrong, especially regarding relationships with others? Your answer to this kind of ethical dilemma will reflect your value priorities.

Philosophers and theologians have grappled with theories of ethical behavior for centuries. Several schools of thought about ethics have emerged. Some of the more common ones guiding Western thinkers are listed here. Note the value assumptions of each.

Libertarianism:	the highest value is to promote individual liberty
Utilitarianism:	the highest value is that which promotes the greatest general happiness and minimizes unhappiness
Egalitarianism:	the highest value is equality, which means justice and opportunities distributed equally
Religious values:	the highest values are based on faith and spiritual truth, such as loving God and one's neighbor
Prima facie values:	universal ethical principles, such as honesty and respect for others, exist and are considered to be self-evident and obvious to rational individuals of every culture

Sometimes, these value assumptions are placed together to support a claim, as in Thomas Jefferson's Declaration of Independence, the document that argued for separation of the thirteen original colonies of the United States from the rule of the King of England. Read the following excerpt from the Declaration noting how all of the value assumptions just listed are included (emphasis added).

The Declaration of Independence of the Thirteen Colonies

In CONGRESS, July 4, 1776

The unanimous Declaration of the thirteen united States of America,

When in the Course of human events, it becomes necessary for one people to dissolve the political bands which have connected them with another, and to assume among the powers of the earth, the separate and equal station to which the Laws of Nature and of Nature's God entitle them, a decent respect to the opinions of mankind requires that they should declare the causes which impel them to the separation.

We hold these *truths to be self-evident, that all men are created equal, that they are endowed by their Creator with certain unalienable Rights, that among these are Life, Liberty and the pursuit of Happiness.*—That to secure these rights, Governments are instituted among Men, deriving their just powers from the consent of the governed,—That whenever any Form of Government becomes destructive of these ends, it is the Right of the People to alter or to abolish it, and to institute new Government, laying its foundation on such principles and organizing its powers in such form, as to them shall seem most likely to effect their Safety and Happiness.

Note that the Declaration contains references to all of the values we listed—liberty, happiness, equality, an acknowledgment of divine endowments, and self-evident truths. While there are substantial similarities among these factors, different individuals give priority to one guiding principle over another. This document provides a good example of how members of a culture may espouse common values yet continue to dialogue about the relative importance of those values with regards to societal issues. (See Exercise 2.1 on p. 46.)

STOP AND THINK

Most people hold values that reflect several of the ethical schools of thought, and they express these values differently, depending upon the issue. An individual may be in favor of free trade (libertarian), equal educational opportunity (egalitarian), creation of national parks (utilitarian), working for faith-based charities (religious values), and a business policy of treating every customer with respect (prima facie values). It is hard to categorize most people as followers of one system exclusively over another because of complex individual differences.

Is there one particular school of thought that you embrace on most issues?

In any society, conflicting positions on issues are often based on differences in ethical value assumptions. For example, libertarians might argue that when someone has created a business on private property, that person has the right to regulate activites that take place on that property, such as smoking. People concerned about the effects of smoke on nonsmokers may give the utilitarian argument that even private restaurants and bars should ban smoking for the greater good of those who want to go to or work in those establishments.

While there are clear differences between the ethical schools of thought, there are also individual differences even within a particular ethical perspective. Issues involving conflicting values usually generate conclusions that answer the question "Where do we draw the line?" For example, one doctor who fought successfully to ban smoking in workplaces to protect the health of nonsmokers (a stand that could be seen as supporting the utilitarian value of the highest good for the most people) argued for a more libertarian view when it came to banning smoking outside. Dr. Michael Siegel "wrote dozens of scientific articles on the dangers of secondhand smoke. His testimony in court and at countless city council meetings helped push public policy toward tighter restrictions on smoking."[1] However, in 2007, Siegel and others who fought hard to get rid of smoking in the workplace objected to similar attempts to ban smoking outdoors. As scientists, they did not believe that the claim that smoking outdoors causes the same secondhand smoke problems that justified the indoor smoking ban was convincing. In speaking of the zeal and success of the antismoking campaigns, Siegel stated, "It's getting to the point where we're trying to protect people from something that's not a public health hazard." At risk, he and other like-minded tobacco control advocates assert, is not only the credibility of public health officials, but also the undermining of a freedom prized in democracies—do as you wish as long as you don't harm others.[2]

Siegel was a strong and effective advocate for creating smoke-free indoor workplaces on utilitarian grounds; he drew the line—on libertarian grounds—when antismoking groups tried to ban smoking outside. In taking his stand, he showed that people with different priorities can solve problems by drawing lines in which conflicting values can be reconciled with a workable compromise. In this case, Siegel believes that the desires of both smokers and nonsmokers can be met without compromising public health.

Many laws also reflect an attempt to "draw the line" in a way that incorporates several value assumptions. One such law was enacted in 1997 in Texas to help state universities reconcile the conflicting goals of admitting high-achieving students from excellent high schools and also honoring and encouraging hard-working, bright students from disadvantaged backgrounds. The value conflicts and priorities represented by the decision to admit the top 10 percent of students from every high school in the state are detailed in an article at the end of this chapter.

[1]"Outdoor Smoking Bans Rile Anti-Tobacco Leader" Randy Myers and Suzanne Bohan. *Contra Costa Times,* January 5, 2007.
[2]Ibid.

SKILL

A critical thinker is aware of his or her value priorities and how they affect dialogue and decision making. (See Exercise 2.2 on p. 47.)

IDEAL VALUES VERSUS REAL VALUES

Men acquire a particular quality by constantly acting in a particular way.

Aristotle

Ethical behavior is easier to discuss than it is to carry out. We have complex needs and emotions, and situations are also complicated. Even with good intentions, we sometimes find it difficult to make ethical choices.

Because of the effort involved in living up to our standards, most of us can make a distinction between our ideal values and our real values. An **ideal value** is *a value that you believe to be right and good*. A **real value** is *a value that you believe to be right and good and consistently act upon in your life*. As critical thinkers, it is important for us to understand and be honest about our own behavior and to distinguish our words from our actions.

People may say they value good citizenship; they believe people should be informed about candidates and issues and express their viewpoints by voting, but they may continue to vote without studying issues and candidates. In some cases, the value of citizenship is only an ideal. For the value to be real, it must be carried out in the life of the individual claiming it as a value.

The more that our values become an integral part of our identities, the easier they are to act upon when we face tough decisions. For example, people in positions of leadership have to make decisions that impact others, sometimes for decades to come, and the way they view themselves guides their choices. Abraham Lincoln was on an extensive 12-day train journey to Washington, DC, to take his place as the sixteenth president of the United States, and he arrived 10 days before his inauguration. He was offered wonderful private accommodations from several prominent leaders but instead chose to stay at the Willard Hotel, close to the White House, stating, "The truth is, I suppose I am now public property; and a public inn is the place where people can have access to me."[3] Lincoln's view of himself as belonging to and representing the best interests of the public helped him make decisions that were consistent with his ideal values.

Lincoln had had strong and capable opponents in the campaign that led to his securing the Republican presidential nomination. His opponents had been as negative in their rhetoric about Lincoln as today's rivals are when they compete for political nominations. However, when he chose a cabinet, Lincoln did not seek "yes-men" who supported his own beliefs and who were happy that he had won the election. Instead, he chose his strongest enemies to become leaders in his cabinet.

[3]Doris Kearns Goodwin, *Team of Rivals* (New York: Simon & Schuster, 2005), p. 312.

In fact, as John Nicolay later wrote, Lincoln's "first decision was one of great courage and self-reliance." Each of his rivals was "sure to feel that the wrong man had been nominated." A less confident man might have surrounded himself with personal supporters who would never question his authority; James Buchanan, for example, had deliberately chosen men who thought as he did.

Later, Joseph Medill of the Chicago Tribune asked Lincoln why he had chosen a cabinet composed of enemies and opponents. He particularly questioned the president's selection of the three men who had been his chief rivals for the Republican nomination, each of whom was still smarting from the loss.

Lincoln's answer was simple, straightforward, and shrewd: "We needed the strongest men of the party in the Cabinet. We needed to hold our own people together. I had looked the party over and concluded that these were the very strongest men. Then I had no right to deprive the country of their services."[4]

In our public and professional lives, we are seen as having integrity when we act upon our ideal values. In our personal lives, we also encounter choices that challenge us to act upon our ideal values and to make them consistent with our actions. Consider the following dialogue:

> Stephanie, 21, is a virgin and had planned to stay that way until she's married. But now she finds herself very attracted to somebody...did I say "very"? She'd hoped that her values, the rules, would protect her from temptation. Now she is set adrift without a paddle because she discovered that values don't function like an automatic, invisible protective shield.
>
> "Just in case I start dating him, do you have any advice on how to stay a virgin?"
>
> "You mean you have values until temptations ride into town; then the values sneak out during the night? The town ain't big enough for both values and temptations. Values keep us steady through times of deep temptation. They are our road map through the minefields of challenge. It is easy to say you have values and easier still to live up to them when you're by yourself in the middle of the ocean."
>
> "That's true."
>
> "Values are truly only shown to exist when they are tested. If it is meaningful for you to reserve sexual intimacy for marital vows, if you feel that doing so elevates sex and you, that is admirable."
>
> "Yeah, but how do you make the values do their thing to keep you from doing something else?"
>
> "Values only have the power you infuse into them with your respect for them and yourself, and your will. Values without temptations are merely lofty ideas. Expediting them is what makes you, and them, special. That requires grit, will, sacrifice, courage, and discomfort.

---

[4]Ibid., pp. 318–319.

But it is in the difficulty that both the values and you gain importance. The measure of you as a human being is how you honor the values.

"When you begin dating him, clarify your position of intercourse only within marriage. If he tries to push you away from that position, you know he values you only as a means of sexual gratification. If he gets seductive and you're lubricating from your eyeballs to your ankles, this is the moment when you choose between momentary pleasure and long-term self-respect."

"That is the real choice I'm making at that point, isn't it?"

There is no fast lane to self-esteem. It's won on these battle-grounds where immediate gratification goes up against character. When character triumphs, self-esteem heightens.

One caller asked, "What if I'm too weak?" I answered that the road to unhappiness and low self-esteem is paved with the victories of immediate gratification.[5]

(handwritten margin note: immediate gratification = short term happiness)

SKILL

A critical thinker can compare and contrast ideals with actual practices. (See Exercise 2.3 on p. 48.)

ETHICS IN ARGUMENTATION

> *It is terrible to speak well and be wrong.*
>
> Sophocles, *Electra* (c. 418–414 B.C.)

Ethical concerns are central to any message. Those who seek to influence votes, sales, or the personal decisions of others need to

- Be honest about their conclusions and reasons
- Not leave out or distort important information
- Thoroughly research any claims they make
- Listen with respect, if not agreement, to opposing viewpoints
- Be willing to revise a position when better information becomes available
- Give credit to secondary sources of information (See Exercise 2.4 on p. 48.)

ETHICAL DECISION MAKING

> *Every man takes care that his neighbor shall not cheat him. But a day comes when he begins to care that he does not cheat his neighbor. Then all goes well.*
>
> Ralph Waldo Emerson, "Worship,"
> *The Conduct of Life* (1860)

[5]Dr. Laura Schlessinger, *How Could You Do That?* (New York: HarperCollins Publishers, Inc., 1996), pp. 151–152.

The first step in clearheaded decision making is knowing your principles and standards. In considering difficult decisions, several "tests" can be useful to apply to your known principles. These tests can help you assess how well your decision adheres to your standards.

1. The Role Exchange Test. The **role exchange test** asks you to empathize with the people who will be affected by the action you take. You try to see the situation from their point of view. You ask yourself how the others affected by your decision would feel and what consequences they would face.

You also ask whether it would be right for the other person to take the action if you were going to be the one experiencing the consequences of the decision. Using your imagination, you change places with the person or persons who would receive the effects of your decision. In short, you decide to treat the other person as you would want to be treated in his or her place.

For example, you see your brother's girlfriend out with other men. You hesitate to tell him because of the hurt it would cause and because you feel it's not really your business to interfere. However, when you do the role exchange test, you decide to tell him because you realize you would want to know if you were in his situation.

2. The Universal Consequences Test. The **universal consequences test** focuses on the general results (consequences) of an action you might take. You imagine what would happen if everyone in a situation similar to yours took this action. Would the results be acceptable?

Under the universal consequences test, if you would find it unacceptable for everyone in a similar situation to take this action, then you would reject the action.

For example, imagine that you are asked to join a community program for recycling cans, bottles, and paper. You enjoy the freedom of just throwing everything together in the trash, but you stop and assess the consequences if everyone refused to recycle. Your assessment causes you to join the program.

3. The New Cases Test. The **new cases test** asks you to consider whether your action is consistent with other actions that are in the same category. You choose the hardest case you can and see if you would act the same way in that case as you plan to act in this one. If you would, then your decision is consistent with your principles.

For example, you are deciding whether to vote to continue experiments that may be successful in finding a cure for AIDS but involve injecting animals with the HIV virus. Your principle is that cruelty to animals is not justified in any circumstance. To formulate a new, harder case, you might ask yourself if you would allow the research to be conducted if it would save your life or the life of your child. If you would, then you might reconsider your voting decision and reassess your principles.

Another example involves the issue of whether a photographer should turn over negatives to the police if it would help detectives identify and prosecute murder suspects (see the article at the end of this chapter about this dilemma). You may believe that freedom of the press cannot be compromised and, therefore, the photographer should be able to keep the negatives out of the investigation. Using the new cases test, imagine that someone you love dearly was the murder victim and that these photographs are the link to catching the murderer. Would that knowledge change your value priorities in this case?

✳*4. The Higher Principles Test.* The **higher principles test** asks you to determine if the principle on which you are basing your action is consistent with a higher or more general principle you accept.

For example, let's say your roommates are not doing their share of the housework so you are considering not doing your own share. However, because you value promise keeping and integrity, you realize that it is important to keep your part of the bargain regardless of whether they are doing their part. You decide to keep doing your share and to talk with them about keeping their part of the agreement. (See Exercise 2.5 on p. 49.)

SKILL

A critical thinker uses ethical standards in argumentation and decision making.

When we make ethical decisions, the actions we take are congruent with our values. When our actions go against what we believe is right, we are prone to rationalize our behavior, rather than to admit we are not always ethical. Consider the following list of common rationalizations used to justify unethical conduct.

COMMON RATIONALIZATIONS

Ethics in Action

I. **"If It's Necessary, It's Ethical."** Based on the false assumption that necessity breeds propriety. Necessity is an interpretation not a fact. But even actual necessity does not justify unethical conduct. Leads to ends-justify-the-means reasoning and treating assigned tasks or desired goals as moral imperatives.

II. **"If It's Legal and Permissible, It's Proper."** Substitutes legal requirements (which establish minimal standards of behavior) for personal moral judgment. Does not embrace full range of ethical obligations, especially for those involved in upholding the public trust. Ethical people often choose to do less than they are allowed to do and more than they are required to do.

III. **"I Was Just Doing It for You."** Primary justification of "white lies" or withholding important information in personal or professional relationships, especially performance reviews. Dilemma: honesty and respect vs. caring. Dangers: Violates principle of respect for others (implies a moral right to make decisions about one's own life based on true information), ignores underlying self-interest of liar, and underestimates uncertainty about other person's desires to be "protected" (most people would rather have unpleasant information than be deluded into believing something that isn't so). Consider perspective of persons lied to: If they discovered the lie, would they thank you for being considerate or feel betrayed, patronized or manipulated?

IV. **"I'm Just Fighting Fire with Fire."** Based on false assumption that deceit, lying, promise-breaking, etc. are justified if they are the same sort engaged in by those you are dealing with.

V. **"It Doesn't Hurt Anyone."** Rationalization used to excuse misconduct based on the false assumption that one can violate ethical principles so long as there is no clear and immediate harm to others. It treats ethical obligations simply as factors to be considered in decision making rather than ground rules. Problem areas: Asking for or giving special favors to family, friends or politicians, disclosing nonpublic information to benefit others, using one's position for personal advantages (e.g., use of official title/letterhead to get special treatment).

VI. **"It Can't Be Wrong, Everyone's Doing It."** A false "safety in numbers" rationale fed by the tendency to uncritically adopt cultural, organizational or occupational behavior systems as if they were ethical.

VII. **"It's OK if I Don't Gain Personally."** Justifies improper conduct done for others or for institutional purposes on the false assumption that personal gain is the only test of impropriety. A related more narrow excuse is that only behavior resulting in improper *financial gain* warrants ethical criticism.

VIII. **"I've Got It Coming."** Persons who feel they are overworked or underpaid rationalize that minor "perks" or acceptance of favors, discounts, or gratuities are nothing more than fair compensation for services rendered. Also used to excuse all manner of personnel policy abuses (re: sick days, insurance claims, overtime, personal phone calls or photocopying, theft of supplies, etc.).

IX. **"I Can Still Be Objective."** Ignores the fact that a loss of objectivity always prevents perception of the loss of objectivity. Also underestimates the subtle ways in which gratitude, friendship, anticipation of future favors and the like affect judgment. Does the person providing you with the benefit believe that it will in no way affect your judgment? Would the benefit still be provided if you were in no position to help the provider in any way?

From *Ethics in Action,* January–February 1991. Reprinted by permission of the Joseph and Edna Josephson Institute of Ethics, www.josephsoninstitute.org.

STOP AND THINK

Are there situations you can think of in which something may be legal but is not ethical? What about situations in which something is not legal but is ethical?

Examples of the Common Rationalizations

I. If it's necessary, it's ethical. "I need to have three years experience to get this job, so I'll put that on my resume, even though I only have two years."

II. If it's legal and permissible, it's proper. "Since my parents are divorced, my mom claims me on her income tax. Even though my dad makes a huge salary and also supports me, the state only counts my mom's salary in figuring out my college funding, so the state pays for my entire tuition, room, and board. It's probably not fair to take the money that other students need, but that's the law."

THE FAR SIDE® BY GARY LARSON

"Wait a minute, Stan. ... These are good hubcaps. If we don't take 'em, it's a cinch some other bears will."

III. I was just doing it for you. "I didn't tell you that your boyfriend/girlfriend was cheating on you because I didn't want you to feel bad."

IV. I'm just fighting fire with fire. "My roommate took my jacket without asking, so I'm taking his camera."

V. It doesn't hurt anyone. "My sister wrote my essay for the online class, but that doesn't hurt anyone else."

VI. It can't be wrong, everyone's doing it. "Lots of people are leaving work early, so why shouldn't I?"

VII. It's OK if I don't gain personally. "When my shift was over, I took some pizzas from the restaurant to give to some kids who were playing on the street."

VIII. I've got it coming. "I don't get paid what I think I'm worth, so I spend time at work to catch up on my email."

IX. I can still be objective. "It's okay for me to receive expensive gifts from people in my district. That won't affect how I vote on their concerns."(See Exercise 2.6 on p. 50.)

LIFE APPLICATION: TIPS FOR COLLEGE AND CAREER

When you find yourself involved in a heated discussion or debate notice if different value assumptions are held on both sides of the issue. If possible, point these out and show the importance of clarifying the different values in order to increase understanding.

When expressing your own views, be aware of the value assumptions held by others that may differ from your own. If you are trying to persuade people who have different value assumptions than you do, acknowledge and show respect (if possible) for the values they may have and explain why you give a higher priority to different values. If they see that you understand their viewpoints, they are more likely to give a fair hearing to yours.

CHAPTER EXERCISES

Exercise 2.1   Purpose: To examine other value systems and how they affect decision making.

1. Examine a value system such as those given in the previous section on ethics. You might study the principles of a specific religion or a political philosophy, such as Christianity, Buddhism, or socialism. Try to list the value assumptions and principles for that system and include examples of how belief in the system affects decision making.

2. Note any similarities or differences between the system you have studied and the other systems listed on page 36. Share your findings with the class.

Exercise 2.2 *Purposes:* To discover how policy debates are influenced by ethical standards. To discover personal standards and principles that determine how ethical dilemmas are resolved.

1. Consider the systems of ethics discussed in this chapter. Individually, or in groups, come up with examples of situations in which the principles of one of these systems clash with the principles of another. You may want to bring in recent local or campus controversies, such as the one detailed on page 55 of the Articles for Discussion.

    Discuss the conflicting value principles represented by your examples.

2. Consider your own definition of ethical behavior; it may fit into one of the ethical schools of thought outlined in this chapter, or it may be a combination of several approaches. Then, using your own principles, try to be completely "ethical" for one week. As often as possible, ask yourself, "What is the best way to respond to this situation?" Keep a daily record of your ethical challenges. Then, report your successes and failures in dealing with these situations.

    Here are some examples of common ethical dilemmas: Should you defend a friend who is being criticized by another friend? Should you give money to a homeless person who approaches you? Should you tell the truth to someone even if it hurts his or her feelings? Should you tell your instructor that several students cheated on a test while she answered a knock at the classroom door? Should you tell callers your roommate isn't home if she asks you to? Should you complain about rude treatment in a store? Should you copy a friend's CD of your favorite music rather than buying your own copy?

    Your own situations will be unique. If time permits, share some ethical dilemmas that you have encountered with the rest of the class.

3. Consider the following situations alone or with a group:

    a. You and your friend are taking the same required history class; you are taking it on Mondays and Wednesdays and your friend is taking it Tuesday evening. You have given up much of your social life to study for this class because the tests are hard. One Monday after the midterm, your friend calls you and wants to know what was on the test since he partied too hard over the weekend and didn't study. You have a good memory and could tell him many of the questions. Do you tell him what was on the test?

    b. You go to a garage sale and notice a diamond ring that is being sold for $10. You know that the ring is worth far more than that. What do you do?

    c. The manager of the fast-food restaurant where you work is selling food that is not fresh or prepared according to the standards of the company. You have complained to her, but she has done nothing despite your complaints. You need this job and the location, hours, and pay are perfect for you; in fact, this boss has tailored your working hours to your class schedule. Nevertheless, you are concerned about public safety. What do you do?

d. You are a member of a city council and you have a serious problem of homelessness in your city. A business owner offers you $100,000 in aid for the homeless if you will let him build an office building over a popular park. How do you vote?

Exercise 2.3   Purpose: To understand the difference between ideal and real values.

List five of your ideal values and five of your real values.

1. Describe what it would take for these ideal values to become real values for you. Think about why you have not made these ideal values real in your life.

2. Then explain what changes in your habits and your priorities would be involved in order for these values to become real for you.

Example

"One of my ideal values is physical fitness. I believe it is important for everyone to keep his or her body strong through exercise and good eating habits.

"As a student, I don't take the time to exercise every day or even every other day. Since I quit the swim team, I hardly exercise at all. When I do have spare time, I sleep or go out with my girlfriend. Also, I eat a lot of fast foods or canned foods because I don't cook.

"For this ideal value to become real for me, I would have to graduate and have more time. Or, I would have to make the time to exercise. The best way would be to combine going out with my girlfriend with exercising. She likes to skate and play basketball, so we could do that together. Getting more exercise is a real possibility. Eating right is probably not going to happen soon. I would have to learn to cook or to marry someone who would cook for me. At this point in my life, I can't see how I could have a healthier diet, even though it is an ideal for me. But it's just not important enough for me to change at this time."

Exercise 2.4   Purpose: To examine the ethical dimensions of an argument.

Listen to a political speech or a sales pitch, or read an editorial essay. Then evaluate the message, stating whether the writer or speaker met the criteria given for ethical argumentation.

You might also use one of your own essays or speeches; analyze it to see whether you were as honest as you could have been and whether you credited secondary sources of information.

Exercise 2.5   Purpose: To be able to utilize tests for ethical decision making.

Option one: Think about an ethical dilemma you have faced or are facing. If you did the exercise on acting ethically for a week, you may have a recent example. You may also use the examples listed in that exercise. In addition, you might consider a difficult ethical dilemma from your past. Then follow the directions given here.

Option two: Think about an ethical dilemma your community or nation is facing; you might also consider an international ethical dilemma. Some examples include the use of scientific information gained by Nazi experimentation on Holocaust victims, the apportionment of funds to poverty-stricken nations, the exporting of cigarettes to other nations, and the rationing of health care. Then follow the directions.

1. On your own or in class groups, take the dilemma through each of the four tests. Write about what each test tells you about the course your decision should take.

2. Come to a conclusion about the decision. Justify your conclusion by referring to the cumulative results of the tests.

Example

My friend helped me get a job at his company and, after only a few months, I was told that he and I were both being considered for a promotion to management. He worked at the job for a year and he's getting married soon, so he really needs this job. I wouldn't even have known about the possibility of working there if he hadn't told me about it and arranged an interview for me. The dilemma: Should I take the promotion if it's offered to me or refuse it, knowing that it will then go to him?

The role exchange test asks me to look at the situation from his point of view. It would hurt him in two ways if I took this promotion: Mainly, he would lose the income and the chance for advancement that go with this position. Also, he would be hurt because he helped me get this job, and then I took a promotion he might have had. There's nothing wrong with my looking out for my own future; but in this case, it would be at his expense.

The universal consequences test asks me to look at general consequences of my decision and determine if it would be acceptable for everyone in this situation to take a similar action. A positive general consequence might be that all of the best people would be given promotions regardless of who needs the promotion most. The negative general consequence would be that people would routinely put their own desires ahead of what might be more fair and what might be best for other people, a "me-first" mentality.

The new cases test asks me to pick the hardest case I can and see if I would act the same way in that case, to determine whether I am consistent. To me, the hardest case would be if my parent would be given the promotion if I didn't take it. I don't live with my parents anymore, but I would step down if it meant that either of them could have the promotion.

The higher principles test asks me to look at my own ethical standards to see if my actions fit into those standards. This test is hard to use, because I value both my own advancement and my friend's welfare. But I can find the higher principle of fairness; I don't feel that it would be fair for me to take a job that he would have had since he is the person responsible for my being in the position to take it.

In conclusion, I won't take this job if it is offered to me. It would be hurtful to my friend who cared enough about me to help me get a job. Also, I wouldn't want to live in a world where people always climbed over one another to achieve success. If it were my parents, I wouldn't take a job that they wanted, even if it would benefit me personally. Finally, I believe in the principle of fairness, and I don't think it would be fair to take a promotion from a friend who gave me the opportunity to work for his company.

Exercise 2.6   Purpose: To understand common rationalizations used to excuse unethical behavior and to see how these apply to specific cases.

1. Give examples for each of the rationalizations presented earlier. For example, for I. If it's necessary, it's ethical, you might cite unethical behavior on the part of campaign managers carried out to ensure the election of their candidate.

2. Try to come up with a variety of situations—personal, social, and political—in which these rationalizations are used. If the class is doing this exercise in groups, share the examples with the entire class.

    Consider whether you rationalize any of your behavior in the ways mentioned on Josephson's list of common rationalizations.

3. Look for examples of people and groups facing ethical dilemmas that stick to their ethical positions, even at great cost, as in the following example.

SALVATION ARMY TURNS DOWN $100,000 DONATION

Salvation Army spurns $100K donation as gambling money. Marco Island, Fla.—The Salvation Army will not accept a $100,000 donation from a Florida Lotto winner because its local leader didn't want to take money associated with gambling.

David Rush, 71, announced the gift last week. He held one of four winning tickets in the $100 million Florida Lotto jackpot drawing of December 14 and took a $14.3 million lump-sum payment.

Major Cleo Damon, head of the Salvation Army office in Naples, told Rush that he could not take his money and returned the check, which another official had accepted.

"There are times where Major Damon is counseling families who are about to become homeless because of gambling," said spokeswoman Maribeth Shanahan. "He really believes that if he had accepted the money, he would be talking out of both sides of his mouth."

January 2, 2003, Associated Press, Contra Costa Times.

CHAPTER HIGHLIGHTS

1. Value assumptions are beliefs about what is good and important or bad and unimportant; because these beliefs are taken for granted, they are part of the foundation of a person's argument.

2. Conflicts between value assumptions need to be addressed before fruitful discussions over value-saturated conclusions can take place.

3. Ethics are standards of conduct that reflect values.

4. There are several schools of thought about ethics, including libertarianism, utilitarianism, egalitarianism, religious principles, and prima facie norms.

5. Ideal values are held by an individual in a theoretical sense; real values are held theoretically and also practiced.

6. Ethics are evident in our behavior as we advocate for ideas and make decisions.

7. Several tests have been developed to help people make ethical decisions. These include the role exchange test, the universal consequences test, the new cases test, and the higher principles test.

8. Ethical decision making is undermined when common rationalizations are used to support unethical practices.

KEY TERMS

Claims (p. 29)
Reasons (p. 29)
Warrants (p. 29)
Backing (p. 30)
Values (p. 32)
Value assumptions (p. 32)
Value conflicts (p. 32)
Value prioritization (p. 33)
Ethics (p. 36)
Morals (p. 36)
Libertarianism (p. 36)

Utilitarianism (p. 36)
Egalitarianism (p. 36)
Religious values (p. 36)
Prima facie values (p. 36)
Ideal value (p. 39)
Real value (p. 39)
Role exchange test (p. 42)
Universal consequences test (p. 42)
New cases test (p. 42)
Higher principles test (p. 43)

CHAPTER CHECKUP

Short Answer

1. Using an example, explain value conflicts.

2. Why is it important to examine value assumptions before discussing issues in which values are involved?

3. What are some ethical principles to be used in argumentation?

4. What is the difference between an ideal value and a real value?

Matching

A. libertarianism	D. role exchange test
B. utilitarianism	E. new cases test
C. egalitarianism	F. universal consequences test

5. A test that asks you to empathize with the people who will be affected by any action you take

6. A belief system in which behavior is considered most ethical when it allows for individual freedom

7. A belief system that claims behavior to be ethical when the same opportunities and consequences apply to all people

8. A test that asks you to consider whether your action is consistent with other actions in the same category

9. A belief system that claims the highest value is that which promotes the greatest general happiness and minimizes unhappiness

10. Under this test, if you find it unacceptable for everyone in a similar situation to take this action, then you would reject the action.

ARTICLES FOR DISCUSSION

In this first article, Rick Reilly, who writes a column for *Sports Illustrated*, asks his readers to think about how they would have coached a particular game; as it turns out, the coaches' decisions set off a firestorm in a local community. Your answer will reveal your own value priorities and could lead to some interesting class discussions. For a fascinating exploration of this topic, go to the *Sports Illustrated* Web site, and see what other readers had to say.

YOU MAKE THE CALL

Is It Good Baseball Strategy or a Weak Attempt to Win?

Rick Reilly

This actually happened. Your job is to decide whether it should have.

In a nine- and 10-year-old PONY league championship game in Bountiful, Utah, the Yankees lead the Red Sox by one run. The Sox are up in the bottom of the last inning, two outs, a runner on third. At the plate is the

Sox' best hitter, a kid named Jordan. On deck is the Sox' worst hitter, a kid named Romney. He's a scrawny cancer survivor who has to take human growth hormone and has a shunt in his brain.

So, you're the coach: Do you intentionally walk the star hitter so you can face the kid who can barely swing?

Wait! Before you answer. . . . This is a league where everybody gets to bat, there's a four-runs-per-inning max, and no stealing until the ball crosses the plate. On the other hand, the stands are packed and it is the title game.

So . . . do you pitch to the star or do you lay it all on the kid who's been through hell already?

Yanks coach Bob Farley decided to walk the star.

Parents booed. The umpire, Mike Wright, thought to himself, Low-ball move. In the stands, Romney's eight-year-old sister cried. "They're picking on Romney!" she said. Romney struck out. The Yanks celebrated. The Sox moaned. The two coaching staffs nearly brawled.

And Romney? He sobbed himself to sleep that night.

"It made me sick," says Romney's dad, Marlo Oaks. "It's going after the weakest chick in the flock."

Farley and his assistant coach, Shaun Farr, who recommended the walk, say they didn't know Romney was a cancer survivor. "And even if I had," insists Farr, "I'd have done the same thing. It's just good baseball strategy."

Romney's mom, Elaine, thinks Farr knew. "Romney's cancer was in the paper when he met with President Bush," she says. That was thanks to the Make-A-Wish people. "And [Farr] coached Romney in basketball. I tell all his coaches about his condition."

She has to. Because of his radiation treatments, Romney's body may not produce enough of a stress-responding hormone if he is seriously injured, so he has to quickly get a cortisone shot or it could be life threatening. That's why he wears a helmet even in centerfield. Farr didn't notice?

The sports editor for the local Davis Clipper, Ben De Voe, ripped the Yankees' decision. "Hopefully these coaches enjoy the trophy on their mantle," De Voe wrote, "right next to their dunce caps."

Well, that turned Bountiful into Rancorful. The town was split—with some people calling for De Voe's firing and describing Farr and Farley as "great men," while others called the coaches "pathetic human beings." They "should be tarred and feathered," one man wrote to De Voe. Blogs and letters pages howled. A state house candidate called it "shameful."

What the Yankees' coaches did was within the rules. But is it right to put winning over compassion? For that matter, does a kid who yearns to be treated like everybody else want compassion?

"What about the boy who is dyslexic—should he get special treatment?" Blaine and Kris Smith wrote to the Clipper. "The boy who wears glasses—should he never be struck out? . . . NO! They should all play by the rules of the game."

The Yankees' coaches insisted that the Sox coach would've done the same thing. "Not only wouldn't I have," says Sox coach Keith Gulbransen, "I didn't. When their best hitter came up, I pitched to him. I especially wouldn't have done it to Romney."

Farr thinks the Sox coach is a hypocrite. He points out that all coaches put their worst fielder in right field and try to steal on the weakest catchers. "Isn't that strategy?" he asks. "Isn't that trying to win? Do we let the kid feel like he's a winner by having the whole league play easy on him? This isn't the Special Olympics. He's not retarded."

Me? I think what the Yanks did stinks. Strategy is fine against major leaguers, but not against a little kid with a tube in his head. Just good baseball strategy? This isn't the pros. This is: Everybody bats, one-hour games. That means it's about fun. Period.

What the Yankees' coaches did was make it about them, not the kids. It became their medal to pin on their pecs and show off at their barbecues. And if a fragile kid got stomped on the way, well, that's baseball. We see it all over the country—the over-caffeinated coach who watches too much Sports Center and needs to win far more than the kids, who will forget about it two Dove bars later.

By the way, the next morning, Romney woke up and decided to do something about what happened to him.

"I'm going to work on my batting," he told his dad. "Then maybe someday I'll be the one they walk."

Sports Illustrated, August 14, 2006. Copyright © 2006 by Time, Inc. Reprinted by Permission of Time, Inc.

QUESTIONS FOR DISCUSSION

1. What is the value conflict illustrated by the decision the coaches had to make in this case?
2. What are the various arguments given for the decision by the coaches, the opposing team coaches, the parents, the local journalists, and Rick Reilly?
3. What do you think the best call would be in a case like this? What does your decision say about your value priorities?

The following article illustrates a strong ethical dilemma that faces both campus newspapers and other forms of media. In this case, a murder was committed on campus and a newspaper photographer took pictures of the scene. The police wanted these pictures to help them identify the suspects; the photographer did not want to turn his work over to the police because he believed that would compromise the freedom of the press. Can you see that this issue involves a conflict between libertarianism (freedom of the press) versus utilitarianism (the police concern about promoting the general welfare by identifying and prosecuting criminals)?

STAFFER GETS SUBPOENAED

Steve Logan

Police services Lt. Paul Lee delivered a subpoena to *Advocate* photographer Soren Hemmila Thursday morning to appear in Superior Court in Martinez at 1:30 P.M. Tuesday.

Lee delivered the subpoena through District Attorney William Clark and the San Pablo Police Department in connection with photographs taken of the scene after Christopher Robinson's murder on campus September 25.

Hemmila and the *Advocate* have refused to turn over unpublished photos, taken shortly after the murder, to the San Pablo Police Department.

California's shield law is designed to help news organizations protect sources and information from outside forces, including law enforcement agencies. The law also states a journalist cannot be held in contempt of court for refusing to turn over unpublished work.

Hemmila believes the photographs are protected by the shield law.

The *West County Times* reported Thursday that San Pablo police believe the photos could give them important information in prosecuting the case of the three suspects who have already been taken into custody and charged with Robinson's murder.

Hemmila said he arrived on the crime scene just as the police were putting up yellow tape. Among the photographs taken, but not published, [were] shots of the crowd in the background.

Hemmila said San Pablo Det. Mark Harrison first came to ask for the negatives "nicely," on Monday.

"I don't like being part of the investigation in this case," Hemmila said Thursday after receiving the subpoena. "I'm willing to do what it takes to protect our rights."

The subpoena said the photographs will be helpful to the police in three ways. Section one said the credibility of an eyewitness who commented in last Friday's story which ran in the *Advocate* needs to be evaluated.

Section two said the photographs will show the crime scene closer to the time of the shooting, which will allow the prosecution to evaluate the weight of the physical evidence which included expended casings at the scene.

Section three said the photographs may show whether the attack was "planned, a surprise attack, or a chance encounter that turned violent."

Hemmila said it would set a bad precedent if the *Advocate* turned over the photos.

"If we make it a [practice] to turn over the negatives to police agencies, they'll expect it in the future and they'll expect it from other publications.

"I don't want the public to think that journalists are part of law enforcement or acting in their behalf."

The Advocate, October 11, 1996. Reprinted by permission of the publisher.

1. The subpoena argued that photographs were necessary to the investigation because they may show whether the attack was "planned, a surprise attack, or a chance encounter that turned violent." If the knowledge gained from the photographs would show that the crime had been planned, would it justify turning them over?

2. Hemmila was concerned about setting a bad precedent if the *Advocate* turned over the photos. What would that precedent be and would you consider it a bad precedent?

3. Although many states have shield laws that protect journalists from releasing information and sources, there is no federal law in place. In recent years, journalists have asked the U.S. Congress to create a national shield law to protect photographs, notes, and anonymous sources. Supporters of such a law are concerned that the ability to gather sensitive information would be weakened without this protection. Those opposed to such legislation are concerned about the need to find out about issues affecting national security, such as imminent terrorist threats; they are also concerned, in an age of bloggers, that almost anyone could call him- or herself a journalist and thus receive special protection.

    Some news agencies frown upon the use of anonymous sources because almost any claim can be made by quoting them. The Associated Press policy allows the use of anonymous sources only when the material is information—not someone's opinion—that is essential to the report and when the source will give the information only if he or she is protected. In addition, the source must be reliable.

    What do you think about national shield laws; what legislation, if any, should be enacted?

The following is an interview from National Public Radio's *Weekend Edition.* The interviewees were Dr. Michael Wilkes and medical ethics specialist Dr. Miriam Shuchman. The interviewer is identified as Liane. They are discussing whether it is ethical to prescribe a placebo and pretend it is a healing drug if it actually makes the patient feel better.

NATIONAL PUBLIC RADIO

Liane: Michael, have you ever been tempted to be less than perfectly honest with a patient?

Michael: Absolutely. There's always that temptation, Liane. Telling the truth in medicine is one of the most difficult things to do. There is an issue that came up recently when another physician suggested that I prescribe a placebo, or sugar pill that had no biologic effects, for a patient. A 70-year-old man had just moved to town, and he came to see me to get a refill of a prescription for a sleeping pill that he'd been given for a long time. In fact, it turned out he's been taking the pill every night since his wife died several years ago. As I spoke with him, it became clear to me that he recognized that he was addicted to the sleeping medicine. In fact, he said he wanted to stop, but every time he tried to stop taking the medicine, he couldn't sleep and ended up taking a sleeping pill. Now, a doctor at the hospital suggested that I use a placebo. He said that he'd had great luck using this kind of placebo for exactly these types of addictions. The problem was that there was no way that I could use the placebo without deceiving the patient. So the issue here for me was whether doctors are justified in telling these little white lies in order to benefit the patient.

Liane: Miriam, as an ethics specialist, what do you say? What does medical ethics tell us is right in this situation?

Miriam: Well, I think the conflict for the doctor here is that he's really seeing two duties. One is not to lie to a patient, and the other is to always do what's beneficial for the patient, not to do harm. So, in this case, the doctor who suggested the placebo may think that it's most beneficial to prescribe the placebo, it won't have any side effects, and the little white lie he thinks is not as important.

Liane: So, should people be concerned that when they go to their doctor that the doctor might be prescribing a placebo?

Miriam: Absolutely not. First of all, the use of placebos in clinical practice is very rare. They're mostly used in research where people are told they're going to be receiving a placebo. And second, there are doctrines and policies around this. It's called informed consent, and what it means is that before a patient can agree to a given treatment or procedure, the doctor is obliged to inform them about the risks and benefits of that treatment, and most doctors are aware of that.

Michael: You know, it's probably worth mentioning here that experts feel that about 30 percent of the medicines that we currently prescribe really have no biologic activity. They work through the power of suggestion. Cough medicines are a great example of this sort of drug. Now that doesn't mean that cough medicines don't work. What I'm trying to suggest is that they work through an effect on the mind rather than on the body, say, on the diaphragm or in the lung tissue or muscles themselves. Anyway, I feel there are too many times when doctors aren't being truthful with patients because they feel they know what's best for the patient.

Liane: We talked about placebos, but what about lying? How often do doctors lie to their patients?

Miriam: Liane, I can't give you a statistic on that, but I don't think it happens very often. Doctors don't intentionally mislead their patients. But what does happen is that patients aren't given the information they really need to make decisions. Doctors don't give them the chance to ask the questions that would get them that information.

Liane: Michael, what happened to the man who was hooked on the sleeping pill?

Michael: Liane, we talked about it for a long time at the hospital. The bottom line was I chose not to use a placebo. The downside of that decision is that the man is still addicted to the medicine although I'm slowly weaning him off by using some behavior modification techniques.

Liane: *Weekend Edition* medical commentators Drs. Michael Wilkes and Miriam Shuchman.

"WESUN—Physician's Candor vs. Patient's Interest" by Liane Hansen, broadcast 11/8/92. Reprinted by permission of National Public Radio, Inc.

QUESTIONS FOR DISCUSSION

1. What is the value conflict discussed by the doctors in this excerpt?

2. Do you believe there are times when a doctor should withhold the truth from a patient? Why or why not?

3. Dr. Miriam Shuchman said that doctors don't give patients the chance to ask the questions that would inform them more fully about their conditions. To what extent do you believe doctors should ensure that patients understand the seriousness of the illnesses they have?

In recent years, peanut allergies have been increasing and can have deadly consequences for those who are affected by them. As a result, school districts have been grappling with how to keep allergic children safe without imposing massive restrictions on nonallergic peanut butter lovers. The controversy has sparked debate in communities across the United States and Canada. The following article details how the problem is seen in one Connecticut school.

PEANUT ALLERGIES PIT PARENT AGAINST PARENT IN SCHOOL DEBATE

Brigitte Greenberg, Associated Press

ELLINGTON, CONN.—For eight-year-old Tim Larew, a sudden and horrible death lurks in one of the most popular of childhood snacks: a peanut butter-and-jelly sandwich. "It's devastating to know that what the average child eats on a daily basis can kill your child," said Kathy Larew, Tim's mother. The second grader at Windermere Elementary School is allergic to all nut products, as well as milk, eggs and soy.

Scores of school systems are grappling with ways to balance the dietary needs of allergic kids like Tim with the rights of others who cherish PB&Js. Some Canadian public schools have responded by banning peanuts and nut products from school lunches altogether. For those with an allergic child, it's a matter of life and death. A touch, a taste, sometimes even a whiff of the stuff can cause a child to stop breathing and go into shock—even die. At Windermere, protecting Tim means creating a peanut-free zone and asking parents to avoid sending peanut-laced items to school, among other accommodations.

But for those moms and dads whose finicky kids live on peanut butter, it's a matter of equal rights. The issue has become so sticky that many parents at Windermere, afraid of being labeled insensitive, were willing to speak only on the condition of anonymity.

"My child matters, too," said one mother. "I don't think it's correct to change 23 kids for one." Another mother complained, "I think the schools are so afraid of lawsuits that they're ignoring the rights of other kids." Instead of absolute bans, which can arouse antagonism without guaranteeing safety, many schools now offer peanut-free cafeteria tables, no-sharing policies for foods that may contain traces of peanuts and instructions for teachers on handling allergy emergencies.

According to the Food Allergy Network (http://www.foodallergy.org/), a Fairfax, Va.–based advocacy and support group, about 125 Americans a year die because of allergic reactions to foods, with peanuts one of the biggest dangers.

If someone with an extreme allergy to peanuts were to accidentally eat even the smallest amount of nut product, she could die within minutes. The cause would be a medical term called anaphylactic shock, in which the throat swells shut, cutting off breathing. Dr. Hugh Sampson, director of the Jaffe Food Allergy Institute at Mount Sinai Hospital in New York, estimates 1.5 million people in the United States are allergic to peanuts. About 20% of them are so allergic that their lives are at risk, he said.

Food allergies have become so widespread that the U.S. Department of Agriculture's school lunch and breakfast programs require schools to offer substitutions for allergy-inducing foods. When Kathy and Bob Larew learned of Tim's allergies, they were determined to give him a normal childhood and enrolled him in public school. But how could they keep Tim safe among hundreds of grade-schoolers? The issue landed in the lap of Frank Milbury, Windermere's principal. Milbury had to come up with reasonable accommodations for Tim or risk defending himself against a discrimination lawsuit under the Americans with Disabilities Act of 1990 and the Rehabilitation Act of 1973, which ensure access to federally funded services—including education—for people who have handicapping conditions.

"If there is something such as an allergy that would prevent that child from gaining an education, you really have to make sure the child is not forced to deal with that allergic substance," Milbury said. Like most parents with allergic children, the Larews didn't want to play the lawsuit card and asked for voluntary measures. So over the summer, Milbury sent a letter asking parents to avoid classroom snacks containing peanuts, peanut butter or nuts. Kathy Larew gave parents a list of acceptable alternatives, including pretzels, chips, fruit and certain crackers.

The letter didn't go over well with everyone in this school, about 25 km northeast of Hartford, Conn. "It can get ugly," Larew admitted. Anne Munoz-Furlong, founder of the Food Allergy Network, said the issue has pit parent against parent in communities around the country. "It comes down to: My kid's life or your kid's peanut butter sandwich. That's how divided an issue this can become," she said. Parents have resisted such bans for a variety of reasons. Some vegetarians argue peanut butter is a good source of protein while others say children's picky appetites rule out alternatives. Others fear liability if they forget to read a label or accidentally put a brownie with nuts in their child's lunch box.

When some parents with children assigned to Tim's class complained, Milbury allowed transfers to other classes. Others who decided to stay had to deal with new routines.

Upon entering class each morning, all the children must wash their hands with a sanitary wipe. At snack time, the rule is "no sharing." A peanut-free zone has been created in the cafeteria. A teacher's aide makes sure that only kids with "safe" lunches sit next to Tim and that no one with a questionable item passes by too closely. Teachers, the school nurse and staff have received special training. Medication is always kept nearby and the school runs 911 drills each year. So far, there have been no mishaps.

Tim is largely unaware of the controversy. Still, he sometimes feels a stigma at special occasions.

"Sometimes I go to parties after the food is done, or I just bring my own piece of cake," he said. "Sometimes I do feel shy. It's hard."

QUESTIONS FOR DISCUSSION

1. What is the basic value conflict represented by this article? What are the arguments of people on both sides of the conflict?

2. How could the values on both sides of this issue reflect one or more of the ethical systems discussed in this chapter?

3. What is your own viewpoint about the controversy represented by this article? What reasons do you have for your position?

4. If you were a PTA president at the school discussed in this article, how would you advise the administration and the parents to handle the situation?

A classic problem in higher education involves college admissions; in state universities, particularly, lawmakers and educators both struggle to create policies that balance admissions and include excellent students from traditionally high-achieving high schools while also rewarding excellent students from disadvantaged schools. In Texas, a law was created that gave anyone in the top 10 percent of his or her high school class automatic admission to any state university. The law was created when federal legislation prohibiting racial preferences was enacted.

Jay Brody, on his Web site collegeapps.about.com (12/22/06), articulates the conflict concerning the Texas statute: "While the law does provide opportunities to the disadvantaged, some believe that it works against applicants who attend strong high schools, take tough courses, but aren't in the top 10 percent of their classes. Others think that the law doesn't do enough, and that there are better ways to help disadvantaged applicants."

TEXAS COLLEGE ADMISSIONS LAW UNDER FIRE

Kids in Top 10% Get in Automatically

Holly K. Hacker

DALLAS—It's been praised for keeping public universities in Texas racially diverse. It's been criticized for hurting talented students with less-than-stellar grades.

Now almost 10 years old, the Top 10% Law on college admissions still kindles emotion and debate. Three bills seeking to limit or kill the law have been filed for the January legislative session.

The law is simple: Texas students in the top 10% of their high school class are automatically admitted to any public university in the state. Legislators passed it in 1997 after a federal court effectively banned racial preferences in college admissions.

It ensures that every high school can send students to the state's premier campuses. Otherwise, some lawmakers worried, minority students at high schools lacking strong college prep programs could be shut out.

But critics say the law is too simple and that it's wrong to admit students based solely on class rank, especially those from highly competitive high schools where tough course loads and lots of extracurricular activities are the norm.

With black and Hispanic students still underrepresented at the University of Texas and Texas A&M, critics question whether the law has worked as intended. And they note that a 2003 Supreme Court ruling again allowed universities to consider race in admissions, making the Top 10% Law moot.

What the two sides say

Attempts to restrict or repeal the law have failed. Supporters of the new bills hope to prevail this time.

"If at first you don't succeed, try and try again," said Rep. Beverly Woolley, a Houston Republican who has filed a bill to throw out the Top 10% Law.

"A lot of kids in my district, they go to really tough schools . . . yet the competition is so strong," Woolley said. "They're really bright students, but they're not in the top 10%."

Others say the law needs to remain.

"I haven't seen a change I'd support yet," said Sen. Royce West, a Dallas Democrat who authored the law and has defended it over the years.

West said the law rewards students with a strong work ethic and that it has helped achieve racial and geographic diversity. The University of Texas and Texas A&M University draw students from more high schools across Texas since the law took effect.

"It's an opportunity for urban Texans and rural Texans—for all Texans—to make sure they have the ability to attend the flagships in the state," West said.

Problems for school

The University of Texas at Austin is Exhibit A for those seeking changes. In 1998, 37% of University of Texas freshmen were admitted under the law. This year, it's 66%. Count only in-state students, and the number edges up to 71%.

Campus leaders say those students have done well, and they don't want the law thrown out. But they do seek some kind of cap.

"It's a capacity problem for us," University of Texas President William Powers said. "We're admitting over 70% of our Texas students on one criterion. . . . We just need more flexibility."

The law has overwhelmed a few University of Texas programs, such as the College of Business. The program is so popular that it can't admit every Top 10% student who applies. And to leave room for others, there's a 75% cap on the number of business spaces for Top 10% students.

Because students still have to apply to individual colleges, admissions officers keep busy.

"We still have to read 17,000 applications," said Gary Lavergne, who heads admissions research at the University of Texas at Austin. And with the law, he said, "We are very sensitive to the competition for the spaces that are left. We have to be very careful, and we are."

Texas A&M also gets lots of Top 10% students, though less than the University of Texas. This year, 44% of freshmen were admitted to Texas A&M under the law.

The other students

University of Texas officials say that, contrary to what some people think, Top 10% students do as well academically as other students. Also, many parents believe that if their child doesn't get into University of Texas under the law, they're shut out. Not true.

"If a Texas resident has a completed application on time, we don't say no. We offer other options," said Bruce Walker, admissions director. For instance, students can start at another University of Texas System school and, with high enough grades, transfer to the University of Texas at Austin. At Texas A&M, students who don't make the top 10% still get in automatically if they finish in the top quarter of their high school class with high SAT or ACT scores.

QUESTIONS FOR DISCUSSION

1. What values are the Texas legislators attempting to reconcile with their state college admissions policies?

2. How would you define the value conflict between those who support the Texas law and those who oppose it?

3. What do you believe are the most important factors for college admissions officers to consider when they put together a freshman class?

4. Should the college admissions factors be the same for private and public institutions or should public colleges have different considerations? What are your reasons for your conclusions on this issue?

IDEAS FOR WRITING OR SPEAKING

1. See if your college has a code of ethics about cheating and plagiarizing. If so, write about this code; take a position on the principles given (agree or disagree with them) and give support for your conclusions. If your college does not have a code of ethics, write one and justify (give reasons for) each of the principles you include.

2. "The Legacy I'd Like to Leave"

   Imagine that you are 80 years old. Your son, daughter, niece, nephew, husband, wife, friend, or coworker is making a speech about you at a party held in your honor. In this speech, he or she mentions your fine qualities and the things you have accomplished in your life. He or she talks about the special traits you have that are treasured by those who know and love you.
       Write the speech, using this format:

   a. List the personal qualities you'd want to have and how they have been specifically evidenced in your life.

   b. List the accomplishments you will have achieved. Again, be specific in your descriptions.

   c. Then analyze what you would need to do (either internally or externally, or both) to merit that kind of tribute in your old age. What ideal values would have to become real for you? What choices would you have to make about your career, your personal life, and your priorities?

3. Write an essay in which you take a position (agree or disagree) on one of the following quotes. Support your conclusion about the quote with specific reasons.

   a. "To educate a person in mind and not in morals is to educate a menace to society." President Theodore Roosevelt

   b. "In looking for people to hire, you look for three qualities: integrity, intelligence, and energy. And if they don't have the first, the other two will kill you." Warren Buffet

c. "The great secret of morals is love." Shelley, *A Defence of Poetry* (1821)

d. "We must never delude ourselves into thinking that physical power is a substitute for moral power, which is the true sign of national greatness." Adlai Stevenson, speech, Hartford, Connecticut, September 18, 1952

e. "Can ethics be taught? At some point in life, ethics must be taught. People are not born with innate desires to be ethical or to be concerned with the welfare of others." Dr. Katherine Smith and Dr. L. Murray Smith

f. "I believe we are the sum total of all that we do, i.e., what we 'do' is who we 'are.' This is true because as adults we make deliberate choices in our actions. Therefore, our actions describe our inner selves, what sacrifices we're willing to make, what evil we're willing to perpetrate. It is with awareness that we persist in negative, ugly, and destructive deeds in one or more areas. Our actions are the blueprint of our character." Dr. Laura Schlessinger

g. "When the Nazis came to power, I looked to the universities that prided themselves upon their intellectual freedom, and they failed me. I looked to the German press, which prided itself on the freedom of the press, and it failed me. Until at last the churches stood alone, and that for which I once had little regard earned my respect." Albert Einstein, after World War II

h. "To sin by silence when they should protest makes cowards of men." Abraham Lincoln

i. "The purpose of ethics in business is to direct business men and women to abide by a code of conduct that facilitates, if not encourages, public confidence in their products and services." Dr. Katherine Smith and Dr. L. Murray Smith

j. "To know what is right and not to do it is the worst cowardice." Confucius

4. *Part A:* List some values you hold. These can be character traits such as honesty, fairness, and compassion. You can also list concerns such as peace, freedom of speech, family ties, ethnic identity, health, wealth, competition, or cooperation.

To isolate some of your values, consider the professions that interest you. If you want to be a high school coach, you may value sports, young people, and/or education. If you want to be an artist, you may value beauty and creativity.

Also, consider how you spend your free time. Different values may be expressed by those who spend time reading science fiction, shopping, volunteering at a nursing home, socializing, or working on a political campaign.

Try to list at least three values reflected in your life.

Part B: Next choose a controversial issue and take a position on this issue; your position should reflect a value you hold. Examples of controversial topics with a value dimension include capital punishment, surrogate parenting, homelessness, nuclear power, active and passive euthanasia, socialized medicine, welfare, immigration, and environmental policies. You might look up issues that are currently being considered by the Supreme Court; many of the court's rulings establish the precedence of one value over another.

After you have chosen an issue and taken a position reflecting your value, arrange your ideas in the following manner:

a. Give several reasons to support your position. Give both moral and fact-based reasons. Use examples and evidence to strengthen your reasons.

b. State some good reasons why you think a person might believe the opposite of what you believe. For example, if you are against compulsory drug testing for athletes, state why someone might argue in favor of it.

c. Conclude by indicating if and how your initial belief was changed by considering the opposite viewpoint. Or, conclude by stating why your initial belief was not changed, despite your fair consideration of the arguments against your belief.

FILMS FOR ANALYSIS AND DISCUSSION

Many film, theater, and television plots involve different value assumptions, priorities, and conflicts. When you go to a movie, notice the value conflicts that are shown through the plot and expressed by the various characters. Here are a few examples.

Million Dollar Baby (2004, PG-13) follows the dreams of Maggie (Hilary Swank) to become a boxing contender under the tutelage of Frank (Clint Eastwood), the only man she thinks can help her realize her dream. Through pure determination and negotiation, Maggie breaks the hardened Frank and convinces him not only to train her, but also to manage her career as a female boxing champion. This film is full of inner conflicts, of both values and ethics, for each character we encounter. Initially, Frank is conflicted by the prospect of training a "girl boxer," afraid she is too old and will not only lose every fight she's in, but also get seriously hurt in the process. As the film progresses, Frank faces an unsettling ethical dilemma that will change the course of both Maggie's and Frank's lives forever.

Similar Films and Classics

Sister Act (1993, PG)

In this film, Whoopie Goldberg plays Deloris Van Cartier, a lounge singer trying to make it big. She has many decisions to make that involve value conflicts, including whether to stay with her mobster boyfriend, who is still married, whether to enter a witness protection program when she witnesses a murder, whether to become involved in a convent choir, and whether to leave the choir before an important performance.

The Mighty Ducks (1992, PG)

This film reveals, in the opening segment, a painful event that shaped the life of Gordon Bombay, who has since become a successful lawyer. After a charge of drunk driving, Gordon is assigned to work with young players and the experience forces him to examine the values he learned at a young age. Note especially how he is given an opportunity to display the congruence between his real values and ideal values toward the end of the film.

Do the Right Thing (1989, R)

In this acclaimed Spike Lee film, which takes place primarily on one hot day in Brooklyn, many different characters represent specific beliefs and values. Note how their various beliefs affect their behavior in relationships and in the decisions they make.

Chariots of Fire (1981, PG)

This film about British sprinters competing in the 1924 Olympics is filled with value conflicts. Eric Little has to decide whether to compete or devote himself completely to his missionary goals; he also has to decide whether to compete on a Sunday, a day that he holds sacred. The Olympic committee has to decide whether or not to change the time of the race to accommodate Eric, the top contender for the 100-meter race. In addition, a teammate has to decide whether to let Eric compete in his place in the 400-meter slot.

The Fountainhead (1949)

This classic film, based on the book by Ayn Rand, concerns an idealistic architect who must decide between his artistic vision and the compromises necessary to sustain work in his field.

3

Reality Assumptions

It's Eleven O'Clock. Do You Know Where Your Assumptions Are?

A critical thinker understands that people have different assumptions about the world that form the basis for opinions; he or she also examines these assumptions.

A critical thinker understands basic patterns of deductive reasoning.

A critical thinker uses reasoning to test logic, discover truth, make decisions, avoid stereotyping, and understand argument.

This chapter will cover

- Reality assumptions

- Patterns of deductive reasoning

- Using deductive reasoning to test logic, discover truth, make decisions, avoid stereotyping, and understand argument.

We learned in the last chapter that when an issue involves a conflict of values, we need to examine the value assumptions and priorities that are foundational to the argument under consideration; in other words, there is no point in bringing in evidence to support a point of view until we address the issue of the clashing values.

If someone believes that legalizing drugs is morally wrong, that person will probably not be moved by a lot of statistics that show that we could save money and cut down on crime by legalizing drugs. Someone with a strong value assumption on an issue is not usually swayed by a discussion of practical benefits of a policy or an action that contradicts his or her values. When a discussion neglects to consider conflicting value assumptions on both sides of an issue, stalemates occur, and new and improved evidence does little to help these stalemates.

The critical thinker who wants to argue on a value-saturated issue needs to clearly and directly address the conflict in values and try to persuade those on the other side to rethink their value assumptions on that issue.

REALITY ASSUMPTIONS

As we discussed in Chapter 2, another foundational aspect to any argument is the underlying assumptions about reality that the various advocates for an issue hold. **Reality assumptions** are beliefs about what is true and factual about the world, and so they are sometimes called *factual assumptions* or *descriptive assumptions*. They are based on the unique experience and education of each individual. Reality assumptions are sometimes directly stated by a writer or speaker, but they are usually implied.

REMINDER

An *assumption* can be defined as a belief, usually taken for granted, that is based on the experience, observations, or desires of an individual or group. Conflicts in value assumptions address the questions "What is right?" and "What should we do or be?"; conflicts in reality assumptions address the questions "What is true and factual?" and "What do we take for granted or as a given fact?" Critical thinkers need to be aware of the assumptions that are basic to arguments they are hearing or making.

The fascinating element of assumptions is that they are often hidden to the people arguing for different conclusions. Finding hidden assumptions in arguments is like reading or watching mysteries; you accumulate clues from what people say and then make guesses about the important things they believe but aren't directly *stating*. For example, consider the different reality assumptions in the following excerpt from an article about the usefulness of standardized tests for predicting college success:

George Mason University professor and radio commentator Walter Williams has stated that high school students should not apply to colleges where average SAT scores are at least 200 points higher than theirs.[1] While Williams does not assume that the SAT and ACT tests are necessarily reflective of a student's intelligence; he does assume that they signify less preparation for the literary and mathematical demands of college. Other educators hold very different assumptions. Muhlenberg College does not require SAT or ACT scores and [its] dean of admissions and financial aid Christopher Hooker-Haring believes that the SAT may merely predict the degree of struggle for first-year college students. He lists other qualities that the SAT does not measure that will help a student survive the adjustment of the first year, including "work ethic, determination, motivation, love of learning, and grit."

Let's look at Walter Williams's argument, using the Toulmin model that was introduced in Chapter 2. His **claim** is that high school students should not apply to colleges at which average SAT scores are 200 points higher than theirs. His **reason** is that the student will not likely succeed based on the **warrant** (assumption) that the SAT and ACT scores are accurate predictions of how well a student is prepared for the literary and mathematical demands of such a college.

Christopher Hooker-Haring, on the other hand, would offer the **claim** that students should not use standardized test scores as a measure of future success. His **reason** is that the tests may predict only the degree of struggle for first-year students. His **warrant** (assumption) is that what will get a student through the challenges of the freshman year is his or her character qualities that are not measured by the tests.

Note that both educators share similar values—the value of education and the value of students surviving the first year successfully. Their differences are about what actually will help students succeed. They have different reality assumptions about what is true and factual for freshman students.

When two people or two groups hold different assumptions, they need to stop and examine those assumptions that frame their arguments rather than continuing to build arguments on those assumptions. As hidden assumptions are brought to the surface, light is shed on the different positions taken on an issue. Then "all the cards are on the table," and people have the opportunity to modify assumptions or to see more clearly why they have a strong conviction about an assumption.

SKILL

A critical thinker examines the reality assumptions of self and others that form the foundations of arguments.

[1]Jay Matthews, *Washington Post,* Tuesday, April 2, 2002, p. A07.

DETECTING REALITY ASSUMPTIONS

One reason that some assumptions are hidden from us is that they are so deeply ingrained; they may surface only when we come across a person or a group that holds different assumptions. We may be confronted with a different set of assumptions than our own when we are involved in a classroom debate. Because assumptions are often based on what we have experienced in our own environments, they often surface when we are in unfamiliar situations, such as when we travel to a new place and are exposed to a different culture.

Most North Americans assume that if an interview or meeting is set for 1:00, then the arrival time should be slightly before 1:00, but people from other cultures may view time more loosely. The expected arrival time could be anywhere between 1:00 and 3:00 for members of some cultures. Because of the differing assumptions across cultures, North Americans who are sent abroad by their organizations are often given training about the assumptions commonly made in the country they will be visiting.

When traveling to another country, we can be sensitive to what is expected of us as visitors. In defending our conclusions on an issue, however, we need to bring the differing assumptions to light so that the discussion is clear and rational.

Examples of Differing Reality Assumptions

- Some people assume that anyone can change and therefore any prisoner can be rehabilitated. Other people assume that there are individuals who are "career criminals" with no hope of being rehabilitated.
- Some people assume that the way to increase employment is to lower taxes. Other people assume that the way to increase employment is to establish more government programs that would provide jobs for the unemployed.
- Some people assume that homosexuality is a condition established in the genetic code before birth. Other people assume that homosexuality is a result of a set of environmental circumstances.
- Some people assume that ethical behavior and empathy for others can be taught in school. Other people assume that if such behavior hasn't been taught in the home, then schools won't be able to teach it.

Other assumptions involve differing definitions of words:

- One person assumes that *love* is an emotion that may or may not be permanent. Another person assumes that *love* is a commitment that is not based on emotional changes.
- One person assumes that *censorship* is any restriction on speech or writing; another uses *censorship* to mean a complete banning of ideas or publications.

In an article on the dispute among obesity experts over the definition of fat, Steve Rubenstein writes:

> The United States defines a fat person as anyone with a "body mass index," or BMI, of 27.6 or higher. The World Health Organization defines a fat person as anyone with a BMI of 25 or higher. As a result of these different definitional assumptions, Americans don't actually weigh any more, according to the latest numbers. But, in keeping with the leaner international threshold for fatness, more of them are fat.[2]

REMINDER

Individuals continually make assumptions about reality. We need to examine the assumptions we make and try to detect the assumptions that others make. When we have a foundational disagreement about reality assumptions, we should discuss those assumptions before we discuss any arguments built upon them. For example, if we believe that people can be rehabilitated, we must understand why we believe that and be able to defend our basic belief. We also need to understand why someone else would believe that people cannot be rehabilitated.

When we realize that an argument involves differing reality assumptions, we need to search for evidence that will prove or disprove the assumptions. Much research is conducted to determine whether commonly held assumptions are true or are simply persistent myths. For example, many people assume that going outside with wet hair may help cause a cold, even though most medical experts have long maintained that colds are caused by a virus and not by wet or cold conditions. However, since the assumption persists, some researchers are trying to gather hard evidence to discover if there is any truth to it. The renowned Mayo clinic reports on one such study:

> Other beliefs about how you catch a common cold—such as going outdoors with wet hair or getting chilled—are starting to be seriously studied. In a small study at the Common Cold Centre in Wales, scientists tested 180 healthy volunteers. Half submerged their bare feet in ice water for 20 minutes, and half stayed dry. Within five days, nearly one-third of the chilled participants developed sore throats and runny noses, whereas only 9 percent of their warmer counterparts did.[3] Cnn.com/mayoclinic.com

[2]Steve Rubenstein, "Millions Suddenly Became Fat Without Gaining Any Weight," *San Francisco Chronicle,* October 11, 1996, p. A6.
[3]Special to cnn.com/mayachnis.com Diseases and Conditions Common Cold. September 8, 2006 (no author given).

Here are some other examples of new information used to question common assumptions:

- It has often been assumed that older students who commute and work off campus might be at a disadvantage. However, a recent study by Carol A. Lundberg, professor of education and organizational leadership at Azusa Pacific University challenges that assumption. Her study found that older students are not negatively affected by spending less time on their campuses. They are as academically successful as traditional-age students, and their social needs are met through the workplace and through other social connections. Also, they tend to have better relationships with faculty and administrators.[4]

  the study of birds

- Fifty years ago, most ornithologists had determined that the ivory-billed woodpecker was extinct. This assumption was thrown into question when a forestry student reported spotting a pair of the large, black-and-white marked birds in a southeastern Louisiana wildlife area in April 1999. As a result of the spotting, an international team of experts using state of the art video and audio detection and recording equipment was commissioned in 2004 to spend 30 days searching for this bird, considered by many to be a "part of our natural heritage and symbolic of the lost wilderness of the Southeast."[5]

- People who buy gift cards may be unpleasantly surprised when their assumptions about the value of the cards prove false, as noted in the following example:

  Last Christmas, Norman Vinson bought his wife Arlene several $50 gift cards at the Brea Mall. The cards seemed easy enough to use, but when she tried to pay for $109 worth of lingerie at a mall department store with two of the cards and $9 in cash, her cards were declined because they weren't worth enough. The couple called the toll-free number on the back of the cards to check the balances. They learned they were being charged a $2.50 monthly service fee for not using the entire value of the cards within six months. And the phone calls, it turned out, cut the cards' value further by 50 cents each. "Here's the whole thing about the whole shootin' match: You go in and buy a $50 gift card, and you assume you're buying someone a certificate that they can use for $50," said Vinson. That's not necessarily true, he has learned. . . . Gift cards can come with many strings attached.[6]

- Psychologists often disagree about the major influences shaping human behavior. One columnist refutes the assumptions of some modern schools of thought as follows:

---

[4]Carol A. Lundberg, "The Influence of Time—Limitations, Faculty, and Peer Relationships on Adult Student Learning: A Causal Model," *The Journal of Higher Education,* volume 74, November/Dec. pps. 665–688, 2003.
[5]"That's Not All Folks: Search on For Birds, Eric Pianin, *Miami Herald,* December 30, 2001.
[6]Lisa Munoz, *Orange County Register,* September 22, 2003. "Gift Cards May Bite Recipient."

Post-Freudian psychology posits that every human behavior has an antecedent, and that it was acquired (learned) by way of some social interaction. If this is true, it follows that a child's behavior is shaped largely by how he/she is "parented." This is fiction. Nonetheless, it has had a powerful effect on today's parents, and especially mothers, many of whom live on the razor's edge of a gnawing fear that every bad thing their children do reflects upon them, that it "tells" of some dreadful parental (most likely maternal) sin of omission or commission.

The flip side of this is that today's parents—again, especially moms— are convinced that their children's accomplishments are evidence they are doing many constant good works in their children's lives.... Don't get me wrong. The way a child is raised, the quality of discipline and love he receives from those who care about him, makes a difference, but it is not the whole story. The fact that every child has a mind of his own means not only that right and proper parenting does not produce a child who will not misbehave, but also that right and proper discipline may not cure misbehavior. In other words, sometimes the best discipline does not "work," even when parents work diligently at it. This is evidence not of some biological dysfunction, but of a dysfunction that is even more fundamental to being human—the will to rebel, to prove that no one is qualified to tell you what to do.... There's nature, and there's nurture, and then there's free will, and the most powerful of the three is definitely the latter.[7]

We frequently confront assumptions about the past; these may be especially strong because of lasting images created by the media. The following excerpt discusses how our cultural views of the decade of the 1950s in the United States may have been skewed:

The sunny, eternally optimistic images of the 1950s depicted in such TV comedies as "Leave It to Beaver" and "The Adventures of Ozzie and Harriet" could leave one to believe that the decade was carefree and fun. Fatherly Dwight Eisenhower was the president; the country was enjoying post–World War II prosperity. All was calm and copacetic in the suburbs. In reality, the '50s were also marked by turmoil and fear. The Cold War was raging between the United States and the Soviet Union. The threat of communism led to the blacklist. Women's roles were changing. Teens began confronting authority. And the civil rights movement began to gain ground.[8]

Sometimes politicians make assumptions that are offensive to their constituents; in one election, candidates offended female researchers by continually referring to what they would do about breast cancer if they were elected

[7]John Rosemond, June 18, 2003, All About Kids Parenting Magazine. "Living with Children."
[8]"TV film festival explores turmoil of '50s," Susan King, *L.A. Times,* September 4, 2001.

to office: "Scientists are repelled by what they see as the condescending assumption in these campaigns; that mentioning breast cancer is a sure way to win the female vote."[9]

THE IMPORTANCE OF EXAMINING ASSUMPTIONS

In our age of accelerated research in many fields, some ideas that were once generally accepted have come into question. Researchers discover that what was assumed to be factual may not be true; it may have been true at one time or it may never have been true at all. When we build arguments on assumptions that are not grounded in fact, our arguments are faulty and the actions we recommend will not achieve our desired ends. We may sound logical and reasonable, but we are leading others and ourselves astray.

A number of years ago, officials in King County in the state of Washington found that, contrary to their assumptions, they had almost twice as many suicides as homicides in their county:

> The Seattle–King County Department of Public Health reported that suicide is a major public health problem, the second most common cause of death among adults ages 20–24. In recent years, the suicide rate has continued to climb in that county.

A common assumption has been made that the often rainy weather in the Pacific Northwest contributed to the suicides, but a public health study found that, instead, the highest number of suicides were committed in July. The real causes of suicide were determined to be, first and foremost, terminal or chronic illness. Other factors included a decline in the quality of life, unemployment, marital and financial problems, and relationship problems.

> The Seattle-King County medical examiner stated that most people assume homicide is a bigger problem than suicide because suicides are rarely reported by the media.[10]

Researchers and investigative reporters often uncover questionable assumptions such as the ones this article discovered in King County. When we examine assumptions with the goal of discovering what is true, we can take more useful action. Some of the reality assumptions that were discovered to be *false* about King County include:

1. Homicide is more common than suicide.
2. The area's gloomy weather contributes to high suicide rates.

---

[9]Gina Kolata, "Vying for the Breast Vote," *New York Times*, November 3, 1996.
[10]Jennifer Bjorhus and Peyton Whitely, "New Report Debunks Myths on Suicide," *Seattle Times*, February 15, 1996.

Change in approach based on examination of assumptions

In this case, supervisors considering the research from the Seattle–King County Department of Public Health may decide to put more funding into preventing suicides instead of concentrating their efforts mainly on homicides. In so doing, they can focus on fighting the most common causes of suicide. Rather than looking for antidotes to gloomy weather, they can support efforts to control pain for those who suffer from terminal or chronic illness; also, county officials can offer more services to people who are unemployed or struggling with financial and relationship problems.

Assumptions should be examined in the light of the best information available; then decisions can be optimally helpful and productive.

Another example of the need to examine assumptions relates to the use of prescription medicine. Because of the availability of numerous new medications and treatments, doctors and pharmacists have to consider more factors in treating patients than they may have in the past. Because harmful, and even fatal, side effects can occur when two different drugs are prescribed to the same patient, pharmacists have to make judgment calls about whether to assume that doctors know about interactions between the drugs they have prescribed.

One investigative report warns consumers not to assume that pharmacy computer systems that check for drug interactions are always accurate. Dr. David Kessler, past commissioner of the federal Food and Drug Administration (FDA), is quoted as saying, "It is simply untenable...to walk into a pharmacy and receive a bottle of pills and no other information. It is not good patient care."[11]

To prevent patients from making harmful assumptions, pharmacists now ask patients to wait for consultations about the medications they are receiving.

The FDA advocates increased communication between consumers and health care providers to avoid harmful assumptions concerning prescriptions:

> The large number of drugs on the market, combined with the common use of multiple medications, makes the risk for drug interactions significant. "Consumers need to tell doctors what they're taking and ask questions, and health professionals could do a better job at trying to get the information they want," says Timothy Tracy, Ph.D., a professor in the school of pharmacy at the University of Minnesota, Twin Cities campus. He says there is a pervasive attitude that the term "medications" only refers to prescription drugs. "So rather than asking patients what medications they take, doctors should make the questions specific: 'Are you taking any over-the-counter medication? Are you taking any herbal treatments or vitamins?'"[12]

---

[11]Susan Headden, *U.S. News & World Report*, August 26, 1996. "Danger at the Drugstore."
[12]www.cfsan.fda.gov/-dms/qa-sup19.html "Tips for the Savvy Supplement User: Making Informed Decisions and Evaluating Information." January, 2002 (no author given).

The Food and Drug Administration also advises consumers to be wary of common assumptions concerning dietary supplements. On the FDA Web site, the following checklist is given:

Check your assumptions about the following:

* #1 Questionable Assumption—

"Even if a product may not help me, it at least won't hurt me." It's best not to assume that this will always be true. When consumed in high enough amounts, for a long enough time, or in combination with certain other substances, all chemicals can be toxic, including nutrients, plant components, and other biologically active ingredients.

* #2 Questionable Assumption—

"When I see the term 'natural,' it means that a product is healthful and safe." Consumers can be misled if they assume this term assures wholesomeness, or that these foodlike substances necessarily have milder effects, which makes them safer to use than drugs. The term "natural" on labels is not well defined and is sometimes used ambiguously to imply unsubstantiated benefits or safety. For example, many weight-loss products claim to be "natural" or "herbal" but this doesn't necessarily make them safe. Their ingredients may interact with drugs or may be dangerous for people with certain medical conditions.

* #3 Questionable Assumption—

"A product is safe when there is no cautionary information on the product label." Dietary supplement manufacturers may not necessarily include warnings about potential adverse effects on the labels of their products. If consumers want to know about the safety of a specific dietary supplement, they should contact the manufacturer of that brand directly. It is the manufacturer's responsibility to determine that the supplement it produces or distributes is safe and that there is substantiated evidence that the label claims are truthful and not misleading.

* #4 Questionable Assumption—

"A recall of a harmful product guarantees that all such harmful products will be immediately and completely removed from the marketplace." A product recall of a dietary supplement is voluntary and while many manufacturers do their best, a recall does not necessarily remove all harmful products from the marketplace.[13]

As critical thinkers, we need to actively discover and then question the assumptions underlying arguments so we are not building arguments on a

[Handwritten margin note: Not building arguments on false foundation]

[13]Ibid.

[handwritten marginal note:] know why believe in what we believe

false foundation. Conversely, when we critically examine what it is we take for granted, we have the advantage of gaining a strong and solid conviction for those ideas and principles we believe to be true. Knowing why we believe what we believe helps us be more credible and effective when we present an argument. Examining the reality assumptions of others helps us understand and assess their arguments more clearly.

CLASS EXERCISE

What are the assumptions?

Purpose: To detect unstated reality assumptions.

One way to detect reality assumptions is to create a brief outline of an argument you hear. Use the elements of the Toulmin method as illustrated in the following examples:

> *Trials and executions should be televised—the public has the right to know what's going on in our courts. Information about the judicial system needs to be more widely disseminated.*

Analyzing this brief argument with the skills we've discussed so far, we could outline the argument as follows:

> *Conclusion/claim:* Trials and executions should be televised.
> *Reason:* The public has the right to have more information about the courts and the judicial system.
>
> *Value assumption/warrant:* Freedom of information is an important value.
>
> *Reality assumption/warrant:* Televising trials and executions would inform the public about our judicial system.

Let's look at another brief argument, outlining the conclusion, reasons, value assumption, and reality assumptions.

> *All teenagers should have the Hepatitis B vaccination starting at 12 years old. Hepatitis B is a sexually transmitted disease that can be fatal. It can also be transmitted through intravenous drug use.*

> *Conclusion/claim:* All teenagers should have the Hepatitis B vaccination.
> *Reasons:* Hepatitis B is a sexually transmitted disease that can be fatal. It can also be transmitted through intravenous drug use.

Value assumption/warrant: Health and prolonged life are important.

Reality assumptions/warrants: All teenagers are at risk of being sexually active or using drugs. Children are at risk for these activities starting at age 12. A vaccination will protect teenagers from the effects of this disease.

Using these examples, can you create different arguments based on different assumptions about reality?

Now, look at the following statements and find possible assumptions that are being made by the speaker. Often, you can find more than one possible reality assumption.

After you have completed this exercise, discuss whether you agree with the assumptions you discovered.

1. This is a receptionist position, so we need a mature woman for the job to make our clients feel comfortable as soon as they walk in here.
2. You can't go to the party in that outfit. Everyone will think you're completely clueless about how to dress, and no one will want to be seen with you.
3. The death penalty is proof that we value revenge more than we value people. We should save and rehabilitate people rather than giving up on them.
4. Charlene is really successful—she's only 28 and she's making $120,000 a year!
5. There is good news in that rape is on the decline in this county—there are 20 percent fewer police reports this year than last year at this time.
6. Bolger's coffee is the best—it's mountain grown. That gives it great taste.
7. The people in that city don't care about the homeless—their city council voted against contributing $80,000 to a county fund to help the homeless.
8. They won't trade their lunches if you give them Twinkle cupcakes, and Twinkle will give them the energy they need to do well in school.
9. You're going to love this blind date—I've known him since fourth grade and he's a great friend of mine.
10. Let's put the county dump in Smallville—it hasn't had a turn as a dump site yet.
11. Let's just live together—why do we need a piece of paper to prove our love?
12. The newspaper didn't print my editorial—I guess the editors don't really believe in free speech.
13. He should try out for the NFL right after high school. If he makes it, he won't need a college degree.

For more practice, see Exercise 3.1 on p. 97.

DEDUCTIVE REASONING

If we lose a sense of the value of truth, we will certainly lose something, and we may very well lose everything.

Bernard Williams, philosopher

The Chronicle of Higher Education, November 14, 2003

In the first part of this chapter, we examined reality assumptions. We saw that sometimes our assumptions about reality, about what is true and what is false, contrast with those of others. How can we know the truth about a given issue?

Philosophers, theologians, scholars, and critically thinking people are all concerned with truth, and many have tried to define truth over the centuries. Vincent Ryan Ruggiero, author of *Beyond Feelings,* gives this definition:

> The truth about something is what is so about it, the facts about it in their exact arrangement and proportions... to look for the truth is to look for the correct answer, the answer that completely expresses reality in the matter. Whatever difficulty we may find in discerning or stating the truth is beside the point.[14]

Being a critical thinker means having a curious and questioning attitude about reality and particularly about the reality assumptions you hold and that others present to you in arguments. Critical thinkers realize that their knowledge and perceptions are limited, and they look for solid evidence before accepting or advocating a viewpoint. When new information becomes available, they revisit and reexamine their reality assumptions about an issue, always striving to discern the truth.

In many of our routine daily decisions, we don't spend a lot of time questioning our thinking. However, as we face the important decisions of our life as people in relationships, and as students, professionals, citizens, and consumers, we do need to question why we believe what we believe, and whether our beliefs are true.

How can we examine how we think and question our own reasoning or the reasoning of others? How can we overcome our own subjective perceptions? What tools are available to help us look critically at information, make reasonable decisions, and know that we are being "logical" in our thinking?

Those who study reasoning have come up with two general frameworks for testing the logic of our reasoning and for discovering truth; these frameworks are inductive and deductive reasoning. **Inductive reasoning** involves finding truth through making observations. The observations might be made through statistical polling, controlled experiments, or relevant examples and analogies. Our observations, when made carefully, can lead us closer to the truth of a

[14]Vincent Ryan Ruggiero, *Beyond Feelings: A Guide to Critical Thinking* (Mountain View, CA: Mayfield Publishing, 1990), 25.

matter. Good inductive reasoning tells us what will *probably* occur in a given situation based on what observation tells us *usually* occurs. We will look at inductive reasoning in Chapters 4 and 5.

While inductive reasoning gives us *probabilities* of what is true in a given situation, **deductive reasoning** is structured in such a way as to give us *certainty* about what is true in a given situation. The conclusion's certainty is established when deductive arguments contain true premises (reasons) stated in the correct form.

Validity in Deductive Arguments

Fallacious and misleading arguments are most easily detected if set out in correct syllogistic form.

Immanuel Kant

When you use the correct form, your argument is logical. In a **deductive argument**, formal patterns are used to reveal the logic of our reasoning. These patterns give us a tool for "quality control"; when the correct deductive form is followed, we call the argument **valid.** The basic patterns of deductive reasoning, which will be discussed in this section, help us test whether our thinking is valid and therefore logical. The pattern of a deductive argument can be considered its form; the statements placed in the pattern can be considered its content. Correct form makes an argument valid, which is a formal term for "logical"; accurate content makes it true. When the form is valid and the content is true, the argument is called **sound.**

An important framework for deductive reasoning is the syllogism. A **syllogism** is a deductive argument in which a conclusion is inferred from two premises. Let's look at the classic example of a syllogism given by Aristotle more than 2,000 years ago:

All men are mortal. (This categorical statement is called the **major premise.**)

Socrates is a man. (The **minor premise** expresses an instance of the principle set out in the major premise.)

Therefore, Socrates is mortal. (Conclusion—the conclusion is inferred—follows from—the major and minor premises.)

This pattern of deductive reasoning can be coded in letters as follows:

All As are Bs.
m is A.
Therefore, m is B.

In this deductive argument, the first premise (all As are Bs) is a universal or **categorical statement**, a statement in which members of one class are said to be included in another class.

This categorical statement is the major premise. The second statement that gives a particular instance of the principle set out in the major premise is the minor premise. The final statement is the conclusion that can be logically inferred from the major and minor premises.

Let's look at some other common examples of deductive reasoning, noting their specific patterns. A **conditional** or **hypothetical syllogism** contains at least one hypothetical (if–then) premise. In a conditional (hypothetical) premise, we are asserting that if the first part of the statement is true, then the second part is also true. We call the first part (represented by A) the antecedent, and the second part (represented by B) the consequent. Here are some common forms of conditional/hypothetical syllogisms.

1. *Modus ponens.* The term **modus ponens** means "the way of affirmation" or affirming the antecedent.

If A, then B. (major premise; we are stating that the antecedent leads to the consequent).

A (minor premise; we are asserting that the antecedent is true).

Therefore, B. (conclusion; if the antecedent is true, the consequent is also true).

Examples

If our team wins the playoff game, it will be in the championship game.
Our team did win the playoff game.
Therefore, our team will be in the championship game.
If the weather report says that it will rain today, I will need my raincoat.
The weather report says that it will rain today.
Therefore, I will need my raincoat.

Keep in mind the difference between a statement or assertion and an argument. Remember that in a deductive argument, the conclusion is inferred (drawn or understood) from the premises that are given. A common error is to take one premise alone as constituting an argument. The first premise given earlier, "If our team wins the playoff game, it will be in the championship game" is only a statement. This statement, called a hypothetical statement, sets up a condition. The condition needs to be fulfilled (or not fulfilled) for the argument to be complete. Conditional (or hypothetical) statements are used commonly in our lives in the form of warranties, contracts, threats, or predictions.

Your instructor may have given you a contract at the beginning of the semester that states the following:

1. If you get 80 percent of the points required, you will receive a B.

This is a conditional or hypothetical statement. It doesn't assert that you have 80 percent of the points in the class or that you have a B. But if you add another statement:

2. You have 80 percent of the points required (and that is true), then we will arrive at the conclusion that:

3. You will receive a B in the class.

Note that if the first two statements in this format are true, then the conclusion must be true. When the conclusion must be true, we have deductive certainty.

STOP AND THINK

What are some examples of hypothetical statements have you heard?

Here is another valid conditional/hypothetical syllogism:

2. Modus tollens. The term **modus tollens** means denying the consequent.

If A, then B.
Not B. (Here the consequent is denied.)
Therefore, not A. (Since the consequent is denied, the antecedent must also be denied in the conclusion.)

Examples

If I have strep throat, then the culture will be positive.
But the culture is not positive.
So, I don't have strep throat.

If I have to get up now, my alarm will go off again.
But my alarm hasn't gone off again.
Therefore, I don't have to get up now.

3. Chain argument. A third form of the conditional argument is often called a **chain argument**:

If A, then B.
If B, then C.
Therefore, if A, then C.

Examples

If you lower the fat in your diet, you will lower your cholesterol.
If you lower your cholesterol, you will reduce the risk of heart disease.
Therefore, if you lower the fat in your diet, you will reduce your risk of heart disease.

If evidence of the defendant's DNA is found at the crime scene, then we can connect him with the crime.

If we can connect him with the crime, then we can have him stand trial.
Therefore, if the defendant's DNA is found at the crime scene, then we can have him stand trial.

If I want to get a good grade in this class, I need high quiz points.
If I need high quiz points, I need to get to class on time.
Therefore, if I want to get a good grade in this class, I need to get to class on time.

REMINDER

Deductive arguments must follow the correct pattern in order to be considered valid. If our reasoning follows the steps outlined in these forms, our arguments are considered valid. If they do not follow the correct form, we have not provided adequate support for the conclusion, even if the conclusion happens to be true.

4. Disjunctive syllogism. Another common pattern of deduction is found in the **disjunctive syllogism**: If one possibility is true, then the other possibility is false. The pattern for this syllogism is structured as follows:

Either A or B.
Not B.
Therefore, A.
Either Ramon took the car to work or he took the bus.
But Ramon didn't take the bus to work.
Therefore, Ramon took the car.

Closely related to the disjunctive syllogism is an argument by elimination. An **argument by elimination** seeks to logically rule out various possibilities until only a single possibility remains. The following valid patterns are arguments by elimination:

Either A, or B, or C.
Not B or C.
Therefore, A.

Either A, or B, or C.
If B or C, then D.
Not D.
Therefore, A.

Either Rachel bought dinner, Roy bought dinner, or Sammy bought dinner.
If Roy or Sammy bought dinner, then they skipped baseball practice.

But Roy and Sammy did not skip baseball practice.
Therefore, Rachel bought dinner.

USING TOULMIN'S METHOD TO UNDERSTAND DEDUCTION

We don't speak in syllogisms, but we can test the logic of our reasoning by placing it into a syllogism. In fact, many of our assertions are what philosophers call enthymemes; an **enthymeme** is a syllogism with a premise implied rather than directly stated. The missing parts—the assumptions of the speaker or writer—are expected to be supplied by the listener or reader. When we discover the missing part, the implied premise, we can place the argument in one of the standard deductive patterns.

[handwritten margin note: We speak in enthymemes hiding premises or assumptions]

As we discussed in previous sections, British philosopher Stephen Toulmin has developed a method of dissecting arguments that helps us isolate the implied premises. His method identifies claims (which are the same as conclusions), reasons, those supports for the claims that are directly stated, and warrants, those connections between reasons and claims that are taken for granted (the reality assumptions). The warrants are the implied premises; they are the "glue" that attaches the reasons to the claims.

When the warrant is clarified, the reasoning of the speaker or writer is more fully revealed, and we are able to see if the reasoning is valid.

For example, you may say, "You shouldn't take that class—the teacher gives too much homework." (This preceding statement is the enthymeme.)

> *Claim/conclusion:* You should not take that class.
> *Reason:* The teacher gives too much homework.
> *Warrant/reality assumption:* If too much homework is given, a class should not be taken.

Written as a conditional argument, the reasoning would be revealed:

> If too much homework is given by a teacher, a class should not be taken.
> Too much homework is given by that teacher.
> Therefore, that class should not be taken.

Someone might respond to this argument by saying, "I like having a lot of homework—it helps me learn the material." This response challenges the warrant that if too much homework is given, a class should not be taken; the objection is not to the logic of the reasoning but to the assumption that too much homework is a negative factor.

For another example, let's say that you and a friend are planning to drive to a movie. You may say, "We're almost out of gas—we need to stop on the way to the movies." This enthymeme could be dissected as follows:

Claim/conclusion: We need to stop for gas on the way to the movies.
Reason: We're almost out of gas.
Warrant/reality assumption: If we're out of gas, we need to stop and get
some more.

We can also see the reasoning pattern by putting the enthymeme into a hypothetical syllogism, as follows:

If we're almost out of gas, we need to stop and get some more.
We're almost out of gas.
Therefore, we need to stop and get some more.

Let's say, though, that your friend responds to your comment, "We need to stop at a gas station on the way to the movies" by stating, "No, we don't need to stop; we're fine."
Using Toulmin's model, your friend's argument is as follows:

Claim/conclusion: We don't need to stop.
Reason: We're fine. (We have enough gas to get to the movies.)
Reality assumption/warrant: If we have enough gas to get to the movies, we don't need to stop.

The enthymeme "No, we don't need to stop; we're fine," could be expressed in a conditional syllogism as follows:

If we already have enough gas to get to the movies, we don't need to stop
for more.
We already have enough gas to get to the movies.
Therefore, we don't need to stop for more.

This sample disagreement points out an important element of deductive reasoning; a deductive argument may be valid (i.e., follows the correct pattern), as are both of the preceding arguments, without being true. The untrue premise can be seen as a faulty reality assumption. The conclusion may follow from the premises, but one or both of the premises may not be true, and the truth is what we are seeking.

Toulmin's method emphasizes the need to pursue truth in argumentation. The claims and reasons of each person need evidence or what Toulmin calls **grounds.** In this case, both you and your friend would have to provide evidence that you do or do not have enough gas to make it to the movies. He might give examples of how the gauge was close to empty before, but he was still able to travel the distance it would take to get to the movies. You may have kept track of how many miles you have gone since the last time the tank was filled and do the math to determine if you have enough gas left to get to the movies. Or you could take your chances and find out if you have enough gas by not filling up and seeing if you make it to the movies.

Both of you have reasoned logically, and the syllogisms outlining your reasoning are both valid. But only one of you has a sound argument in which both the major and the minor premises are true. When the premises of a valid syllogism are true, the truth of the conclusion is guaranteed.

When we know that an argument is sound, we can accept the conclusion of that argument with confidence. We can make good decisions based upon the information given in a sound argument because the argument is both logical and true, as conveyed by the following chart.

	True	**False**
Valid	Sound Argument: Correct Form True Premises	Unsound Argument: Correct Form, Untrue Premises
Invalid	Unsound Argument: Incorrect Form, True Premises	Unsound Argument: Incorrect Form, Untrue Premises

REMINDER

1. Understanding the process of deductive reasoning helps you realize what you are assuming to be true when you state your position on issues.
2. When an argument is valid and the premises are true, the conclusion must be true, and the argument is called sound.

THE USES OF DEDUCTIVE REASONING

Why is it useful to learn the patterns of deductive reasoning? Using deductive reasoning can

1. Illuminate and clarify our beliefs (reality assumptions) and help us consider whether those beliefs are rational. If we find that our beliefs are rational and logical, we may act on them. If they are irrational, we can challenge them.
2. Help us discover truth, particularly in situations in which there is a right and wrong answer.
3. Help us make decisions, particularly when there are established rules and guidelines.

4. Help us avoid stereotyping and distortion of information.
5. Help us understand argument.

Deductive Reasoning Helps Us Uncover and Question Reality Assumptions

As we discussed in the previous section, deductive reasoning can help us examine everyday reality assumptions. Sometimes, when we examine our assumptions, we see that they are logical and true, and we feel more confident about our reasoning. Other times, we uncover assumptions that are not based in truth but on unquestioned "folk wisdom." In his book *The Psychology of Persuasion,* Robert Cialdini talks about a friend who was having trouble selling some turquoise jewelry. She had priced the jewelry reasonably, put it in a central location in her store, and told her sales staff to push it.

> Finally, the night before leaving on an out-of-town buying trip, she scribbled an exasperated note to her head saleswoman, "Everything in this display case, price × 1/2," hoping to just be rid of the offending pieces, even at a loss. When she returned a few days later, she was not surprised to find that every article had been sold. She was shocked, though, to discover that, because the employee had read the "1/2" in her scrawled message as a "2," the entire allotment had sold out at twice the original price.[15]

Cialdini explains what happened in a way that reveals how we need to examine our reality assumptions in order to be more critical thinkers:

> The customers, mostly well-to-do vacationers with little knowledge of turquoise, were using a standard principle—a stereotype—to guide their buying: "expensive = good." Thus the vacationers, who wanted "good" jewelry, saw the turquoise pieces as decidedly more valuable and desirable when nothing about them was enhanced but the price.
>
> ...It is easy to fault the tourist[s] for their foolish purchase decisions. But a close look offers a kinder view. These were people who had been brought up on the rule "You get what you pay for" and who had seen that rule borne out over and over in their lives. Before long, they had translated the rule to mean "expensive = good." The "expensive = good" stereotype had worked quite well for them in the past, since normally the price of an item increases along with its worth; a higher price typically reflects higher quality. So when they found themselves in the position of wanting good turquoise jewelry without much knowledge of turquoise, they understandably relied on the old standby feature of cost to determine the jewelry's merits.[16]

[15]Robert B. Cialdini, *The Psychology of Persuasion* (New York: William Morrow, 1993).
[16]Ibid.

In this situation, the customers relied on a reality assumption, which can be expressed in the major premise of the following syllogism:

If an item is expensive, it must be good.
This jewelry is expensive.
Therefore, this jewelry must be good.

They literally paid a price for not questioning the truth of this assumption.

Clarifying and questioning our reality assumptions can also help us grow beyond self-imposed limitations. Our assumptions about reality may keep us from trying new things that we really are capable of accomplishing; by uncovering faulty reality assumptions, we can make necessary changes in our lives.

For example, someone we'll call Linda might say, "I can't take that speech class." Her friend LeVar asks why and Linda responds, "I can't take the class because I'd have to give speeches." Linda's confident friend says, "So what?" to which Linda says with great emotion, "If I have to take a speech class, I'll just fall apart and die!" LeVar, knowing the principles of deductive reasoning, helps Linda look at her logic through the pattern of chain argument.

If I take a speech class, I'll have to give speeches.
If I have to give speeches, I'll get nervous.
If I get nervous, I'll fall apart and die.
Therefore, if I take a speech class, I'll fall apart and die.

Considered in this light, Linda is able to see that, although her reasoning is valid, it is not true. She is "catastrophizing" her situation, making it much more serious than it is. Certainly, it may be uncomfortable for her to give a speech, but it is not a life-threatening situation. She can see that discomfort need not be catastrophic. The way we speak sometimes both reveals and creates our thoughts about situations. Using the tools of deductive reasoning to objectify her thoughts, Linda may be able to adjust her thinking to reality, rather than continuing to function with exaggerated fears. (See Exercise 3.2 on p. 98.)

Using Deductive Reasoning to Discover Truth and to Make Decisions

What eludes logic is the most precious element in us, and one can draw nothing from a syllogism that the mind has not put there in advance.
Andre Gide, *Journals*, June 1927

Deductive reasoning is most useful when the major premise is known to be true, to be a "given." Then we can test the truth of individual cases that may fall under the category or condition of the major premise.

For example, using a categorical syllogism, we can assert that some As do fit into an all-encompassing category (B) and give us valuable information. Let's consider some biological truths in this light. All women with an HCG (human chorionic gonadotropin) level above 5 are pregnant. Any cold-blooded vertebrate of the class *Reptilia* including tortoises, turtles, snakes, lizards, alligators, crocodiles and extinct forms are considered reptiles, and all persons with a blood alcohol level of .08 in the state of Illinois are legally drunk. Because of these known "alls," solid conclusions can be drawn: Doctors can tell individual women if they are pregnant; veterinarians, scientists, and pet store owners can identify reptiles; and police officers in Illinois can ascertain whether individual drivers are legally drunk. You might discover that you and several members of your immediate family have type A blood. Because this is a known truth, if you need a blood transfusion, family members can be approached to volunteer.

Hundreds of conditions and illnesses have been studied inductively (through observation), and the results of the studies have given us truth that can be used in diagnosis. When the symptoms of a particular condition or disease are known, doctors and patients use these given truths to diagnose individual cases.

For example, in Figure 3–1, readers can use a medical guide to see whether they have a serious condition. The chart is based upon the truth about insect bites and stings. The individual reading the chart tries to confirm or deny the symptoms that apply to his or her specific case.

Note that this chart reveals major premises (what is known to be true about insect bites in descending order of danger) and also the conclusion for each case. The chart allows patients to reason deductively by fitting in their own symptoms as the minor premise. Then patients can know how serious their condition may be and what conclusion is justified (i.e., what action to take).

A reader of this chart can easily use a chain argument to discover if a given condition might be serious and can make a good decision about treatment.

Example

Let's say a spider has bitten your friend. If she is wheezing and having difficulty breathing, you can reason deductively as follows:

If wheezing and breathing difficulties follow an insect bite, the bitten person is experiencing a serious allergic reaction.
Marites is wheezing and having breathing difficulties.
Therefore, Marites is experiencing a serious allergic reaction, and

If someone is experiencing a serious allergic reaction, he or she should see a doctor at once.
Marites is experiencing a serious allergic reaction.
Therefore, Marites should see a doctor at once.

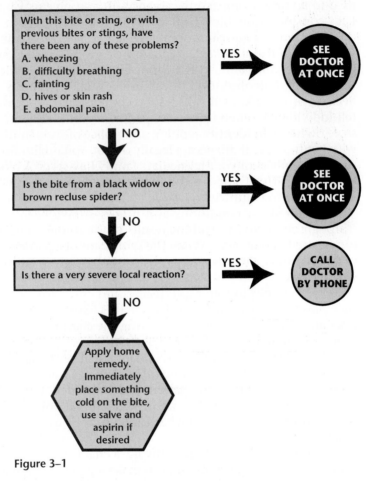

Insect Bites or Stings

Figure 3–1

STOP AND THINK

Can you create syllogisms that would fit other symptoms described in this chart?

Deductive reasoning is also used to establish whether an individual case fits into a specific legal category.

The application of most laws can be clarified through deductive reasoning. For example:

If you went through a red light and caused an accident, you are liable for the damages.

You went through a red light and caused an accident.
Therefore, you are liable for the damages.

There are also specific rights and responsibilities in most business transactions. For example, hotel guests and hotel owners each have specific rights,
and each may be liable for violating those rights. Lawyers in disputes between
business owners and customers refer to the legal regulations when determining whether or not they have a case or a defense.

Deductive reasoning is also used to discover the truth about criminal cases
and what the law requires a jury to conclude about the innocence or guilt of a
defendant.

Consider a prosecutor and a defense attorney presenting arguments to a jury.
One noted criminal case involved two young men who shot and killed their parents. There was no question that the boys committed the crime. The argument in
their trial centered on their motivation: Was the killing a premeditated act by two
children hoping to receive an inheritance, or was it an act motivated by years of
abuse and a desperate sense of helplessness and rage? Reconstructing the positions of both the prosecution and the defense in simple terms, we might note the
following argument. The prosecutor's basic argument could be outlined as follows:

If children murder their parents in cold blood, they deserve to be punished
to the full extent of the law.
These children murdered their parents in cold blood.
Therefore, they deserve to be punished to the full extent of the law.

The defense attorney admitted that the children murdered their parents,
but she added information that brought her to a different conclusion about
sentencing:

If children murder parents because they fear abuse, there are mitigating
circumstances to the murder.
If there are mitigating circumstances, then the children deserve a lighter
sentence.
Therefore, if children murder parents because they fear abuse, they deserve
a lighter sentence.

When jurors can follow the logic of the arguments presented, they can
examine the evidence for both the prosecution and the defense in order to
make their determinations. (See the first article at the end of this chapter for
an interesting difference of opinion between the U.S. Supreme Court and a
state supreme court on issues of sentencing guidelines.)

On a lighter note, deductive reasoning can also reveal truth in various
instances of daily living, especially those involving cultural rules and traditions. Numerous examples of this usage include the rules for sports and games;
traditions for births, weddings, and funerals; codes of conduct; and general

agreements about sportsmanship and fairness. When people make comments regarding various activities and situations, they are often made as enthymemes, those statements that imply, but do not directly state, a complete syllogism.

Note the statements that follow and how they can be "decoded" as conclusions of valid deductive arguments.

Conversation between two golfers:
"Why isn't Fred finishing the round?"
"He was disqualified because of his clubface." (enthymeme)

Decoding

The rules of golf state that no foreign material shall be applied to the clubface for the purpose of influencing the movement of the ball.
If foreign material is applied to the clubface for the purpose of influencing the movement of the ball, the play shall be disqualified. (major premise = the rule)
Foreign material was applied to the clubface used by Fred. (minor premise = the specific violation of the rule)
Therefore, Fred is disqualified. (conclusion)

As stated earlier, Fred can argue whether the minor premise is true or even whether someone may have tried to disqualify him by applying material to his club; however, the *logic* of the rule still applies, and Fred would have to argue that the minor premise is not true in his case.

"My son and his fiancée have finalized their wedding date, so we can reserve the restaurant for the rehearsal dinner."

Decoding

In our wedding tradition, the groom's parents arrange and pay for the rehearsal dinner. (major premise)
We are the groom's parents. (minor premise)
Therefore, we arrange and pay for the rehearsal dinner. (conclusion)

Again, these statements highlight how reasoning is used logically. This syllogism is valid and makes sense within the context given. However, the truth factor may change the reality. If the son and his fiancée decide to elope, or to have a small, family wedding, different traditions would apply.

CLASS EXERCISE

Purpose: To discover the logical reasoning behind the following enthymemes.

A. Decode the following statements as syllogisms. Then discuss whether there are instances in which they may not be true.

Example

One player to another in a Scrabble game: "You have to take those letters off—you can't use Maine as a word."

Decoding

Proper names are prohibited in Scrabble.
Maine is a proper name.
Therefore, Maine is prohibited as a Scrabble word.

1. Usher to guest at wedding: "If you're with the bride, you need to sit on this side."
2. Teacher to student: "You got marked down a grade because you were one day late turning this paper in."
3. Former Red Sox Manager Don Zimmer was fined $5,000 for running across the infield and lunging at Pedro Martinez.
4. After Martinez grabbed Zimmer by the head and tossed him to the ground at Fenway Park, he was fined $50,000.
5. During a game of blackjack: "With 22 points, you're out of this round."
6. Teacher to young students: "You must use your `inside' voices because we're back in the classroom."
7. Concession worker at theatre: "Please finish your coffee before you go into the theatre."
8. Steward to airplane passengers: "It is time to shut off cell phones and other electronic devices because we are taking off now."
9. Garden shop employee to customer: "If you have a shady yard, you don't want to buy these flowers."
10. Financial planner: "We always advise our customers to diversify their assets—have some stocks, some bonds, a variety of investments, to cover the fluctuations in markets."

B. Watch a television program that features a civil trial, such as *People's Court* or *Judge Judy*. Write the plaintiff's argument, the defendant's argument, and the judge's verdict as a syllogism. Comment on the validity and truth of the judge's ruling.

REMINDER

Deductive arguments follow formal patterns of reasoning and are aimed at establishing the certainty of a conclusion. The conclusion's certainty is established when deductive arguments contain true premises (reasons) that are stated in the correct form.

Using Deductive Reasoning to Combat Prejudice and Stereotyping

Much of Aristotle's early work on syllogisms involved categorization of elements of the natural world. These categories help us understand our world by seeing distinguishing features of different species, as exemplified by the following categorical syllogism:

> All animals that nurse their young and have hair are mammals.
> Brown bears nurse their young and have hair.
> Therefore, brown bears are mammals.

Deductive reasoning works well in biology, medicine, engineering, electronics, and law because the categories are well established and agreed upon by experts in each field. Because we are applying individual cases to previously determined "truths," we can know for certain that our conclusions are true within these contexts.

A critical thinker needs to distinguish between major premises (reality assumptions) that fit into these limited truth categories and major premises that have not been and often *cannot* be proven. Although we can say what all mammals have in common, we cannot generalize about groups of people based on ethnicity, religion, gender, political affiliation, profession, or economic status because we cannot study every member of these groups. When we try to fit all Democrats, Cubans, teenagers, or musicians into an all-encompassing mold, we suffer from what general semanticists call a "hardening of the categories," a belief in rigidly held but untrue reality assumptions.

Prejudicial statements involve deductive reasoning that is untrue and unproved, but often logically valid. Let's say that you hear someone comment: "Of course Lisa's a terrible driver—she's a woman!" This enthymeme could be placed into a syllogistic format as follows:

> All women are terrible drivers.
> Lisa is a woman.
> Therefore, Lisa is a terrible driver.

You can see that if the premises of this syllogism were true, then the conclusion would be true. But the major premise given here could never be proven true; we cannot know *all* about any group of individuals.

Stereotyping is a form of classifying people, places, or things according to common traits. Stereotyping works for identical inanimate objects. For example, all computers of a certain model should perform exactly the same functions. If you have a computer that does not perform to specifications, you have a defective model. The manufacturer will likely repair your model or replace it so you have the model you expected. You can easily fashion a sound deductive argument about a new computer:

We cannot study every individual

All new ZX model computers are (2.5)gh machines.
My computer is a new ZX model.
Therefore, my computer is a (2.5)gh machine.

Manufacturers often print logos and numbers on machines to highlight the stereotypical mold into which they fit, so that shoppers know exactly what they can expect from the particular model chosen.

When we stereotype people, however, we are classifying them in ways that do not meet the truth criteria in deductive reasoning. Even if Lisa has been in a number of accidents and has difficulty driving, it's not because she is a woman. The term *woman* refers only to the trait of being female. Every female and every male have numerous individual characteristics that distinguish them from others and make it impossible to fit them into a convenient mold. Because it is impossible to know and study all members of any human ethnic, religious, gender, political, economic, or interest group, a stereotype about people on this basis can always be challenged as untrue and therefore unsound. (See Exercise 3.3.)

SKILL

A critical thinker uses reasoning to discover truth and prevent stereotyping.

Questionable Premises: Using Deduction to Understand Argument

Deductive reasoning is an important tool for constructive argumentation. As we noted in the first chapter, an issue involves controversy, that is, more than one plausible side of an argument. Understanding the process of deduction helps us outline our own reasoning and the reasoning of others, so that we can see if it is, first of all, logical (following correct form), and, second, grounded in truth.

Consider this syllogism:

All drivers who speed are subject to a fine.
You are speeding.
Therefore, you are subject to a fine.

In this example, you might agree with the major premise but question the minor premise.

For our purposes, we will call the questionable premise the **premise of contention.** Critical thinkers will argue about the premise of contention rather than about the conclusion. That is to say, critical thinkers will argue about reality assumptions, the reasons that form the basis of conclusions.

When people argue about conclusions, stalemates are inevitable. Adults end up sounding like children arguing over who left the door open:

argue
about
premise
not
conclusion

"You did it."
"No, I didn't."
"Yes, you did."
"No, I didn't."...

Parents who weren't at the scene of the crime have little basis for a rational judgment on an issue like this. Only real evidence (fingerprints, videotapes, or witnesses) would help them get to the truth.

The same frustrating process occurs in some sexual harassment cases, often called "he said, she said" issues. If there are no witnesses, tapes, letters, or other forms of evidence, then the accuser has no proof of being a victim and the accused has no proof of being innocent. Focusing on conclusions without accompanying evidence statements creates no-win arguments.

So what can we reasonably do in arguments that seem to lead to stalemates? Let's take the highly charged issue of abortion. At demonstrations, we may witness a scene that is hardly more sophisticated than the one between children noted previously, as the advocates for both sides focus on conclusions:

"Unborn children are worthy of protection."
"No, they're not."
"Yes, they are."
"No, they're not."...

If we can use deductive reasoning to uncover the beliefs of both sides, we can then focus our efforts on fruitful areas of inquiry. For example, we might outline the "pro-life" argument as follows:

All human life is valuable and worthy of protection.
An unborn child is a human life.
Therefore, an unborn child deserves protection.

Those who are "pro-choice" would find the minor premise to be the premise of contention; the contentious factor is whether or not an unborn child is a human life. In a similar manner, we might outline the pro-choice reasoning:

Tissue masses have no civil rights.
A fetus is a tissue mass.
Therefore, a fetus has no civil rights.

Which is the premise of contention in this syllogism?

Both syllogisms are valid since the conclusions follow logically from the premises. But the premise of contention in both cases is the minor one. So, each side needs to focus efforts on proving that its minor premise is true.

Note here that the arguments sound different depending on the terminology used—*unborn child, fetus, tissue mass, human life.* Chapter 7 will focus on the power of words to shape our perceptions of an issue.

The Born Loser Reprinted by permission of Newspaper Enterprise Association, Inc.

REMINDER

In deductive arguments, a critical thinker will (1) outline his or her argument and the argument of the other person, (2) determine if the arguments are valid, (3) find the premise(s) of contention, and then (4) argue that his or her premises are true.

LIFE APPLICATION: TIPS FOR COLLEGE AND CAREER

When you are listening to a discussion in class or at a meeting, try to find and understand the reality assumptions that are held by various speakers. Also look for reality assumptions that form the basis of policies at work and at school (e.g., note the assumptions behind a policy that requires uniforms for certain jobs) and that form the rules for games and sports.

If you are arguing for a change in policy, try to present the old policy in the form of a logical syllogism and then show why the new policy would be more useful.

CHAPTER EXERCISES

Exercise 3.1   Purpose: To find assumptions made by professionals in various fields. Consider your major area of study. What are some assumptions made by people in that field? If you study dance therapy, then you must assume that dance can be psychologically helpful to people. If you study ecology, then you must believe that the environment is a system that needs to be balanced.

Example

"I am studying early childhood education because I assume children need some structured experiences before they get to kindergarten. I also assume they learn best if they have lots of time to be creative and explore. And I assume they need lots of interaction with other kids to learn to share and relate.

"I have argued with some of my teachers who assume children should learn to read before kindergarten. We know that children can learn to read early and they can learn some math, but my assumption is they'll burn out if they have to study so young. And I also assume they'll catch up and be happier than kids who had to read so soon."

Exercise 3.2 Purpose: To examine how reality assumptions affect decisions.

Think of several decisions you have made recently (voting, consumer, relational) and try to find the reality assumption behind the decision. Express the reality assumption as a major premise in a deductive argument.

Example

"My boyfriend was invited to my family reunion, which lasted over a weekend. We went out to breakfast and lunch with my parents each day, and I noticed that he never offered to pay for anything; he let my parents pick up the tab in every case. I was really upset and decided that he wasn't marriage material. My reality assumption fits into a chain argument: If a man is serious about a relationship, he will want to impress a woman's family. If he wants to impress a woman's family, he will offer to pay for meals when they go out. Therefore, if a man is serious about a relationship, he will offer to pay for meals when they go out.

"I was really angry on our way back to school, and I told him I thought he was really selfish. He was surprised and hurt and said that he would have been glad to pay, but he thought it would be rude to offer, since he was a guest. He was actually raised to believe that it is insulting to hosts to offer to pay for meals. Then I realized that he always pays when we go out and doesn't even ask me to pitch in. Acting on my reality assumption would have broken us up."

Exercise 3.3 Purpose: To construct syllogisms from prejudicial statements.

Most prejudicial statements can be unraveled as valid arguments with false premises. Think of a prejudicial statement that has been directed at you (or a friend) in the past. Reconstruct that statement into syllogistic form.

Example

"My friend is on welfare because her husband left her and her two children. She can't find a job that would make enough money for her to afford child care. When people find out she is on welfare, they tell her she should be working and not sponging off of society. Their reasoning is that

All people on welfare are lazy.
You are on welfare.
Therefore, you are lazy.

"There might be some people who fit into this description, but it's unfair to put all people who need welfare into this category. I think if people understood my friend's situation, they would be less judgmental and more sympathetic."

CHAPTER HIGHLIGHTS

1. Reality assumptions are beliefs about what is true and false; these beliefs are often taken for granted, and they are part of the foundation of a person's argument.

2. Reality assumptions need to be brought to light and examined so that those who make them do not build arguments on untrue or unconsidered premises.

3. Reality assumptions can be discovered and examined through deductive reasoning and through the Toulmin model of argumentation.

4. In deductive reasoning, the conclusion is inferred from the premises. When the premises follow correct syllogistic patterns, the argument is considered valid. A conclusion inferred from true premises that are expressed in valid form creates a sound argument.

5. Critical thinkers focus on whether premises lead to reliable conclusions.

6. Deductive reasoning helps us discover and examine our underlying assumptions, find both logic and truth in an argument, make clear decisions, avoid prejudice and stereotyping, and understand argument.

KEY TERMS

Reality assumption (p. 68)

Inductive reasoning (p. 79)

Deductive reasoning (p. 80)

Deductive argument (p. 80)

Valid (p. 80)

Sound (p. 80)

Syllogism (p. 80)

Major premise (p. 80)

Minor premise (p. 80)

Categorical statement (p. 80)

Conditional syllogism (p. 81)

Hypothetical syllogism (p. 81)

Modus ponens (p. 81)

Modus tollens (p. 82)

Chain argument (p. 82)

Disjunctive syllogism (p. 83)

Argument by elimination (p. 83)

Enthymeme (p. 84)

Grounds (p. 85)

Stereotyping (p. 94)

Premise of contention (p. 95)

CHAPTER CHECKUP

Short Answer

1. How can deductive reasoning be used in daily life?
2. What is the difference between a value assumption and a reality assumption?

Sentence Completion

3. When the premises of a deductive argument follow the correct form, we call the argument _____.
4. When the premises of a deductive argument follow the correct form and are also true, we call the argument _____.
5. A deductive argument containing two premises and a conclusion is called a _____.
6. Beliefs about what is true or false that are often taken for granted are called _____.
7. While inductive reasoning looks at probability, deductive reasoning aims to establish _____.

True-False

8. General semanticists call stereotyping a "hardening of the categories."
9. When we build an argument on assumptions that are not grounded in truth, our arguments are faulty and the actions we recommend will not achieve our desired ends.
10. The premise of contention is the area of agreement in an argument.

ARTICLES FOR DISCUSSION

As we have seen, deductive reasoning can be used to argue about the truth of premises; when truth is discovered, good decisions can be made. Judges use deductive reasoning to make rulings and to sentence defendants according to their best interpretation of legal guidelines. When rulings are questionned, appeals of convictions and sentences can be made to higher courts up to the highest court of a country.

This first article involves a case that was ruled upon by a judge; the ruling was appealed to a state supreme court and upheld, and it was then sent to the U.S. Supreme Court, where it was reversed. Notice how the law was interpreted differently by the state and federal courts.

STATE'S CRIMINAL SENTENCING SYSTEM UNCONSTITUTIONAL, SUPREME COURT RULES

Bob Egelko

California's sentencing law violates the right to a jury trial because it allows judges to add years to a prison term based on their own fact-finding, the U.S. Supreme Court ruled Monday in a case that will force the state to re-examine basic questions of crime and punishment.

The 6–3 ruling could take four years off the 16-year sentence of a convicted child molester from Contra Costa County who challenged the law, and it could shorten the terms of several thousand other prisoners who were given maximum sentences by judges.

It also requires the state to change its sentencing law while it struggles to contain the soaring costs of an overcrowded prison system.

"This is an opportunity to take an in-depth look at how things are functioning," said new Attorney General Jerry Brown, who as governor signed the 1977 law that the Court struck down. "In the meantime, there will be a significant number of cases that will have to be retried."

The 1977 law was designed to promote uniform sentences—equal times for equal crimes—by eliminating parole boards' authority to set terms for most prisoners. Instead, the law gave judges the power to choose among three sentences for each crime.

The case before the Supreme Court was brought by John Cunningham of San Pablo, a former Richmond police officer who was convicted of sexually abusing his son from December 1999 to October 2000. The boy, who turned 10 during that period, said his father had molested him two or three times a week, sometimes accompanied by threats or beatings.

Cunningham insisted he was innocent, saying his son had a history of lying. His convictions are final, however, and the ruling concerned only his sentence.

Under California law, Cunningham's crime—continuous sexual abuse of a child—was punishable by 6, 12 or 16 years in prison. The law required the judge to choose the middle term unless facts about the defendant or the crime justified the longer or shorter term. Those facts were determined by the judge after the jury conviction.

The judge in Cunningham's case imposed the maximum sentence after finding that the boy had been particularly vulnerable and that Cunningham had committed the crime with great violence and posed a danger to society. None of those issues had been submitted to the jury.

The pre-1977 law set a much broader range of sentences—one to 15 years, for example, or 10 years to life—and let the parole board decide when a prisoner was ready for release. The law was attacked from both the political right, which said board members were being duped into premature paroles, and the left, which said sentences were prolonged arbitrarily or for political reasons.

The 1977 law has made sentences more predictable. But the state prison population, then just over 20,000, now totals 172,000, while the crime rate has changed little.

Monday's ruling followed Supreme Court decisions in 2004 and 2005 that overturned sentencing laws in other states as well as the federal sentencing rules. In those cases, the court found that the law improperly subjected a defendant to a longer term based on a judge's assessment of the facts.

The California law, "by placing sentence-elevating fact-finding within the judge's province, violates a defendant's right to trial by jury," Justice Ruth Bader Ginsburg said in the majority opinion, which rejected a 2005 state supreme court ruling upholding the law.

Although a jury must find a defendant guilty beyond a reasonable doubt, Ginsburg noted, a California judge can increase the standard sentence based on facts that the judge finds more likely than not to be true.

Dissenting Justice Samuel Alito said the state law allowed a judge to choose a reasonable sentence within the range established by the legislature, similar to the system that the Supreme Court imposed when it struck down the federal sentencing law in 2005. Justices Anthony Kennedy and Stephen Breyer joined his dissent.

The Court did not order specific changes in the law, saying that was up to state legislators. Defense lawyers generally favor the option that many states adopted after court rulings: allowing a jury to decide all facts affecting sentences.

The uniformity promoted by the 1977 law "can still be achieved. You just have to add one procedural protection for defendants," said Jeffrey Fisher, a Stanford law professor who filed arguments with the court on behalf of the National Association of Criminal Defense Lawyers.

But David LaBahn, executive director of the California District Attorneys Association, said prosecutors prefer an approach that would eliminate the current requirement that judges in most cases choose the middle of the three sentences. Judges would then have free rein to select any of the three options without invading the domain of the jury, whose verdict would have made all three choices available, he said.

Fisher countered that such a system would make sentencing less predictable.

Brown said he would like to increase the authority of the parole board, and perhaps judges, to tailor prison terms.

"We need greater individualization of sentences because some inmates require more punishment than others," the attorney general said.

With prison costs contributing heavily to the state's budget deficit, both Gov. Arnold Schwarzenegger and state Sen. Gloria Romero, D-Los Angeles, the Senate majority leader, have proposed commissions to advise legislators on sentencing.

Romero said Monday that the ruling made the creation of an independent commission more urgent. Schwarzenegger issued a statement saying he would "work to ensure that this decision will not be a threat to public safety."

About 15 percent of the felons sentenced to prison in California receive longer terms, according to state statistics. But only a small percentage of those—which no one could estimate Monday—will be affected by the ruling. Most state inmates were sentenced under plea agreements under which they agreed to the prison term and waived the right to appeal even if the sentencing laws were later overturned.

The remainder can seek resentencing to middle terms. They include Cunningham, whose term would be reduced to 12 years.

Those reductions would not be automatic, however. In Cunningham's case, Deputy District Attorney John Cope of Contra Costa County said he would ask the sentencing judge to convene a new jury to find facts that would justify the 16-year term.

But Cunningham's lawyer, Peter Gold, said such a hearing would amount to retrying the case. LaBahn of the District Attorneys Association said such hearings might violate the constitutional ban on double jeopardy.

The case is Cunningham vs. California, 05-6551.

How they voted:

How the U.S. Supreme Court voted Monday in a 6–3 ruling striking down California's sentencing law:

Majority: Ruth Bader Ginsburg, John Paul Stevens, Antonin Scalia, David Souter, Clarence Thomas, Chief Justice John Roberts.

Dissent: Samuel Alito, Anthony Kennedy, Stephen Breyer.

QUESTIONS FOR DISCUSSION

1. What was the logic of the judge who first ruled on this case and the California Supreme Court that upheld his ruling? Can you put their logic into a syllogism?

2. Under which guidelines did the U.S. Supreme Court reverse the state court's ruling? Try to phrase the Supreme Court ruling in a syllogism.

3. In light of what the judge discovered in the case of Cunningham vs. California, do you believe that the sentence was appropriate to the crime? Why or Why not?

4. How do facts established "beyond a reasonable doubt" vary from facts based on a "preponderance of the evidence?" What reality assumption is behind the need to prove a case beyond a reasonable doubt?

5. One of the U.S. Supreme Court justices stated that California could keep its determinate sentences but change the law by giving judges "broad discretion" to impose any of the three possible sentences. Do you believe that provision would be an improvement to state laws?

In the following article, columnist Leonard Pitts Jr. discusses and challenges current assumptions about racism held by many in the academic community. As you read it, notice the logical bases of his arguments. Try to put them in the form of categorical or conditional syllogisms.

CAN BLACKS BE RACIST?

Leonard Pitts Jr.

"Black people cannot be racist."

It's been maybe 20 years since the first time I heard some member of the black intelligentsia say that on an afternoon talk show. Naturally, all hell broke loose.

Years later, all hell still awaits repair.

I base that assessment on the response to something I did in a recent column. Namely, I defined racism as "this practice of demeaning and denying based on the darkness of skin."

Man, what'd I want to go and say that for? The flood of letters has been unrelenting, dozens of aggrieved Caucasians wanting your poor, benighted correspondent to know that racism, thank you very much, is also felt by those whose skin is not dark at all. Several folks figured I must be one'a them black folk who considers black folk incapable of racism. One individual went so far as to contend that yours truly, like most blacks, hasn't a clue what racism really is.

Well, golly, where to begin?

First, my take on the "blacks can't be racist" argument: Unassailable logic, unfortunate rhetoric.

People who make that argument reason as follows: Yes, blacks can be prejudiced or bigoted, but not "racist" because racism involves systemic oppression—the wielding of power. As blacks neither wield power nor control the system, the reasoning goes, it's beyond their ability to be racist.

I get impatient with people who make the argument in those terms, terms that seem, frankly, calibrated to produce more confrontation than insight. Most people who hear the point framed in that way are, understandably, unable to get past those first inflammatory words: "Blacks can't be racist."

So let's frame it another way. Let's allow that black folks can, indeed, be racist. Or prejudiced, intolerant, biased, bigoted or any other word that floats your boat. Black people are, after all, members of the human race and, as such, are heir to all the idiocy by which human beings are beset.

But with that established, let's also say this: It's an affront to common sense to suggest there is equivalence between black-on-white bigotry and its opposite. This is the point the black intelligentsia's rhetoric has obscured and people like my correspondents have denied, avoided and ignored. As an aggregate, bigoted blacks have much less power to injure whites than vice versa. They also have less history of doing so. These are incontrovertible facts that render hollow the yowling demands that the racism of blacks be accorded a place in the national consciousness commensurate with that of white people.

Hey, when you find a black bigot, feel free to censure and ostracize him or her as the circumstance warrants. I don't care. Just don't pretend the transgression is what it is not. Don't claim it represents a significant threat to the quality of life of white Americans at large.

Because if it represents such a threat, then where are the statistics demonstrating how black bias against whites translates to the mass denial of housing, bank loans, education, employment opportunities, voting rights, medical care or justice? And please, spare me the anecdote about Jane, who couldn't get into school, or Joe, who lost his job, because of affirmative action.

Not the same. Not even close. There are, in fact, reams of statistics documenting that racism has fostered generation after generation of Joes and Janes—not to mention Jamillas, Rasheeds and Keshias—in the African American community. And those numbers come not from the NAACP, the Nation of Islam, the Congressional Black Caucus or any other group with an ax to grind but, rather, from the federal government and from university think tanks. Yet even with those bona fides, some people find evidence of white racism's power dishearteningly easy to ignore.

They have to, I suppose. Otherwise, they wouldn't be able to continue pretending an equivalency that does not exist. And somewhere inside, even THEY must recognize that fact.

Put it like this: If given the option of going through life as a white man suffering the effects of black racism or the reverse, I know which one I'd choose.

Tribune Media Services, January 11, 2002. Copyright © 2002 by Tribune Media Services. Reprinted by permission of The Permissions Group on behalf of TMS Reprints.

QUESTIONS FOR DISCUSSION

1. Pitts makes the following comment:

[M]y take on the 'blacks can't be racist' argument: Unassailable logic, unfortunate rhetoric.

People who make that argument reason as follows: Yes, blacks can be prejudiced or bigoted, but not `racist' because racism involves systemic oppression—the wielding of power. As blacks neither wield power nor control the system, the reasoning goes, it's beyond their ability to be racist.

Can you phrase his commentary as a deductive argument? Why does he call the argument unassailably logical but unfortunate in its rhetoric?

2. When Pitts claims that blacks can be racist, how is he defining the word *racist*?

3. What point is Pitts making in this column about the difference between black and white bigotry?

Andrew Lam is a writer and commentator on cultural issues. In the following article, he discusses how he realized that his definition of "garbage" changed when his cousin came to visit him from their native Vietnam. Notice as you read that Lam also is made aware of how his value assumptions changed when he became assimilated to his new country.

WASTED FOOD, DISCOVERED SOULS

Andrew Lam

Last week, I took a cousin newly arrived from Vietnam for a tour of downtown San Francisco, hoping to impress him with America's architectural grandeur. But the tall and shiny high-rises were all too overwhelming for him, and my cousin became very quiet.

Then, as we walked past a large garbage bin filled with papers and boxes, he suddenly stopped and stared, "Brother," he said. "In Vietnam this stuff is all money."

This relative of mine is not an environmentalist. His comment simply reflects his own frugal, third world background. Everything is useful; nothing ever goes to waste.

Back home, he told me, a family could live for a week recycling these papers. "I can't believe they throw all this stuff away," he said, shaking his head. And I felt a slight tug of guilt. My garbage, too, is often full of papers and cans and discarded food.

Yet I am not unfamiliar with his feelings of indignation. I, too, came from that agrarian-based ethos in which land is sacred and everything yielded from the good earth must be treasured. Indeed, what I throw away today would have astounded me years ago.

When my family and I first came to America two decades ago as refugees, my job was to spy on the supermarket across the street from our apartment. When they threw away expired food, my brother and I would spring into action. One night, as we dragged a carton full of outdated frozen pizzas, TV dinners, and cookie dough across the parking lot, we were stopped by a policeman.

Red-faced and stuttering, we offered to return the food to the garbage bin, but the policeman shrugged. "Help yourself, boys," he said, and walked away. But my brother and I never went back. If we were once shocked by America's opulence, we have long since learned to take it for granted that, well, there's plenty more where that came from.

But my cousin got me thinking: Perhaps a sure sign of successful assimilation into an over-developed society is when an immigrant tosses away his sense of frugality and his deep appreciation for what once sustained him.

At home after our excursion, my cousin helped me prepare dinner. A few pieces of apple and pears accidentally fell from my chopping block onto the floor. Immediately, he stooped to pick them up. "You don't have to do that," I wanted to say, but something in his meticulous gesture stopped me.

Instead, as I watched him, a distant and long-cherished memory emerged. I am five years old standing at the edge of a golden rice field at harvest time in the Mekong Delta where my family came from, and watching farmers stoop to gather rice.

I had wanted to show my cousin America's grandeur, but it was he who showed me something else far lovelier. There, on the shiny tile floor of my kitchen, my cousin, too, was busy gathering bits of our old identities—scattered pieces of our soul.

Reprinted by permission of the author. Andrew Lam is an editor with Pacific News Service. He is working on his first short story collection.

QUESTIONS FOR DISCUSSION

1. What are the differing assumptions of Andrew Lam and his cousin about both the high-rise buildings and the contents of the garbage bins in San Francisco?

2. Lam states, "I, too, came from that agrarian-based ethos in which land is sacred and everything yielded from the good earth must be treasured. Indeed, what I throw away today would have astounded me years ago." How do you think Lam's assumptions about garbage were changed?

3. America is referred to as an "over-developed" society in this article. Do you believe that a society can be overdeveloped? To what extent can development and appreciation of the land harmoniously coexist?

The following humorous article, created by *The Onion*, provides a good example of how deductive truth is subject to change when new information is discovered.

Pluto was considered the 9th planet from 1930 until 2006. This smallest and most distant planet had always been somewhat different from the other planets because it was tiny, solid, and moved in a less circular, more elongated orbit than the other eight. While the other planets moved within the boundaries of the constellations of the zodiac, Pluto's path was above and below that band.

Classification is critical to any field of study, and in August 2006 the International Astronomical Union redefined the term "planet" and then reclassified Pluto as a "dwarf planet" based on their decision that a planet should be large enough that its gravity would clear out its region in space. That demoted Pluto to the status of "dwarf planet," a category that it shares with the former asteroids Eris, Ceres, and other objects yet to be discovered.

BEARER OF BAD NEWS

NASA Launches Probe to Inform Pluto of Demotion

In August, the International Astronomical Union downgraded Pluto to a dwarf planet. The panel of experts met to officially redefine the characteristics of a planet. To deliver the news to the distant orb about its newly lowered status, scientists at NASA's Kennedy Space Center launched a special messenger probe in September.

"It's tough, but we thought giving it to Pluto straight was the right thing to do," NASA Chief Engineer James Wood said. "After all, it put in 76 years as our ninth planet—it just didn't seem fair to break the news with an impersonal radio transmission beamed from Earth."

The Consoler probe is scheduled to reach Pluto in 2016. Upon landing on the planetoid's surface, the probe will relay to Pluto the news of its demotion, then orbit the tiny celestial body and radio messages of gratitude for its eons of planetary service to convince Pluto that it is still a highly valued part of the solar system's configuration.

"Pluto is more than 3.5 billion miles from the sun," Wood said. "Launching that probe felt like the best way to avoid alienating it any further."

Wood said Consoler will "take pains" to explain to Pluto that the reasons for the demotion "had nothing to do with anything it did personally."

"It was a great planet, and it will be a great dwarf planet," Wood said of Pluto's tenure. "No one is questioning its orbit around the sun, and of course Pluto's gravity and pressure gradient force is plenty sufficient to maintain hydrostatic equilibrium. Pluto still has three moons: Charon, Hydra and Nix. No one's going to take that away from it."

Scientists at NASA have taken precautions that word of the demotion will not reach Pluto before Consoler does. The New Horizons probe, which will pass by Pluto in July 2015, has been instructed to maintain radio silence. It is, however, programmed to congratulate nearby Eris and Ceres for their promotion from asteroids to dwarf planets.

"The Consoler probe will reach Pluto on a Friday, if our calculations are correct," Wood said. "It's always better to do this kind of thing right before the weekend."

QUESTIONS FOR DISCUSSION

1. Consider this major premise of a categorical syllogism:

   A planet is a large spherical object that orbits a star and does not emit light. What needs to be added to this premise to exclude Pluto from being classified as a planet?

2. The first official AIU list of the Sun's planets includes Mercury, Venus, Mars, Jupiter, Saturn, Uranus, and Neptune. For 76 years, students were taught that there were nine planets. How does this new categorization exemplify the tentative nature of our knowledge?

3. What changes in curriculum need to be made when a new discovery makes our former assumptions outdated?

4. Read more about it: Trace the reasons why Pluto was considered a planet for so long and all of the factors creating the change. Also, look for areas of new discovery set in motion by the changed definition of planets and dwarf planets.

IDEAS FOR WRITING OR SPEAKING

1. Explain three or four assumptions made by your culture, subculture, or family. These assumptions can be about use of time and/or resources; holiday traditions; the roles of men, women, and/or children; or the place of work, family, and citizenship.

Example

"One assumption of my family is that everyone will go to college. My parents were expected to go to college by their parents, even though their parents didn't have the money to go themselves.

"It was never directly stated that we had to go to college; it was just taken for granted that we would. My parents would start sentences by saying, 'When you go to college...' or 'After you finish college....'

"When my little brother decided to get a job right after high school, everyone was in shock. It never occurred to us that we wouldn't all go straight to college. After he worked two years in a warehouse, my brother did decide to attend college. Maybe he was living up to the family's expectations, but I think he was hoping for an easier life!"

2. Choose a social, political, or religious movement or group and write about three assumptions that guide this group. Take a position, agreeing or disagreeing with the assumptions of this group. Begin with an introductory paragraph that contains your conclusion (thesis statement). Then write a paragraph for each assumption you discuss. End with a paragraph that summarizes your beliefs about the underlying assumptions of this group.

   Some possible topics for this assignment: Greenpeace, the Young Republicans, the Democratic Party, the Libertarian Party, Christianity, Hinduism, Judaism, Islam, feminism, Action for Children's Television, The National Rifle Association, Mothers Against Drunk Drivers, the Society for the Prevention of Cruelty to Animals, and Amnesty International.

3. Using the same organizational format as Idea 2, explore the assumptions made by both sides of a controversial issue. For example, you might explore the assumptions of people who support and people who are against tuition for community colleges. One assumption of those who support tuition might be that people work harder when they have to pay for education; an assumption of those against tuition might be that fees are an unnecessary and prohibitive burden on the poor and that they are therefore "classist."

   Find several assumptions on both sides of your issue. Then explain which assumptions are the most reasonable and why.

FILMS FOR ANALYSIS AND DISCUSSION

Martin Scorsese's *The Departed* (2006, R) is a film that keeps the audience guessing even though much information seems to be provided at an early stage. Within the first few minutes of the film, we find out that there is a police informant within the Boston mafia (Leonardo DiCaprio), and someone working for the mafia in the Massachusetts' State Police Department (Matt Damon). Although the men have not met, their actions determine the fate of both their lives. What is assumed to be the truth almost never is in this film, and, even when the credits roll, the answers aren't delivered in a nicely wrapped package.

Similar Films and Classics

Crash (2005, R)

The film involves a number of characters of different racial, ethnic, professional, and socio-economic backgrounds. Note the many assumptions and stereotypes made by the characters and how they all turn out to be wrong.

The Verdict (1981, R)

The Verdict is a fascinating story in which a lawyer realizes that the willingness of all parties to settle out of court will hurt his client and hide the truth of the medical malpractice that brought the lawsuit. Note the self-protective assumptions made by most of the defendants.

To Kill a Mockingbird (1962)

This story, told from the point of view of a woman remembering the events of her childhood, makes many statements about stereotyping and harmful reality assumptions. The main character's father, a lawyer who defends an unjustly accused black man in 1932 Alabama, is the voice of reason about the trial and other life lessons. The father Atticus tells his daughter, "You never know someone until you step inside their skin and walk around a little."

Twelve Angry Men (1957)

This classic story, which has since been made into a TV movie, tells of the struggles of a jury to reach a unanimous verdict in a murder trial. Each juror makes different reality assumptions and sticks to them until a second look at the evidence creates a breakthrough. This is an excellent example of the various perspectives that emerge when a group decision needs to be made.

4

Inductive Arguments: Statistical and Causal Generalizations

Prove It to Me: What Are the Statistics?

A critical thinker understands the basics of polling and the legitimate uses of statistical research in supporting conclusions.

A critical thinker understands the structure and uses of inductive reasoning, including statistical and causal generalizations.

This chapter will cover

- The use of statistical evidence in arguments

- The reporting of statistical data

- The use of causal generalizations

In the last three chapters, we focused on the foundations of arguments, including issues, reasons, conclusions, value assumptions, and reality assumptions. We looked at deduction as a tool to help us discern the logic and the truth of the statements we make and to base our decisions on sound reasoning.

As we discussed in the first chapter, anyone can have an opinion (conclusion) and give reasons for that opinion. But the critical thinker evaluates the quality and credibility of the reasons before offering or accepting a conclusion. Inductive arguments aim at establishing strong, if not absolutely certain, conclusions. Inductive strength is based on good evidence from which we can draw useful generalizations.

In this chapter, we will consider the kinds of evidence and the quality of the evidence used to support inductive generalizations; we will learn principles for evaluating both statistical generalizations and causal generalizations.

INDUCTIVE REASONING

Thus far, we have looked at the concept of deductive certainty and the criteria for developing a sound deductive argument. Ideally, all of the issues that we face could be resolved with certainty by following correct reasoning. In our human state, however, very few conclusions can be proven beyond a shadow of a doubt. Even our criminal court system asks only that a conclusion be proven "beyond a *reasonable* doubt." That means the evidence does offer strong support for the conclusion with the reservation that there may be an *unusual* exception. When we offer evidence that gives weight (but not complete certainty) to a conclusion, we are reasoning inductively.

Inductive arguments are evaluated on the basis of their strength. A strong inductive argument does not guarantee the truth of the conclusion but rather provides strong support for the conclusion.

If we can present evidence to prove that a premise (assertion, statement) is very *likely* to be true, we have valuable information on which to base our decisions. In addition, if we know there can be exceptions, we can understand them when they are encountered.

The process of **induction** occurs when we use facts or research findings to make generalizations. Stated in coded form, we offer proof that *most* As are Bs. Therefore, if I encounter an A, it is probably a B. However, I realize that there are exceptions. Robert Pirsig explains the difference between induction and deduction in his book *Zen and the Art of Motorcycle Maintenance*:

> Two kinds of logic are used, inductive and deductive....If the cycle goes over a bump and the engine misfires, and then goes over another bump and the engine misfires, and then goes over a long smooth stretch of road and there is no misfiring, and then goes over a [third] bump and the engine misfires again, one can logically conclude that the misfi is caused by the bumps. That is induction....

past experiences — personal or not

If, from reading the hierarchy of facts about the machine, the mechanic knows the horn of the cycle is powered exclusively by electricity from the battery, then he can logically infer that if the battery is dead the horn will not work. That is deduction.[1]

Most of the issues we face on a daily basis involve inductive reasoning. We gather facts from our background experiences and our reading and research—experiential and empirical data—to come to conclusions that make sense to us because of their strength. We then use these conclusions to guide our actions. For example, let's say a woman receives a call from her sister who tells her that she has developed breast cancer. The woman does some research and talks to her own doctor. Her inductive reasoning goes like this:

> Researchers claim that most women who have a family history of breast cancer (P) will develop breast cancer (Q). (Most Ps are Qs).
> My mother (m1) developed breast cancer (Q).
> My sister (m2) developed breast cancer (Q).
> My two aunts (m3 and m4) had breast cancer (Q).
> Since m1, m2, m3, and m4 constitute family members, I have a family history (P); I (m5) am P.
> Therefore, it is likely that I (m5) will also develop breast cancer (Q). (Conclusion—m5 will probably be Q, because most Ps are Qs.)

Conclusions based on strong inductive reasoning

Can you see that the conclusion "It is likely that I will also develop breast cancer" is not a certainty, but a strong possibility? The woman who reasons in this way can now examine her choices in a logical manner. She can do a reasonable risk assessment about her chances of developing cancer and also her chances of recovery if she were to develop this form of cancer. Some women faced with this family history have had healthy breasts removed before cancer could develop. These women will never know if they might have "dodged the bullet" and avoided the disease without having taken these measures. But they reasoned that, in their individual cases, the probability was high enough and the consequences grave enough to justify their actions.

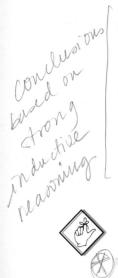

REMINDER

Critical thinkers use the process of induction to draw reasonable conclusions and to make thoughtful decisions.

---

[1] Robert M. Pirsig, *Zen and the Art of Motorcycle Maintenance: An Inquiry into Values* (New York: William Morrow, 1974), 99.

When you use **inductive reasoning**, you look at evidence and draw conclusions that are not certain, but likely. These conclusions are called *inductive generalizations*. All inductive generalizations are *possible*, but within the range of possibility, some are much more *probable* than others because they are based on good, convincing evidence (see Figure 4–1).

Many deductive premises are derived from previous inductive arguments with strong evidence. For example, a parent may present the following major premise of a deductive argument to a son or daughter heading off to college:

> *If you charge more on your credit card than you can afford, you will get yourself into debt.*

The student—let's call him David—leaves for school and is suddenly faced with the responsibility of handling finances above the tuition and housing that his parents have paid and a small scholarship that gives him the money for books. David gets a part-time job at a DVD store to cover the expenses of clothing, entertainment, gas, insurance and repairs for his car, and any other goodies he may wish to buy.

David has been careful not to use the credit card that was sent to him, but he does keep it in his wallet, just in case. As the school year goes by, some unexpected expenses use up most of his salary, and David starts using the credit card: He has to have a brake job on his car, he wants new clothes for a dance, and he meets someone that he'd like to take out for dinner and a movie once a week.

When some of David's friends ask him to join them on a vacation during the winter break, he knows he can't afford to go but decides to charge the trip anyway. When he returns from his vacation, a bill from his credit card company reveals that his monthly payment has gone up for the third time.

If he took the time, David might reason:

> The first time I overcharged, I owed more to the credit card company every month.
> The second time I overcharged, I owed so much that I had to extend my working hours to pay the credit card bill.
> The third time I overcharged, I realized that my monthly payment would be used just to pay the finance charge, and it would take several years to pay off what I owe.
> Because of all of these incidents, I'm in debt.
> Therefore, if I overcharge on credit cards, I will be in debt.

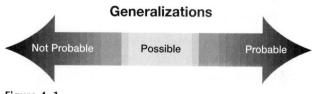

Generalizations

Not Probable   Possible   Probable

Figure 4–1

David has come to this conclusion *inductively,* through a series of experiences. He has learned from his mistakes that it is harmful to overcharge on his credit cards. Probably, David will pass his wisdom on to his own future children, in the form of a *deductive* argument:

> If people overcharge on their credit cards, they will be in debt.
> I overcharged on my credit card.
> Therefore, I was in debt.

His children may be wise enough to learn from their father's experience and avoid making the same mistakes. But they may be like many of us and come to the truth inductively, through personal trials and errors.

Inductive generalizations, such as those discovered in David's case, are also foundational to more formal decision-making situations. For example, once a jury in a criminal trial hears the arguments of both prosecution and defense, the members of the jury begin to use inductive reasoning to examine the evidence. They receive some information that is definitely true; for example, they may know that a murder has been committed. They may also receive undeniably factual information about the DNA of the victim and of the defendant and about the legal issues involved in the case.

However, the jury will hear different interpretations about what may be concluded from the given factual information. Both sides will try to convince the jury of the strength of their arguments by presenting the statements of experts and of witnesses; by citing research, statistics and forensic evidence; by using examples of similar cases; and by searching for a pattern or sequence of events that would explain that the defendant did (or did not) commit the crime. Their interpretations of the various types of evidence will be expressed as inductive generalizations.

In this chapter and the next, we will focus on methods of examining and assessing the strength of evidence used to support conclusions in inductive arguments, whether the issue is the guilt or innocence of a defendant, the qualifications of a political candidate, the usefulness of a product or service, or the importance of a social cause.

When you understand various forms of inductive reasoning, you are better equipped to evaluate the quality of the evidence people give for their conclusions. You can then support convincing arguments and refute poorly supported arguments. You will be ready to strengthen and defend your own reasoning and to make good decisions based on that reasoning.

STATISTICAL EVIDENCE

Statistical evidence, which leads to the form of inductive reasoning known as **statistical generalizations,** refers to data collected by polling and research studies. Pollsters and researchers use systematic methods to get results with great predictive value; that is, they can tell us what probably will happen in a given situation. For example, a Gallup poll or a Harris poll generally reflects how people will vote and who will be elected to political office.

Why do we carry out research aimed at generating accurate statistics? One motivation for doing research is to have a sense of control over our individual and collective futures; as critically thinking people, we want to act clearly, deliberately, and responsibly. We want to be prepared for future events. We can anticipate the future, which is unknown, by reasoning from known facts and observations; that is the process of reasoning inductively.

On a daily basis, we use statistics to make predictions and decisions in our personal lives. For example, if you've been on three blind dates arranged by your cousin and they have all been terrible, you will probably predict that a fourth date arranged by this person will turn out the same way. If you have noticed that a particular route home from school is usually congested during commuting hours, you might choose to take another route or schedule your classes for less busy times. Or, you might watch a baseball game and predict that because the batter has a .350 average and has been doing well the last few games, he will make at least a base hit right now. You're surprised if he strikes out. On the other hand, a batter with a .220 average who has just recovered from an injury would not be likely to get a good hit. If he does, you are again surprised.

As individuals, we reason inductively by generalizing from observations we make about our own circumstances and experiences. As a society, we use more formal research methods to get accurate information about social issues such as rates of disease, drug and alcohol usage; patterns of criminal activity; likely election results; and public opinion about government policies. We use this information to make decisions about our future direction; statistical research helps us decide which programs should be funded or denied funding, which should be modified, and the goals we wish to achieve.

THE MANY USES OF STATISTICS

Numerous professions in our culture use statistics. Lending companies use statistics on interest rates to support their arguments that people should get car and home loans or refinance existing loans. Real estate agents show statistics on public school test scores to clients to convince them to buy a home in a particular neighborhood. Weather forecasters use statistics to help them make predictions, and seismologists use statistics about past earthquakes to predict the progression of future earthquakes. Political advisers use statistics to decide the popularity of candidates and policies. Advertisers collect evidence on the size and nature of magazine and newspaper audiences to decide where to place their advertisements. The Nielsen ratings give commercial advertisers a good idea of what television channels are being watched for a given period.

New ways to gather statistics are often discovered. One method, called a "Q" score, has become the industry standard for measuring how audiences feel about politicians, products, celebrities, broadcast and cable programs, brand names, and even performers of the past. Q scores actually summarize the various perceptions and feelings that consumers have into a single, but revealing, "likeability" measurement. This research looks beyond the numbers of viewers to programs and assesses how connected people are with a program or product.[2]

The categories of performers who are assessed by Q scores include a wide range of public figures such as actors and actresses, reality show contestants, musicians, consumer reporters, athletes, authors, chefs, comedians, models, directors, and business executives.

Q score companies promise to deliver information that goes beyond the Nielson ratings and to let producers and advertising executives know how viewers feel about individual celebrities as well as cartoons, brands, and specific programs. The assumption is that people will be attentive to advertisements or programs that are connected to their favorite candidates, actors, athletes, and other famous figures. Producers and advertisers pay thousands of dollars to receive Q score information that identifies which celebrity would be a good spokesperson for their products, an attractive, recognizable model for a commercial, or a desirable star for a television show.

One columnist notes the impact of the Q score as follows:

> The research into who watches television, when and why, has produced an entire sub-industry of pollsters and numbers-crunchers. One of the best-kept secrets, and at the same time one of the most valued tools of network executives, is the so-called "Q" score.
>
> That's short for TvQ, the periodic report's title, with the "Q" standing for qualitative. Essentially, average viewers are asked which stars and shows they recognize, then asked to rate them in terms of best-liked personalities and programs. The results are invariably hush-hush, but they are prized by network execs as a measurement of what shows create audience favorites, even if they're low-rated.[3]

STOP AND THINK

How might advertisers or television and film producers use some of the information gathered from Q scores?

Just as Q score researchers and the Nielson Company help television executives decide which programs and personalities are worth keeping, other companies track statistics concerning target populations for products and services.

[2]Jennie L. Phipps, "TVQ and Cable Q Measure Series' Popularity with Targeted Viewers," *Television Week*, April 21, 2003.
[3]Jonathan Burlingame, "Television," *Contra Costa Times*, January 12, 1990, p. 10 C. Reprinted by permission of the author.

baby boomers like & dislike

For decades, businesses have catered to the baby-boomer market, those 76.1 million individuals born between 1946 and 1964. Advertisers continue to use music, celebrities, and ideas that appeal to them to sell cars, vacations, and "age-defying" products. Since the 1960s, baby boomers have been considered the major target audience influencing the economy. Now, as the baby boomers are aging, business leaders and marketers are turning their attention to a new group, the Tween market. Generally defined as children between the ages of 8 and 14, statistics show that Tweens have lots of disposable income. Research by the Canadian Television network YTV cited purchasing power in that country alone totaling $1.8 billion, with projected increases of 10 percent each year, and the research firm NPD Funworld (a marketing organization) credits Tween spending with bringing $3 billion of new money to the marketplace.[4] As a result of their spending power, Tweens are rapidly becoming a primary focus of advertisers and programmers.

Business leaders also use statistics when they counsel companies on "best practices." For example, Canadian writer Dan Corbett of National Quality Institute advises his readers to create work environments that reduce stress, citing the high costs that result from unpleasant workplaces. He writes:

> A study by the Canadian Policy Research Network shows that high stress levels are a significant factor in absenteeism. In the study, employees who reported high levels of work-life conflict missed an average of 13.2 days versus 5.9 days for those with low conflict levels.... Another recent study, sponsored by Health Canada and conducted by Linda Duxbury of Carleton University and Chris Higgins of the University of Western Ontario, concludes that workplace stress "adds up to an enormous toll, for employees and their organizations." Corbett quotes his associate Geri McKeown to confirm his conclusions. "We know now that the workplace environment is a major determinant of health; you can't separate it from the individual. During the past decade, workload has become overwhelming for people. Many organizations have focused on the needs of the client at the expense of their own employees, and that's not a model for sustainability.[5]

Corbett advises companies to reduce stress by helping employees make decisions that affect them directly; he also counsels them to distribute workload more reasonably and fairly, and to add rewards and recognition to their systems, such as financial incentives and fitness centers.[6]

The baseball commission did statistical research on steroid use and found that between 5 percent and 7 percent of players tested positive, prompting

---

[4]"Tweens Take Over: Y Generation Is the Wunderkind of Brand Marketing" by Paul A. Peterson, TDMonthly, June, 2003.
[5]"Healthy Workplace Check-Up: On the Road to Excellence," National Quality Institute, February 17, 2003 www.nqi.ca
[6]Ibid.

them to create a drug policy that imposes fines and suspensions. "In my view of the world, it's hard to say use is rampant based on these results," said Robert Manfred, baseball's vice president for labor relations. "But 5 percent is not an acceptable number to us. From our perspective, it's still a problem that we'll continue to work on until we reach zero.... This system [of drug testing] was set up to identify the scope of this problem," Arizona Diamondbacks general manager Joe Garagiola Jr. said. "Not to be lost sight of is 93 to 95 percent of the tests were clean. That suggests, by and large, players get it on this issue.... Still, 5 to 7 percent is significant. Everyone recognized this was a problem. That's why the players association agreed to it."[7]

Government agencies also conduct statistical studies to determine the best use of taxpayer dollars. If the statistics tell us that the rate of teenage pregnancy is down but the rate of teenage drug use is up, then government and community efforts can be focused on current drug problems. If student scores in math and science are declining but scores in English and history are high according to international criteria, then more attention can be usefully directed to improving education in math and science.

Sometimes the results of statistical research offer evidence that local, national, or international spending priorities need to be changed. Several states, for example, have created more stringent rules for young drivers based on statistical findings. In Illinois, research on auto accidents showed that, even though only 6 percent of drivers were 16 years old, they accounted for 16 percent of crash fatalities. As a result, the state strengthened its graduated license program by requiring young drivers to increase their training to 50 hours, including 10 hours of night driving. Parents or legal guardians must sign a letter verifying that young drivers applying for a license have completed the requirements.

As we've discussed, statistics are used to create relevant policies that address real problems. Individuals also use statistical research to make decisions about personal choices; for example, statistics are used to advise students about issues that take a toll on success in college and on their health and well-being. The following data on college drinking are offered by a peer counseling Web site for Cal Poly University:

> Here are a few sobering statistics on how drinking too much, too often can put a serious damper on your dreams of achieving academic glory—or even your dreams of just graduating:
> According to the Core Institute, an organization that surveys college drinking practices, 300,000 of today's college students will eventually die of alcohol-related causes such as drunk driving accidents, cirrhosis of the liver, various cancers and heart disease.
> 159,000 of today's first- year college students will drop out of school next year for alcohol- or other drug-related reasons. The average student

[7]Jim Salisbury, "Baseball Fails Goal on Steroid Test Results" *Contra Costa Times,* November 14, 2003. Copyright © 2003. Reprinted by permission.

spends about $900 on alcohol each year. Do you want to know how much cash the average student drops on his or her books? About $450.

Almost one-third of college students admit to having missed at least one class because of their alcohol or drug use, and nearly one-quarter of students report bombing a test or project because of the aftereffects of drinking or doing drugs.

One night of heavy drinking can impair your ability to think abstractly for up to 30 days, limiting your ability to relate textbook reading to what your professor says, or to think through a football play.

90% of all campus rapes occur when alcohol has been used by either the assailant or the victim.

At least one out of five college students abandons safe sex practices when they're drunk, even if they do protect themselves when they're sober.

55% of female students and 75% of male students involved in acquaintance rape admit to having been drinking or using drugs when the incident occurred.

60% of college women who are infected with STDs, including genital herpes and AIDS, report that they were under the influence of alcohol at the time they had intercourse with the infected person.

According to the Centers for Disease Control, 1 in 1,500 college students is HIV positive, and the fastest-growing populations of American people infected with HIV are teenagers and young adults.[8]

HOW THE RESEARCH IS DONE

As we have seen, in this age of the proliferation of statistical information, most people and professions are influenced by the findings of research studies, and these studies are frequently used as a basis for making significant decisions. Check your local or national newspaper on any given day, and you will probably notice several articles about recent studies. How do we determine the quality of the statistical evidence we hear or read? To answer this question, we need to have a basic understanding of how the research is carried out.

When someone creates a research study, he or she needs to consider three questions:

1. What do I want to find out?
   This is called the **characteristic of interest.**
2. Whom do I want to know about?
   This is called the **target population.**
3. Whom can I study to get accurate answers about my entire target population?
   The sample

[8]Cal Poly peer counseling website. hcs.calpoly.edu/peerhealth/alcohol/info_students_stats. html

This is called the **sample.** We usually can't study everyone in a given target population, so we have to observe some representative members of the population. For polling, the minimum sample size is usually 1,000.

SKILL

Understand the basic structure of statistical research.

Examples

Characteristic of interest: What are the most popular television programs in the United States?
Target population: Residents of the United States who watch television.
Sample: At least 1,000 randomly selected Americans who watch television.

Characteristic of interest: Who will win the next U.S. presidential election?
Target population: Americans who are eligible to vote.
Sample: At least 1,000 randomly selected Americans who are eligible to vote.

Characteristic of interest: Whether Canadian parents want screens on all Internet sites that advise of violent or sexual content.
Target population: Canadians who are parents.
Sample: 1,000 randomly selected Canadian parents.

The characteristic of interest and target population are fairly easy to identify. The quality of statistical research depends largely on the sample drawn from the target population. For a study to be accurate and reliable, several things must be true about this sample.

The Sample Must Be Large Enough

Any sample studied must be sufficiently large to justify the generalizations drawn from the research. Otherwise, we are dealing in poor experimental design or even stereotyping. If someone says, "Men are terrible cooks—both my brother and my boyfriend have burned dinners this year," she is generalizing from a couple of cases. Her outline would look like this:

Characteristic of interest: Whether men can cook well.
Target population: One-half of the human race.
Sample: My brother and my boyfriend.

Sometimes when we stand back and look at what someone is claiming and the evidence she uses, we can see how inadequate the argument is. Yet how often do we talk like this or agree when others talk like this?

A real problem in both statistical and experimental research is having the resources to study a sufficient sample. Researcher Frank Sulloway discusses this problem:

> Small studies are less reliable than large studies. The typical behavioral study involves about 70 subjects. Owing to statistical error, studies routinely fail to confirm relationships that are known to be true for larger populations....Everyone knows that girls at age eighteen are taller than they are at age fourteen. In samples of only 70 subjects, this lawful relationship will be validated statistically less than half the time! Common sense dictates that findings should count more if they are based on 10,000 subjects than if they are based on 100.[9]

Sulloway suggests that when only small samples can be studied, researchers combine the results of several studies in order to draw more reliable generalizations.

STOP AND THINK

Assess the adequacy of sample size relative to a target population by outlining the following claims that are based on inadequate samples. State the target population, the characteristic of interest, and the sample.

"Asians are so good at math; there are four of them in my algebra class and they have the top scores."

"People who live in that part of town are so weird—I saw two women with green hair there last week."

"Men have such a hard time showing their feelings—my dad has never cried in front of us."

There are many theories about why we so easily jump to hasty conclusions about a whole group of people (target population) based on a small sample of people. One theory is that we feel more secure in this complex world when we can place everyone in a neat category. Another theory is that we are not trained or motivated enough to be careful about our generalizations. Many of us enjoy giving our opinions, but we're not willing to expend the time and energy to find the data that are required to prove them. So we give opinions about topics we really are just guessing about; other people do the same thing and we call it "conversing" and "socializing" and everybody's happy. If we happen to hear reliable evidence about a topic of interest to us, we add that to our conversation too.

[9]Frank Sulloway, *Born to Rebel* (New York: Pantheon Books, Random House, Inc., 1996).

Most of us get defensive about our pet stereotypes and indefensible positions and don't like people to shake us up. However, as we become critical thinkers, our positions will be taken more carefully and backed up with the kind of evidence that gives us real confidence about the opinions we share with others.

REMINDER

The sample must be large enough—that is, enough people must be studied—to justify the generalizations made by the researchers.

The Sample Must Represent the Target Audience

When a sample is **representative**, the people studied are like the people about whom you wish to generalize. For example, if you want to study the effects of fluoride on children in the United States, it would not be enough to study only children who live in the Northeast. If you draw a conclusion from your research, it must reflect the entire target group.

For a sample to be representative, it must have the same significant characteristics in the same proportions as the target group; this principle is illustrated in Figure 4–2. If the sample does not have these characteristics, then it is not representative and is called **biased**. A biased sample does not provide adequate evidence to support a conclusion.

A common problem with modern social science research is that many researchers are college professors who use their students as "volunteers" for

[handwritten margin note: Sample must include a good representation of audience otherwise BIASED]

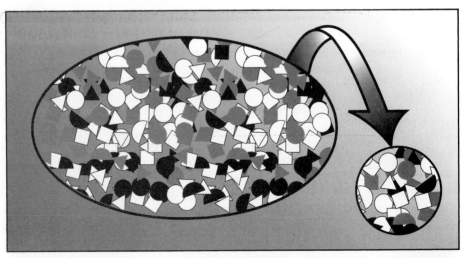

Figure 4–2 A representative sample has the same significant characteristics in the same proportion as the target population.

their studies. While some extrapolations from student samples to the general population are reasonable, other findings may relate more specifically to college students on a particular campus rather than to larger segments of the population. Student populations generally reflect a limited age grouping, and students on a given campus may be more politically liberal or conservative than the general population. Their ideas about an upcoming election can't be generalized to (be said to represent) the larger public. And if the sample studied comes from only one class—say, political science—it may not even be representative of the college as a whole.

The Sample Must Be Random

Randomness is closely linked to the representativeness of a sample. It has been found that you can draw solid conclusions about a large target population by using a much smaller, but representative and randomly selected, segment of that population. **Randomness** means that every member of the target population has an equal chance of being chosen as part of the sample. For example, pollsters might choose a random method of interviewing residents of a particular city by calling every tenth name in the local directory. Statisticians have discovered that a truly random sample is generally representative of the target population.

Using random samples of the target population makes the results of a study accurate with a small percentage of possible error. Polls could show that a certain candidate will get approximately 25 percent of a vote with a "margin of error" of 5 percent, which means he or she will probably get 20 percent to 30 percent of the vote. This margin of error will decrease as the random, representative sample increases in size.

CHECKLIST FOR POLLS AND STATISTICAL STUDIES

> *A well-designed poll can provide a reasonably accurate snapshot of thoughts and opinions of a population. When fundamentals are not followed, however, polls can quickly become both misleading and unreliable.*
>
> Stone Analytics, Inc. www.secondmoment.org

You might think, at this point, that the requirements of a good statistical study are hard to meet; yet, despite the difficulties involved with the need to find random, representative, and sufficiently large samples of a target population, it can be and is done frequently. For example, you can review polling predictions about election results and find them to be quite accurate. In addition, research organizations, like a Q score company provide useful information about candidates and other well-known individuals.

Performer Q measures the familiarity and appeal of personalities in a variety of categories to determine targeted audience attraction.

Performer Q data enable our clients to make informed decisions about a specific personality's demographic appeal and/or examine the field of possible alternatives.

Performer Q studies are conducted as follows:

- Studies are fielded every six months in January & July.
- Each study measures over 1,700 personalities, whose names and descriptions are submitted by full-study subscribing clients. Individual orders are also accepted.
- Each personality is rated by a nationally representative sample of 1,800 children, teens, and adults.[10]

SKILL

Analyze the quality of statistical evidence by noting the size, representation, and randomness of the sample.

Questions to Ask About Statistical Reports

When you need to critically evaluate reports of statistical studies, consider the following questions:

1. **What is the sample size?** For national public opinion polls, it is a general principle that at least 1,000 randomly selected individuals who are representative of the target population will give reliable results.

   When a research study involves carefully supervised testing and training of subjects or expensive material (like the studies discussed in Chapter 5), a much smaller sample might be optimal. For example, it is unreasonable and undesirable to have hundreds of subjects test an experimental drug that may be helpful in treating a particular disease but may also have significant side effects.

2. **Is the sample representative in all significant characteristics and in the proportion of those characteristics?** For example, if 10 percent of a state's voters are age 65 or older, are 10 percent of the sample voters in this age range? If the sample is not representative, then the study is considered biased.

3. **Have all significant characteristics been considered?** Sometimes it is hard to know exactly which factors about the target population are significant. Does the sex and age of the target matter? What about ethnicity and educational level?

[10]http://www.qscores.com/performer.asp. Marketing Evaluations, Inc. The Q Scores Company.

4. **If the study is a poll, are the questions biased?** In other words, are they slanted to bring about a particular response? For example, consider the following "loaded" questions:

 a. Do you believe that the government has a right to invade private lives by taking a census?

 b. Do you approve of preventing thousands of senior citizens from enjoying a safe, affordable, and lovely retirement home in order to protect a moth?

 Because these questions are biased toward the obviously "correct" answer, the information gathered from them is unreliable.

REMINDER

The answers that pollsters receive (and media report) greatly depend on precisely what the pollsters ask and how they ask it....The answers are sometimes determined (and always influenced) by the questions—the exact wording of the questions posed by the interviewers, the order in which the questions are asked, and in some cases even the way in which they are asked (in person or via the telephone). For this reason, the answers are seldom very meaningful unless you also know about the questions that elicited them.[11]

5. **What is the credibility of the polling organization or research institute?** In most cases, we read about a study in a magazine, newspaper, or textbook. Since we get an abridged version of research from these sources, it is helpful to note whether polls were conducted by credible organizations such as Gallup, Harris, and Roper and whether research studies were done under the auspices of universities or reliable "think tanks."

6. **Is the survey biased because of the vested interest of the company that paid for it?** If a company is paying for a survey to promote a product or service, there may be bias involved in the design and the results. Journalist Patricia Rodriguez notes the findings and sponsors of several recent surveys conducted by polling organizations:

 • Americans believe the best learning and information source today is the Internet. (Sponsored by Internet provider Prodigy)
 • The majority of Americans polled plan to travel during the holidays. (Sponsored by online travel service Expedia.com)

[11]David Murray, Joel Schwartz, and S. Robert Lichter, *It Ain't Necessarily So* (Lanham, MD: Rowman & Littlefield Publishers), 2001, 98.

Calvin and Hobbes   Bill Watterson. © Watterson. Distributed by Universal Press Syndicate. Reprinted with permission. All rights reserved.

- Movies, CDs, and video games are tops on teens' holiday wish lists. (Sponsored by Sam Goody, which sells movies, CDs, and video games)
- Two out of three doctors who offer nutritional advice to their patients recommend that said patients eat more yogurt. (Sponsored by Dannon, which makes, you guessed it, yogurt)[12]

You can use the preceding checklist to help you feel more confident about using statistical evidence to support conclusions. It can also help you refute inadequate and unreliable evidence.

USING SURVEYS AS EVIDENCE

Sometimes, surveys can yield helpful, accurate information. Consider the survey cited in an article from the office of the Inspector General on identity theft investigations:

> Question: *I'm a student; why do I need to be concerned about identity theft? I don't have a lot of money or assets; why would I be a target for identity theft?*
>
> Answer: Being a student does not safeguard you against identity theft, one of the fastest-growing consumer crimes in the nation. Identity thieves don't steal your money; they steal your name and reputation and use them for their own financial gain. They attempt to steal your future! Identity theft literally steals who you are, and it can seriously jeopardize your financial future.

---

[12]Patricia Rodriguez, "Be on guard for ridiculous survey results," Knight Ridder Newspapers, December 18, 2001.

Imagine having thousands of dollars of unauthorized debt and a wrecked credit rating because of identity theft. Also, the unfortunate reality of identity theft is that it is you, the victim, who is responsible for cleaning up the mess and reestablishing your good name and credit. The experience of thousands of identity theft victims is that this frustrating experience often requires months and even years.

In fact as a student, you may even be more vulnerable to identity theft because of the availability of your personal data and the way many students handle this data. A recent national survey of college students found that:

- Almost half of all college students receive credit card applications on a daily or weekly basis. Many of these students throw out card applications without destroying them.
- Nearly a third of students rarely, if ever, reconcile their credit card and checking account balances.
- Almost 50 percent of students have had grades posted by Social Security number.

All of these factors make students potential identity theft victims.[13]

In contrast to the useful warnings taken from the Inspector General surveys, one method of research that may lead to interesting speculations but is not generally considered accurate or reliable is the mail-in survey. Let's imagine that a magazine asks its readers to respond to questions about how they spend their money. If the magazine has a circulation of 10,000 and it receives only 2,000 replies, which would be a high response rate, it can't really draw any information from those 2,000 answers because the sample is no longer random. Those who answered are a select group—they have something in common, which is that they are readers of this particular magazine who had the time and inclination to answer the questions and send them in. You can't use this survey to generalize about how most people spend money. Another problem is that survey questions often do not reflect what people would really do in a given situation; they reflect only what people would like to think they would do. If you ask someone if he or she uses money for necessities before luxuries, the person might answer yes, but his or her checkbook could reveal a completely different reality.

In addition, it's possible for someone to send in several surveys to skew the results or just as a prank. Survey results can be more controlled than these examples indicate, but you are safe to conclude that most mail-in surveys you read about in magazines and newspapers are not representative and therefore don't provide reliable support for your conclusions.

---

[13]"Don't let identity thieves steal your future," www.ed.gov/about/offices/list/org/missedidtheft.

130   *Chapter Four*

REMINDER

Arguments using statistical evidence need an adequate sample that is randomly selected from a representative group in the target population. When you find studies like this, you can accept them as accurate and use them for your personal decision making and argumentation.

STATISTICAL GENERALIZATIONS

Keep in mind that although you may get information from a well-conducted study, the conclusion will not be true in every case. Statistical evidence reflects only what can *generally* be expected; conclusions about such evidence are called statistical generalizations. They add *strength,* not certainty, to your conclusions. For example, it might be discovered that most hyperactive children in a study responded well to dietary changes; this finding does not mean that every child will respond in the same way. Or, we might read about a study showing that most sports magazine readers are men, but that does not mean every reader is male. Knowing that most of the readers are men helps the magazine recruit the most appropriate advertisers.

Remember that inductive strength is based on good evidence from which we can draw useful generalizations (see Figure 4–3). In short, we can get important information from statistical research that helps us make decisions or gain knowledge in a general way. Still, we need to allow room for the complexities of individual people and not expect that what is generally true will be true for everyone.

[handwritten margin note: Statistical evidence will not be true in every case]

Little or No Support for Conclusion   **Some Support for Conclusion**   **Strong Support for Conclusion**

Figure 4–3   A good inductive argument provides strong support for the conclusion.

CLASS EXERCISE

Purpose: To analyze the quality of one reported study.

Read the following report of a research study, keeping the following questions in mind:

1. What is the conclusion of the researcher?
2. How representative of the target population was his sample? Was the sample size adequate?

3. Which methods did he use to gather his data? Are these methods reliable?

4. In the second paragraph the reporter implies that these research results would be duplicated in other classrooms. Do you agree or disagree and why?

5. To what extent is the headline given to this article a responsible one?

AT A LECTURE—ONLY 12 PERCENT LISTEN

Bright-eyed college students in lecture halls aren't necessarily listening to the professor, the American Psychological Association was told yesterday.

If you shot off a gun at sporadic intervals and asked the students to encode their thoughts and moods at that moment, you would discover that:

- About 20 percent of the students, men and women, are pursuing erotic thoughts.
- Another 20 percent are reminiscing about something.
- Only 20 percent are actually paying attention to the lecture; 12 percent are actively listening.
- The others are worrying, daydreaming, thinking about lunch or—surprise—religion (8 percent).

This confirmation of the lecturer's worst fears was reported by Paul Cameron, 28, an assistant professor at Wayne State University in Detroit. The annual convention, which ends Tuesday, includes about 2,000 such reports to 10,000 psychologists in a variety of meetings.

Cameron's results were based on a nine-week course in introductory psychology for 85 college sophomores. A gun was fired 21 times at random intervals, usually when Cameron was in the middle of a sentence.

Reprinted from *San Francisco Sunday Examiner Chronicle.*

THE REPORTING OF STATISTICAL STUDIES: TRUTHS, HALF-TRUTHS, AND DISTORTIONS

Newspapers like to stress the importance of the news they report, not to qualify or minimize its possible significance.[14]

As we have noted, studies are not usually reported in the popular media in their complete context. Instead, excerpts from a study are given, and sometimes the reader or listener gets an incomplete or distorted picture of what was

[14]Murray, Schwartz, and Lichter, *It Ain't Necessarily So*, Lanham, Maryland: Bowman & Littlefield Publishers, 2001.

really discovered by the research. Reporters are pressured to give us dramatic news that compels us to read, and they don't want to stress the uncertainty about results of a study that may exist in the scientific community.

One of the most important responsibilities of those reporting studies is to give us a true picture of what was discovered so that we can draw reasonable generalizations. Both raw numbers and percentages should be used so that we can assess the significance of any findings; for example, a report might claim that a new study shows a 50 percent drop in the rate of teenage pregnancies. But on closer examination, we might discover that the sample was taken from only one high school in which the number of pregnant girls went from 4 to 2. Obviously, the sample size is too small to make any relevant claim about teenage pregnancy rates. Conversely, a large sample size may find 200 more teenage pregnancies for a given year across a particular state, yet the researcher could claim a seemingly small 5 percent increase in pregnancies if 4,000 had occurred in the previous year.

Advertisers may also "lie with statistics." For example, a bicycle store could place an ad thanking the public for "doubling" the volume of sales this year. That ad could mean, in reality, that sales of the bicycles went from 5,000 to 10,000 for the year or that sales went from 1 to 2.

Statistics can also be distorted by the terms a journalist uses to characterize their significance. For example, if a politician receives a 40 percent disapproval rating on how he is handling education reform and a 36 percent approval rating with the rest of the respondents undecided, a reporter could say, "*Many* voters disapprove of the governor's handling of education, and *only* 36 percent of those polled approve." Conversely, a reporter could "spin" the statistics in the other direction by saying that "*only* 40 percent of voters disapprove of the governor's policies on education, while 60 percent either approve or are undecided."

Reporters may also choose to discuss poll results without giving the actual numbers to readers. Using the previous example, a reporter could leave out the specific data and just state that "there is increasing disapproval and uncertainty among voters concerning the governor's policy on education."

Another problem with reports of statistical studies is that headlines may distort the actual findings of the study. An article summarizing a study of the effect of video games on college life presented a balanced look at the positives and negative findings of the researchers. Unfortunately, the headline "Study Surprise: Video Games Enhance College Social Life" slants the information and could be misleading to readers who scan the headline or who read only the first part of the article. The headline "spins" the report as essentially good news about video games as a social and interactive activity; it takes a discerning reader to note some of the problems associated with students who spend a large amount of their time playing video games, including lower grades and test scores for younger game players, that are given in the latter part of the article. (See Exercise 4.1 on p. 145.)

[handwritten margin note: raw data is essential for reasonable generalizations]

CAUSAL GENERALIZATIONS

Scientific research may at first glance sound specialized or even forbidding as a topic, but in fact it is research results—of a remarkable variety, from health news to environmental alarms to the latest findings on child-rearing practices— that increasingly construct the public agenda.[15]

Statistics and controlled studies (which will be discussed in the next chapter) are often used to draw inductive generalizations about the causes of conditions or events. We attempt to determine causal connections for several reasons: First, we seek to eliminate current difficulties and prevent future problems that arise for individuals; second, we want to resolve general problems that affect large groups of people; and finally, much great investigation is motivated by sheer human curiosity.

On an individual level, we look for causes in order to eliminate problems that arise in daily life. We might seek to understand why our car is making a certain sound, why our checkbook doesn't balance, why our dog seems lethargic, or why we lost a job or an important relationship. If we find a cause, then we hope we will find a cure for our present difficulties as exemplified in the following column by the late Ann Landers.

ANN LANDERS

Dear Ann Landers:

If it weren't for one of your recent columns, I might be either dead or paralyzed. I owe you a large debt of gratitude.

For about a week, I had been experiencing temporary numbness in my left arm and hand. The numbness was sometimes accompanied by periodic paralysis of my left hand. My first thoughts were that I either hit my crazy bone or had perhaps been using my computer too much.

As I read your column describing the symptoms of a stroke, I immediately recognized that my numbness matched the early warning signs you had mentioned. I dropped the newspaper and went directly to the emergency room. The CAT scan revealed a large mass of blood in the crevice between my brain and my skull.

Fortunately, the operation to drain the fluid was a complete success and the doctors say there should be no lasting effects. For this, I am extremely thankful. Please know I am enormously grateful to you, Ann, for the perfect timing of that column.

[15]Ibid., p. 1

We look for causes of societal problems in our efforts to ensure that these problems do not occur again. This search for causes occurs when we have car, train, and plane accidents; outbreaks of food poisoning; a trend of lower test scores; or a disease that is becoming an epidemic.

In addition, we seek causes in order to eliminate potential problems that affect the general public: Seat belts and air bags were created and altered as a result of understanding the causes of the kinds of human injury that can occur after the impact of a collision; baby furniture and toys are modified or recalled based on our understanding of their harmfulness to children; the government may look at inflationary trends caused by the infusion of more money into the country before it takes action to stimulate a failing economy; and premarital counselors can advise engaged couples about the major causes of divorce and help them address important issues before they get married.

Consider the following examples of studies that were done to enhance our decision making on a variety of topics.

On the decision to require and support helmets for bicycle riders:

Each year in America, 3000 kids die from traumatic brain injuries. The 29,000 who survive may face lifelong problems. Yet many injuries could be avoided if all kids on wheels wore helmets. They reduce the risk of head injury by 85%, brain injury by 88%. For this year's National Safe Kids Week, Johnson & Johnson and Bell Sports are giving $1 million in helmets to kids in need. (*Parade Magazine,* April 28, 2002)

On the need to prevent deterioration of the coral reef:

A new study released by WRI reports that nearly two-thirds of Caribbean coral reefs are under increased threat from human activities. With the parade of destructive hurricanes that has swept through the Caribbean this year, the region can ill-afford to damage [its] coral reefs, which function as vital natural barriers to coastal erosion and other storm damage.

Lauretta Burke and Jonathan Maidens, coauthors of *Reefs at Risk in the Caribbean,* evaluated human hazards to Caribbean reefs in four broad categories: coastal development, watershed-based sediment and pollution (like runoff of fertilizers and pesticides from farms), marine-based pollution and damage, and overfishing.

Due to these perils, Burke and Maidens concluded that about one-tenth of Caribbean coral reefs are at very high levels of threat, one-third at high threat, one-fifth at medium threat, and one-third at low threat. High threat levels signify that considerable destruction of coral has already occurred or is likely to occur in the next five to ten years.

"Coral reefs are a foundation of the Caribbean's economic and social health," said Burke. "Immediate action must be taken to protect these reefs and ensure the health, safety, and livelihoods of the societies that depend upon them."

The authors estimate that in 2000 Caribbean coral reefs provided the region with goods and services valued at between US$3.1 billion and US$4.6 billion from fisheries, dive tourism, and shore-line protection services. Continuing degradation of the region's coral reefs could reduce net annual revenues from dive tourism—which provided an estimated US$2.1 billion in 2000—by as much as US$300 million per year by 2015.

"The continued degradation of the region's reefs would lead to a loss of fishing livelihoods, malnutrition due to lack of protein, loss of tourism revenues, and increased coastal erosion," said Maide. (Coral Reef Destruction Threatens Caribbean Countries, by Peter Denton WRI.org From World Reserves Institute, October 2004, Volume 2, No. 9.)

On causes for South Korea's having the world's highest traffic accident rate of 10,300 people killed and 426,000 injured in crashes every year in a country of 46 million people and also on causes of other social problems that South Koreans face:

South Koreans call it ppalli ppalli ("hurry hurry")—doing everything quickly, from leaving planes to eating, walking and driving.... "Ppalli ppalli was the main driving engine behind the nation's rapid industrialization," said Yoo Suk-choon, a sociologist at Seoul's Yonsei University. South Korea was reduced to ashes during the 1950–53 Korean War, but has built itself into the world's 11th-largest economy.

However, government officials and social critics blame ppalli ppalli for many ills: traffic jams, corruption, slipshod construction and the reckless expansion by corporations on borrowed money, which proved a disaster during Asia's 1997–98 financial crisis. Today, after decades of rushing, there are calls for a more leisurely lifestyle.

The government, supported by labour groups, is pushing legislation to introduce a five-day work week. Most Koreans still work a half-day on Saturdays. "Korean workers need to live more humanely," said Park Kwang-woo, a policy coordinator at the Korean Confederation of Trade Unions, the country's largest labour group. (Sang-Hun Choe, Associated press)

On the harmful effects of party drugs:

The good times may roll right into the emergency room for users of cocaine, speed, or ecstasy. Specialists think that these "party drugs" can trigger strokes, and that the risk may be especially high for those with unsuspected defects in the blood vessels that supply their brains. Up to 8% of the population may have such abnormalities, Andrew W. McEvoy, M.D., tells WebMD.

McEvoy reports in the May 13 issue of the *British Medical Journal* that he found such blood vessel defects in 10 of 13 young adult patients he treated who had strokes after using these drugs. Most of these patients survived, but cocaine may contribute to more than half of the deaths from certain types of strokes, he says. McEvoy is a research fellow at the National Hospital for Neurology and Neurosurgery in London.

McEvoy tells WebMD that he became interested in the drugs-stroke connection when he noticed that his hospital was treating more young adults who had strokes after taking one of the popular "party drugs." He tested blood vessels in the brains of 13 of these patients and found that only one had completely normal vessels....

Kurt Nolte, M.D., has studied autopsies of people who died of stroke. He found that nearly 60% of younger patients whose strokes were not caused by brain injuries had cocaine in their blood. He is a forensic pathologist in the office of the medical investigator at the University of New Mexico School of Medicine in Albuquerque. "Each time an individual uses a stimulant, such as cocaine or [speed], he or she takes a risk," Nolte says.

"Party Drugs" May Blow Your Mind—or at Least Your Brain," Staff writer, Web MD Medical News, Archive, May 12, 2000.

As we can see from these excerpts, we are constantly using research findings to determine causal connections that help us make personal and policy decisions on a variety of topics.

Over the past few centuries, philosophers and scientists have developed specific theories of cause and effect. These theories help us make **causal generalizations,** which can then be used as evidence to support a conclusion. Keep in mind, however, that what is believed and accepted as causal today may change as new information becomes available. The following section will review the most common theories of causation.

HUME'S CONDITIONS FOR CAUSE AND EFFECT

The British philosopher David Hume (1711–1776) created a theory of cause and effect. He reasoned that we are justified in saying that one thing is the cause (x) of an effect (y) if the following three conditions are met:

1. X, the cause, *preceded y*, the effect, in time.
2. X and y are *contiguous* (in contact with one another) in time and place.
3. There is a *history* of (1) and (2); that is, there is a history of x preceding y and of x and y being related in time and place.

The first condition is clear; if one thing causes another, the cause must come before the effect. But we should also note that sometimes the cause and effect appear to occur at the same time; for example, as soon as I pull the plug on my lamp, the light goes out.

The second condition specifies the need for a relationship in time and space between a cause and an effect. For example, in outbreaks of diseases caused by "sick buildings," a connection is made between workers (often on particular floors) who experience the onset of the same illness. The reminder that causes and effects must be connected guards against superstition and unlikely causes.

The third condition helps us justify a causal effect by pointing to a regular tendency. A florist can reason that every year, on certain holidays, the demand for flowers goes up. A public school teacher can chart a tendency for a consistent reduction in math skills over summer vacation. A doctor can anticipate that a patient will be nauseated as a side effect of many types of chemotherapy. A driver can note which roads are regularly jammed during the week because of rush hour. Conversely, if there is no history of regularity between a particular cause and a particular effect, then a critical thinker should wait for such a trend to surface before accepting an alleged causal connection.

Even when all of Hume's criteria are met, it is hard to distinguish between a correlation (two events occurring together in a regular pattern) and a specific causation. We can, for example, look at studies that show a connection (correlation) between violent criminals and their abusive parents. But it is difficult to explain fully why some of these violent criminals from abusive homes have siblings who are nonviolent, productive, and functioning members of society. In other words, it is easier to see the connections and associations in time and space between two conditions than it is to prove that one of the conditions caused the other.

However, when we come across a strong correlation between two conditions or activities, we should consider whether there is a possible area of causation to be explored. Consider these statements by MIT research scholar and author Frank Sulloway:

> There is an old maxim that "correlation is not causation." Although this is certainly true, it is also true that, under some circumstances, correlations provide a reasonably reliable guide to causation. For example, the correlation between winning a million dollars in the lottery and having more money to spend is very high, and these two outcomes are obviously related in a causal manner. We must employ common sense in deciding whether, and to what extent, correlations suggest a causal relationship. Even when correlations do not warrant the assumption of causality, they generally suggest that *some other variable, itself associated with the two correlated variables,* is causally involved in the observed relationship. As we introduce additional variables into a statistical analysis, we can often pinpoint the most likely source of "causation."[16]

---

[16]Salloway, *Born to Rebel*, pp. 72–74.

Theories of technical causation, which we turn to now, can help us better understand causal connections between conditions.

TECHNICAL CAUSATION

Another format for determining causation specifies two different types of conditions between causes and effects.

A **necessary condition** is a condition (state of affairs, thing, process, etc.) that must be present if the effect is present. Equivalently, if the necessary condition is absent, then the effect cannot occur.

One of the necessary conditions of life as we know it is oxygen. Some of the necessary conditions of a fire are oxygen, a flammable material, and a form of ignition. If we know the necessary conditions of an event, then we can prevent it from happening. Remove any of the necessary conditions and the effect does not take place. A necessary condition is a prerequisite for the effect. Thus we can speak of a necessary condition as a cause, or one of the causes, of an event.[17]

A **sufficient condition** is a condition (state of affairs, thing, process, etc.) that automatically leads to the production of another event. If the condition is present, then the effect will definitely occur. The sufficient condition creates the effect.

Swallowing cyanide is a sufficient condition for death. The difference between a necessary and a sufficient condition is that although a necessary condition must be present, it will not produce the effect by itself. The sufficient condition is able to produce the effect by itself. Usually the sufficient condition is really a set of necessary conditions, all of which must be present at the same time and place. For instance, a combustible material, oxygen, and the combustion point are all necessary conditions for a fire. Together all three constitute the sufficient condition for a fire. If we know the sufficient condition of an event, then we can produce it at will. Thus we can speak of a sufficient condition as a cause of an event.[18]

STOP AND THINK

It has been said that holding elections is a necessary but not a sufficient condition for establishing a democracy. To what extent, if any, do you agree with this statement?

MULTIPLE CAUSES

Finding the exact cause of an event or an effect can be very difficult, even in technical matters. We often must look at **multiple causes**, a combination of causes leading to a specific effect. A particular business might be successful

[17]Nicholas Capaldi, *The Art of Deception* (Buffalo, NY: Prometheus Books, 1987), 158.
[18]Ibid.

because of a combination of the needs of the community, the location of the store, and the advertising campaign. A person may die because of a combination of a weak heart, a diet with a large proportion of fat, and an overexertion in exercise. The weak heart could be further traced back to a family history of heart disease. Taken in combination, these factors may be sufficient to cause death.

There are multiple causes to social problems. For example, a number of researchers have found that teen alcohol and drug use occurs at higher levels in affluent areas.

> It's not just a matter of children having more money to spend, though that is a factor. Disconnected families and pressures to succeed push youths to destructive behaviors, say researchers, sociologists and others trying to help these children. Adults in many wealthy areas are often loathe to acknowledge that such problems exist in their world. "The amount of denial on this issue is phenomenal," said Madeline Levine, psychologist and author of *The Price of Privilege*.[19]

Other researchers agree that the pressures to succeed, the glamorous appeal of drugs to students who don't see the social problems they create, the absenteeism and denial of parents, and the numerous extracurricular obligations of students all are factors in the higher incidence of alcohol and drug use. "The association of wealth and teen substance abuse holds true internationally," said Shirley Beckett Mikeel, deputy director for the Association of Addiction Professionals. She has worked with groups from France, England, Egypt and New Zealand."[20]

The phenomenon of multiple causes makes it difficult to provide evidence beyond a reasonable doubt in many cases. For example, over the years people have sued tobacco companies because, they claim, the tobacco caused them to develop lung cancer. However, despite convincing evidence about the harmfulness of tobacco, people have difficulty proving that tobacco is the only cause, sufficient by itself, for the development of lung cancer. Until recently, lawyers for the tobacco companies argued successfully that there are, in any given case, other possible causes for a person's susceptibility to lung cancer and that other people who smoke a similar amount of tobacco have not contracted the disease.

The difficulty of establishing causal connections and then proving them in court is chronicled by Jonathan Harr in his book *A Civil Action*, which he spent eight years researching and writing. The book deals with the case of eight children in Woburn, Massachusetts, who contracted leukemia as the result, their families claim, of toxic pollution from industrial plants near their homes. The lawyer, Jan Schlictmann, who took on the polluting corporations

[19]Eric Louis, "Lap of Luxury Breeds Higher Rates of Teen Subsance Abuse," *Contra Costa Times,* February 19, 2007.
[20]Ibid.

in court, believed in the truth of his clients' case but also knew that the case would be difficult to prove.

> The children's illnesses and the contamination of two water wells that served their homes had been documented. What was missing was proof that the two industrial plants, owned by Beatrice Foods Co. and W.R. Grace and Co. were responsible for the contamination and that the chemicals had caused the children's illnesses....
>
> He hired geologists to prove that Beatrice and Grace had contaminated the wells. And he hired medical experts to establish a link between leukemia, the cause of which was unknown, and the contaminated water.
>
> The millions spent in preparing for trial virtually bankrupted Schlictmann and his firm.... [In court] he had to confront an unsympathetic judge and high-paid corporate attorneys who used every motion and procedural sleight of hand to block his way.
>
> A split decision that absolved Beatrice of responsibility and held little promise of final victory over Grace forced Schlictmann to settle the case for $8 million. The settlement gave a measure of satisfaction and compensation to the Woburn families, but it wasn't enough to pay Schlictmann's bills.[21]

The Woburn case, which generated 159 volumes of depositions and trial testimony, is a good example of the difficulty in proving a causal connection against the doubts generated by good defense lawyers. In gathering the necessary expertise to make a case, Schlictmann spent so much money that his car and furniture were repossessed and the bank foreclosed on his home. Most lawyers have to believe that they can prove their cases with a "preponderance of the evidence" before they will take such risks.

The practice of allowing juries to assign a portion of blame for an injury to the plaintiff and a portion to the defendant is a response to the difficulty jurors have determining the precise cause of a problem. In one case, a male psychologist was accused of causing pain, suffering, and suicidal tendencies in a female patient with whom he had had sexual relations. The psychologist admitted to having had sex with his patient, but he produced explicit love letters she had sent to him. In addition, his attorneys presented information about the patient's previous sexual history; the psychologist, as defendant, was not required to reveal details of his own sexual history. As a result of the evidence presented by the defense, the jury softened the verdict by assigning 18 percent of the blame to the patient and 82 percent of the blame to the psychologist. They reasoned that although he had broken his professional ethics, she had contributed to that breakdown. (See Exercise 4.2 on p. 145.)

---

[21]Willy Morris, "Civil Author Nearly Beaten by Case," *Contra Costa Times*, October 10, 1996.

Immediate Causes

In searching for causes, we should also consider the notion of an immediate or situational cause of a problem. We can ask, "What factor makes the difference between an event happening or not happening?" (In folk wisdom, this might be expressed as "the straw that broke the camel's back.")

The **immediate cause** is preceded by other factors that led up to the effect. If someone causes an accident because of driving drunk after a party, we have the immediate cause of the collision. Remote causes of the accident would be the lack of a designated driver for drinkers at the party, and the decision of the driver to have alcohol rather than soda; had there been a designated driver or a sober driver, the accident probably would not have happened. Less immediate causal factors are called **remote causes**.

In a discussion of the human costs that result when a community does not have affordable housing, Theresa Keegan refers to remote causes of a young man's death: "To this day, I can still recall the regrets uttered during an interview almost a decade ago by a caring, loving mom whose 16-year-old son had been stabbed to death. She had been working, not for personal fulfillment, but simply to keep a roof over their heads. And her working meant he was left on his own. Regret didn't even begin to describe her grief. A lack of affordable housing wasn't cited as a cause on his death certificate, but that's what can happen when the struggle for basic shelter dictates our actions."[22]

In many cases, critical thinkers have to ask the question, "Where do we draw the line in our search for causes?" (See Exercise 4.3 on p. 148.)

Where do we stop researching?

MILL'S ANALYSIS OF CAUSE AND EFFECT

British philosopher John Stuart Mill (1806–1873) formulated several specific methods (which he called canons) to help us systematically discover causes; Mill's canons are foundational to what we now called controlled studies (which will be covered in Chapter 5). Let's look at two of these methods, the method of agreement (or similarity) and the method of difference.

Method of Agreement

Using the **method of agreement**, a cause is found by noting that X is the only factor always present when Y (the problem or the good effect) occurs; therefore, X causes Y.

Let's say a family of four is on vacation and goes to Chicken King for lunch. Dad orders nuggets, fried chicken, fries, and a root beer. Sister has the same thing except she isn't thirsty so she doesn't order the root beer. Mom used to be a vegetarian, so she can't handle the fried chicken, but the nuggets

[22]Theresa Keegan, "Lack of Affordable Housing Is Costly," *Contra Costa Times,* June 1, 2003.

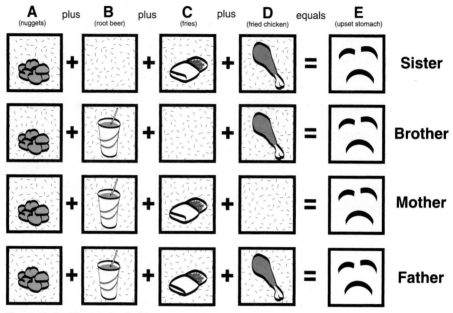

Figure 4–4   The Method of Agreement.

don't look like chicken, so she has them with the fries and the root beer. Brother orders the same as Dad, but hates potatoes, so he doesn't order the fries. That night, they all wake up with painful cramps and stay up most of the night dealing with upset stomachs. The chart of this particular scenario could look something like Figure 4–4.

Using the method of agreement, it can be easily seen that the one thing that is present in every individual's meal is the order of nuggets. The evidence leads to the inductive generalization that the nuggets caused the family members to have upset stomachs.

Method of Difference

Using the **method of difference**, the cause is found by noting that the only difference between the event or effect (called **Y**) happening or not happening is whether one element—**X**—is present.

Using our previous example, let's look at one particular member of the family again. Dad recovered from the illness but the next day decides to eat at Chicken King again. He might have decided never to set foot in that, or any other Chicken King, but instead he experimented, using the method of difference. He ordered the same meal as the day before but he decided not to have the nuggets. The chart of the scenario could look like Figure 4–5.

That night the father had no symptoms, and the next day notified the Chicken King manager that by using the method of difference following the method of agreement, he believes the nuggets caused his family's stomach aches.

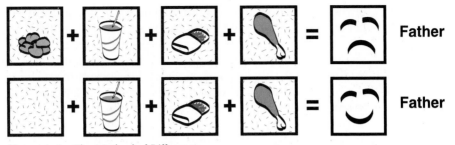

Figure 4–5   The Method of Difference.

In this example, the sample is of course too small and the surrounding conditions too uncertain for a valid generalization. However, it does serve to highlight the contrast between the method of agreement and the method of difference. These methods are used, separately and together, to conduct valid research experiments.

Scientists and other professionals use the method of difference to make useful discoveries. For example, if a patient reports to a psychologist that he is depressed, he might be asked to keep a journal, detailing the times of most and least depression. If the psychologist discovers the most depression (Y) occurring on Sunday night and Monday morning, then she might conclude that the depression is related to a return to work (X) after the weekend. Although the return to work may not turn out to be the cause, it provides a useful avenue of inquiry.

A famous example of the use of the method of difference occurred when Edward Jenner, a nineteenth-century British physician, was investigating a cure for smallpox. He discovered that a certain group of people—dairymaids—rarely got the disease. What was the difference between the dairymaids and the larger population?

On further investigation, Jenner discovered that most of the dairymaids had had cowpox, which is similar to smallpox but not usually deadly to human beings. Because they had had cowpox, they were immune to the smallpox; the cowpox had "vaccinated" them against smallpox. So cowpox (X) caused the positive effect (Y) of immunization from the illness. From this discovery, Jenner came upon the notion of vaccinating people against smallpox.

USING DIFFERENCE AND SIMILARITY TOGETHER TO DETERMINE CAUSE

Often the method of agreement (similarity) and the method of difference go together. Both methods are evident in Robert Cialdini's discussion of fixed-action patterns in animal behavior:

> When a male animal acts to defend his territory, for instance, it is the intrusion of another male of the same species that cues the

territorial-defense tape of rigid vigilance, threat, and if need be, combat behaviors. But there is a quirk in the system. It is not the rival male as a whole that is the trigger; it is some specific feature of him, the trigger feature. Often the trigger feature will be just one tiny aspect of the totality that is the approaching intruder. Sometimes a shade of color is the trigger feature. The experiments of ethologists have shown, for instance, that a male robin, acting as if a rival robin had entered its territory, will vigorously attack nothing more than a clump of robin-redbreast feathers placed there. At the same time, it will virtually ignore a perfect stuffed replica of a male robin without red breast feathers.[23]

In the case of these male birds, X (the presence of red-color feathers) makes the difference between the territorial response happening or not happening. And whenever the red feathers are present, whether or not there is a real threat to the robin, he will react in the same way.

If a patient is having allergic reactions, a doctor may begin a systematic search for the causes of the ailment. The patient might be told to stop eating food typically involved in allergies (for example, wheat, sugar, and dairy products). Then, after a period of time, the suspected allergens are introduced one at a time; if the allergic reactions reoccur, the patient is advised to eliminate the food that triggered the reactions. If the patient continues to eliminate this food and finds that the allergic reactions are gone, then the process of reasoning from evidence to a cause has been successful in this case. X is the only food that caused the reaction Y; and in every case in which X is eaten, the reaction occurs.

Mill's basic concepts are foundational to the scientific method in which experiments are conducted in order to discover or eliminate strong support for causal connections. The data from these studies can help us make reliable causal generalizations, as we will see in the next chapter.[*]

LIFE APPLICATION

Be aware that any personal, local, or national problem has multiple causes, and avoid placing blame simplistically on only one factor. Make it a habit to look for both remote and immediate causes of problems, especially when you are in a position to come up with or vote on possible solutions.

Use strong statistics to make rational decisions concerning risks. As *Time* magazine writer Jeffrey Kluger suggests, focus on probable outcomes of your daily actions rather than worrying about remote possibilities:

> *Shadowed by peril as we are, you would think we'd get pretty good at distinguishing the risks likeliest to do us in from the ones that are statistical long shots. But you would be wrong. We agonize over avian flu, which to date has*

---

[23]Robert B. Cialdini, *The Psychology of Persuasion* (New York: William Morrow, 1993), p. 3.
[*]Two of Mill's methods that we did not cover here—the method of residue and the method of concomitant variation—are also useful in discovering causal links. You may wish to read about these methods to further your understanding of theories of causation.

killed precisely no one in the U.S., but have to be cajoled into getting vaccinated for the common flu, which contributes to the deaths of 36,000 Americans each year. We wring our hands over the mad cow pathogen that might be (but almost certainly isn't) in our hamburger and worry far less about the cholesterol that contributes to the heart disease that kills 700,000 of us annually.[24]

CHAPTER EXERCISES

Exercise 4.1   Purpose: To become aware of how reporting of scientific research may distort information.

1. Look at articles on research in your local or national newspaper. See if the headlines accurately summarize the research. Then note whether the reporter is making claims that are not clearly supported by the research.

2. Compare and contrast two or three articles on the same research study to see how the information is presented and therefore is likely to be received differently by the readers.

Exercise 4.2   Purpose: To understand the need to consider multiple causes when addressing social problems.

Read the following excerpts from articles on various issues. For each one, identify the multiple causes of the problem as given in the article; discuss what policies are currently addressing these causes. If no policies are mentioned, come up with your own suggestions for dealing with the various causative factors.

ASIAN WOMEN IN U.S. FACE HIGHER CANCER RISK

Eileen Glanton

For 49 years, Rose Hsu lived a dream.

The daughter of Chinese immigrants, she coasted through childhood in San Francisco's Chinatown, excelled in school, married a doctor and moved to the suburbs.

Then, in 1994, Hsu got breast cancer and discovered a medical truth doctors already knew: Although Asian nations have the world's lowest incidence of breast cancer, Asian women in the United States have the same risk as white women. An Asian woman's chance of getting breast cancer increases by more than 80 percent within a decade of arriving in this country.

The biological factors are abundantly clear, says Regina Zeigler, a National Cancer Institute physician who led a 1993 study on Asians and breast cancer.

---

[24]"How Americans are Living Dangerously," by Jeffrey Kinger, November 26, 2006, Time.com

"A woman coming to the U.S. from Asia probably gives up a naturally healthy diet for American processed foods," Zeigler said. She may exercise less and undergo stress in navigating a new culture. And a language barrier may prevent her from seeking medical help or understanding public service announcements.

More elusive, though, are a host of cultural factors—modesty, day-to-day philosophy—that narrow Asian women's odds of beating the disease.

Health officials are learning that the best way to battle those factors is to step out of the doctor's office and into the community.

The American-Italian Cancer Foundation, based in Manhattan, does most of its work in the city's poorer minority neighborhoods. Staff members drive a mammography van to churches, community centers and health fairs, where they perform free mammograms.

"We seek out underserved, uninsured women, and those in culturally cloistered neighborhoods," says Gilda Zane, the group's executive director. "Immigrant women have their own language, their own culture, and they don't go out. So we have to try to get in."

Mei Tsing recently visited the Chinatown Health Clinic in Manhattan for her second mammogram in four years.

Experts would say the 63-year-old woman should have first had the test 20 years ago, and should receive it every year or two. But before Tsing trades her oversized Columbia University sweatshirt for a paper robe, she discounts the idea of visiting any doctor that often.

"I have other things that worry me more," says Tsing, whose mammogram turned up no problems.

That's a common, and dangerous, philosophy among immigrant women.

"They worry about making a life for their family, not about a lump that doesn't hurt," Zane says.

But finding such a lump is critical. Breast cancer is the most common type of cancer among adult women, but its sufferers boast strong survival rates— more than 70 percent live at least five years after diagnosis. The most likely survivors are the women who catch the disease before it can spread.

After several years of gentle pestering by her family physician, Hsu had her first mammogram in March 1994. The test turned up a cancerous tumor, tiny enough to remove through a lumpectomy.

"I was lucky, really," Hsu reflects.

MULTIPLE CAUSES OF SUICIDE

Although the nature-versus-nurture debate still rages in some psychiatric circles, most researchers who study suicide fall somewhere in the middle. "You need several things to go wrong at once," explains Victoria Arango of the New York State Psychiatric Institute, which is affiliated with Columbia-Presbyterian

Medical Center. "I'm not saying that suicide is purely biological, but it starts with having an underlying biological risk." Life experience, acute stress and psychological factors each play a part, she asserts. At the root of the mystery of suicide, however, lies a nervous system whose lines of communication have become tangled into unbearably painful knots.

Carol Ezzell, "Why? The NeuroScience of Suicide," Scientific American.com, February 2003. www.sciamdigital.com/index.cfm

---

SELF-SEGREGATION

Students Stick with Same-Race Groups

Gina Pera

Why do most teens hang out with friends of the same race? It's just "more comfortable" to be with people who share your background, say thousands of teens in essays submitted to *USA Weekend*. In fact, we got more mail on this topic than any other in the survey. Most also agree that adolescents possess a strong need to belong, and race provides the most obvious visual identity. At the same time, seven in 10 say they have a close friend of another race.

Here are the other reasons survey respondents cite most often:

Peer Pressure. At some schools, making friends of another race creates problems with same-race friends. "If I talk to a person of another race, some black friends will say, 'You're stuck up,' " says Chavonda Pighet, 15, a black student at South Robeson High School in Rowland, N.C. Her friends tell Chavonda that she should pick one group or the other. "But that's not right. I try to spend time with both."

Fear of Rejection. Venturing beyond the comfort of a familiar group is a risk. For some, it comes at too high a price. "People of other races ask too many questions about my culture, which is Mexican-Indian and Native American," says Swift Sanchez, 14, of Forks (Wash.) High School. "They try to watch what they say, but they slip and say racial things." Twin sister Fawn agrees. "If I make a mistake around some white people, they say 'Look at that stupid Indian.' "

Safety in Numbers. Some kids fear for their safety, says Anthony Harris, 14, of Chicago's Luther High School South. "They think all black people sell drugs, all Mexicans carry knives, all white people listen to heavy metal," says Harris, who is black. As a result, teens seek the protection of the group "just in case something happens, like a fight."

Ignorance. Teens, who face big changes as they grow up, want to feel secure, says Luke Kozikowski, 13, of St. Stanislaus School in Chicopee, Mass. So the races separate to avoid conflict. "But then they feed on each other's fears." The only way to really feel comfortable with different kinds of people, says Kozikowski: "Take a chance and get to know them one at a time."

Gina Para, *USA Weekend*, August 18–20, 1996. Copyright © 1996. Reprinted by permission of the author.

CURB TEEN SMOKING BY VALUING KIDS

Caroline Allison Wolter

There is no universal reason why young people smoke. However, before trying to discourage those who are already smoking, we need to understand what motivates them to begin. Discontent, boredom, peer pressure and escape are only the beginning. Deeper issues are likely to be at the root of this self-destructive behavior. Kids aren't born with these issues. They are learned and integrated from the day they are born.

I feel it is a difficult, if not nearly an impossible, task to discourage teenagers from smoking once they have begun. They may cut back or sneak cigarettes, but chances are they won't quit. Why? Because smoking is only a symptom of deeper feelings of low self-esteem and inadequacy, which are more likely the root causes.

If we can't help teen smokers now, we should focus on what we can do. Parents, teachers and society must value children from the day they are born. Their behavior needs to change before the teens have a chance of not smoking. This means we must allow kids to be kids. People need to be more honest with themselves and their children.

USA Weekend, August 18–20, 1996. Copyright © 1996. Reprinted by permission of the author.

Exercise 4.3   *Purpose:* To distinguish immediate from remote causes of an event or effect.

1. Do some research on a social or national event and try to isolate the causes, both immediate and remote, of this event. For example, if you researched U.S. entry into World War II, you would go beyond the attack on Pearl Harbor, as far back as World War I, to see all the influences that both compelled and restrained U.S. involvement. Other examples would be immediate and remote causes of homelessness, an outbreak of wildfires, sexually transmitted diseases, the state of a political party, the rise of corporate conglomerates, the war in Iraq, or the foster care system. How far back can problems related to these topics be traced?

2. Study the arguments used by the prosecution or by defense attorneys in a trial that attempts to prove a cause-effect relationship between events. Examples would be trials against manufacturers of faulty products, such as silicone implants or dangerous toys, or trials in which one person claims that damage was done to them by another person or by a company, such as complaints about the effects of secondhand cigarette smoke or video display terminals. Investigative news programs, such as *Frontline, 60 Minutes,* and *20/20* often feature stories about such trials, and they make transcripts of their programs available to the public. Look at the statements made by the attorneys for both the prosecution and the defense, and find examples of arguments claiming or denying a cause-effect relationship. Summarize these arguments and comment on their persuasiveness both to the jury and to you as a critical thinker.

CHAPTER HIGHLIGHTS

1. The strength of a conclusion is based on the quality of evidence used to support the conclusion.

2. Statistical evidence can be gathered from polling a sample of a target population about a given topic, which is called the characteristic of interest.

3. Samples used to collect data must be sufficiently large, randomly chosen, and representative of the target population. When a sample is not representative, the study is biased.

4. Surveys can yield useful information when they are based on statistical research; however, mail-in surveys usually yield inadequate statistical evidence because they do not reflect a random and representative sample.

5. Studies reported in both print and electronic media are abridged; critical thinkers will read them carefully and do further investigation of the findings before using them to support conclusions or decisions.

6. Philosophers and scientists have developed several theories of causation; among these are Hume's conditions for cause and effect, theories of technical causation, and Mill's canons of cause and effect.

KEY TERMS

Induction (p. 113)
Inductive reasoning (p. 115)
Statistical evidence (p. 116)
Statistical generalization (p. 116)
Characteristic of interest (p. 121)
Target population (p. 121)
Sample (p. 122)
Representative (p. 124)
Biased (p. 124)

Randomness (p. 125)
Causal generalizations (p. 136)
Necessary condition (p. 138)
Sufficient condition (p. 138)
Multiple causes (p. 138)
Immediate cause (p. 141)
Remote causes (p. 141)
Method of agreement (p. 141)
Method of difference (p. 142)

CHAPTER CHECKUP

Short Answer

1. What are some uses of statistical generalizations?
2. What problems can occur with the reporting of statistical evidence?
3. Why is it helpful to look at multiple causes of a problem?
4. Why are mail-in surveys unreliable sources of evidence?

Sentence Completion

5. A _____ sample is random and adequate in size.

6. Finding a cause by noting the factor that is always present when the effect occurs is called the method of _____.

7. A condition that must be present if the effect is present is called a _____ condition.

Matching

A. Characteristic of interest

B. Sample

C. Target audience

8. The group about which a researcher wishes to generalize. *target*

9. Members of a target population who are studied by a researcher. *sample*

10. The specific question that a researcher wants to answer. *A*

ARTICLES FOR DISCUSSION

In the United States, there is increasing community concern about the epidemic of methamphetamine use. According to one source, "Few local governments, especially in rural areas, have the resources to deal with the devastating effects. Robberies and burglaries have increased because of meth, as have domestic violance, assaults, and identify theft. Child welfare officials report an increase in out-of-home placements because of meth. Meth-lab burn victims end up in hospitals at a tremendous cost to hospitals and state Medicaid programs. Hallucinations, weight loss, skin sores, disfigured or destroyed teeth, and brain damage are among the physical results of meth use."

"Meth Epidemic Moves From Rural Places to Cities," http://www.ruralschools.org/news/survey.html (Organizations concerned about Rural Education, accessed August 11, 2007.)

One group that has been sharing information on the national methamphetamine problem is the National Association of Counties. They did a study of 45 states, that is summarized from this excerpt from a county Coroner's office.

THE METH EPIDEMIC

The swift rise of the use and distribution of methamphetamine . . . has overwhelmed our communities and government services. The increasing widespread production, sales, and use of methamphetamine (also sometimes known as "speed"), is now affecting urban, suburban and rural communities nationwide. County governments across the nation are on the front lines in responding to the methamphetamine crisis. This insidious drug causes a whole host of problems including legal, medical, environmental, and social ones. County and city services (and the taxpayers) must pay for investigating meth labs and distribution cases, making arrests of offenders, holding these suspects in jails, prosecuting them, providing treatment services, probation services, and cleaning up toxic lab sites along with social services costs.

In an alarming number of methamphetamine arrests, there is a child in the home. Social workers and law enforcement officers find that the children are frequently suffering from neglect and abuse. The National Association of Counties (NACo) recently conducted surveys of law enforcement and county child welfare officials in order to determine the impact of meth on government services and their communities. The results were from 500 counties from 45 states. Here is a summary of their results:

- Meth is a growing problem that is now national in scope. Of the 500 responding law enforcement agencies, 87% report increases in meth-related arrests starting three years ago. A number of states, including California, reported 100 percent increases. Seventy percent found robberies or burglaries have increased because of meth use...The Sheriff's Office has experienced a growing number of theft and burglary cases committed by meth addicts especially involving thefts from cars, commercial burglaries, mail theft, and identity theft. Some counties have also experienced a 62 percent increase in domestic violence because of meth use.
- Meth is the leading drug-related local law enforcement problem in the country. Fifty-eight (58%) percent of the counties surveyed stated meth was their largest drug problem.
- Meth related arrests represent a high proportion of crimes requiring incarceration. Fifty percent (50%) of the counties estimated that 1 in 5 of their current jail inmates were housed because of meth related crimes. The problem was even worse in the other half of counties surveyed...Jails are also experiencing a rise in inmate populations, especially in female inmates. One Sheriff from a northern California county stated his female inmate population has risen 30% in the last couple of years due to methamphetamine.
- Other crimes are increasing as a result of meth. Seventy percent of the responding counties stated that along with burglaries, robberies, and domestic violence, assaults and identity thefts have also increased.

In addition to the resulting crime, the production of methamphetamine produces a number of environmental issues as well. The makeshift labs vary in sophistication and can be located in barns, garages, back rooms of businesses, apartments, hotel rooms, storage facilities, vacant buildings, residences, and vehicles, including RVs. This drug, which is smoked, injected, or ingested, is synthetic, cheap, and relatively easy to make in these labs. They frequently will use pseudoephedrine, the ingredient in cold medicines, and common fertilizers and solvents. The materials are dangerous and highly explosive. During my law enforcement career, I have been to a number of meth lab sites where explosions from the manufacturing process had set the residence aflame. In addition, the chemical waste products from this manufacturing process are frequently dumped into the ground, sewer systems, or alongside roads. Even more disturbing is the impact that meth is having on children. The NACo study also found that meth is a major cause of child abuse and neglect.

- Forty percent of all the child welfare officials in the survey reported increases in out-of-home placements of children due to meth in the last year.
- During the past 5 years, 71% of the counties in California alone reported an increase in out-of-home placements due to meth, as did Colorado.

In addition, 59% of county officials stated that the particular nature of the meth user parent has increased the difficulty of family reunification.

The rising number of foster children due to meth use is greatly impacting county welfare systems and the need for more foster parents. As these children are moved around in an overburdened social service system, their parents may be in jail, awaiting treatment, or not seeking treatment. One study found that these children often stay in out-of-home placement three times as long as other children. In addition, many of these children have special needs.

Law enforcement and social service providers in Santa Cruz County are already studying this drastic burden on county services to devise some solutions. However, this widespread problem will take a commitment from all of us, including the public, to solve it with the appropriate resources that will be required.

The Meth Epidemic, Santa Cruz County Sheriff-Coronor's Office, www.scsheriff.com/MethArticle.htm Copyright © 2005.

QUESTIONS FOR DISCUSSION

1. What statistics cited in the article show that methamphetamine addiction is a serious and growing problem?
2. What are the overt and hidden costs of addiction to society as a whole?
3. The article mentioned specific increases in difficulties associated with methamphetamine use in a community—what were some of these new or newly aggravated problems?
4. What should be done on a national and local level to combat methamphetamine use?

A recent PBS *Frontline* program covered the efforts of one reporter to investigate the causes of the methamphetamine epidemic that had been plaguing his Oregon community for years and is rapidly spreading across the United States. Reporter Steve Suo compared statistics in addiction rates and saw that they went up and down in a consistent pattern across the country; he then searched for the causes of the consistent ups and downs of these rates. He also persisted in tracing the reasons why it took so long for the problem to be addressed seriously on federal levels of government.

You can download a transcript of their program and watch it on www.pbs.org/wgbh/pages/frontline/meth/view/ If you choose to read the transcript or watch the program, consider the following additional questions:

5. What factors in the *Frontline* program indicate that meth addiction is an international issue?

6. Why was the US Congress slow to understand and enact legislation to curb the meth problem?

7. How did the interests of pharmaceutical companies affect the proposed solutions to the meth problem?

8. Frontline added several personal stories to their coverage of the methamphetamine problem. Why is it important to connect statistics with examples of how an issue impacts individuals? How does the combination of data and narrative make the argument that meth is a serious problem?

"The Meth Epidemic" http://www.pbs.org/wgbh/pages/frontline/meth/view/, Posted February 2006

Following is an executive summary of a report that was commissioned and funded by the Independent Women's Forum. The Forum did not do the research or the writing in order to maximize objectivity. This report is based on original research conducted by the Institute for American Values' 16-member Courtship Research Team, led by Norval Glenn, professor of sociology at the University of Texas, and Elizabeth Marquardt, an affiliate scholar at the Institute. Professor Glenn also served as the project's research director. To access the complete survey, including methodology and recommendations, you can visit the website at www.iwf.org.

HOOKING UP, HANGING OUT, AND HOPING FOR MR. RIGHT: COLLEGE WOMEN ON DATING AND MATING TODAY: EXECUTIVE SUMMARY

An 18-month study of the attitudes and values of today's college women regarding sexuality, dating, courtship, and marriage—involving in-depth interviews with a diverse group of 62 college women on 11 campuses, supplemented by 20-minute telephone interviews with a nationally representative sample of 1,000 college women—yields the following major findings.

1. **Marriage is a major life goal for the majority of today's college women, and most would like to meet a spouse while at college.** Eighty-three percent of respondents in the national survey agreed that "Being married is a very important goal for me," and 63 percent agreed that "I would like to

meet my future husband in college." Contrary to what we might think, today's college women have high marital aspirations and many are actively thinking about marriage.

2. **But there are important aspects of the college social scene that appear to undermine the likelihood of achieving the goal of a successful future marriage.** For example, since 1980, women have outnumbered men attending college. In 1997, the sex ratio on-campuses nationally was only 79 men for every 100 women.

3. **In addition, relationships between college women and men today are often characterized by either too little commitment or too much,** leaving women with few opportunities to explore the marriage worthiness of a variety of men before settling into a long-term commitment with one of them.

4. **"Hooking up," a distinctive sex-without-commitment interaction between college women and men, is widespread on-campuses and profoundly influences campus culture, although a minority of students engage in it.** Three-fourths of respondents agreed that a "hook up" is "when a girl and a guy get together for a physical encounter and don't necessarily expect anything further." A "physical encounter" can mean anything from kissing to having sex. In the national survey, 40 percent of women said they had experienced a hook up, and one in ten reported having done so more than six times. Women who had hooked up reported a range of feelings, positive and negative, about the practice. For example, 61 percent of college women who said that a hook up made them feel "desirable" also reported that it made them feel "awkward." Hooking up commonly takes place when both participants are drinking or drunk.

5. **To say "we hooked up" could mean a couple kissed, or had sex, or had oral sex, but no one will know for sure.** Indeed, it appears that the ambiguity of the phrase "hooking up" is part of the reason for its popularity. Although premarital sex is much more acceptable now than in the past, women are still wary of getting a bad reputation. Saying "we hooked up" allows women to be vague about the nature of the physical encounter while stating that it happened.

6. **"Dating" carries multiple meanings for today's college women.** We found four widely used and different meanings for the term, two of which were more common. A college couple who is "dating" is sometimes in a fast-moving, highly committed relationship that includes sexual activity, sleeping at one another's dorm most nights, studying together, sharing meals, and more, but rarely going out on "dates." These fast-moving commitments and hooking up operate as two sides of the same coin. At the same time, "dating" is also often synonymous with "hanging out," in which women and men spend loosely organized, undefined time together, without making their interest in one another explicit, unless they hook up, at which point dating and hooking up become the same thing.

7. **College women say it is rare for college men to ask them on dates, or to acknowledge when they have become a couple.** Only 50 percent of college women seniors reported having been asked on six or more dates by men since coming to college, and a third of women surveyed said they had been

asked on two dates or fewer. Young women and men more often "hang out" rather than go on planned dates, and if they live in a coed dorm, their dorm is where they most often meet members of the opposite sex. They report that because they can hang out or hook up with a guy over a period of time and still not know if they are a couple, women often initiate "the talk" in which they ask, "Are we committed or not?" When she asks, he decides.

8. **College women from divorced families differ significantly from women who grew up in intact families regarding marriage aspirations, getting advice from parents, and hooking up.** Women from divorced families appeared more eager to marry, and wanted to marry sooner, but were less likely to believe that their future marriages would last. They were also less likely to report that they were raised with firm expectations about relationships with men, and less likely to report that their parents had told them to save sex for marriage. They were more likely to have hooked up, and if they did hook up, were more likely to have done so often—of women who had hooked up at least once, 37 percent of college women whose parents had divorced reported hooking up more than six times, compared with 23 percent of women from intact families.

9. **There are few widely recognized social norms on college campuses that help guide and support young women in thinking about sex, love, commitment, and marriage.** College women say they want to be married someday, and many would like to meet a future husband at college. Yet it seems that virtually no one even attempts to help them consider how their present social experience might or might not lead to a successful marriage, or how marriage might fit with other life goals.

10. **As a result, the culture of courtship, a set of social norms and expectations that once helped young people find the pathway to marriage, has largely become a hook up culture with almost no shared norms or expectations.** Hooking up, hanging out, and fast-moving ("joined at the hip") commitments are logical, though we believe seriously flawed, responses to this disappearance of a culture of courtship. The options available to college women are obviously strongly influenced by choices that other young men and women make, but each young woman today tends to see her choices as wholly private and individual. For example, while most college women expect to marry for life and 88 percent would not personally consider having a child outside of marriage, 87 percent agree that "I should not judge anyone's sexual conduct except my own." Consequently, when women are hurt or disappointed by the hook up culture, they typically blame themselves.

11. **The lack of adult involvement, guidance, and even knowledge regarding how young people are dating and mating today is unprecedented and problematic.** Parents, college administrators, and other social leaders have largely stepped away from the task of guiding young people into intimate relationships and marriage. Few older adults are aware of what hooking up or dating means for college students today, and the institutional arrangements of space on many campuses, such as coed dorms, clearly help to facilitate the hook up culture.

Based on these findings, we offer the following recommendations.

1. **Recognize that older adults, including parents, college administrators, and other social leaders, should have important roles in guiding the courting and mating practices of the young.** The virtual disappearance of adult participation in, or even awareness of, how today's young people find and marry one another should be seen as a major social problem, and should end.

2. **Recognize that college women typically do not yearn for a series of "close relationships," but instead the majority seek long-term commitment and marriage.**

3. **There appears to have been a reduction in male initiative in dating on college campuses. Recognize that the burden of dating and mating should not fall on women alone, and that there is a need for greater male initiative.**

4. **Support the creation of socially prescribed rules and norms that are relevant to and appropriate for this generation, and that can guide young people with much more sensitivity and support toward the marriages they seek.** When it comes to inherently social acts such as romance and marriage, social rules do more than restrict individual choice, they also facilitate it. The absence of appropriately updated social norms, rituals, and relationship milestones leaves many young women confused, and often disempowered, in their relationships with men. Socially defined courtship is an important pathway to more successful marriages.

Hooking Up, Hanging Out, and Hoping for Mr. Right: College Women on Dating and Mating Today Norval Glenn and Elizabeth Marquardt, Principal Investigators. An Institute for American Values Report to the Independent Women's Forum. Copyright © 2001 by Institute for American Values. Reprinted by permission of the publisher.

QUESTIONS FOR DISCUSSION

1. How did the institute that commissioned the study and the researchers who did the study choose a study design that would maximize the accuracy of the findings?

2. Were the findings of the researchers similar to what you have observed about dating practices on college campuses? If not, what differences have you noticed?

3. Have you seen changes in the dating and mating rituals during your own lifetime? If so, what are the changes and why do you think they occurred? If not, do you know someone of an older generation who has observed such changes?

4. Given the research findings, to what extent do you agree with the recommendations of the researchers?

IDEAS FOR WRITING OR SPEAKING

Using the following format, create a persuasive speech or essay on an issue of your choice. Use statistical research to support your conclusion.

1. Find an issue that interests you. The more interest you have in the issue, the more conviction you will have in your writing or speaking.

2. Write out your conclusion about the issue. Your position on the issue should be clearly articulated and will form your thesis statement.

3. Begin your essay or speech with an introduction that provides a context for your issue and your position. You may also use important statistics to gain the attention of your readers or listeners. Put your thesis statement at the end of your introduction.

4. Identify and expand upon the reasons that support your conclusion. Present these reasons in the body of the essay or speech. Concentrate on statistical evidence. You may also include examples and expert testimony to complete your support.

5. Use the conclusion of your essay or speech to restate your major points and to reemphasize the importance of your conclusion. Remind your readers or listeners of the points you brought out in your introduction, bringing these points full circle in your closing thoughts.

LONGER-TERM WRITING ASSIGNMENT

The purpose of this assignment is to give you an in-depth understanding of a social, national, or international problem and the many factors that enter into changes in policy. This may be done as a long-term project for an individual or a group.

Begin by asking yourself, "What is a continuing community, campus, national, or international problem that concerns me?" Or, take the advice of English professor Bruce Reeves, and fill in the blank on the following question: "If we can send a man to the moon, why can't we _____?" For example, you might think, "If we can send a man to the moon, why can't we solve world hunger?" Or, "Why can't we stop the drug cartels?" "Why can't we provide jobs for everyone?" "Why can't we have peace in the Middle East [or somewhere else]?" "Why can't we rid our town of pollution from the local factory?"

Then, begin researching the problem. You will learn more about research in the next chapter, but begin with the knowledge you have gained in this chapter. Look up statistics that relate to your problem, being careful to note how the research has been carried out.

After you read Chapter 5, begin the rest of your research, using a minimum of six sources of information, including studies done about this problem and the opinions of experts who have written or spoken about it. If the problem you are studying is local, try to interview officials who are in a position to address the problem or who have worked on the problem.

Take notes on the background of the problem, including the history of the problem, the scope of the problem, and the impact or effect of the problem. Consider whether there are multiple causes contributing to the problem.

As you research this problem, consider past efforts to solve it. To what extent were those efforts successful? Where there have been failed policies, explain why they have failed.

Note also any current or recent proposals about this problem. For example, if you are writing on the difficulty of ending homelessness, consider why past proposals have not been approved or successfully implemented. Also, consider the chances of success for any current proposals.

When you have finished studying this problem, create a proposal for a solution to this problem. Support your proposal, showing how it will resolve the difficulties that previous proposals have come up against. Also, explain how it will not create more problems than it solves.

If you find that you can't come up with a solution to the problem, then explain what variables make it too difficult to solve. State what would have to change for a resolution to be possible.

In sum, your paper or speech should include a complete explanation of the background and scope of the problem, the harm it creates, the policies that have not worked against this problem, and your proposed solution to the problem or analysis of why it can't currently be solved. Also, include a bibliography of all sources you used in researching this problem.

FILMS FOR ANALYSIS AND DISCUSSION

The Constant Gardener (2005, R) stars Ralph Fiennes as a widower searching for the truth about the death of his beloved wife, played by Rachel Weisz. As it turns out, the truth involves corrupt corporations covering up deaths all over Africa, and he might be their next target. The film combines flashbacks of Weisz discovering the corruption with present scenes of Fiennes researching the cover-up of both his wife's death and much more. This is a topical film about finding truth through the researching of causes and effects.

Similar Films and Classics

Erin Brockovich (2000, R)

This true story is about a unemployed single mother who gets involved in one of the biggest class action lawsuits in American history. Note the search for causes of poisonings afflicting community residents and the series of events that lead Erin to be a focal point of the investigation.

A Civil Action (1998, PG-13)

Actor John Travolta plays Jan Schlittman, a lawyer who agrees to represent eight families whose children died from leukemia; he attempts to link the deaths to two large corporations that leaked toxic chemicals into the water supply of Woburn, Massachusetts. Note the personal cost to Schlittman that is discussed in Chapter 4 in our section on *Multiple Causes*.

The China Syndrome (1979, PG)

This film explores a young reporter's discovery of an accident at a nuclear power plant and how the incident is covered up by those who wish to keep it a secret. Note how difficult it is to seek the truth about an incident when those with vested interests do not want full disclosure.

5

Inductive Generalizations: Controlled Studies and Analogies

Who Said So? And Who Are They Anyway?

A critical thinker understands the credible use of controlled studies, expert testimony, and generalizations from analogies to support arguments.

This chapter will cover

- The use of controlled studies in arguments

- The criteria for credibility of controlled studies

- The use and misuse of expert testimony in supporting conclusions

- The use of analogies in inductive generalizations

In the previous chapter, we considered the use of statistical studies and causal generalizations as evidence (reasons) to support conclusions. In this chapter, we will focus on the inductive generalizations that come from *controlled studies;* we will also look at the importance of *expert testimony.* We will then examine another commonly used form of inductive reasoning, that of generalizing from *analogies.*

Researchers use controlled studies to make observations and draw conclusions about many subjects, including human and animal behavior and solutions to medical problems. These studies are called *controlled* because they use specific methods for comparing groups of subjects. Other researchers can duplicate these methods so that the accuracy of the findings can be verified.

The conclusions drawn in carefully controlled scientific studies are inductive generalizations; a good study shows us what will *probably* or *usually* occur in a given circumstance.

Some of the elements of controlled studies are the same as those used by polling organizations. A researcher still works with the three questions discussed in Chapter 4:

1. What do I want to find out? (the characteristic of interest)
2. Whom do I want to know about? (the target population)
3. Whom can I study to get accurate answers about my target population? (the sample)

As with polling, researchers usually can't study everyone in a given target population, so they have to observe *some* members of the population. The number of subjects depends on how precise an answer the researcher needs. Preliminary results leading to *additional* studies can be gathered from a very small sample. For example, if a researcher discovers that 20 women with kidney problems have a negative reaction to the drug ibuprofen, his or her findings can be used to justify the funds for a larger study.

In medical research, the design of a study is called the **protocol**. Two groups of **subjects** (people or animals) who are alike in all *significant* (relevant) aspects need to be studied in order for the research to have the element of **control**. Control involves weeding out extraneous factors that could affect the outcome of a study.

RESEARCH DESIGN

A good research design includes the following:

1. A **question** to answer: This is the characteristic of interest concerning a targeted population. A researcher begins with a question, such as, "What is the effect of the new drug Z on migraine headaches?"
2. A **hypothesis**: This is a speculation about what will be discovered from the research: "The drug Z will shorten migraine headaches caused by restricted blood vessels."

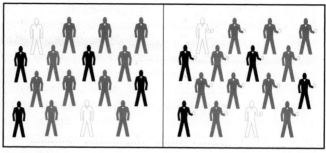

Control Group   Experimental Group

Figure 5–1   The experimental group receives the special treatment, called the variable.

3. A **sample** of individuals to study: The sample should be randomly selected and representative of the target population. The sample is divided into two groups (see Figure 5–1).

   a. A **control group**: A group of subjects from the sample who get no treatment or a placebo (sugar pill).

   b. An **experimental group:** A group of subjects from the sample who are exposed to a special treatment called a *variable;* for example, this group would be given the drug to assess its effects in comparison with similar people who are not given the drug or who are given a placebo.

4. **Data:** The observations made by the researcher as he or she completes the study.

5. **Conclusions:** After the study is carried out, the researcher compiles the data and draws conclusions; the researcher interprets the meaning and significance of the data.

In addition, researchers carefully consider the implications of the findings, which means that they will speculate about further research that can be done to answer questions related to the study.

Significant results may be discovered when the only difference between the control group and the experimental group is that the experimental group is exposed to a special treatment, such as a new drug; this special treatment is called the **independent variable**. Researchers can draw accurate conclusions and eliminate alternate explanations for the results of their research if the studies are carefully designed to fit the criteria described on the preceding pages. The generalizations they draw may be used as evidence in inductive arguments.

results are discovered when an independent variable is used

SKILL

Understand the basic components of a controlled study.

STOP AND THINK

How is a controlled study based on Mill's method of difference? *basically, it is the same — the difference is analyzed*

CRITERIA FOR EVALUATING RESEARCH FINDINGS

Science is always simple and always profound. It is only the half-truths that are dangerous.

George Bernard Shaw, *The Doctor's Dilemma* (1913)

Junk science makes junk law.

Dr. James Dobson

Interesting findings from research studies are often reported in newspapers and magazines or on television programs. Most of these reports don't give complete information about the research design. Before accepting the results of research as reliable, the following questions should be asked:

1. How large was the sample? As we discussed in Chapter 4, a small sample can suggest areas for further research; for example, a recent study on prevention of heart disease involved only 47 subjects but was the cause of considerable hope in the scientific community. *L.A. Times* reporter Thomas H. Maugh III notes the following:

> A small clinical trial has shown for the first time that it is possible to use drugs to remove plaque from clogged arteries, a finding that could lead to radically new ways to treat heart disease, the No. 1 killer in the United States.
> Infusions of a genetically engineered mutant form of high-density lipoprotein, the so-called good cholesterol, over a five-week period were shown to reduce plaque volume in patients suffering from chest pain.
> "This is an extraordinary and unprecedented finding," said Dr. Steven Nissen of the Cleveland Clinic Foundation, who led the study reported in the *Journal of the American Medical Association*.[1]

Preliminary studies that show great promise should receive our attention and the funding and resources of our universities and hospitals. One reporter asked Dr. Nissen if he would proceed to conduct more research after the initial small studies proved hopeful. Nissen replied:

> Absolutely. And I think it is important for everyone to understand that this is not an available therapy. It's investigational. But we are so encouraged by these results that now we have a good reason to do

[1] *L.A. Times,* November 5, 2003. "Drug for Heart Disease Called Breakthrough," Thomas H. Maugh II.

studies in thousands of patients. And I'm really very confident that when we go ahead and study this in a larger group, we're going to find that targeting the HDL, the good cholesterol, can actually turn around this disease, and it can do it much faster than we ever believed.[2]

Scientists can be enthusiastic and hopeful about promising studies. As critical thinkers, however, we need to remember that more complete studies need to be conducted before we can use the research findings as factual support for our conclusions.

Studies with an inadequate sample are sometimes reported in the news media because of their fascinating results. If you read about a remarkable study, be especially careful to pay attention to information about the sample used by the researcher. Consider the following research reported under the heading "FYI, True Love Is the Best Drug." Was the sample large enough to justify the conclusion expressed by the headline?

> While the verdict may still be out on whether love is stronger than hate, new research suggests it is at least healthier. In a study of older, happily married couples, Ohio State University researchers found that abrasive arguments weakened the couples' immune systems, making them more vulnerable to illnesses and infectious diseases. Scientists had asked 31 couples ages 55 to 75 to discuss the issues that caused problems in their marriage. Blood samples were taken at regular intervals and monitored for changes in hormone levels and immune function. The more negativity the couples expressed toward each other, the more their immune systems weakened.[3]

Remember that newspapers, magazines, and television programs want to present interesting information to readers and viewers. Most reporters are not trained in research design, so they are not usually skilled at examining methodology; their primary job is to create a good story. The "story" they create can be found in the headline used to summarize the article, which often claims far more than is merited by the limited study.

2. Is the study reliable? As we discussed in Chapter 4, if a sample is not representative of the target group, then the study is biased and not reliable; the results cannot be generalized to a larger population. In the previous example about married couples, the reporter generalized about all couples from a small group of couples, ages 55 to 75. Remember that representativeness means having the same characteristics in the same proportion as the target population. Consider the following claim made in an article entitled "Marijuana-like Substance in Brain Could Help Treat Parkinson's, Researchers Say":

[2]Ibid.
[3]Staff and wire reports, "FYI, True Love Is the Best Drug," *Contra Costa Times,* September 10, 1996, p. E1.

Neuroscientists have found that a substance similar to the active ingredient in marijuana but produced naturally in the brain helps to control mobility—and may offer a novel target for treating Parkinson's disease. Stanford University researchers reported today in the journal *Nature* that marijuana-like "endocannabinoids"—one of the many chemicals used in the brain to transmit signals from one neuron to another—form part of the neural machinery that directs normal movement.[4]

The article later notes that this experiment was done only on mice, that it will take years of research to reach the human testing stage, and that

THC, the active ingredient in marijuana, activities the same class of receptors as the natural chemicals but has effects throughout the brain, and no demonstrated benefits in terms of improved mobility . . . one thing the findings don't suggest is that smoking marijuana might help alleviate Parkinson's.[5]

3. Are there alternative explanations for the findings? Have all of the important factors of the data been considered? There might be explanations for findings in research other than the ones given by the researchers. For example, if the members of the experimental group know they are receiving the treatment, they may report positive changes based solely on their expectations (that is, if Joanne knows she received the new drug that cures headaches, she may expect to feel better and then actually feel better). To control for this kind of error, researchers generally try to conduct **blind studies** in which the participants are not told whether they belong to the experimental group or the control group.

Also, researchers may unconsciously exaggerate the improvement they see in the experimental group, especially if the study results are very important to them. For this reason, **double-blind studies** are often conducted; in these studies, neither the experimenter nor the participants know which is the control and which is the experimental group.

One recent study conducted in three Illinois cities compared the accuracy of eyewitness identifications of suspects between the traditional and "reform" method of identification. In the traditional method, several individuals—including the suspect—are lined up and viewed simultaneously by the witnesses. In this method, the police are aware of the suspect's identity. The traditional method is blind, but the reform method is double blind—in the reform method, witnesses look at people or pictures one by one, and the officer or officers present do not know the identity of the suspects and aren't working on the case.

[4]sfgate.com, Carl T. Hall,"Marijuana-like Substance in Brain Could Help Treat Parkinson's, Researchers Say," *Chronicle Science Writer,* Wednesday, February 7, 2007.
[5]Ibid.

Of the 319 simultaneous lineups conducted, the suspect identified by police was chosen 59.9 percent of the time. Of 229 sequential lineups, the suspect was chosen only 45 percent of the time.

Sheri Mecklenberg, general counsel to the Chicago Police and director of the study, said she found the results surprising and hoped they would generate further study. "This is important for everyone. What police, defense attorneys and prosecutors want is better witness identification," she said.

But the study was criticized by Gary Wells, a professor of psychology at Iowa State who has published more than 100 articles on the topic. Wells' chief concern was that the simultaneous lineups were conducted by investigators working the cases. That makes the results hard to compare, Wells said.

"The reason that we so vehemently push the double-blind is because of a concern that the lineup administrator unintentionally influences the person's choice, leads them to pick the suspect," he said.[6]

In addition to the problems associated with bias, it is also difficult to design research studies that help us discover the causes of problems. For example, we wouldn't want researchers to take identical twins and encourage one to become a smoker to see if her lungs deteriorated over time while her nonsmoking sister's lungs remained clear. So we often are hampered by limited information, evidence we can collect from past *occurrences*, as we seek to discover reasonable causal generalizations. Same sample groups are difficult to study, as discussed by columnist Linda Seebach in the following excerpt:

American education suffers from an excess of experiment and a shortage of research. The difference is that research studies are carefully designed to test an educational theory by comparing one group of students who have tried a new method with a similar group who have not.

The difficulty is that such research is expensive and complicated. New medicines are tested for safety and efficacy by "double-blind" tests in which neither doctors nor patients know who is getting the experimental drug. But education can't be conducted blind; children, and their parents, know perfectly well what is going on in their classrooms.

Recruiting children for a research study can lead to errors, if the parents who consent are unlike those who don't in some way the researchers don't know about.

So the staple fare of education journals is success stories told by enthusiastic teachers reporting on their own classroom experiments. The stories are true, they may even be inspiring, but they don't prove any general principles.[7]

---

[6]asweeney@suntimes.com. "Traditional Police Lineup Works Better: Study," by Annie Sweeney, *Chicago Sun Times,* March 29, 2001. Copyright Chicago Sun-Times 2006.
[7]Linda Seebach, "Education Lacks Enough Research," *Contra Costa Times,* September 1, 1996.

4. Are the results statistically significant? When a finding is labeled **statistically significant**, it is probable that the reported effect will occur again in similar circumstances. For example, let's say there are 100 persons in an experimental group and 100 persons in a control group, and 13 more in the experimental group react to the treatment (the variable). With that proportion of difference in reaction, researchers can conclude that there is a 95 percent probability that the variable (and not a chance occurrence) caused the effect, and they can call their study statistically significant.

5. Have other researchers been able to duplicate the results? There is always a first discovery of a link between a variable and an effect on people. However, if a study reveals an important finding, then other researchers may try similar experiments to verify the results of the research and look for applications of the discovery. When others have tried to do the same experiment and failed, the results are considered unreliable.

Duplicate studies are often conducted on products that make incredible claims, and these studies often refute the claims of the original researchers; for example, many companies declare, often through infomercials, that their research has come upon the "fountain of youth." One such product was discussed as follows on a medical talk show:

> *Jill:* I'm calling to find out about human growth hormone, HGH. I have friends on it that say wonderful things about it and that it is a fountain of youth. Then I read an article about HGH and a lawsuit. I am wondering what the lawsuit is about and if HGH is dangerous?
>
> *Dr. Dean:* Be very careful. I would think most of what they're experiencing and telling you about is probably a placebo effect.
>
> A few years ago, there was a study that claimed all kinds of benefits from HGH. Then they repeated the study carefully in a double blind fashion—it turns out that it is not a good thing. It will give you sore and aching muscles that will grow tumors. This is not the fountain of youth, nor does it increase strength. It is one of those things that got out of hand.
>
> The lawsuit you have heard about is where the company who makes HGH agreed to pay a criminal fine and restitution, like $50 million, because they promoted growth hormone for a medical use that was not approved by the FDA.
>
> As part of their fine, they have to educate physicians about the approved indications, which are for growth hormone deficient people, usually kids, and people with kidney disease. There are some other syndromes that it has been approved for as well.[8]

The original study that caused companies to sell "growth hormone therapy" to stop or reverse aging was conducted on only 21 men, 12 of whom were

[8]Dr. Dean Edell, "Growth Hormone Is Not the Fountain of Youth," www.healthcentral.com (accessed April 15, 1999).

given growth hormone and experienced significant side effects. Because so many people spent money on the magic bullet aging cures promised by companies, actions were taken against those making such claims and promises based on inadequate research:

> In January 2003, the FDA sent a warning letter to *Be Youthful,* of Edmonton, Canada, objecting to claims that their Be Youthful HGH product was effective against depression, chronic fatigue, high blood pressure, and high cholesterol levels.[9]

> In April 2003, *Nature's Youth*, LLC, of Centerville, Massachusetts, voluntarily destroyed approximately 5,700 boxes of "Nature's Youth HGH" with a market value of about $515,000. The destruction took place after the FDA notified the company that claims made for the product were unsubstantiated and therefore illegal. The company had claimed that the product, which it described as a growth-hormone releaser, would enhance the body's natural production of Human Growth Factors and Insulin-like Growth Factor-1; improve physical performance; speed recovery from training; increase cardiac output; and increase immune functions; and was "your body's best defense against aging."[10]

In 2005, Edmund Chein, M.D., who operates the Palm Springs Life Extension Institute (PSLEI) in Palm Springs, California, was placed on five years' probation during which he must (a) pay $10,000 to the State of California for costs, (b) take courses in ethics, prescribing practices, and recordkeeping, (c) refrain from making unsubstantiated advertising claims, and (d) either have his practice monitored or participate in an intensive professional enhancement program. The clinic's Web site states that PSLEI specializes in "optimized total hormone balancing by returning hormone levels to values consistent with a younger person." The grounds for discipline included inappropriately and negligently prescribing HGH plus insulin to a patient who was neither deficient nor diabetic.[11]

6. Does the researcher claim that the study proves more than it was designed to prove? Some researchers may be too hopeful or excited about the implications of a study they conducted; for example, if a small sample of cancer patients has been helped by an experimental drug, the researcher needs to limit the report of results to the findings of this particular study. A news organization may also report the results of a study in such a way as to magnify its significance. For example, a headline read "Lab Helps Find Gene Link to Migraine. Research Connects Defect on Chromosome 19 to Familial Headaches." In the opening paragraph, the results are summarized as follows:

> Scientists have for the first time linked a form of migraine headache to a defective gene by using DNA snippets supplied by Lawrence

---

[9]"Growth Hormone Schemes and Scams," by Stephen Barrett, M.D., Quack Watch, July 9, 2006
[10]Ibid.
[11]Ibid.

Livermore Laboratory and a lab-developed "map" of the gene's chromosome.[12]

The article goes on to discuss the fact that 20 million people in the United States suffer from migraine headaches; the traits of a migraine headache are described in detail. The reader is not told that this research may not be directly relevant to finding cures for common migraine headaches until the ninth paragraph:

> But the finding, published in the journal *Cell,* applies to a type of migraine that is "exceedingly rare" and atypical because it involves attacks of paralysis and brain deterioration, according to Neil Raskin, a UC-San Francisco neurology professor and immediate past president of the American Association for the Study of Headache. "I've only seen two patients [with that disorder] ever and I'm an old man," he said.[13]

When a study is promising, the researcher can suggest studies that would be needed to make further discoveries about the effectiveness of a treatment. As critical thinkers, we need to carefully consider the evidence presented in an article that pulls us in with promises of a greater research breakthrough than has actually occurred.

7. Has the research been done by a respected institution? Research from a well-established institution such as the National Institutes of Health or Stanford University is generally considered credible. Be careful in your judgments, however, if research from one reliable source contradicts research from another reliable source; it is best to withhold judgment or to accept conclusions tentatively in these cases.

8. Are the researchers biased? Even if the research organization is well respected, it may have a vested interest in the outcome of the study.

In a study on the effects of prostate medicines, note how one of the pharmaceutical companies that funded the research found fault with it. Do you think the criticism of the study it funded reflects bias?

> The first head-to-head comparison of the nation's two most popular medicines for prostate trouble found that one gives significant relief while the other is virtually worthless.
>
> The two medicines, Hytrin and Proscar, are taken by millions of older men to relieve the symptoms of an enlarged prostate gland.
>
> The study found that Hytrin eases men's discomfort by about one-third, while Proscar works no better than dummy sugar pills.
>
> ...The study was financed by Merck & Co., which makes Proscar, and Abbott Laboratories Inc., the maker of Hytrin.

---

[12]Peter Weiss, "Lab Helps Find Gene Link to Migraine," *Contra Costa Times,* November 5, 1996, p. A7.
[13]Ibid.

Although both companies approved the study's design, Merck discounted its significance as publication approached in today's issue of the *New England Journal of Medicine.*

Dr. Glenn Gormley, a Merck research official, said that in hindsight, the study was not set up properly to answer the question of which drug is better.[14] (See Exercises 5.1 on p. 191 and 5.2 on p. 192.)

REMINDER

Inductive reasoning is the process of making generalizations from specific observations.

CONTROVERSY IN RESEARCH FINDINGS

If you have studied the previous section you probably have an appreciation of how difficult it is to do research that yields accurate results. Good studies require time and money to complete. Even studies that use the scientific method and produce clear results are sometimes criticized by scientists or others who find flaws in the researcher's methods or conclusions. You may be familiar with studies of the effects of a substance on rats that show that the substance causes cancer. Studies like these may be criticized on the basis that researchers were comparing human and rodent metabolism when they drew their conclusions; findings of such studies are also routinely criticized because the proportionate doses given to the rats are often much higher than most humans would ingest.

Read the following excerpt from an article about another controversial research study that has been criticized by some groups and praised by others:

> Two recent studies that conclude that abortions have little negative psychological impact on women have renewed debate over a politically charged issue that, many researchers concede, appears unlikely to be resolved soon.
>
> Representatives of anti-abortion groups contend that the studies are methodologically flawed and biased because the researchers favor abortion.
>
> In particular, the critics say the studies did not follow women for a sufficiently long time after their abortions to assess accurately the occurrence of delayed effects; that they used a sample of women unrepresentative of the general population; or that they employed inappropriate measures of psychological distress.[15]

The problem of divided opinion about the validity of a study is a difficult one, but as consumers of information, we can either withhold judgment until

---

[14]Daniel Q. Haney, "The Battle of Prostate Medicines," *Contra Costa Times,* August 22, 1996, p. B1.
[15]Chris Raymond, *The Chronicle of Higher Education,* February 7, 1990, p. A6.

As consumers of information, we can wait until research satisfies us

more conclusive evidence is presented or give credence to a study with evidence we believe is strong enough to influence our current decisions. For example, if we read that one study showed that a low-fat diet contributed to reduced cholesterol rates and another study showed no significant relationship, we might still choose to believe that there is a good chance of reducing cholesterol with the low-fat diet. The critical thinker realizes that researchers are not in agreement about the ultimate prevention and cure of elevated cholesterol levels, but he or she chooses to make some dietary changes based on limited research because "It can't hurt and it might actually help my heart."

A more difficult problem with research is avoiding errors that could affect the results of a study. Consider the following commentary on the subject of research studies conducted by young scientists:

> Errors may occur through improper laboratory practices, faulty equipment, accidental mix-ups, poorly designed experiments, inadequate replication of research results, or any number of other reasons, some involving negligence and others occurring through no fault of the scientist.
>
> …[E]rror is, in fact, inherent in any endeavor carried out by fallible human beings. The great possibility of error is one of the reasons why judgment is so important in science and why a scientist who has avoided error, designed good experiments, exercised good judgment, and discovered something new about the nature of things in the universe can experience such a thrill of achievement.[16]

John Ioannidis, an epidemiologist at the University of Ioannina School of Medicine in Greece, says that small sample sizes, poor study design, researcher bias, selective reporting and other problems combine to make most research findings false. But even large, well-designed studies are not always right, meaning that scientists and the public have to be wary of reported findings.[17]

Given the possibility of error in experimentation, the question arises: "Whom should I believe?"

prove to be wrong

> "We should accept that most research findings will be refuted. Some will be replicated and validated. The replication process is more important than the first discovery," Ioannidis says.
>
> But Solomon Snyder, senior editor at the Proceedings of the National Academy of Sciences, and a neuroscientist at Johns Hopkins Medical School in Baltimore, . . . says most working scientists understand the limitations of published research.
>
> "When I read the literature, I'm not reading it to find proof like a textbook. I'm reading to get ideas. So even if something is wrong with

---

[16]Francisco J. Ayala, "Point of View: For Young Scientists, Questions of Protocol and Propriety Can Be Bewildering," *The Chronicle of Higher Education*, (November 22, 1989): A36.
[17]"Most Scientific Papers Are Probably Wrong," Kurt Kleiner, August 30, 2005, NewScientist.com news service.

the paper, if they have the kernel of a novel idea, that's something to think about," he says.[18]

As critical thinkers, we must live between two extremes. One is an attitude of cynicism and anti-intellectualism that says, "Scientific research studies can never be trusted because there are too many possibilities for error." The other extreme is an attitude of passive reverence for the scientific method that says, "Scientists are the geniuses who are trained to carry out the studies that have brought us so many great advances, so I am not intelligent or educated enough to question any research I read." Both of these attitudes are inappropriate for the critically thinking individual. Research can be trusted if it is carried out in the correct manner, and you are quite capable of understanding the basic elements of research and evaluating specific studies you read or hear about. Use the factors we have discussed in this chapter to evaluate the credibility of research studies and implications for important decisions you need to make.

Remember that when we evaluate new or controversial findings, we also need to consider the credibility of the publication or news station reporting the study. Do the reporters have a reputation for being thorough and careful before they report on a study? Is there a science editor for the newspaper or magazine who knows which studies deserve to be reported and how they can be accurately summarized? We also need to consider the credibility of the institution that did the study: Was it carried out by a questionable sexuality researcher who spends a lot of time on the talk-show circuit? Was there possible bias in the research, as in a tobacco company finding that cigarettes improve lung capacity? Or was it done by a reputable research institution with no known biases?

A general rule of thumb is, if you are going to use information or report information to others, you need to verify your sources, just as a good journalist would. Then you can present the information to others with confidence and credibility.

SKILL

Read and discuss original studies before making decisions based on controversial research findings.

We can't possibly keep up with all advances in any given field of research. As critical thinkers, we can look at the credibility of the reports we hear or read, do more intensive study of those reports in which we are interested, and note the most recent findings on any interesting research. (See Exercise 5.3 on p. 193.)

Read the following article about a study on seasickness as a humorous review of some basic elements of controlled studies.

[18]Ibid.

SICKENING EXPERIMENT ON HUMAN SUBJECTS

Steve Rubenstein

Scientists were paying people $200 to throw up in San Francisco this week. It was too good a deal to miss.

They do these sorts of things at the University of California at San Francisco. Researchers are always looking for guinea pigs willing to try experimental drugs. In this case, the drug was a new anti-seasickness pill. The ad said you could make $200 for popping the pill and taking an eight-hour boat ride.

There was only one condition. You had to be the nauseous type. Somehow I qualified.

Dozens of people, many with holes in their pants, signed up for the voyage. It was encouraging to see so many selfless people pitching in for science.

"People will do anything for $200," explained one researcher. "Even this."

Before sailing away, we had to take a physical. It was a snap. The main thing the doc seemed interested in was whether I was the throw-up type. It's no good testing seasickness pills on people who don't get seasick.

"How do you feel on boats?" the doc asked, in that concerned demeanor of his calling.

"Terrible," I said. "Lousy. I head straight for the rail."

It was the right answer. The doc's face lit up like the penlight in his breast pocket. He put my chart in the active file. I was in.

On the appointed day, we men and women of science assembled at the hospital to take our pills. Since it was a scientific study, only half of us would be getting capsules containing the actual drug. The other half would receive capsules containing sugar, a placebo. A researcher handed out the pills randomly.

We weren't supposed to know which capsule was which, of course. That wouldn't be scientific. But the capsules, made of clear plastic, were easy to tell apart. The drug looked like tiny time pills, and the placebo looked like sugar. Someone sure screwed up, the doc said, especially because many people believe seasickness is a state of mind.

"What did you get?" we guinea pigs asked each other.

"Placebo," said one sad-eyed soul. "Darn. I'm a goner."

We were to swallow the pill precisely at 8 a.m. The researcher took out her digital watch.

"Place the pill in your right hand," she said. "Prepare to swallow."

We three dozen strangers stood abreast, pills in hand, united in time and place.

"Five, four, three, two, one. Swallow."

Gulp.

Into the buses we marched, and off to Fisherman's Wharf. We had a job to do.

The seas looked calm, which did not sit well with one of the passengers on the boat. His name was Kirt, and he turned out to be the president of the company that was trying to market the new drug. He had paid $80,000 to UCSF to conduct the impartial study—which he cheerily denied would be any less impartial because of his busybody presence on the boat—and said the last thing he wanted to see was calm seas. Sick people is what he wanted.

"I don't want everyone to throw up," he said. "I just want the right people to throw up. The placebo people."

And then we shoved off on our mission. Eight nauseating hours on the high seas.

"Don't worry," the skipper told Kirt. "I'm going to get these people sick for you."

The San Francisco Chronicle, May 25, 1990. Copyright © 1990 by The San Francisco Chronicle. Reprinted by permission of the publisher.

QUESTIONS FOR DISCUSSION

1. What controls did the researchers use for this study?

2. Since this article is humorous, and probably exaggerated, we can't claim it as serious evidence of faulty research. Given that disclaimer, what areas of potential error in results did the author point out?

3. If you were to set up a study to test a new anti-seasickness pill, how would you design your research? (See Exercise 5.4 on p. 193.)

CHECKLIST FOR MAKING, EVALUATING, REPAIRING, AND REFUTING ARGUMENTS

Make things as simple as possible—but no simpler.

Albert Einstein

argument
↓
conclusion
↓
reasons
↓
evidence

So far, we have looked at the structure of argument. We've noted that an argument contains a conclusion or claim about an issue. The conclusion/claim is supported by reasons, sometimes called premises. We have seen that in both deductive and inductive arguments, the quality of the evidence is what distinguishes a strong argument from a weak one.

When making an argument, you want to be prepared to defend each part of it. You should anticipate the objections others may make to your argument and "repair" any weak aspects.

Following is a checklist that you can use to make, evaluate, and repair your own arguments; you can also use it to refute the arguments of others.

For a deductive argument:

1. Check that the argument is valid; put your reasoning into a syllogism, using the correct structure.

   If a proper syllogistic form has not been used, repair the argument by using a correct form.

Let's say Marina's friend Sam told her that he wanted a job at the college bookstore, but he didn't get it.

Example of invalid argument: *reason*

If he didn't show up for the interview, he didn't get the job. *Conclusion*
He didn't get the job.
Therefore, he didn't show up for the interview. *should be conclusion*

This is invalid because the form the speaker used is wrong:

If A, then B.

B

Therefore, A

Her friend may have shown up and still not received the job.

The correct form is:

If A, then B.

A.

Therefore B.

The argument is repaired by using the correct form:

If he didn't show up for the interview, then he didn't get the job.
He didn't show up for the interview.
Therefore, he didn't get the job.

2. Check that your premises are true and accurate.

Ask yourself, "Does the major or minor premise assume any facts that have not been proven?"

If so, repair the argument by backing up any assumptions with evidence.

Example: When Marina gives Sam her logical assessment of the situation, he replies: "You're wrong. I did show up for the interview, but they needed someone who had experience as a cashier and that's why I didn't get that job."

Both Marina's major and minor premise were untrue. Now the reasoning would be:

If someone doesn't have cashier experience, they won't get the job at the bookstore.
Sam doesn't have cashier experience.
Therefore, Sam didn't get the job at the bookstore.

3. If your conclusion follows from true premises that are stated in the correct form, your argument is *sound*. Now that Marina has repaired her reasoning with the correct form and true premises, her argument is sound.

Refuting a deductive argument:

1. Point out any reasoning that is not valid, i.e. that does not follow proper syllogistic forms.
2. Point out any premises that aren't true.
3. Point out cases in which the premises may be true and the argument may be valid, but the conclusion can still be false; in other words, point out any other possible facts that make the argument questionable.

Example

If Rachel got the part of Antigone, then Rebecca didn't get the part.
Rachel got the part of Antigone.
Therefore, Rebecca didn't get the part.

This appears to be a sound argument, but it can be "trumped" by more current and reliable information. If the director decided to change his original plan and double-cast the part of Antigone, then both Rachel and Rebecca could have gotten the part.

More up-to-date or more accurate information often trumps information that was considered true at one time but is no longer true. Laws change, cures for diseases are found, and new technology emerges, making it possible to refute many claims with new evidence.

For an inductive argument:

1. Check that the evidence you are using to support your claims—statistics, examples, controlled studies, expert testimony, and analogies—is reliable and accurate.

   Use the checklists on pages 126–128 to evaluate statistical and causal generalizations and on pages 163–170 to evaluate controlled studies.
2. Check that the conclusions you draw are based on a preponderance of the evidence.
3. Determine whether you are using the most current research from credible sources; be willing to adjust your argument when more accurate or reliable information becomes available.

   Research as many sources as possible before coming to a final conclusion or making a decision.

   Repair inductive arguments by replacing faulty or dated evidence with the most credible and current support.
4. When an inductive argument is based on strong evidence, it is considered a **cogent argument**.

   For both deductive and inductive arguments, imagine how people with different assumptions or beliefs might respond to your reasons and conclusions. Then be prepared to answer their objections. If you find an area of objection that weakens your argument, find the source of the problem from the checklist and strengthen your argument by repairing the damaged part.

be prepared for questions

In refuting an argument, use the same checklists to find weaknesses in reasoning and evidence.

Defending and Refuting Arguments

Purpose: to practice examining and strengthening arguments

As a group, write an argument outline, using the format that follows. In small groups, come up with as many objections to the argument as possible. Be prepared to defend your group's argument from the objections that will be raised by other groups. You may do this as an impromptu class exercise or as a prepared debate.

Defenders:

We believe _____ based on the following evidence _____.

Refuters:

We have noted the following errors in your reasoning and evidence:

When each group has created an argument and checked it, groups can present to the class. The other groups should then offer objections and allow the defenders to repair (or refute) them.

Consider doing some classroom parliamentary debates (see Chapter 10 for rules). This form of debating provides great practice for making, repairing, and refuting arguments.

USE OF AUTHORITY: EXPERT TESTIMONY

In addition to drawing generalizations from controlled studies, writers and speakers frequently find strong support for their conclusions from the testimony of experts. An **expert** is an individual who has education, significant experience, or both in a given area; experts are usually recognized and respected by their peers in their specific fields of endeavor. An expert is considered to be someone who is aware of and up-to-date on current research in his or her field. We turn to experts in many areas of our daily lives: We consult doctors, dentists, lawyers, mechanics, counselors, and salespersons, all of whom are supposed to have more knowledge and experience in their fields than we do.

We also rely on friends and acquaintances who have become knowledgeable about various subjects because they spend time on and keep up with these subjects; for example, we might consult a friend we respect who has read all about the candidates for an upcoming election. We listen to what she says because she has credibility as an informed voter. When we buy a car or a stereo, we might consult a friend who works on his car or who has had several stereos because we see him as having more expertise than we do. Even for small purchases, like clothing, we may ask a friend to help us if we believe this person has a significant knowledge of fashion trends.

The phenomenon of consulting acquaintances before we make decisions has been called the **two-step flow** of information (see Figure 5–2). Our expert friends, who are called **opinion leaders**, first (step 1) get their information from the media (television, the Internet, magazines, newspapers, and books), and then (step 2) pass this information on to us. In our information-saturated age, this method makes sense; we can't be informed about everything, so we become experts in the areas we spend our time on and others become experts in other areas, and we share information. We learn from one another's experiences, mistakes, and successes and save time (and sometimes money) in the process.

Sharing information

Advertisers and campaign managers are well aware of this two-step phenomenon as they carefully choose the magazines and television shows to best reach their target audiences. If they can get the opinion leaders to vote for their candidates or to use their products, the rest of us will follow. News of the person or product will travel by word of mouth to the secondary audiences. (See Exercise 5.5 on p. 194.)

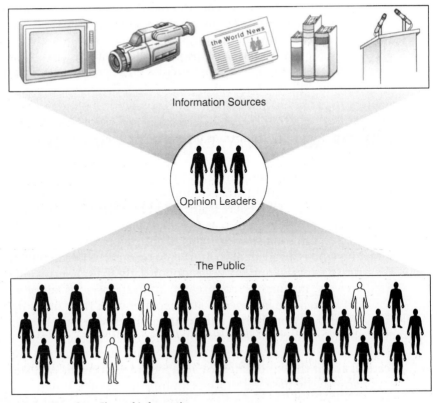

Figure 5–2   Two-Step Flow of Information

two step flow is acceptable for personal decision making but not for critical political decision

Use of a network of friends may work well for personal decision making, but it won't work to quote these friends in papers or speeches. You can't say "Vote for candidate X for senator; my friend Mark, who reads all the major newsmagazines, thinks he has the best foreign policy" and expect your audience to be convinced.

Nor can you say "I know a woman who works for a pharmacy, and she thinks that 80 percent of the people who get prescriptions for Valium are drug addicts" as evidence that Valium users are addicted to drugs. It may be true that this drug is carelessly prescribed, and it may be true that candidate X is the best person for senator; however, the writer or speaker needs to use support that is generally recognized as valid in order to present a strong argument.

An expert who can be used to add strength to arguments has relevant academic credentials and/or significant experience in the area in question. Individuals who are seen as experts in a field are recognized by their colleagues or by the general public, or both. This recognition often comes as a result of publishing articles or books, earning advanced degrees or positions, coming up with valuable discoveries, or attaining success or acclaim in their areas of expertise.

People who fit these categories have credibility in their fields, and their opinions are generally considered reliable sources of evidence for a particular argument.

The author of the following passage is a professional tracker. Trackers like Tom Brown Jr. are experts in deciphering markings such as footprints; often, they are called upon to study crime scenes. They can draw inductive generalizations about an event by looking for predictable "signs." After years of intense observation, Tom Brown is able to ascertain whether a person who left footprints is right or left-handed; he can also determine the person's approximate weight, among other factors. Tom can discern accurate information from a crime scene even after rain has covered the area.

AN OPINION WITH SUBSTANCE

Tom Brown Jr.

I took the class into the woods and stopped by a drainage ditch. The bottom was covered with soft sandy soil. It was also covered with animal prints. I asked the class to notice all the prints that were visible. They named two animals and guessed at two more. There were eleven, not counting the dog.

When I ask for prints, I'm not just looking for clear sharp markings of large well-known animals. I'm searching for an explanation of every mark on the ground....As I study the markings a picture begins to form in my mind of what passed the spot I am checking before I arrived. My mind begins to place animals in space and time.

Something began to take shape as I noticed the age of the different tracks....

"Wow!" I yelled. "Look at that." It had all come together, and I began to explain the scene to the class as I pointed to the markings that were the tracks of a dog and a rabbit, which had been on this spot at the same time.

"Dog came down, saw the rabbit before it smelled him. Maybe a cross wind. He jumped after the rabbit. Here is his first set of four running prints." I pointed. "Here, here, here, and here. Here is the rabbit moving up the side of the ditch to that sweet new grass." Again I pointed to markings that looked almost as if someone had scraped the dirt with a branch. "The rabbit sees the dog, does a boogie here, and races down the hill. He made two gigantic leaps. See where he jumped? See where the dog leaped for him and missed? Skidded here, regained his balance, and followed up the other side, there."...

"How did you do that?" Kay asked.

"I sat for days on the edge of a field and watched rabbits feed, breed, bear young, and avoid danger. After each happening, I would study the marks that had been left in the earth. I can tell when a rabbit is sitting or standing, agitated or calm. Whenever a dog came through the field and happened on a chase, I would follow its every marking, remembering what my eyes had seen just moments before. After a great amount of time, I began to recognize those signs as I happened onto them."

From pp. 215–216 in *The Search: The Continuing Story of the Tracker* by Tom Brown, Jr., and William Owen. Copyright © 1980 by Tom Brown, Jr. and William Owen. Reprinted with the permission of Simon & Schuster Adult Publishing Group. All rights reserved.

SKILL

Recognize legitimate and illegitimate uses of expert testimony.

PROBLEMS WITH EXPERT TESTIMONY

When listening to an argument, a critical thinker should consider some common problems associated with expert testimony:

1. Use of experts in the wrong field of expertise
2. Use of experts who are not recognized as experts
3. Use of experts who are paid for their testimony
4. Use of experts who are biased
5. Experts who do not realistically limit their own expertise
6. Expert testimony that is contradicted by equally expert testimony

1. Use of experts in the wrong field of expertise. The most visible form of this problem occurs in advertisements in which a person who is respected in one field is used to endorse a product out of his or her area of expertise. It is a legitimate use of authority for an athlete to promote sports equipment, but some ads capitalize on good-looking or popular celebrities by using them to promote cars, shampoos, or cereals.

In a famous ad campaign, an actor in a white coat and stethoscope announced, "I'm not a doctor, but I play one on TV." Ads frequently feature people in doctors' uniforms and hospital settings giving advice on medications. The words *doctor dramatization* may be written on the screen as a disclaimer. However, consumers might easily overlook these vague words or take them to mean that a real doctor is dramatizing his recommendation of the product.

Be careful of slick expert advertisements by nonexperts, which are generally accompanied by impressive costumes and backgrounds. If real expertise isn't mentioned in an endorsement, don't assume there are credentials lurking somewhere in the person's background.

Sometimes there are professional credentials for a celebrity endorsing a product, but those credentials don't directly relate to the product being promoted. For example, Dr. Phil McGraw, who has a degree in psychology, has written a book entitled *The Ultimate Weight Solution: The 7 Keys to Weight Loss Freedom.* His book is a major bestseller and is promoted on his own popular television talk show as well as on NBC's *Today* show. While it can be argued that there is a psychological component to weight loss that Dr. Phil legitimately discusses in his book, he has come under criticism for using his name and image to endorse a line of nutritional supplements, including vitamins, power bars, and meal-replacement drinks. *New York Times* writer Sherri Day notes the following:

> Of course, celebrity licensing and endorsement deals have long been a mainstay of consumer marketing, but few talk-show hosts have so closely associated the products they endorse with the content of their television programs. McGraw's licensing deal with *Shape Up* crosses another barrier, one that has been regarded as sacred: Unlike books or videos, the products can directly affect viewers' health. And because McGraw carries the honorific "doctor"—though he is a clinical psychologist and not a physician—his critics say that consumers are more likely to trust his recommendations.
>
> "As soon as we heard the prospect of him going into the nutritional food category, it was kind of like 'What?'" said Sid Good, the president of Good Marketing, a consumer products consultant in Cleveland. "It's always different when you step into the medical field. There are a different set of assumptions that we make as consumers in terms of what our expectations are and the appropriateness of who's giving us the advice."[19]

2. Use of experts who are not recognized as experts. Most areas of expertise today are in the midst of increasingly new discoveries. If someone is considered an expert based on experience or education completed years ago and

[19]Sherri Day, "Dr. Phil Risks Credibility Selling Diet Supplements," *New York Times,* November 4, 2003.

if the person has not kept up with his field, then he or she is questionable as an expert. When a finding by an expert is quoted, a date should accompany the quotation so we know when the discovery was made.

The importance of current information accounts for the advice to look up recent research when you want to support a position. Books are good sources of support; however, in some fields, a book that is even a few years old becomes obsolete due to new information. Some of your textbooks are in the tenth or eleventh edition because of the need for updating information. Social science books need to be constantly updated because of changing political, economic, and cultural realities; for example, a history book that is just a year old will not have included a newly elected president or new borderlines between countries. Although foundational theories are essential, current ideas and events in any field are also important.

Sometimes a person's credentials are distorted. Having "doctor" in front of one's name can mean that one is a physician, a dentist, a recipient of a doctoral degree in an academic field, a chiropractor, or a psychologist. As a critical thinker, you need to understand what a title means, the reputation of the institution that conferred the title, and, if possible, the credibility the titled person has with his or her colleagues. The claims made by this person can then be considered in light of a reasonable assessment of his or her position as an expert.

3. Use of experts who are paid for their testimony. One fairly obvious consideration in listening to evidence based on expertise is to find out whether the authority is paid for the testimony or endorsement. Some people are paid to promote products. A salesperson may genuinely believe that a brand new truck will meet your needs, but he is not the only person to ask about it because of the conflict of interest built into his role. Similarly, an expert witness, such as a psychologist who is called to testify on behalf of a defendant in a trial, may fully believe in the defendant's case but lose credibility if she is paid for her testimony. If you suspect that an expert may be advising you based on "what's in it for him," get a second opinion, as did columnist Thomas Sowell in the following excerpt:

> The other day, the lights suddenly went out in the bathroom. After our amateur attempts to find out what was wrong got us nowhere, my wife found an electrician in the *Yellow Pages* and had him come over.
>
> He did all kinds of investigating in all kinds of places and came up with the bad news: None of the usual things was wrong. What was wrong was probably that a wire had gone bad somewhere in the walls.
>
> He conjured up a picture of a broken live wire dangling somewhere in those walls, ready to ignite something, so that we could wake up in the middle of the night with the place engulfed in flames. My wife was upset and I didn't find the prospect all that great myself. What could we do?
>
> The electrician said that he would have to open up the walls and just track down the place where this dangerous wire was. His estimate of how much it would cost was not cheap.

I thanked him and paid him for his time, but said that obviously we would have to get a second opinion before undertaking something that drastic. He said he understood, but urged that we get that opinion very soon—today—because of the danger involved.

This time I decided that the *Yellow Pages* were not the way to go. I phoned a very reputable contractor I know who had done some work for us a couple of years earlier and asked for his recommendation of an electrician.

Enter electrician number two—and exit electrician number two less than five minutes later. The lights were back on and not a wall had been touched. What was wrong was so simple that the first electrician undoubtedly realized immediately that we must not know anything about electrical systems if we had not fixed it ourselves.[20]

4. Use of experts who are biased. Many people feel so strongly about an issue that they join with others who have similar beliefs, forming clubs, unions, and associations. They often are or become experts in their areas of interest, but their expertise is sometimes accompanied by a strong bias.

For example, those who lobby together for gun control may become highly knowledgeable about laws and regulations across the various states; similarly, members of the National Rifle Association gain expertise on the various statutes affecting gun ownership. Neither of these groups can be considered impartial and unbiased in a discussion of gun control. This does not mean a critical thinker should not listen to them; in fact, most editorials and televised debates on this issue and on other controversial issues involve individuals with strong biases, and many of these individuals try to present a balanced viewpoint. However, critical thinkers keep in mind that they are hearing the facts from particular points of view, and they listen for possible exaggeration of the benefits of, or problems with, proposed policies.

Another form of bias may be inherent in a particular approach to an area of expertise. Various methods of psychology are practised by different counselors, and various approaches to medical treatment are taken by different physicians. One doctor may treat hyperactivity with medication, while another may favor eliminating foods to which the hyperactive child may be allergic. Because of the different viewpoints espoused by experts in the same discipline, critical thinkers try to learn as much as possible and to get a number of professional opinions before making an important decision. (See Exercise 5.6 on p. 195.)

5. Experts who do not realistically limit their own expertise. Contemporary societies value and rely upon expertise; we have made great progress in many areas of learning, and we have experienced impressive technological advances. It is important to recognize however, that even experts cannot know *everything* about a given field. That is why doctors, lawyers, engineers, educators, and almost all other professionals specialize in limited areas within their fields. Even then, conferences are continually held to discuss and

[20]Thomas Sowell, "Who Do Poor Turn to in a Pinch," *Contra Costa Times,* July 29, 1996, A-10.

share new findings and sometimes to refute commonly held assumptions about a particular body of knowledge. An expert who serves the larger community well will limit his or her pronouncements to what is known to be true and will withhold judgment or give a variety of possibilities for the areas that are still unknown or controversial. When experts in a field go beyond what they know for certain to be true, people's lives can be severely impacted, as illustrated in the following excerpt from Thomas Sowell, syndicated columnist and author of the book *Late-Talking Children:*

> Phone calls and e-mails from parents began coming to me immediately after *Dateline NBC* broadcast a feature on very bright children who are years late in beginning to talk....
>
> What ignited all this interest was the story of Carol Gage's son Collin, a bright but late-talking little boy on whom "experts" had hung a variety of dire labels. Now 7 years old, Collin is talking and his intellectual abilities and social development are beginning to belie the labels.
>
> All too many parents of similar children have encountered similarly hasty and dogmatic "experts"—in the school system especially. One of the mothers who contacted me told of her son's being put into classes for retarded children, even though his IQ later turned out to be 149. Tragically, false diagnoses like these are all too common.
>
> A man in the group I studied had an IQ of 180 but, when he was a child, his mother was warned that someday he might have to be "put away." Nuclear physicists Albert Einstein and Edward Teller were both suspected of being mentally retarded as small children, because they both talked late. So was famed 19th century pianist Clara Schumann.
>
> No one really understands why some children who are very bright are also very late to begin speaking. But the worst problem is not ignorance. It is arrogance and dogmatism on the part of too many professionals to whom desperate and trusting parents turn for help. Some children have been declared "retarded" or "autistic" on the basis of less than 10 minutes' observation.
>
> There is no disgrace that our knowledge is not what we would like it to be. The disgrace is the pretense that it is, at the expense of vulnerable children and their distressed parents.[21]

6. Expert testimony that is contradicted by equally expert testimony. One characteristic of the Information Age is the proliferation of research carried out by individuals, corporations, universities, and think tanks. The outcome of one study may be diametrically or partially opposed to the findings of another study done by an equally prestigious person or group. In addition, we are seeing that today's discovery can sometimes be tomorrow's mistake; that is, current research often makes research of a few years ago obsolete, and even dangerous. Such was the case for the pregnant women of the 1950s who were

[21]Thomas Sowell, "Experts Who Aren't," *Contra Costa Times*, April 5, 1999.

routinely given the drug DES to prevent miscarriages; this drug was later found to have done significant damage to their daughters and grandchildren.

When we consider these problems, we can understand why some people have become cynical about all medical pronouncements; they may fear catching hepatitis from drinking fountains because "next year, they'll find out that hepatitis is transmitted through water." This attitude is not reasonable, but there is wisdom in choosing a *healthy* skepticism.

A healthy skepticism looks at pronouncements from authorities and considers their credentials, whether they have support from their colleagues, and whether their ideas make sense.

Researcher Frank Sulloway explains a useful way to interpret contradictory research findings. In his book on birth order and personality, he discusses why we can trust his findings about the personalities of firstborn children, despite some studies whose results contradict these findings:

> The question we need to ask about any topic of research is whether significant results exceed "chance" expectations, especially in well-designed studies. *Meta-analysis* allows us to answer this question.
>
> ... [Seventy-two] of the 196 studies on birth order display significant results that are consistent with my psychodynamic hypotheses. Fourteen studies yield contrary results. The remaining 110 studies are not statistically significant in either direction. What does this mean? In any group of 196 studies, chance will produce about 10 spurious confirmations, give or take a random fluctuation in the error rate. We can be 99 percent confident that chance will produce no more than 21 spurious confirmations. The likelihood of obtaining 72 spurious findings is less than 1 in a billion billion! In spite of occasional negative findings, the literature on birth order exhibits consistent trends that overwhelmingly exceed chance expectations.[22]

Sulloway's statistical analysis, summarized in Table 5–1, shows us that when many studies are combined, we can draw good generalizations about the meaning of the research.

By contrast, when two respectable experts or institutions disagree and there is no clear-cut weight of evidence, critical thinkers have two options: They can remain neutral until more confirming studies are completed or they can do more personal research. Personal research includes finding relevant journal articles in the library or on the Internet, interviewing people in the field, and calling the institutions that have done the studies to request copies of their findings (because, as previously discussed, they are usually summarized only briefly by the standard media sources).

Personal research becomes crucial when we need to make decisions about our own lives and we encounter contradictory opinions. Such was the case for

[22]Frank Sulloway, *Born to Rebel* (New York: Random House, 1996).

Table 5–1   Summary of 196 Controlled Birth-Order Studies, Classified According to the Big Five Personality Dimensions

Behavioral Domain (by Degree of Confirmation)	Outcome[a]	Likelihood of Outcome by Chance[b]
OPENNESS TO EXPERIENCE		
Firstborns are more conforming, traditional, and closely identified with parents.	21 confirming (2.2 expected) 2 negating 20 no difference	Less than 1 in a billion
CONSCIENTIOUSNESS		
Firstborns are more responsible, achievement oriented, organized, and planful.	20 confirming (2.3 expected) 0 negating 25 no difference	Less than 1 in a billion
AGREEABLENESS/ANTAGONISM		
Laterborns are more easygoing, cooperative, and popular.	12 confirming (1.6 expected) 1 negating 18 no difference	Less than 1 in a billion
NEUROTICISM (OR EMOTIONAL INSTABILITY)		
Firstborns are more jealous, anxious, neurotic, fearful, and likely to affiliate under stress.	14 confirming (2.4 expected) 5 negating 29 no difference	Less than 1 in a billion
EXTROVERSION		
Firstborns are more extroverted, assertive, and likely to exhibit leadership.	5 confirming (1.5 expected) 6 negating 18 no difference	Less than 1 in a million (but studies conflict)[c]
All Results Pooled	72 confirming (9.8 expected) 14 negating 110 no difference	Less than 1 in a billion billion

Note: Data are tabulated from Ernst and Angst (1983:93–189), using only those studies controlled for social class or sibship size. Each reported finding constitutes a "study."

[a]Based on a "chance" confirmation rate of 5 percent.

[b]Based on the meta-analytic procedure of counting confirming studies versus all other outcomes (Rosenthal 1987:213); one-tailed tests. With the expected number of confirming studies set to a minimum of 5, all statistical comparisons are significant at $p < .005$ For Openness, $z = 13.19$; for Conscientiousness, $z = 12.14$; for Agreeableness, $z = 8.44$; for Neuroticism, $z = 7.68$ for Extroversion, $z = 5.01$; for all results pooled, $z = 20.39$.

[c]In this one instance I have compared positive and negative studies together, versus those showing no difference, and employ a two-tailed test.

Source: Frank Sulloway, *Born to Rebel.* Copyright © Springer-Verlag New York, Inc. Reprinted with permission.

reporter Daniel Borenstein, who was being treated for cancer of the head and neck. He started by seeking treatment from his friend, a medical oncologist:

> At first, I didn't appreciate that there are different types of oncologists. Randy is a "medical" oncologist, the sort of doctor who administers chemotherapy to treat cancer. As I learned, one must not confuse him with a radiation oncologist.
>
> Although choosing Randy as my doctor for my chemotherapy was easy because he was a good friend, I realized soon after I started my treatment that I would need to pick a radiation oncologist—and make key decisions about where to radiate. I had no idea that I would travel across the country searching for the answers.
>
> On May 25, 2005, after two rounds of chemotherapy, I had my second body scan, the first one since starting treatment. The results: The visible cancerous node had shrunk to 30 percent of its original size. And its "brightness" on the scan, the measure of the intensity of the cancer, was similarly about one-third the pretreatment level.
>
> "It's a huge, huge success for the chemotherapy," Randy told me when I saw him the next day.
>
> Randy had been reviewing the latest studies on treatment for head-and-neck cancer like mine. As he put it, "I want to hit you with the kitchen sink once" to minimize the chances of the cancer returning. The original plan was three rounds of chemotherapy, which would take nine weeks, followed by six to seven weeks of daily radiation treatment. But Randy was adjusting my therapy, making it more intense than originally planned.
>
> First, he explained, studies showed that the radiation would be more effective if given concurrently with additional chemotherapy. So—and here was the big surprise—when I underwent the radiation phase, I would also receive more chemo. The radiation therapy would be daily Monday through Friday for six to seven weeks. The concurrent chemo would be administered weekly....
>
> Randy was not a radiation expert. So we agreed that, before I started my radiation at Alta Bates' Herrick campus in Berkeley, I would go to the UC San Francisco medical center for a consultation.
>
> Imagine my surprise when Jeanne Quivey, a leading radiation oncologist at UCSF, told me that the preradiation chemotherapy I had endured was a waste of time.
>
> Since then, I've come to fully appreciate that medicine can be as much an art as a science; that some doctors want to be on the cutting edge and others want to use the most-proven treatment.
>
> To Quivey, there was no doubt about the best tool for fixing my cancer. "We think the curative treatment is the radiation," she said. At her institution, patients like me were treated primarily with radiation, sometimes with simultaneous chemotherapy.
>
> She was quite clear: Chemo in advance of radiation does not add to the cure rate for cancers like mine. Actually, she added, one study

found it was harmful. Until there was a change in the survival rate, UCSF would not use chemotherapy before radiation.

Searching to make sense of this surprise, I noted that there seemed to be a split in the medical community on the treatment. Quivey was unyielding. "There might be a split in the community," she said, "but the data is on my side."

This wasn't just a theoretical dispute. This was a core disagreement about the underlying rationale of my therapy that also extended to other key questions, such as how much of my head and neck to irradiate, what chemotherapy to give me at the same time, and what drugs, if any, I should receive during the treatment to protect my salivary glands from the radiation.

What if Quivey were right? What if Randy were wrong? There was no compromise position between them. How could I receive treatment from a medical oncologist and a radiation oncologist if they weren't working from the same playbook?

Randy was surprised to hear my account of the appointment with Quivey. To be sure, he had warned me that he was using new therapies. He had told me the data were still evolving. And if we waited for conclusive studies on survival rates, that would be years down the line— way too late to help me.

Moreover, Randy wasn't just making up the three-drug preradiation chemo regimen as he went along. It was being studied and used at one of the leading hospitals in the nation—the Dana-Farber Cancer Institute, affiliated with Harvard University, in Boston. I had seen some of the research, and Randy had been following it carefully. We decided I should see Roy Tishler, the radiation oncologist on that research team.... Meanwhile, I started reading medical studies, including the one Quivey cited as showing advance chemo could be harmful. That research, it turned out, looked at patients who were treated from 1965 to 1993. Those patients didn't receive the three-drug treatment I was given. One of those drugs, Taxotere, wasn't available back then.

As the doctors debated my future, there was good news about the effects of the chemotherapy I had received. My third body scan showed no cancer activity. It didn't mean I was cancer-free, only that the levels were below what the scan could detect.

The one thing the doctors all agreed on was that I still needed the radiation—and the sooner, the better. But the devil was in the details.[23] (Note: Daniel Borenstein had several other issues to decide after receiving contradictory advice from 7 doctors he consulted. Fortunately, he chose treatment that has left him alive and in remission.)

In addition to controversy in study results, there is also controversy in expert witness testimony at congressional hearings, public forums, and criminal trials.

[23]"Learning to Decipher Language of Treatment," by Daniel Borenstein, *Contra Costa Times*, February 11, 2007.

When government officials and juries have to rely on circumstantial evidence that is interpreted by experts, they may not know whom to believe. They need to rely on their best assessment of the credentials of the experts and the soundness and strength of the evidence they present. (See Exercise 5.7 on p. 196.)

REASONING BY ANALOGY

Another interesting and common form of inductive generalizations involves reasoning from analogies. When someone uses analogies to support an argument, he or she is drawing a comparison, saying in essence: I have evidence that this policy works well in one or more cases; therefore, I infer that it will work well in other, similar situations.

Have you ever taken a test with questions like those in Figure 5–3?

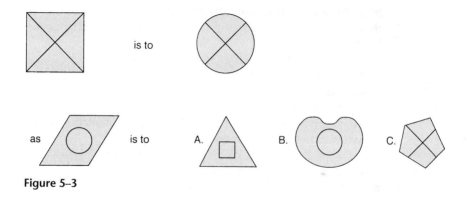

Figure 5–3

This test measures the ability to **reason by analogy.** If you answered B, you correctly identified the analogous drawing; both drawings contain two figures (X and 0) that have the same relationship to the figure that encloses them.

When speakers or writers use analogies, they describe something (an object, event, idea, or process) and compare it to something else. The *claim* is that the two things are alike in important ways. Reasoning by analogy can be coded as follows:

A is to B as C is to D.

Reasoning by analogy, comparing one idea or plan to another, is one of the major forms of evidence used by speakers and writers. For example, schoolteachers, police officers, firefighters, city planners, and other professionals often share ideas with others who do similar work, because they know that what worked in one community might work in another. Conferences and conventions for people in the same profession are all about sharing what is useful in one context, under the assumption that it will also be useful in another.

We will consider effective reasoning by analogy for the remainder of this chapter. In the next chapter, we will focus on faulty analogies and other errors in reasoning.

The human mind's ability to reason by analogy begins at an early age and continues throughout life. A child may reason, "Camp is just like school—I have to get up early and do what the counselors tell me." A friend may help parents understand a child's jealousy of a new baby brother or sister by comparing the arrival of the new baby to a spouse bringing home a new mate. An elderly person may complain, "This nursing home is like prison—the food is lousy, I have to follow too many rules, and no one comes to visit me."

Reasoning by analogy is useful in two ways:

1. We are able to explain a new or difficult idea, situation, phenomenon, or process by comparing it to a similar idea or process that is more familiar.
2. We are able to give reasons for a conclusion by showing that our idea or program has worked at another time or in another place. We are also able to show that an idea or policy we don't favor has not worked well in another context.

REMINDER

When we reason by analogy, we assume that since something holds true in one context, it will also hold true in another, similar context.

Reasoning by analogy is commonly used in argumentation. Good analogies add inductive strength; if an idea or policy has been shown to be useful in some situations, we can argue that it will also be useful in other similar situations.

When we report studies of experiments on animals and draw conclusions or predictions for humans, we are reasoning by analogy.

Example

A researcher may report that when rats are confined to an overcrowded cage, they exhibit antisocial behavior; a conclusion is then drawn about humans, comparing crowded rats to city dwellers. The researcher may imply that crime may result from overcrowded conditions.

When we look at a specific past event to justify a conclusion about a current policy, we are reasoning by analogy.

Example

Someone may argue that Prohibition didn't work in the 1920s—people still found a way to make alcohol and an underground criminal network was supported. In the same way, it is argued, making drugs illegal today simply means that people will get them from dealers at a high price.

When we compare a system in one place to a system in another, we are reasoning by analogy.

Example

Politicians may cite the prescription drug affordability in Canada as a way to argue for better prescription drug access in the United States.

In a commentary on teen curfews, law professor Dan M. Kahan challenges criminologists "who ridicule curfews as empty gestures that do little to address the root causes of juvenile delinquency." Kahan believes that curfews are effective because they free juveniles from the pressure to appear tough by hanging out at night and breaking the law to impress their peer group. Using inductive reasoning by analogy, Kahan states:

> Many cities that have adopted curfews, including New Orleans, San Antonio and Dallas, have reported dramatic drops in both juvenile criminal activity and juvenile criminal victimization.[24]

When you notice someone supporting a position by comparing one idea, situation, or plan to another, stop and evaluate whether the comparison is valid. If it is, you have a good analogy, which may be used to add inductive strength to your conclusions. (See Exercise 5.8.)

LIFE APPLICATION

Use studies to help you make important life decisions. If you or a loved one has been recommended to take a course of action in relation to a particular condition or disease, check out the most recent studies concerning the suggested treatment. Prepare questions to ask the doctors based on your research.

Use current research to make other decisions. Whether deciding to take a job in a particular industry, to buy a certain product, or to pursue a program of graduate study, gathering the information that is easily available from online journals, magazines, and experts in a field helps you choose reasonable courses of action.

CHAPTER EXERCISES

Exercise 5.1   Purpose: To understand and use criteria for evaluating research.

Analyze the following examples in light of the criteria given for evaluating research findings. Then answer the following questions:

1. To what extent did each study meet the criteria for evaluating research? What are the strengths and weaknesses of each design?

[24]Dan M. Kahan, Comentary for *The Washington Post,* reprinted in the *Contra Costa Times,* November 17, 1996, p. A17.

2. Are there factors the researchers overlooked in designing their studies? If so, what is needed to improve the design?

3. Does one study have a better design than the other? If so, how?

A researcher is interested in a new treatment for controlling the effects of the AIDS virus. He designs a study, called the protocol, which involves two groups of patients who have recently (within the past six months) tested positive for the virus. One group receives the new drug and the other group receives a placebo. There are no special dietary changes, and no other treatments are given to the two groups. The only difference between the groups is that one is taking the drug and the other is not. The subjects in the experiment don't know whether they have the real drug or the placebo; that way the alternate explanation that they felt better because they expected to feel better (the placebo effect) is eliminated. As progress with the two groups is monitored, the researchers should be able to determine if the new drug has any positive effect.

A researcher wants to find out if test performance in college is improved when students eat a breakfast that is high in carbohydrates. She chooses two randomly selected groups of students and asks them to follow a breakfast plan for a semester. Because she does not want them to know that she is trying to discover the effect of diet on test scores, she tells them the test is for cholesterol ratings.

The control group is given a skimpy breakfast of a low-carbohydrate drink. The experimental group is given a breakfast loaded with carbohydrates that includes toast and cereal. Each subject keeps a diary of what he or she had for breakfast. Teachers are asked to report on the morning test scores of the groups of students. At the conclusion of the semester, the test scores are compared to see if the experimental group did better than its peers in the control group.

Exercise 5.2   Purpose: To experience what goes into the design of research studies.

Design a study of your own. Pretend you have unlimited money and people and decide what you want to find out. Then create a study with a control group and an experimental group. You can be serious or humorous—the research topic is not important. The only important thing is your understanding of the scientific method.

This is a good exercise to do with a partner, because you can get more ideas on how to control against alternative explanations for your results.

You might also try to carry out your study with a small sample and to report your findings to the class, including your design, your results, and your conclusions. Remember that a small sample can point to an interesting study to be carried out with a larger, more representative group.

Examples of Questions to Study

- Does garlic cure the common cold?
- Does listening to quiet music lower students' heart rate before a test?

- Would more people buy a green or a maroon camera case?
- Do people get more or less work done when they are sitting in an attractive room versus an unattractive room?
- Do young children learn math better if they work with real items (coins or beads) or with worksheets?
- Do people who have no seasickness when sailing also have no seasickness when on a motorboat?
- Do people who have not eaten for a few hours buy more food at a supermarket than those who have just eaten?
- Do athletes perform better after watching comedians?

As you can see, the possibilities of what inquiring minds would like to know are endless. Once you decide on your question and determine your hypothesis, state how you would find a control group and an experimental group, how you would guard for error, and how you would analyze your results.

Exercise 5.3 *Purpose:* To explore the effect of reported research on decision making.

For a few days, consider how decisions you have made are based on information you've read about or heard about. Did you choose to have or not to have a surgical procedure because of research findings you read? Have you invested in a particular stock or mutual fund based on reports of a successful track record? Do you read safety and performance studies in consumer magazines before buying a car?

Are any of your decisions about the food you eat (fat content, cholesterol content, sugar or salt content, balance of food groups) based on research? If so, do you remember what the research said and where you read or heard about it? If you take vitamins, ask yourself why you take them and what research led you to make vitamin supplementation a daily habit.

What about exercise options? Do you regularly exercise, and if so, have your decisions about what kind to do and what equipment or clothing to wear been based on research studies?

To complete this exercise, answer the following:

1. What is the habit you have acquired, the action you have taken, or the item you have purchased?
2. What factors led you to make the decision to acquire the habit, take the action, or buy the item?
3. What have been the effects (if any) of your decision? To what extent has your life been enhanced by your decision? How might your life be different if you had not made the decision?

Exercise 5.4 *Purpose:* To gather data from personal research.

Choose one of the following options for a personal experiment.

1. Chart your study habits for a week or two. Note if you have a regular time and place for studying. Is the equipment you need readily available (pens,

paper)? Do you review notes shortly after class? Do you study alone or with others? What distractions intrude upon your study time (television, radio, phone, snack breaks, visitors)? After you have charted your habits, look at your record and draw conclusions about where time is well used, where it is wasted, and how it could be put to better use.

2. Chart your eating and exercise habits for a week or two. Then look at your record and draw some conclusions about your lifestyle. Does your record reflect healthy nutritional choices; a rushed, erratic schedule; or a combination of both? Do you exercise regularly? Try to predict what will happen to your health if you continue to eat and exercise in this way.

3. Try a lifestyle experiment on yourself. Change an aspect of your daily life: Set and stick to consistent study habits; do a certain aerobic or bodybuilding exercise; reduce your intake of fat or sugar; or eliminate caffeine, tobacco, or a food you crave (some nutritionists believe that people are allergic to foods that they crave). Keep a record of how you feel after adhering to your new program for two weeks or a month, and report the results to your instructor. (It might also be interesting for several people to work together on this, forming an experimental group.)

Exercise 5.5   Purpose: To gain a practical understanding of how the two-step flow influences decision making.

Consider some voting or buying decisions or some decisions about medical treatment you've made lately. Did you consult an expert or a knowledgeable friend before making your choices? If not, on what basis did you make your decisions?

Try to list your three most recent decisions and trace any outside influences on those decisions.

Examples

"I used to read a popular weekly newsmagazine in order to be informed. A friend of mine who is a professor told me about another magazine he likes better because it gives more in-depth coverage of issues. I switched to this other magazine and I really like it. I enjoy getting a broader report on current events." (from a retired businessman)

"I developed a breast infection—very common for nursing mothers—and didn't want to make a trip to the doctor for antibiotics. The doctor wouldn't prescribe the drugs without seeing me, so I called a friend of mine who is an expert in herbs. She suggested home remedies, which I took for several days; they did keep me from getting worse. But I wanted to get better faster, so I gave in and made the appointment." (from a mother of an infant)

"My friend is a photographer, and so I consulted him about what to look for in a digital camera. I thought I knew which one I wanted to buy until he pointed out some features that were lacking in my choice. When I told him everything I needed and the price I could afford, he came up with two good choices for me to consider." (from a college student)

Exercise 5.6 *Purposes:* To discover examples of bias in books, magazines, or televised programs. To consider biased viewpoints.

1. Try to isolate an incident of possible bias in your reading or viewing. You might go through your textbooks and note any examples that seem to support a particular viewpoint or political stand. When you watch a television interview show, note whether the host gives equal time and courtesy to all points of view, or whether he or she seems to favor one side over the other. If you watch a debate, note the slant or "spin" given to both sides of the issue. Many newsmagazines are considered to have a bias, either conservative or liberal or radically left or right; find an issue that is covered by two magazines with different biases and contrast the presentation of the issue.

Examples

A. The book *The Perfect Wife: The Life and Choice of Laura Bush* by (*Washington Post* reporter) Ann Gerhart really slams Laura Bush in the parenting of her twins:

"They just want to do like every other teenager does," she [Laura] has insisted often. This declaration is dead opposite from most parents' insistence, which is, of course, "I don't care what the 'other kids' do. You are not other kids."[25]

I think the writer has misinterpreted this quote for her own purposes of making Laura seem like a bad parent. It could just as well be interpreted that her kids want a normal life, left alone by the media and not having to have Secret Service follow them around everywhere. In fact, this is what Hillary Clinton also wanted for her daughter, and the press generally left Chelsea alone.

The author also paints the Bush twins as much worse than Chelsea in their behavior. She writes:

"Chelsea went to parties and had boyfriends, but she had a gift for keeping her mishaps out of the public eye."

I have seen the same tabloid coverage of Chelsea and the Bush twins as far as their partying exploits go. Although Chelsea appears far more interested in politics, she has had her share of hanging out with celebrities and having fun. Also, the reporter doesn't take into account the difference between an only child and twins and how only children have fewer opportunities to act out. I don't admire the Bush twins, but the more I read of this book, the more it seems that this reporter is not trying to be fair and give different possible interpretations to Laura's parenting style and her comments. She just seems to want to slam her and I think the sarcastic title of her book (sarcastic because the book is a negative portrayal of Laura), shows the writer's bias.

[25]"Laura's Girls," by Ann Gerhart, *Washington Post,* January 7, 2004, CO1.

B. I recently received a "questionnaire" about whether I thought a large superstore should be allowed to locate in our county. I tend to favor allowing the superstore to be here, but I also understand the concern our county supervisors have about megastores hurting our smaller grocery stores and grocery chains. I saw my favorite local coffee shop lose a lot of business when a big coffee chain came to our town.

The questionnaire I received didn't mention this other side of the issue—the welfare of small stores hurt by the power of large superstores to take most of their business. Instead, these were a couple of the questions they asked:

- Which do you think is the most important problem facing our county?

  Education, Crime, Property Taxes, Affordable Housing, Jobs, Growth, or Big Box Stores? (Obviously all of the other issues are going to come out higher than big box stores).

- Should the decision to have large-scale retailers be made by consumers or by the Board of Supervisors? (This question doesn't take into account the responsibility the board has been given by the people for issues such as growth, small business concerns, traffic, and the desire of some towns in the county to keep a small-town look).

- Could our county use more than $500,000 in new sales tax revenue and 500 new jobs from a superstore?

  Yes, No, or Don't Know (Clearly the obvious "yes" vote here can be used to say that people favor the store.)

Whoever came up with this survey seems to want to use it to argue that the will of the people is being ignored by the "power-hungry" board of supervisors. Otherwise, the questions would be more neutral and would reflect both sides of the issue.

2. Take an issue and create viewpoints for several characters. For example, you could imagine the responses of a police officer, an addict, a drug pusher, a parent, and a politician to the notion of legalizing drugs. What natural biases might influence their responses? Working alone or in groups, write out each of their possible responses and see where the similarities and differences are. This exercise works well as a role play followed by a class discussion.

Exercise 5.7   Purpose: To recognize controversial expert testimony.

Find an example of expert testimony contradicted by equally expert testimony; editorial pages sometimes contain pro-con arguments of this nature, or you can find them in *USA Today* on the debate page, on numerous network and cable programs such as public broadcasting's *Newshour,* CNBC's *Hardball* with Chris Matthews, Fox's *On the Record,* ABC's *Nightline,* or online at network and cable television Web sites. State the basic areas of disagreement and the reasons given for each side's conclusions. Then decide which of the arguments you would support and explain why.

Also, you might focus on how evidence is found that allows for a new trial; for example, DNA evidence is used frequently to reexamine the guilt or innocence of people convicted of crimes.

Exercise 5.8   Purposes: To understand the usefulness of analogies as learning tools. To increase familiarity with the common use of analogies.

Although we are considering analogies as they relate to persuasion, analogies are also useful in conveying information. Ask a teacher you respect how he or she has used analogies to explain a difficult process to students. Find two or three examples of these kinds of analogies and share them with the class.

Exercise 5.9   Purpose: to gain experience in evaluating the credibility of websites.

One of the biggest challenges for critical thinkers is to evaluate Web sites and decide which are credible and which are not.
Use the following tool to evaluate Web sites so that you base your arguments and decisions on reliable information.

Web Site Evaluation Tool

Web site name:_____

Subject:_____

URL:

_____

Author (if available): _____
Date of Access (today's date):_____

Sponsoring organization: _____
Date on Web site: _____

Domain name: ☐ .com ☐ .edu ☐ .gov ☐ .org ☐ other

Criteria #1—Credibility

Does the site display the name or logo of the institution or organization responsible for the

---

Continued

Web page?

☐ Yes

☐ No

Is there a source of works cited?

☐ Yes

☐ No

Do you recognize the author(s) or institutions as an expert in the subject?

☐ Yes

☐ No

Based on this information, the Web site is:

☐ Credible

☐ Not credible

Criteria #2—Bias

What does the domain name tell you about the site?

Is there a hidden message?

What is the purpose of the Web site?

☐ Business/commercial

☐ Entertainment

☐ Informational/News

☐ Persuasive

☐ Personal Page

☐ Other:

Based on this information, the Web site is:

☐ Biased

☐ Not biased

Criteria # 3—Accuracy

Are the grammar and the spelling correct?

☐ Yes

☐ No

Is the information consistent with information from other sources and your previous knowledge?

☐ Yes

☐ No

Based on this information, the Web site is:

☐ Accurate

☐ Not accurate

Criteria #4—Currency

Is the information up-to-date?

☐ Yes

☐ No

When was the information last revised?

[Date]

Continued

Based on this information, the Web site is:

☐ Current

☐ Not current

Criteria #5 —Usefulness

Are there links to other sites related to the topic?

☐ Yes

☐ No

Is the information presented easy to understand?

☐ Yes

☐ No

Is the site easy to navigate?

☐ Yes

☐ No

Based on this information, the Web site is:

☐ Useful

☐ Not useful

Based on your overall observations, is this a worthwhile Web site for your research needs?

☐ Worthwhile

☐ Not worthwhile

CHAPTER HIGHLIGHTS

1. Scientific discoveries are often made through controlled studies; a well-designed study can be repeated by other researchers and thus can lead us closer to the truth about an issue.

2. A good research design includes a characteristic of interest, a hypothesis, and a sample, which is divided randomly into a control group and an experimental group.

3. The only significant difference between a control group and an experimental group is the treatment received by the experimental group.

4. The data gathered from a study are used to draw conclusions and to suggest areas for further study.

5. A critical thinker will review a study according to specific criteria to determine the extent to which the study is valid or biased.

6. The findings of many studies are considered controversial by experts in the field. When studies are controversial, critical thinkers withhold judgment or accept findings provisionally.

7. When using authoritative testimony as a support for conclusions, critical thinkers should consider whether the expert is educated and/or experienced in a field that is relevant to the issue under discussion.

8. Problems with using expert testimony include the use of experts in the wrong field of expertise, the use of experts who are not recognized as experts, the use of experts who are paid or biased, the use of experts who don't realistically limit their expertise, and the use of expert testimony that is contradicted by equally expert testimony.

9. Reasoning by analogy, comparing one idea or plan to another, is a form of inductive evidence used both to explain and to persuade.

KEY TERMS

Protocol (p. 161)

Subjects (p. 161)

Control (p. 161)

Question (p. 161)

Hypothesis (p. 161)

Sample (p. 162)

Control group (p. 162)

Experimental group (p. 162)

Data (p. 162)

Conclusions (p. 162)

Independent variable (p. 162)

Blind studies (p. 165)

Double-blind studies (p. 165)

Statistically significant (p. 167)

Cogent argument (p. 176)

Expert (p. 177)

Two-step flow (p. 178)

Opinion leaders (p. 178)

Reason by analogy (p. 189)

CHAPTER CHECKUP

Short Answer

1. What are some questions to ask about a study to determine whether it is valid or biased?
2. How should critical thinkers respond when a study is controversial?
3. What distinguishes someone as a genuine expert in a given field?
4. How are generalizations from analogies useful in supporting conclusions?

Sentence Completion

5. A speculation about what will be discovered from the research is called the _____.
6. A group of subjects who are given no treatment is the _____.
7. The researcher's interpretation of the meaning and significance of the findings is called the _____.
8. A group of subjects who are exposed to a special treatment is called the _____.
9. A randomly selected and representative part of the target population is the _____.
10. A sugar pill or other treatment that is meant to have no real effect on the subjects of the study is called a _____.

ARTICLES FOR DISCUSSION

The following article gives a humorous look at the frustrations of a reporter who is constantly exposed to contradictory reports, and who sets out to determine what he can believe. The bulleted section at the end of the article is an excellent checklist for critically examining the research we read.

FOOD NEWS BLUES

Anthony Schmitz

Not long ago I set a coffee cup on the table and opened the newspaper to a piece of good news. "New Study Finds Coffee Unlikely to Cause Heart Ills," read the headline. One thing less to worry about, I thought, until I remembered a story from a few weeks before. That morning the headline warned, "Study: Heart Risk Rises on 4, More Cups Coffee Daily." My paper does this all the time. Concerning the latest dietary findings, it flips and flops like a fish thrown to shore.

"Medical research," it declared one Wednesday, "repeatedly has linked the soluble fiber in oats with reductions in serum cholesterol." By Thursday of the next week all that had changed. "Studies Cast Doubt on Benefits from Oat Bran," the headline cried. Once again the paper offered its readers a familiar choice. Which story to believe? This week's, or last week's, or none at all?

The paper in question is the *St. Paul Pioneer Press*. It's a respectable provincial daily, not unlike the papers in Houston, Detroit and dozens of other cities. One day, recently, the news editor, Mike Peluso, said he'd take a crack at explaining his paper's flip-flops.

Peluso is compact, graying, more grave than jocular. He met me at the newsroom door. "You want a cup of coffee?" he asked, pointing at a vending machine. No, I said, trying to recall whether this week coffee was good or bad. Peluso shrugged and headed for his cluttered cubicle. Beyond its flimsy walls reporters jabbered into phones.

I arranged the coffee and oat bran clippings on a paper-strewn table. Peluso examined them one by one. He grimaced. He sighed. He swallowed black coffee from a paper cup.

"How do you reconcile the conflicting claims?" he asked himself. "One month coffee can't hurt you, the next month quit coffee and your heart will tick forever."

Exactly.

Peluso shook his head. "I don't know, I don't have any answers for that. You've got to talk about the real world here."

For Peluso, the real world looks something like this: News of a hot nutrition study gets beamed into the newsroom from wire services such as Associated Press, the *New York Times* or the *Baltimore Sun.* Peluso and his staff poke at the story, trying to find flaws that argue against putting it in the paper. By and large it's a hamstrung effort. Never mind that the reporter who wrote the piece is thousands of miles away. She'd defend the story anyway. The paper's own health reporter is scant help; he's been on the beat two months.

Meanwhile, Peluso knows that his competitors—another daily paper, plus radio and television news—won't spend a week analyzing the study. They'll run it today. Which is to say Peluso will, too. But the story the reader sees won't be as detailed as the piece that came over the wire. Compared with the *New York Times* or the *Washington Post,* the *Pioneer Press* is something of a dwarf. Stories get trimmed to fit. Subtleties and equivocations—the messy business of research—don't always make the cut.

"Look," said Peluso, "we're not medical authorities. We're just your normal skeptics. And it's not like we're inventing the research. We're simply reporting on it. We present what's there and let people draw their own conclusions."

"So what should readers make of all the contradictory advice you offer them?"

Peluso sighed again. "I don't know," he said. "You've got to take everything with a grain of salt until the last word comes in. I hate to tell people I don't believe everything I read, but the fact is anybody who believes everything they read is nuts."

Researchers whose work makes news soon learn that the match between science and journalism wasn't made in heaven. Richard Greenberg, a microbiologist who directs the office of scientific and public affairs at the Institute of Food Technologists, has watched what happens when the scientific method collides with journalistic technique.

"The first thing you've got to remember," says Greenberg, "is that science is not fact. It is not truth. It is not holy scripture. It's a compendium of information. You try to put all the research together and come to a consensus. Just because somebody runs a study that comes to a particular conclusion doesn't change everything that's gone before."

Scientists don't generally reach consensus in time for the next deadline. After 30 years of study, coffee's link to heart disease remains an open question. Four plus cups a day may slightly increase the risk, though some research suggests only decaf is linked to heart problems. Similarly, a decade's worth of oat bran experiments have served only to get a good argument going. Some studies suggest oat bran isn't any better at lowering cholesterol than white bread. If you eat enough of either, the message goes, you won't have room for fatty food. Others say oat bran has innate—though so far inexplicable—cholesterol-lowering properties.

While on their way to answering the big questions about fat or cholesterol or fiber, researchers often pause and dicker merrily about the design flaws in one study or the dicey statistical analysis in another. "Among ourselves," says one epidemiologist, "we're more interested in the detail of how things are done than in saying right now whether oat bran's good for you."

For journalists it's exactly the opposite. The arcana of statistical analysis and research design are boring at best, baffling at worst. The big question is whether oat bran will keep your heart ticking.

"The reporter and headline writer are trying to distill the meaning of the latest piece of research," says Greenberg. "They're trying to grab the eye of the reader. They're searching for absolutes where there are no absolutes. And this is what happens. One day you read caffeine is bad. Then you read that if you take the caffeine out, coffee is OK. Then you hear that the solvent that takes out the caffeine is dangerous. Then you find out the caffeine isn't dangerous after all. It so confuses the public they don't know whom to believe. And the truth is, there wasn't really any news in any of these studies. Each of them was just another micromillimeter step toward scientific consensus."

For Greenberg, news exists in those rare moments when scientists weigh the evidence and agree to agree—when the American Heart Association, the National Cancer Institute or the National Academy of Sciences pronounces that you ought to eat less fat, or more vegetables.

But by the terms of journalism, scientific consensus is a dead-letter file. If everybody agrees, there's no conflict, there's no news. In comparison, debates such as those about coffee or oat bran are a newsroom gold mine. Contradictions and conflict abound. Better still, almost everyone has oatmeal or coffee in the cupboard.

"You can't convince an editor not to run this stuff," says Howard Lewis, editor of the newsletter *Science Writers.* "My advice is that they do it for the same reason they run the comic strips and the astrological columns. But I feel it's all a hoax. Usually they're not accomplishing anything except sowing panic or crying wolf."

A Purdue communications professor raised a stir few years back when he suggested that research news might be more harmful than helpful. Writing in the journal *Science, Technology and Human Values,* Leon Trachtman observed that 90 percent of the new drugs touted in newspaper reports never reached the market or were driven from it because they were ineffective, too toxic or both. Readers relying on this information would have made wrong choices nine times out of 10.

So who's served, Trachtman asked, by publicizing these drugs before there's a scientific consensus on them? "When there's no consensus, why broadcast contradictory reports?" Ultimately, he said, readers are paralyzed by the pros and cons. He asked whether the result will be contempt for research, followed by demands to stop wasting money on it.

Not surprisingly, Leon Trachtman got blasted for implying that a scholastic elite ought to be making decisions for us. Among the critics was David Perlman, a science editor who writes regularly about health and nutrition. Often, Perlman says, research leads to public debates. Will avoiding fatty foods really lengthen your life? Should government experts try persuading people to change their eating habits? It's debatable. But citizens can hardly take part if they're capable of nothing more than numbly accepting expert advice. "To abdicate an interest in science," says Perlman, citing mathematician Jacob Bronowsky, "is to walk with open eyes toward slavery." Perlman trusts people's ability to sort through well-written news.

"It's not just the masses who are confused," says Trachtman. "It's the same for well-trained scientists once they're out of their field. I think people ought to establish a sensible, moderate course of action, and then not be deflected from it every morning by what they read in the paper."

But let's face facts. Do you have the resolve to ignore a headline that declares, "Sugar, Alzheimer's Linked"? If you can't help but play the game, you can at least try to defend yourself from nonsense by following these rules:

- *Count the legs.* First, ask if the group studied bears any relation to you. Don't let research done only on four-legged subjects worry you. Pregnant rats, for instance, are more likely to bear offspring with missing toes after getting extremely high jolts of caffeine. What's this mean for humans? Probably nothing. There's no evidence that drinking moderate amounts of caffeine causes human birth defects.

  If research subjects have two legs, read closely to see if they're anything like you. Early research that helped launch the oat bran fad involved only men, most of whom were middle-aged. All had dangerously high blood cholesterol, which reportedly fell after they ate a daily cup-plus of oat bran—enough for a half-dozen muffins. Fine, unless you're female, have low cholesterol already, or can't stand the thought of eating half a dozen bran muffins every day.

- *Check for perspective.* Even if you're a match for the group being studied, don't assume the results are significant. "Check if the journalist gets the perspective of other people in the field," says Harvard epidemiologist Walter Willett. "People who have watched the overall flow of information are in a good position to say, 'Well, this really nails it down,' or 'That's interesting, but it needs confirmation.'"

- *Ask how many guinea pigs.* Quaker Oats research manager Steven Ink, who's written a guide to nutrition studies, says the best research uses at least 50 subjects. By this standard, we should look askance at the recent study showing that eating 17 tiny meals a day lowers cholesterol. Only seven people took part. But rules of thumb don't always work. A small number can be meaningful if the effect observed is large and consistent. You don't need to feed 50 people cyanide to figure out that it's going to be bad for everyone.

  What's more, Ink advises, subjects shouldn't be fed quantities of food that no one in his right mind would eat. One example is the recent study showing that trans fatty acids such as those in margarine may be bad for your heart. Subjects ate three times more trans fatty acids than the average American.

  Finally, any group tested should be compared to a similar group. Early studies that linked coffee to heart disease were skewed because coffee drinkers differed greatly from the control group. The coffee drinkers were more likely to smoke and eat a high-fat, high-cholesterol diet. Both habits carry bigger heart risks than does drinking coffee.

- *Wait for confirmation.* "Don't let one study change your life," says Jane Brody, the *New York Times* health writer. She waits for three types of food research to agree before changing her eating habits.

  First, she looks for studies of large groups that show a link between a food and good or bad health—Italy's big appetite for olive oil and its low rate of heart disease for instance. Then she watches for lab evidence in test animals that suggests how the food causes its effect in people. Finally, she considers human experiments in which two groups are compared—one eating the food, the other not eating it, with neither group knowing which is which.

  Applying this rule to her own meals, Brody skimps on butter and favors olive oil. She eats plenty of fruits and vegetables, lots of potatoes, rice, beans and pasta, and modest amounts of lean meat. "This plan won't make you sick, has a good chance of keeping you well, and is immune to these fads that are here today and gone tomorrow," Brody says.

- *Hunt for holes.* No matter how carefully you read, you'll have to rely on the information your newspaper chooses to supply. If the big mattress ad on an inside page gets dropped at the last minute, the editors may suddenly have room for an exhaustive treatment of the latest coffee study. But if a candidate for national office gets caught with his pants down, the space required for a thorough exposé may mean the coffee piece gets gutted.

When editors at the *St. Paul Pioneer Press* got hold of a wire service report debunking oat bran, they found room for the first two-thirds. The third that didn't fit held a stern critique by other experts. They charged that the study contained too few people (20 female dietitians), didn't control the rest of what they ate, and started with subjects who had unusually low cholesterol.

"The reader really has to be skeptical," says Frank Sacks, the Harvard researcher whose oat bran study was under attack. "Take my case, for instance. The reporter really ought to say that this is a new finding, that it needs to be replicated. This is a warning sign that you have to wait a while. Reporters hate that when you say it. They call it waffling. But the truth is your hot new finding might not be confirmed down the line. You hate it when that happens, but it happens time and again.

"The real conservative advice is not to take any of this stuff in the newspaper with a whole lot of credence," says Sacks. "You could just wait for the conservative health organizations like the American Heart Association to make their recommendations and then follow their advice."

I called the American Heart Association to get its line on oat bran and coffee. "We don't have an opinion," said John Weeks somewhat plaintively.

"We get calls every day from the media," said Weeks. "They want to know what we think about every new study that comes out. And we don't have an opinion. We don't try to assimilate every new study. Our dietary guidelines would be bouncing all over the place if we did. Once the evidence is there, we move on it. Until then, we don't."

The Heart Association is sticking with the same dietary advice it's dispensed since 1988, when it last revised its model diet. Eat less fat. Eat more grains, vegetables and fruit. The evidence that oat bran lowers cholesterol is so limited that the association makes no specific recommendations about it. Concerning coffee, the group has nothing to say.

Weeks' advice for whipsawed newspaper readers has a familiar ring. "What people need to keep in mind," he said, "is that one study does not a finding make."

"You mean," I asked, quoting Mike Peluso's newsroom wisdom, "I'm nuts to believe everything I read?"

Said Weeks, "That's exactly correct."

Anthony Schmitz, *In Health* (November 1991), © 1991. © Anthony Schmitz. Reprinted with permission of the author.

1. Comment on the following paragraph from the article:

   "But by the terms of journalism, scientific consensus is a dead-letter file. If everybody agrees, there's no conflict, there's no news. In comparison, debates such as those about coffee or oat bran are a newsroom gold mine. Contradictions and conflict abound. Better still, almost everyone has oatmeal or coffee in the cupboard.

   Should newspapers and magazines report controversial studies or wait until there is scientific consensus for the findings of the studies? What are your reasons for your answer?

2. What habits, if any, have you changed because of research that was reported by the popular media? (Consider dietary and exercise habits as well as advice on car safety, product safety, durability of consumer goods, and so on.) To what extent has the advice been helpful?

3. What is the best approach to the reading of research in the popular press? Should you believe nothing, everything, or some things? Do you agree with the guidelines for reading research that are given in this article?

4. Do you believe that scientific journals such as the *New England Journal of Medicine* should be more readily available to the public by being sold in bookstores and supermarkets? Would people buy these publications, and if so, would they be capable of understanding them? Give reasons for your answers.

In the following article, we read about a controversial new treatment for post-traumatic stress disorders. The treatment, if given shortly after a traumatic event, limits the negative memories that some victims suffer for years. Some professionals and victims are very excited about the positive potential of this treatment, and others fear it may create a dangerous outcome.

"COULD A PILL HELP FADE TRAUMATIC MEMORIES?"

Suppose you could erase bad memories from your mind. Suppose, as in a recent movie, your brain could be wiped clean of sad and traumatic thoughts.

That is science fiction. But real-world scientists are working on the next best thing. They have been testing a pill that, when given after a traumatic event like rape, may make the resulting memories less painful and intense.

Will it work? It is too soon to say. Still, it is not far-fetched to think that this drug someday might be passed out along with blankets and food at emergency shelters after disasters like the tsunami or Hurricane Katrina.

Psychiatrist Hilary Klein could have offered it to the man she treated at a St. Louis shelter over the Labor Day weekend. He had fled New Orleans and was so distraught over not knowing where his sisters were that others had to tell Klein his story.

"This man could not even give his name, he was in such distress. All he could do was cry," she said.

Such people often develop post-traumatic stress disorder, or PTSD, a problem first recognized in Vietnam War veterans. Only 14 percent to 24 percent of trauma victims experience long-term PTSD, but sufferers have flashbacks and physical symptoms that make them feel as if they are reliving the trauma years after it occurred.

Scientists think it happens because the brain goes haywire during and right after a strongly emotional event, pouring out stress hormones that help store these memories in a different way than normal ones are preserved.

Taking a drug to tamp down these chemicals might blunt memory formation and prevent PTSD, they theorize.

Some doctors have an even more ambitious goal: trying to cure PTSD. They are deliberately triggering very old bad memories and then giving the pill to deep-six them.

The first study to test this approach on 19 longtime PTSD sufferers has provided early encouraging results, Canadian and Harvard University researchers report.

"We figure we need to test about 10 more people until we've got solid evidence." said Alain Brunet, a psychologist at McGill University in Montreal who is leading the study.

It can't come too soon.

The need for better treatment grows daily as American troops return from Iraq and Afghanistan with wounded minds as well as bodies. One government survey found almost 1 in 6 showing symptoms of mental stress, including many with post-traumatic stress disorder. Disability payments related to the illness cost the government more than $4 billion a year.

The need is even greater in countries ravaged by many years of violence.

"I don't think there's yet in our country a sense of urgency about post-traumatic stress disorder" but there should be, said James McGaugh, director of the Center for the Neurobiology of Learning and Memory at the University of California at Irvine.

He and a colleague, Larry Cahill, did experiments that changed how scientists view memory formation and suggested new ways to modify it.

Memories, painful or sweet, don't form instantly after an event but congeal over time. Like slowly hardening cement, there is a window of opportunity when they are shapable.

During stress, the body pours out adrenaline and other "fight or flight" hormones that help write memories into the "hard drive" of the brain, McGaugh and Cahill showed.

Propranolol can blunt this. It is in a class of drugs called beta blockers and is the one most able to cross the blood-brain barrier and get to where stress hormones are wreaking havoc. It already is widely used to treat high blood pressure and is being tested for stage fright.

Dr. Roger Pitman, a Harvard University psychiatrist, did a pilot study to see whether it could prevent symptoms of PTSD. He gave 10 days of either the drug or dummy pills to accident and rape victims who came to the Massachusetts General Hospital emergency room.

In follow-up visits three months later, the patients listened to tapes describing their traumatic events as researchers measured their heart rates, palm sweating and forehead muscle tension.

The eight who had taken propranolol had fewer stress symptoms than the 14 who received dummy pills, but the differences in the frequency of symptoms were so small they might have occurred by chance—a problem with such tiny experiments.

Still, "this was the first study to show that PTSD could be prevented," McGaugh said, and enough to convince the federal government to fund a larger one that Pitman is doing now.

Meanwhile, another study on assault and accident victims in France confirmed that propranolol might prevent PTSD symptoms.

One of those researchers, Brunet, now has teamed with Pitman on the boldest experiment yet—trying to cure longtime PTSD sufferers.

"We are trying to reopen the window of opportunity to modulate the traumatic memory," Pitman said.

The experiments are being done in Montreal and involve people traumatized as long as 20 or 30 years ago by child abuse, sexual assault or a serious accident.

"It's amazing how a traumatic memory can remain very much alive. It doesn't behave like a regular memory. The memory doesn't decay," Brunet said.

To try to make it decay, researchers ask people to describe the trauma as vividly as they can, bringing on physical symptoms like racing hearts, then give them propranolol to blunt "restorage" of the memory. As much as three months later, the single dose appears to be preventing PTSD symptoms, Brunet said.

Joseph LeDoux, a neuroscience professor at New York University, is enrolling 20 to 30 people in a similar experiment and believes in the approach.

"Each time you retrieve a memory it must be restored," he said. "When you activate a memory in the presence of a drug that prevents the restorage of the memory, the next day the memory is not as accessible."

Not all share his enthusiasm, as McGaugh found when he was asked to brief the President's Council on Bioethics a few years ago.

"They didn't say anything at the time but later they went ballistic on it," he said.

Chairman Leon Kass contended that painful memories serve a purpose and are part of the human experience.

McGaugh says that's preposterous when it comes to trauma like war. If a soldier is physically injured, "you do everything you can to make him whole," but if he says he is upset "they say, 'suck it up—that's the normal thing,'" he complained.

Propranolol couldn't be given to soldiers in battle because it would curb survival instincts.

"They need to be able to run and to fight," Pitman said. "But if you could take them behind the lines for a couple of days, then you could give it to them after a traumatic event," or before they're sent home, he said.

Some critics suggest that rape victims would be less able to testify against attackers if their memories were blunted, or at least that defense attorneys would argue that.

"Medical concerns trump legal concerns. I wouldn't withhold an effective treatment from somebody because of the possibility they may have to go to court a year later and their testimony be challenged. We wouldn't do that in any other area of medicine," Pitman said. "The important thing to know about this drug is it doesn't put a hole in their memory. It doesn't create amnesia."

Practical matters may limit propranolol's usefulness. It must be given within a day or two of trauma to prevent PTSD.

How long any benefits from the drug will last is another issue. McGaugh said some animal research suggests that memory eventually recovers after being squelched for a while by the drug.

Overtreatment also is a concern. Because more than three-quarters of trauma victims don't have long-term problems, most don't need medication.

But LeDoux sees little risk in propranolol.

"It's a pretty harmless drug," he said. "If you could give them one or two pills that could prevent PTSD, that would be a pretty good thing."

Klein, the Saint Louis University psychiatrist, said it would be great to have something besides sleep aids, antidepressants and counseling to offer traumatized people, but she remains skeptical about how much long-term good propranolol can do.

"If there were a pill to reduce the intensity of symptoms, that would be a relief," she said. "But that's a far step from being able to prevent the development of PTSD." Only more study will tell whether that is truly possible.

QUESTIONS FOR DISCUSSION

1. Dr. Roger Pitman used the drug propranolol in his pilot studies. What was he trying to discover, and how did he conduct his research?

2. While Pitman was concerned about using propranolol to prevent post-traumatic stress, other researchers are hoping to be able to cure PTSD through the drug. What is the design of their research, according to this article?

3. What are the main areas of controversy and concern over the research and treatment possibilities discussed in the article? Do you share those concerns?

4. If you were involved in a traumatic incident, would you want the option to be treated with propranolol? Why or why not?

IDEAS FOR WRITING OR SPEAKING

1. *Research paper or speech.* The purpose of this assignment is to help you become familiar with using research to support your conclusions. Many highly intelligent people will give good reasons for their conclusions; however, they may not take the time to study current research findings to support their reasons.

   Your objective for this paper or speech is to find out how well you can substantiate the reasons for your conclusion.

   Since the issue you choose will be controversial, there will be opinions on both sides. You need to show, with your research, that your reasons are stronger than the reasons given by the opposition.

   The steps to take to prepare this essay or speech are as follows:

   a. Choose a controversial issue that you can research. It is important that the issue will have been studied by researchers and discussed by experts.

   b. Take a stand on the issue, or formulate a tentative hypothesis. A hypothesis states what you believe your conclusion will be after you conduct your research.

   c. Find at least four sources of research to support your conclusion. These sources include reports of studies done on the issue and articles and comments by experts that can be culled from professional journals, newsmagazines, or broadcast interviews. If you know an expert, you can arrange for an interview and record the comments as authoritative testimony.

      Also, find some experts arguing for the opposing side of the issue, so that you can address their reasoning in your essay or speech.

   d. Complete a rough draft of your essay or speech, which should include your issue, conclusion, reasons, and evidence to support your reasons. Also, in the body of the essay or speech, address the strongest reasons given by those who draw the opposite conclusion, and say why these reasons are not strong enough to justify that conclusion.

   e. Write the final form of your speech or essay, adding an introduction and conclusion. The introduction should highlight the importance of your issue; you can use quotes, statistics, analogies, or anecdotes to gain the attention of your audience. The conclusion should summarize your reasons and reemphasize the importance of your issue and the validity of your findings.

2. *Pro-con paper or speech.* The purpose of this assignment is to have you understand, firsthand, that issues are controversial because there is usually valid reasoning on both sides. In addition, when you complete this assignment, you will be a more experienced researcher and a more discerning thinker about the quality of reasons given to support conclusions. To complete this assignment, do the following:

a. Choose a controversial issue. For this assignment, it is best if you do not feel strongly about the issue because you need to be objective about the good reasons on both sides. However, do choose an issue that is interesting to you, so you are motivated to read about it.

b. Write your issue in question form, so you can clearly see the pro and con sides of the issue by answering yes or no to the question. For example, you might write: "Should high school principals be able to censor articles from student newspapers?" Those who answer yes are on the "pro" side of this issue; those who say no are on the "con" side.

c. Find eight sources of research on your issue. Four should be pro and four should be con. The sources may be journal articles, newspaper or magazine articles, books, transcripts of radio or television broadcasts in which experts testify, or personal interviews you conduct with an expert on the issue. (Some experts will give you their time, so don't hesitate to call for an interview.) A bibliography of these sources should be handed in with your finished product; use standard bibliographical form.

d. Study the research that you compile and choose three reasons for supporting the pro side of the issue and three reasons for supporting the con side. These reasons should be the best you can find for each side. Write out the reasons for each side, using evidence to support each reason.

e. Finally, take a position on the issue and state why you found the reasons for that position to be more sound. (You can see now why you should start off being as neutral as possible on this issue.) Acknowledge the strengths of the other side while explaining why you found your chosen side's position to be stronger. Conclude your essay or speech by commenting on what you learned in the process of studying both sides of an issue.

FILMS FOR ANALYSIS AND DISCUSSION

It's hard to look at McDonald's the same way after seeing Morgan Spurlock's *Super Size Me* (2004, PG), a film that documents Spurlock's month-long journey of eating only what is on the McDonald's menu to find out who's responsible for the overweight trend in America. Note especially how Spurlock does research on himself; listen for the expert opinions he hears. This film is also a good review of causal and statistical generalizations.

Similar Films and Classics

Who Killed the Electric Car? (2006, PG)

This documentary looks at the forces pushing for and against the consumer adoption of the electric car. Note especially how the use of electric cars versus SUVs affects the environment, the dependence on foreign oil, consumers and the automobile industry.

Thank You for Smoking (2005, R)

This film looks at how a lobbyist, Nick Naylor, tries to make the argument for the tobacco industry despite all of the evidence about the harmfulness of cigarette smoking. Note especially how Nick argues for his points against all common sense and reason.

6

Reasoning Errors

I Know What I Think—Don't Confuse Me with Facts

A critical thinker recognizes errors in reasoning.

This chapter will cover

- Fallacies (errors in reasoning) in the form of reasons that do not provide adequate support for conclusions

- Fallacies in the form of statements that lead listeners away from the real issue

- Useful approaches for handling fallacies

Understanding an argument is a complex process, as we have seen. We need to know what someone is concluding (claiming) about a particular issue or problem and the reasons for his or her beliefs. And we need to assess the strength of an argument by considering the quality of evidence used to support a conclusion.

When we look at an individual's support for his or her beliefs, we may perceive that something doesn't make sense, but we may not have words for whatever seems faulty in the reasoning. This chapter will teach you some terms that are used to characterize typical errors in reasoning. These errors occur so often that they have acquired a name of their own: **fallacies.**

Keep in mind, as you read this chapter, that the fallacies discussed are simply labels we give to faulty reasoning. Don't be concerned about labeling every faulty reason perfectly. Instead, use this discussion of fallacies as a general tool to help you analyze the quality of reasons given for a conclusion. Knowing common fallacies can help you avoid using them in your own arguments and to refute faulty reasoning in the arguments of others.

Fallacies can be categorized as (1) reasons that seem logical but don't necessarily support the conclusion or (2) statements that distract listeners from the real issue.

INADEQUATE REASONS AS FALLACIES

Reasons that sound good and logical but are not adequate support for the conclusion are the first fallacies to consider. These are tricky because they use the form of good reasoning, but they don't have real substance.

The major categories for insufficient reasons are faulty analogies, false cause, ad hominem, two wrongs make a right, slippery slope, straw man, and hasty conclusions.

Faulty Analogies

As we discussed in the last chapter, analogies can be legitimately used to create inductive strength for an argument. If we can show that an idea or policy has been useful in some instances, we can generalize that it will be useful in another, similar situation.

Because analogies are used commonly, we must be careful not to accept them uncritically. The key to an accurate analogy is that *the two things being compared are similar in all significant aspects*. If there are significant differences between the items being compared, then we have a **faulty analogy.**

Sometimes the comparison is easy for a critical thinker to make. Let's look at a typical use of analogy in advertising, that of comparing a product to an experience:

> *Springsoft fabric softener smells great. It's like hanging your clothes out in the fresh air.*

Similarities between a fabric softener and hanging clothing in the fresh air are that both are used while getting clothes dry and both presumably smell good.

Differences can be noted as follows:

Springsoft	**Fresh Air**
Smell induced by chemicals	Smell from fresh air
Recurrent cost involved	One-time clothesline cost
Quick when used with dryer	Time consuming

You can see that comparing *Springsoft* with fresh air is not accurate in all of the dimensions that are significant to a consumer. It would be more accurate to ask consumers to buy *Springsoft* because it has a nice fragrance and makes clothes feel softer. So why don't advertisers just state the facts?

Advertisers, politicians, salespeople, lawyers, teachers, and other advocates usually realize that a powerful picture is worth more than a detailed argument. A swim instructor may know that asking children to put their arms out straight is more effective when she adds, "like Superman does." Campaign managers realize that a powerful negative image leveled against an opposing candidate may have greater impact than a reasoned case against him. Likewise, parents who want to believe that they are doing the best for their children may respond to the idea of infusing fresh air and sunshine into their clothes, especially since the fresh air and sunshine come in an easy-to-use product.

Faulty analogies occur when we compare one situation or idea to another and disregard significant differences that make the comparison invalid. For example, to compare plans for overcoming racism in the United States to plans that work for the Finnish people would be fallacious: Finland has people of many fewer races than does the United States. Or, someone might suggest that we look at the low rate of theft in some countries and adopt a similar prevention plan. The problem is that some of these countries have punishments that are not likely to be adopted by North American voters and legislators, such as the removal of a hand for stealing.

People may use faulty analogies to excuse their actions. One example occurred when 78 students at Dartmouth College were charged with cheating. While discussing the upcoming homework, their professor had clicked on a Web site that contained the answers. The professor had promised that he would secure the site, but he forgot to do so, and these students presumably got their answers directly off the Web. In an article in the *Boston Globe,* writer David Abel comments on how the students used faulty analogies to justify their actions:

> Some of the students compared their predicament to a professor leaving the answers to an exam on a classroom blackboard. Others likened it to a professor leaving the answers in an unlocked desk drawer. Either way, the two analogies reflect an increasing concern among educators ranging

from elementary teachers to Ivy League professors: Cheating is getting a lot easier.

...For Scot Drysdale, the chairman of Dartmouth's Computer Science department, the past few weeks have been tense, with a groundswell of students countering the cheating charges, claiming the professor set them up.

But Drysdale never bought into the copying-off-the-blackboard analogy. In his view, despite the ease of clicking onto a Web site, some effort, however minimal, was necessary to find the answers, kind of like opening a desk drawer.

"Sure it was easy," he said. "But they still had to go looking for it. That's the point."[1]

Faulty analogies are used frequently when social issues are discussed. You might hear someone claim there is no problem with violence on television or in movies. The person taking this position might say, "I watched television shows all my life and I turned out just fine." The problem with this reasoning is that the quantity of programs and the standards for violent content are different from the programming of 20 or 30 years ago. The speaker may or may not be right about the effect of televised violence, but this comparison does nothing to prove his or her point.

Faulty analogies are often accompanied by a limited understanding of significant changes that make our current world different from the world of previous generations.

We also encounter faulty analogies in personal relationships when one person gives advice to another. For example, if a grandparent tells you that he or she used to walk five miles in the snow to get to school, suggesting that you or your children should do the same, you would have to consider the difficulty of implementing this plan in a culture where parents are afraid to let their children even play in the front yard without supervision.

Or let's say a friend of yours is advising you about how to prepare for a speech you have to give for a class. He or she might say, "Just relax and don't prepare too many notes. That's what I did and I got an A." That method may work for your friend but may be totally inappropriate for you; you may be the kind of person (like most of us) who needs to have good notes and to practice a speech before giving it to a class.

A common problem with people who give advice is their assumption that what worked for them will work for you—a classic case of faulty analogy.

When you see someone supporting a position by comparing one idea, situation, or plan to another, stop and evaluate whether the comparison is valid. If it is, you have a good analogy and a good reason to listen to the speaker. If it is not a valid comparison in some important way, then you have a faulty analogy. (See Exercise 6.2, p. 251.)

---

[1]David Abel, "Peek Performance: Does the Internet Create More Cheaters, or More Skillful Ones?" *Boston Globe,* March 19, 2000, p. C-1.

REMINDER

A faulty analogy follows this format:

1. A is being compared to B. There are some points of similarity between A and B.
2. However, the differences between A and B are strong enough to make the comparison invalid. In everyday language, a faulty analogy is "like comparing apples to oranges."

Critical thinking response: Point out the significant differences that make the comparison between A and B too weak to use as support for the argument.

False Cause: Post Hoc Ergo Propter Hoc

False cause, also called **post hoc ergo propter hoc** (post hoc for short), is an interesting fallacy that is committed frequently in reasoning about personal, social, and political issues. The Latin translates to "after this, therefore because of this" and refers to the practice of stating that because one event followed another, the first event caused the second event. As we discussed in Chapter 4, cause-effect reasoning is sometimes relevant and valid; it is used extensively in psychology (a person may have a fear of abandonment because he or she was abandoned as a child), in history (Jewish people became merchants in parts of Europe because they were not allowed to purchase land), in business (sales increased after a new advertising campaign), in medicine (you are tired and run down because of low blood sugar), in politics (she had 78 percent of the votes and lost 50 percent after the last-minute smear campaign by her opponent), and in economics (the economy began to recover when interest rates were lowered).

In all these cases, research and reasoning could prove one event came after another and that, in all probability, the first event was a cause of the second event. The fallacy of post hoc occurs when there is no real proof that one event *caused* another event; there is only evidence that one event came *after* another event. **Correlation**, a close connection between two events, is not the same as **causation**. With no evidence of causation, we fall into superstition, as described by the following lyrics:

> Very superstitious, ladders 'bout to fall
> Thirteen month old baby, broke the lookin' glass
> Seven years of bad luck, the good things in your past.

From "Superstition" by Stevie Wonder. Copyright © 1972.

Stevie Wonder refers to the superstitious beliefs that bad luck is caused by people walking under ladders or breaking mirrors. Through his lyrics, he advises his listeners that superstitions reflect wrong thinking and create needless suffering. The same can be said for positive superstitions that keep people bonded to unproven beliefs, such as the notion that a lucky penny or rabbit's foot brings good fortune or success.

Superstition is the clearest example of false cause. Superstitious thinking is uncritical thinking. A superstitious person may reason fallaciously, "I got fired because I walked under that ladder yesterday" or "The reason I failed the test is that I didn't forward the 'good luck' email that was sent to me last week." What's especially dangerous about superstitious thinking is that if a person really *believes* he is somehow "cursed," he may *act* as if he is cursed and make the curse come true because of his expectations. (See the article by Michael Crichton on page 259 for several examples of such deadly thinking.)

However, the post hoc fallacy is often more subtle than mere superstition; it consists of reasons that are not supported by adequate evidence. For example, politicians are fond of blaming budget deficits and unemployment rates on their predecessors ("I didn't get us into this mess—the previous administration did"). The problem is that this reasoning ignores the more complicated factors that need to be understood in order to change the current situation for the better. The blaming process is often at the root of a post hoc fallacy, and it short circuits constructive action that could alleviate a problem.

Here are some examples of post hoc fallacies based on shifting the blame and therefore not taking responsibility:

"The reason our team lost is because we weren't playing at home."
"I failed the class because the teacher hated me."
"I saw how you put your television set in the car. The reason it doesn't work is that it was poorly placed in your car after you left our repair shop."
"I ate three pieces of pie at Joanne's house because I didn't want to hurt her mother's feelings."
"I can't find my soccer ball because a large green and brown monster came and ate it while I was sleeping." (Small children can also use fallacies.)

Although many post hoc fallacies are based on blame and rationalization, some are based on a lack of information to substantiate a valid reason—in other words, sometimes we just don't know the real cause of a particular problem.

In our frustrated attempts to find reasons and therefore solutions or explanations for situations, we may rush to assign blame without fair and careful analysis. Then our investigations are weakened because we may be tempted to address surface and not deeper causes for problems, and we may look for singular rather than multiple causes.

For example, if we say that homelessness is usually the result of a lack of confidence in the ability to work (false cause in many cases), then we look for a solution to fit the false cause. So homeless people are given motivational lectures and training. Some individuals may be helped by this approach, but we still have the basic problem of homelessness. Some of the homeless may be mentally unfit for employment or seminars; some may be displaced homemakers who

Solutionized over a false cause

would rather be in the parks with their children than shuffled off to training; some may be fully equipped to work, but lack a mailing address and phone number that would help employers contact them; some may be perfectly happy in a homeless condition; and some may welcome job training but find it difficult to get hired. Problems are complex and a single cause doesn't address them accurately. We would do better to get at the root and diverse causes of social problems, rather than try to find quick fixes to what may not be the complete problem. (See Exercise 6.3, p. 252.)

REMINDER

False cause follows this format:

1. A occurs before B.
2. With no other evidence than the fact that A occurred before B, it is said that A caused B.

Critical thinking response: Point out that the correlation between A and B does not confirm a causal link between them. Give examples of other factors that could have caused B.

Ad Hominem: Attacking the Person

Ad hominem is a Latin term meaning "to the man" or **attacking the person.** Ad hominem occurs when a person is attacked on a personal quality that is irrelevant to the issue under discussion. For example, someone might say that a woman is not qualified for a position on a city council because she's a homemaker, or someone might say that an actor has no right to take a position about environmental issues.

In these cases, the people should not be judged because of their professional affiliations: A homemaker could do as well as anyone else in city government, and an actor is also a citizen who has the right to speak out (even if he or she does have the advantage of a larger audience than the average person).

The use of ad hominem arguments has been a staple of political rhetoric for a long time. Consider the following accusations that were used in the presidential campaign of 1800, which is said to have been characterized by "ugly insults coming from both sides":

> President John Adams was accused of being "a fool, a gross hypocrite and an unprincipled oppressor." His opponent, Thomas Jefferson was called "an uncivilized atheist, anti-American, a tool for the godless French."[2]

[2]Abby Collins-Sears, "Shortcomings of Founding Fathers Studied," *Contra Costa Times,* February 20, 1996, p. A-3.

People may resort to an ad hominem argument when they can't think of strong reasons to counter someone else's arguments; they may also use ad hominem in a desperate attempt to discredit someone whose motives they distrust. Such was the case for trial lawyer and television commentator Gerry Spence, who writes about his own unfortunate use of ad hominem argument in the courtroom:

> As a young lawyer, I stared at the ceiling numberless nights fretting about how to meet the power of an opposing lawyer in a case for a terribly injured client. My client had been brain-damaged by a defectively designed crane and was left without a sense of who or where he was. He deserved justice. But the insurance company refused to pay a penny. As they often do, they brought in their famous lawyer to defend the manufacturer. To get justice for my client, I had to win against this man.
>
> … I found myself completely obsessed with my fear of this handsome charmer, who was the epitome of wrong to me. I talked to every lawyer who would talk to me about him. The more I listened, the more I discovered that he had no apparent Achilles' heel. Moreover, everyone seemed to like him, even those whom he had beaten. I lay awake at night devising scores of arguments to the jury. At last I came up with this one:
>
> "Ladies and gentlemen,
>
> "Mr. Randolph Hightower is a mighty nice man. But when this case is over he will suffer neither loss nor gain from anything you do. His fee from his client will be the same, win or lose. No matter what your verdict, when this case is over he will simply pull out another file and try another case for the same client he represents here today. And when Mr. Hightower walks into court tomorrow, despite what the facts may be in that case, he will have the same nimble smile for the next guy, the same perfect demeanor, the same kindly exterior. It frightens me. No matter what the facts, no matter where justice lies, no matter how evil his client or his cause, he will always remain the same—kindly appearing, marvelously poised, unpretentiously compelling—in short, wonderful.
>
> "I am afraid you will like him more than you like me, for, in truth, he is more likeable than I. I am afraid you will feel closer to him than you do to me, for indeed, he seems like the kind of man you would like to have as a friend, while I am sometimes abrasive and difficult to approach.
>
> "I am afraid that you will therefore decide the case in his favor, because you like him, when justice demands that you decide for my client. That is my fear. I have thought about it a lot."
>
> Later, I actually made this argument to the jury. To my bitter shock, the jurors found against my client. Afterward, one of the jurors was kind enough to speak to me about my argument.

"Mr. Spence, didn't you trust us?"

"Why, of course," I quickly replied. "Why do you ask?"

"Because you took great pains in telling us that you were afraid we would approach this case as a personality contest. This case was not a personality contest, Mr. Spence. We decided this case on the facts, not on who the nicest lawyer was."

Suddenly I realized I had proven beyond doubt that I was not nice. Too late, I realized that I had spent my time defending against the lawyer, rather than presenting the justice of my case to the jurors....I realized I didn't have the first idea who my opponent was. As the years have passed, I now know him as a genuinely nice man who saw himself as merely representing his client's interests to the best of his ability.[3]

Some logicians believe that discussing an opponent's personal qualities is always a diversionary tactic. However, there are times when attacking the person is valid, because the area of attack is pertinent to the issue under consideration. For example, it is relevant to say that you won't vote for someone for class treasurer (or Congress) because you know she can't balance her checkbook and has overspent her credit cards. It is relevant to refuse to vote for a certain person to be a deacon in your church if he is continually gossiping about other church members. It is relevant to question an environmentalist who travels to speaking engagements about global warming on private jets. It is relevant to refuse to vote for a candidate who promises to care about the elderly but lacks a record of supporting legislation aimed at helping senior citizens. In these cases, personal character and conduct are relevant to the position being sought.

It is hard to determine the relevance of some aspects of personal character. A frequent point of discussion in the 1996 and 2000 presidential elections was whether or not the integrity of a candidate was an important factor for voters to consider. The debate generated interesting speculations about what traits and behaviors constitute the character of a leader.

For example, during former President Clinton's impeachment trial, public opinion was divided over the effect of his actions on his ability to govern. A national debate focused on questions such as "Is the president's personal life, even if conducted in the Oval Office, any business of the citizens?" "Is there a correlation between being dishonest with a spouse and being untrustworthy as a public servant?" "Is lying to the public an impeachable offense when the lying is about personal conduct?" Most of these questions boiled down to the general question, "Does character count?" If so, then a leader's personal character and moral authority is relevant to citizens. If not, then questions of personal character can be seen as ad hominem attacks.

Many citizens contended that a president's personal life is irrelevant and that he should be judged on the basis of job performance. The Senate's finding

---

[3]Gerry Spence, *How To Argue and Win Every Time* (New York: St. Martin's Griffin, 1996), pp. 35–36.

that the president's behavior did not "rise to the level of impeachment" seemed to be a support for this position.

However, in the subsequent 2000 election year, most writers and political analysts believed that Vice President Al Gore, recognizing that character was a relevant criterion to much of the electorate, chose Senator Joe Lieberman as his running mate to add ethical credibility to the ticket. *Boston Globe* columnist Thomas Oliphant wrote that Gore used Lieberman's "recognized morality to buck the Clinton monkey on his back."[4] Before Gore's announcement of his choice of running mate, he was behind in the polls by 17 points. After the announcement, he was only 2 points behind—a very dramatic difference. Rowland Nethaway, senior editor of the *Waco* (Texas) *Tribune-Herald*, gave his analysis:

> Despite the usual plus and minus error points, the results clearly show that Bush and his running mate Dick Cheney dropped dramatically after Gore selected Lieberman—a man best known for taking the microphone on the Senate floor and condemning Clinton for immoral, harmful, and deceitful behavior.
>
> The big bump in Gore's poll numbers appears to be based on his selection of a man who said Clinton had "compromised his moral authority."
>
> Surely that's why Gore selected Lieberman....
>
> Known as the moral conscience in the Senate, Lieberman has teamed up with Bill Bennett, a Republican moralist, to condemn the coarsening of American values by Hollywood, in music and on television.
>
> If Bush picked Dick Cheney to buy some foreign policy experience and gravitas, Gore apparently picked Lieberman to buy some morality and integrity.[5]

In the 2007 race for the Democratic presidential nomination, there were some heated exchanges early on between the camps of candidates Hillary Rodham Clinton and Barak Obama, particularly after Hollywood producer David Geffen held a huge fundraiser for Obama and referred to the Clintons as liars. However, as the campaign got underway, it seemed that both senators wanted to project integrity and move away from the ad hominem attacks. Glenn Thrush made these observations from Selma, Alabama:

> Sens. Hillary Rodham Clinton and Barack Obama nearly trampled each other yesterday trying to seize the high road in their first joint appearance as 2008 rivals.
>
> After an ugly spat earlier this month—and a bitter behind-the-scenes tussle for black support—both Democrats viewed a ceremony

---

[4]Thomas Oliphant, "Breaking Barrier of Bigotry," *Boston Globe*, August 8, 2000.
[5]Rowland Nethaway, "Al Buys a Conscience and a Conservative Too," *Cox News Service*, August 10, 2000.

commemorating the 1965 civil rights march here as a chance to prove they aren't at each other's throats.

With the exception of one nasty comment by an Obama supporter, the theme of nonviolence ruled the day.

"It's excellent that we have a candidate like Barack Obama, who embodies what all of you fought for here 42 years ago," said Clinton referring to the landmark "Bloody Sunday" march across the Edmund Pettus Bridge that led to the Voting Rights Act.

Obama, for his part, said Clinton was "doing an excellent job for this country and we're going to be marching arm-in-arm."[6]

If someone attacks the character, appearance, personality, or behavior of another person, ask yourself, "Is this aspect of the person a relevant part of the issue?" If it is relevant to the issue under discussion, it may be used as evidence. If it is not relevant to the issue, then you have discovered an ad hominem fallacy. (See Exercise 6.4, p. 253.)

REMINDER

Ad hominem follows this format:

1. Person A makes a claim or asks you to act or vote in a specific way.
2. Person B attacks person A on an irrelevant personal trait rather than on the claims that person A makes.

Critical thinking response: Discuss how the personal traits of person A are not relevant to the claims, proposals, or candidacy of person A.

Two Wrongs Make a Right

Closely related to the ad hominem fallacy is the fallacy called **two wrongs make a right**. This fallacy occurs when someone rationalizes that one person's or one group's action is justified because some other person's or group's action is just as bad or worse. This fallacy is often used to excuse behavior on the grounds of other bad behavior.

Examples

"You can't blame me for going out with someone else when you're so moody all the time."

"It's not fair to give me a ticket—at least three people were going even faster than I was."

"Yes, I hit my sister, but only after she stuck her tongue out at me."

---

[6]"Hillary, Obama March Together," by Glenn Thrush, March 5, 2007, newsday. com.

"Of course I cheated on the test—everyone else was cheating too."
"Why should I pay my taxes when the money is misused by our governor?"
"I downloaded only 20 copyrighted songs—other people have taken many
    more than that."

Making excuses for our own wrongful actions by pointing out the wrongful actions of others does not justify them.

There are times, however, when a wrongful action can be justified by the wrongful action of another. In these cases, we can provide relevant and legitimate reasons for taking an otherwise wrong action, as the following examples show:

Parent to child: "Why did you grab your brother—you really scared
    him!"
Child to parent: "I'm sorry he got scared, but I had to grab him
    because a car was coming right at him."

Storeowner to manager: "Why did you open the safe for that criminal?"
Manager: "Because he had a gun and might have hurt everyone in the
    store if I didn't."

In these cases, the wrongful action is justified by the circumstances.

A subcategory of both the ad hominem fallacy and the two wrongs make a right fallacy is the **look who's talking** fallacy. This fallacy is committed when someone denies a claim because he or she believes that the speaker who is making the claim is hypocritical.

Examples

Judy: "I wish I could lose some weight."
Erik: "I know that exercising is supposed to help."
Judy: "Why should I listen to you—I don't see you moving off the couch!"

Parent: "Taking drugs is really harmful and is not a way to solve your
    problems."
Child: "How can you say anything to me about that? Didn't you do
    drugs when you were in high school?"

The fact that a speaker may not now or in the past have "practiced what he or she preaches" does not mean that what he or she has to say is without merit. In fact, someone who has made mistakes in the past may have the most credibility in advising others to avoid his or her own mistakes. For example, many effective substance abuse counselors were once users themselves, and their personal experiences often give them valuable insight into their clients' thinking and behavior. However, even if someone doesn't follow his or her own advice, the advice may still be good.

It is valid to point out hypocritical *behavior* without denying the sound arguments of others, as in the following examples:

Janelle: "I'm irritated that my lab teacher is so concerned about our being there on time. Half the time, she shows up late herself."

Norma: "That is stupid. But there's no point in being late if it will affect your grade."

Sean: "Steve keeps telling me I need new tires, so he won't go anywhere in my car!"

Jose: "He's right about the tires, but he should be just as concerned about the brakes in his car."

In these cases, no one is denying the validity of the teacher's rules or Steve's comments, just pointing out the hypocrisy of their behavior.

REMINDER

Two wrongs make a right (plus look who's talking) follows this format:

Person A acknowledges a wrong or unfair action but rationalizes the action by pointing out someone else's equally wrong or unfair action, *or*

1. Person A points out Person B's mistake or bad behavior.
2. Person B responds by pointing out another action that is equally bad or worse, arguing that it cancels out his or her own bad behavior. In the case of look who's talking, the equally bad behavior involves hypocrisy.

Critical thinking response: Acknowledge the equally bad or worse behavior, but remind the person that it does not justify his or her own actions.

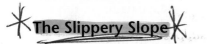

The Slippery Slope

Slippery slope refers to the domino effect. If you push one domino in a pattern, then all the others will fall. A slippery slope argument states that if one event occurs, then others will follow, usually in an inevitable and uncontrollable way. Any domino effect argument involves a prediction about the future and is therefore based on speculation. Still, this form of reasoning can be valid, even when opponents call it a slippery slope, if the interpretations are soundly based on existing facts and reasonable probabilities. For example, in the 1970s, people used to discuss the possibility of a domino effect in Southeast Asia; they believed that when the United States left Vietnam, then not only Vietnam but also Cambodia would fall to the communists. This concern proved to be valid.

When school-based health clinics were introduced, some parents complained that this was the first step in birth control devices being distributed by schools. This argument, which was dismissed as a slippery slope argument, did prove to be valid. Many school-based health clinics now offer birth control and reproductive counseling.

There are also cases in which an individual is refused a reasonable privilege because it would probably call for the privilege to be extended to too many others. For example, let's say you are a day late paying your auto registration. The clerk would probably still have to charge you a penalty because "If I make an exception for you, I would need to make an exception for everyone."

The slippery slope fallacy occurs when undesirable consequences of a single act are predicted and not substantiated by evidence. For example, many people fight the idea of making tobacco advertisements illegal despite overwhelming evidence concerning the harmfulness of this substance. The slippery slope argument given is that if cigarette advertising is made illegal because tobacco harms people, then pretty soon advertising for eggs and milk would be curtailed because of the cholesterol content of these products.

The problem with this argument is that eggs and milk are not analogous to cigarettes; although there is a high cholesterol content in these products, they are also extremely nutritious in other ways, whereas no nutritional or health value has been found for cigarettes. Therefore, it's not likely that advertisements for eggs or other healthy products would be disallowed just because tobacco ads would be.

Another example of the use of the slippery slope fallacy concerns Gregory K., a severely abused child in Florida who successfully sued to "divorce" his parents so that he could live with his foster family, which wanted to adopt him. The boy's parents were divorced, the father was an abusive alcoholic, and the mother was so neglectful of the child that he had been placed in foster homes for several years. Lawyers for the boy feared for his life should he return to this environment. Lawyers for the state social workers, however, claimed that allowing a boy in this circumstance to sue his parents could lead to other children suing to leave their parents because they were denied the latest style of shoes or video games. As one writer stated, revealing the fallacious slippery slope nature of this argument:

> If the lawyers really believe that, it doesn't say much for their own profession. Are there attorneys who would handle some brat's Ninja Turtle—deprivation case? Not likely, especially if the kid didn't have a fat retainer fee in his piggy bank. And are the lawyers saying there are judges who would take a frivolous suit seriously, and not toss it out as nonsense?
>
> No, if the Florida boy wins his case what we'll probably see are other suits filed by kids who will be saying that they have had it with parents who are dope heads, drunks, sadists; parents who don't know how to take care of children and are unwilling or incapable of learning. And that they've had it with social service agencies that don't provide real social services."[7]

In an interview about cloning, Margaret McLean, director of Biotechnology and Health Care Ethics at the Markkula Center for Applied Ethics at Santa

[7]Mike Royko, "When Mother and Father Don't Know Best," *This World*, May 3, 1992, p. 4.

Clara University talked about how the public fears a slippery slope in the potential applications of cloning technology:

> People reacted when nuclear transfer technology produced [the cloned sheep] Dolly. This birth announcement was quite unexpected. There were fears that we'd do such things as clone babies to harvest their organs. But we don't do these kinds of things now. Things like this— where we think of life merely as a means to an end—would be leaps off the slippery slope and into the abyss.[8]

There are also examples in personal communication in which the slippery slope fallacy occurs. If you ask for a day off work to take your sick dog to the vet and your employer says, "I can't give you the day off because then everyone would want the day off," you have probably encountered this fallacy. Not everyone is going to want the day off, and most people would not take advantage of your situation to ask for similar time off. Your need for time off is not based on negligence (as is the case with people who pay bills late and are penalized); your need is based on an emergency.

REMINDER

The slippery slope follows this format:

1. Someone proposes an idea or plan of action.
2. Someone else predicts that implementation of the idea or action would create a series of undesirable, and even catastrophic, consequences. No evidence is given to support this prediction.

Critical thinking response: Remind the speaker or audience that predictions about the future are always speculative and that there is no evidence that the predicted dire consequences would take place if the idea or plan were implemented.

Straw Man

Straw man is a clever and subtle, but quite common, way of distorting and then attacking an opponent's argument. Someone using the straw man technique will take his or her opponent's claims and exaggerate or distort them. He or she then proceeds to destroy this newly created, false, more easily attacked argument (the weaker, easily defeated "straw" man). It is as if a boxer is in the ring with a real, living opponent and an opponent made of straw. The boxer knocks out the straw opponent and declares victory, while the real opponent still remains untouched.

---

[8]Charan Sue Wollard, "Margaret McLean," *San Jose Mercury News*, March 5, 2000, p. 7.

For example, in advocating for gun control of semiautomatic weapons, a debater might claim, "I believe that AK47s should be outlawed—no one needs that level of firepower to be protected." A fair response would be to address whether or not AK47s have a legitimate use and then to discuss that legitimate use. A speaker who uses the straw man argument might instead respond as follows: "As we can see, my opponent is against the use of firearms for self-protection—and so she would allow criminals to possess firearms and deny ourselves their use." The argument has been extended to a discussion of whether *any* firearms can be owned by citizens. If the speaker can convince his audience that his opponent would like to ban all firearms from private citizens, he has a much stronger rebuttal. The problem is that the issue is confined to AK47s, and so his extended straw man argument only confuses the debate.

Philosopher Gary N. Curtis writes about a common straw man called "extreme man":

> Extreme positions are more difficult to defend because they make fewer allowances for exceptions, or counter-examples. Consider the statement forms:
>
> - All P are Q.
> - Most P are Q.
> - Many P are Q.
> - Some P are Q.
> - Some P are not Q.
> - Many P are not Q.
> - Most P are not Q.
> - No P are Q.
>
> The extremes are "All P are Q" and "No P are Q." These are easiest to refute, since all it takes is a single counter-example to refute a universal proposition.[9]

In other words, when we take a reasonable, moderate, arguable position of another person and make it sound like an extreme position, we can more easily refute the extreme position. In most social and political issues, there are moderate and extreme positions. Few people are at the extreme end of the spectrum, with no exceptions to their positions. For example, on the question of immigration, the extreme positions would be the complete ending of new immigration on one end and allowing immigration with no restrictions at all on the other end. Consider the following exchange that starts out as a reasonable discussion:

Paul: We can't keep allowing illegal aliens to settle here without going through the process that other immigrants have gone through. The increase in population is draining our state's resources.

[9]Gary N. Curtis, "Logical Fallacies: The Fallacy Files," www.fallacyfiles.org.

Rochelle: But the immigrants take the jobs that citizens won't take—
they pay sales tax and they strengthen the economy.

Paul: So you're saying just open the borders completely and let everyone have free health care and free education.

Rochelle: I didn't say that. But it sounds like you don't want to let any
new people come to this country. How selfish can you get?

Can you see that Paul and Rochelle started off with moderate positions but then characterized each other's position at the extremes, the "all" or "none" positions. This happens frequently in communication on an issue about which people are passionate. Curtis states that using this fallacy creates not only a "straw man," but also a "straw demon" out of the other person's argument.

Let's look at some other examples of straw man. Notice how the second speaker changes the issue into one that is easier to refute than the real issue under discussion.

Angela: I think we should wait until we've graduated and have jobs
before we get married.

Giorgio: So having tons of money is more important to you than our
being together. How can you be so materialistic?

Choral director: I'd like to introduce some contemporary music into
our concerts.

Member of choir: So you want to throw out hundreds of years of classical
music just to appease a new audience! That's a terrible idea.

Often a straw man is used to argue against a restriction deemed important to a particular group. For example, if a bookstore decides to sell only "family-friendly" books, it may be accused of censorship or of banning books rather than making a free market choice to restrict what it sells. Similarly, a radio station may decide against playing certain music that does not appeal to its intended audience; the station manager may be accused of censoring that music, when, in fact, she has not prevented people from buying the music or listening to it on another station.

The effect of a straw man can be to confuse the issue and the audience. A critical thinker combats this fallacy by pointing to the limits of the original issue and showing how they have been extended to an entirely different issue.

REMINDER

Straw man follows this format:

1. Person A takes a position on an issue.
2. Person B defines Person A's position in an exaggerated or distorted way and then proceeds to refute it.

Critical thinking response: Remind Person B of the limits of Person A's position on the issue and ask him or her to respond to the real position taken by Person A.

Hasty Conclusions

Labels are devices for saving talkative persons the trouble of thinking.
John Morley, "Carlyle," *Critical Miscellanies* (1871–1908)

When we want to know the answer to a serious problem or event, we may be tempted to draw a **hasty conclusion,** or hasty generalization—that is, to make a claim on the basis of insufficient information. In Chapters 4 and 5, we looked at polls and controlled studies that did not provide good evidence because conclusions were based on a sample of evidence that was too small or that was not representative of a target population. When a pollster does not study a sufficient number of voters, she cannot draw a valid conclusion about election results. Similarly, when a researcher makes claims about how a drug will affect *all* people based on a small study of college students, he is drawing a hasty conclusion.

Hasty conclusions can also be encountered when people take a stand or make a claim based on limited evidence. When someone defends a position without adequate support for that position, faulty reasoning has occurred; we may say that the person is "jumping to conclusions." Professionals usually strive to be careful about their judgments—reporters make sure that their sources are reliable, doctors perform tests before they diagnose a serious condition, and police officers gather sufficient evidence before making an arrest. Sometimes, however, there is a "rush to judgment" as was the case when a high school student was arrested and accused of stabbing another youth; the arrest was based on his having a black sweatshirt (as a witnesses attested the perpetrator wore) in his car. Before the young man was cleared by four alibi witnesses who testified that he was at a home working on a school project, his name was released to the media, and he was confined to jail, with $30,000 bail, and he was reported to be the prime suspect.

One citizen who was disturbed by this incident posted an editorial with the title *Forever Changed*:

> An innocent family has been forever changed due to what Pleasant Hill police Lt. Enea has referred to as "unfortunate." How can those sworn to serve and protect Anthony Freitas and our entire community call jailing an innocent high school student, without even checking out his alibis, "unfortunate"?
>
> Was it his "misfortune" to own a black sweatshirt (which had no hood or pockets). Was it his "misfortune" to have a job that required the use of a box cutting tool?

Have the police reports been made public record? We have to wonder what process was used in identifying Anthony as a suspect (while the true perpetrator was roaming free).

Why did it take Pleasant Hill investigators six days to speak with the fourth adult alibi? How do we prevent this "misfortune" from happening to our children? The Freitas family has incurred considerable financial, as well as mental, "misfortune." Will there be restitution?

The entire Pleasant Hill community should seek answers or throw out their black sweatshirts.[10]

We may also jump to conclusions in our personal lives when we hear a few facts or make a few observations and then make a sweeping generalization. For example, someone may be treated poorly by a few people in an organization and jump to the conclusion that all people in that organization are rude. Or someone may have spoken to a Republican who has no sympathy for the unemployed and jump to the conclusion that all Republicans are cold and heartless. Drawing generalizations on a small sample of information is the basis of prejudice. When we are prejudiced, we stereotype people and situations instead of taking the responsibility for considering the realities of each situation. The antidote to prejudice is more information and experience, but we sometimes fail to get more information; we draw hasty conclusions because it is the easier route to take. It's easier to just take someone's word for it when he or she says "you can't trust that company" or "this candidate doesn't care about the environment" than it is to do our own research. Other times, we are more comfortable living with our uncritical assumptions because they have become a part of our thinking patterns: If we stereotype people and situations, then we think we know what to expect from them.

If we believe that only Republicans or Democrats or Independents can govern best, then we know whom to vote for without having to think about individual qualifications. A teacher may classify students as good, mediocre, or poor based on a few assignments, rather than giving them the chance to succeed over time. You can see how uncritical interpretations can have lasting negative effects for both individuals and society.

One important type of hasty conclusion is called the **self-fulfilling prophecy.** When someone makes a self-fulfilling prophecy, he or she starts with an unproven conclusion, such as, "I'm no good in math," and then acts as if this conclusion is a fact (he or she doesn't bother to study math and fails the tests), proving the assertion that he or she is poor in math.

There are two types of self-fulfilling prophecies—those that other people make about us and those we make about others or ourselves. If you think back to labels given to you by teachers, peers, or parents in early years, you may find that they have become fulfilled in your life.

---

[10]"Forever Changed," Hector Merino, *Contra Costa Times*, January 5, 2007.

For example, if you were told that you were going to do well in sports, you probably assumed that was true and had the confidence to succeed; on the other hand, if an art teacher told you that you were a terrible artist, you probably accepted this evaluation and gave up on art. You assumed that the conclusion was true and then acted as if it were true. Finally it *became* true.

Examples

"You'll never be able to learn geometry."
"I always strike out."
"He's a really selfish guy."
"I'll never learn to swim."
"You can't talk to those punks."
"That textbook is too hard to understand."
"You'll love new Bolger's instant crystals!"

The self-fulfilling prophecy has been operative on a societal level in forms such as bank runs and escalating tensions between ethnic and political groups. On personal levels, self-fulfilling prophecies are responsible for limitations we place on ourselves and our abilities.

As critical thinkers, we are responsible for knowing if personal or group limitations are the results of careless predictions. Then we are empowered to change our attitudes and our actions. (See Exercise 6.5 and 6.6 on p. 253.)

REMINDER

A hasty conclusion follows this format:

A generalization is made on a sample that is too small or not broad enough to be representative of all of the elements of the target population, *or*

1. A limited number of observations are made about A (A may represent a group or an individual).
2. A sweeping generalization about A is drawn from these limited observations.

Critical thinking response: Check the amount and quality of evidence before making or accepting a conclusion.

SKILL

Recognize when reasons given to justify a conclusion are not sufficient.

FALLACIES THAT MISLEAD

To this point, we have examined errors that occur when the reasons given for a particular conclusion do not clearly support the conclusion. The second category of fallacies is characterized by reasons that lead the listener away from the real issue. Common examples of this type of fallacy are red herrings, ad populum, appeal to tradition, appeal to pity, false dilemma, equivocation, and begging the question.

The Red Herring

The **red herring** fallacy gets its name from the old practice of drawing a herring—a smoked fish—across a trail to distract hunting dogs from following their prey. In this manner, the hounds were led away from their prey; this technique was used by criminals who didn't want to be found and had access to smoked fish. Similarly, when someone can distract your attention by getting you on the defensive about a different issue than the one under discussion, that person has taken you off track of the real, or original, issue.

Children are particularly skillful at using red herrings; it's one of their best defense mechanisms against parental demands.

Examples

Mother: Get that sharp stick out of here!

Child: That's not a stick. It's a laser beam. I need it to perform surgery on some space aliens.

Father: Joey, it's time to brush your teeth and get in bed.

Joey: You didn't tell that to Suzy.

Father: (getting off track) Suzy's older than you.

Joey: But I'm taller than she is.

If this child is successful, he will have gained extra time, and he might even be able to stall long enough for his parent to forget what time it is.

What a child does purely in the pursuit of having his or her way, he or she may learn to do as an adult in defense of a larger cause.

Example

When Reform Party founder H. Ross Perot was running for president of the United States, he was questioned at a conference of newspaper editors. *Philadelphia Inquirer* columnist Acel Moore wanted specific answers about Perot's proposals concerning the drug problem in the United States.

Acel Moore: Let this audience know. I haven't heard it.

Mr. Perot: Do we have to be rude and adversarial? Can't we just talk?

Mr. Moore: If you're going to be a candidate for the President of the United States, I think you should have to go through that process. And part of the process is being asked questions of a very specific nature, and coming forth with some responses.[11]

Red herrings are used often in politics because there are many topics politicians may not wish to discuss. They may not have knowledge of the topic, or they may be unprepared to answer difficult questions about it because in taking a stand, they are sure to alienate or anger some part of their electorate. You can often encounter red herrings in political interviews and press conferences.

Examples

Interviewer: Your position on immigration has been confusing to some people. Can you clarify your position on giving driver's licenses to illegal immigrants?

Politician: Immigrants are valuable members of our society. We're a country founded on immigrants. As a matter of fact, my family immigrated here only a few years before I was born.

Reporter: Mr. Secretary, why won't the president admit that he wrote those memos with his signature on them?

Secretary: Why are you reporters always attacking this president and defending his opponents?

If the politician can get the interviewer to turn the discussion to his own experience as an immigrant, he will have avoided answering a question that he doesn't want to answer. And if the secretary can get the reporters to defend themselves, they will have been led away from the issue of whether the president wrote the memos. People use red herrings to move the dialogue away from an issue that is uncomfortable for them to a different issue that can be more easily discussed.

People also use red herrings to defend against a reasonable criticism:

Brielle: I was upset when you didn't come to my game Friday.

Manu: I guess that makes me the worst friend ever and that's why you don't like me.

Dylan: I can't believe you "forgot" to tell me that you put a dent in my car yesterday.

Kevin: You care more about that car than about your friends.

When reasonable statements or claims are "extended" by the other person, confusion and fighting are likely. It's important for speakers to stay with the original subject and not be pulled into a defensive exchange on an irrelevant or tangential subject.

[11]Ted Koppel, "The Unknown Ross Perot," *Nightline,* April 23, 1992.

REMINDER

A red herring follows this format:

1. One person brings up topic A.
2. The other person brings up topic B under the guise of being relevant to topic A (when topic B is actually not relevant to topic A).
3. If the second person is successful, topic A is abandoned.

Critical thinking response: Remind the speaker of the original topic. You may also offer to discuss topic B at another time.

Ad Populum: Jumping on the Bandwagon

The **ad populum** fallacy is another one we seem to learn from early childhood. This fallacy consists of a false appeal to the authority of "everyone." We are told that a course of action should be taken, or an idea should be supported, because "everyone" is doing it or believes it.

American society has been said to produce individuals who are *other directed*, which means that the opinions and approval of others are important motivating factors. The other-directed person is contrasted with the individual who is *inner directed* and derives his or her motivation and approval mostly from internalized sources.[12] Some of our societal cliches reveal this tendency, such as "keeping up with the Joneses," "the in-crowd," or simply "everybody's doing it."

Advertisers capitalize on our tendency to jump on the bandwagon and follow the crowd by using slogans such as "Who wants Trident? I do, I do!" and "The Pepsi Generation." Or, assertions are made without any proof, such as "This is the way America vacuums," or "This is where America goes for dinner." Infomercials feature representatives of every possible audience member in order to convince viewers that "people like you" are using and benefiting greatly from a product. Sometimes advertisers don't even use words; they just show large numbers of people who are happily consuming their products. If you stop and think about these "reasons" for buying products, they seem silly. So why do advertisers continue to use them? Because they work; many people want to identify with the right products, to be cool and accepted.

Examples

"Join the millions of satisfied customers who have purchased a Crocodile pickup. What are you waiting for?"
"That's not fair. All the other kids get to go to the Dismembered Junkies concert!"
"Hey, America: Introducing your new turkey stuffing mix!"
"Everyone is using our wireless service! Sign up today!"

[12]David Riesman, *The Lonely Crowd* (New Haven: Yale University Press, 1950), pp. 19–26.

REMINDER

Ad populum follows this format:

1. An assertion is made that most people approve of or take part in X.
2. Therefore, it is claimed that X is desirable and should be bought or supported.

Critical thinking response: State directly that the numbers of people voting for a candidate, supporting a proposition, or buying a product are not your criteria for decision making. Ask for specific reasons to support a candidate or policy or to buy a product.

THE FAR SIDE® BY GARY LARSON

© 1985 FarWorks, Inc. All Rights Reserved/Dist. by Creators Syndicate   Larson

The Far Side® by Gary Larson © 1985 FarWorks, Inc. All Rights Reserved. Used with permission.

"As if we all knew where we're going."

Appeal to Tradition: "We've Always Done It This Way"

Closely related in its logic to the ad populum fallacy is the **appeal to tradition**, which occurs when a belief or action is supported simply because it conforms to traditional ideas or practices. In both ad populum and appeal to tradition arguments, the conclusions of the speakers or writers may be fine, but the reasons are not relevant to the conclusions. You should drink Pepsi or Coke if you like the taste but not because everyone is drinking it. Similarly, you may not want to change the way you are doing something because it works well for you, not because it has always been done that way; the folk wisdom on that is "if it ain't broke, don't fix it."

Traditions held by families, organizations, and nations are wonderful in their ability to bind us together and give us a sense of belonging. These traditions are not what we are suggesting when we discuss "appeal to tradition" as a fallacy. In fact, in our "new and improved" society, we might note the fallacy of "appeal to change" or "appeal to the novel." Just because a product or approach to a problem is new does not mean that it is an improvement on the old product or policy.

Sometimes a newly elected candidate or manager in a corporation may make changes without considering the reasons why a particular system is in place. Often, nonincumbents campaign on the idea that we need change, but they don't tell us what that change will involve or how the change will be an improvement over the current situation; in fact, there are times when changes solve one problem but then create a host of new problems that leaves us in a worse position than we were before the changes. Neither tradition nor novelty is an adequate reason to vote for a candidate, to support legislation, or to buy a product.

There are times, however, for a reasonable discussion about whether something should be done a different way or with a different person. In such cases, it is not useful to say, "We need to do it this way because we've always done it this way." That statement is an appeal to tradition that short-circuits useful dialogue or needed change.

Examples

"Vote for Smith. We've always had a member of the Smith family in our
    state legislature."
"All the men in our family are lawyers; you will be too."
"Our workers have always been happy working 9 to 5; there's no need to
    change that schedule."

As noted by these examples, the fallacious appeal to tradition gives an irrelevant and distracting reason for an opinion. It may very well be that the company mentioned in the last example should not change its working hours or create flextime for its employees; it may find it needs all the workers available at the same time. However, to offer "we've always done it this way" as a reason does nothing to engender a meaningful discussion of the possibilities of useful change and, in fact, obscures the issue.

REMINDER

An appeal to tradition follows this format:

1. X has been traditional in that it has been done for some time.
2. Therefore, X is claimed to be the best way to do things.

Critical thinking response: Ask for reasons against a proposed change other than that it is not how things have been done in the past. Point out advantages of a new approach or a change from the status quo. Show that the proposed changes will not cause bigger problems.

Appeal to Pity

We all go through hard times and face different challenges in life. Sometimes our difficulties are completely out of our control, such as the death of a loved one, an accident or medical condition that leaves us disabled, or the loss of income due to a company going out of business. However, sometimes our problems are brought on by our own lack of planning or foresight. We may take on too much—a job, family obligations, school, volunteer work, and fun activities—and then appeal to others to bail us out of the natural consequences and conflicts that our schedules bring. Or we may neglect our responsibilities and then want others to fix the problems we have brought on through this neglect.

An **appeal to pity** occurs when someone argues that others should follow a course of action or hold a certain belief for no other reason than that they should feel compassion for the irrelevant claims of the speaker. For example, a student may miss many classes during a semester without good reason but may realize too late that a poor grade will affect his athletic scholarship. An argument is then given to the instructor as follows: "I really need a better grade in last semester's class or I won't be eligible to play and that will affect my whole future." Although the student's claim is true, it is irrelevant to the conclusion that a better grade should be given, since compassion about the poor grade earned is not a justification for raising the grade.

Other appeals to pity may sound like this:

"You really should go out with me because I'll be really upset if you don't."
"I know you're on a diet, but I slaved all day on this feast, so you should indulge just this once."
"You may have a lot to do, but it won't be any fun for me if you don't come to the party."

Not all appeals to compassion or emotion are fallacious. There are times when the appeal is directly relevant and thus provides a good reason for the conclusion of the speaker, as noted in the following examples.

Examples of Relevant Appeals to Compassion

A televised scenario is presented to show starvation in another country and to appeal to those with means to help out: "Look at these children who have no running water and whose mothers have to watch them go hungry. Your contribution of just 50 cents per day would relieve this starvation and perhaps save a life." This is a genuine appeal to compassion for those who are victims of their unfortunate circumstances. (Note that reputable charities are happy to provide financial statements and other information that verifies their credibility.)

Parent to child: "I know you want to go to the ocean for winter break, but Grandma is getting much worse, and this may be our last time to be together as a family. You could bring a lot of joy to her by coming home that week."

Child to parent: "It's really out of the way to take Keisha home, but she got out of class too late for the bus. Since it's so cold out, could we give her a ride?"

We all have emotions and feelings, and sometimes they are relevant to a speaker's conclusion. When they are irrelevant and are used to circumvent rational thought for individual responsibility, they are fallacious appeals to pity. (See Exercise 6.7, p. 254.)

REMINDER

An appeal to pity follows this format:

Person A wants Person B to take a course of action simply because Person B should have empathy for Person A's dilemma. Person A has no legitimate reasons as to why Person B should take this action.

Critical thinking response: Ask for reasons, besides misplaced compassion, why the course of action should be taken. Show sympathy for Person A's problem, and then explain why you cannot agree with his or her position or comply with his or her request.

The False Dilemma

Human cloning: Will it be a lifesaving scientific advance, like penicillin? Or will it prove to be a horrible mistake that unleashes untold devastation upon humanity, like the accordion?[13]

Another error in reasoning, common in both personal and political communication, is the **false dilemma** or the **either-or fallacy.** When someone makes this error, he or she polarizes a situation by presenting only two alternatives, at extreme ends of the spectrum of possibilities. Any other reasonable possibilities besides these two extremes are left out of the statement, and the careless listener may believe that the issue is limited to the two choices given.

[13]Dave Barry, Miami Herald, 12/30/2001 (No clowning, here's your personal cloning manual; copies available).

Hagar the Horrible by Chris Browne. Reprinted with special permission of King Features Syndicate.

Examples

"Do you want four more years of overspending and poor priorities or do you want four years of prosperity and sensible spending?" (*Note:* You may be able to prove that the incumbent candidate can be fairly criticized on his or her spending priorities, but does that mean the only alternative is your new candidate or that the new candidate will be as flawless as is implied?)

"Do you want to give your family the same, boring potatoes for dinner tonight, or do you want to give them the exciting taste of Instant Stuffing?"

"Sure, you can go ahead and date Jesse and end up with a broken heart and bad memories; but wouldn't it be better to go out with me, since I know how to treat you right and show you a good time?"

"If you don't go to college and make something of yourself, you'll end up as an unhappy street person."

Polarization leads a listener away from a reasonable consideration of the complex problems involved in most decision-making situations and presents one conclusion as perfect while the other is seen as disastrous.

Example

My boyfriend used false dilemma when it was time to decide what to do during the weekends. I am a dance lover and I always tried to convince him to go dancing, but he always polarized the situation. He used to say to me: "Do you prefer to go to a crowded place where there is too much noise, people cannot talk because of the loud music, and sweat a lot, or would you prefer to go to a nicer place where you can relax, enjoy a delicious meal, and talk without shouting?"

The false dilemma can be a dangerous fallacy because it leads us to simplistic solutions and encourages us to give our allegiance to a person or idea without considering a solution that would more fully address complex problems.

[handwritten margin note: reduces issues to simplistic solutions]

In an interview in the *Atlantic Monthly,* Barbara Dafoe Whitehead points out the false dilemma that her interviewer proposes when he asks her about the cause of increasing problems in children:

> Journalists Caryl Rivers and Judith Stacey contend that it's poverty, not family structure, that is at the root of many children's problems. How do you respond?
>
> "Poverty is terrible for children, and it causes tremendous hardship. I share with Rivers and Stacey the view that when twenty-two percent of American children are in poverty, there is a serious problem that must be addressed. I don't dispute their contention that poverty is hard on kids and at the root of many children's problems. But it is not an either-or proposition. There is a well-worn debate that pits family structure changes against economic changes and says that one is the reason for children's problems. There's evidence that points in both directions. Family structure causes poverty in some cases and poverty causes families to break down. To me it's an unnecessarily polarized debate and one that I'm not going to enter."[14]

Sociologist Deborah Tannen also confronts the tendency to reduce social problems to a false dilemma. She writes the following in her book *The Argument Culture:*

> I suggest that finding a solution to any major question or issue is virtually impossible when everything is defined in extremes. Our blind devotion to this approach will always get us into trouble, because most people are usually in the middle, and most issues have many sides.[15]

Tannen suggests that in argumentation we would benefit by

> experimenting...with formats other than debate for framing the exchange of ideas. The change might be as simple as introducing a plural form. Instead of asking, "What's the other side?" we might ask instead, "What are the other sides?" Instead of insisting on hearing "both sides," we might insist on hearing "all sides."[16]
>
> The error of false dilemma is easy to make for two reasons:

- We like to think solutions are clear-cut and simple; a simple solution saves us time and effort in understanding all the complexities of a situation.
- Our language encourages polarized thinking by including few words to describe a middle ground between extremes. Look at this list:

[14]Barbara Defoe Whitehead, "What We Owe," *The Atlantic Monthly,* February 1997.
[15]Deborah Tannen, *The Argument Culture* (New York: Ballantine, Random House, 1999), p. 352.
[16]Ibid., p. 26.

```
Beautiful . . . . . . . . . . . . . . . . . .Ugly
Strong . . . . . . . . . . . . . . . . . . Weak
Extroverted . . . . . . . . . . Introverted
Brave . . . . . . . . . . . . . . . . .Cowardly
Happy . . . . . . . . . . . . . . . . . . . . .Sad
```

Although we have words that describe the extremes (poles) of a state of being, we have few words describing a middle ground. To put yourself in the middle of these adjectives, you have to say "sort of happy," "somewhat happy," "average," or "medium."

Since our language is polarized, our thinking tends to be polarized if we don't make the effort to be more accurate. In our statistically oriented culture, we tend to use numbers to let us know where things stand on a polarized continuum. We might say "On a scale of 1 to 10, how happy are you with our plan?" or "On a scale of 1 to 10, how close are we to closing this deal?" We use numbers to fill in where words are lacking.

As a critical thinker, you can tell someone who is creating a false dilemma that you see the situation as more complex than it is being described. You can then draw attention back to the issues, by asking questions such as "What specific changes does your candidate propose to make if she is elected?" or "What is so good about Instant Stuffing?"

REMINDER

A false dilemma follows this format:

1. Someone claims that there are only two polarized explanations of a problem, two polarized solutions to a problem, or two polarized choices to be made.
2. Other reasons for a problem or possible solutions or choices are dismissed, often with a warning of dire consequences "unless the best alternative is chosen."

Critical thinking response: Point out the polarization of the issue and ask the speaker for other choices in between two extremes. Focus on the complexity of the issue; also point out the fact that no single candidate or plan is without flaws.

Equivocation

Change is inevitable, except from vending machines.

If you think nobody cares, try missing a couple of payments.

When everything is coming your way, you're in the wrong lane.[17]

When we look at language in Chapter 7, we will see that words can be misleading because they often have more than one meaning. **Equivocation** occurs when someone uses a different meaning of a word already discussed in order

---

[17]T. Edward Damer, "Attacking Faulty Reasoning: A Practical Grade to Fallacy-Free Arguments" (3rd edition) (Wadsworth, 1995) pages 157–159.

to win a point. You can discover equivocation by noting that a word that is used to mean one thing in a statement is then twisted to mean another thing in a second statement.

Lewis Carrol showed the frustrating experience of talking with an equivocator in his novel *Through the Looking Glass:*

> "We can never have jam today," the Queen insisted.
>
> "But it must come to jam some day," Alice protested. "After all, the rule is, 'jam every other day.'"
>
> "Precisely," said the Queen. "'Jam every other day.' But today is not any other day, you know."[18]

The basic form of the fallacy of equivocation is

a. A statement is made using term X with one meaning.
b. A rebuttal is made using term X with a second meaning.
c. A conclusion is then drawn using term X with the second meaning.

The term *equivocation* comes from the Latin terms *equi* (equal) and *vox* (voice)—and means "with equal voice." When a term is used *univocally* in an argument, it always has the same meaning, but when it is used *equivocally,* more than one meaning is given an equal voice. Here are some examples of arguments that contain this fallacy:

Carla: It is well known that the average family has 2.5 children (premise #1).
Ray: Well, Linda's family is very average (premise #2), so they must have 2.5 children (conclusion).

The problem here is that the key term *average* is used in more than one sense. With the first premise, the term is used in the sense of statistical averages. But the second premise switches to another sense of average, this time meaning "not unusual." By equating the two, the crazy conclusion of a family having a fraction of children is reached. Often the speaker or writer who is equivocating makes an argument that sounds logical; however, the argument can only be reliable if key words maintain the same meaning throughout the argument. The problem with equivocation is that a second meaning of an ambiguous word is taken, as in the following examples:

"You are against murder, so you should be against capital punishment."

Written as a deductive argument, this would be the speaker's case:

All killing is murder.
Capital punishment is killing.
Therefore, capital punishment is murder.

[18]Lewis Carroll, *Through the Looking Glass,* 1862, online library through Project Gutenberg.

To those who believe that all killing is equivalent, this would be a valid argument. To those who distinguish murder as criminal action from capital punishment, the argument involves equivocation.

> "I don't know what the fuss is about natural foods—everything I eat comes from some part of the earth, so there isn't any difference."

This argument can be construed as follows:

> Everything that originates with natural materials can be considered natural food.
> Fast food originates with natural materials.
> Therefore, fast food is natural food.

> *Sister to brother:* "Maybe I did hurt your arm. But you hurt me just as much by telling Dad."

In this case, the sister is changing the meaning of *hurt*, saying that telling a parent about being hurt is equally painful and wrong as inflicting a physical injury.

> *Political candidate 1:* Our country should be focused on children.

> *Political candidate 2:* If your party gets elected, we *will* have children running the country.

Political candidate 2 has used equivocation to change candidate 1's definition of children to an insult to candidate 1's political party.

REMINDER

Equivocation follows this format:

1. Person A makes a statement or takes a position on an issue.
2. Person B takes a term from Person A's statement and attributes a second meaning to that term.
3. Person B then draws a conclusion based on the second meaning of the term.

Critical thinking response: Point out that Person B has changed the meaning of the term as Person A was using it. Define the term as Person A meant it. Offer to discuss Person B's new issue after Person A's issue is discussed.

STOP AND THINK

In the late sixteenth century, Catholics were forbidden to practice their religion in England, and priests were forbidden to enter the country. The Jesuits managed to smuggle priests into England, and they wrote a manual called *A Treatise of Equivocation,* which instructed priests and their flocks on techniques to answer government

interrogators without committing the sin of lying. One example of these equivocation techniques suggested using ambiguity by saying "A priest lyeth not in my
house" (meaning, to the interrogator, that they were not harboring an illegal priest,
but meaning, to the Catholic, that the priest did not tell lies). The Jesuits believed
that equivocating to avoid unfair punishment (which sometimes included death
by public torture) was justifiable. To what extent do you agree with their
assessment?[19]

Begging the Question

The fallacy of **begging the question** is one of the more subtle ways a speaker
or writer distracts attention from an issue. Begging the question takes place in
two ways:

1. The speaker makes a claim and then asks you to prove that his or her
   claim is not correct. Instead of giving reasons for a conclusion, the speaker
   places the burden of proof on the listener or on the person being debated.
   For example:

   "How do you know I can't do psychic surgery?"
   "Show me that space aliens don't exist!"
   "Why do you think they call it Up Close?"
   "Why wouldn't you call 1-800-Dentist to get the best professional care?"
   "Isn't it worth $16 a month to protect your family with $250,000 worth
   of life insurance?"

   Don't be trapped into proving someone else's conclusion. It's hard
   enough to prove your own!

2. The second way a person can beg the question is by building on an
   unproven assumption in his or her argument as if it were a given fact.
   The classic example is "Have you stopped beating your wife?" This question assumes the husband has beaten his wife. Notice how there is no
   way to answer this question with a "yes" or "no" without confirming that
   the speaker's assumption is correct. This form of begging the question has
   also been called a *loaded question* because the question is "loaded" with at
   least one—and sometimes several—questionable assumptions.

Other Examples

"Why are you always so defensive?"
"How can you vote for a dump site that is going to destroy the environment?"
"Why are you supporting a team that is going to lose the Super Bowl?"

[19]Lady Antonia Fraser, *Faith and the Story of the Gunpowder Plot* (New York: Doubleday, 1997).

Loaded questions are used in surveys to get a desired response, and they are also used to "close" sales, as in the following examples:

Survey question: Do you want to continue supporting a candidate who only cares about pleasing special interest groups?

Sales question: "Do you want to charge that now or put it on layaway?" (This question presumes that the customer is planning to buy the item.)

Begging the question does not always mean that a question is asked. People can beg the question when they give reasons to support their conclusions without giving evidence for these reasons. For example, a speaker might say:

Since legalizing drugs would reduce the crime rate, we have to consider where our legislative priorities are.

Can you see that the speaker here has made the assumption (interpretation, inference, guess) that the crime rate would be reduced if drugs are legalized and then has moved on to the next point? It could be that the legalization of drugs would reduce crime, but that possibility has to be supported with evidence before it can be used as a reason.

Begging the question is also called circular reasoning, as in the following example:

If it's on television, it has to be a good show, because only good shows get on television.

The speaker in this example is using the assumption that only good shows get on television as proof that a particular show is good. No evidence has been offered to support the assumption that only good shows get on television.

REMINDER

Begging the question follows this format:

1. A conclusion is claimed to be true.
2. The reasons (premises) given for the conclusion have not been proven by the speaker or writer; instead, the truth of the reasons is assumed by the speaker or writer.
3. Sometimes, the listener is challenged to prove that the conclusion is not true.

Critical thinking response: Instead of trying to answer a question that is based on an unproven assumption, ask the speaker for the evidence that supports his or her claim.

SKILL

Recognize reasons that are irrelevant and lead listeners away from the real issue.

STOP AND THINK

You may find it hard to categorize errors in reasoning under one label or another; some speakers manage to use a whole group of fallacies at once.

Example

"Everyone knows the governor is unreliable; if we keep trusting him not to raise taxes, we could all be in debt by next year."

The statement in the Stop and Think box on this page could be an example of begging the question, since the speaker reasons from an unproven assumption that the governor is unreliable. It could also be ad populum, since the speaker uses the phrase *everyone knows* to support his claim. It could be seen as ad hominem, an attack on the character of a person that is unconnected to an issue. Finally, it could be called a slippery slope argument, because the speaker predicts catastrophic results from the action of trusting the governor.

The bad news is that writers and speakers who are not careful in their reasoning may lump several errors together and leave you to wade through the mess! The good news is that you don't need to be obsessed with finding the exact title of a fallacy and attacking your opponent with it. You only need to see that certain reasons people give to justify their conclusions are insufficient or irrelevant. The labels we give to the reasoning errors are useful only in helping us define and avoid inadequate and faulty support for our conclusions. These labels also provide guideposts for evaluating and refuting the reasons others give.

LIFE APPLICATION

In your academic, professional, and personal life, make it a practice to "stop and think" about arguments that you are hearing, particularly from charismatic, articulate individuals who seem to have a great way with words. Try to discern if their reasons genuinely support their conclusions, or if they are actually inadequate or irrelevant to the issue at hand, despite the convincing manner of the speaker. Use the approaches given in the chapter to question their reasoning in a respectful but firm manner.

Address the negative self-fulfilling prophecies in your own life. Move beyond limitations that are imposed by others or by past thoughts and experiences. If you weren't good in a subject in high school, that doesn't mean that you won't become strong in that subject in college—keep pursuing good instruction in areas of study and skill that you enjoy. As you continue to learn, you will gain new insights and abilities and grow as a person and a professional.

CHAPTER EXERCISES

Exercise 6.1   Purposes: To practice isolating errors in reasoning. To notice overlap in categories of fallacies.

1. Find errors in reasoning in magazine, newspaper, or television advertisements or in letters to the editor. You may discover that a particular inadequate reason may fit the description of several fallacies. Share the errors you find with your class.

2. There are other common fallacies in reasoning. Find examples of other types of fallacies that are not listed in this chapter (from other instructors or textbooks). Explain these to your class.

3. In a class group, come up with two examples of each of the fallacies. Then, as a class, play the game "What's My Fallacy?"

WHAT'S MY FALLACY?

Fallacies Involved

Faulty analogy	Red herring
Post hoc (false cause)	Appeal to tradition
Slippery slope	Begging the question
Hasty conclusion	Ad populum
Ad hominem (attacking the person)	Either-or (false dilemma)
Straw man	Equivocation
Two wrongs make a right	Appeal to pity

Game Rules

Object of the game: To accumulate points by correctly guessing the fallacies of the other teams.

Form class teams of three to six persons each.

Each team should put between 14 and 28 fallacies (1 or 2 for each category) in random order on paper or cards; this step may be done in groups during class, or the team may assign several fallacies to each member to do at home. These fallacies should be no more than a few sentences. For example, a team might say, "How can you vote for him for student body president—he's a vegetarian!" This would obviously be an instance of attacking the person rather than his policies.

Each team needs: one reader, one scorekeeper, one to two referees

Scoring

Each team must have at least 18 errors in reasoning to read to the other teams.

The lead team (each team is the lead team when its members stand in front of the class to read their list of fallacies) earns one point for each appropriate example and loses one point for each inappropriate example.

Guessing teams win two points for each correct answer and lose one point for each wrong answer. You may wish to have one guessing team have a chance to guess the fallacy before moving on to the next team (for example, moving from team 1 to team 2 to team 3), or you may have all of the teams try to guess at one time.

In order to get two points for a right answer, the guessing team must be recognized by the referee of the lead team and say *why* the fallacy was chosen. The answer must satisfy the lead team and the instructor. The instructor may award one point for a close answer.

Your instructor may decide to award points toward a grade for this exercise or may just use the game to help you practice recognizing fallacies.

In most classes, an interesting discussion of what distinguishes one fallacy from another will occur; this discussion will help you recognize fallacious reasoning more easily.

Exercise 6.2   Purpose: To utilize criteria for evaluating reasoning by analogy.

Consider the following analogies and evaluate their validity. Note similarities that make the analogy useful and persuasive and/or significant difference that make the analogy misleading.

1. While discussing the issue of whether schools should ban peanut butter, one mother expressed concern that the school community become aware of the problem and involved in efforts to prevent tragedies associated with the allergy:

   To San Ramon parent Leslie Mague, the issue is terrifyingly simple. Bringing a peanut butter sandwich to school is like bringing "a loaded gun or a land mine: You don't know when it will go off," she said. Her son Braden was 33 months old when an Asian peanut noodle dish sent him into anaphylactic shock. "Within seconds, he swelled up like a balloon," she said.[20]

2. This excerpt is from an introduction given by Ted Koppel of ABC's *Nightline*, when he did a program on the founder of the Reform Party, Ross Perot. Perot ran a very popular third-party campaign for president of the United States in 1992, gaining 19 percent of the popular vote.

   Koppel: How do you figure the phenomenon of Ross Perot? Why do so many people who know next to nothing about the man seem so

[20]Jackie Burrell, "Peanut Allergy Problems Mitigated at Area Schools," *Contra Costa Times,* September 10, 2003, p. a01.

enchanted by him? A few years ago, I mulled over the same question with regard to the enormous popularity of Vanna White. She of *Wheel of Fortune,* you ask? The very one. She is, after all, a lovely woman with an engaging manner and a charming smile, and no one, but no one, lights up letters on a board better than she. But that still doesn't explain the depth and breadth of Vanna's popularity. The world is full, after all, of thousands of equally lovely, engaging, and charming women. What is it, then, about Vanna?

And then it struck me. Of all the people on television whose names we know who are not playing somebody else, we probably know less about Vanna, that is, what she thinks and believes, than almost anyone else, and so we can project onto her what we would like her to believe.

So, too, with Ross Perot. He is enjoying the support of conservatives, liberals, and moderates precisely because, like Vanna, Ross doesn't go into much detail.[21]

3. Homosexual men and women have been traditionally excluded from the armed forces, and the "don't ask, don't tell" policy did not foster an atmosphere of acceptance. When this topic was first debated in Congress, one argument for completely lifting an exclusionary policy is that gay men and women are a minority group just like Hispanic Americans and African Americans and that no other minority group is banned from the military.

In an argument given for keeping gays out of the military, the assertion was made that separate living quarters would have to be provided to keep straight and gay personnel apart, just as similar policies provide separate living quarters for heterosexual men and women in the military.

4. A couple sued a landlord for refusing to rent to them because of their sloppy appearance; they claimed discrimination in the form of "lookism" (prejudice against someone because of how they look). In defending himself, the landlord stated, "You wouldn't hire someone who was out of shape as an employee in a health spa, and you wouldn't want a receptionist for an investment firm who had purple hair. So why should you have to rent an apartment to people who look sloppy?"

Exercise 6.3   *Purpose:* To discover diverse causes for a given phenomenon.

1. Look at the problem of substance abuse in our culture and answer the following questions: What are some of the simplistic (post hoc) reasons given for the problem? What might be some of the deeper causes of this problem, and what solutions are implied by these causes?

2. Do a short paper or speech on the causes of a social, national, or international problem. Take a position on which causes were immediate, which remote, which sufficient, and which necessary for the problem to develop. If some analysts of your problem commit the fallacy of assigning a false cause, say how. Support your position with evidence.

[21]Ted Koppel, "The Unknown Ross Perot," *Nightline,* April 23, 1992.

Exercise 6.4   Purpose: To determine if there are cases in which personal qualities are relevant reasons for rejecting political candidates.

List the elements of personal character that are important for a president or elected representative. What in a candidate's background, if anything, would prevent you from voting for him or her? Are there things about a person that would bother you if they had occurred recently, but you would overlook if they had occurred in his or her past? How far back into someone's background would you look when making your voting decision?

Exercise 6.5   Purpose: To analyze the effect of hasty conclusions and self-fulfilling prophecies.

Think of some personal and some cultural hasty conclusions and self-fulfilling prophecies. How did they come about and how did they become "fulfilled"? What could be done to change attitudes and/or actions now?

Example

"During a Winter Olympics skating competition, one of the medal contenders for pairs figure skating fell during a crucial performance. The commentator for CBS said that a reporter had once written that this skater seemed to be having trouble with jumps. The commentator explained that after the skater read this article, she continually had trouble with her jumps.

"I noticed that this skater seemed hesitant about her jumps during the Olympics. I wondered if a sports psychologist could help her get over what seemed to be a self-fulfilling prophecy. Her coach and her psychologist could help her to form a positive attitude. She could come to believe she's good at jumping by practicing and watching her jumps. The evidence of many successful jumps completed in practice sessions would change her negative expectation and she would perform better in competition."

Exercise 6.6   Purposes: To think of ways to respond to situations more critically. To consider how to avoid hasty conclusions.

Read each situation, noting what the uncritical thinking response would be. Then give an example of what a critical thinking response might be.

Example

A candidate for your state assembly is campaigning door-to-door and asks for your vote. You tell her that your major concern is funding for local schools. She tells you that she is very concerned about this problem also and has given it much consideration.

Uncritical thinking response: Vote for the candidate without further information.

Critical thinking response: Ask the candidate about her specific concerns and the solutions she proposes; follow up with questions about the details of the candidate's proposal. Ask about the sources of funding for any programs she proposes. Also ask her to comment on the proposals of other candidates. Check out the plans of other candidates and weigh them carefully before voting. Also consider the general platform of other candidates to assess the overall consequences of voting for a given candidate.

1. Your friend from your 10:00 class tells you to meet her at the cafeteria early.

   Uncritical thinking response: Arrive at the cafeteria at 9:45, assuming the friend wants to tell her something or to walk to class together.
   Critical thinking response:

2. You are depressed because you seem to be gaining weight. While switching channels on your television set one night, you catch a promotional show on a weight-loss supplement that claims you can lose weight just by taking it twice a day. The commentator for the program says that significant research has been done on this product, showing that it is a real breakthrough. There are several testimonies from the audience about how well this supplement has worked for them to promote rapid weight loss. Also, a famous actor is endorsing the product.

   Uncritical thinking response: Dial the 800 number on the screen and charge the product.
   Critical thinking response:

3. You are invited to a birthday party at your friend's house. She is a good friend, but each time you have attended a party at her house you have had a bad time. Once, you got food poisoning from the fried chicken; another time, it seemed as though everyone had a date except you. You've started to predict that you'll have a terrible time at her parties. What do you do?

   Uncritical thinking response: Stay at home.
   Critical thinking response:

   Add other situations to which you have responded to uncritically. What could you have done differently?

Exercise 6.7   Purpose: To distinguish between legitimate and fallacious appeals to emotion.

Expand your awareness of appeals to pity in two ways:

1. Take the examples given in the section describing Appeal to Pity (page 240) and state the conclusion and reasons given for the mini-arguments they represent. Note the differences between legitimate and fallacious appeals to compassion.

2. In a small group or by yourself, list some of your own examples of legitimate and fallacious appeals to pity. Share these with the class and see if you all agree on which are good reasons to support a conclusion and which involve an irrelevant and thus fallacious reason.

CHAPTER HIGHLIGHTS

1. Errors in reasoning are called fallacies.

2. One type of fallacy involves reasons that sound logical but provide inadequate support for conclusions. These include faulty analogies, false cause (post hoc), ad hominem, two wrongs make a right, slippery slope, straw man, and hasty conclusions.

3. A second type of fallacy is found in reasons that lead listeners away from the real issue. These include red herring, ad populum, appeal to tradition, appeal to pity, false dilemma, equivocation, and begging the question.

4. An error in reasoning may be hard to classify. The important point for the critical thinker is that the recognition of fallacies helps us analyze the quality of reasons given to support conclusions.

KEY TERMS

Fallacies (p. 216)

Faulty Analogy (p. 216)

False cause or Post hoc ergo propter hoc (p. 219)

Correlation (p. 219)

Causation (p. 219)

Ad hominem: Attacking the person (p. 221)

Two wrongs make a right (p. 225)

Look who's talking (p. 226)

Slippery slope (p. 227)

Straw man (p. 229)

Hasty conclusions (p. 232)

Self-fulfilling prophecy (p. 233)

Red herring (p. 235)

Ad populum (p. 237)

Appeal to tradition (p. 238)

Appeal to pity (p. 240)

False dilemma: Either-or fallacy (p. 241)

Equivocation: (p. 244)

Begging the question (p. 247)

CHAPTER CHECKUP

Short Answer

1. What is the difference between fallacies that mislead and fallacies that do not provide adequate support for conclusions?

2. Analogies are a major form of inductive reasoning. What makes an analogy faulty?

3. How does a hasty conclusion relate to the size of a sample?

True-False

4. The post hoc fallacy is concerned with future events.

5. The slippery slope fallacy has also been called the domino effect.

6. An example of the ad hominem fallacy would involve being urged to buy a product because "everyone else is buying it."

Matching

A. Begging the question   B. Red herring
C. Appeal to tradition   D. Ad populum

7. Using various means to change the issue under discussion.

8. Taking a course of action because of the number of other people who appear to be taking this course of action.

9. Putting the burden of proof for your ideas on the listener.

10. Suggesting that because a certain action has been taken in the past, it should continue to be taken.

ARTICLES FOR DISCUSSION

Discovering fallacies is sometimes a complicated process. If you think you've detected a fallacy, first stop and ask yourself, "What is the issue and conclusion of the writer?" Then see if the statement in question fits one of the two criteria for fallacies. Is it an assertion that is irrelevant to the conclusion (and thus does not support the conclusion), or is it a statement that leads the listener away from the real issue under discussion? If the statement fits one or both of these criteria, then you can identify the particular fallacy with confidence.

Consider the following examples, all from editorial pages. When you read two sides of an issue, try to distinguish which points genuinely support the writer's conclusion and which are fallacious. If you discover fallacious reasoning, think about whether the author could have made his or her point with better support.

Here is some background information for the first two letters to the editor: Kerri Strug is a gymnast who performed despite a serious injury to her ankle, thus supporting her team's Olympic victory. To some viewers, it was an act of courage; others believed that the act sent the wrong message. Following are two opinions.

ASHAMED OF STRUG'S SACRIFICE

Sylvia Lacayo

I'd never been more ashamed to be American after I watched in horror the women's gymnastics competition in which Kerri Strug "sacrificed herself" for the team by vaulting on an injured ankle.

Then I saw the next morning's headline on the *Times,* which summarized the event as "Magnificent." To sacrifice children for the greediness of coach Bela Karolyi isn't magnificent. It's not magnificent to expect kids to peak at the age of 18.

Columnist Sam McManis, who reported the "magnificent" story, says they're adults and make their own choices. Strug's 18 years mean nothing, knowing that practically her entire life has been manipulated to please her coaches' desires. To please Karolyi is her only choice.

She may be an adult legally, but her squeaky, Mickey Mouse voice over the reporter's microphone proved she's no adult and her limited life proves she's never been a kid.

Gymnasts are neither kids nor adults. They're pawns in Karolyi's and NBC's ratings supervisors' game of greed and power. It's a game those adults choose to play, but don't say Strug chooses to play it. I'm 19 years old, and I know that leaving the Georgia Dome in a stretcher, crying in pain, could never be my dream.

Reprinted by permission of the author.

KERRI STRUG MADE READER CHEER

Joshua C. Logan

While Sylvia Lacayo "watched in horror" as Kerri Strug "sacrificed herself" and won the gold for the USA women's gymnastics team, I cheered once Kerri finished her vault. She showed strength and courage. If Lacayo had her way, Strug would have quit. But Strug showed that she wasn't going to give up.

Lacayo's attack in saying that Bala Karolyi's "greediness" pushed Strug into the vault is simply ignorant. Why would Karolyi need another gold medal? He was the coach of the greatest gymnast ever. Bela Karolyi did his job and encouraged her to give it her all.

According to Lacayo, Strug's "Mickey Mouse" voice is proof of immaturity. Not only is it mean to make fun, but the assumption is false again. Strug pushed herself and fulfilled her dream as an athlete. Sounds like maturity to me.

I and most Americans, rejoice over Strug and her teammates' victory in Atlanta. Those are the people I want to represent me and my great nation.

Reprinted by permission of John Diestler.

The following letter to the editor was written in response to a question put to readers: "What needs to be done to reduce the number of sex crimes and cases of sexual harassment of women in the military?" What do you make of the writer's response to the stated issue?

KEEP WOMEN OFF THE STREETS

Larry Bunker

End the front line involvement of women in the police and fire-fighting departments. It has been a horrible experiment, and there is really only one solution. They can stay behind the desks and push all the papers they want, but get them off street duty.

Placing female officers as partners in squad cars has not only endangered the lives of veteran police officers but also increased the cases of sexual harassment. Don't kid yourself, we, the taxpayers are paying huge sums of awards resulting from integrating the sexes. If women don't want to be harassed, then keep them away from male occupations.

Another thing, if a policeman is only allowed to use his weapon when in imminent danger, who do you think will draw and shoot first? A six-foot-six ex-football player or a five-foot-two ex-dancer? If you have more mass than the arresting officer, you are more in danger of being shot. Watch out, guys.

What examples do we have in history where women were shown to have the courage, strength, and stamina to fight crime or fight fires? Isn't this just another sad and dangerous way to get more votes?

To those who comment that women have been successful in these areas, I would say that you haven't faced facts. We the public are more than ever responsible for our own safety. I say, stock up on guns and fire extinguishers, you're going to need them.

Reprinted by permission of John Diestler.

In the following editorial, written for the University of Pittsburgh's paper Pitt News, author Shannon Black points out the fallacies of hasty conclusions and the slippery slope that are common to chain e-mails.

E-MAIL CHAIN LETTERS DECEIVE

Shannon Black

Every morning, I check my e-mail in the event that something of dire importance has been sent to me over the course of the night. Instead, I usually find myself sorting through junk mail and chain letters.

The spam doesn't annoy me; I find it more hilarious than believable that a prince from Nigeria needs money to save his family. The e-mails that do bother me are particular kinds of chain letters that are sent to me in bulk.

I have no problem with chain e-mails that threaten me with tragedy or bad luck if I dare to delete them rather than passing them on to 68 people in 10 seconds. I happen to like toying with fate, and oftentimes I find myself waiting a few moments for the promised catastrophe to occur after I press the delete key. Fortunately, despite the massive amounts of chain e-mails I've refused to forward, I've never once been the victim of any of their ominous threats.

The particular chain e-mails that drive me crazy are the ones that can easily be mistaken for propaganda. Such letters attempt to argue a point or state an opinion. I find nothing wrong with spreading e-mails about important news or beliefs; I'm guilty of occasionally sending my friends e-mails about issues that are important to me. Some of the chain e-mails that get passed around, however, are filled with fallacies and bizarre exaggerations.

I have reached a point where I simply cannot stand reading another chain e-mail that tries to prove a point with false information. Perhaps I expect too much from the Internet, but I always hope that people will begin to catch on and stop forwarding glaringly false e-mails. Upon the realization that trying to stop such e-mails is futile, I've decided to fight back by refusing to pass on any e-mail found to be false. In doing this, I've discovered the chain e-mails that are the most popular and that need to be discontinued.

If an e-mail suggests that sending it to a hundred people will save the life of a small child, it's not real. Millionaires and businesses cannot track how many people a letter is sent to. It's highly improbable that the "generator" of the e-mail would ever be able to spend enough time and energy figuring out just how many e-mail addresses a single letter has spread to. E-mails like this can be safely deleted without any guilty feelings.

. . . The story of a brave, young student in a classroom standing up for what he believes, against the tyranny of a biased teacher is a very popular e-mail. If there is a surprise twist at the end with the speaker being a famous, historical person it is probably fabricated. While I'm sure Mark Twain and Albert Einstein stood up for what they believed in, it is not very practical to think that someone took down their speech verbatim before spreading it around the Internet. These can also be tossed.

. . . Not all chain letters are bad. Chain e-mails can be a lot of fun when they are used to send out jokes or update people on current events. They can also, however, be filled with lies and cruel or exaggerated statements. Rather than blindly forwarding them in their original form, take the time to make sure their facts are correct. A quick stop at Snopes.com—a Web site that specializes in debunking Internet myths—can clear away any misunderstandings. If going to Snopes takes up too much time, hitting the delete key doesn't take much effort. I highly suggest it.

From *Pitt News*, "Black's Anatomy," October 12, 2006. Reprinted by permission.

The following article by Australian writer Andrew Fenton discusses whether it is important for celebrities to "practice what they preach" when they urge others to show concern for the environment and for people living in poverty.

RWANDA IS SO HOT RIGHT NOW

Andrew Fenton

How can we believe celebrities flying around in private jets preaching about the big issues, asks Andrew Fenton.

It's really easy to take cheap shots at celebrity hypocrites who support trendy causes. It's fun too.

After all, isn't there a fundamental contradiction in having movie stars living in 32 bedroom mansions in Beverly Hills telling the rest of us to consume less? Or being preached to about anti-consumerism by rock stars whose luxurious, pampered lifestyles depend on the funds generated by ticket, CD and merchandising sales? Is it right that Paris Hilton, the poster girl for decadent, meaningless over-consumption plans to go to Rwanda next month to draw attention to childhood poverty?

This week Leonardo DiCaprio's new film *The 11th Hour* opens in cinemas. It's a grab bag of gloomy scenarios about the impending end of the world overlaid with footage of hurricane Katrina and other natural disasters. Leo solemnly intones a call for our society to radically rethink our over-consumption of natural resources and to start to live more sustainably. The message itself is laudable—it's just Leo undermines his own call for action by constantly jetting around the world, leaving the film wide open to accusations of hypocrisy from right-wing attack dogs like Fox News' Sean Hannity.

"You are lecturing Americans about a planetary emergency, a crisis of global proportions," Hannity told filmmakers Nadia and Leila Conners.

"Yet your co-producer (DiCaprio) is putting a bigger carbon footprint in one hour in his private jet than an average American will put driving an SUV for a year. I am sure there are people at home who are saying, 'when you change your lifestyle, I will consider changing mine.'"

It's a similar story with Jennifer Lopez, George Clooney, Brad Pitt and Julia Roberts, all of whom have enthusiastically and publicly embraced hybrid cars. Problem is, they'd have to drive them around the world a few times to save the same amount of carbon they burn up in just one trip on a private jet.

"We're all trying the best we can, truly we are," an exasperated DiCaprio said recently.

Barbara Streisand—who famously declared a 'Global Warming Emergency' two years ago—is another good example of the perils of preaching one thing and doing another. She's consistently called on the public to start conserving energy and water yet spends $22,000 a year watering her lawns and gardens, and her enormous mansion reportedly has an air-conditioned room solely devoted to her fur coats.

The token nature of trendy celebrity causes reached a zenith in April this year when the *Pimp My Ride* crew made an Earth Day special. As American comedian Lewis Black pointed out at the time, the last people who should be giving environmental lessons are a bunch of guys who spend each episode hotting up cars to the point where they're as fuel inefficient as possible.

That same day Oprah handed out energy efficient light globes to her entire audience—which probably won't go too far towards undoing the damage caused by the day she gave everyone in her audience free cars.

Daily Telegraph Opinion Editor Tim Blair takes a certain malicious glee in exposing the hypocrisy of celebrities on his blog. He cites the Live Earth worldwide series of concerts in July as a particularly egregious example.

"The concept of getting rock stars to tell people to rein in their lifestyles I think was a masterstroke," he says. "I mean, you've got people who are bywords for excess and consumption and destruction and gigantic wasteful lifestyles telling people to reduce their carbon footprints! It's amazing anyone turned up—because it's hard to walk when you're doubled over laughing."

Like many conservatives, Blair reserves particular venom for Al Gore, the former U.S. vice-president and maker of *An Inconvenient Truth.*

"How can you be Al Gore and do this when you're flying around in private jets, charging $150,000 to $250,000 to give a speech telling people to live a more simple lifestyle? It's hysterical."

Blair points out that Gore owns a massive property in Tennessee that consumes a phenomenal amount of power. But, in Gore's defense, it must be said he has realized his 930sqm house with its 20 bedrooms and eight bathrooms does generate some negative publicity and has since installed some solar panels.

As enjoyable as it is to beat up on celebrity hypocrites, there is always the sneaking suspicion that some critics are simply playing the man and not the ball. That is to say, their excessive focus on the hypocrisy of stars is a way of discrediting the message and to excuse inaction by the rest of us on the environment.

"Pointing out eco-celeb's lifestyle contradictions is one of the many strategies that the frightened, confused and lazy use to delay action on the environment," argued environmentalist Erin Courtenay on the *TreeHugger* website last month.

"Too often the criticisms imply that a green-celeb's errors render their environmental message moot and their actions meaningless."

Courtenay makes a fair point in that we need to separate the debate about the need to act on the environment from our discussion of the hypocrisy of celebrities.

But as Blair points out, the only reason we even listen to their environmental message is because of who they are—not because they actually have any real knowledge of the subject.

How can we engage with the underlying scientific debate when the discourse is reduced to trendy slogans uttered by the rich and famous?

Does Leonardo DiCaprio really understand the intricacies of scientific debate about the release of methane from clathrate compounds that are hypothesised as a cause for other warming events in the distant past, including the Permian-Triassic extinction event and the Paleocene-Eocene Thermal Maximum?

Or is DiCaprio just an actor?

"We've totally devalued expertise," says Dr Jackie Cook, from the School of Communications at University of South Australia. "We don't understand knowledge or research any more, we only understand opinion and image. What we have to do is shift from the surface into the depths (of an issue) but image floats faster through the (media's) system than anything else."

Andrew Fenton: Film Writer, *The Adelaide Advertiser*, October 13, 2007. andrewfenton@ hotmail.com. Reprinted by permission.

QUESTIONS FOR DISCUSSION

1. Famous people have the potential to raise awareness about important issues. Writer Jeff Bercovici credits celebrities with much awareness of important global issues. In his article for the Canada Free Press, "Green Fakers: Why Eco-Hypocrisy Matters," he also points out that it "is surprising the way

celebrities react to such charges" (of not practicing a 'green' lifestyle), "sometimes by ignoring them outright, sometimes by spouting lame self justifications, but rarely, if ever, by acknowledging the disconnect and vowing to lead a humbler, cleaner, more sustainable existence." Do you agree with his assessment and the need for celebrities to "practice what they preach"?

2. A quote from the article states: "Pointing out eco-celeb's lifestyle contradictions is one of the many strategies that the frightened, confused and lazy use to delay action on the environment," argued environmentalist Erin Courtenay on the *TreeHugger* website last month. To what extent, if any, do you believe that Courtenay is herself using an ad hominem argument against those who complain about celebrities? Could her point be made in a more effective way?

3. Is it an ad hominem argument or a legitimate concern that those at the forefront of global issues are not experts concerning the policies that they support?

The issue of global warming has become a primary international concern. It was the subject of former Vice President Al Gore's Oscar-winning documentary *An Inconvenient Truth* and is a key topic in scientific conferences. The National Academy of Sciences, the UN's Intergovernmental Panel on Climate Change (IPCC), and other noted scientists and organizations have reached consensus that global warming is a reality and that measures must be taken to prevent catastrophic international consequences. There are also credible scientists, who have been labeled "deniers," who agree that global warming is a reality but raise questions concerning the subissues of the extent of human's role in causing global warming, the consequences that will come from the warming, the extent of the warming to come, and the ability of humans to affect changes.

In the following article, writer and radio host Dennis Prager discusses his objection to the analogy made by writer Ellen Goodman concerning those who raise questions about this issue.

ON COMPARING GLOBAL WARMING DENIAL TO HOLOCAUST DENIAL

Dennis Prager

In her last column, *Boston Globe* columnist Ellen Goodman wrote: "Let's just say that global warming deniers are now on a par with Holocaust deniers."

This is worthy of some analysis

First, it reflects a major difference between the way in which the Left and Right tend to view each other. With a few exceptions, those on the Left tend to view their ideological adversaries as bad people, i.e., people with bad intentions, while those on the Right tend to view their adversaries as wrong, perhaps even dangerous, but not usually as bad.

Those who deny the Holocaust are among the evil of the world. Their concern is not history but hurting Jews, and their attempt to rob nearly six million people of their experience of unspeakable suffering gives new meaning to the word "cruel." To equate those who question or deny global warming with those who question or deny the Holocaust is to ascribe equally nefarious motives to them. It may be inconceivable to Al Gore, Ellen Goodman and their many millions of supporters that a person can disagree with them on global warming and not have evil motives: Such an individual must be paid by oil companies to lie, or lie—as do Holocaust deniers—for some other vile reason.

The belief that opponents of the Left are morally similar to Nazis was expressed recently by another prominent person of the Left, George Soros, the billionaire who bankrolls many leftist projects. At the World Economic Forum in Davos last month, Soros called on America to "de-Nazify" just as Germany did after the Holocaust and World War II. For Soros, America in Iraq is like the Nazis in Poland.

A second lesson to be drawn from the Goodman statement is that it helps us to understand better one of the defining mottos of contemporary liberalism: "Question Authority." In reality, this admonition applies to questioning the moral authority of Judeo-Christian religions or of any secular conservative authority, but not of any other authority. UN and other experts tell us that there is global warming; such authority is not to be questioned.

Third, the equation of global warming denial to Holocaust denial trivializes Holocaust denial. If questioning global warming is on "a par" with questioning the Holocaust, how bad can questioning the Holocaust really be? The same holds true with regard to Nazism and the George Soros statement. Claiming that America in the Iraq War is morally equivalent to Nazi Germany in World War II trivializes the unparalleled evil of the Nazis.

Fourth, the lack of response (thus far) of any liberal or left individual or organization—except to defend Ellen Goodman—or from the Anti-Defamation League, the organization whose primary purpose has been to defend Jews, is telling. Just imagine if, for example, an equally prominent Christian figure had written that denying America is a Christian country is on a par with denying the Holocaust. It would have been front-page news in the mainstream media, the individual would have been excoriated by just about every major liberal individual and group, and the ADL would have cited this as an example of burgeoning Christian anti-Semitism and Holocaust trivialization. But not a word at the ADL on Soros's comments about de-Nazifying America or Goodman's Holocaust-denial comment.

Fifth, and finally, the Ellen Goodman quote is only the beginning of what is already becoming one of the largest campaigns of vilification of decent people in history—the global condemnation of (a) anyone who questions global warming; or (b) anyone who agrees that there is global warming but who argues that human behavior is not its primary cause; or (c) anyone who agrees that there is global warming, and even agrees that human behavior is its primary cause, but does not believe that the consequences will be nearly as catastrophic as Al Gore does.

If you don't believe all three propositions, you will be lumped with Holocaust deniers, and it would not be surprising that soon, in Europe, global warming deniers will be treated as Holocaust deniers and prosecuted. Just watch. That is far more likely than the oceans rising by 20 feet. Or even 10. Or even three.

QUESTIONS FOR DISCUSSION

1. Prager makes the point that those who question issues surrounding global warming are seen as having evil motives. To what extent do you believe that bad motives are attributed to "deniers"?

2. What problems does Prager have with the analogy made by writer Ellen Goodman in which she compares global warming denial to Holocaust denial?

3. Prager further objects to an analogy implied by George Soros. What is that analogy?

4. To what extent do you agree or disagree with Prager's comments on the admonition to "Question Authority"? What criteria should we use to distinguish a credible questioning of research from one based in hateful or selfish motives?

The following article is about the debate that preceded Arnold Schwarzenegger's election as governor of California to replace Gray Davis, who was recalled by a majority of the voters in the state. The national media showed great interest in this election for two reasons. First, a recall of an elected governor is a very rare event. The last recall of a state governor took place in 1921 when Lynn Frazier was recalled as governor of North Dakota. Second, this debate featured a popular actor, known for his role in action movies, particularly the *Terminator* series. Many commentators could not believe that Schwarzenegger, who had only worked on after-school programs for the state, could convince voters that he should be elected to replace the current governor. Schwarzenegger and others who were debating against him used a variety of interesting approaches to impress voters, and the press and the people were given quite a show as the debate proceeded. As you read the following *Newsweek* article on the debate, look for some of the fallacies that the candidates used to promote their own positions, particularly for ad hominem attacks.

ARNOLD'S BIG MO

Karen Breslau

Maybe the producers of the Game Show Network thought they were being clever by airing the first episode of *Who Wants to be Governor of California?* on the same night as the debate featuring the five major candidates vying to replace Gov. Gray Davis. The political debate, critics sneered, was to be a totally canned affair, with participants rattling off rehearsed answers to questions that had been distributed to the public—and the candidates—two weeks ago.

Even Arnold Schwarzenegger, under fire for limiting his debate participation to the only event with pre-announced questions, sent a letter to the organizers, urging them to change the format. But as it turned out, no one who saw last night's free-for-all in Sacramento had to switch channels for comic relief. The debate, ripe with accusations, interruptions, barbs and knee-slapping ripostes, was more entertaining than any game show. At one point, the exasperated moderator said he was going to have to adjust his medication if the unruly candidates wouldn't mind their manners. But whether the program informed California's anxious and befuddled electorate on the eve of the historic Oct. 7 recall election is an entirely different question.

In addition to Schwarzenegger, the debate, sponsored by the California Broadcasters Association and held at Cal State Sacramento, featured his main opponent, Democratic Lt. Gov. Cruz Bustamante, as well as Republican Tom McClintock; commentator Arianna Huffington, who is running as an independent; and Peter Camejo of the Green Party. It was supposed to be Schwarzenegger's Big Mo: a chance for him to show his critics that he really is a man of substance and to face off with McClintock, the plucky state senator who has increasingly drained conservative Republican voters from Schwarzenegger's column and forced him into a virtual tie with Bustamante. Schwarzenegger may have succeeded, at least in part, in his first ambition, but he did little to diminish McClintock. And Schwarzenegger clearly benefited from low expectations. "As long as he doesn't drool, you guys are going to say he did OK," said Chris Lehane, one of several Democratic operatives working the press room on behalf of Gray Davis, who was not invited to the evening's event. (Organizers said the event was designed to introduce voters to his would-be replacements and that Davis had been given equal time at a town hall meeting with voters two weeks ago.) Lehane, who served as Al Gore's press secretary, knows all about low expectations: He watched his candidate sigh and "lockbox" his way to defeat in his debates against the supposedly dim-witted George W. Bush during the 2000 presidential campaign.

Schwarzenegger, of course, did not drool. Looking tanned and dapper, he delivered his now-familiar lines about "cleaning up" Sacramento and bringing relief to California's overtaxed, overregulated business owners with panache and confidence. He offered nothing new in terms of specifics, but then neither did the other candidates—with the exception of McClintock, who is renowned in

Sacramento for his mastery of financial and budgetary arcana. When Bustamante tried to claim credit for a recent reform of the state's bankrupt workers' compensation program, Schwarzenegger cut him off. "That reform was pre-election bogus," he interjected. "You guys put wool over the people's eyes. We have a three-strike system—you did it three times, now you're out." As Bustamante sputtered, the audience burst into applause and cheers. Watching Arnold grin, as he triumphantly planted his elbows on the V-shaped table where the candidates were seated, it wasn't hard to imagine him honing his bomb-throwing skills during 20 years of Thanksgiving dinners with his Kennedy in-laws.

From then on, the food fight was on. The spiciest exchanges took place between Schwarzenegger and Huffington, who has been a gadfly in the superstar's campaign since the day Schwarzenegger filed his candidate's papers and Huffington knocked over a microphone stand as she rushed to get in the picture with him. As Huffington railed against corporate corruption and tax loopholes during her answer to one question, Schwarzenegger chided her for her own income-tax shelters, which recently made the front page of the *Los Angeles Times*. "Arianna, your personal income tax has the biggest loophole. I can drive my Hummer through it." More hoots and howls from the audience. A few minutes later, Huffington began criticizing the Bush administration's tax policy. "If you want to campaign against Bush, go to New Hampshire, you are in the wrong state," Schwarzenegger chided. As the audience cackled, Schwarzenegger seemed more frat boy than gubernatorial candidate. "Maybe you need more decaf." As Huffington struggled to retake the stage, Schwarzenegger continued to talk over her and Huffington took her shot. "This is the way you treat women," she finally blurted. "We know that."

By this point, the audience was howling and the moderator became an umpire. Ruling that Huffington had committed a "direct and personal attack," an apparent violation of the mysterious rules, the ump gave Arnold a free throw. "I just want to say I have a perfect part for you in *Terminator 4*," he shot back. "That's all I can say." At this point, the moderator had practically given up trying to shush the crowd. "Ladies and gentleman, this is not Comedy Central," he shouted over the hubbub. "I'm serious."

Arnold's laugh line may have brought down the house, but it could also hurt him with women voters, who are already skeptical of his candidacy, according to most polls. Huffington appeared in the press room during the postdebate spinning session to profess her outrage at Schwarzenegger making light of a scene in *Terminator 3*, in which his character stuffs the head of a murderous female robot down the toilet. Asked earlier about his choice of words, Schwarzenegger told reporters he thought the exchange had been "entertaining" and wondered if he and Huffington should take their show "on the road." "I don't find it at all entertaining," Huffington responded. "I'm going to expose him for the phony he is."

The fireworks between Huffington and Schwarzenegger all but overshadowed the impressive performance of McClintock, who rattled off statistics and policy reforms with a thoroughness no other candidate could match—all while he gracefully fended off repeated rumors that he would soon drop out of the race to clear the field for Schwarzenegger....

"I wasn't impressed with any of them," said Courtney Buehler, a freshman who stood on the staircase outside the debate hall, straining for a glimpse of Arnold. Buehler said she had recently registered as a Republican and was considering voting for Schwarzenegger but wasn't persuaded by his performance. "I think he's intelligent, but he doesn't have the experience," she said. "I guess I'll vote for McClintock."

Newsweek, September 25, 2003. Copyright © 2003 by Newsweek, Inc. Reprinted by permission of PARS International Corp. on behalf of the publisher.

QUESTIONS FOR DISCUSSION

1. The writer of this article states that the debate was highly entertaining but questions whether it provided any useful information for voters to use to make their decisions about replacing their current governor. What factors contributed to the free-for-all atmosphere of the debate?

2. The exchanges between Schwarzennegger and Huffington were quite heated. Which fallacies do you see in their comments to each other? Are there any claims they made about each other that could be considered legitimate? If so, which ones?

3. When the moderator ruled that Huffington had committed a "direct and personal attack" against Schwarzenneger, he gave Arnold a "free throw" to respond with his own response. Do you think that was the way to handle her ad hominem attack? If so, why? If not, what should the moderator have done?

4. The one candidate that the writer claims had specific ideas (McClintock) seemed overshadowed by the candidates with stronger personalities. Should public debates have rules that make sure that a serious discussion of policies and programs can take place? If so, what should these rules be?

5. Can you identify any other fallacies that were committed by the participants in this debate?

IDEAS FOR WRITING OR SPEAKING

1. Write an argumentative essay or speech about a current issue in which you include several examples of fallacious reasoning. At the end of the essay or speech, identify the fallacies you have committed. Share your papers or speeches with the class and see if your errors in reasoning can be isolated.

2. Write a critique of an editorial or essay from a newspaper or magazine. Point out the fallacies made by the writer of the editorial. Also, discuss valid reasoning on the part of the writer.

3. Choose an issue about which you have strong opinions. Read some viewpoints by people who oppose your opinion on this issue; errors in their reasoning will usually be obvious! List and explain several errors made by your opponents or one major error that weakens their arguments.

Next, look critically at your own viewpoint. What errors are committed by those who favor your position on this issue? List and explain these errors.

FILMS FOR ANALYSIS AND DISCUSSION

The hilarious and heartbreaking comedy *Little Miss Sunshine* (2006, R) is a master class in resiliency and overcoming self-fulfilling prophecies in our personal lives. The film's focus is the Hoover family, a dysfunctional but loving group of misfits who travel from New Mexico to California on their way to the "Little Miss Sunshine" beauty pageant. Along the way, they encounter a plethora of obstacles, both physical and emotional, that send them on a slippery slope of bad judgments and crazy thinking.

Bulworth (1998, R)

This film tells the story of a politician who has put out a contract on his own life in order to collect on an insurance policy for the sake of his family. Note especially the ad hominem attacks he makes, as well as the use of "two wrongs make a right" and "straw man."

Fargo (1996, R)

Fargo follows a murder investigation carried out by Marge Gunderson. Marge is a logical and systematic investigator, and her rationality is offset by the fallacious reasoning of most of the other characters in the film. Note especially Two Wrongs Make a Right, Ad hominem, Post Hoc, Red Herring, and Begging the Question.

Bringing Up Baby (1938)

This classic film is an entertaining look at hasty conclusions and red herrings. The comedy follows a serious paleontologist and an heiress with a pet leopard in a search for a priceless bone.

7

The Power of Language

What's in a Name?

A critical thinker examines the power of language and how it can be used or misused in an argument.

This chapter will cover

- The power of words to frame arguments

- How words influence perception

- Vagueness, ambiguity, doublespeak, and weasel words

If language be not in accordance with the truth of things, affairs cannot be carried on to success.

Confucius, *Analects* (6th C.B.C.)

In his definition of man, Kenneth Burke said, "Man is the symbol-using animal."[1] Language is the powerful system of symbols that enables us to communicate in ways no other creatures can. Speechwriters for politicians or businesspersons can be paid thousands of dollars for a short speech. Those who are willing to pay these enormous fees know that the words that are used and the way they are organized can make or break a campaign, a merger, or a crucial proposal.

On a smaller scale, many professionals attend workshops that focus on how to present ideas—how to sell stereos, clothing, or food by using the correct phrasing. For example, some large supermarket chains train their checkout clerks to ask, "Is plastic okay?" They assume that if people are asked if they want paper or plastic bags, they will opt for the more expensive paper bags. By asking in a way that narrows the customers' responses to a polite yes or a less polite no, they hope to cut down on the expenses of using paper. Other salespeople may show some items to a customer and ask, "Will you be using cash or credit today?" before the potential buyer has even decided whether to make a purchase.

Employees who work in front office or public service positions are often trained to handle the public by speaking in ways that reflect courtesy and diffuse anger. You may have noticed that in a well-managed office or store, you can complain and receive sympathetic words from a receptionist or clerk (even if you don't get what you want from them). For example, a receptionist may say, "I'm so sorry that you've had to wait so long for the doctor; we've had a number of emergencies today."

In our personal lives, we think about phrasing things to get the desired results. Teenagers and adults may rehearse their opening words carefully before calling a potential date. Children think about and practice how to ask their parents for treats or money. You may have experienced a time when you sat in your room or car rehearsing what you were going to say to someone; we usually engage in that kind of preparatory behavior when we are dealing with a stressful situation—an important job interview, a fight with a loved one, a proposal of marriage, or a request for a change in salary or working hours. We believe, consciously or unconsciously, that our choice of words and the way we say those words can influence others.

This chapter will explore the influence that words have on people, especially as citizens and consumers. We will look at the way words can help us clarify issues and, conversely, how words are sometimes used to make issues more obscure and difficult to understand.

[1]Kenneth Burke, *Language as Symbolic Action: Essays on Life, Literature, and Method* (Berkeley: University of California Press, 1966), p. 3.

DENOTATION AND CONNOTATION

What's in a name? A rose by any other name would smell as sweet.
Shakespeare, *Romeo and Juliet*, 1595–1597

The first principle to understand is that words, as symbols, are extremely powerful. To comprehend this idea, consider two terms, *denotation* and *connotation*.

The **denotation** of a word is the specific object or act that a word points to or refers to. Words such as *dog, van, walk, swim* and proper nouns such as *Marisa* all point to objects, actions, or persons; the words denote these objects, actions, or persons. In some academic fields, the term *denotation* is used to mean the word's dictionary definition.

Connotation refers to all the images—positive, negative, or neutral—that are associated with any given denotation. The connotations of words include their emotional meanings, which may be different for different individuals.[2]

If you think about these definitions, you can see that although denotations are the same for everyone, connotations vary from person to person. For example, for citizens of the United States, Thanksgiving denotes a national holiday that takes place on the fourth Thursday in November. According to this excerpt from an editorial writer, the holiday has diverse connotations:

> Thanksgiving has different and sometimes multiple images for each of us. The Pilgrims and Indians dining at Plymouth. A joyous (or stressful) gathering of family and friends. Travel. A day off work. Time away from school. The beginning of the end for the American Indians. The official start of the shopping season. Soup kitchens and food banks.[3]

(Handwritten margin notes:) denotation / definition / literal / primary meaning

(Handwritten margin notes:) connotation / an idea of feeling / a word involves

STOP AND THINK

Think of the name of a holiday that you celebrate. What images are associated with that day for you? How might the name of that holiday evoke different images for other people?

Connotations are so powerful that various organizations have been asked to change their names when they are perceived to be offensive to a particular group. A council of local governments in the Washington, D.C. area passed a resolution requesting that the Washington Redskins football team change its

---

[2]For our purposes, we are using the definition of *connotation* used by general semanticists who study the effects of words on thinking and behavior. Some scholars employ different meanings of this term; you may wish to consult a formal logic text for definitions of this term that are used in that context.

[3]Pat Craig, "Let's Not Forget the Little Things," *Contra Costa Times*, November 28, 1996, p. A-27.

name because of the connotations that were perceived to be insulting to Native Americans. Carol Schwartz, one of the authors of the resolution, said that she is a football fan and loves the team but has been bothered by the name, which she claims dates back to a time when bounties were placed on American Indians and bloody scalps, or "red skins," were proof of a kill. "The use of this degrading and dehumanizing term for a team name is offensive and hurtful to Native Americans and to many people who reject racial stereotypes, racial slurs and bigotry as socially and morally unacceptable," her resolution reads.[4]

Karl Swanson, the spokesman for the Redskins, made it clear that the resolution would not influence the team to change its name. He said he had expressed the team's positions clearly in a letter sent to Ms. Schwartz, accusing her of spreading "misinformation" about the origin of the team name. Mr. Swanson says the name *Redskins* refers to the American Indian practice of painting the faces and bodies of warriors with red clay prior to battle. He said the Redskins have always depicted Indians in an honorable fashion and that the team has repeatedly found a "striking amount" of support from fans and the general population.[5]

Another group that has requested name changes is PETA, People for the Ethical Treatment of Animals. Leaders of this group believe the names of some cities and towns promote negative connotations of animals:

> People for the Ethical Treatment of Animals on Tuesday asked Contra Costa supervisors to consider changing the unincorporated town's name to "Unity," in tribute to the Union Oil Company, which employed many East Bay residents through much of the 20th century. The name Rodeo, PETA says, conjures images of a brutal anachronistic sport that glorifies animal cruelty.
>
> …One town leader found "Unity" far less desirable than "Rodeo." The town's name (pronounced ro-*day*-o) is Spanish for "roundup." It acknowledges the annual cattle event that took place every March, after the grazing season, early in the town's history, said Diane Leite, an advisory committee chairwoman.
>
> The *Californio* lore certainly carries a more positive connotation than renaming Rodeo after an oil refinery, she said. After 100 years of heavy industry, the town's land is difficult to develop because of toxic exposure. "We were a cattle town, and it's something to be proud of," she said. "I don't think we should name our town after the oil industry."
>
> PETA's campaign coordinator Lisa Franzetta acknowledged the irony of an animal rights group pushing to commemorate a refining facility. But, she said, the town is certainly free to come up with an alternative. PETA has sought politically correct titles before. The group recently asked officials in Hamburg, Germany, to consider the name

[4]"Council Votes for Redskins to Change Name," by Matthew Cella, *The Washington Times*, January 10, 2002.
[5]Ibid.

"Veggieburg," Franzetta said. And, to no avail, they suggested Fishkill, N.Y. try on "Fishsave" for size.[6]

People may write to advice columnists to get help in responding when they feel insulted by a label, as the following excerpt from a "Miss Manners" column illustrates:

Question: A group of women was giving testimony before a congressional committee regarding an issue of serious concern to them. When it came his turn to question them, a certain Southern senator said, "Mr. Chairman, we've got a lovely group of ladies here. We thank you for your presence. I have no questions."

The senator surely thought he was being gentlemanly, but the women felt they were being patronized and did not hide their displeasure at being referred to as "lovely ladies."

Is it ever correct for a government official, or anyone for that matter, to make such remarks? If not, what would be the proper response to discourage such offenses from being recommitted? This sort of thing seems to occur frequently.

Was the senator rude, or were the women overly sensitive?

Answer: The senator was rude, but not in the purposeful sense of delivering an insult. The manners he used were once considered gracious in any setting, although they are now widely recognized to suggest, when employed in a clearly nonsocial situation, that the chief contribution of ladies is to be decorative.

There is, however, a grandfather clause, by which elderly people who are obviously unaware of changes are not taxed for mild offenses that are well meant. Miss Manners is thinking of closing this down soon, because there has now been ample time for gentlemen to understand changes that began a quarter of a century ago. In any case, politicians usually do not wish to avail themselves of the excuse that they are unaware of what is going on in the modern world.

You did not tell Miss Manners which senator it was, so she will kindly presume that he was not being wily and purposely trivializing their appearance—and in such a way that they probably looked petty and ill-tempered in bristling. It would have been better to reply graciously, "How kind of you, Senator; we gather this means that you fully support what we are saying."[7]

In addition to having emotional reactions about how we are labeled as members of a group, we also have strong feelings about individual names. The

[6]Peter Felsenfeld, "PETA Thinks Rodeo Not PC, Asks Town to Change Its Name." *Contra Costa Times,* October 22, 2003)

[7]Judith Martin, "Time to Say Goodbye to Patronizing Phrases," *Contra Costa Times,* August 14, 1995, p. A-2.

name *Terry*, for example, simply refers to a given person (denotation); still, I may have a positive connotation for the name while you may dislike the name because of a negative experience you had with someone named Terry in your life. *Washington Post Magazine* writer Gene Weingarten says that it is possible to track the historical roots and the popularity of names back to 1900 on a federal database. He writes the following about his concerns that current names are too trendy:

> Increasingly, people are no longer naming children for their ancestors or heroes or even favorite actors or athletes—names with some sense of history or reverence or accomplishment—and are choosing trendy names that to them seem hip or creative.... When you do this, your victim is your own child. I know of a kid, born in the mid-1960's, who used to introduce himself thus: "Hi, my name is Caribou, but you can call me Mike."... For as long as humans have been responsible for naming their offspring, there have been bad names. The 1910 list of names shows many Clarabellas. Ova was somewhat popular, as was Fanny. And a bunch of boys regularly got saddled with Elmer and Thurston. But these are mostly names that have slid into disfavor over the years.... Adolph, for example, was a reasonably popular name that plummeted in popularity after about 1930.[8]

Names and labels help us clearly understand the difference between denotation and connotation. For example, names connected to heritage are often filled with meaning for individuals and cultures. At the end of this chapter, one writer talks about the significance of the names given to him and his friends by their Vietnamese parents and how much is lost when these names become "Americanized." Try Exercise 7.1 (p. 299) to see if you and another person have a disagreement about the connotations of names.

THE POWER OF CONNOTATION

As we have discussed, we have personal connotations for words based on our unique past experiences as individuals; we also have cultural connotations associated with names and words. When the child star Shirley Temple was at the height of her career, thousands of parents named their daughters Shirley after her, but in the succeeding generations, very few did.

Lawyers, generally aware of the power of connotations, will be careful about the words they use to make their cases to a jury. For example, the lawyer for defendant Alex Kelly, who was accused of raping a 16-year-old girl "skillfully managed the information that was presented to the jurors. He often referred

---

[8]Gene Weingarten, "Madisonness," *Washington Post Magazine*, September 21, 2003.

to Kelly's father, who has a plumbing business and real estate investments, and posted a $1 million bond for his son, as 'a plumber.'"[9]

Semanticists, who study the meaning of words, use a tool that allows them to assess the cultural connotations of a word. This tool is called a **semantic differential.** Researchers give a list like the following to groups of people in order to assess the connotative meaning of a word. The word is rated on a scale from one extreme to the other.

semantic meaning of words; different cultural connotations

Fast	…	…	…	…	…	Slow
Strong	…	…	…	…	…	Weak
Beautiful	…	…	…	…	…	Ugly
Active	…	…	…	…	…	Passive
Brave	…	…	…	…	…	Cowardly
Good	…	…	…	…	…	Bad
Powerful	…	…	…	…	…	Powerless

Meaning is based upon three dimensions: Is the word good or bad? Is it active or passive? Is it powerful or weak? Note that all of the polar dimensions given in the semantic differential fit into one of these three categories.

woman is lady

In several classroom studies of the words *lady* versus *woman*, it was discovered that most students see the term *lady* as good, passive, and weak, while the word *woman* is seen as neither good nor bad, but as active and strong. Advertisers commission studies of words to discover if the name they will give to a car, cola, or laundry detergent has positive connotations for their target audiences.

STOP AND THINK

Look at names given to products and businesses. What images do you believe the companies want to have associated with their products or services? Which names do you consider successful, and which names don't work?

We can say that a name or word is just a label and has no effect on us, but consider the following examples:

- When you go into a gift or novelty store, you are likely to see a section of "over the hill" paraphernalia for people who are turning 30, 40, 50, or 60. You know that, logically, when you have a birthday, you are essentially the same biochemical and emotional being you were the day before. Yet when the label *30* or *40* is attached to you, you may suddenly experience a sense of anxiety or mild depression because of the connotations (images) associated with that age. Conversely, ask young children how old they are and they will usually be quite conscious of whether they are 5 or $5\frac{1}{2}$ or $5\frac{3}{4}$ and will use these minute distinctions as status symbols among

[9]William Glabberson, "For Juries, the Truth vs. the Whole Truth," *New York Times,* November 16, 1996.

their peers. People who reach the age of 21 in the United States (the age of full adult privileges) will sometimes say with surprise, "I don't *feel* 21," or "I don't feel different." The main difference is in the label.

- If you believe that abortion is wrong, do you want to be described as *anti-abortion, anti-choice,* or *pro-life?* Do you want to use the word(s) *fetus, products of conception, unborn, preborn,* or *baby?*
- If you believe that abortion is a right, do you want to be described as *pro-abortion, anti-life,* or *pro-choice?* Do you want to use the word(s) *fetus, products of conception, unborn, preborn,* or *baby?*
- Colorado's governor vetoed a "lettuce libel" law that would have let farmers sue anyone who falsely insulted their agricultural products. Now, the produce police have struck in Louisiana, where a new law prohibits "disparagement of any perishable agricultural or aquacultural food product."[10] Could this lead to a Crawfish Anti-Defamation League?
- Leonore Hauck, a managing editor for the *Random House* dictionary division, discussed how definitions change to reflect current sensibilities. "One of the definitions of 'girl' in 1947 was 'a young, unmarried woman.' Today we say, 'a young, immature woman, esp. formerly, an unmarried one.' The word 'formerly' shows you how the meaning has changed, and a note warns the reader, 'Many women today resent being called girls.'"[11]

However, even more recently, the term *girl*—when used by women in a casual conversation—has become acceptable again. "We've taken back the word and are using it the way we want-girl power, girl talk," said Jane Pratt, the 34-year-old editor of her eponymous new magazine, *Jane.* "It's about girls supporting each other and reveling in what's fun about being a girl. . . . Girl power means something different from feminism." Now *girl* crops up throughout pop culture. "Girls rule" emblazons T-shirts. A college women's crew scrawls, "You row, girl" on the side of the team van.[12]

- The Food and Drug Administration "ordered milk labels changed to give Americans a better idea of how much fat is in that glass. Those jugs of 2 percent milk that were labeled 'low-fat' were to be renamed 'reduced fat.' Only 1 percent milk can be called 'low-fat,' while skim milk, the healthiest choice, can be advertised as 'fat-free' or 'nonfat' milk. The change came after consumer advocates complained that Americans were misled into believing milk with 2 percent fat was healthier than it actually is."[13]

In addition, the FDA warns milk and ice cream manufacturers not to use the terms *no hormones* or *hormone free* on their products. Warning letters from the FDA explain that these are false claims because all milk contains

[10]Amy Bernstein, "Eye on the '90s," *U.S. News and World Report,* December 23, 1991, p. 17.
[11]Patricia Holt, "The Woman Who Decides What Goes in Webster's," *San Francisco Chronicle,* October 24, 1991, p. E-5.
[12]Carla Hall, It's a "girl" Thing for Women, *Los Angeles Times,* November 19, 1997, P. A1.
[13]"Milk Cartons to Reflect Clarification of Fat Context," 2002, MooMilk.com (no author).

naturally occurring hormones, and milk cannot be processed in a manner that renders it free of hormones.[14]

- In a budget battle in the state of California, former Governor Pete Wilson apologized to Americans of Welsh ancestry for using the term *welshing on his agreement:*   ~~Contry west of UK - Wales~~

> "If I have offended you or the Welsh community by my comments, I apologize," Wilson said, in an August 9 letter to Rees Lloyd, lawyer for the Twm Sion Cat–Welsh-American Legal Defense, Education & Development Fund.
>
> The term "welsh" is used in a derogatory manner to mean failure to pay what is owed, to go back on one's word, Lloyd said Sunday from the group's Glendale headquarters.
>
> "I recognize the distinct history and pride that makes the Welsh heritage unique, and can assure you that it was not my intention to offend you or your ancestry in any way," Wilson wrote.
>
> Lloyd said the governor's apology ends the dispute.[15]

- Studies investigating the way in which authority status affects perceptions of size have found that prestigious titles lead to height distortions. In one experiment conducted on five classes of Australian college students, a man was introduced as a visitor from Cambridge University in England. However, his status at Cambridge was represented differently in each of the classes. To one class, he was presented as a student; to a second class, a demonstrator; to another, a lecturer; to yet another, a senior lecturer; to a fifth, a professor. After he left the room, each class was asked to estimate his height. It was found that with each increase in status, the same man grew in perceived height by an average of a half inch, so that as the "professor" he was seen as two and a half inches taller than as the "student."[16]

- Dennis Baron, professor of English and linguistics at the University of Illinois at Urbana-Champaign, notes the following: "McDonald's wants Merriam-Webster to take its McJob and shove it. McDonald's CEO Jim Cantalupo is steamed that the latest edition of *Merriam-Webster's Collegiate Dictionary* defines "McJob" as low-paying, requiring little skill, and providing little opportunity for advancement. Three years ago, the *American Heritage Dictionary of the English Language* ran a similar definition, and the *Oxford English Dictionary* includes "unstimulating" in the mix of descriptors branding McJobs as dead-end. Cantalupo calls such negative definitions "a slap in the face" to American restaurant workers. . . . Merriam-Webster announced that it was sticking by its definition,

---

[14]"FDA Warns Milk Producers to Remove "Hormone Free" Claims From the Labeling of Dairy Products" U.S. Food and Drug Administration www.fda.gov, September 12, 2003.
[15]Associated Press report, *Contra Costa Times,* August 14, 1995, p. A-7.
[16]Robert B. Cialdini, *The Psychology of Persuasion* (New York: William Morrow, 1993), p. 223.

which reflects the way McJob has been used for at least 17 years. Dictionary editors regularly include words far more controversial and offensive because their job is to record how the rest of us use our language, and we don't always use it politely.[17]

- In the continuing debate over immigration, people of varying points of view choose different terms to describe the issue. Note the difference in connotation in the following terms: *guest workers, undocumented workers, migrant workers, undocumented folks, undocumented immigrants, illegal immigrants, illegal aliens.* The term chosen by a speaker or writer is a strong indicator of the viewpoint he or she takes on this issue.

REIFICATION: WHEN WORDS TAKE ON MORE POWER THAN REALITY

making something abstract more real

Imagine yourself subject to a classroom experiment. You are sitting in class, about to see a film. To make the session more festive, your instructor gives you crackers and a homemade paté to munch as you view the movie. You enjoy the hearty taste of this snack, and when the film is over and the lights go back on, you ask for the recipe. Your teacher then informs you that you have been eating dog biscuits with canned cat food on top.

If you are like many people, you may experience a sense of nausea and disgust, though some cat food and dog food is perfectly edible for humans and is more nutritionally balanced than most fast food. But the labels put on this food, the words themselves, not the actual products, might make you sick.

In the same way, some people feel special when they are served expensive caviar or sweetbreads. The fact that they are eating fish eggs or cow organs has no jarring effect on them because there are such powerful, positive connotations associated with the names of these foods.

Reification occurs when words themselves become more powerful and influential than objective reality. It involves treating words—which are abstract symbols—as if they were concrete realities. It leads to human foibles such as those found in the following examples and readings:

- Paying more money for "name brands" that may have the same ingredients as generic brands of products.
- Feeling confident when wearing designer label jeans or unworthy when wearing possibly higher quality jeans that don't carry the popular label.
- Feeling like you can't succeed in a math or writing course because a teacher in fourth grade said you were "poor in math" or because of one previous grade.
- Feeling overweight even when you are at or below your ideal weight because you were called fat years ago. (Karen Carpenter, a singer who died

[17]Dennis Baron, "McLanguage Meets the Dictionary." *Chronicle of Higher Education,* 50 (17): B-14.

Calvin and Hobbes © Watterson. Dist. by Universal Press Syndicate. Reprinted with permission. All rights reserved.

of complications of anorexia nervosa, was reportedly very upset about a critic who referred to her as overweight, and that label may have contributed to her obsession with her weight.)

- Two people having a perfectly pleasant conversation at a party until one person mentions that he or she works as a therapist, professor, doctor, minister, or judge, which then makes the other person uncomfortable.
- In "primitive" cultures, being subject to stomach cramps because you know that someone is sticking needles in a doll with your name on it. Or in "sophisticated" cultures, creating hotel elevators that go from floor 12 to floor 14, leaving out the (presumably unlucky) thirteenth floor. (Note that this arrangement is especially true in hotels that house gambling casinos, presumably filled with people concerned about maximizing their "luck.")

THERE'S A SUCKER BORN IN EVERY MEDIAL PREFRONTAL CORTEX

Clive Thompson

When he isn't pondering the inner workings of the mind, Read Montague, a 43-year-old neuroscientist at Baylor College of Medicine, has been known to contemplate the other mysteries of life: for instance, the Pepsi Challenge. In the series of TV commercials from the 70's and 80's that pitted Coke against Pepsi in a blind taste test, Pepsi was usually the winner. So why, Montague asked himself not long ago, did Coke appeal so strongly to so many people if it didn't taste any better?

Over several months this past summer, Montague set to work looking for a scientifically convincing answer. He assembled a group of test subjects and, while monitoring their brain activity with an M.R.I. machine, recreated the Pepsi Challenge. His results confirmed those of the TV campaign: Pepsi tended to produce a stronger response than Coke in the brain's ventral putamen, a region thought to process feelings of reward. (Monkeys, for instance, exhibit activity in the ventral putamen when they receive food for completing a task.) Indeed, in people who preferred Pepsi, the ventral putamen was five times as active when drinking Pepsi than that of Coke fans when drinking Coke.

In the real world, of course, taste is not everything. So Montague tried to gauge the appeal of Coke's image, its "brand influence," by repeating the experiment with a small variation: this time, he announced which of the sample tastes were Coke. The outcome was remarkable: almost all the subjects said they preferred Coke. What's more, the brain activity of the subjects was now different. There was also activity in the medial prefrontal cortex, an area of the brain that scientists say governs high-level cognitive powers. Apparently, the subjects were meditating in a more sophisticated way on the taste of Coke, allowing memories and other impressions of the drink—in a word, its *brand*— to shape their preference. (emphasis added)

Pepsi, crucially, couldn't achieve the same effect. When Montague reversed the situation, announcing which tastes were of Pepsi, far fewer of the subjects said they preferred Pepsi. Montague was impressed: he had demonstrated, with a fair degree of neuroscientific precision, the special power of Coke's brand to override our taste buds.

The *New York Times Magazine,* October 25, 2003. Copyright © 2003 by Clive Thompson/ Featurewell.com. Reprinted by permission of David Wallis as agent for Clive Thompson.

The "magical" power of words is also discussed by social psychologist Robert Cialdini as he explains why businesses create contests in which participants are asked to write short essays praising their products:

> Another common way for businesses to cash in on the "magic" of written declarations occurs through the use of an innocent looking promotional device. Before I began to study weapons of social influence, I used to wonder why big companies such as Procter & Gamble and General Foods are always running those "25-, 50-, 100 words or less" testimonial contests. They all seem to be alike. The contestant is to compose a short personal statement that begins with the words, "Why I like..." and goes on to laud the features of whatever cake mix or floor wax happens to be at issue. The company judges the entries and awards some stunningly large prizes to the winners. What had puzzled me was what the companies got out of the deal. Often the contest requires no purchase; anyone submitting an entry is eligible. Yet, the companies appear to be strangely willing to incur the huge costs of contest after contest. The type of product doesn't matter; the process is the same. Participants voluntarily write essays for attractive prizes that they have only a small chance to win. But they know that for an essay to have any chance of winning at all, it must include praise for the product. So they find praiseworthy features of the product and

Very interesting; believing in one's own abstract idea of a product

describe them in their essays. The result is...hundreds of thousands of people in America who testify in writing to the product's appeal and who, consequently, experience that "magical" pull to believe what they have written.[18]

Sometimes reification can cause life-or-death consequences; superstitious and confused thinking can get people into deep trouble. Consider the story of a 25-year-old Frenchman, Lucien Schlitz, and his 19-year-old first mate, Catherine Plessz, who set out on a long cruise for the tropics aboard a 26-foot steel cutter called the *Njord*. They started in the Mediterranean Sea, which was so rough that it put the boat on its side. The boat righted itself, but later a freak wave swept over the boat and both Lucien and Catherine found themselves in the water. Through desperate efforts, both managed to get back on board, but they no longer had a rudder (steering mechanism), so they were adrift.

The boat was still whole even though it had been knocked around by the storm. It would seem, to our clear, dry heads, that the logical thing would be to remain on board with the comforts of food, water, and blankets and to wait for help. But Lucien's mind was stressed and fatigued and he began to think obsessively about the life raft. He was terribly concerned that it wouldn't inflate, so he pulled it open, nearly losing it to the wind in the process. Since it measured six feet across, he couldn't fit it in the cockpit, so he moored it to the back of his steel boat.

> Soon after that, by mental processes that would surely be a feast for any psychologist, the only solution that seemed left to Lucien and Catherine was to take refuge in the *life* raft which represented safety (emphasis added)—still, as we see it, in a pattern of psychological aberration which explains the inevitability of everything they did.... Lucien and Catherine had now sought safety in their life raft after throwing into it some tinned food, some distress flares, two 20-litre jerricans of water, a compass and the leather sack with their money and their papers. Then the line linking them to the *Njord* parted.[19]

Over the next days, Lucien and Catherine needlessly suffered great thirst, hunger, sleep deprivation, and cold from being frequently tossed into the water by the waves upsetting the raft. On the twelfth day,

> just as they had decided that survival was too difficult and they would make a quick end to it by drinking all the rest of their water at once for a last sensation of well-being, they were spotted at fifty yards, despite 8 foot troughs, and rescued by a cargo ship.[20]

---

[18]Baron, p. 80.
[19]Bernard Robin, *Survival at Sea* (Camden, ME: International Marine Publishing Company, 1981), p. 112.
[20]Ibid., p. 114.

This extended example reveals that we can give a word or phrase (in this case, *life raft*) power of its own and make faulty decisions based on that word or phrase.

SKILL

Recognize the power we can attach to words. Pause and consider the facts, knowing how labels can be deceiving.

MEANINGS ARE IN PEOPLE

General semanticists, who study the effects of words on people, have articulated some key principles to guide our responsible use of words.

Their main principle is the following: *The word is not the thing.* They use the analogy of a map (the words) showing a particular territory (reality). The map can give us information about the territory, but it is only a visual representation of the territory and it can never show all the details of the territory. Our responsibility as thinkers is to realize that words are limited and to check out the territory before we draw hasty conclusions. If Lucien and Catherine, the sailors just discussed, had had the strength and wisdom to think over their options, they would have realized that, though their inflatable raft was *called* a life raft, their lives were more secure if they remained on board their cutter and sent up flares from there, saving the raft for use as a second vessel. In fact, the sailboat *Njord* was found adrift, but sound and dry, many days before Lucien and Catherine were rescued from their ordeal.

The meaning of words lies in people and not, magically, in the words themselves. Misunderstandings of words and phrases can be clearly seen when people speak different languages, as illustrated in the following news feature.

CASE CLOSED: BLADDER THREAT, NOT BOMB

Drunken German Served 9 Months

Warren Richey

FORT LAUDERDALE, FLORIDA—A drunk German tourist who triggered a bomb scare as he tried to tell a frightened flight attendant that he really, really, really had to go to the bathroom was a free man on Wednesday after more than nine months in prison.

Johann Peter Grzeganek, 23, told a judge in federal court in Fort Lauderdale that it was all a misunderstanding.

He said when he warned a flight attendant that when it was "going to explode," he was referring to his bladder, not the plane.

The pilot wasn't taking any chances. He turned the plane around, dumped his fuel, and returned to Fort Lauderdale airport.

The plane was searched. No bomb.

Grzeganek was charged with knowingly making a false bomb threat on an aircraft in flight, a crime that carries a 20-year minimum mandatory sentence with no parole.

Faced with the prospect of growing old in prison, Grzeganek agreed to plead guilty to four lesser charges.

Unable to make his bond, he remained in prison waiting for his day in court, which arrived Wednesday.

Prosecutors came to the sentence hearing prepared to ask Chief U.S. District Judge Norman Roettger to keep Grzeganek behind bars for two to three years.

Roettger had a different idea. The chief judge, who understands German, read in court a letter Grzeganek wrote from his cell.

Grzeganek, who speaks little English, admitted to having been drunk the night of the flight. He said he drank heavily in part because he fears flying.

He also said he needed to use a bathroom. When the need became an emergency, he sought relief. The plane was in a steep climb at the time. An English-speaking flight attendant stopped him. He told her in German, according to his letter, "I have to go to the bathroom, my bladder is full and going to explode."

The attendant, Beate Westerhouse, testified it appeared Grzeganek was drunk and preparing to urinate in the aisle.

Westerhouse told him to get back in his seat.

"He said, 'No, no, no, the roof would go'" Westerhouse said.

"I took this to mean that something would make the roof explode," she said.

Roettger asked if she had ever heard the German phrase: "Then the roof flies." It is a colloquialism, Roettger said, that means a person needs to use a bathroom.

Roettger sentenced Grzeganek to time served.

Fort Lauderdale Sun-Sentinel. Copyright © 1993. Reprinted by permission of the publisher.

Cross-cultural confusions are not unusual. Some linguistic theorists and scholars believe that our language profoundly shapes our perception of culture. Edwin Sapir and Benjamin Whorf created the Sapir-Whorf hypothesis, which states that language both reflects and affects our view of reality. To some extent, we are trained to see the world based on the language we learn. For example, most languages have words that represent and create a unique awareness of the world. Georgina Pattinson writes for BBC News about Adam Jacot de Boinod's book *The Meaning of Tingo*, in which the author gives many examples of words and phrases with no English equivalent. The Japanese have the term *katahara itai*, which indicates the action of laughing so much that one side of your abdomen hurts; the German's say *Kummerspeck*—literally, "grief bacon"—to describe the excess weight gained from emotion-related overeating, and the Dutch have the word *Ultwaaien* for "walking in windy weather for fun." Albanians have 27 separate expressions for a moustache. For Hawaiians, a *kualanapuhi* is an officer who keeps the flies away from the sleeping king by waving a brush made of feathers. *Tingo* comes from the Easter Island language of Pascuense and means "to borrow objects from a friend's house, one by one, until there's nothing left."[21]

Jacot de Boinod used over 280 dictionaries and 140 websites to compile his list of words and phrases, and he is convinced that a country's dictionary says more about culture and national character than a guide book. Hawaiians, for instance, have 108 words for sweet potato, 65 for fishing nets, and 47 for banana.[22]

We can see that phrases and words do frame experience for individuals and cultures. If someone sees subtle differences in moustaches and sweet potatoes, he or she is seeing a different reality than someone who doesn't. Most professions also involve learning a complex vocabulary. While many laypersons may know the words *cells* and *carcinoma* (cancer of the epithelial cells), doctors, researchers, and other medical professionals learn to distinguish squamous cell carcinomas from adenocarcinoma of glandular cells and from carcinoma of transitional cells. Their training teaches them to recognize and identify abnormalities so that they can prescribe the best courses of treatment for their patients. They have been taught to "see" the world differently. In a similar way, musicians, athletes, lawyers, stockbrokers, dancers, and a host of other specialists expand their perceptions of reality through technical vocabularies.

Our frames of reference, our unique windows on the world, are influenced by our culture, our expectations, personalities, values, experiences, ages, genders, and education. Even when people speak the same language, misunderstandings frequently occur because of what words mean to different individuals. Dictionary definitions are useful for providing knowledge, but they often fall short in creating understanding among people. For example, *Webster's New International Dictionary* may define *love* as "a deep and tender feeling of affection for, or attachment or devotion to, a person or persons," but we can't rely on that definition when a significant other says, "I love you."

We need instead to find out what the word *love* means to an individual. Does it mean, "I want to marry you," "I enjoy your company," "I love every person and you're a person," "I will always be with you no matter what happens," or something else?

SKILL

Realize that meanings are in people. Ask, "What do you mean?" whenever a word or phrase is unclear or is a potential source of misunderstanding.

[21]Georgina Pattinson, *BBC News Magazine,* 26 September, 2005. "Tingo, Nakkele, and Other Wonders,"
[22]Ibid.

The skill of clarifying what a word or phrase means to someone else may seem so simple as to be insulting to your intelligence, and yet it is one of the most valuable and underused skills we have. We are inclined to make assumptions when we hear a phrase, a political speech, or a commercial message; we tend to believe that what the other person means is what we would mean if we had used those words.

Assumptions are common with the use of relative terms, such as *cold, hot, probable, generous, inexpensive,* or *beautiful*; there are also relative phrases, such as *a short distance, light housekeeping,* or *an easy test*. These words seem to have a general meaning but often mean different things to different people. For example, if your friend wants you to meet her at class "early" and gives you no further explanation, it's possible that one of you may arrive a few minutes before class starts and the other may be waiting there for an hour.

Our tendency to project our own meaning onto the words of others explains why we are so often disappointed with blind dates ("This person is wonderful"), political candidates ("I care about the 'little people' in America") or products ("Pimples virtually disappear!"). We really want to believe there is the perfect date, political solution, or pimple formula for us. Sometimes we don't take time to question what the people who say these words really mean, as illustrated in the following article.

SURE I'M COMMITTED...OOPS...BYE-BYE

Dr. Laura Schlessinger

Simply saying words such as *committed* or *love* does not mean there actually is commitment or love. Then why say the words? Because of the instant gratification brought upon by such declarations; gratifications like sex or enhanced (temporary, of course) sense of self. Listen to Cliff.

Cliff, thirty-nine, is in a difficult situation right now. He's been dating a twenty-seven-year-old woman for two and a half months. That's ten weeks of weekends they spent together, amounting to about twenty days of actual contact time.

"We had a committed relationship and it seemed like our relationship was made in heaven. Then she was diagnosed with lupus and I went over to talk with her and tried to explain my feelings."

"What feelings are those, Cliff?"

"That I can't marry her because of her health condition."

"I guess you only enjoy relationships when they look like they're made in heaven, and don't come burdened with the realities of earth."

"Well, I suppose. Maybe 'made in heaven' was a poor choice of words."

"No, I imagine it accurately expresses that you like your relationship pretty and neat."

"Well, yeah."

"Cliff, I don't know if you're ever going to find a perfect situation with nothing unpleasant or challenging to deal with, but I guess you could just move on and keep trying."

"If we were already married, it would be a life-long commitment and that would be different."

"You already used the word *committed* before. You said you were committed already."

"I didn't mean that really."

"I guess you really meant the sex was good and she was fun."

"Is there a way to explain my feelings to her?"

... "Realistically, there isn't much between you. Your predicament shows why infatuation and recreational sex should not be used as criteria for the notion of commitment. You are at the point of committed to good sex, good times, good fun, good feelings."

... Cliff had sex, which I think ought to be serious business, and told his lady he was committed; when there was an opportunity to show that the commitment meant something, he showed it meant nothing.

Often, the cause of projecting our personal meanings to words spoken by others may lie in our emotional need to believe that something is true; other times, we are just untrained or too busy or lazy to pursue the reality of what is being said to us. And sometimes speakers or writers make things so confusing that it takes a grand effort to understand them. Consider a report that reads: "We have confirmed that the overturning of the presidential veto to create an amendment protecting the flag has been enforced."

In states where voters are given choices about public policies through propositions, there is often confusion in the wording of these propositions. For example, a number of years ago, in California, if you voted *yes* on a particular proposition, that meant you were saying *no* to nuclear power plant expansion; if you voted *no,* that meant you were saying *yes* to this expansion. More recently a *yes* vote on a proposition meant that you were voting *no* to big box stores, and a *no* vote meant that you were voting *yes* to big box stores. When ballot measures are confusing, voters may end up casting votes they don't really mean.

To help us defend against words that don't clearly represent reality, we will examine four common problems with language: vagueness, ambiguity, doublespeak, and weasel words. We will focus especially on the deliberate exploitation of these problems by advertisers, salespersons, politicians, and others.

THE PROBLEM OF VAGUENESS

A word or phrase is *vague* when its meaning is unclear. **Vagueness** is a common problem in public discourse. Some politicians will use only vague, abstract terms that have generally positive connotations and not define what they mean, hoping that each listener will like the sound of the promises being made. When asked for specific details about their plans, they may commit the fallacy of "ignoring the question" (see the first example that follows). Conversely, sincere politicians will say they have a plan for "increased aid to the needy" and then define what they mean by *aid,* what they mean by *the needy* and then what, precisely, they have in mind.

Good reporters will notice vague language and press politicians and other policy makers to explain themselves. If they explain using only more vague, abstract terms, be careful about supporting them (because you don't know what you're supporting).

Example

Reporter: Mr. Candidate, you mentioned you have a comprehensive plan to deal with our terrible traffic problems. Can you tell us what is involved in this plan?

Candidate: Gladly. I plan to use all available resources to create a wide-range solution to this problem that has plagued us for years.

Reporter: Can you be more specific? Are you planning expansions, and would these cause greater tolls or taxes for the citizens?

Candidate: As I've said, the program will be really comprehensive and each citizen will be considered and served. If I'm elected, you're going to see some incredibly positive changes.

This candidate appears bright enough to describe his program in glowing terms, but he is unwilling or unable to detail what he is actually proposing. Perhaps the candidate hasn't formulated a plan, or perhaps he avoids giving details about his plans for fear of alienating special-interest groups.

Example

Family: Can you tell us if this operation on our mother's hip is dangerous and also, will she have use of her leg afterward?

Surgeon: All surgery has risks and these things are always hard to predict.

Family: Well, can you give us typical recovery rates and times?

Surgeon: Each person is different, but you can rest assured we are doing everything in our power to help.

In this example, everything the surgeon said may be true, but she has not provided any statistics or details to help the family feel at ease. Health care professionals are busy people, and they can't afford to make promises they may not be able to keep; still, you need to press for information so you can make the best decisions for your health and the well-being of your loved ones.

Darlene: Paul, I really love you, and I think it would be good for our relationship if we started seeing other people.

Paul: What are you saying? Do you want to break our engagement?

Darlene: No, nothing like that. I just think it would be healthy for us to date other people.

> *Paul:*   Are you interested in seeing someone else?
> *Darlene:*   No, not at all. I think we'd both just grow more if we were able to experience a variety of relationships.
> *Paul:*   What does that mean?
> *Darlene:*   Well, it means I still love you but I just think it would be great for our relationship if we saw other people too.

In this situation, Darlene is either confused about what she wants or is sure of what she wants but doesn't know how to tell Paul. He needs to keep pressing for specifics for the sake of his mental health and so that he can have the information he needs to assess the relationship.

Examples of Commercials with Vague Wording

"Get your clothes a whiter white and a brighter bright!"
"Smoke Winters—with cool, smooth flavor!"
"It's the real thing!"
"The Hugo Company: We care about people."

By this time, you should be identifying vagueness in language, and how advertisers, like politicians, use positive connotations to excite the audience. But the question remains: What are they talking about?

The preceding examples are meant to show how frustrating it can be to get people to move from the nonspecific to the concrete so that we can really understand what they are saying. Some people are purposefully vague; others just have a hard time expressing themselves or knowing exactly what they want to communicate. Still, critical thinkers need to persist in understanding what is meant by vague words and phrases; then, any decisions about voting, having surgery, continuing a relationship, or buying a product can be made rationally.

AMBIGUITY IN LANGUAGE

Ambiguity in language can also cause problems in communication. A word or expression is ambiguous when it has two or more different meanings. Unlike vague terms, ambiguous terms do have specific definitions, but they are phrased in a way that makes the correct definition unclear to the reader or listener. Often, riddles use ambiguity to create a puzzling situation; one common riddle asks you to turn the following drawing into a six by adding just one line:

IX

The answer, reflecting one of several types of "sixes" is

SIX

Ambiguity is also the problem in these humorous, but real, headlines compiled by Jay Leno and others:

"Drought Turns Coyotes to Watermelons."[23]
"Need Plain Clothes Security. Must Have Shoplifting Experience."[24]
"Foreclosure Listings: Entire State of New Jersey Available."[25]
"Red Tape Holds Up New Bridges."[26]
"Police Begin Campaign to Run Down Jaywalkers."[27]
"Hospitals Are Sued by 7 Foot Doctors."[28]

In England, similarly ambiguous signs have been seen:

"Automatic Washing Machines: Please remove all your clothes when the light goes out." (Notice in a Laundromat)
"After tea break, staff should empty the teapot and stand upside down on the draining board." (Notice in an office)
"The farmer allows walkers to cross the field for free, but the bull charges." (Notice in a field)

On a more serious note, ambiguity in language is confusing and causes numerous communication problems. We discussed in Chapter 6 how ambiguity is central to the fallacy of equivocation, in which a speaker changes the meaning of a key term in order to win a point. Ambiguity can also create difficulties when no argument is involved, as in the following example:

Former FBI director J. Edgar Hoover was reading a typed copy of a letter he had just dictated to his secretary. He didn't like the way she had formatted the letter, so he wrote on the bottom, "Watch the borders," and asked her to re-type it. The secretary did as she was instructed and sent it off to all top agents. For the next two weeks FBI agents were put out on special alert along the Canadian and Mexican borders.[29]

Drabble® by Kevin Fagan. Reprinted by permission of United Feature Syndicate, Inc.

[23]Jay Leno, *Headlines* (New York: Warner Books, 1989), p. 99.
[24]Ibid., p. 148.
[25]Ibid., p. 48.
[26]"Ms-Sam-Antics Daffynitions," 2001, mssamantics.us/wordplay/newspaper.htm
[27]Ibid.
[28]Ibid.
[29]Roger von Oech, *A Whack on the Side of the Head* (New York: Warner Books, 1990), p. 114.

Ambiguous language can be especially perplexing between cultures. As we discussed previously, many expressions common to speakers of one language group (or subculture) are misunderstood by members of other cultures. When asked if they would like more coffee, some English-speaking people respond, "No, thanks. I'm fine." People who are learning the language can't understand what seems to be a report on the state of one's health as an answer to a question about more coffee.

As in all cases of possible confusion in language, a critical thinker should consider alternative meanings to words and phrases and clarify terms by asking, "What do you mean?" (See Exercise 7.2).

DOUBLESPEAK, INCLUDING WEASEL WORDS

[handwritten: Words that are intentionally misleading or ambiguous]

We have seen how vagueness and ambiguity in language can be used either unintentionally or deliberately to make issues cloudy. Words can also be deceptive in other ways. In this section, we will look at doublespeak and its subcategory weasel words.

Doublespeak is "language used to lie or mislead while pretending to tell the truth. . . . It is used by the highest elected officials, by bureaucrats in state and local government, by members of industry, academia, and other areas of society in order to deceive, to make the bad seem good, the negative appear positive, the disastrous seem tolerable."[30] If language is the map, as general semanticists like to say, and reality is the territory, then doublespeak is the creation of a map that distorts the territory. Those who hear doublespeak are deceived and misled about the territory because of the deceptive map.

In his popular book *Doublespeak,* William Lutz claims that doublespeak is

a very conscious use of language as a weapon or tool by those in power to achieve their ends at our expense. While some doublespeak is funny, much of it is frightening. We laugh and dismiss doublespeak as empty or meaningless words at our own peril, for, as George Orwell saw so clearly, the great weapon of power, exploitation, manipulation and oppression is language. It is only by being aware of the pervasiveness of doublespeak and its function as a tool of social, economic and political control that we can begin to fight those who would use language against us.[31]

One of the most common forms of doublespeak is **euphemism,** which means the use of a less direct but more acceptable term to describe an event, person, or object. In their daily use, euphemisms are not usually meant to deceive and to distort, but to soften harsh realities. We use euphemisms to explain disease and death to children when we make such statements as, "Aunt Sofia isn't

[handwritten: euphemism: use of a mild word to describe something]

---

[30] Position Paper, National Council of Teachers of English, 1988.
[31] William Lutz, *Doublespeak* (New York: HarperCollins, 1989), pp. xii–xiii.

feeling well today, so she's in the hospital," or "Grandma passed away." We may use euphemisms to sound better when we describe ourselves as *slender* (instead of skinny), *full-bodied* (instead of fat), or *under a lot of stress* (instead of irritable). Euphemisms may also be employed by advertisers to avoid being sued for using terms that have been trademarked. Complications may also arise when organizations try to trademark euphemisms. For example, the NFL has a trademark on the term Super Bowl, and advertisers are forbidden to use the phrase to promote products like televisions and snack foods. Many advertisers turned instead to euphemisms such as "The Big Game." Much to the bewilderment of both advertisers and sports writers, the NFL is now trying to trademark the "Big Game" euphemism, so that others can't make any specific reference to the Super Bowl.

Euphemisms are common in education. A teacher might use the euphemism "We're going to have a quiz" to announce a 50-item exam, reasoning that students would not panic studying for a "quiz" as much as they would for a "test" and therefore they would do better. Yet, students might prefer a 10-item test to a 50-item quiz. Similarly, parents may be told that their child is "having some problems with math" to soften the blow of a failing grade.

Euphemism as doublespeak is common in business and government. In some cases, the euphemisms chosen become another category of doublespeak, which Lutz terms *inflated language*. Inflated language is designed to make the commonplace seem extraordinary or to make simple things more complex than they are. Following are some examples compiled by the National Council of Teachers of English:

Fired: dehired, nonrenewed, nonretained, selected out
Layoffs: negative employee retention, workforce adjustments, headcount
　　reductions, career alternative enhancement program
Pain: discomfort
Death: terminal living, negative patient care outcome (or "That person is
　　no longer a patient at this hospital.")
Poor: economically nonaffluent, economically marginalized
Prisoner: client of the correctional system
Lazy: motivationally dispossessed

Doublespeak is a form of personal and corporate denial of painful realities. No company wants to be seen as "firing" employees because that term has negative, cruel connotations. People want to be seen as compassionate, so they use terms that present the company in the best possible light. Many professionals use euphemisms to soften or inflate reality. For legal reasons, detectives may term someone a *person of interest* until they can gather enough evidence to change the term to *suspect*. Celebrities use doublespeak for "damage control" when they have said or done something that has solicited negative reactions; for example, when Justin Timberlake grabbed Janet Jackson's dress and exposed her breast during a halftime performance at the Super Bowl, he explained that there had been a "wardrobe malfunction." Real estate agents refer to tiny houses as "darling cottages" or "dollhouses"; they may describe dumps that are falling off of foundations as "needing a little tender loving care."

Reflecting on his experience trying to rent a home in Los Angeles, writer John S. Brady said that he ran into "some truly stunning feats of linguistic gymnastics":

> In the able and utterly shameless hands of one property owner seeking to lure prospective renters, a rundown bungalow fronted by a lumpy, sun-scorched patch of dirt through which, by the looks of it, the entire population of Southern California's moles had at one time or another passed, became a "quaint Craftsman-style house with a spacious yard." An equally creative landlord advertised a place with a "sunny garden." There was only one problem. This particular garden consisted of a lone rose pushing its way valiantly, but ultimately vainly, through the cracks in the concrete pad off the kitchen.[32]

Another form of doublespeak has been called **spin.** Spin is the favourable appearance given to matters—often political—by "spin doctors."[33]

Spin is used to put the words and behavior of people in a positive light so that a positive reaction may result or a negative reaction may be minimized. Often spin is linked with the notion of damage control. When politicians or celebrities say or do something that may hurt them in the public eye, they seek to reframe the truth in a more acceptable way. Just as someone puts spin on a ball (like a bowling ball, baseball, or billiard ball) to change direction, spin doctors cast a spin on words and actions to influence their direction.

Sometimes spin comes in the form of vague phrases that deflect responsibility, such as "I don't recall saying that," "I can't imagine saying that," "We need to move on from that," "I won't be discussing that," "I won't stoop to discussing those allegations," "I can't comment on that," "You're misinterpreting what I said," or "That was the alcohol speaking, and I'm going to enter rehab."

Professor Steven Doloff has created some linguistic fallacies—along with their Latin names—that illustrate political and journalistic spin quite well:

1. Si anas est, tetrinnit: "If it's a duck, expect it to quack": This is when politicians use any question at all asked by an interviewer to recite a self-serving prepared statement on some issue. Even though the lack of connection between the question and the answer can sometimes be quite striking, this tactic is nevertheless exceedingly common. Defenders of this verbal groundshifting might say that the interviewees are only "reframing" bad questions....Politicians, however, almost never take overt issue with even the most biased questions (by saying, for example, "I think that's a misleading or unfair question because..."). In fact, they frequently say, "That's a very good question" and then go on to deliver their unrelated responses.

[32]John S. Brady, "Waiting for the Big One" *Chronicle of Higher Education,* November 4, 2003.
[33]www. phrasefinder/uk.org

Change of fact occurring based on daily speculation

2. *Ludicra exercitatio facilis est; res civilis, difficilis:* "Athletics is simple; politics, complex": This is when journalists cover political events as "sports," focusing almost exclusively on daily public-opinion polls and speculating on one side or another's constantly shifting chances of "victory." Because poll statistics are "facts" in a very shallow kind of way, they are offered as easily understood "news" of daily winners and losers. Does this kind of political handicapping help the public? Yes, if people literally are betting on election or legislative results; no, if people want any informative analyses of politicians, platforms, positions, or political track records to assist them in choosing for whom to vote.

keen = enthusiasm; giving to the public a preoccupation that will generate interest

3. *Homo in speculo interrogat:* "The person in the mirror has a question": This is when news interviewers attribute to the public a preoccupation with something that the media themselves are <u>keen</u> on because they hope it will generate a marketable amount of public interest. When reporters declare to politicians or other celebrities that "many people" are saying something provocative or asking some embarrassing personal question about them, what they really mean is "we are saying or asking those provocative things because it's our job to think up hot-button questions." I can't figure out why celebrities don't regularly respond to such queries with, "I haven't heard anyone except you guys say or ask that. Exactly who are you quoting, anyway?"

one word emotionally charged used all over again

4. *Verbum unum mille argumentationibus aequiparat:* "One word is worth a thousand arguments": This is when public speakers mine their speeches, arguments, or remarks with one emotionally charged or coded word or phrase, timed to explode at frequent intervals. The purpose is to regularly return to such words and reduce the audience's potentially complicated feelings about a controversial subject (presumably under rational discussion) to an irrational gut response. That term could be socialist or fascist or liberal or welfare mother or stormtrooper or ACLU or Rush. Maximum use of the term is the point—not cogent argument, which is much harder to do.[34]

In argumentation it is often said that "Whoever defines the terms, wins the debate." Policy makers often struggle to choose the words that will put the best spin on their policies or actions. The Bush administration used the word *surge* to describe the order for 21,500 more soldiers to go to Iraq in 2007. Democrats countered by calling the surge an *escalation*; Secretary of State Condoleeza Rice countered by changing the term to *augmentation*, "an augmentation that allows the Iraqis to deal with this very serious problem that they have in Baghdad."[35]

Frank Luntz, a pollster, focus group master, and author of the book *Words That Work: It's Not What You Say, It's What People Hear*, said that

> the word "surge" puts focus only on the numbers of soldiers in Iraq, rather than the mission or what Bush is billing as a change of strategy. "Escalation" causes people to link the Iraq war to the unpopular

[34]"Caveat audiens—"let the listener beware," Steven Doloff, *The Humanist*, January 1997.
[35]Lynn Sweet, "Surge? Escalation? Augmentation? It depends on who's talking." The Sun-Times Newsgroup, suntimes.com (accessed January 14, 2007).

Vietnam conflict. Luntz usually advises Republicans, but the insights about the political use of language are so useful in his book that the new Senate majority whip, Sen. Dick Durbin, made sure that everyone on his press staff got copies.... Each Saturday afternoon, Durbin and the other Senate Democratic leaders teleconference with congressional guests booked on Sunday talk shows. They brief the guests about major themes the leaders want to emphasize and suggest ways to talk about the message, such as calling sending more soldiers to Iraq an escalation and not a surge.[36]

Interestingly, Democrats were also advised not to go on the *Colbert Report*, because Colbert's questions are so incisive that few politicians can be interviewed by him and come out in a positive light.

Doublespeak and spin are used in our personal lives also. If you have children or siblings, you know that a fight is explained differently from each person's viewpoint. A "light tap" to one person ends up being a "big hit" when described by the other. Some women in the business world have complained that when they have made an unpopular decision they are labeled as "aggressive," whereas a favored male counterpart would have been labeled "assertive" or "a strong manager." We may describe a friend of ours who rants and raves at small provocations as "just excitable" or even "dynamic." A favorite line used to control reactions and soften the blow of a breakup is "It's not you. It's me. I'm just not ready for a relationship."

Sometimes it is suggested that a culture should change words to create better connotations. For example, Gail Sheehy, author of popular books on the stages of life, would like to eliminate the word *aging*. "Let's don't even call it *aging* anymore," Sheehy exclaims. "The very word carries pejorative baggage. Let's refer to successful aging as *saging*—the process by which men and women accumulate wisdom and grow into the culture's sages."[37] (See exercise 7.3.)

Other forms of doublespeak include **jargon**, the use of specialized language to exclude or impress people who don't understand the terminology, and **gobbledygook**, which is vague language used to confuse and overwhelm those who hear it. These forms of doublespeak have been labeled *crazy talk* by the late writer and semanticist Neil Postman. He defined crazy talk as talk that reflects "bad" purposes.[38] Postman cited Werner Erhard, the founder of the very successful Erhard Seminars Training (a self-help workshop) as using crazy talk in the following excerpt from an interview:

Sometimes people get the notion that the purpose of Erhard Seminars Training is to make you better. It is not. I happen to think that you are perfect exactly the way you are.... The problem is that people get stuck acting the way they were instead of being the way they are....

[36]Ibid.
[37]Gail Sheehy, *New Passages* (New York: Random House, 1995), p. 420.
[38]Neil Postman, *Crazy Talk, Stupid Talk* (New York: Delacorte, 1976), p. 83.

> The purpose of est training is to transform your ability to experience living so that the situations you have been trying to change or have been putting up with clear up just in the process of living.[39]

Another example of crazy talk is the wording given by some telephone solicitors who tell you that they represent a popular charity. One ploy is to use the vague phrase "I am part of a commercial fundraiser for charitable purposes." In many cases, these individuals are taking the lion's share of your donation for themselves and giving only a small percentage to the group they claim to represent. Critical thinkers should listen carefully between the lines and ask questions about where the funds will go before deciding whether to give money to such solicitors.

Advertisers also use inflated language and gobbledygook to impress consumers. They want to present their products as necessary and in some cases even miraculous, and they have developed the tools to do so in the form of creative doublespeak. According to Carl Wrighter, an advertising copywriter, "Today's advertising industry is the most potent and powerful mass marketing and merchandising instrument ever devised by man."[40] He claims that, even if you think that you're smart enough to see through advertising tricks, you may overlook the subtle power of weasel words.

According to *Webster's New International Dictionary*, a **weasel word** is "a word used in order to evade or retreat from a direct or forthright statement or position." Let's look at how advertisers use these words so that they can make great claims and not have to prove them.

According to Wrighter, the most commonly used weasel word is *help* or *helps*. An ad might claim, "This cream will help prevent acne," or "Our new formula helps the pain to go away." "This mouthwash helps stop the germs," or "This pill helps you feel drowsy so you can sleep." Notice that no one is claiming that the products will prevent acne, make pain disappear, stop germs, or guarantee sleep. They only promise to *help* do those things.

By only promising to help, advertisers relieve the manufacturers of any responsibility for the actual effectiveness of their products. Wrighter says that we don't really hear the word *help;* we hear only the promise, perhaps because we want to believe there are perfect products that will solve our problems. He also believes that 75 percent of advertising uses the word *help*. If that's true, you should be able to detect this weasel word easily. Watch also for modifications of this word such as "significantly helps" or "greatly improves."

Salespeople sometimes use a technique of doublespeak called "What if I could"... Business writer Kelley Robertson gives the following examples used to entice customers to consider buying a product or service:

> "What if I could show you how you could save money, would that be of interest to you?"
> "What if I told you that you could capture more market share, would you like to hear how we can help you do this?"

[39]Ibid.
[40]Carl Wrighter, *I Can Sell You Anything* (New York: Random House, 1972), p. 2.

"What if our system saved you time, would that be of value to you?"
"What if I matched our competitor's price, would you buy it?"[41]

Robertson suggests that salespeople try to directly anticipate and address obstacles that prevent people from buying.

"The real key is to address your prospect's objections during the sales process. This means asking the right questions early in the sales process and positioning your product, service, or solution so that you answer their objections before they express them."[42]

Another prominent weasel word is *like*—the word *like* is used to **romance the product**, which means to make you think about something bigger, better, or more interesting than the product and to associate the product with that better thing. You might think of "romancing the product" as creating a faulty analogy.

(handwritten margin note: like = faulty analogy)

Wrighter gives several examples of romancing the product such as an old Mateus wine ad that claimed that drinking Mateus is like taking a trip to Portugal. When the ad appeared on television, depicting a romantic Portuguese holiday, the target audience was meant to forget that they would be drinking it in their own homes—no beaches, music, or wonderful meals would accompany it like they do in the ad. Other powerful images from the past include "It cleans like a white tornado" or "It's like a great taste explosion in your mouth." Some products are romanced with a name, such as Softique (for tissues) or Beverly Hills, Obsession, or Diamonds (for perfume). Lipton specialty teas have names such as Gentle Orange, Mountain Berry Apple, and Lemon Soother. One ad compares drinking the tea to experiencing a deep massage. Ads for cars romance their product by showing exciting drives through rough terrain or even on the edges of buildings. Often these rides feature encounters with beautiful men and women who are drawn to the person with the great car. (See Exercise 7.4, p. 301.)

Wrighter cites other words besides *help* and *like* that are used to make consumers think that a product is more promising than it actually is. Here are some of the most common:

- *Virtual* or *virtually:* This word means "almost, but not in fact."

"Virtually foolproof"
"Virtually never needs service"
"Virtually trouble-free"

An ad for a "medication tracking system" reads as follows:

Do you worry when a loved one forgets to take daily medication? Or takes too many pills because he or she loses track of the dosage schedule? You can help by giving Medi-Track. This caring gift makes it virtually

---

[41]Kelley Robertson, "Avoid the What Ifs," http://www.businessknowhow.com/marketing/sales-questions.
[42]Ibid.

impossible for medication users to lose track of their schedule—no matter where they happen to be.

- *Acts* and *works:* These words are other forms of *helps* and are often used with the word *help.*

  "Works like magic"
  "Works to help prevent"
  "Acts against"
  "Acts on the cough control center"

- *Can be:* When advertisers say their product *can be* useful they make no definite claim that it will be useful. *Can be* simply means that it is possible. Variations are *could be, might be,* and *may be.*

  "Shine toothpaste can be of significant value when used in a monitored dental program."

- *Up to: Up to* implies a range from zero to the figure that is given. Consumers tend to hear only the larger number.

  "You may have won up to $500."
  "Dude deodorant gives you protection for up to 12 hours."
  "Come to our sale and get up to 50 percent off."

- *As much as:* Similar to *up to, as much as* means that you might get the ultimate benefit described, but you might not.

  "As much as 20 percent greater mileage."
  "Blabble gum gives you as much as an hour more chewing satisfaction than the leading brand."

Also, Wrighter suggests that you be aware of vague terms such as *refreshes, comforts, tackles,* and *fights.* These vague terms have positive connotations that may or may not have a basis in reality when referring to a specific product. Some terms that are commonly used because of their appealing sound but that have no definite meaning include

"Fortified"	"Flavor and Taste"
"Style and Good Looks"	"Different, Special, Exclusive"

Sometimes these terms are strung together:

  "Phitrin: New. Improved. Bigger. Better."

SKILL

Recognize when words are used to deceive and confuse readers and listeners.

Recognizing the problem of misleading commercial claims, the federal government has been making attempts to set clearer standards about the meaning of labels given to foods. Consumers have been confused about the meaning of terms such as *fresh, light, low-fat,* and *cholesterol-free.*

Federal regulations set guidelines for labeling the fat and cholesterol content of products such as yogurt or cheese. One way that food companies can get around these regulations is to shrink the "serving size" given on the package. If the serving size is small enough, then the product can be called "lower in fat" than an identical product with a larger serving size.

[handwritten margin note: serving size = if small, lower fat for example]

We as consumers can't rely on government agencies to clarify our thinking about commercial messages. We need to recognize doublespeak in all of its forms and keep in mind William Lutz's admonishment about advertising:

> Every word in an ad is there for a reason; no word is wasted. Your job is to figure out exactly what each word is doing in an ad—what each word really means, not what the advertiser wants you to think it means. Remember, the ad is trying to get you to buy a product, so it will put the product in the best possible light, using any device, trick, or means legally allowed. Your only defense against advertising is to develop and use a strong critical reading, listening, and looking ability.[43] (See Exercise 7.5, p. 302)

LIFE APPLICATION

Consider the need to "decode" the language of others. When they speak abstractly, ask questions rather than assuming that they mean the same thing you would mean if you used their words. Particularly when you receive an abstract instruction or critique, ask for specifics. For example, if your boss says, "you're not being very careful lately," ask how you can specifically be more careful (rather than assuming a negative interpretation and becoming defensive).

When you speak with others, try to be as clear and unambiguous as possible. Instead of using abstract language about a problem—for example, telling your significant other that he or she is being selfish—make specific requests: "I'd like you to call me more often and spend more time with me on the weekends." People don't know what you'd like unless you ask. If they can't or won't give you what you need, that's important for you to know.

Be direct and polite with requests and complaints. Minimize "qualifiers" that weaken your credibility, such as "if it's not too much trouble" or "I was thinking maybe you might" or "I sort of have a feeling that sometimes"...

Practice the words you will use in a job interview. There are common questions that are frequently asked, such as "Why do you want to work here?" "Tell us about yourself." "What are your greatest strengths and weaknesses?" (When asked about weaknesses, don't use a hidden strength, such as "I'm a perfectionist" or "I can't

---

[43]Lutz, *Doublespeak,* p. 102.

say no to extra work." Most interviewers know those pat answers. Instead, talk about a minor weakness that you have overcome or are in the process of overcoming. That will address the real question without damaging your credibility.

CHAPTER EXERCISES

Exercise 7.1   Purpose: To understand and experience the power of connotations.

1. Meet with a friend, family member, or ideally a "significant other" (boyfriend or girlfriend), and try together to pick out a name for a boy and for a girl that you would both be happy to give to a child. See if in your discussion you can isolate how the connotations of some names are different for both of you because of your memory of different people (denotations).

   When you find a name that you can both agree on, state why. What are the positive connotations that you have for the name, either because of past associations or because of the sound or meaning of the name?

2. Ask your parents or someone else's parents what they had in mind when they chose a name for their son or daughter. Specifically, ask them how they decided upon the name and what connotations they associated with that name.

   Since children often live up to parental expectations, try to assess whether the name had any effect on the child as he or she was growing up. Did the name imply strength, weakness, friendliness, masculinity, or femininity, or did it call forth images of a famous person?

Example

"Shahruz. The very feeling of power, strength, and courage that simple word "shah"—meaning king in English—implies is the reason why most Persian and Urdu male names begin with the word "shah." It is the same reason my parents chose to name my brother "Shahruz," which means "king of the day."...My brother's name was chosen by my maternal grandmother. She chose it mainly since it was "different" from all the other typical Pakistani names she had heard. At the same time, it signified power and strength—two qualities many of us believe that males have or should have. The "ruz" part of his name, meaning "day" in the English language, symbolizes a sort of eternity for kingship. When we say "king of the day," it implies that the reign of the king is endless; that his leadership will go on for day after day until the end. And my eight-year-old brother *does* behave as a royal. Because of his age, I am not certain that his behavior and actions were due to his attempt to live up to his name. However, his qualities and personality match that of any king—leadership, pride, style, authority, courage, and strength. While these characteristics sound positive and necessary, I personally believe that sometimes they can get a little out of hand. Too much leadership and authority in a child can be seen as bossiness, too much pride can make them be known as a show-off, and too much style can be seen as materialism. While my brother is nothing to these extremes, many royal figures are seen as such. Yet any name in my culture including the word "shah" is seen as only positive. The images associated are of high standard and while times have changed and the role and behavior of royalty has changed, the connotations have remained much the same." (by a student)

Exercise 7.2   Purposes: To recognize how vague or ambiguous terms can be misleading and how we can avoid the problems associated with assumptions about meanings. To realize that meanings are in people, not in words.

1. Give an extended example, or several examples, of the use of abstract, ambiguous, or vague terms that are not defined by the writer or speaker. You can find these examples in editorials, political speeches, advertisements, or perhaps when you converse with friends. List the abstract, vague, or ambiguous terms or phrases used and tell how different people could interpret these words in different ways. If possible, extend the exercise by asking someone who is using vague terms to clarify what he or she means by those terms. For further practice, see the discussion questions and suggestions for speech or essay writing at the end of the chapter.

2. Think of some examples of verbal misunderstandings that have occurred in your life or in the life of someone you know. How could the confusion have been avoided? Consider a time when you misunderstood someone's words or instructions.

Example

"I missed an English class and called a friend to get the assignment. She said we had to turn in a copy of a résumé that we might use to apply for a job. Then she said, 'You also need a cover.' I assumed she was using the word cover the way I use it, so I bought a report cover. What she really meant was that we were supposed to have a cover letter introducing ourselves to an employer. The cover letter goes with the résumé.

"I could have avoided these problems by asking what she meant when she mentioned a cover. Or I could have repeated back to her what the assignment was; then she might have caught my error."

3. This exercise should be done in classroom groups.

Assume you have been selected as a citizen's advisory committee to the Supreme Court. Your task is to form a clear definition of one (or more) of the following words or phrases: *obscenity, life, cruel and unusual punishment, competency, marriage,* or *adult.* Your definition will be used to guide future decisions on issues related to these terms.

In your discussion, try to come to a consensus. Whenever possible, resolve disagreements by presenting evidence to clarify positions. You may also give personal examples to increase the understanding of one another's viewpoints.

After you have used the time allotted (at least 20 minutes), choose a member of your group to present your results to the class as a whole. The spokesperson should discuss

- The definitions the group agreed upon.
- The difficulties in coming to consensus and why they occurred. Consider especially how the differing values and experiences of group members affected their desired definitions.

Exercise 7.3   Purpose: To recognize euphemisms and how they are applied.

Try to think of euphemisms that you've heard or used. What are some euphemisms for the following: *selfish, cheap, war, lies, kill?* How about for a badly damaged car that someone wants to sell?

Now try an exercise that British philosopher Bertrand Russell created and called "Conjugating Irregular Verbs." Take a personal characteristic or action and express it favorably, neutrally, and unfavorably, as follows:

Favorable	*Neutral*	*Unfavorable*
I'm slender.	You're thin.	She's skinny.
I'm frugal.	You're careful with money.	He's cheap.

Complete these "conjugations," which all start with a favorable description. Add neutral and unfavorable descriptions for each one.

1. I have high self-esteem.
2. I'm curious about my neighbors.
3. I like to relax.
4. I'm pleasantly plump.
5. I don't like to stifle my child's creativity.
6. I'm not a perfectionist about cleaning.
7. My car has a lot of character.

Exercise 7.4   Purpose: To identify gobbledygook and phrases that romance the product.

An ad for Mercury Sable automobiles featured a silhouette of a dancing couple behind a car.

Explain how the following words, which accompanied the ad, were used to romance the product, and point out the vague gobbledygook that is used to describe the "new" changes in the car.

We dressed in silence.
And drove.
When we walked in,
She said something to the piano player.
Next thing, I hear this song we used to love.

She takes my hand. We dance. And something
that was there before, was back. Only stronger.
Mercury Sable.
The new, remarkably sophisticated Sable.
Its body has been totally restyled.
Its interior so thoroughly redesigned
even the controls are easier to read and reach.
It has standard driver and optional passenger air bags.
It rides smoother. Quieter.
And makes driving more of a pleasure.
The car that started it all,
does it again.

Exercise 7.5   Purpose: To discover weasel words in persuasive messages.

1. Analyze some television, radio, or magazine advertising; campaign literature; or junk mail, specifically looking for doublespeak and weasel words.
Bring samples to share with your class.

    Try to include campaign messages in your search. Look for literature
that comes in the mail dealing with upcoming elections.

    Which particular weasels did you find most often? What effect did
the weasel have on the message—that is, why do you think that the writer
of the message used that weasel?

    Use the following sample ads to get you started:

Having a party and don't know what to serve? Try Tony's Barbequed
Party Wings for that spicy hot partytime action. Our secret sauce has 37
of the world's finest ingredients mixed to virtual perfection and applied
with tender loving care to each piece. So, spice up your next party with
Tony's Party Wings; you'll feel like you're flying high with satisfaction.

    Is your smile an average dull white in an average dull world?
Make the change and brighten your outlook. For that all-day smile,
your teeth deserve the best. Flash toothpaste with ZX-19 can help
whiten and brighten your teeth for up to 8 hours. Stand out from the
crowd—join the Flash generation, and change your dull world into a
Flash world.

    Vote for Richmond for school board. She knows about the latest
classroom technology and can help make our school district the most pro-
gressive in the state. As a parent herself, J. Richmond cares about excellence in education and she shares your concerns. Having J. Richmond on
the board is like having a friend attending the meetings for you.

2. In class groups, create some ads or an extensive "infomercial" for a product. Try to use as many weasel words as possible and use images that
romance the product. Present your commercials to the class either live or
on videotape and see if all of your strategies are detected.

CHAPTER HIGHLIGHTS

1. Critical thinkers should be aware of the power of words to both clarify and obscure issues.
2. Language has a persuasive impact on people because of connotations, the images associated with words and phrases.
3. Reification occurs when words take on more power than reality.
4. The meaning of words is in people.
5. Four common problems with language are vagueness, ambiguity, double-speak, and weasel words.

KEY TERMS

Denotation (p. 271)
Connotation (p. 271)
Semantic differential (p. 275)
Reification (p. 278)
Vagueness (p. 286)
Ambiguity (p. 288)
Doublespeak (p. 290)

Euphemism (p. 290)
Spin (p. 292)
Jargon (p. 294)
Gobbledygook (p. 294)
Weasel word (p. 295)
Romance the product (p. 296)

CHAPTER CHECKUP

Short Answer

1. What should a critical thinker do when the meaning of a word is not clear?
2. How is vagueness used by candidates and advertisers?
3. How are weasel words used to sell products?

Sentence Completion

4. The images associated with a word make up the word's _____.
5. The process of words becoming more powerful than objective reality is called _____.
6. Meanings aren't in words; meanings are in _____.
7. Language used to lie or mislead while pretending to tell the truth is called _____.
8. A less direct but more acceptable term to describe an event, person, or object is a(n) _____.

9. The specific object or act that a word refers to is the word's _____.

10. When a word or expression has two or more meanings and the meaning is unclear, we say that it is _____.

FREE-RANGE? NATURAL? SORTING OUT THE POULTRY LABELS

Suzanne Hamlin

So why did the chicken cross the road?

If it was a free-range chicken, it was probably trying to find the meaning of life.

Consumers, too, are looking for answers, along with lower-fat, higher-protein alternatives to red meat. Poultry consumption is at record levels. In 1993, the last year for which Agriculture Department figures are available, the typical American ate 47 pounds of chicken, up from 26 pounds in 1975. And chicken and turkey together accounted for 32 percent of the total amount of meat consumed in the United States in 1993, up from 19 percent in 1970.

Which raises more questions: What does "free range" mean anyway? Is there a difference between a free-range chicken and an all-natural bird? What qualifies as organic and what as farm-raised?

Welcome to the arcane world of federal labeling regulations, which apply to poultry processors who sell at least 20,000 birds a year. The widespread assumption is that a free-range chicken is a happy-go-lucky bird, gamboling about the barnyard at will, pecking at organic grains until its rendezvous with a wood-burning grill.

But to the labeling division of the Agriculture Department, which sets the definitions and standards for poultry, a free-range bird is one that has access to the outdoors. Period. So a free-range chicken, turkey or duck could be munching on potato chips and drinking antibiotic cocktails and still be legal.

"Free range" was originally a menu term and is generally attributed to Larry Forgione, the chef at An American Place, his restaurant in Manhattan. In the early 80s, when he was at the River Cafe in Brooklyn, he used the term "to describe healthy chickens that were raised on small, local farms," he said.

But Kathy Leddy, a spokeswoman for the agency's labeling division, said that as long as chickens have some way to get out of the coop, they can be considered "free-range" or "free-roaming." When asked how the agency knew if producers were in compliance, she said that they must provide drawings or photographs with arrows pointing to the coops' doors.

A half-dozen large processors contend that free-range may not be such a good thing after all. Randy Day, the vice president for quality assurance at Perdue Farms Inc. in Salisbury, Md., said that sanitary and heated housing and nutritionally balanced feed formulas were the best thing that had ever happened to chickens. "Chickens that roam around outside pecking for food grains in manure are not chickens I would want to eat," he said.

The free-range chicken may or may not be "all natural," a term sanctioned by the Agriculture Department and now in wide use on package labels. Does "all natural" guarantee that a bird has never been fed antibiotics or coloring agents and has not been injected with salt and water?

Ms. Leddy said that it does not.

"The term was first approved by the USDA in 1982 for processed food," she said. "It meant that if additives were part of the product, they could not be artificial."

"For poultry to be 'all natural,' it means that if anything is injected into the chicken at the processing plant, it must be natural," she said. "Salt and water can be added, but not something like sodium phosphate." But "all natural" does not cover a chicken's diet or living conditions before it reaches the processing plant. Many of the chickens sold in this country have been fed coloring agents like marigold petals to make their skin more yellow.

And the majority have had antibiotics added to their feed. They are taken off the antibiotics seven to 14 days before they are killed. Producers contend that this makes them "antibiotic free," a term that is not, incidentally, an official Agriculture Department designation. But if the chicken has never been fed antibiotics, the processor can note that on the package.

What about chickens labeled "no growth hormones used"? That is just stating the obvious. Although the Agriculture Department has approved the use of growth hormones in beef, it has not sanctioned their use in veal, pork or poultry. But drugs, as opposed to hormones, is another matter.

Bacitracin, an antibiotic that is also a growth drug, is part of the feed formula of many chickens, including those processed by Perdue and Bell & Evans. The Agriculture Department, while acknowledging that bacitracin can be a growth drug, characterizes it as an antibiotic, which processors contend is necessary to eliminate disease.

Producers say that new big-breasted breeds, not growth drugs, are the reason birds are bigger these days. Perdue, for one, is proud of its big chickens, bred to grow faster and consume less feed.

"The American public wants more white breast meat," said Day of Perdue, "and we deliver 15 percent more on our birds." The Agriculture Department says that the average four-pound broiler needed 10 weeks and 10 pounds of feed to grow to maturity in 1960. By 1990, a 4-pounder could be produced in six weeks with eight pounds of feed.

And why do some chickens and turkeys labeled "fresh" appear to have just come in from an Arctic storm? They have so many ice crystals in their cavities that pliers are needed just to remove the giblet bag.

To the Agriculture Department, "fresh" is a broad term; it can be applied to any bird that has been stored or transported at anywhere from 36 degrees to zero. It's only when poultry dips below zero that it is considered frozen.

In poultry, "organic" is a term that has no meaning, at least not to the Agriculture Department. Using the strict dictionary definition ("Having the characteristics of, or derived from, living organisms"), all poultry is organic. But neither the Agriculture Department nor any other Federal agency has ever defined the term, so no national standard exists. On poultry labels, only the phrase "raised on feed without pesticides" can be used, the Agriculture Department says.

Stress brought on by harsh living conditions is not monitored by the Agriculture Department, although a chicken cooped up in very little space is probably going to be one tough bird. The poultry industry recommends—but does not require—that each bird be allotted seven-tenths of a square foot of floor space in the chicken coop. The Agriculture Department does not address that issue at all. Unlike laying hens, chickens raised for the table are not kept in individual cages; they can zip around in their seven-tenths of a square foot as freely as they want.

So what can consumers do? There are at least two options. They can write or call the poultry processor at the address given on [a] package and ask, in depth, about the feed formula and living conditions. They can also trust their own sense of taste. A stressed-out, waterlogged, ice-covered chicken just isn't going to deliver in flavor, no matter how much extra-virgin olive oil it's cooked with.

Many poultry perfectionists, including the Manhattan chefs Eberhard Muller and Gray Kunz, like Murray's Chickens, a special breed raised in Shomkin, Pa., and processed in South Fallsburg, N.Y. Available in markets on the Eastern Seaboard for nine months now, Murray's look and taste like real chickens. They are given more space than most to roam, the processor says, and are fed a protein diet that contains no animal byproducts, no bacitracin and no coloring agents.

Murray's does not advertise its chickens as free-range or organic because, "they are neither," said Steve Gold, who owns the company with Murray Bresky.

"At present, there is no legal standard for organic chicken," he continued, "and if we put our chickens outside during a Pennsylvania winter, they would freeze to death."

QUESTIONS FOR DISCUSSION

1. Suzanne Hamlin states that a free-range chicken, turkey, or duck "could be munching on potato chips and drinking antibiotic cocktails and still be legal," since "free range" means only that a bird has access to the outdoors. Cite some other examples from this article that illustrate differences between consumer perception about poultry labels and reality.

2. To what extent do you believe that labeling should be standardized more strictly? Should consumers be given more written information about products that contain labels such as *free-range, all natural,* and *organic?*

In the following essay, Andrew Lam writes about how the Vietnamese names of his friends, which have strong and beautiful meanings, are ridiculed and ultimately forsaken so that the friends can identify with and fit into American culture. It is a great example of how meanings are in people and positive meanings are sometimes lost to assimilation.

WHAT'S IN A NAME?

Andrew Lam

Wang, Dung, Mai Suan, Noc, Trang, Than, Phat. What are these? Names, Vietnamese names. While in my native tongue they suggest colors of clouds and precious jade, in English they are twisted into a funny word, a grunt or even a cough.

Vietnamese names are often turned ugly in America, their magic snuffed out like a birthday candle. My name, Dung, spelled D-U-N-G, which means bravery in Vietnamese, is but animal excrement in English.

Van, Truc and Trang—meaning cloud, bamboo and elegance—the three pretty girls who walk down the high school hallway, suffered constant pestering from classmates who would yell, "Look out, here comes a van, a truck and a train!"

One summer, Van, Truc and Trang, after leafing through *Vogue* and *Mademoiselle* magazines, emerged Yvonne, Theresa and Tanya. They even looked different, wearing more fashionable clothes and makeup.

My sister Noc became Nancy when our landlord, having failed to pronounce her name, threw up his hands and said, "Never mind, let's call you Nancy, as in Nancy Kwan, the actress."

And there's Qua, a friend from college, who wanted to finalize his naturalization process with an American name. But which one? He was drinking milk when he was filling out the application, and saw a picture of a lost boy named Kevin on the milk carton. Qua shrugged. Kevin he became the day he swore his allegiance to the United States of America.

Thus like street urchins, we children of Vietnam gathered our new identities from anything deemed worthy. Then over the seasons, through the years, many of us have learned to embody our new names. For they have given us an assurance of being Americans, part of this country.

Indeed, sometimes I wonder if any of us would have assimilated so well into this country without our new names. After all, it was Huai who, under the tropical sun, and amid exploding B-52 bombs, mourned for slain relatives. Now, Lucy is busy decorating her beautiful suburban home in the Silicon Valley.

Tao, the jack fruit vendor's daughter, who once expected to follow her mother's footsteps, became Christine a decade later, and found herself in a different kind of market instead. Wall Street. Through her computer linkups, Christine, the stockbroker, now negotiates across time zones, oceans, continents.

But what of our old names? Huang, Yung, Mai Sung, Ngop, Jiang, Than, Phat. In our old language, they are kept safe, but more. I should like to think their magic is instilled in us, in us who must adapt and change, but who still cherish the memory of a world full of iridescent clouds and precious jade.

QUESTIONS FOR DISCUSSION

1. Andrew Lam, an associate editor for the Pacific News Service, came to America when he was 11 years old. As recounted in this story, he and his friends all went through name changes. What made them change their original names?

2. To what extent, if any, do you agree with Andrew's statement "Sometimes I wonder if any of us would have assimilated so well into this country without our new names"?

3. Some people are going in the opposite direction from Andrew and his friends and using names from their country of origin. Why do you think they are making this change?

4. Ask relatives or friends who have changed their names why they chose to do so. To what extent did they act under peer pressure, a desire to embrace their new country, or a desire to disassociate with their native country?

The following article discusses the use of the word *many* as a weasel word that enables a writer to make claims without being specific.

WEASEL-WORDS RIP MY FLESH!

Jack Shafer

How many "many's" are too many for one news story?

Like its fellow weasel-words—some, few, often, seems, likely, more—many serves writers who haven't found the data to support their argument. A light splash of weasel-words in a news story is acceptable if only because journalism is not an exact science and deadlines must be observed. But when a reporter pours a whole jug of weasel-words into a piece, as Louise Story does on Page One of today's *New York Times* in "Many Women at Elite Colleges Set Career Path to Motherhood," she needlessly exposes one of the trade's best-kept secrets for all to see. She deserves a week in the stockades. And her editor deserves a month.

Story uses the particularly useful weasel-word "many" 12 times—including once in the headline—to illustrate the emerging trend of Ivy League–class women who attend top schools but have no intention of assuming the careers they prepared for.

She informs readers that "many of these women" being groomed for the occupational elite "say that is not what they want." She repeats the weasel-word three more times in the next two paragraphs and returns to it whenever she needs to express impressive quantity but has no real numbers. She writes:

> Many women at the nation's most elite colleges say they have already decided that they will put aside their careers in favor of raising children. Though some of these students are not planning to have children and some hope to have a family and work full time, many others, like Ms. Liu, say they will happily play a traditional female role, with motherhood their main commitment.
>
> Much attention has been focused on career women who leave the work force to rear children. What seems to be changing is that while many women in college two or three decades ago expected to have full-time careers, their daughters, while still in college, say they have already decided to suspend or end their careers when they have children.
>
> Many students say staying home is not a shocking idea among their friends. Shannon Flynn, an 18-year-old from Guilford, Conn., who is a freshman at Harvard, says many of her girlfriends do not want to work full time....
>
> Yet the likelihood that so many young women plan to opt out of high-powered careers presents a conundrum....
>
> What seems new is that while many of their mothers expected to have hard-charging careers, then scaled back their professional plans only after having children, the women of this generation expect their careers to take second place to child rearing....
>
> Sarah Currie, a senior at Harvard, said many of the men in her American Family class last fall approved of women's plans to stay home with their children....
>
> For many feminists, it may come as a shock to hear how unbothered many young women at the nation's top schools are by the strictures of traditional roles....

None of these many's quantify anything. You could as easily substitute the word some for every many and not gain or lose any information. Or substitute the word few and lose only the wind in Story's sails. By fudging the available facts with weasel-words, Story makes a flaccid concept stand up—as long as nobody examines it closely.

For instance, Story writes that she interviewed "Ivy League students, including 138 freshman and senior females at Yale who replied to e-mail questions sent to members of two residential colleges over the last school year." Because she doesn't attribute the preparation of the e-mail survey to anyone, one must assume that she or somebody at the *Times* composed and sent it. A questionnaire answered by 138 Yale women sounds like it may contain useful information. But even a social-science dropout wouldn't consider the findings to be anything but anecdotal unless he knew (1) what questions were asked (Story doesn't say), (2) how many questionnaires were distributed, and (3) why freshman and seniors received the questionnaires to the exclusion of sophomores and juniors. Also, (4) a social-science dropout would ask if the *Times* contaminated its e-mailed survey with leading questions and hence attracted a disproportionate number of respondents who sympathize with the article's underlying and predetermined thesis.

To say Story's piece contains a thesis oversells it. Early on, she squishes out on the whole concept with the weasel-word *seems*. She writes, "What seems to be changing is that while many women in college two or three decades ago expected to have full-time careers, their daughters, while still in college, say they have already decided to suspend or end their careers when they have children."

To say the piece was edited would also be to oversell it. Story rewrites this seems sentence about two-thirds of the way through the piece without adding any new information. "What *seems* new is that while many of their mothers expected to have hard-charging careers, then scaled back their professional plans only after having children, the women of this generation expect their careers to take second place to child rearing." [Emphasis added.]

Halfway through, Story discounts her allegedly newsworthy findings by acknowledging that a "person's expectations at age 18 are less than perfect predictors of their life choices 10 years later." If they're less than perfect predictors, then why are we reading about their predictions on Page One of the *Times*? While bogus, "Many Women at Elite Colleges Set Career Path to Motherhood" isn't false: It can't be false because it never says anything sturdy enough to be tested. So, how did it get to Page One? Is there a *New York Times* conspiracy afoot to drive feminists crazy and persuade young women that their place is in the home? Did the paper dispatch *Times* columnist John Tierney to write a pair of provocative columns on this theme earlier this year (early May and late May) and recruit Lisa Belkin to dance the idea around in an October 2003 *Times Magazine* feature titled "The Opt-Out Revolution"?

Nah.

I suspect a *Times* editor glommed onto the idea while overhearing some cocktail party chatter—"Say, did you hear that Sam blew hundreds of thousands of dollars sending his daughter to Yale and now she and her friends say all they want in the future is to get married and stay at home?"—and passed the concept to the writer or her editors and asked them to develop it.

You can see the editorial gears whirring: The press has already drained our collective anxiety about well-educated women assuming greater power in the workplace. So, the only editorial vein left to mine is our collective anxiety about well-educated women deciding not to work instead. Evidence that the *Times* editors know how to push our buttons can be found in the fact that as I write, this slight article about college students is the "Most E-Mailed" article on the newspaper's Web site.

Jack Shafer is *Slate*'s editor at large. http://www.slate.com, September 20, 2005. Copyright © 2006 by Washingtonpost.Newsweek Interactive Co. LLC. Reprinted by permission of United Media on behalf of the publisher.

QUESTIONS FOR DISCUSSION

1. Why does Jack Shafer call Louise Story's article a "bogus trend story"?

2. Some research that led to Story's conclusions are cited in this critique. What problems does Shafer point to in the research?

3. Sarah Currie, a senior at Harvard, is quoted as saying that many of the men in her American Family class last fall approved of women's plans to stay home with their children. How might the men in this class reflect a biased sample?

4. Shafer says that halfway through her article, Story qualifies her findings; how does she qualify them and what is the qualifier's effect on her thesis?

5. Why do you believe the *New York Times* put this story on page one, and why do you believe it was the most emailed story on the *Times'* Web site at the time of Shafer's writing?

IDEAS FOR WRITING OR SPEAKING

1. Respond to one of the following quotes from British novelist George Orwell's *Politics and the English Language*. Take a position on the quote and support your position using essays; newspaper, magazine, or journal articles; advertisements; books; films; videos; or interviews.

   a. "In our time, political speech and writing are largely the defense of the indefensible."

   b. "The whole tendency of modern prose is away from concreteness."

   c. "The great enemy of clear language is insincerity."

   d. "In our age, there is no such thing as 'keeping out of politics.' All issues are political issues, and politics itself is a mass of lies, evasions, folly, hatred, and schizophrenia."

   e. "Political language...is designed to make lies sound truthful and murder respectable, and to give an appearance of solidity to pure wind."

2. Write or speak about a proposal for change, using both abstract objectives and concrete proposals. The abstract terms should be used to express the ideals you seek to achieve with your proposal; the concrete explanations are used to let your readers or listeners know exactly what your proposal entails and the "real-world" impact you expect it to have. For example, you might state that you would like to see increased employment opportunities in the inner cities (general objective). Then you can explain exactly how you would go about increasing employment, detailing programs and how the programs would be organized, funded, maintained, and evaluated. (concrete proposals)

   You may want to organize your essay or speech using one of the speech formats discussed in Chapter 10.

3. *Sales Pitch.* Listen to a "hard-sell" sales pitch by a professional salesperson. You might go to a car lot or stereo store, or just invite a door-to-door salesperson to speak with you. Then list and analyze the reasons that you are given in favor of buying the product or service. Answer the following questions:

   a. Were you given valid and well-documented reasons for buying the product or service?

   b. Did the salesperson use deception or try to mislead or confuse you with vagueness or any of the forms of doublespeak covered in this chapter?

   c. Which arguments were persuasive and which were not? Explain why.

4. *Useless Item Survey.* Find something that you bought and never or rarely used. Then answer the following questions:

   a. What motivated you to buy this item?

   b. Why have you never or rarely used it?

   c. Why do you still have it?

   d. Have you learned anything useful from this useless purchase?

5. *Ad Campaign.* An article in the business magazine *Investment Vision* advised readers to consider investing in products with ad campaigns that created powerful positive images. The article reminded readers that corporations spend $129 billion yearly on ads and that the most effective are those with a clear concept. The best campaigns, it believes, focus on one or two words associated with the product, such as *thrive* for Kaiser hospitals, *the world on time* for Federal Express or *dependable* for Maytag.

   Assuming that companies desire positive connotations for their products, study the ad campaigns of several companies.

   a. Discuss each image and how it is achieved through the ads, focusing especially on the words used to create a concept.

   b. Decide which campaigns are more successful at creating strong, positive connotations. Support your conclusions with reasons.

6. Using the same format as in the ad campaign (idea 5), study a present or past political campaign; focus especially on the use of language to present desired images of the candidates.

   For example, when Senator, presidential candidate, and former First Lady Hillary Clinton was first running for senator from the state of New York, her advisers struggled with how the campaign literature should present her. Should the buttons and bumper stickers feature "Hillary Clinton," "Hillary Rodham Clinton," "Mrs. Clinton," or "Hillary Rodham"? Each name might hold different connotations for voters. Finally, the campaign managers decided to go with a more general and vague approach; her name became, simply, "Hillary."

FILMS FOR ANALYSIS AND DISCUSSION

A very topical and funny film called *In Good Company* (2004, PG-13) takes place in the corporate world of mergers and acquisitions but is also a good study in weasel words. The film follows family man Dan Foreman (Dennis Quaid) and his new boss, 26-year-old Carter Duryea (Topher Grace). Both men are going through personal crises as well as trying to handle the pressures in the competitive and always changing business world. We meet Carter in a meeting about how to market cell phones to the untapped demographic of "under 5 year-olds." Carter's answer is colorful dinosaur phones with their own unique roar/ring tone. This high satire continues with Carter's first meeting with his new staff after his company "Globecom" takes over the magazine Dan works for, *Sports America*. As Carter downs his fifth Starbucks latte, he delivers a hilarious speech about "synergy," a buzzword that Globecom uses to describe cutting costs within the company while simultaneously driving up revenue. Unfortunately, in the name of "synergy," many of the people Dan has worked with his whole career need to be fired, or in Globecom's words "let go…because it sounds better." Intertwined with the satire is a real-life look at where loyalty and honor exist in a culture that focuses on meeting the bottom line.

Similar Films and Classics

Mean Girls (2004, PG 13)

This film follows high school student Cady Heron as she goes from being home-schooled in Africa to entering the world of public high school in the United States. Her first friends at her new school encourage her to break into the popular clique, the Plastics, and find out their dark secrets. Note how Cady learns to use new words and phrases to fit in with the Plastics and how her behavior changes as she starts using the language of the popular mean girls. When Cady decides to leave the mean girl group, she also makes decisions about words she will no longer use.

The N-Word (2004, Not rated.)

This documentary, featuring many popular celebrities, discusses the powerful, inflammatory nature of the N-word. It is a good example of the rules that govern language usage, as the interviewees discuss when, where, how, by whom—and whether the N-word should be used.

Lost in Translation (2003, R)

This film is about two individuals who meet and become friends during a visit to Japan. It shows both the confusion and the humor when the two tourists grapple with language and cultural differences.

Crazy People (1990, R)

This comedy features an ad-man who is undergoing a breakdown because of his desire to use honest language, rather than weasel words, in his advertising campaigns. When he is sent to a psychiatric hospital to recover, he meets a delightful group of fellow patients; they all work on new product slogans that promote truth in advertising and achieve great success in the process.

Suggestion in Media

Is What You See What You Get? Do You Really Want It?

A critical thinker is aware of the presence and power of suggestion in electronic and print media.

This chapter will cover

- Suggestion in electronic media

- Suggestion in print media

- Advertising and marketing strategies

- Impacts of electronic communication

> *The hand that rules the press, the radio, the screen and the far-spread*
> *magazine, rules the country.*
> > Learned Hand, memorial address for Justice Brandeis, December 21, 1942

THE LOST ART OF THE PUBLIC SPEECH

Bob Greene

Speeches—eloquent, painstakingly crafted, carefully thought out, and meticulously paced, full-length speeches—are an endangered American species.

The speech has historically been one of the most important means of serious communication. If a person had an essential message to deliver, that message was conveyed in a speech. That's what politicians and great thinkers did when they had something to say: They labored over a speech until it was ready, and then they delivered it out loud to an attentive audience.

No more. The speech is already an anachronism. Twenty or 30 years ago, the serious speech was still a routine part of American life, and now the serious, influential speech is so rare that it's startling when one comes along.

The people you would most expect to want to continue the tradition of the speech—politicians with a national audience—are rushing to help devalue the speech. Next time you watch network TV news, pay close attention to how national politicians talk. They have begun to speak almost exclusively in those cute little bursts expressly written to be picked up by television producers—predigested 8- to 12-second nuggets that don't resemble anything an actual person would ever say during a real-world conversation....

This goes on especially on the floor of Congress....Except in the most uncommon of circumstances, reporters and camera crews are only going to pick up the luminescent little word-pellets that have been custom-constructed for them....

If Abraham Lincoln wanted to make a point today, he would deliver the Gettysburg Sound Bite.[1]

Public arguments, which formerly consisted largely of political speeches and debates, can now be found on commercials, talk shows, interview programs, segments of news programs, and sometimes even comedy shows and dramas. Arguments that appear in print include advertisements, essays, and editorials; they can also be found in abundance on the blogs and Web pages of the Internet. Citizens and consumers have a wide array of options for getting information on an issue, a candidate, or a product; on any given day, we may read a newspaper or magazine, watch television, surf the Internet, download a podcast, and listen to the radio. While these multiple means of accessing information provide incredible resources for us, they also compete for our attention. Increasingly, as we seek to determine what is true or false and

---

[handwritten marginalia: how to make right choice it so much time is wasted on filtering information]

which policies, candidates, and products are in our best interest, we have to walk through the minefields of misinformation, clever but empty sound bites, exaggerated product promises, and glitzy personal and commercial promotions. This chapter will consider how media influence, shape, and alter the many messages we receive.

The print and electronic media use a variety of persuasive techniques that critical thinkers should understand. Most of these techniques come under the heading of *suggestion*; there are also technologies that seek to understand and access the unconscious motivations of target audiences, which will we consider later in the chapter.

SUGGESTION IN DAILY LIFE

Suggestion means presenting ideas or images in such a way as to reveal certain aspects or qualities and to conceal others. We use the power of suggestion to create impressions in our personal lives, impressions that help us look or seem better or different than we actually are.

You might stuff any debris under the seat of your car if you are unexpectedly asked to drive an attractive person home, so that you appear neater than you really are. Women (and some men) use suggestion when they wear makeup to look older, younger, or prettier. Balding men might wear hats or comb their remaining hair so it looks thicker than it is. Most of us choose clothing that makes us look better by concealing flaws.

People use the power of suggestion in the professional world also, such as when a real estate agent tells a client to bake something sweet for an open house so the home will seem warm and inviting; or when salesclerks are told to look busy, even when there is no real work to do; or when a car salesperson asks you to sit inside a car and feel comfortable, hoping that the suggestion of ownership and the smell and feel of a new car will induce you to buy. Dr. Alan Hirsch, neurologic director of the Smell and Taste Treatment and Research Foundation in Chicago, did a study on the effect of smell at a Las Vegas casino. When interviewed by National Public Radio's Neal Conan, he said,

> What we found was, in the presence of a pleasant odor, there was an increased amount of money people placed in slot machines. The increase was of 45.11 percent, which was highly significant because when we looked at the control area where there was no odor, there was only a two percent change compared to the weekends before and the weekends after.[2]

British professor Mark Griffith cited Hirsch's research in an article he wrote for a British Web site, in which he discussed the trend of marketers to stimulate all of a consumer's senses in order to create brand loyalty:

[2]*USA Today,* 1993.

Like memories, sensory perceptions are unique to each of us and have the capacity to emotionally stimulate, leaving the chance to build brands by leveraging the five senses wide open. Some commercial operators have already got the hang of sensory appeal. For instance, some supermarkets bake fresh bread on the premises so passersby smell the aroma, are struck with hunger and are drawn inside. One major British bank introduced freshly brewed coffee to its branches with the intention of making customers feel at home. The familiar smell was used to help relax the customers. Other examples include a leading chain of toiletry stores which pumped the smell of chocolate through its air conditioning system in the run up to Valentine's Day, and a well-known clothes shop which filled its flagship stores with the smell of freshly laundered shirts.

...Like smell, sound also evokes memory and emotion. Meaningful sound is a cheap but very effective way of appealing to another of a customer's senses and of powerfully enhancing a brand's message or appeal. A pop song from your youth can help bring back the excitement felt in your teens....

Sound effects and noise in the gambling environment are very important in getting people to gamble. Sound effects—especially in activities like slot machine playing—are thought to be gambling-inducers. Constant noise and sound gives the impression of a noisy, fun and exciting environment. Walk into any casino in Las Vegas and you will experience this. It's also common for slot machines to play a musical tune or buzz loudly if you win, with low denomination coins hitting a metal payout tray making lots of noise. This is all deliberate. It gives the impression that winning is far more common than losing (as you cannot hear the sound of losing!). So next time you're in a room full of 1,000 slot machines, remember that the sound of 20 of them paying out is more audibly noticeable than the 980 machines that are losing money for the punter (gambler).[3]

Another way that suggestion is used in everyday life concerns the design of stores. Joseph Weishar, author of *Design for Effective Selling Space,* claims that retailers can use store design to exert absolute control over the responses of their customers. Weishar says that shoppers move in predictable patterns; for example, 80% of customers turn right when they walk into a store. Savvy retailers place the items they most want to sell to the right of the store entrance. In addition, they find ways to move customers to the back of the store, often by featuring sales in that area; since most people don't leave the same way they came in, a trip to the back ensures a round trip through the store. The highly successful Disney stores feature a large video screen against their back wall, knowing that kids will try to move their parents

[3]Mark Griffiths, "Scenting Success," http://www.inside-edge-mag.co.uk/casinos, (accessed February, 2006), Inside Poker, insidepokermag. co. uk.

back there; these stores also create a fun, vibrant atmosphere that appeals to their target audience.[4]

Sharon Zukin, professor of sociology, has written a book about how shopping has changed American culture. She believes that people who buy things they don't need aren't necessarily greedy, but instead are seduced by the suggestive emotional experience of shopping, whether it is online or in a store:

> Even if we don't make a purchase, the social space of stores is a material image of our dreams. Low prices? Wal-Mart, where men and women of all income levels shop together, offers us a vision of democracy. Brand names? Sony and Band-Aids represent our means to a better life. Designer labels? The Armani suit or Miss Sixty jeans will win us the job or a social partner. The seduction of shopping is not about buying goods. It's about dreaming of a perfect society and a perfect self.[5] (See Exercise 8.1, p. 356.)

TELEVISED SUGGESTION

The media does set the agenda about what will and will not get discussed.
Sherry Bebitch Jaffe, Center for Politics and Policy

Television producers, directors, editors, and advertisers have always used the power of suggestion. The following guidelines help you view television with an understanding of the subtle, but consciously detectable, elements of suggestion. For news programs and talk shows, be aware of

1. The selection of issues
2. The use of time
3. The selection of guest and panel members
4. What is included or excluded on a set
5. The nonverbal element of clothing
6. The use of language
7. The use of camera angles and cuts
8. Camera distance and framing

The Selection of Issues

Hundreds of global and national issues could be covered on any given day. The average network and local newscast is 24 minutes long, including sports and weather (with 6 minutes of commercials). Many stories are written but not aired because of these time limitations. So the selection of which stories are

---

[4]Joseph Weishar, *Design for Effective Selling Space*, (Texas: McGraw Hill), 1992.
[5]Sharon Zukin, "Attention Shoppers: Your Dreams in Aisle 3." *The Chronicle Review,* December 19, 2003.

"THAT'S 73% WHO ARE DISGUSTED BY TABLOID JOURNALISM BUT CAN'T TALK TO US WHILE 'CURRENT AFFAIR' IS ON."

Dunnigan's People Ralph Dunnigan. © Tribune Media Services, Inc. All rights reserved. Reprinted with permission.

important and the decision about the order in which they will be presented give network news editors enormous power. The very fact that a story is on the morning or evening news makes it seem important to us; we never really know what other issues are not being covered.

Mike Wallace, host of CBS network's popular *60 Minutes* (an investigative reporting program) stated that on news-related programs, the reporter's interest often decides whether a story is profiled. In other words, both reporters (by choosing stories) and editors (by deciding which stories are aired) have the power to decide what is and what is not worthy of coverage.

Another important factor in determining the content of programming is *numbers* or *ratings*. The shows that get the largest audiences (determined by independent research companies, such as Nielsen) also get the largest share of advertising revenue. In effect, if a program wants to stay on the air, it has to attract a large audience.

One method used to attract viewers is **sensationalism.** When broadcasters use sensationalism, more exciting stories are chosen over less exciting but perhaps more newsworthy ones, and the most bizarre, visually interesting, or *sensational* elements of these stories are featured. A local station might focus on the day's fires and auto accidents, showing all the gory details, and bypass stories on upcoming propositions or elections. Stories involving celebrities get prime coverage in both local and national newscasts and sometimes receive hours of repetitive coverage on cable stations. For example, Gail Shister wrote for the *Philadelphia Inquirer* about the extensive coverage of the death of Anna Nicole Smith:

> War? What war?
> The sudden death of former Playmate Anna Nicole Smith last week drew more coverage on cable news than Iraq, according to figures released Tuesday by the Project for Excellence in Journalism.
> In just two days, Smith's demise consumed 21 percent of all programming monitored by PEJ on CNN, MSNBC and Fox News Channel for the week—including a mind-boggling 50 percent Thursday (the day she died) and Friday.
> Policy debate over Iraq and the '08 presidential race came in second and third at 15 percent and 10 percent, respectively, over the week.[6]

Coverage of Anna Nicole continued for weeks with some cable programs devoting their entire hours to the various issues surrounding her death.

Celebrity trials are also prominently featured on news programs. According to the *Tyndall Weekly* media monitor, a seven-minute court appearance by Kobe Bryant, which was a mere legal formality, ranked as the number one news story on the national network evening news and the fourth biggest story of the week. The *Rocky Mountain Media Watch,* in noting the hype given to Bryant's Colorado trial, stated, "Media hype-fests squeeze critical stories out of the news."[7] In addition to the disproportionate coverage given to trials, a host of television shows that reenact and even create sensational stories has developed over the past decade.

The apparent success of sensational coverage of the news (and of an ever-increasing line-up of "reality" programs) is one factor behind the claim that the primary purpose of television news, whether broadcast or cable, is to entertain rather than to inform. The late professor and media analyst Neil Postman was concerned about the blurring of news and entertainment. He wrote "It would seem that right now, Americans are more interested in entertainment than any other aspect of personal life…even in school now teachers are more and more trying to be entertaining because television has taught the young that learning, whatever it is, must always be fun. And if it's not fun, then it's not worthwhile and you should just change the dial…go to another station."[8]

Whatever the objectives of a given program, we as critical thinkers can choose to view news broadcasts with discernment rather than passively absorbing them. We can stop and ask ourselves if a story being covered is one of the most important stories of the day or just one of the most exciting stories.

[6]Gail Shister, Anna Nicole Smith Found to Overwhelm Iraq War Coverage, *The Philadelphia Inquirer*, February 14, 2007.
[7]Jason Salzman, "Look Out. It's Hurricane Kobe!," *The Rocky Mountain News,* "Speakout," September 28, 2003.
[8]Stephen Marshall, "Prelude to Vegas: Neil Postman Gets Interviewed," Channel Zero, 1996.

discernment = ability to judge well

The Use of Time

Two elements of time can influence listeners. One is the time placement of a story. A story given prime (early) coverage on a news program will seem very important to the audience. On network news, when the worldwide events of the day are given only 24 minutes, any item rating coverage attains instant credibility with viewers. On cable news networks, where there are frequent interruptions for "breaking news," the items highlighted in these segments are seen as truly significant.

Former anchorman Dan Rather was interviewed about the power of network news and asked why CBS once used some of its precious evening broadcast time to cover a frog that could jump 30 feet. Rather laughed and said that when a frog can jump 30 feet, that is news! He skirted the question gracefully, but the issue remains: What is worthy of national broadcast in a limited time frame, and, more importantly, who decides?

David Brinkley addressed the question of who decides what to broadcast at a meeting of the Radio-Television News Directors Association. He commented on the fact that most Americans don't read newspapers to be informed, choosing to watch television news instead. "All they know about public policy," he said, "is what we tell them."[9]

The quantity of time is also a factor on television and radio. On network news programs or short radio news updates, both of which have little time, a story given significant coverage is seen as vital. On the other hand, 24-hour cable news networks have a different problem; they have to find enough stories to fill an entire day. As veteran news anchor Walter Cronkite states, "They're forced to continually fill air time, so they often wind up devoting too much attention to stories that aren't truly important in the overall scheme of things."[10] When we keep seeing coverage of the same story on cable news of, for example, a sensational celebrity trial, it takes on import that it may not merit.

Talk shows frequently feature guests who discuss different aspects of the same problem; that gives viewers a variety of perspectives and adds interest to the issue. However, when one guest is given more time than another to make his or her points, that guest has a greater chance of influencing the audience.

In addition, we begin to feel better acquainted with the person who is given more time; the factor of familiarity may unconsciously persuade us to feel closer to that person's position, especially on a topic that is new to us. (See Exercise 8.2, p. 357.)

The Selection of Guest and Panel Members

When you watch a debate or talk show on an issue, notice the credentials of the persons being interviewed. If the producer or editor either is not careful or has a bias, one side may be represented by attractive, articulate spokespersons

[9]Marlin Maddoux, Free Speech or Propaganda? (Nashville: Thomas Nelson Publishers, 1990) p. 73.
[10]Chuck Barney, "Good News: Cronkite's Still Involved," *Contra Costa Times*, February 25, 2004.

and the other by intensely emotional, abrasive people. Are the persons selected really in leadership positions in the causes they represent and are they respected by their colleagues? If there is only one "professional" on the panel (often a doctor, psychologist, writer, or lawyer), does he or she represent only one side of the controversy and therefore lend credibility only to that side?

Be fair by keeping in mind the principle that if a controversy rages for a long time, that usually means reasonable people are disagreeing about important definitions or principles. Don't judge an issue by an abrasive spokesperson who may or may not represent the norm of persons who support his or her side. The producer may have chosen a more colorful and interesting, but much less representative, person to discuss either side. Unfortunately, when more aggressive guests are featured on programs about important topics, they obscure the issues by talking over each other. As Walter Cronkite states, "I think most of that stuff is meant to be entertainment, not journalism. All that screaming and hollering is absolute anathema for me. I tune out as soon as I can't understand what they're saying, and that's too bad because some of these people are pretty well informed."[11]

anathema = something/someone one strongly dislikes

Related to the selection of people who are interviewed about an issue is the treatment of each spokesperson by the interviewer. Note whether the interviewer is equally positive (or negative) in the interrogation of the guests. Sometimes, a biased interviewer will direct positive, easily answered questions, often called "softball" questions, to one guest and more negative, probing, "hardball" questions to a guest who represents the other side of the issue. For example, if the interviewer likes the guest, he or she could say, "Some people seem confused by your stand on this particular issue; could you explain more about your current thinking about it?" (softball question). On the other hand, if the interviewer doesn't like the guest, the question might sound like this: "How can you explain the obvious contradictions in your position on this issue?"(hardball question). You can see the power an interviewer has to make a guest feel (and thus seem to the audience) comfortable and respected or uncomfortable and defensive.

What Is Included or Excluded on a Set

When an interview is given, notice the environment in which it is set. For example, on a commercial for encyclopedias, we might be impressed by a "teacher" who is surrounded with books and diplomas.

The director of a commercial can create the impression of an academic background that may have nothing to do with anyone's credentials. The actress who portrays a teacher on an encyclopedia commercial doesn't have to be a teacher. Advertisers know that the impression of authority—created by a setting of a doctor's office, a classroom, or a law library—can have a positive impact on our response to the commercial message. (See Exercise 8.3, p. 358.)

[11]Ibid.

The Nonverbal Element of Clothing

How someone is dressed is an important factor in creating a suggestion of his or her character and appropriateness for a given role. For example, both the Republican and Democratic parties have "schools" for their candidates in which training is given on campaign techniques; part of this training covers proper dress in various situations. Spouses are also encouraged to attend sessions on how to dress themselves and how to help their mates dress to create the right impressions. Even small details such as appropriate length and color of socks are covered in these workshops.

Clothing style is an essential element of advertising as well. Actors who are portraying pilots, doctors, managers, or other professionals are dressed to fit the part.

Several years ago, John Molloy wrote the best-selling books *Dress for Success for Men* and *The Woman's Dress for Success Book* about his extensive studies on how styles and colors create impressions. His books are filled with research about how changing the look or color of one's clothes, jewelry, accessories, and hairstyle has helped individuals perform better at job interviews, sales calls, or other difficult communication situations. Many producers, advertisers, candidates, or spokespersons are familiar with techniques such as Molloy's and use them to create positive suggestions on their audiences. A number of television programs, such as TLC's *What Not to Wear* or *Flip This House*, have emerged to encourage people to "make over" their clothing, hair style, and homes to create good impressions on others. The hosts of these programs often write their own books; for example, Clinton Kelly and Stacy London have a book called *Dress Your Best* that advises readers what to wear to convey certain impressions at work and for formal and casual events. (See Exercise 8.4, p. 359.)

The Use of Language

Setting and appearance send messages nonverbally; the use of a reporter's language can also affect our perception of an issue. Some years ago, when a terrorist bombing would occur, news reporters would say, "Such and such a group takes *credit* for the bombing." Other reporters and the public took offense at the word *credit,* which has a positive connotation. The late Eric Severeid, a respected commentator, did a segment on the harm done by such words. Because of similar protests, the commonly accepted statement is now "Such and such a group claimed *responsibility* for the bombing." In recent years, some reporters have chosen to change the term *suicide bombings* to *homicide bombings* to reflect the fact that the suicide bombers seek to kill innocent civilians.

One media critic gave the example to illustrate how a reporter's use of words can distort the facts of a situation:

I might say, "I've been a journalist for thirty years." Now a newspaper could pick that up and report: "Charles Wiley said he has been a journalist for thirty years." That's fact. Just straight reporting. Or the reporter could say, "Marlin's guest *admitted* he's been a journalist for thirty years." Or he can say, "He has *conceded* he's been a journalist for thirty years." Or he could go to the final step and say "Wiley *confessed* he's been a journalist for thirty years." You see how one word changes the whole meaning."[12]

Sometimes, a journalist with a bias will use certain labels to characterize a person or an issue in a poor light. One clever way to discredit someone is to quote an enemy of that person. For example, if a journalist (broadcast or print) doesn't like the success of a third party candidate, she can quote someone else who has called the candidate a "spoiler." On the other hand, if the journalist likes the third party candidate, she can quote someone who calls him "a fresh alternative for change." In that manner, the reporter is only reporting the facts of what someone else has said about the candidate. In addition, certain labels can be attributed to a person, thereby coloring how a neutral audience might perceive him or her. On the positive side, someone might be labeled a "moderate." More negative labels include "liberal," "conservative," "ultraliberal," "ultraconservative," "ideologue," "millionaire," and "extremist." To discredit a politician, a reporter might describe him or her as "embattled" or "trying to head off criticism"; programs that are disliked may be labeled as "costly."[13]

[handwritten margin note: quotes from different sources]

SKILL

Recognize the techniques of suggestion used by electronic media.

The Use of Camera Angles and Cuts

Sometimes, directors tell camerapersons to shoot a person from below; this angle gives the speaker more authority, as if the viewers are "looking up to" the individual. Commercials use this technique to command attention and respect for a particular actor who is telling us to buy something, or to show how large and impressive an authority figure looks to a common person. One commercial used this technique to illustrate how big a parent looks to a toddler.

Conversely, when the camera angle is above the speaker, the impression is that the viewers are looking down on the speaker; in this case, the speaker may look insignificant or even dishonest.

The ability to use cuts (switching from one camera to another) to create positive or negative impressions about a speaker during a debate or talk show, or even in a news report, gives television directors great power. For example, a director can cut to a shot of an audience member's reaction to a speaker, thereby

---

[12]Martin Maddoux, *Free Speech or Propaganda?* (Nashville: Thomas Nelson Publishers, 1990), p. 54.
[13]Bob Kohn, *Journalist Fraud* (Nashville, TN: WND Books, 2003), p. 148.

giving the impression of approval or disapproval of what the speaker has said. Also, during convention coverage, directors can cut to one audience member who appears bored with a candidate and thus unfairly represent the majority of audience members. Conversely, C-SPAN has used wide-angle shots to show the audience that while a congressperson or senator is making an impassioned speech, the chairs in the room are empty.

Cuts in editing are used to select a short segment of a longer interview for broadcast. Sometimes, these cuts distort the statements that have been made by taking them out of context. The **sound bite** is a brief selection of a longer speech, usually heard out of context; both politicians and editors use sound bites to create impressions on viewers.

[handwritten margin note: Statements are which become out of context]

Advertisers also use distorted camera angles and quick cuts from scene to scene in order to command attention. These unusual, quickly moving scenes, coupled with increased volume, make sure that viewers pay attention to commercials.

Camera Distance and Framing

Directors of programs may deliberately or unconsciously use camera shots to influence audiences. Close-ups control our emotions by adding an element of intimacy. We feel closer to a person and identify more readily with the person's viewpoint when we can see him or her as, literally, close to us. We may believe that the speaker is telling us the truth because he appears to be looking us in the eye. In fact, the speaker is looking at the camera or at the interviewer and only appears to be making eye contact with us. Conversely, educator John Splaine writes, "A camera angle from the side will suggest that a pictured person, who is responding to an incriminating question, might not be telling the truth."[14]

A wide-angle shot can make us feel distant from an individual. We feel uncomfortable with someone who seems far away from us, and that may translate into a lack of trust for his or her position on a given issue. When a scene is shot from a helicopter, the people below are seen as far away and alien, sometimes appearing more like ants than human beings.

In addition, **framing**—the deliberate or unconscious use of camera shots to influence audiences—can make a critical difference. One loud demonstrator shown close up at a rally can create a distorted image if there are hundreds of other people protesting quietly. During the coverage of the chaos in Los Angeles following the verdict of the Rodney King trial, television viewers saw two Korean men standing in front of their businesses pointing handguns; a Korean community leader criticized the reporters for leaving out the rest of the scene, which consisted of groups of looters heading for the stores. By showing only the two men with handguns, viewers were given a false impression and the storeowners were literally "framed."

---

[14]John Splaine, "Critically Viewing the Social Studies: A New Literacy," *Louisiana Social Studies Journal,* XVI, no.1 (Fall 1989): 16.

Critical thinkers need to be vigilant in their awareness of the impressions that can be created electronically. (See Exercise 8.5, p. 359.)

SUGGESTION IN PRINT MEDIA

Four hostile newspapers are more to be feared than a thousand bayonets.
Napoleon I, *Maxims* (1804–1815)

The broadcast media, television and radio, used to be subject to what was called the **Fairness Doctrine**, which meant that if broadcasters allowed air time for one side of an issue, they had to allow time for other points of view as well. The Federal Communications Commission (FCC) created the doctrine because of the limited channels available for broadcasting. Under the Fairness Doctrine, a network or affiliate was considered a "public trustee" and, as such, could not air an interview, documentary, or news program on one side of an issue and refuse to offer an equivalent opposing viewpoint. Likewise, a station could not air a message by one legitimate political candidate without allowing time for his opponent; the idea was that controversial issues should be handled in a fair and balanced way on the public airwaves. However, with frequency changes and the proliferation of cable channels toward the end of the twentieth century, the public began to have many more choices of programs, and the concerns that prompted the Fairness Doctrine were greatly eased; in 1987, the courts declared that since the Fairness Doctrine was not mandated by Congress, the FCC did not have to continue to enforce it. Since that time, Congress has tried to create legislation mandating the Fairness Doctrine, but that legislation was vetoed by Presidents Reagan and George Bush Sr. Some members of Congress want to bring back the doctrine to make sure that a balance of viewpoints on controversial issues is maintained. However, as Val Limburg writes in a treatise on the doctrine, "The public relies instead on the judgment of broadcast journalists and its own reasoning ability to sort out one-sided or distorted coverage of an issue."[15]

As a result of their history with the Fairness Doctrine, most television and radio networks and affiliates are sensitive to the importance of a balanced approach. However, even with a station policy of giving time for different viewpoints on an issue, broadcasters can still choose which guests appear and can manipulate programs using the techniques detailed in the previous section. And, as networks proliferate and competition for viewers and listeners increases, some radio and television networks are moving toward presenting either more liberal or more conservative programming, hoping to capture a larger, more loyal target audience.

Unlike the broadcast media, the print media have not had a history of governmental pressure to be fair; however, journalism did try to live by a certain

[15]Val Limburg, "Fairness Doctrine" Accessed March, 2007, www.museum.tv/archives/etv/F/htmlF/fairnessdoct/fairnessdoct.htm.

ethic that was codified in 1923 by the American Society for Newspaper Editors. Their ethic reads as follows: "Sound practice makes clear distinction between news reports and expressions of opinion. News reports should be free from opinion or bias of any kind." Schools of journalism traditionally taught reporters to focus on the facts and to use the questions "Who?" "What?" "When?" "Why?" "Where?" and "How?" to inform readers thoroughly about a news item. Over the years, with the proliferation of news sources, the line between straight news and commentary has been blurred; in fact, today's newspapers and news magazines often gain a reputation for a certain perspective that caters to their readers. Some commentators are concerned about the effect of **spin**, the presenting of stories with a subtle editorial bias, on reader's perceptions. In noting the need for some kind of fairness doctrine for the press, media scholar Ben Bagdikian stated that "most daily newspapers have not faced up to the fact that they are monopoly institutions and therefore have an obligation to speak for the entire community and to be sensitive to every segment of it."[16]

While some local and national newspapers strive to create a balance of views on controversial issues, many newspapers and magazines present primarily conservative or liberal perspectives. They feature columnists who largely subscribe to the publisher's political and social viewpoints. As critical thinkers, we can be responsible readers and see through biased presentations when we examine the following elements of print journalism:

1. The use of headlines
2. The use of "leads" or openings to a news story
3. The balance of reporting on an issue
4. Fairness in editorial essays and letters
5. Photo composition

The Use of Headlines

> *The vast majority of people who read newspapers gain their understanding of the news by glancing at the headlines and subheads. To influence the headlines is to influence public opinion.*
>
> Bob Kohn, *Journalistic Fraud, August, 2003*

Most readers know that the sensational headlines featured on papers found in supermarket checkout lines are not credible. When we read a headline proclaiming that a famous star has "8 new babies," we can assume that her cat had a litter of kittens or another equally silly explanation for this amazing news. Few of us believe that a 13-year-old really did elope with a two-headed alien. Obviously, these tabloids have little credibility and should not be used as resource material for research papers.

Less sensational headlines can also distort information and mislead readers in subtle ways. Headlines in respectable newspapers and magazines are

---

[16]Ben Bagdikian, *The Media Monopoly* (Boston: Beacon Press, 1973).

important because many readers are "scanners"—they skim the paper, reading headlines and then going back to read only the articles of interest to them.

A headline that is scanned and recorded in the memory of a reader can give a misleading picture of information without actually being false. For example, let's say a reporter did a detailed story about an antinuclear protest that was held at a local power plant. The story covers the issues brought up by the demonstrators and the responses made by the plant spokesperson.

An editor who did not approve of this protest could use the headline "No One Arrested at Power Plant Demonstration." Bringing in the idea of arrest by stating that there were no arrests is a subtle way of implying that arrests had been anticipated or that the protesters were not peaceful.

A joke illustrating how "spin" can be used against someone was going around midway through Bill Clinton's first term in office: The president went on a fishing trip with members of the press corps. After their boat left shore, the president realized he had left his tackle on the dock, so he stepped off the boat, walked to shore, picked up his tackle, and walked back over the surface of the water. The next day's headline read "Clinton Can't Swim."[17]

Presidents and other governmental leaders are subject to criticism on a variety of issues. It goes with the territory, because no official can please everyone. As previously noted, newspapers and newsmagazines may have an editorial bias and feature largely liberal or conservative viewpoints on their opinion pages. Many readers turn to these opinion pages to read strong perspectives about an issue. However, when large newspapers bring their editorial bias into their front pages, where the "straight news" is supposed to be, and when they slant stories with the wording of headlines, the readers may accept the slanted viewpoint as the simple truth. For example, columnist Andrew Sullivan pointed out that in October 2002, a routine Commerce Department study revealed that the economy had grown by 3 percent. The report, favorable to the Bush administration, was headlined differently by three news organizations:

ECONOMY RACES AHEAD AT 3.1 ANNUAL RATE IN SUMMER—*Associated Press*
ECONOMY GROWS AT 3.1 PERCENT PACE—*Washington Post*
ECONOMY GREW AT 3.1% IN 3RD QUARTER, SLOWER THAN EXPECTED—*New York Times*[18]

Editors can shape the news and give a positive or negative spin on events by the use of carefully constructed headlines.

In addition, headlines are often read as summary statements about events or discoveries. A headline that makes strong and unusual claims (particularly on the front page) draws readers to buy the paper or to read the article.

Headlines can also come in the form of the titles editors give to letters written by readers. Sometimes these titles are representative of the position

---

[17]Deborah Tannen, *The Argument Culture* (New York: Ballantine Books, Random House, Inc., 1998), p. 54.
[18]Kohn, *Journalistic Fraud*, p. 84.

of the person who wrote the editorial, but sometimes they are used to distort or ridicule the position of the writer. In this way, an editorial page may appear to give balanced perspectives on issues, but in reality does not. For example, someone may write a letter to the editor of a newspaper or magazine that is critical of Candidate X, alleging that the candidate won a recent election by making untrue statements about his opponent. If an editor disagrees with the letter writer, she might write the headline to the letter as "Reader Upset by Candidate's Victory." If she agrees with the writer, she might headline the letter: "Smear Campaign May Have Lead to Candidate X Election Win."

The Use of "Leads"' or Openings to a News Story

> *The power of the press in America is a primordial one. It sets the agenda of public discussion; and this sweeping political power is unrestrained by any law. It determines what people will talk and think about—an authority that in other nations is reserved for tyrants, priests, parties and mandarins.*
>
> Theodore White, *The Making of a President*, 1972

Closely related to the headline of a story is the introductory sentence, called the lead sentence or, simply, the **lead**.* The lead sentence is meant to give the reader the "gist" or the essence of the story. Many busy readers rely on the leads to inform them of the important news of the day. If a particular story is of interest to the reader, he or she can read on for more detailed information, but the details are expected to add on to the main idea of the story that has presumably already been presented in the lead.

Editors usually create the headlines to a story by reading the lead and briefly summarizing its contents. If the lead is slanted, it is likely that the headline will also be slanted. For example, in an article on a study of chocolate, the lead claimed that chocolate might mimic the effects of marijuana and boost the pleasure people get from eating it. The headline then followed the lead by claiming that "Report on Chocolate May Bring a Real High." Since the writer of the lead did not give the real essence of the finding (that the substances researchers found in chocolate were too minute to produce a high), the headline gave distorted information.[19]

As we discussed previously, traditional schools of journalism train writers to focus on the essential facts about an event by answering the following questions: Who was involved? What happened? When did it happen? Where did it happen? Why did it happen? How did it happen? These are called the 5 Ws and the H in journalism, and good journalists answer all of them close to the beginning of the story, usually in the first sentence. An unbiased news writer will try to cover the 5Ws and the H in a factual manner without injecting opinion.

---

*The lead may also refer to the lead story, the "big story" that is featured and usually placed in the upper right column of the front page.

[19]Associated Press, "Report on Chocolate May Bring a Real High," *Contra Costa Times*, August 22, 1996, p. B-1.

However, the lead can be slanted by a reporter or an editor who wishes to have readers interpret the news with a particular perspective. For example, the *Who* can be emphasized if the reporter likes the *Who* and the *Who* has done a good thing, or the *Who* can be minimized if the writer doesn't want to credit the *Who* with a good action. Let's say that a governor, Governor Smith, has managed to balance her state budget and make positive steps toward reducing a deficit that she inherited from a previous administration; she accomplished this by getting all of the state assembly members to accept her new proposals. A newspaper that doesn't like Governor Smith could run a lead that downplays her involvement in the budget balancing. The lead could read as follows: *Members of the state assembly worked together to create a balanced budget, easing the anger of many voters over the budget mess that has plagued this administration.* By giving credit to the state assembly alone and implying that the budget mess was this administration's fault, the reporter has been able to avoid giving any credit (or even mention) to the governor. In fact, the way the lead reads, the governor seems to have caused the budget problems, and her efforts seem to be completely irrelevant to the progress that was made.

The *What* can also be distorted by a journalist who has an agenda beyond reporting the news factually. Let's say a paper likes Candidate X and dislikes Candidate Y. Recent polls have shown Candidate Y is leading Candidate X by 10 points. A straightforward lead might be: *A recent Gallup poll shows that Candidate Y leads nearest opponent Candidate X by 10 points.* A lead (and the headline derived from the lead) that puts a positive spin on the candidacy of Candidate X could spin the facts as follows: *Candidate X and Candidate Y are the top candidates in a close race for the eighth district's congressional seat.*

In a critical piece on the different coverage of the *What* in the Israeli-Palestinian conflict, *U.S. News and World Report* columnist John Leo writes:

> "He kept bleeding" was a large front-page headline in the April 4 *Washington Post.* The story was about a wounded Palestinian who died in Bethlehem after Israeli forces refused to let ambulances into the fire zone. The Israelis said snipers were still active. Also they may have been suspicious of the local ambulance corps after explosives were discovered under the stretcher of a 3-year-old boy. Maybe the Israelis were just being monsters, as the press increasingly seems to think. But the level of "he kept bleeding" and "they've killed my wife" coverage of the Palestinian-Israeli war is quite high. Another *Washington Post* headline was "Father, son dead: Family wonders why." This is a very unusual way to cover combat, particularly when there are no neutral observers around to back up stories supplied by angry partisans. The British press is filled with this stuff, and the hostility to Israel is impossible to miss. American reporters are more professional, but focusing on highly emotional "they've killed my wife" coverage is dicey. It tells us nothing about what we need to know—whether the killing of civilians was incidental or intentional, massive or minor. After all, "they've killed my wife" journalism can be churned out after "collateral damage" in almost any battle in any war.

In contrast, I don't see much emotional coverage of the Israeli civilians intentionally blown up by Palestinian bombers. Most attacks pass without any notice in the press. The coverage we do get is dry and matter-of-fact. In February, for instance, CNN's Web site mentioned the "killing of two Israelis" by a suicide bomber. The bomber was identified, but there were no names of the 15-year-old victims, no details about the horrific damage to other teens by flying nails embedded in the bomb, and not even a mention that one of the two dead was a U.S. citizen. Palestinian bombers, on the other hand, tend to get more vivid treatment, often with endearing photos and warm, human-interest touches. The *New York Times* reported that one bomber "raised doves and adored children," though this adoration apparently did not extend to the children being bombed.[20]

Clever writers with a bias can slant any of the 5Ws and the *How*. As critically thinking readers, we need to "read between the lines" whenever we sense that we are receiving an editorial opinion disguised as a straight news story. (See Exercise 8.6, p. 306.)

The Balance of Reporting on an Issue

All I know, is just what I read in the papers.

Will Rogers

Whereas network news and interview programs have a shortage of time, newspapers and newsmagazines have limited space. The editors decide which stories are important enough to cover and on what page. Generally, if a story is on the front page it is perceived by readers as more important than a story placed further back in the paper. Many busy readers only have time to read the front page, so the stories featured there take on the most prominence.

In addition to the location of stories in a newspaper, the location of facts within the story is also important; misplacement can create a distorted view of the events covered. When significant facts are not covered in or close to the lead of the story, the reader can be misled, as we discussed in the last section concering an article on the effects of chocolate. If a writer wants to put a good spin on a damaging story, the damaging elements can be minimized in the lead and placed toward the end of the story, since many readers don't have time to read all the way to the end; crucial facts can thus be lost to the majority of readers.

It is also important for news stories to give different perspectives on divisive issues; if more space and space closer to the lead of the story are given to one viewpoint and other viewpoints are minimized, ignored, or placed toward the end of the story, readers don't get the full picture surrounding a controversial topic.

Finally, major newspapers and newsmagazines need to cover all stories that have significance for their readers. Editors have the power to decide

[20]John Leo, "No Way to Cover a War," *U.S. News and World Report,* April 29, 2002.

whether a story even makes the press, and because of the space shortage, some stories won't be covered. Sometimes, for example, coverage of minor candidates to an election is stopped in favor of giving more space to the front-runners. In many cases, the decision about whether to run or pull a story would be difficult for even the most impartial editor. In other cases, a story may be pulled primarily because of the bias of an editor; if, for example, an editor does not agree with a group staging a large protest, the story of the protest may not be covered at all. (See Exercise 8.7, p. 360.)

Fairness in Editorial Essays and Letters

As we have discussed, some newspapers and magazines try to balance their editorial pages by printing both liberal and conservative viewpoints, sometimes on alternate days. Other papers get a reputation for being primarily liberal or conservative because of the stands taken by their editorial writers. In addition, local newspapers often print their suggestions as to how readers should vote in an upcoming election. It is important for critical thinkers to realize that reporting is not always objective and fair and that the editorial pages are set aside to reflect the opinions of readers and essayists.

    Notice whether the essays on the editorial page seem to favor one political viewpoint over another. In addition, examine the letters to the editor that are published. They should reflect differing, rather than homogeneous, opinions on the same issue.

SKILL

Recognize the use of suggestion in print media.

Photo Composition

If a picture is worth a thousand words, then photojournalists have a strong communicative advantage. They can influence our perceptions of people or events with the photographs they print.

    Most of us would agree that outright lies using photographs are unethical; for example, when photographers for *TV Guide* used image processing to create a cover featuring the head of Oprah Winfrey with the body of actress Ann-Margaret, readers and fellow journalists alike were disapproving. As technology has advanced, so has the ability to alter images to make them look real. A staff photographer covering the war in Iraq for the *Los Angeles Times* was fired for altering a photograph to make it more visually striking. When Brian Walski sent his altered photograph to his own director of photography, the director didn't notice anything wrong. It took a *Hartford Courant* employee to notice that something was amiss, and even he wasn't able to confirm the alteration until he magnified

A photograph can "frame" a scene in different ways. In the first shot, the speaker appears to be addressing a substantial audience. In the second shot, we see that there are very few audience members. (Photos by John Diestler.)

the picture 600 percent. Walski, a highly respected, veteran photographer, apologized for the fabrication; he and other reporters believe that his judgment may have been affected by his sleepless days in a war zone. Nonetheless, his boss, Colin Crawford, felt compelled to fire him. "What Brian did is totally unacceptable and he violated our trust with our readers," Crawford said, "We don't feel good about doing this, but the integrity of our organization is essential. If our readers can't count on honesty from us, I don't know what we have left."[21] Crawford was right in knowing that we don't like to be deceived by our technology, and reputable news organizations do not knowingly print altered images.

But more subtle forms of manipulation can occur through photocomposition. A responsible photographer could take a wide-angle shot of a rally, thus giving the viewer a sense of the general scene. A less scrupulous, or less careful, photographer could shoot instead a few unruly persons, which would discredit the general group of peaceful participants. Conversely, he or she could focus the camera on a fight between one police officer and one participant, which would give an impression of general police brutality. In addition, captions beneath photographs can influence our perceptions of a person or event.

Newspapers and newsmagazines should treat photographs as documentary information that helps us get the general feel of an event. When you sense that a photograph is making an editorial statement, stop and consider what viewpoint is being suggested through the picture.

THE POWER OF MEDIA TO SHAPE INFORMATION

Journalists may take us seriously as news consumers but generally ignore our wider role as citizens. They do not encourage communication, strengthen the public dialogue, or facilitate the formulation of common decisions, but may in fact do just the opposite by framing news in objective and episodic formats.

Scott London,"How the Media Frames Political
Issues,"1993, ScottLondon.com

Writers and producers of news and feature stories have enormous power to shape the information that is broadcast or published. As we have discussed, selection of issues, camera angles, questions asked, choice of wording, placement in a program or publication, balance of reporting, and people interviewed all have an effect on how we view the topics that are presented to us.

Shanto Iyengar, director of the Political Communication lab at Stanford University, has written extensively on the problems concerning media framing of issues. He calls most television reporting "episodic" news framing, reports on single concrete events. Episodic reporting is contrasted with "thematic" framing, which is reporting that includes a general context for political and social issues and events.

[21]Kenneth F. Irby, "L.A. Times Photographer Fired Over Altered Image," Poynteronline, April 2, 2003.

[Handwritten margin note: Society vs. Individual responsibility / Thematic is broader]

Iyengar's studies found that subjects shown "episodic" reports were less likely to consider society responsible for the event, and subjects shown "thematic" reports were less likely to consider individuals responsible. In one of the clearest demonstrations of this phenomenon, subjects who viewed stories about poverty that featured homeless or unemployed people (episodic framing) were much more likely to blame poverty on individual failings, such as laziness or little education, than were those who instead watched stories about high national rates of unemployment or poverty (thematic framing). Viewers of the thematic frames were more likely to attribute the causes and solutions to governmental policies and other factors beyond the individual's control.[22]

Those who study the effects of media often debate the extent to which programs *create,* rather than *reflect,* reality for readers and viewers. Certainly, producers and directors of feature films use all of the technical and artistic elements available to them to bring audiences into their world. We attend movies to be entertained and sometimes enlightened; we expect to laugh or cry at comedies and dramas and marvel at the special effects of action films. We are aware that our emotions and perceptions are being manipulated, and we want to be affected by what we see and hear on the screen.

But the interesting question for the media-literate individual is "To what extent are my thoughts and feelings being manipulated by what purports to be news?" Are reporters giving us a window to the significant events happening in the world or are they, to some extent, creating the scenes we are shown? Are they presenting "just the facts," or are they really shaping the facts so that news stories and features become a subtle form of argumentation?

William Dorman, professor of journalism and government at the California State University in Sacramento, believes that meaning is actively shaped by print and electronic journalists:

> Media manufacture meaning; they do not simply serve as a neutral conveyor belt for information about what happens in the world. The important word here is *manufacture.* In my view, journalism is as much a manufacturing process as, say, the shoe industry. To be sure, there are important political, ethical and even moral differences—but the idea of a manufacturing process in which choices are made about what gets produced and how is precisely the same. Journalists select what will be covered and determine *how* it will be presented, including what elements will be included or left out, what elements will be emphasized or left in the shadows, what language will be used, and so on. These are human choices made by human beings working in a social system in which there are punishments and rewards. Indeed, I encourage my students to use the label **Representer** synonymously with the term Reporter."[23]

Professor Dorman encourages his students to do "frame hunts." Students find clippings from newspapers, magazines, blogs, or books; they may also

[22]Scott London, "How the Media Frames Political Issues," scottlondon.com (accessed March, 2007 Original, January, 2003).
[23]William Dorman, "Using Frame Analysis in the Classroom," handout.

comparing news is
importance ⊗
socially or
culturally
(results
may be different

record a segment of a radio or television program that features media framing of a person or event. One common method for discovering a frame is to find a news item that is covered in two or more publications and note the difference in the reporting of that item.

Following is an example that Professor Dorman has used in his classroom. As you read each item, imagine that you have no particular feelings about Senator McCain and his campaign for the presidency of the United States. How might you view McCain and his chances of winning his party's nomination differently depending on which account you had read?

McCain Embarks on 2-Day Iowa Bus Tour

John McCain fired up the "Straight Talk Express" bus from his first presidential campaign on Thursday in hopes of getting his second bid back on course after an early season slump.

"We've got to build the momentum," the Republican senator said, even as he brushed off polls that show him trailing rival Rudy Giuliani. "I'm very happy with where we are right now. We're fine."[24]

McCain Fighting to Recapture Maverick Spirit of 2000 Bid

In the seven years since John McCain and his "Straight Talk Express" nearly derailed George W. Bush's White House ambitions, the blunt-spoken senator from Arizona has become the very picture of the highly managed presidential candidate he once scorned.

And along the way, he lost Stuart Hume and Mike Moffett.

The New Hampshire GOP activists counted themselves among McCain's loyalists in 2000, admiring his rejection of party dogma. But both men have turned elsewhere this time around.[25]

Another example of getting an angle or framing a story occurred in a feature for the *Contra Costa Times*. This newspaper serves a county close to Berkeley and San Francisco in northern California, which has a diverse population. The feature profiled a variety of middle school students and the challenges of their lives. Two of the preteens had lost parents, one watched a mother survive addiction to cocaine, one struggles with attention-deficit disorder, and one is the child of immigrants. Following each child's story were suggestions of how people in the child's part of the county could volunteer to help preteens and make a difference in their communities.

[24]Liz Sidoti, "McCain Embarks on 2-Day Iowa Bus Tour," Associated Press Writer, http://www .sfgate.com/cgi-bin/article.cgi?file=/n/a/2007/03/15/politics/p101013D23.DTL&type=printable (accessed March 15, 2007).
[25]Michael D. Shear, *Washington Post*, "McCain Fighting to Recapture Maverick Spirit of 2000 Bid," http://www.washingtonpost.com/wp-dyn/content/article/2007/03/14/AR2007031402301_pf.html (accessed March 15, 2007).

The parents of one of these children felt that their daughter had been misrepresented. The headline for her story read: "Lorene: Chafing at the Bit." Following are some of the quotes characterizing her:

> Lorene is popular. Tall and slender, with straight blonde hair, clear green eyes and perfect teeth, she's one of the most popular girls in the seventh grade class at Orinda Intermediate School. "The queen bee of her little hive of popular girls," one teacher said, scornfully, "Lorene does well enough in her classes, but it is the social aspects that dominate her school hours."[26]

The article goes on to mention detentions, attitude problems, disrespect for family members, and a privileged life affected by divorce. A subheadline at the bottom of the three-page spread on Lorene reads: "Affluent Teens: Money Can't Buy Them Emotional Security." Although Lorene is not mentioned in this section, the implication is clear: She, and other "privileged" teens are at risk for depression and substance abuse when their families don't provide them with emotional security. Her parents expressed their dismay at this implication in a subsequent editorial.

"KIDS" SECTION PORTRAYS LORENE UNFAIRLY

Dennis and Sandy C.

In the "Kids at the Crossroads" insert in the November 17 edition of the *Times,* our daughter Lorene was the young person interviewed from Orinda.

When the *Times* reporter originally approached us, we were led to believe that the principal at Orinda Intermediate School had recommended Lorene as an outgoing, communicative student who would be a good candidate for the interview. The principal has told us that the *Times* never contacted her for her recommendations.

We were led to believe that this was an honor and that the article would be upbeat and positive. Little did we realize that the *Times* had an agenda to portray an Orinda teenager as an over-privileged, callous, uncaring person.

Our family and friends were outraged by the article. Our daughter was in tears after reading the portrayal of her and her family. After hours and weeks of interviews, the *Times* chose to print only the comments that would support its preconceived notions.

The Times omitted most that was good about Lorene and the loving part that both her parents play in encouraging her self-confidence and quest for independence. Her father spent a portion of one interview explaining how most teenagers experience a brief period of aloofness with their parents as they make the transition from adolescence to adulthood. The thrust of this discussion was

---

[26]Pam King, "Kids at the Crossroads," *Contra Costa Times,* November 17, 1996, p. 15.

about the transitory nature of this phenomenon. The *Times* chose to portray this as a way of life for Lorene.

Let's set the record straight. Lorene is a well-adjusted, loving, intelligent, goal-oriented 12-year-old. She gets all A's and B's, is on two basketball teams, a soccer team and a volleyball team. She has a large cross-section of friends and is sensitive to the needs of the less fortunate. She spent last Thanksgiving serving dinners to the homeless at the Richmond Rescue Mission and adopted a family to help last Christmas.

She is an actress and has an impressive resume of training classes, modeling, stage performances and voice-overs. Rarely does someone so young feel this focused. The *Times* was well aware of Lorene's wonderful traits, yet in the "Kids at the Crossroads" article, Lorene's fine grades, concern for the needy, and aspiring goals are never once mentioned.

Lorene is an asset to her family, her school and her community. She does not use drugs or alcohol, she is not violent, she does not have problems in school and she has the comfort of a loving family. How dare the *Times* insensitively slant the reporting to suggest otherwise.

The *Times* has done a child and her community a disservice. Shame on the *Times* for discrediting the reputation of a "Kid at the Crossroads."

Reprinted by permission of the authors.

When this editorial was researched for purposes of publication, Lorene's mother was asked to give further incidences of the distortion of information. Sandy C. said that the reporter never directly lied in the story, but that she presented the facts in such a way as to create a false image of her daughter. As an example, she mentioned a quote that was highlighted at the top of one page in which Lorene stated, in reference to staying for several weeks at her father's home, "I probably won't miss my mother. I'm looking forward to the freedom. I can do anything I want." Sandy said that those words were spoken in an obviously kidding, bantering voice. She and Lorene were joking and laughing together at the time; she felt that the reporter clearly understood the context of the quote, but presented it as something an arrogant, self-centered child would say. In fact, Sandy stated that when her daughter read the quote and several others talking about how she enjoys "putting one over on the adults in her life," Lorene was incredulous; she cried and said she felt betrayed by the reporter. She feels that she doesn't get away with any negative behavior.

In another incidence of framing, Lorene is characterized as being suspended for "slamming a classmate up against a wall." Her mother said that, in fact, a boy had hit Lorene in the face at which point she pushed him away hard and he hit the wall. Sandy agreed to the suspension and the need to punish any use of physical force; however, she is upset by the characterization of Lorene as a violent bully.

One of Lorene's teachers, Maureen W., wrote the following comments after she read the article:

I am disturbed by the insinuation that most Orinda children are rich, selfish snobs. As in all communities, we have individuals who may fit that description. I have taught at Orinda Intermediate School for seven years. I have taught in several other school districts in Contra Costa County over my twenty plus years of teaching. In my years of teaching at both high schools and the intermediate schools, I have met all types of individuals. To generalize that the Orinda individual is morally insensitive is astonishingly stereotypical. If this article's intention was to harm Orinda children, you have succeeded. How devastating for a young person and her family to read such a negative article. Shame on you."[27]

Ms. W.'s letter was sent to the editor but was not published. Another unpublished letter in response to the article on Lorene came from her soccer coach, Tom A.:

My take on Lorene's part of this article was to portray Orinda as an enclave of spoiled, wealthy kids from dysfunctional families. That exists here; Orinda is an easy target. Certainly this will reinforce some peoples' opinions. Perhaps that was the reporter's goal.

Lorene and her family, however, are not as they were presented, and I hope that folks in and around the area won't believe everything they read."[28]

Many stories, such as Lorene's, are reported factually, but with the particular frame the reporter wants to create. Certain elements are emphasized; other factors may be completely omitted. As a critical thinker, it is important for you to consider the way in which a story is presented and people are characterized. Whenever possible, read or watch a story from different sources before making interpretations about the information presented. (See Exercise 8.8, p. 360.)

A BAG OF MARKETING AND ADVERTISING TRICKS

It takes an educated or very discerning person to be aware of and pay attention to the many methods used to persuade viewers to think or act in a certain way. The old saying "Let the buyer beware" means that when we are subjected to various pitches by advertisers and politicians, we should have the power to say no to their claims and to resist being persuaded against our will. Increasing our awareness of the persuasive techniques used by print and electronic media gives us more power as thinkers, voters, and consumers.

---

[27]Maureen W. © Reprinted by permission of the author.
[28]Tom A., reprinted by permission of the author.

Advertisers and marketers are continually devising new ways to persuade target audiences. Let's consider some of their common techniques:

1. Fuzzy words
2. Logical fallacies
3. Stylized images and sounds
4. Celebrity associations and endorsements
5. Product placement
6. The Gestalt principle
7. Eye tracking
8. Neuromarketing

Fuzzy Words

We discussed the persuasive elements of language extensively in Chapter 7 and to some extent in Chapter 6 as well. However, it's useful to look at some examples that are specifically used by marketers and advertisers. **Fuzzy words** are weasel words that create an impression without specifically defining a concrete meaning for the words or phrases used. An example would be the words "Made in America" on a product label. The implication of the label is that the consumer is supporting American workers and manufacturers, but what may really be meant is "some of this product is made in America." An ad may proclaim, "Four out of five doctors recommend the main ingredient in our product." It sounds as if four out of five doctors recommend the product, but on careful inspection, the ad is citing only the main ingredient as the recommended item; this technique is often used when the main ingredient is a common one, such as aspirin. Advertisers also use fuzzy words like "crisp" or "full-bodied" or phrases such as "you're worth it" to make their products seem appealing while promising nothing. They may also make claims with no context or point of comparison, such as "Snappy has 25% more peanuts per jar" or "There's nothing like the feel of Silky tissues."

Logical Fallacies

Advertisers are great at presenting arguments that are so engaging and well designed that consumers may forget to consider that their claims are illogical or unsupported. For example, one technique frequently used is to show "before-and-after" images of an individual; a frowning woman with no makeup is shown next to her smiling self with professional makeup, and the difference in her look is attributed to a new skin formula. The "PC versus Mac" ads use a similar formula: PC is shown as older, out-of-shape, and rumpled in his corporate clothing, while Mac is young, cool, and casually dressed. It is hoped that consumers will make the same connections and overlook the false dilemma/either-or fallacy with which the computers are being contrasted. The either-or fallacy is also committed when food companies claim to have authentic products like "the real salsa" versus their competitors whose salsa is cast as illegitimate.

We've seen that *romancing a product*—associating the product with wonderful scenes of fun and excitement that seem to accompany people who buy the product—is really a faulty analogy. The advertisers don't directly state that owning their car or using their shampoo will dramatically improve your life, but their commercials create an association of enjoyment and fulfillment that is connected to buying the product.

Advertisers also may commit the fallacy of "begging the question"; for example, a disembodied voice may ask, "Why are so many people switching to our wireless service?" without giving any statistics to support their claim that people actually are switching.

Stylized Images and Sounds

When millions of dollars are spent on commercials and print ads (for example, $2.6 million for a 30-second Super Bowl ad), companies want slick and polished images showcasing their products. Under hot lights, the ice cubes in a cool drink would melt, so perfectly shaped plastic cubes are used. Professional "dressers" are hired to ensure that food looks great; a dresser may go through dozens of hamburger buns to choose the perfect one to complement a hamburger for an ad. Filtered lighting is used to create atmosphere, and items are often made to seem bigger than they actually are. Freckles, blemishes, and weight can all be removed and adjusted with image-editing programs. Someone promoting a new cholesterol medication may be shown dancing happily through a field to soft, inspiring music; it is hoped that the required warnings of side effects, including possible fatalities, will be ignored as viewers are entranced by the engaging sights and sounds of the commercial.

Television and radio advertisers also get and keep our attention with loud music or words and frequent camera cuts. You may have noticed that you can do homework during a television program, except when the commercials come on; they seem to grab your attention. This process happens to children, too. The next time you are watching television with a young child, notice how alert the child becomes during almost any commercial. We respond to loud, fast-paced programming with frequent image changes. Even public television programs such as *Sesame Street* use this technique of 15- to 30-second spots to keep attention levels high. Commercials shown on programs airing after midnight are particularly loud; people who fall asleep in front of a television set may be startled awake by the blaring of a commercial message (invariably advising late-night viewers to improve their lives by using their product or service). No advertiser wants to play to a sleeping audience.

Celebrity Associations and Endorsements

Advertisers have always used popular celebrities—athletes, singers, and other famous figures—to entice target audiences. Sometimes, the celebrity has some credibility, such as a former Olympic athlete who uses a pain reliever to help soothe an injured knee or an actress who lets the public track her progress on a particular weight loss program. In other cases, celebrities are used to push products because it is assumed that people will buy the products in order to feel associated with the celebrity.

It's hard for consumers to avoid being targeted. During the rebellious 1960s, students shook off the oppression of expensive clothing and started wearing jeans as a way of distancing themselves from the values of corporate America. In response, designer jeans were created, marketed, modeled by celebrities, and sold for very solid profits. When subsequent generations started ripping their jeans, ripped jeans were likewise marketed, and some people even pay hundreds of dollars for them. There has been a recent movement toward supporting Fair Trade and shunning corporations that exploit international workers. Undaunted, corporations have responded by marketing their products to a new target audience called *conscience consumers*. British writer Jane Mortinson gives an example of this phenomenon in an article on the collaboration of rock star Bono and the American Express company:

> When Bono walked into the head office of American Express 18 months ago, the company practically laid out the red carpet. The campaigning rock star had something that one of the world's biggest financial services groups was very much looking for: a way of reaching the growing band of so-called "conscience consumers."
>
> This month, Amex launched its RED card, part of an initiative in which consumer companies are backing Bono's Global Fund, which helps women and children affected by HIV and Aids in Africa. Amex's contribution is to donate 1% of all spending on the card to the charity. The woman charged with making sure the launch of the card in Britain is a success—with the plan then to roll it out globally—is Laurel Powers-Freeling, the American head of Amex's UK consumer card business.
>
> Powers-Freeling says the company, more often associated with power lunches than global poverty, had an immediate meeting of minds with the singer. "It was an interesting moment for us because one of the things we at American Express have been observing for a while is this trend towards what we now call the conscience consumer. The people saying, 'I have to spend money anyway, so if there's a way of using the power of my purse for good, great, but I don't want to give up anything to do so.'"
>
> More exciting for Amex perhaps was the chance to reach a whole new market. Since joining the company just over a year ago from Marks & Spencer, Powers-Freeling has sought to make Amex more of an "everyday" card. Product red—as the initiative likes to be known— offers something potentially far more valuable than a large target market: the chance to become worthy by association. "What I want is obviously more Amex cards and for more people to feel it is part of their lives, that they have an affinity with it," Powers-Freeling says in

her no-nonsense voice, which still bears the twang of her midwestern upbringing after 20 years in Britain.

The principle of paying more—or at least doing without Air Miles or loyalty bonuses—to feel good about yourself is not new. Amex estimates there are already 1.5 million "conscience consumers" in the UK, people who buy products associated with a social or ethical benefit, be it Fair Trade coffee or organic bananas. This is expected to swell to 3.9 million within three years.[29]

Product Placement

Technological advances have made it possible for consumers to avoid television advertising by recording shows before watching them; people without TiVos or recording equipment can leave the room during commercials. Advertisers have fought back with **product placement**, embedding their products into the actual story lines or sets of programs. Those who watch *American Idol* see each of the judges drinking from a very large *Coke* glass. Sitcoms and dramas also include product placements from cereals to electronics.

Some analysts trace the rise of embedded products to the film *E.T.* and the marked rise in sales for Hershey's Reese's Pieces candy that followed the new candy's placement in the film. *E.T.* is one of the most popular films of all time, grossing $800 million so far. Advertisers are asked to pay big money for the kind of exposure movies and television programs can provide. In his column *Desperate Advertisers*, Buzz McClain discusses the increasing trend of advertisers to place their products in all forms of media:

> *Advertising Age* magazine says it costs some $26 million to "integrate" a product on a popular television series today. For companies that want a shot on NBC's *The Apprentice*, a per-episode exposure can cost up to $2 million.
>
> One Fort Worth national furniture retailer recently approached a program about displaying its wares and was dismayed to discover it would cost $5 million for the privilege. He turned down the opportunity.
>
> But not everyone does. Advertisers spent $4.2 billion on TiVo-proof (you can't zip through it) product placements and brand integration last year, according to research group PQ Media of Stamford, Conn. Nearly half of that—$1.9 billion—was in television, with $1.3 billion in feature films. Recorded music—particularly hip-hop and rap—and video games also reaped millions by incorporating branded entertainment.[30]

[29]Jane Martinson,"The Amex chief providing backing for Bono," *The Guardian*, business.guardian .co.uk (accessed March 17, 2006).

[30]Buzz McClain,"Desperate Advertisers," *The Star-Telegram*, http://www.1stapproach.com/ press-desperate_advertisers.html (accessed October 6, 2005).

Placing their products in films, television programs, and other media may help advertisers, but it can negatively affect the artistic vision of the writers and directors. When huge amounts of money are being spent on product placements, the marketers want to make sure that their merchandise is quite obvious to the audiences, and that can be annoying as writer Jon Folland notes on the Web site nativ.tv:

> [W]hen watching *Casino Royale*, the new James Bond movie, I was driven to distraction by the brazen overuse of such advertising.
>
> Having paid enough money for tickets and watched 15 minutes of adverts, I was ready to watch the film. But where did the adverts end and the film begin? The film was a relentless parade of products embedded in appropriately naff scenarios. This wasn't subliminal, this was in-your-face advertising. How many times do characters in the film need to look closely into their mobile phones before you lose the immersive experience of a really good film and start getting angry at the blatant use of product placement?[31]

In addition to embedding products in various forms of media, marketers also like to place their products in attractive retail settings. Supermarkets charge companies more for placing products at eye level or at the checkout stand where they are more likely to be noticed and bought. Many studies have been done to show how consumers move through stores and which aisles are more likely to bring product sales. Wal-Mart stores have a "power aisle"; research has shown that customers will spend more time looking at items on this aisle, particularly if they had seen ads for the products on display there. Phil Vischer, creator of the popular *VeggieTales* series, writes about the marketing of his videos:

> The average Wal-Mart shopper would look at the average product situated along a Wal-Mart store's prime circulation path—the fabled "power aisle"—for just over two seconds. In the case of a video, if they hadn't already heard something good about it, forget it. They wouldn't even pick up the package. And that's only if you were lucky enough to get your product positioned along the power aisle in the first place. Get stuck "spine-out" in the in-line section, and the average shopper wouldn't see your video at all. You might as well be in the dumpster out back.[32]

The Gestalt Principle *organized whole perceived as more than the sum of its parts*

In addition to using a variety of attention-getting devices, advertisers and political media coordinators are keenly interested in holding attention, even for just a few seconds more than their competitors. To hold attention, they

---

[31]Jon Folland, "What Can I Remember About Casino Royale? Sony, Omega, Aston Martin…The plot? Not sure." www.nativ/tv (accessed November 20, 2006).
[32]Phil Vischer, *Me, Myself, & Bob* (Nashville, TN: Thomas Nelson Publishers, 2006), pp. 143–144.

have to "grab" the audience in some way, and many utilize the principles of Gestalt theory.

A principle of Gestalt psychology states that "the whole is greater than the sum of the parts." Our minds strive toward congruence and completion of information. If a message strikes us as incomplete, we will fill in the missing details ourselves. Consider the following passage that has been circulating on the Internet:

> Aoccdrnig to rsceareh at Cmabrigde Uinervtisy, it deosn't mttaer in what order the ltteers in a word are; the only iprmoetnt thing is that the frist and lsat ltteer be in the rghit pclae. The rset can be a total mses and you can still raed it wouthit a porbelm. This is bcuseae the human mind deos not raed ervey lteter by istlef, but the word as a wlohe.

If you were able to understand the passage, it is because you took each word as a whole and filled in the incorrect parts, as Gestalt theory has postulated.

The **Gestalt principle** also takes effect when we perceive movement on a theater screen even though the projector is in reality showing only a quick series of still images. Cartoonists rely on the Gestalt principle when they use the technique of cell animation; the cartoonist draws a series of frames in which the character moves slightly from frame to frame. The viewer supplies the missing information and perceives realistic movement. Providing missing information is central to the process of human perception, whether this information is visual or auditory. Consider the following Gestalt techniques that are commonly used but seldom questioned by us as consumers of the message.

1. Questions or Slogans That the Consumer Is Taught to Answer. Early in advertising history, Winston cigarettes used a simple jingle: "Winston tastes good like a cigarette should. Winston tastes good like a (clap, clap) cigarette should." For a long time, television and radio listeners heard this jingle sung in a joyful manner.

Then one day, the jingle proceeded as follows: "Winston tastes good like a cigarette should. Winston tastes good like a (clap, clap)." Listeners who had heard the jingle before could hardly help completing the song in their minds, thus joining in with the advertisers to laud the praises of this cigarette. They had been trained over time to know the ending of the commercial, and when the standard ending was left out, they filled it in.

We are generally taught as children that it is rude not to answer a question asked of us, and this carries over into adulthood. Assertiveness trainers put considerable focus on teaching clients that they don't need to answer every question they are asked.

Advertisers capitalize on our early training by asking us questions, knowing we probably will instinctively formulate answers in our minds. Here are some examples:

Aren't you hungry for King Burgers now?
Why do you think they call it Up Close?
Doesn't your child deserve a gift of love?

2. *Images That Don't Make Sense.* Again, our minds try to make sense out of things that are together but don't seem to go together. Leon Festinger's theory of cognitive dissonance, discussed further in Chapter 9, states that the need for "congruence" (consonance, harmony) is not only a human need but also a drive, just as powerful as our drive for food and water. We are motivated by this drive and so we take action when things don't make sense. We try to make sense out of them.

For example, you may be disturbed by a couple who don't seem suited for each other; their presence together may cause you to try to figure out what they see in each other. Even children love challenges called "What is wrong with this picture?"

Advertisers capitalize on our fascination with the incongruent by sometimes putting things together that don't seem to go together. They know that if we are puzzled, we will give more attention to or spend more time on the ad, even if we aren't aware of doing so. They also know that if we become familiar with a product's brand name, because we've spent more time or given more attention to its claims, then we are more likely to buy the product.

One cigarette advertiser created a series of print ads showing two scenes of people interacting; there was no clear indication of what was going on between these people or why they were together. Often, the people were shown laughing, but the readers were not told what they were laughing about.

Incongruous scenes may be combined with sexual insinuations, making them doubly fascinating to viewers. Some researchers and graphic designers claim that certain images can attract and maintain the attention of viewers; these images include children, dogs, cars, death, guns, war, and sex. Michael Hoff, one of the leading producers of nonfiction television programs (including *Real Ghostbusters*, *Top 10 Creepy Creatures*, *Deadly Duels,* and *I, Detective*) believes that the combination of subliminal elements sells his "don't touch that dial" programming: "Sex, death, and weirdness are the critical elements of any good television show," Hoff explains with a sly smile. "If you've got all three, man, you've got a hit."[33]

Eye Tracking

Retailer John Wanamaker is credited as saying, "Half of my advertising dollars are wasted—I just don't know which half." It has been hard for advertisers to know what works and what doesn't, but innovative technologies for studying intricacies of consumer behavior are being pioneered, and their findings are sold to companies that hope to use their advertising budgets more wisely. One

[33]Chuck Barney, "Michael Hoff's 'Oooh-Whee' TV," Knight-Ridder/Tribune News Service, February 27, 2004.

"eye-tracking" company does extensive research on how consumers look at ads so that its clients can design advertising for maximum impact on their target audience; the new technology is explained on its Web site, eyetracking.com:

> Using a lightweight headset with three small cameras, it is possible to record exactly where a person is looking as he or she is interacting with some kind of visual display. For example, say a person is navigating a website, looking to purchase an item online. With **eye-tracking**, it is possible to see exactly where this person is looking for specific information about the item, how they compare different items, and where they look to navigate to the shopping cart or other areas of the site.
>
> The user's point of gaze is superimposed on a video recording of the website as they interact with it. In this way, it is possible for developers to interact with the interface through the eyes of the user. It is possible to see objectively if a user has difficulty locating information, if they miss critical information, or have trouble navigating.
>
> The eye patterns can also be plotted on a bitmap in order to look at a viewing history spanning several seconds or longer. GazeTraces™ document the scanning behavior of a single participant scanning a single screen display or portion of it. This allows you to see clearly what on the page first caught the attention of the user, what elements he missed, and what elements may have been confusing.[34]

The Eye Tracking company analyzes television, internet, and Web page viewing, packaging, and even brand positioning for sponsorships and then delivers suggestions to their clients as to how to optimize the attention of target audiences. The company also claims that it can assess customer's emotional reactions to an advertised product:

> A recently patented process measures changes in the pupil diameter to determine the emotional state of a user as they engage with your product. Changes in the pupil indicate in real time and objectively whether he or she is reacting favorably to your product.[35]

The Poynter Institute summarized research observations made while studying the eye movements of Web surfers, finding that ads get viewed (or not) in large part as a result of page placement and several specific design elements. Some of the findings seemed obvious, such as the fact that 55 percent of viewers scanned an ad placed on top of the page, while only 14 percent saw the one at the bottom. Some others, not so obvious, include the following:

> Text ads did far better than graphic ads.
> Ads that blended into the content generally did much better. Ads, for example, inset into text columns did extremely well.

[34]"Eye Movement and Point of Gaze," Eye Tracking, Inc., accessed 3/2007
[35]"Revolutionary Metrics," Eye Tracking, Inc., www.eyetracking.com, 3/2007

Visual breaks between content sections tend to act as visual dams, creating a high drop-off rate for further viewing.

Contrasting background colors tip viewers off to the fact that the image is an ad—and hurt results. White or no background differentiation fared much better.

Performance improved in a direct relationship to ad size—larger ads commanded more and longer attention.[36]

Neuromarketing

For many years, scholars have debated the existence of **subliminal persuasion**, the use of messages that cannot be perceived by the conscious mind but that are registered unconsciously.

You may remember hearing about the merchandising trick drive-in movies allegedly used to play on customers. One frame of delicious-looking hot-buttered popcorn was spliced into a movie (remember that movies are shown on a fast-moving, frame-by-frame basis). Researcher James Vicary claimed that this frame, shown beneath the level of the viewers' conscious awareness, was correlated with an increase in popcorn sales at intermission time. This claim raised serious concerns and caused lawmakers to suggest legislation banning subliminal splicing; however, no examples of this practice were ever substantiated, and Vicary later admitted that he had falsified his research. The stir over his claims, however, created a huge industry of tapes filled with subliminal messages; people bought these tapes because they were promised that listening to them would help them relax, lose weight, and learn languages while they slept.

There remains controversy about whether subliminal persuasion exists; for those who believe it does exist in various forms, there is controversy about whether or not it is effective. However, researchers are continually studying the human brain, and their findings are offered to marketers in various fields who want to increase brand-name recognition and gain and hold the attention of target audiences in as many ways as possible. We have noted attempts to use the senses—colorful images; loud, catchy music; appealing smells—to attract consumers and make products memorable to them.

In addition to the standard marketing techniques, a new technique called **neuromarketing** uses recent advances in MRI scanning of the brain to assess how consumers will respond to products and advertisements.

If scientists can determine internal reactions to products and brand names, reactions that the consumer registers unconsciously, then companies may have a tool for genuine subliminal persuasion. *New York Times* reporter Clive Thompson explored the new field of "neuromarketing" by visiting psychiatrist Clint Kilts at his neuroscience facility called BrightHouse Institute:

---

[36]Poynter: September 8, 2004. Eye Tracking Study Reveals Ad Viewing Behavior…Marketingvox.com Observations on Advertising)

The BrightHouse Institute's techniques are based, in part, on an experiment that Kilts conducted earlier this year. He gathered a group of test subjects and asked them to look at a series of commercial products, rating how strongly they liked or disliked them. Then, while scanning their brains in an M.R.I. machine, he showed them pictures of the products again. When Kilts looked at the images of their brains, he was struck by one particular result: whenever a subject saw a product he had identified as one he truly loved—something that might prompt him to say, "That's just so me!"—his brain would show increased activity in the medial prefrontal cortex.

Kilts was excited, for he knew that this region of the brain is commonly associated with our sense of self....M.R.I. studies have found increased activity in this region when people are asked if adjectives like "trustworthy" or "courageous" apply to them. When the medial prefrontal cortex fires, your brain seems to be engaging, in some manner, with what sort of person you are. If it fires when you see a particular product, Kilts argues, it's most likely to be because the product clicks with your self-image....

Kilts stabbed his finger at another glowing yellow dot near the top of the brain. It was the magic spot—the medial prefrontal cortex. If that area is firing, a consumer isn't deliberating, he said: he's itching to buy. "At that point, it's intuitive. You say: 'I'm going to do it. I want it.'"...

M.R.I. scanning offers the promise of concrete facts—an unbiased glimpse at a consumer's mind in action. To an M.R.I. machine, you cannot misrepresent your responses. Your medial prefrontal cortex will start firing when you see something you adore, even if you claim not to like it....

Neuromarketing may also be able to suss out the distinction between advertisements that people merely like and those that are actually effective—a difference that can be hard to detect from a focus group. A neuromarketing study in Australia, for instance, demonstrated that supershort, MTV-style jump cuts—indeed, any scenes shorter than two seconds—aren't as likely to enter the long-term memory of viewers, however bracing or aesthetically pleasing they may be....

In response to his critics, Kilts plans to publish the BrightHouse research in an accredited academic journal. He insisted to me that his primary allegiance is to science; BrightHouse's techniques are "business done in the science method," he said, "not science done in the business method." And as he sat at his computer, calling up a 3-D picture of a brain, it was hard not to be struck, at the very least, by the seriousness of his passion. There, on the screen, was the medial prefrontal cortex, juggling our conscious thinking. There was the amygdala, governing our fears, buried deep in the brain. These are sights that he said still inspire in him feelings of wonder. "When you sit down and you're watching—for the first time in the history of mankind—how we process complex primary emotions like anger, it's amazing," he said. "You're like, there, look at that: that's anger, that's pleasure. When you see that roll off the workstation, you never look back." You just keep going, it seems, until you hit Madison Avenue.[37]

Researchers from MIT, Stanford, and Carnegie Mellon University have also used brain scans to look at how consumers think about products in order to understand and predict what they will buy. Jonathan Potts reports on this research:

> For the first time, researchers have used functional magnetic resonance imaging (fMRI) to determine what parts of the brain are active when people consider whether to purchase a product and to predict whether or not they ultimately choose to buy the product. The study appears in the journal *Neuron* and was co-authored by scientists at Carnegie Mellon University, Stanford University and the MIT Sloan School of Management.
>
> This paper is the latest from the emerging field of neuroeconomics, which investigates the mental and neural processes that drive economic decision-making. The results could have a profound impact on economic theory, because the decision of whether to purchase a product is the most basic and pervasive economic behavior. *Spreading widely*
>
> Previous imaging studies have found that separate parts of the brain are activated when people are confronted with financial gains versus financial losses. The authors of this latest study believed that distinct brain regions would be activated when people were presented with products they wish to purchase (representing a potential gain) and when they were presented with those products' prices (representing a potential loss). The researchers wanted to see if they could then use this information to predict when a person would decide to buy a product, and when they would pass it up.
>
> Twenty-six adults participated in the study, in which they were given $20 to spend on a series of products that would be shipped to them. If they made no purchases, they would be able to keep the money. The products and their prices appeared on a computer screen that the participants viewed while lying in an fMRI scanner. The researchers found that when the participants were presented with the products, a subcortal brain region known as the nucleus accumbens that is associated with the anticipation of pleasure was activated. When the subjects were presented with prices that were excessive, two things happened: the brain region known as the insula was activated and a part of the brain associated with balancing gains versus losses—the medial prefrontal cortex—was deactivated.

---

[37]From Clive Thompson, "There's a Sucker Born in Every Medial Prefrontal Cortex," *New York Times*, October 26, 2003.

Furthermore, by studying which regions were activated, the authors were able to successfully predict whether the study participants would decide to purchase each item. Activations of the regions associated with product preference and with weighing gains and losses indicated that a person would decide to purchase a product. In contrast, when the region associated with excessive prices was activated participants chose not to buy a product.[38]

Other technological advances, currently used for mostly positive purposes, can also be used to deceive. For example, scientists at the Massachusetts Institute of Technology have created realistic videos of people saying things they actually have not said. The videos seem so authentic that viewers cannot detect any tampering when people are simulated speaking languages that they do not speak. The technology involves the use of artificial intelligence to teach a machine what a person looks like when talking—using a few minutes of videotape, the computer captures images that represent the full range of motion of the subject's mouth. With an accurate picture of the mouth, the computer can superimpose it on a person's face and, having also learned electronically to imitate the person's every sound, can make the person say new things. The technology could also be used to create more realistic video games. But scientists and media critics also fear that this new technology might be used to discredit or embarrass people by having them appear to say things they haven't said; it could also be used to have people with credibility seem to be endorsing products or programs. Some scientists predict that there will have to be a whole new field of experts who will have to testify at trials as to whether a video has been forged with this new technology.[39]

SKILL

Be aware of the use of advertising and marketing techniques

We can't realistically be aware of all of the ways we are targeted as citizens and consumers. But critical thinkers do have some defenses against the barrage of tricks and tools used to get us to cast our votes and spend our money:

- Become aware of your attention span when you are listening to or viewing an advertisement. Are you drawn to a particular image, but can't explain why?
- When making decisions as a consumer, consider why you are buying a particular brand. Do you really believe this brand is the best or is it just a

---

[38]Jonathan Potts, "Researchers Use Brain Scans to Predict When People Will Buy Products," www.cmu.edu (accessed January 6, 2007). (also cited on *Medical News Today*.)
[39]Gareth Cook, "At MIT, They Can Put Words in Our Mouths," *The Boston Globe*, May 15, 2002, p. A1.

or if you really like; tastes better?

name you recognize? Read labels to see if the ingredients in your "brand" really differ from less expensive brands.

- When making decisions as a voter, be clear about the reasons you are supporting a particular candidate or proposition. Have you "bought into" a slogan or into someone's claims without thinking? Do you clearly understand the issues and the various conclusions about the issues?

The key to walking through the minefields of print and electronic persuasion is to be armed with facts and logical reasoning about your decisions as a citizen and a consumer. Critical thinkers avoid basing their judgments on the consciously or unconsciously applied manipulations of campaign managers and advertisers. A good offense is your best defense. (See Exercises 8.9 and 8.10 on p. 361.)

STORYTELLING AS PERSUASION

So far, we have focused on persuasive techniques used by television, radio, print journalism, and advertising. Critical thinkers also need to be aware of the enormous power of storytelling—in the form of movies and televised fiction—to influence our beliefs about the world. Often, when an issue is presented in story form, it has tremendous persuasive power and may reach people who have not responded to "logical" arguments; we are particularly vulnerable to the arguments hidden in stories because we see storytelling as primarily entertaining and we aren't on the lookout for subtle manipulations of our emotions and perceptions.

People who feel strongly about an issue often have had a personal understanding and connection to the issue; those who speak out against drunk driving or drug abuse, or in favor of funding for a particular disease often have had significant experience and thus a depth of emotion that fuels their expertise on the topic. But strong emotions about a topic can be stirred even in a neutral audience through the vicarious experience that a movie provides. If someone wants, for example, to gain support for animal rights, a film about lovable animals that are being abused can do a lot to garner public sympathy. In similar fashion, if someone wants to paint a person or a group as villainous, a powerful argument to that effect can be made through a fictional portrayal. Good filmmaking allows an audience to experience the perspective of the main characters and to see life as they do; too often, however, the audience does not easily separate fact from fiction and believes that the story presented is the unabridged truth.

A disturbing trend can take place when fictional films about historic events are taken as an accurate portrayal of those events. For example, Oliver Stone has made powerful films about former Presidents John Fitzgerald Kennedy (*JFK*) and Richard Nixon (*Nixon*). By interspersing true events with fictional speculations about these men, Stone creates a compelling narrative. The problem is that moviegoers who are not familiar with true historic events don't separate the truth from the fiction and take Stone's movies as documentaries. Some libraries even place these films in the history reference sections rather than in the movie collections, adding to their perception as historic, rather than fictional, narratives.

The president of Wellesley College, Diana Chapman Walsh, felt the need to "set the record straight" about the portrayal of Wellesley in the film *Mona Lisa Smile* after she had received letters from concerned alumnae. Walsh said the film gave a "distorted and demeaning portrayal of our alma mater." College administrators had read an early version of the script that they said emphasized students' intelligence and their close relationships with faculty advisors, and this positive portrayal prompted them to give permission for Revolution Studios to film on campus. When the movie came out, the administrators noted that the screenplay had been changed and now characterized the college as "rigid and hidebound and the students as rich and spoiled." The film characterizes Wellesley as a place where it is dangerous for faculty to show independence and portrays administrators as frightened and as having "claws under their gloves." Some people on campus were upset enough to consider suing for libel; they realized that many moviegoers who see this film would assume that it is an accurate historic picture of Wellesley in the 1950s. The studio's spokesperson countered, "We did not set out to make a documentary." However, to many viewers, it may seem to be just that.[40]

When we see movies set in a specific historical time period, we need to be alert to the differences between what really happened and what the screenwriters added to make the story more interesting. With those precautions, we can maintain an objective perspective that helps us stay grounded in reality.

CITIZENS, CONSUMERS, AND RELATIONSHIPS IN AN AGE OF TECHNOLOGY

A challenge to critical thinkers in the exploding Age of Information is to make conscious, deliberate choices about how they want to use the available technological innovations as citizens, consumers, and people in relationships.

At one time, most people lived in agrarian societies, connected deeply to the land. Families and communities worked together, and though the life was difficult, relationships were close and enduring. Couples usually grew old and died on the same piece of land they bought as newlyweds.

During the industrial revolution, factories and other businesses created a work environment in which fathers and sometimes mothers left the home for most of the daylight hours. Many people still follow this pattern; one or both parents leave home in the morning and congregate at some time in the evening when athletic practices, after-school programs, and a host of other extracurricular activities are completed.

[40]Sara Lipka, "Wellesley's President Isn't Smiling Over College's Portrayal in Film," *The Chronicle of Higher Education* January 14, 2004.

The technological advances of recent decades give us an abundance of new choices, allowing many people to work at least in part from home and forge unique lifestyles. There are also many new choices concerning media that provide endless opportunities to explore issues, products, and relationships.

In response to the average person's ability to navigate and design his or her world through technology, *Time* magazine's Person of the Year in 2006 was "You."

> The "Great Man" theory of history is usually attributed to the Scottish philosopher Thomas Carlyle, who wrote that "the history of the world is but the biography of great men." He believed that it is the few, the powerful and the famous who shape our collective destiny as a species. That theory took a serious beating this year.
>
> …(2006) is a story about community and collaboration on a scale never seen before. It's about the cosmic compendium of knowledge Wikipedia and the million-channel people's network YouTube and the online metropolis MySpace. It's about the many wresting power from the few and helping one another for nothing and how that will not only change the world, but also change the way the world changes…We're looking at an explosion of productivity and innovation, and it's just getting started.…For seizing the reins of the global media, for founding and framing the new digital democracy, for working for nothing and beating the pros at their own game, TIME's Person of the Year…is You…This is an opportunity to build a new kind of international understanding, not politician to politician, great man to great man, but citizen to citizen, person to person.[41]   *generation me*

As Lev Grossman points out, we have numerous and incredible choices, not only because of Web 2.0 but also because of cell phones, iPhones, digital cameras, TiVos, Wii, and other electronic devices exploding on the world market. Commuters can be entertained all the way to and from work with iPods, books on CDs, or an abundance of FM or AM radio stations. A person who is unable to walk can still go grocery shopping online. A parent who is torn between seeing his favorite team's playoff game and his daughter's piano recital can TiVo the game and watch it later in the night, skipping the commercials. A student who needs to take care of a sick parent can do research from home; she can look up great sources for a history paper and then check out various Web sites to find out the latest breakthroughs, treatments, and support groups for her parent's medical condition. A musician can go to iTunes and download numerous renditions of a song. Friends can connect every day from anywhere in the world by phone or email or on My Space or Facebook. Citizens concerned about any social issues are able to read numerous articles from the best papers and magazines in the world. Voters can check their favorite sources before casting a vote, and consumers can do comparison shopping before buying a product or choosing a hotel or airline. Dinner and theatre reservations can be made from home, and hundreds of movie and

[41]Lev Grossman, "Time's Person of the Year; You," *Time*, December 13, 2006.

DVD reviews can be accessed to help us decide what to see or buy. People invited to a wedding can go to a department store's Web site, find out exactly what a bride and groom want, and have it delivered with a personalized message the next day.

The choices we have also come with some interesting consequences. Your local grocery store and your online bookstore both know exactly what you like to buy and read and will continue to tempt you with your favorite products in the form of individualized coupons or email offers. Unscrupulous hackers and scam artists will invade your privacy and try to invade your wallet as well. Predators can use increasingly sophisticated means to lure naïve children and teens. Someone may post malicious lies about you on a Web site and hurt your chances of being hired for a job or getting into graduate school. Critical thinkers have to be aware of the minefields of cyberspace and realize that every transmission that is made is out there forever.

And there is one more consideration. With all of the fascinating and entertaining choices available to us, we need to be mindful of how we want to use our time. The same tools that can make us closer to our friends and family, more aware of what's going on in the world, and more able to be efficient in our work can also isolate us from others. Roommates don't have to agree on what music to play; they can each listen to different tunes on their personalized iPods. Parents may be glued to their own PCs while children are talking, texting, instant messaging, or playing video games into the wee hours of the morning. As critical thinkers, we should heed the advice of the late professor and writer Neil Postman who warned us to be careful of "amusing ourselves to death." With vigilance about our personal choices, we can use our amazing electronic tools to impact our lives and our world for the good.

LIFE APPLICATION

There is a saying that you can tell about someone's priorities if you can see his or her calendar and checkbook. We all have a limited amount of time and resources. Be conscious and deliberate about your use of technology. If you don't have a plan, others—including people, programmers, advertisers, and Web masters—will have a plan for you. Decide how you can best use your time and money and set your own electronic and spending limits accordingly.

CHAPTER EXERCISES

Exercise 8.1   Purpose: To discover and analyze examples of suggestion in personal and professional contexts.

1. For the brave and honest only: Think of five ways you use the power of suggestion in your life—to create an impression on a boss, friend, mate, teacher, parent, or in general. Or, observe or interview other people, asking how they arrange their world to create impressions.

Example

Some of the ways that I have used suggestion in my life to impress people include dressing nicer for things such as job interviews to give the impression that I fit right in. I have also used big words in conversation and in job interviews along with my physical appearance to make myself appear to be a lot more intelligent than I am. When trying to present an image or an idea I am a lot more careful about what I say. Also, I tend to be a lot quieter than I really am. I also tend to speak more softly, and I help people out a lot more than I would normally do. This gives the impression that I am helpful and hard working when in reality I usually have to force myself to do work around my house. (from a student)

2. Interview a professional, telling him or her about the concept of suggestion and asking in what ways he or she uses it in business. Examples include asking a manager of a supermarket if certain products are arranged at kid level to appeal to children and if items at the checkout counter are chosen for a particular reason. Or ask stereo salespersons or department store managers how their stores are arranged to give a desired impression to customers.

   Another approach to this exercise is to begin by analyzing the layout of a store or an office (for example, a supermarket, department store, electronics store, bank, doctor's office, or toy store). Come to some conclusions about why the business is laid out in that particular way; support your conclusions with reasons. After you have made some assumptions about the layout, interview the manager of the store to find out if the layout is meant to influence customers in any way.

Exercise 8.2   Purpose: To compare the effect of different selection and ordering of news stories.

1. Watch the evening news on several stations, either local or national, for one or two nights. You may have to switch back and forth from one channel to another if the coverage is simultaneous (unless you can hook up two sets in the same room, or have a classmate watch a different station). Then, consider the following elements.

   Note the selection of issues, the order of the stories shown, and the time given to each story. If different stories were covered, which station covered the more important story, in your opinion? Note also any "slant" given to a story by the comments or facial expressions of the anchorpersons. Did some stations feature more sensational stories or more in-depth coverage of stories than others?

   You may not notice much difference in the selection of issues on the commercial networks; try comparing a commercial network with public television's or C-SPAN's coverage. See if you can identify any major differences between them.

After compiling your research, answer this question: If you were an editor on one of the broadcasts, what changes, if any, would you make in the coverage of the news? Which stories would you give more, less, or no coverage? Which stories would get top priority on your network?

2. In class groups, assume you are the program editors for a local edition of the evening news. Look at the story topics that follow and put them in order from most to least important. The most important will be covered at the top of the program and the least important may be cut in the interest of time.

To make your task easier, set some criteria before you order the stories. Possible criteria include international or national value, usefulness to the local populace, and relevance to the largest number of people. In essence, you are to decide what the people in your audience should know. Think about other important criteria and then list your criteria in order from the most to the least important.

   a. There is an update on hopeful signs in new Mideast peace initiatives.
   b. A murder-suicide occurred at a downtown hotel.
   c. Polls on an upcoming campaign show the front-runner falling behind.
   d. There is a serious drought in a neighboring country.
   e. A death-row inmate has been executed, and there was a protest involving 300 people.
   f. Someone has written a book claiming that a famous star, thought dead for a number of years, is alive and well.
   g. A major freeway accident is causing hour-long delays in the evening commute.
   h. A local day-care center has been charged with child abuse.
   i. A new drug for treating AIDS, which has been used with some good results in Canada, has been banned indefinitely in the United States, pending Food and Drug Administration approval.
   j. There is massive starvation in another country, and relief efforts are hindered by a lack of funds.

Exercise 8.3   Purpose: To understand the altering of settings to create impressions on viewers.

1. Analyze the setting of a place that you frequent—it could be your classroom, the business that employs you, a store, a restaurant, or your home. What impression does the room convey? If you put a camera in different places in the same room, what different impressions would be created? Do the people in charge of this environment consciously set it up the way it is? If so, what is their purpose?

2. Analyze the set of a commercial or television program—why do you think it looks the way it does? How have the set designers "framed" the environment and what impression does it convey?

Exercise 8.4 *Purpose:* To understand personal-image engineering in order to be more discerning about the image engineering done by political candidates, salespersons, or actors promoting products.

1. Stop and write down everything you are wearing that is visible to others. Include makeup, jewelry, and accessories and consider your choices of colors. What impression are you trying to convey to others with your "look"? If you generally dress while you're half asleep, stop and think about how someone else might judge you based on your clothing.

   You can extend this exercise to the classroom by having a few classmates write down the impression they get from your appearance. Compare their answers with the impression you'd like to make. How did you do as an image engineer?

2. Note how the actors in some commercials are dressed; what impression are they trying to create? If you have access to a televised trial, or even to television programs such as *People's Court,* you can note the appearance of the plaintiffs and defendants and draw conclusions about why they are dressed as they are. How does their image affect their credibility? How might a different image give viewers (and the judges) different impressions?

Exercise 8.5 *Purpose:* To find examples of suggestive techniques used by broadcast media.

1. Watch an interview program and analyze the suggestive elements we've mentioned in this section: the selection of issues, the use of time, the selection of guest and panel members, what is included or excluded on a set, the nonverbal element of clothing, the use of language, the use of camera angles and cuts, and camera distance and framing. Is there anything about the presentation of the material that creates suggestions? If so, what do you think might be the motive of the producers, directors, or editors in charge of the broadcast?

2. Watch (or tape, if possible) several commercials. Using the list of techniques as a guide, isolate the ways in which the advertisers are trying to persuade you to buy their product or use their service. If you live with children, see if they are particularly attracted to commercials and if they respond to the advertising appeals on children's programming.

3. Watch a situation comedy that features laugh tracks. Notice if you or the people you watch with are influenced to laugh by this fabricated element of suggestion.

4. Analyze the opening of a television or radio program. How does the opening work to keep you tuned in to the program?

5. Notice the camera cuts and angles in a feature film; scenes from most films are shot from a number of angles and then carefully pieced together in post-production. How did the director and film editors choose cuts and angles to create impact for the audience?

Exercise 8.6   Purposes: To gain awareness of misleading headlines and leads and how they distort information. To find examples of imbalanced reporting and editorializing.

1. Look for examples of headlines and leads that distort the meanings of stories. Bring the headlines and/or leads to class for discussion, or write a paper in which you explain the following:

    a. How does the headline and lead distort the information in the story?

    b. Why do you think that headline and lead were chosen?

    c. What would be a more appropriate headline or lead for this story; why do you think a more impartial heading or lead was not chosen?

2. Look for examples of imbalanced reporting or editorializing, or for the use of misleading photographs. Bring the stories, photographs, or editorial essays to class or write a paper in which you explain the following:

    a. How is the story, photograph, or editorial biased?

    b. How could bias have been prevented? What would be a more fair representation of the information?

Exercise 8.7   Purposes: To see that news coverage varies depending on the source. To consider the different priorities held by various sources.

1. Compare your local newspaper, a large city newspaper, and a national paper. What stories are covered on the first few pages? Why do you think different stories are featured by the various papers?

2. Choose an issue that is getting wide press coverage. Find articles on this issue in several different newspapers or magazines. Compare the coverage in each one, and then write an essay in which you address the following questions:

    a. What elements of coverage framed the story in different ways? Analyze the summary of the story given in the first one or two paragraphs, the quotes selected from the persons interviewed, the amount of coverage given to both sides of the issue, and the use of headlines, leads, and photographs.

    b. Which source reported the issue most fairly, in your view? Give examples to support your position.

Exercise 8.8   Purpose: To become aware of the subtle ways in which a story may be shaped to influence readers or viewers.

This exercise, created by Professor William Dorman, encourages what he calls "frame hunts."

Bring in a clipping from a newspaper or magazine or a segment from a story covered on television and try to convince other students that the story has a frame or slant of some sort. The class should vote thumbs up or thumbs down on each case. At the end of the semester, or of this section of the course, have a "Frame Off" in which the "Frame of the Year" is selected from all the frames submitted throughout the course.

Exercise 8.9   Purpose: To be able to detect suggestion in advertisements.

Find examples of television commercials or advertisements in magazines or newspapers that employ one or more of the forms of persuasion discussed in this chapter. Share your findings with class members. For this exercise, many heads are better than one because of the different perceptual abilities people have. One person may discover a musical trick used in a television commercial; another person may detect subtle images in a print ad. Look also for "testimonials" from "average" people who are really paid actors promoting a product; signs that testimonials come from paid testimony are flawless delivery of lines, carefully chosen clothing, and disproportionate raving about the product; columnist Dave Barry calls these actors "Consumers from Mars."

Exercise 8.10   Purpose: To gain a deeper understanding of suggestion, persuasion, and neuromarketing.

Read more about it! This chapter gives you a basic understanding of the principles of suggestion and persuasion and a glimpse at some of the new technologies used to enhance merchandising. Many other books and articles have been written on the subject. If you find these subjects interesting, do further research on them, including interviews with reporters, graphic designers, advertisers, or instructors of journalism and broadcasting.

You may want to focus your research on the controversial questions associated with subliminal persuasion: Does it currently exist? If so, how does it influence audiences? Share your research findings with your class.

CHAPTER HIGHLIGHTS

1. Professionals use the power of suggestion to create impressions about products, ideas, and candidates.

2. To be more critical of televised suggestion, viewers should be aware of the selection of issues; the use of time; the selection of guest and panel members; the set; the clothing of television personalities; and the use of language, camera angles, camera cuts, camera distance, and framing.

3. To be more critical of suggestion in print media, readers should be aware of the use of headlines, the use of "leads" or openings to a news story, the balance of reporting on an issue, the degree of fairness in editorial essays and letters, and photo composition. All of these elements taken together form the overall frame given to a particular story.

4. Suggestion and subliminal persuasion involves information meant to affect people on an unconscious level. Messages of this kind can be detected with training.

5. Advertisers and marketing experts use a number of persuasive techniques including fuzzy words, logical fallacies, stylized images and sounds, celebrity associations and endorsements, product placement, the Gestalt principle, eye tracking, and neuromarketing.

KEY TERMS

Suggestion (p. 317)	Representer (p. 336)
Sensationalism (p. 320)	Fuzzy words (p. 341)
Sound bite (p. 326)	Product placement (p. 344)
Framing (p. 326)	Gestalt principle (p. 346)
Fairness doctrine (p. 327)	Eye tracking (p. 348)
Spin (p. 328)	Subliminal persuasion (p. 349)
Lead (p. 330)	Neuromarketing (p. 349)

CHAPTER CHECKUP

Short Answer

1. Explain the concept of suggestion, using a few examples.
2. How does the selection of issues by writers, producers, and editors affect the audience's knowledge of current events?
3. How can headlines shape the perceptions of newspaper readers?

Sentence Completion

4. Until recently, broadcasters were compelled to allow airtime for both sides of controversial issues, under the law known as the _____ _____.
5. The practice of choosing more exciting stories over those stories that may be more newsworthy is called _____.
6. The deliberate or unconscious use of camera shots that influence audiences is known as _____.
7. A principle stating that our minds strive toward completion of information is the _____ principle.

True-False

8. Newspapers have to allow equal space for opposing viewpoints.
9. The existence of unconscious subliminal persuasion has not been proven.
10. Language can shape reader's perception of issues.

ARTICLES FOR DISCUSSION

The following article discusses a disturbing phenomenon that occurred when documentary filmmakers, who claim to be giving us a genuine portrayal of real events, distorted images in their films. In both cases discussed, the filmmakers altered their images to manipulate our perceptions, thereby breaking the rules that make documentaries credible sources of information.

DOCUMENTARIES: TRUE LIES?

Mary F. Pols

Winged Migration, an Oscar nominee for best documentary, is a spectacularly beautiful movie about birds that migrate vast distances. Everyone should see it.

But to my mind, it is not now, nor has it ever been, a true documentary film.

It features staged scenes, birds raised by humans but never identified as such, and misleading manipulations in editing and special effects that distort reality. It lost the best documentary Oscar to *Bowling for Columbine,* an audience-pleaser that apparently also played fast and loose with the truth, not to enhance the beauty of our experience, but for political purposes.

Both these films represent a troubling deviation from the rules that have traditionally governed documentaries, starting with the essential: Movies in this category are meant to be nonfiction. They are supposed to tell the truth. When we find out they don't, it casts a pall over the whole documentary community, in much the same way the Jayson Blair fiasco—the most recent example of vile ambition and ego leading an alleged journalist to write fiction instead of truth—has muddied not just the venerable *New York Times* but the entire journalistic community.

There's a movement afoot, started by people disgusted with Michael Moore's liberal politics, to persuade the Academy of Motion Picture Arts and Sciences to take back his Oscar for *Bowling for Columbine.* Even though I disagree with their motive, their arguments that the film is not a true documentary are, lamentably, quite compelling.

Some of the complaints are rabid, tedious and sound like the childish taunting we all remember from schoolyard days. But if you watched *Bowling for Columbine* under the impression that Charlton Heston stormed into Colorado two days after the Columbine shootings, waved a rifle over his head and shouted, "From my cold dead hands," you owe it to yourself to do some research (start with www.revoketheoscar.com).

A summary: Heston came to Denver months, not days, later. The scene with the rifle happened in North Carolina in an entirely different year. The speech we see him give, taunting the mayor of Denver, was patched together to make Heston look like an ogre. And those are just some of the manipulations documented on the Web site.

The offenses in *Winged Migration* are made in defense of nature, which seems more honorable. But they, too, whittle away at the standard of truth for documentary film. When I saw *Winged Migration,* I knew only that it was an Oscar nominee and that the filmmakers had gone to great lengths to bring cameras into the skies alongside the birds, building special gliders, planes and hot-air balloons. A card during the opening credits announced that no special effects were used in the movie.

Instantly, I was transfixed. I felt I was flying with the birds, then dying with them. A flock passes over what looks like a refinery, and one gets stuck in the muck. It struggles to get out and fails. The other birds fly away without it. Without commentary, the filmmakers move on. It's devastating.

As it is when hunters begin shooting birds out of the sky. We've been in flight with these creatures and without warning, they are falling to Earth. By the time a batch of crabs attacked a bird with an injured wing, I was wiping away tears. What I loved about the film was the way it involved us in the birds' lives, then introduced, so naturalistically, the dangers that face them in a world ruled by mankind.

So when the director, Jacques Perrin, came to show *Winged Migration* at the San Francisco International Film Festival in April, I had a million questions for him, starting with the bird in the oil slick. Did they rescue it?

"It's not oil," Perrin said. "It's milk, in the ground, with vegetable color. So the birds were happy to be there. It was not a reality."

What about the refinery?

"All the fabric of the industry you saw? It's all cinema. We make a painting."

I interrupted him. Perrin speaks English with a fairly thick French accent, so I wanted to make sure I was hearing him correctly. "You mean a matte painting?"

"Yes. And also the smog. It was like Hollywood cinema. The attitude of the animals, they are real, but I make a movie."

He explained that it would not be right for him to kill birds on-screen or to profit from their deaths. The filmmakers actually rescued the bird being attacked by crabs. What you see on the screen are crabs consuming a fish.

As for the geese that drop from the sky after being shot by hunters, Perrin said he spliced together footage from two locations to create the effect he wanted. A crew went to Canada and filmed a government program to thin the snow goose population. Back in France, Perrin noticed that the birds his group had raised (he hired more than 100 veterinary students to imprint with the birds before they were born) had a habit of flapping wildly in celebration whenever they returned home. That's what you see when you think you're seeing injured birds tumbling to Earth.

"We make the sound and you have the impression this is hunting," Perrin said. "This is not hunting. They are very happy at that moment."

To be clear: I wouldn't want Perrin to kill birds on camera. But I felt betrayed once I knew all this. Because of the disclaimer in the beginning, that no special effects were used, and because the film was a best documentary nominee, I assumed that what I was seeing was real. Reality gave the film its power. When it was revealed to not be real at all, that power was diminished.

I called Jon Else (*Sing Faster: The Stagehands' Ring Cycle* and *The Day After Trinity*), an Oscar-nominated documentary filmmaker who heads the UC Berkeley Graduate School of Journalism documentary program. We talked about both films. Else loved *Bowling for Columbine* but was disappointed to discover that the truths he thought he was seeing weren't reliable. Ditto for *Winged Migration*, which he said is "no more a documentary than *All the President's Men*."

The documentary that really invented the medium as we know it today, Robert Flaherty's 1922 film about the Inuit, *Nanook of the North,* contained stagings, although no one knew about it at the time. (To get better light, Flaherty cut an igloo in half and posed his "stars" inside.) Else says he's willing to cut some slack for the man who was creating a new medium. But in modern-day documentary filmmaking, re-creations, fictions and stagings should be clearly labeled or described as such, he said. The audience has to know what it's seeing.

"The erosion of truth in documentary is a serious problem," Else said. "I think that probably the Academy or the independent documentary association needs to address it.

"We thrive on the currency of fact. I don't know how else to say it. If you counterfeit that, it's sort of like counterfeiting money.

"We documentary filmmakers have been cashing in for decades upon the fact that people believe what we put on the screen to be truer than most moving images. . . . When people put things on the screen that are clearly intended to be true but are not, that clearly threatens the whole documentary community."

As an example of this erosion of trust, I felt so discombobulated after talking with Perrin that I watched a third best documentary nominee, *Spellbound,* with suspicion. It seemed too good to be true that the filmmakers had picked eight amazing National Spelling Bee finalists, including two who made it to the final four, to profile before the actual event took place. I wondered about Jeff Blitz and Sean Welch's methods, so I gave them a call.

It turned out that they did have to go back and do interviews with three of their eight chosen subjects to flesh out the documentary, which, by the way, is wonderful.

"I think historically, you have to take certain liberties in terms of how the different stories that are being told within the nature of those time frames," Blitz said. "So if I shot the first part of the day talking to someone's mother, the second part of my day talking to someone's dad, there is nothing that would bind me in my final film from putting all of mom's interview before or after dad's interview."

No offense in that.

"I think that the real kind of test is whether you feel that you are making a portrait of the truth of a scene or as it was found by you," Blitz said. "Some of the questions that people have about Michael Moore's film, people wonder if Michael found the truth to be one thing and then found it to be a more effective movie if it was shown to be something else."

Exactly. Blitz and Welch had done what the best documentaries do; give a rich and moving view of real life. But I doubted them. That's what happens when other documentary filmmakers play with the truth.

Mary F. Pols is the *Times* movie critic.

1. What are some examples given of distortion in the documentary films *Winged Migration,* and *Bowling for Columbine?*

2. Why do you think the filmmakers altered the film to create the effects that they did? If the audience perceived the films as genuine portrayals of real events, what "political purposes" might they serve?

3. Comment on the writer's statement "I wouldn't want Perrin to kill birds on camera. But I felt betrayed once I knew all this. Because of the disclaimer in the beginning, that no special effects were used, and because the film was a best documentary nominee, I assumed that what I was seeing was real. Reality gave the film its power. When it was revealed to not be real at all, that power was diminished."

4. Do you agree with Jon Else when he states that "recreations and stagings should be labeled as such" so that the audience can know what is real and what is fictional in a documentary?

In documentary films, we expect to be given a true account of actual events. We don't want fiction injected into what purports to be a film about reality. However, we don't mind a bit of reality, such as a realistic setting, injected in what we know is a story.

Even stories, however, have the power to create public perception about people and organizations. The following article discusses how the treatment of the military by the movie industry often affects viewers' perceptions. It is helpful to filmmakers to have access to real military bases and equipment, and they can usually get that access if the movie is not designed to put the military in a bad light. Similarly, the public information director for the Los Angeles Police Department, Mary Grady, says that she personally receives pitches five or six times a week from producers wanting to use the LAPD in either a reality program or a fictional treatment. The police department, like the military, is selective about what kinds of access they will sanction, and they have set up an entertainment and trademark unit to specifically deal with the huge volume of requests received from Hollywood. As Grady says, "We want to work with Hollywood. When they were filming *Hollywood Homicide* over at the Hollywood station, I can't tell you how excited people were to have the department be a part of that. There are more than 9,000 hard-working people in this department who put themselves out there every day. And they deserve to be afforded some respect."[42]

---

[42]Glenn Whipp, "LAPD Protecting Its Image by Rejecting Negative Movies," *Los Angeles Daily News,* February 22, 2003.

WHEN MOVIES GO TO WAR, PENTAGON TAGS ALONG

Not Every Story Gets Military OK, But Some Need the Assistance

Jennifer Brown

In an early script for *Forrest Gump*, the likable but dim character went to Vietnam in a unit full of slow-witted soldiers like himself.

"They had everybody of reduced intellect except the lieutenant," said Phil Strub, who coordinates the Pentagon's film liaison office. "And the Army said it never would have happened that way."

So Strub's office used some creative persuasion on the producers. And in the final version, Gump's fellow soldiers were smarter.

It was just one part of a big movie. But to the Defense Department, the things Americans learn in movie theaters endure, so it often uses the carrot of its cooperation to ensure that films reflect accurately, and positively, on the military.

"We feel strongly that the images people see of the military in Hollywood are the most formative images," said Major Nancy LaLuntas, director of Marine public affairs in Los Angeles.

"[We've] maintained all along that if we have the ability to accurately influence those images, the American public will have a better image of the military."

Of course, some filmmakers balk at the interference. For example, *A Few Good Men*, starring Tom Cruise and Jack Nicholson, was made without help from the Pentagon, which had objected to the portrayals of some Marines.

The Pentagon gets a few hundred requests each year for tanks, aircraft carriers, active-duty officers to play extras, or just technical advice to make a story more accurate.

Filmmakers send scripts with wish lists to the military film offices—one in Washington, and four in Los Angeles for each of the military branches.

The Pentagon then uses its leverage to try to persuade filmmakers to change parts of the story deemed inaccurate or too negative.

How much filmmakers are willing to revise depends on how much help they need, Strub said. A movie like *Top Gun*, about fighter pilots, could not have been made without the military—because "you can't just rent aircraft carriers."

Usually, he said, both sides bend.

"We say, 'These are areas that are unrealistic. We know this isn't a documentary, we know this isn't news, but you've got to have some plausibility,'" said Strub.

Pentagon approval certainly makes life easier, said Amy Lemisch, who coproduced *Renaissance Man*, starring Danny DeVito as an English teacher hired to educate U.S. troops.

"I've talked to a lot of people who didn't get approval...and we were lucky," Lemisch said. "They gave us the locations. They gave us the attention. They gave us military extras."

Filmmakers pay the Pentagon the costs of operating the expensive equipment, such as helicopters, planes, or tanks, that they use. The military says the charges cover only costs, and do not bring in a profit.

Moviemakers' demands for help from the Pentagon's film liaison office—opened in 1949—have increased since 1986's *Top Gun*.

But while many get the Pentagon nod, scores did not, including *Crimson Tide*, about an armed mutiny on a submarine. "Firing a gun on a submarine is stupid and would never happen," Strub said.

Of course, there may be more to the rejections than just being unrealistic, since the military helps with some extremely unrealistic movies if it likes the plot line.

The spy plane in 1996's *Executive Decision* has a tunnel that opens through the top, allowing heroes Steven Seagal and Kurt Russell to crawl through into a hijacked passenger plane.

"It couldn't have happened," Strub said. "But we'll say, 'Oh all right.' If that's a capability we can let bad guys think we have, why not?"

QUESTIONS FOR DISCUSSION

1. To what extent do you agree with Major Nancy LaLuntas, who stated, "We feel strongly that the images people see of the military in Hollywood are the most formative images." What images of military life have you received from film?

2. Comment on the following statements from the article: "Filmmakers send scripts with wish lists to the military film offices—one in Washington, and four in Los Angeles for each of the military branches. The Pentagon then uses its leverage to try to persuade filmmakers to change parts of the story deemed inaccurate or too negative."

As technological advances have made it possible for consumers to avoid viewing commercials, advertisers have found new strategies for reaching target audiences. One of the most powerful and ethically questionable involves aiming ads at young children. In the following article, the writers expose methods used to create consumerism and brand loyalty in children; they also urge parents and governmental leaders to act against such aggressive marketing.

THE PARENT'S BILL OF RIGHTS: HELPING MOMS AND DADS FIGHT COMMERCIALISM

Jonathan Rowe and Gary Ruskin

Paul Kurnit is the president of KidShop, an advertising firm that specializes in marketing to children, and he has plans for our kids.

"Kid business has become big business," Kurnit says.[1] To make kid business even bigger, he preaches what he calls "surround marketing": saturation advertising that captures kids at every possible moment.[2]

"You've got to reach kids throughout the day—in school, as they're shopping at the mall, or at the movies," says Carol Herman, a senior vice president at Grey Advertising. "You've got to become part of the fabric of their lives."[3]

This is what parents today are up against—corporate advertisers who seek to entwine themselves with children's lives. By most measures, the advertisers are succeeding. Each week, the typical American child takes in some 38 hours (yes, a full work week) of commercial media, with its endless ads and come-ons.[4] And that's not counting the ads that commandeer their attention from billboards and the Internet, the omnipresent brand logos, and the advertising that increasingly fills the schools.

The merchandise pushers have invaded the commons of childhood, the free open spaces of imagination and play, and turned it into a free-fire zone of commercial importuning. In some quarters, this appalling situation is seen as success. "There have never been more ways in the culture to support marketing towards kids," enthuses Kidscreen, a publication for ad firms and corporations that target kids.[5] That there's a market for such a publication is revealing.

Corporate advertisers have contrived to wedge themselves into the space between parents and their children. They enlist the best psychologists and market researchers money can buy to lure kids to products and values many of us don't approve of and even abhor. Parents find themselves in a grim daily battle to keep these forces at bay.

On their own, parents cannot contend with the nation's largest corporations and their weapons of mass childhood seduction. It's time Washington stood up for parents. It's time politicians recognized that raising children is the most important task of our society.

It's time, in other words, for a Parents' Bill of Rights.

Not that long ago, parents actually had control over the front doors of their homes. Sure, a kid might hide a racy magazine under the mattress, but little came into the house without the parents' okay. Even outside the home and school, for adults to approach kids with the thought of influencing them was considered an antisocial act, and offenders could be put in jail.

The invention of electronic media changed all that. The history of the last century, in fact, could be written as the story of how marketers contrived to bypass parents and speak directly to impressionable children. The front door became a permeable membrane, admitting the advertising industry to its promised land. Children are "natural and enthusiastic buyers," a child psychologist wrote in the 1938 book *Reaching Juvenile Markets*. For advertisers, he went on, there was a "tremendous sales potential."[6]

Psychologists, who are supposed to help children, were now employed to help ensnare them. No longer were such adults considered predators; because they wore suits, sat in offices, and operated at a distance through the media, they were respectable executives and even "pioneers." In the 1930s, the medium was radio; sponsors of children's shows included Ralston cereal and Ovaltine—products that parents actually might want their kids to have—and the ads themselves seem almost tame by today's standards. The young ear is not as impressionable as the eye, and advertisers were still concerned that Mom or Dad might be listening.

Then came television and the beginning of the modern era in the assault on kids. Television is inferior to radio as a storytelling medium; radio engages the imagination, while television numbs it. But as an advertising medium, television is unsurpassed. Children want what they see, and with television advertisers could offer an endless parade of things to want. After Welch's grape juice became a sponsor of *The Howdy Doody Show* in the 1950s, sales of grape juice to families with young children increased almost five-fold.[7]

With television, moreover, the ads weren't just between the shows. They could be in the shows as well. The Disney Corporation created a series about Davy Crockett, starring the actor Fess Parker in a coonskin cap. In short order, kids throughout the country were nagging their parents for the mock coonskin caps that coincidentally began to appear in stores. Crockett gear became a $300 million business—roughly $2 billion in today's dollars.[8]

Increasingly, advertisers had children to themselves. Few parents sat through *The Mickey Mouse Club* or the Saturday-morning cartoon shows. Even shows for general audiences held untapped possibilities. If kids are the most impressionable audience in the house, why not enlist them as sales agents in regard to everything the family bought? "Eager minds can be molded to want your products!" enthused a firm that produced "education" materials for schools. "Sell these children on your brand name, and they will insist that their parents buy no other."[9]

Corporations were literally alienating children from their parents, shifting children's loyalties more toward the corporations themselves. Rejection of parental authority became a persistent and embedded theme, even in such seemingly innocuous shows as Howdy Doody. Television figures became surrogate parents who pushed consumption at every turn. Dr. Frances Horwich, the kindly "principal" of *Ding Dong School*, popped vitamins and urged her preschool viewers to tell their mothers to pick the bottle with the pretty red pills at the drugstore.

Perhaps it was not entirely accidental that the generation weaned on such fare would become, a decade later, the "Me Generation" of the 1960s. Advertisers were thinking long-term. "Think of what it can mean to your firm in profits," Clyde Miller wrote in *The Process of Persuasion*, "if you can condition a million or ten million children who will grow into adults trained to buy your products as soldiers who are trained to advance when they hear the trigger words 'Forward, march.'"[10]

These developments did not go unnoticed. In his landmark book *The Lonely Crowd*, David Riesman observed that corporations had designed a new role for children, as "consumer trainees." In the process, Riesman said, they had turned traditional values upside down. Earlier in the century, children's publications had promoted such qualities as self-discipline and perseverance. "The comparable media today," he wrote, "train the young for the frontiers of consumption—to tell the difference between Pepsi-Cola and Coca-Cola, as later between Old Golds and Chesterfields."[11] (The latter were popular cigarette brands.)

Some parents did resist. In the 1950s there often were a few kids in the neighborhood who weren't allowed to watch TV. But most parents then, as now, were reluctant to deny their kids what their friends had. Moreover, parents themselves were caught up in the commercial euphoria of the post-war years, when a new car or television seemed a just reward for the hardships of the Depression and a world war.

Soon the commercial saturation of childhood became the new norm, and people hardly noticed anymore. An entire industry arose to mold young minds to crave products, and to cast parents in the subordinate role of financier of these fabricated wants. James U. McNeal, a former marketing professor at Texas A&M University, is perhaps the most influential advocate of modern marketing to children. "[T]he consumer embryo begins to develop during the first year of existence," McNeal writes, with no hint of embarrassment or shame. "[C]hildren begin their consumer journey in infancy and certainly deserve consideration as consumers at that time."[12]

It is not comforting to know, as we cuddle our newborns, that there exists an industry of James U. McNeals eager to prod them on to their "consumer journey." Nor is it comforting to know that there are marketing consultants, like Cheryl Idell of Western Initiative Media Worldwide, who advise corporations on how to harness the "nag factor" to increase sales. Idell contends that nagging spurs about a third of family trips to fast-food restaurants, and of purchases of videos and clothing.

And what about the naggees? In the writings of people like McNeal, parents exist as deep pockets to be siphoned by kids, whose role is to influence purchases. This mentality has become the dominant force with which parents must contend. They encounter it at every turn: They take the kids to a sports event and are barraged by ads. They buy a video for them and find that it is choc-a-bloc with "product placements"—brand-name products that are built into the story.

Parents feel the heavy breathing of the marketers even on their littlest ones. *Teletubbies*, for example, is an animated TV show aimed at toddlers as young as one year. The producers portray it as educational. But Marty Brochstein, editor of the Licensing Letter, is more candid, calling Teletubbies a "major big bucks opportunity."[13] The show has done promotions with Burger King and McDonald's. If that's education, it's not the kind most parents have in mind.

The morphing of advertising into life extends even to the schools. Corporations have taken advantage of tight school budgets to turn classrooms and hallway walls into billboards for junk food and sneakers. As for the Internet, it's a marketer's dream, a technology that children roam unsupervised, and that offers endless opportunities for getting into children's minds. "Kids don't realize they're reading advertisements," says Lloyd Jobe, CEO of Skateboard.com.[14]

Marketers know exactly where to find children, too. The collection of children's personal information, and the invasion of their privacy, has become commonplace. American Student List LLC (www.studentlist.com/lists/main.html), a list broker, sells a list of "20 million names of children ranging in age from 2 to 13," along with their addresses, ages, genders, telephone numbers, and other personal information.

For advertisers, it all has been a bonanza: Market researchers estimate that children ages four to 12 influence some $565 billion of their parents' purchasing each year, and McNeal calls children the "superstars in the consumer constellation."[15] For kids, however, the role of consumer "superstars" has meant an epidemic of marketing-related diseases. American kids are fatter than ever, and rates of obesity and type-2 diabetes are soaring. Teenage girls have become obsessed with their bodies, due largely to the images of physical perfection that barrage them from fashion magazines, TV, movies, and ads. More than half of all high school girls say they were on diets during the previous month. Likewise, eating disorders are now the third leading chronic illness among adolescent girls.[16,17]

Drinking, too, is a problem. A study by the National Institute on Media and Family found that the more a beer company spends on advertising, the more likely are seventh- to twelfth-graders to know about that beer—and to drink it.[18] Perhaps not coincidentally, alcohol is a factor in the four main causes of death among young people ages 10 to 24: car crashes, other accidents, homicide, and suicide.[19]

The merchants of death are adept at using marketing to undermine the good influence of parents. Tobacco marketing is especially successful at counteracting parents who encourage their children not to smoke.[20] Each day, another 3,000 children start to smoke; the lives of roughly a third of them will be shortened by smoking-related illnesses.

Added to all this is the production of misery and dissension in the home. Our children are being coached and prodded in the arts of petulance and nagging by those whose sole purpose is to turn them into conduits for their parents' money. As the anthropologist Jules Henry once noted, advertising has become an "insolent usurper of parental function, degrading parents to mere intermediaries between children and the market."[21]

A survey by the Merck Family Fund found that 86 percent of Americans think that young people today are "too focused on buying and consuming things."[22] *Business Week*, no enemy of corporate America, perhaps put it best: "Instead of transmitting a sense of who we are and what we hold important, today's marketing-driven culture is instilling in [children] a sense that little exists without a sales pitch attached and that self-worth is something you buy at a shopping mall."[23]

You might think our representatives in Washington would show some concern, but politicians in both major parties seem reluctant to stand up to commercial predators. Back in the late 1970s, for example, the Federal Trade Commission (FTC) proposed an end to advertising to children too young to grasp that ads aren't necessarily true. In response, Congress stripped the FTC of any authority to enact rules against advertisers who take advantage of the vulnerabilities of impressionable youth. J. Howard Beales III, the FTC's chief of consumer protection in the current administration, is an economist perhaps best known for his scholarly defense of R. J. Reynolds and its infamous "Joe Camel" ad campaign. David Scheffman, the new head of the FTC's bureau of economics, also worked for the tobacco industry.

Parents deserve a little more respect. Their job is hard enough without the marketing culture treating them as cannon fodder. The technology of seduction has increased tremendously in sophistication and reach, and corporate seducers have gained new legal rights. Yet the means for parents to contend with these intrusions, and to talk back to the intruders, have scarcely grown at all. In many respects, they have diminished.

The time has come to right the balance. The government can't do parents' job for them, but it certainly can give them the legal rights they need to stand up effectively to corporations that target their kids. Parents should not be second-class citizens. They should not feel under siege by a culture designed to shake them down for money, and to usurp the function of instilling values in their kids.

The time has come for a Parents' Bill of Rights.

NOTES

1. Paul Kurnit, "Griffin Bacal's Paul Kurnit Finds Mainstream Marketers Cozying Up to Kids," *Kidscreen* (January 1, 2001).

2. Janice Rosenberg, "Brand Loyalty Begins Early: Savvy Marketers 'Surround' Kids to Build Connection," *Advertising Age* (February 12, 2001).

3. "Selling to Children," *Consumer Reports* (August 1990).

4. "Kids and Media @ the New Millennium," The Henry Kaiser Family Foundation, November 1999.

5. Ed Kirchdoerffer, "Keeping Up with Today's Kids," *Kidscreen* (January 1, 1999).

6. E. Grumbine, *Reaching Juvenile Markets* (New York: McGraw-Hill, 1938). Quoted in Norma Odom Pecora, *The Business of Children's Entertainment* (New York: Guilford Press), 24.

7. Ibid.

8. Faye Fiore, "America as Disney's Land: The Fantasy vs. the Reality," *Los Angeles Times*, September 25, 1994.

9. Vance Packard, *The Hidden Persuaders* (London: Penguin Books, 1957), 133.

10. Ibid.

11. David Riesman, *The Lonely Crowd* (New Haven: Yale University Press, 1950), 98.

12. James U. McNeal, *The Kids Market: Myths and Realities* (New York: Paramount Market Publishing, 1999), 37–38.

13. Gary Strauss, "Teletubbies' Appeal Spins Marketing Gold: Britain's Latest Fab Four Tugs U.S. Purse Strings," *USA Today*, October 27, 1998.

14. Dulcie Leimbach, "When Ads Aimed at Kids Come to Life," *New York Times*, December 13, 2000.

15. Faye Rice, "'Superstars' of Spending: Marketers Clamor for Kids," *Advertising Age* (February 12, 2001).

16. Centers for Disease Control and Prevention, Surveillance Summaries, *Morbidity and Mortality Weekly Report* 49 (2000): 1–5. Cited in Mary Story et al., "Individual and Environmental Influences on Adolescent Eating Behaviors," *Journal of the American Dietetic Association* (March 1, 2002).

17. "Position of the American Dietetic Association: Nutrition Intervention in the Treatment of Anorexia Nervosa, Bulimia Nervosa, and Eating Disorders Not Otherwise Specified," *Journal of the American Dietetic Association* (July 1, 2001).

18. National Institute on Media and the Family news release, April 19, 2001 (www.mediaandthefamily.org/press/20010419-2.shtml).

19. L. Kann, et al., "Youth Risk Behavior Surveillance, United States, 1999," *Morbidity and Mortality Weekly Report* 49 (2000): 1–96.

20. John P. Pierce, et al., "Does Tobacco Marketing Undermine the Influence of Recommended Parenting in Discouraging Adolescents from Smoking?" *American Journal of Preventive Medicine*, 23, no. 2 (2002): 73–81.

21. Jules Henry, *Culture Against Man* (New York: Random House, 1963), 76.

22. Merck Family Fund, "Yearning for Balance," 1995 (www.globallearningnj.org/global_ata/Yearing_for_balance.htm).

23. David Leonhardt and Kathleen Kerwin, "Hey Kid, Buy This!" *Business Week* (June 30, 1997).

http://www.alternet.org/story/15754. Reprinted by permission of the authors.

1. Jonathan Rowe gives some historic background concerning marketing to children. To what extent do you agree with his conclusion that marketing has gotten worse in recent years?

2. Do you believe that there should be limits on advertising to children? If so, what should they include and how could the limits be enforced?

3. Should schools accept money from corporations in exchange for allowing them to advertise and sell their products? If so, should there be any limits on these sales?

IDEAS FOR WRITING OR SPEAKING

1. Respond to one of the following quotes by the late author, media critic, and professor Neil Postman; Postman wrote many important books on media and American culture, including his classic *Amusing Ourselves to Death.* Support your thesis statement with evidence from radio, television, advertising, newspapers, magazines, journals, books, or Websites.

   "Indeed, we may have reached the point where cosmetics has replaced ideology as the field of expertise over which a politician must have competent control."[43]

   "The shape of a man's body is largely irrelevant to the shape of his ideas when he is addressing a public in writing or on the radio or, for that matter, in smoke signals. But it is quite relevant on television."[44]

   "It would seem that right now, Americans are more interested in entertainment than any other aspect of personal life.... Las Vegas would do just fine as a symbol [of America]."[45]

   "How many people when seeing a newscast about say a serious earthquake or an airplane crash will actually start to cry or grow silent at the tragedies of life? Most of us don't because right after the story of the airplane crash there's going to be a thing for Burger King or if not that a story about the World Series or some other event that basically would say, 'Now listen, don't take this thing about the airplane crash too seriously, it's just something to amuse you for the moment, and we certainly don't want you to be morose when we get to the United Airlines commercial because we'd like you to be in a sort of upbeat mood to sell you a trip to San Francisco.'"[46]

---

[43]Neil Postman, *Amusing Ourselves to Death* (New York: Viking Press, 1985), p. 4.
[44]Ibid., p. 7.
[45]Neil Postman quoted by Stephen Marshall, "Prelude to Vegas," online interview @ channel zero.
[46]Ibid., p. 26.

2. Analyze one of the more successful television programs and draw some specific conclusions about why it is successful. Support your conclusions with reasons. Consider the images the program projects about the people it represents.

   Another approach to this assignment would be to contrast programs that are popular now with shows (or films) that were popular in the past. Write about the different cultural, economic, or historical elements influencing these shows or films; it would be interesting to take programs from different decades for this assignment. Here are some questions to think about as you watch these programs: What was acceptable in the past but is in some way unacceptable now? What is acceptable now that would have been considered unacceptable in the past?

3. Discuss the influence of television programs on culture. To what extent does television *reflect* cultural norms and to what extent does it *create* them? Given your answer, what considerations, if any, should television producers make before approving new projects?

   To narrow your topic, you might consider the effects of television on children, using these statistics from the Henry J. Kaiser Family Foundation study of viewing habits, published in late 2003. According to their findings, 65 percent of children live in homes where the TV is left on at least half the time or more and 36 percent live in homes where the TV is on "always" or "most of the time."[47]

   Another Kaiser report stated, "It is well established that the stories children and adolescents watch on television can influence their lives in important ways." For example, heavy exposure to violence can lead to heightened risk of aggression, and constant bombardment of commercials can affect spending patterns. "Similarly," the study continues, "media portrayals involving sexuality can contribute to the sexual socialization of young people."[48]

4. Consider the statement: "You can tell the ideals of a nation by its advertisements."[49] What does our current advertising say about our culture's ideals? Consider values, roles of men and women, the view of the elderly, the importance of technology, and the use of time and space. Support your position with at least six examples from both print and electronic media.

5. Writer Joseph Giordano states, "An important cause of distorted and damaging TV stereotypes is the tendency of some media executives to view ethnic culture as an 'immigrant phenomenon,' a transitional phase in the process of Americanization rather than a continuing influence on people's language, religious lives, arts, politics, food preferences and so on."[50]

[47]Kaiser Family Foundation report, October 28, 2003. "New Study Finds Children Age Zero to Six Spend As Much Time with TV, Computers and Video games As Playing Outside."
[48]Gayle Vassar Melvin, *Contra Costa Times*, February 10, 1999.
[49]Norman Douglas, *South Wind* (London: Nartin Secker & Warburg, 1917), p. 64.
[50]Joseph Giordano, "Promoting Pluralism," *Media and Values*, Winter 1987.

Should the media strive to emphasize our similarities, differences, or both? Provide reasons for your answer.

6. In discussing ethnic and religious traditions, Giordano also states, "At times, these traditions conflict with surrounding values, but they are also sources of strength and understanding. How they work in second-, third-, and fourth-generation families can provide a rich store of story ideas and authentic characterizations for writers, directors, and actors."[51] Write a proposal for a television program or a feature-length film centered around a tradition that provides strength and cultural understanding to an individual or group. How could a program like this be used to increase cultural understanding in a pluralistic society?

7. Critics have accused television news as functioning primarily as a form of entertainment. Watch several news programs and respond to these critics. To what extent do you agree or disagree with them and why? Give specific examples to support your answer.

8. Collect your junk mail for two or three weeks without opening it. Then analyze it by answering these questions:

   a. How did you recognize it as junk mail?
   b. What techniques does the sender use to entice you to open the envelope?
   c. Once opened, what techniques are used to prompt you to read further than the first line?
   d. Are these techniques effective? Consider graphic design, placement of key words, the way you are addressed, special offers, enticements, and deadlines.

9. Write an essay or speech about your viewpoint on the following quote by former Senator John Danforth, Republican from Missouri:

   What people see when they turn on the TV is violence. What they see is sex. What they see is total disrespect for family and for authority, and what they see is stereotypes. And this is, in my opinion, a very large part of the problem. The medium of television right now is disgusting. So are many of the movies that people see. And I think that one way to start on this problem is to have a summit meeting perhaps called by the President which brings together people who are leaders of broadcast, the broadcast networks, people who are leaders of cable television, of the motion picture industry, and ask them what responsibility they have for this country, other than squeezing every last dime they can out of it.[52]

[51]Ibid.
[52]From the *MacNeil-Lehrer Newshour,* televised May 9, 1992. Interview with Senator John Danforth.

FILMS FOR ANALYSIS AND DISCUSSION

The dead-on satire *Thank You For Smoking* (2006, R) is a testament to the spin culture of American media. Aaron Eckhart plays Nick Naylor, a lobbyist for Big Tobacco and a master of spinning the truth so that it always lands in favor of his employer. The first scene of the movie shows Naylor convincing a talk show crowd that he cares about lung cancer victims because he doesn't want to lose them as clients. This is satire that takes no prisoners, smartly observing how media can make truth a relative term.

Similar Films and Classics

The Truman Show (1998, PG)

This movie is a humorous but also serious look at how the line between reality and fantasy can become blurred by television programming. Since his birth, Truman has been placed on a beautiful Hollywood set and everyone he interacts with is a paid actor. Truman doesn't know that millions are watching the reality show of his life and that what he considers his real world is being limited and exploited by the producer of his popular show.

Broadcast News (1987, R)

This film follows the struggles of a network news producer who resists the growing trend towards 'news as entertainment' and must decide between style and substance in both her professional life and her romantic life.

Network (1976, R)

An aging news anchor has lost his strong ratings and is given two weeks notice by his network. His reaction to the firing provides an excellent and comic commentary on the effects of sensationalism.

Meet John Doe (1936)

John Doe, a man who writes a letter protesting social ills and threatening a dramatic suicide is the creation of Ann Mitchell, a fired reporter who is expressing her own frustrations. When the public shows great concern for the fictional letter writer, the paper has to rehire Ann and also hire a man to impersonate her fictional character. The film provides food for thought about how entire political and social movements can be fueled by a story made up by a reporter and covered up by her paper.

9

Fair-Mindedness

It's You and Me, Kid, and I'm Not So Sure About You

A critical thinker is aware of egocentrism, ethnocentrism, and the role of emotions on judgment.

A critical thinker listens and responds to opposing viewpoints with empathy and fair-mindedness.

This chapter will cover

- Defense mechanisms that cloud our thinking

- The effect of conformity on critical thought

- Rational approaches to emotional reasoning

- Points of logical vulnerability

- Active listening techniques that foster open-mindedness and empathy

Centuries ago, we learned, contrary to our previous beliefs, that the earth is not the center of the universe. We discovered that the sun does not revolve around the earth; instead our earth, along with the other planets, revolves around the sun.

The fact that we tended to see our earth as predominant reveals the self-centered (not necessarily selfish) nature of our perception of reality. That self-centered perspective did not die out with our ancestors; we still tend to view the world from our own individual and group perspectives. Fortunately, however, along with our limited viewpoints, we also have the ability to discover new information and to make "course corrections" in our theories and our behavior.

Just as our ancestors made corrections to their theories and actions when confronted with inescapable facts, we as a culture are regularly changing our ideas and behavior when new understanding warrants changes. For example, in the face of increasingly credible threats to our environment, we are rejecting the assumption that the earth is infinitely supplied with renewable resources. Instead, we are focusing on conservation and preservation of our environment as a crucial issue, viewing our resources as precious rather than expendable and searching for alternative sources of energy.

Advances in media technology have enabled us to get a more complete picture of the global interdependence of not only our physical environment but also the world's people. When we see how others live and the problems they face, we can be less ethnocentric. **Ethnocentrism** (sometimes called **sociocentrism**) is the tendency to view one's own race or culture as central, based on the deep-seated belief that one's own group is superior to all others.[1] We can only hold on to ethnocentrism when we can consider other cultures as less important or deserving than our own. Such an attitude of superiority is harmful to the dialogue that must proceed as decisions are made that involve a diverse and increasingly interdependent world.

A critical thinker can counter ethnocentrism by developing the trait of fair-mindedness. **Fair-mindedness** involves

1. A respect for people whose ethnicities and traditions are different from our own,
2. A willingness to hear and understand other viewpoints, and
3. An openness to change when new information or insight warrants that change.

Egocentrism, the individual version of ethnocentrism, has been defined as a tendency to view everything else in relationship to oneself; one's desires, values, and beliefs (seeming to be self-evidently correct or superior to those of others) are uncritically used as the norm of all judgment and experience. Some psychologists believe that this tendency is rooted in early childhood, when we

[1]Richard Paul, *Critical Thinking* (Rohnert Park, CA: Center for Critical Thinking and Moral Critique, 1990), p. 549.

typically engage in what is called "mine is better" thinking. We see our own toys, family, pets, and sports teams as better than everyone else's, and this perception can continue throughout life if it remains unquestioned. Egocentrism has been called one of the fundamental impediments to critical thinking.[2] To be a logical, fair, and less egocentric thinker, we can learn several skills. We can learn:

1. To recognize the basic defense mechanisms we use to distort reality and to deceive others and ourselves
2. To recognize areas where we, for whatever reasons, have trouble being rational
3. To understand and have empathy for someone else's viewpoint

There is nothing wrong with taking strong, even immovable, stands on issues; we don't want to be so open-minded that we have no core beliefs or opinions at all. What is unfair is taking a strong stand without having thought carefully and honestly about all the relevant factors involved in an issue. And the most fair, ethical, and persuasive attitude is one of respect and courtesy to those with whom we disagree.

STOP AND THINK

Author and speaker Ravi Zacharias defines one's "worldview" as the cumulative answer to four questions: Where did I come from? What is life's meaning? How do I define right from wrong, and what happens to me when I die? Those are the fulcrum points of our existence.[3] How do different individuals answer those questions?

[2]Ibid., p. 548.
[3]Julia Duin,"Christian Worldview: An Interview with Ravi Zacharias," *The Washington Times,* washington times.com, 2003 (accessed August, 2007).

HOW WE DEFEND OUR EGOS

Are you thinking or are you just rearranging your prejudices?

Walter Martin

People who are fair-minded are aware of the natural weaknesses that come with being an individual human. The best place to start in understanding our weak points in reasoning is to examine human defense mechanisms. Defense mechanisms are "the clever ways we deceive ourselves, protect ourselves, and extract ourselves from uncomfortable situations—they are negative escape hatches that offer us temporary treatments for persistent problems."[4] **Defense mechanisms** are strategies we use to avoid uncomfortable realities. For our purposes, we will consider two major defense mechanisms that interfere with clear thinking.

Rationalization is a defense mechanism that underlies many others; it is our way of justifying or trying to make sense of things that don't make sense. It's a way of explaining things away that should be brought under examination. When, for whatever reasons, we want to avoid an unpleasant truth, or when we want to believe that something is true, we can come up with a justification for our desired belief. Television writers Greg Behrendt and Liz Tuccillo wrote a book of questions and answers for women who make up excuses about why men they like don't call them. Greg's response to almost every question is also the title of the book: *He's Just Not That Into You.* Greg and Liz note how often women rationalize and help one another rationalize when men are clearly not interested in pursuing a closer relationship.

Note how we use our minds to distort reality in the following examples.

Examples

- Jorge's favorite political candidate is found to have cheated on his taxes. He rationalizes his continued support for this person by saying, "He may have cheated on his taxes, but he's made up for it by all the good budget cuts he helped pass."
- Claire finds out that the car she just bought has been criticized by *Consumer Reports* for having a faulty transmission system. She rationalizes by saying, "All cars are meant to fall apart in a few years."
- Jasmine continues to smoke cigarettes, although considerable evidence supports the fact that cigarettes are a causative factor in several diseases. She tells herself and others, "I'm not going to worry about every habit I have. I could die tomorrow by slipping on a banana peel, so I might as well enjoy life today."
- Someone that Thom would like to get to know keeps refusing his requests for a date. He rationalizes by saying, "She must be really busy this year."

[4]Frank Minirth, M.D., and Don Hawkins, Th.M., *Worry Free Living* (Nashville, TN: Thomas Nelson Publishers, 1989), p. 78.

- After committing herself to a strict diet, Ginger has a doughnut for breakfast. She then eats three more, rationalizing, "I already ruined the diet, so I may as well enjoy today and start again tomorrow."
- A clerk at a supermarket forgets to charge a customer for some sodas on the bottom of the cart. When the customer starts to load them into her car and realizes the mistake she might rationalize by thinking, "Oh, well. It's a big company and they will never miss a few dollars." (See Exercise 9.1, p. 404.)

As you can see, rationalization can enter every area of our thinking. Leon Festinger, a sociologist, created a theory to explain why we use this mechanism so frequently. He said that as humans we are subject to a state of mind called **cognitive dissonance.** This state occurs whenever two ideas (or cognitions) are out of sync and create discomfort (dissonance) in our thinking patterns. Dissonance is seen as a state of mental tension. We are uncomfortable when we are confronted with evidence that goes against our worldview, whether it is evidence about a person, an issue, or even our own character. We seek to relieve the mental tension caused by dissonance in one of two ways.

1. We try to increase information (cognitions) that is consistent with what we already believe. We seek out more evidence that favors our viewpoint and speak to people who will reinforce our original viewpoint. Sometimes, we know just what sources will be favorable to our positions regarding an issue or a personal situation. For example, we might find a Web site that is filled with information that supports our beliefs; we might also call on friends who we know will take our side and agree with us. Increasing positive support as a way to avoid dissonance often involves rationalizing, as we have seen in the previous examples. We explain away inconsistencies between our principles and our actions rather than facing them and dealing with them.
2. We may try to also decrease or diminish any information that contradicts our view of a person or an issue. If, for example, we are researching an issue and find a credible Web site that refutes our beliefs, we may just ignore the information on that site and search for one that supports our beliefs. Or, if some of our friends don't like our boyfriend or girlfriend and try to tell us why, we may just avoid those friends. That reduces the dissonance by eliminating any contradictory viewpoints. This second form of dissonance reduction is part of the defense mechanism of denial, which we will discuss shortly.

Interestingly, Festinger believes that the need to resolve mentally inconsistent information is a basic drive, like the drive for food; our minds strive to "survive" unpleasant incongruities.

A mentally healthy person is in a state of congruence; that is, the individual's behavior conforms to his or her beliefs and values. Unfortunately, many of us, instead of striving for true congruence by getting our behavior in line with our values when inconsistencies occur, or by changing our viewpoints about an issue when we are proven wrong, will settle for a counterfeit peace of mind through rationalization. If we keep rationalizing, we can become psychologically unhealthy and removed from reality.

Consider the fate of many people who followed a cult leader named Jim Jones (whose life is chronicled in the 2006 film *Jonestown*) to Guyana and their deaths. When he passed himself off as a man of God and had sexual relations with many of his followers, he rationalized by calling it a form of ritual cleansing. When he humiliated young children for small infractions of his system, Jones (and some of the children's parents) rationalized that he had their best interests at heart.

The more we give up our critical thinking abilities, the harder it becomes to face our errors in judgment, and personal and social tragedies can be the result. As people who vote, buy products, influence others, and form relationships, we need to use information to help us learn and make decisions; rationalization is a form of sloppy thinking we can't afford to use.

A defense mechanism closely related to rationalization is **denial**. Denial is also a state of mind that blocks critical thinking, because it involves the repression of or refusal to recognize any negative or threatening information. Some of us go into denial when we hear we've bounced a check or forgotten to make a payment on a bill. We may tell our creditors they must have made a mistake or that they never sent the bill, when the reality is that we've made a mistake we choose not to face because of fear, pride, or both. Another personal example of denial is summarized in an anecdote from a call-in radio program excerpted from Dr. Laura Schlessinger's book *How Could You Do That?*

> Nancy, forty-seven, called all bent out of shape because her "fella" of six months turns out to be married. Her question was about whether or not it was right for her to tell his wife of the affair...mostly, I thought to punish him, and only somewhat to warn her.
>
> That isn't the whole picture at all. I asked her if she'd been to his place of residence in the six months of their steamy sexual relationship: "No."

Betty by Gary Delainey and Gery Rasmussen.
Reprinted by permission of Newspaper Enterprise Association, Inc.

I asked her if she'd even been given his home number or spoken to him at home on the phone in the evenings: "No."

I suggested that she truly knew all along that he was probably living with someone, married or not, and that she ignored that because she didn't want to give up the immediate gratification: the passion and attention. Furthermore, she had a fantasy going that she'd get him.

She begrudgingly acknowledged I was right.

Frighteningly, she couldn't seem to get with the idea that what she did wasn't right. She was too busy displacing all the blame for the current state of affairs on his adultery, not her own lack of conscience in getting involved with an attached fellow (the impact on his partner/wife/kids) and her lack of courage in finding out truths up front and dealing with them. Motivation for this stupid behavior? Immediate gratification. She made a choice of "right now" over good sense or conscience.

Trying to avoid the self-examination, she calls to find out if it was right or not for her to blow the whistle on him. I told her, "That is a separate issue from what is my deeper concern about you, which is your denial that you made a choice, which got you to this point. If you tell on him, it doesn't change you, and you were not an innocent victim.

…There's no denying that sometimes choosing to own up to your own weakness, badness, selfishness, or evil is tough to do. But it's the only way finally to get control and some peace of mind."[5]

Denial, like other defense mechanisms, comes into play when we experience an emotional reaction to information. Sometimes, denial is normal and helpful to our systems, as when we hear shocking news and give ourselves time, through denial of the facts, to cope with the information.

For example, if you are informed at a doctor's office that you have a life-threatening disease, it may be temporarily helpful for you not to digest this information completely until you are home with supportive family members or in the care of a good counselor. In this case, it might be hard to drive home if you were fully immersed in the truth of your condition.

Denial becomes a problem for critical thinkers when they refuse to acknowledge the truth or the possible truth of an argument presented to them. This problem can be summed up in the cliché "I know what I believe. Don't confuse me with the facts." The facts may be complicated, but the critical thinker needs to sort through them in order to make a reasonable judgment on an issue, or at least to withhold judgment on a complex issue about which he or she is uninformed.

Government officials may also deny important information, such as the seriousness of warnings, as illustrated in the following *New York Times* report:

---

[5]Dr. Laura Schlessinger, *How Could You Do That?* (New York: HarperCollins Publishers, Inc., 1996), pp. 94–95.

WASHINGTON, Sept. 18—The United States intelligence community was told in 1998 that Arab terrorists were planning to fly a bomb-laden aircraft into the World Trade Center, but the F.B.I. and the Federal Aviation Administration did not take the threat seriously, a Congressional investigation into the Sept. 11 attacks found.

The 1998 intelligence report from the Central Intelligence Agency was just one of several warnings the United States received, but did not seriously analyze, in the years leading up to the Sept. 11 attacks that were detailed today at a Congressional hearing.[6]

SKILL

Recognize defense mechanisms we use to deceive ourselves.

Denial and rationalization are often found together as defense mechanisms, when truth is denied and behavior is rationalized. Note both factors in another excerpt from the writings of Dr. Laura Schlessinger:

> I feel sorry for anyone's pain and problems. But when they are the result of betrayals and abandonments coming back to haunt, and the primary issue is not remediation of those actions, I don't feel it to be an ethical obligation to get personally involved.
>
> Trina, twenty-eight, has a sister, thirty-four, who split from her husband and has a new guy who dumped his wife. The sister kicked out her own seventeen-year-old daughter who wasn't going along agreeably with all this and is now living with Grandma. Trina is now wondering about not inviting the live-in guy to a family event.
>
> "Trina," I scolded, "you are displacing responsibility about this situation to him. You want to punish only him, but your sister is the one making the decisions; she chose him and she dumped her own daughter. Your sister's actions are being ignored so you can be appropriately, but safely, righteous. You don't want to upset the family applecart, right?"
>
> "Right."
>
> In discussing what her sister was actually doing wrong, Trina kept trying desperately to pardon her sister (by citing her traits as) low self-esteem, lonely, beguiled, not thinking straight, confused, lost, etc.
>
> Sure, Trina says the guy is a bum, but she's just as sure her sister is merely weak and confused, not really bad. How is that again?
>
> In psychological terminology, Trina is "splitting," i.e., ascribing ever so neatly all the bad behavior to one person and all the good to another. This is a means of coping with the difficult ambivalence of

[6]James Risen, "Threats and Responses: The Investigation; U.S. Failed to Act on Warnings in '98 of a Plane Attack," *New York Times,* September 19, 2002, p. 1.

having love and attachment you feel for someone and not wanting that to be marred by ugly realities.

Well, in real life, all good people do some wrong things and all bad people do some right things. I've heard many women defend abusing men by saying, "But, other than that, he does good stuff!"[7]

On a personal level, we may see all of the shortcomings of people we don't like and deny and excuse the faults of people we care about, as illustrated in the previous example. Similarly, we may see all of the negative aspects of viewpoints and policies we oppose and only good points in viewpoints and policies we support. By polarizing reality in this way, we leave out important considerations and hinder our ability to make the best decisions.

Critical thinkers take the time and energy required to recognize the weak points of their own side of an issue and the good points of their opponents. They search for truth rather than victory and are willing to change when presented with new information instead of insisting on maintaining a position that can no longer be supported.

Even when we are careful to give credit to the good points of all sides of an issue, we may still find that there are times when our emotional reactions cause us to lose rational perspectives. When that happens, we need to be aware of and adjust for our strong feelings, rather than denying that they have an impact on us.

CONFORMITY AND WAYS TO OVERCOME IT

Most people brought up with the reality assumptions of a democratic society like to think of themselves as independent thinkers who make their own decisions. One of the governing values of those who settled the American West was "rugged individualism," the tough-spiritedness that helped people survive physically difficult and socially isolated conditions.

Although our society has been characterized as highly individualistic, fascinating research in social psychology can help us understand some of the areas in which we may tend to conform unconsciously to others rather than thinking for ourselves. Knowing these tendencies can help us guard against them when we need to make important decisions.

In his excellent book, *Influence, The Psychology of Persuasion,* social psychologist Robert Cialdini discusses the principle of social proof, which states that "The greater the number of people who find any idea correct, the more the idea will seem to be correct." He gives many illustrations of how the beliefs and actions of others are used to guide our own beliefs and actions, especially in situations of uncertainty.

[7]Schlessinger, *How Could You Do That,* pp. 94–95.

In general, when we are unsure of ourselves, when the situation is unclear or ambiguous, when uncertainty reigns, we are most likely to look to and accept the actions of others as correct. In the process of examining the reactions of other people to resolve our uncertainty, however, we are likely to overlook a subtle but important fact. Those people are probably examining the social evidence, too. Especially in an ambiguous situation, the tendency for everyone to be looking to see what everyone else is doing can lead to a fascinating phenomenon called "pluralistic ignorance." A thorough understanding of the pluralistic ignorance phenomenon helps immeasurably to explain a regular occurrence in our country that has been termed both a riddle and a national disgrace: the failure of entire groups of bystanders to aid victims in agonizing need of help.[8]

Cialdini goes on to detail situations in which pluralistic ignorance takes place, including the famous case of a Queens, New York, woman who was murdered while 38 neighbors watched from their windows. When the murder occurred, the media were filled with questions about how such apathy could prevail when it would have been so simple for the bystanders to make an anonymous call to police.

Subsequent studies reveal that the cause of the inaction was not apathy, but conformity to the inaction of others. In study after study, people acting alone were usually willing to offer help and assistance to someone in trouble. But when a crowd was present and no one in the crowd took action, that seemed to indicate that no action was necessary; individuals encountering the inaction of others read the cues of the group and also did nothing to help the person in trouble.

Additional studies show that individuals are much more likely to conform to others who seem similar to themselves. Cialdini cites the research of sociologist David Phillips who discovered that immediately following the reports of suicides of young people, there was a remarkable increase in similar suicides among the young. When a suicide story involved an older driver, the statistics on suicides in older drivers immediately increased. Phillips also discovered a similar trend in homicide rates. Cialdini states, "it is clear that widely publicized aggression has the nasty tendency to spread to similar victims, no matter whether the aggression is inflicted on the self or on another."[9]

When others who are similar to us engage in an activity, the activity becomes legitimized. This may account for patterns of high school, junior high school, and even elementary school homicides. Students hear the stories of others who, like themselves, have difficulty in their lives and resolve the difficulty through homicide or homicide followed by suicide. Although they may not conform to their peer group at school, they do conform to their "reference group" of destructive revenge seekers, and they perform "copycat" murders.

[8]Robert B. Cialdini, *The Psychology of Persuasion* (New York: William Morrow, 1993), p. 129.
[9]Ibid., p. 151.

The previously noted examples deal with unusual situations, but the human tendency to conform also can be noted in routine, daily activities. One of Cialdini's students, a highway patrolman, reports on a common accident that can be attributed to "social proof," the idea that if everyone thinks or does something, it must be correct.

> After a class session in which the subject of discussion was the principle of social proof, he stayed to talk with me. He said that he now understood the cause of a type of traffic accident that had always puzzled him before. The accident typically occurred on the city freeway during rush hour, when cars in all lanes were moving steadily but slowly. Events leading to the accident would start when a pair of cars, one behind the other, would simultaneously begin signaling an intention to get out of the lane they were in and into the next. Within seconds, a long line of drivers to the rear of the first two would follow suit, thinking that something—a stalled car or a construction barrier—was blocking the lane ahead. It would be in this crush to cram into the available spaces of the next lane that a collision frequently happened.
>
> The odd thing about it all, according to the patrolman, was that very often there had been no obstruction to be avoided in the first place, and by the time of the accident, this should have been obvious to anyone who looked. He said he had more than once witnessed such accidents when there was a visibly clear road in front of the ill-fated lane switchers.
>
> The patrolman's account provides certain insights into the way we respond to social proof. First, we seem to assume that if a lot of people are doing the same thing, they must know something we don't. Especially when we are uncertain, we are willing to place an enormous amount of trust in the collective knowledge of the crowd. Second, quite frequently the crowd is mistaken because they are not acting on the basis of any superior information but are reacting, themselves, to the principle of social proof.[10]

Conformity occurs when we follow what others are doing rather than relying on our own best judgment. We sometimes find that conformity is a necessary condition for being accepted in a group. When a group member expresses an opinion that is different from the group's opinion, pressure is often applied to get the "deviant" to conform. The pressure may come in the form of reasoning, teasing, bribery, shaming, pleading, complimenting, or, usually as a last resort, shunning. The tendency for individuals to go along with a group's decision has been labeled by Yale psychologist Irving L. Janis as **groupthink.** Groupthink involves faulty decision making by groups that sacrifice sound judgment in order to keep their unity as a group; group members

[10]Ibid., pp. 162–163.

don't offer or consider several alternative solutions to a problem; they don't seek outside, expert opinion; they don't criticize each other's ideas; and they rationalize poor decisions. Janis discovered the principle of groupthink in his study of various actions taken by U.S. government leaders that led to dire consequences for many people. Professor Vincent Ryan Ruggiero discusses Janis's study in his book *Beyond Feelings*:

> The actions were Franklin D. Roosevelt's failure to be ready for the Japanese attack on Pearl Harbor, Harry S. Truman's decision to invade North Korea, John F. Kennedy's plan to invade Cuba, and Lyndon B. Johnson's decision to escalate the Vietnam War. In each case, Janis found that the people who made the decision exhibited a strong desire to concur in the group decision.
>
> …More specifically, Janis identified a number of major defects in decision-making that could be attributed to this conformity. The groups he analyzed did not survey the range of choices but focused on a few. When they discovered that their initial decision had certain drawbacks, they failed to reconsider those decisions. They almost never tested their own thinking for weaknesses. They never tried to obtain the judgments of experts. They expressed interest only in those views that reinforced the positions they preferred, and they spent little time considering the obstacles that would hinder the success of their plans. In each of the cases Janis studied, these defects in thinking cost untold human suffering.[11]

More recently, scholars who have studied the effects of groupthink have also blamed other disasters including the explosion of the space shuttle Challenger on the phenomenon of groupthink.

How can we overcome the effects of conformity and groupthink on our actions?

1. Realize that as humans, we have a tendency to unconsciously accept social proof, the proof that is provided by a broad acceptance of an attitude or action. This tendency may manifest in small social choices or in blind ethnocentrism.
2. Understand that as social beings, we work in groups and seek the acceptance of the group. Be aware of the phenomenon of groupthink and bring it to the attention of the group when appropriate.
3. Watch the tendency to conform to others or to rebel against others; instead, base decisions on good evidence and reasoning.
4. When working with a group, suggest that the group divide into subgroups to brainstorm ideas before discussing them as a whole group. Use outside experts to offer opinions on important matters. Have an impartial leader who establishes an open climate where it is safe to criticize ideas; a good

[11]Vincent Ryan Ruggiero, *Beyond Feelings: A Guide to Critical Thinking* (Mountain View, CA: Mayfield Publishing, 1990), p. 64.

leader will also encourage group members to challenge different solutions to problems and to consider many alternatives before coming to a decision.

EMOTIONAL REASONING AND RATIONAL RESPONSES

Like conformity, **emotional reasoning** causes us to distort the truth of our circumstances and to make poor decisions. We all experience feelings as a result of the words or actions of others. People who reason emotionally *react* to other people and to events, taking their feelings as automatic proof of their own analysis of the situation. People who reason logically also experience their emotions but stop and consider possible interpretations before reacting, so that they can *respond* in a rational and constructive manner.

Cognitive psychologists help people use tools of rationality to overcome debilitative emotions and to reason more clearly. A rational approach to emotions is based on the following principles:

We all face numerous situations every day.
Feelings and reactions to these situations are natural.
Our feelings can be traced back to our thoughts, that is, our interpretations of the events.
If we examine the thoughts/interpretations that produced the feelings, the feelings will often change or be diminished.
When feelings are more in line with reality, our actions will be more constructive.

For example, let's say that you say hello to a coworker who is usually friendly, and she quickly walks right past you without returning your greeting. A natural reaction would be to feel insulted, hurt, or annoyed with her. You might decide that the next time you see her, you're not going to say anything. Although your feelings are normal, your interpretation of the event involves "jumping to conclusions," interpreting the event, assuming your interpretation is correct, and then judging the situation accordingly.

But suppose that you find out that your coworker was rushing past you because she had just been told that her mother was in intensive care following a car accident. Now, the natural reaction would be to feel concern and sympathy. You might decide to see if you could help her in some way.

We can illustrate how our thoughts determine our feelings in a simple chart:

Situation	Thoughts	Feelings
Coworker ignores you.	"She thinks she's superior to me."	Irritation, anger
Coworker ignores you.	"She is upset about her mother."	Concern, sympathy

STOP AND THINK

Critical thinkers realize that all events and behaviors are not personally designed to make their lives difficult; they are able to stop and consider other interpretations and respond accordingly.

It takes a certain amount of character, in the form of self-control, patience, and optimism to stop and question our interpretations before we react. For example, when a flight is delayed, it is common for people to take out their anger and frustration on the clerk at the airline counter, even though it would not be his or her fault that the mechanic found a problem in the engine or that the weather has caused delays. People on the "front lines" of customer service are trained to deal with frustrated and angry outbursts; they are taught not to take the verbal abuse personally and to refer inconsolable or threatening people to the next level of management. Their job is made easier by people who use rational "self-talk" before lashing out, as illustrated here:

Situation	Thoughts	Feelings	Action
Airport delay	"I'm being taken advantage of by the airline."	Anger-rage	Yell at clerk
Airport delay	"There is a problem with the plane or weather."	Irritation	Adjust/cope

The first individual rages at the clerk, which only makes the situation more unpleasant. Note that the second individual is also irritated, but his rational thinking allows him to adjust to the situation rather than making it worse. He might even talk to the clerk about getting a flight on another airline, and his polite manner would make her more receptive to trying to help him come up with a creative solution to his dilemma.

When our thoughts are based on a correct interpretation of reality, our actions will be more useful. Even when our negative thoughts seem reasonable, we are able to act more rationally if we stop and think. For example, let's say that your coworker got an hourly raise that you also deserved.

Situation	Thoughts	Feelings
Coworker gets raise	"I also deserved this raise."	Anger at boss

This situation may seem and may actually be unfair to you, in which case your feelings are justified. But it is also important to consider the best actions to achieve your goals. You might get angry with your boss and accuse her of being unfair, but that is not likely to help you achieve your goals and may even hurt your case. If you can calmly present the situation to her, she may see that she was wrong and correct the wrong; if she doesn't, there is often recourse through her supervisor or through a union representative.

Dr. Phil McGraw has a useful phrase that helps people examine the consequences of their actions. He often asks his troubled guests this question about their reactions to their circumstances: "How's that working for you?" Even when our anger is justified, we need to come up with the best course of action for our lives. Screaming and lashing out at others or giving up in frustration rarely achieves long-term goals.

There are other patterns of thinking that distort reality and make it hard for us to make clear decisions. Following are some of the most debilitating.

1. *Overgeneralizing.* Overgeneralizing involves coming to a general conclusion on the basis of a single incident or a few incidents. People who overgeneralize often use exaggerated terms such as "always," "never," "everyone," and "anything." They label themselves and others as permanently fixed in some character trait because of a few examples, and they overlook any evidence to the contrary. Overgeneralizing causes prejudice and stereotyping of others and also of ourselves.

Examples

"I got a D on my test—I'll never understand math."
"You're always late."
"We'll never have the time to get this done."
"I forgot our anniversary—I'm just a terrible boyfriend."

2. *Mind Reading.* Mind readers assume they know what others are thinking or assume that others should know what they are thinking. Mind reading is based on the psychological process of "projection"—assuming that what would be true for you in any given circumstance is true for the other person.

Examples

"The only reason he married her was for her money."
"You should have known that I wanted that job—it was obvious."
"The reason she said that was because she was jealous."

3. *Filtering.* When we filter, we focus on the negative details of a situation and filter out all the positive—this has also been called "awfulizing" a situation and is a favorite tactic of pessimistic thinkers. When the negative details are all that we allow, they become larger and more powerful than they really are. Often, the filtering implies a helplessness on the part of speakers; they see circumstances as completely out of their control or influence.

Examples

"Our schools are a complete mess. Things have changed so much because of the new policies that education has become impossible."

"I've tried to get a job, but people just aren't hiring; and even if they are, I can't live on the salary I'd get."

"Every time I try to give up drinking, someone has a party; I can't change because our school is just too much of a party school, and I'm not willing to be an outcast."

4. Catastrophizing. Closely related to filtering, catastrophizing occurs when people expect disaster. People who catastrophize imagine and anticipate problems, and they often use the term *what if?* Creative thinkers can come up with any number of potentially catastrophic events. While rational concerns should always be considered before embarking on a new course of action and life does involve some risk, catastrophizing is filled with unsubstantiated fears and a magnifying of negative possibilities. On a personal level, this mode of thinking reflects a lack of trust in one's capacity to adapt to changes.

[handwritten: lack of trust in one's capacity]

Examples

"We can't change the stadium's location. We'll lose all our fans."

"Online classes are a bad idea. There's no way to prevent cheating."

"Junior shouldn't be taking gymnastics. What if he falls and breaks his arm?"

"I'll never be able to get a job with all of the other people in my major."

5. Personalizing. When we personalize, we relate everything that happens to ourselves, and we "take things personally," assuming that general statements or actions are made in reaction to us. We also falsely believe that our characteristics or actions are continually being compared, favorably or unfavorably, against others. Personalizing creates both defensiveness and pessimism.

Examples

"I know he's lied and cheated on other girls too, but he broke up with me because I wasn't good enough for him."

"The C in history just shows how much that teacher hated me."

"Our boss told us that we were all working too slowly, but I know she meant me."

"Every team I'm on is going to lose."

6. Perfectionism. Perfectionists have a false belief that perfection is possible. They end up minimizing their good qualities or the good parts of a situation and focusing instead on how they or others have not measured up. Perfectionists have a hard time accepting their own humanity and the limits of other human beings; their desire to be without fault in any way can make them avoid or stop trying.

[handwritten: Watch!]

Examples

"I'm so upset that I missed two questions—I should have studied harder for the test."

"Yes, we finally have a new theater, but it's going to be another year before the sound system is complete."

"Honey, I know you spent all day cleaning the yard, but you didn't put away your laundry."

"I know we won and I scored the most points, but my brother was Most Valuable Player when he was my age."

STOP AND THINK

Do you or someone you know tend to use emotional reasoning? *no*

WAYS TO DEAL WITH EMOTIONAL REASONING

When you find yourself involved in the irrational reasoning processes outlined in the previous section, there are several things you can do to get back on track.

1. *Be Aware.* Stop and see if you can identify how your reasoning is distorted. Are you catastrophizing, minimizing, or jumping to conclusions?

2. *Map Out the General Beliefs Behind Your Emotions.* Common beliefs related to feelings can be generally seen as follows:

Feeling	General Belief
Anger	My rights have been violated in some way.
Sadness/grief	I have experienced a loss.
Anxiety	I am concerned about something happening in the future.
Guilt	I have violated someone else's rights.
Embarrassment	I have lost standing with others.

3. *Analyze the Specific Situation that Caused Your Thinking.* For example, if you didn't receive a grade or a promotion that you felt you deserved, you may believe that your rights have been violated; that belief generated the feelings of anger. If you are unprepared for an upcoming test or interview, you may feel anxiety.

4. *Consider Other Interpretations of the Situation.* Your teacher may have made a mistake in your grading or you may have misinterpreted the grading criteria. You may feel unprepared for an upcoming test because of missing some class time. Come up with the worst case, best case and most likely case concerning your situation. Sometimes, just asking yourself, "What is the worst thing that can happen?" or "Why does this situation bother me so much?" can bring insight and clarification.

5. *Prepare for Action.* Try to plan for the best possible outcomes and to prevent the worst possible outcomes. For example, you may decide to talk with your instructor about your grade when you are feeling calm and rational. Instead of approaching him with anger and a sense of unfairness, bring your work and grades and ask him to explain how your grade was calculated. If you have a difference of opinion, explain it to him. If you get no satisfactory answer, calmly go to the next level, his supervisor, until you receive the answers or changes you need.

    6. *Accept Good Changes and also Accept Reality.* You can't control other people, and there are many situations that are also out of your control. But you can respond with clear thinking and positive actions that help you make the best of your circumstances, effecting change when possible and moving on when necessary. (See Exercise 9.2, p. 405)

SKILL

Recognize and use logical thinking to counter emotional reasoning.

POINTS OF LOGICAL VULNERABILITY

Professor Zachary Seech has come up with a great description of the trouble spots in our thinking, areas where we have trouble being rational. He calls them **points of logical vulnerability**. We can be vulnerable to a general topic, such as politics, or a specific one, such as our sister's choice of a husband.[12]

    There are topics about which a person, we say, "just cannot be rational." What we mean is that this person has great difficulty being objective on these specific topics. He or she finds it difficult, in some cases, to consider the evidence impartially and draw a sensible, justified conclusion. These topics are the points of logical vulnerability for that person.[13]

    Each person has different "sore spots" in his or her life, and dialogue on a given issue becomes difficult when our emotions blind our thinking on certain points. If you are a die-hard fan of a particular team, you may not be objective about how they will do in the next game. If fast food fits your lifestyle perfectly, you may not be open to any discussion of health problems associated with a steady diet of cheeseburgers and fries. If you are upset because your roommate is getting married and moving out, you may find yourself disliking his or her new mate.

    Points of logical vulnerability affect us so much on a personal level that we are likely to deny or rationalize any evidence that might disprove our opinions. For example, if you dislike a senator because of her views on taxes and then

[12]Zachary Seech, *Logic in Everyday Life* (Belmont, CA: Wadsworth Publishing, 1988), pp. 2–3.
[13]Ibid., p. 2.

(handwritten margin note: points of logical vulnerability are personal / change from person to person)

she supports a tax bill you also support, you might rationalize that "she's just trying to appease us; she doesn't really care about the issue."

Conversely, if you like the senator and she does something you consider wrong, you might rationalize that she was forced into making concessions she would not have personally approved. Our points of logical vulnerability cause us to distort or deny information that goes against our deeply held opinions.

Keep in mind the difference between having strong, well-considered convictions about which you are not flexible (such as your values), and opinions that have not been thought out, but have been based solely on emotions or identification with others who hold those opinions. The latter opinions are probably points of logical vulnerability for you. (See Exercise 9.3, p. 405.)

Antidotes for Points of Logical Vulnerability

You can confront your points of logical vulnerability in several effective ways. The first approach is to apply certain techniques of rational thought to your opinions; the second is to learn to listen actively and accurately to people with differing opinions.

General semanticists study the relationship between words and behavior. They believe that we can improve our mental health by increasing the accuracy with which we speak, and they have come up with several "cures" for irrational statements.

A classic irrational statement stereotypes a whole group of people based on a limited sample of experience on the part of the speaker. Another term for a stereotypical statement is a *sweeping generalization.*

Let's say a man named Harold has had several bad experiences in his relationships with women. The first woman he wanted to marry left him for another man; the second woman he wanted to marry told him she wasn't ready for a commitment and that she needed "space"; the third woman he wanted to marry left town with no forwarding address. In discussing his problems with his best friend, Harold makes the statement: "All women are cruel and selfish."

Now we can understand how anyone with this record of experiences would be upset about his former relationships, but we also can see, as outside observers, that his statement is emotional and would not hold up to critical scrutiny. You can't interact with three women and then claim that all women (about half of the human race) are cruel and selfish.

General semanticists, basing their work on the pioneering writing of Albert Korzypski, apply what he called **semantic devices** to help people be more rational about their statements; they believe that if we speak more logically, we will be able to overcome debilitating emotions and reactions. They would ask Harold to do a few things with his statement "All women are cruel and selfish."

- Eliminate the word *all* since no one can know every single woman. Change the general term *women* into specifics: Woman 1, woman 2, and woman 3 become Patty, Marcia, and Gina. Now he has: "Patty, Marcia, and Gina are cruel and selfish." Not perfect, but more accurate; at least in this case he is not generalizing from three examples to half of the human race.

    Semanticists call this technique **indexing;** you take your general label (women, Catholics, Asians, Americans) and change it to actual people. You also delete the word *all* from your vocabulary when it precedes a general category. One can never know *all* about any given group.
- Next, a general semanticist would ask Harold to change his vague labels of *cruel* and *selfish* to specific behaviors. "Patty, Marcia, and Gina did not marry me, although we were dating and I asked them to marry me. Patty married someone else, Marcia told me she needed 'space,' and Gina left town without contacting me."
- For accuracy and perspective, our semanticist would also ask Harold to put a *date* on his statement. "Patty, Marcia, and Gina did not marry me, although we were dating and I asked them to marry me. Patty married someone else, Marcia told me she needed 'space,' and Gina left town without contacting me. These incidents happened when I was in my late teens and early twenties."
- The final addition to Harold's statement is called the *etc.* because it includes other realities that add balance and fairness to the original statement. Think of a young child who complains with all accuracy, "Joey pushed me!" This statement is clear and unambiguous, yet we don't know what else was going on in the situation. We don't have the total picture or the context in which the event occurred.

    To figure out what was going on, a parent or teacher might ask, "Did you push him too?" It could be that the child who complained was indeed the victim of Joey's aggressiveness, or maybe the complaining child pushed Joey first. Also, it could be that Joey was pushing to get somewhere and was unaware that he had pushed the other child. We can only know what happened in a situation when we get more information.

Think about the times you feel really annoyed with someone's behavior. In recounting your irritation to a friend, do you really try to be fair and objective or do you tend to present the details that best support your right to be annoyed?

When general semanticists recommend the use of the *etc.*, they are recognizing the complexity of situations and that we can rarely say all there is to say about the factors involved that create differences of opinion. They would suggest that Harold add information to his statement to give a more accurate picture of reality:

- Patty, Marcia, and Gina did not marry me, although we were dating and I asked them to marry me. Patty married someone else, Marcia told me she needed "space," and Gina left town without contacting me. These incidents happened when I was in my late teens and early twenties. I knew Patty was ready to get married, but I didn't ask her until she was involved with someone else; I could have still dated Marcia as one of the men she was dating, but I wanted to be the only one; I don't know why Gina left town.

SKILL

Use rational thinking aids to overcome areas in which you have trouble being rational.

If you compare Harold's first statement with this last statement, you might understand why the use of semantic devices improves mental health. A counselor might help Harold arrive at the same kinds of rephrasing. If he continues to see all women as cruel and selfish, he might never try to interact with them again, but if he sees that he has had a few bad experiences, he can learn from his mistakes and continue to grow and develop relationships. As humans, we all endure hurtful experiences; people who can apply reason to their emotional reactions can bounce back more easily. The use of reason increases our resiliency.

The semantic devices are useful in helping us change irrational comments we make about people and issues to more truthful and fair-minded statements. (See Exercise 9.4 on p. 406.)

ACTIVELY AND ACCURATELY LISTENING: DEVELOPING EMPATHY

> *Some psychologists believe that the ability to listen to another person, to empathize with, and to understand their point of view is one of the highest forms of intelligent behavior.*
>
> Arthur Costa, "Teaching for Intelligence" 1988

Many cultures place a high value on competition, and this competition is not restricted to sporting events—it also comes out in debates and discussions on issues. According to Deborah Tannen, author of *The Argument Culture,* the desire to win and the enjoyment we find in having the most persuasive argument may limit our ability to be fair to opposing sides of issues.[14]

Tannen makes a distinction between "having an argument" and "making an argument":

> When you're having an argument, you aren't trying to understand what the other person is saying; you're trying to win the argument. Both of you ignore the other's valid points and leap on weak ones, which is frustrating, because neither of you is listening to the other. In making an argument, you're putting a logical train of thoughts together to persuade someone of your point of view.[15]

When we sense that someone is trying to win an argument and is not willing to listen, he or she loses credibility with us, and we usually tune him or her out. The most persuasive speaker is one who can understand and address

[14]Deborah Tannen, *The Argument Culture* (New York: Ballantine, Random House, 1999), p. 352.
[15]Ibid., p. 354.

the points brought up by those who don't share his or her opinion. To understand and respond to an opposing argument, we must hear what the speaker for the opposition is saying.

Why do we find listening difficult, and why don't politicians listen more fairly in debates? Some of the reasons we don't listen include the following:

principal purpose

- The thrust of debate is to win; therefore, we will tend to listen to the opposition's position only so we can find fault with it. The focus is on victory, not on understanding, especially in public debating forums. Too often a televised discussion or debate models bad behavior; speakers shout over each other, rarely admitting that an argument made by the other person has any merit.
- We are not trained to listen. Some of us have had training in speech, but few have had specific training in effective listening techniques.
- We fear if we really listen to the other person, we will lose our train of thought.
- We fear if we really listen to the other person, we might agree with him or her and that could be unsettling and uncomfortable.
- Effort and energy are required in order to try to understand the viewpoint of another person.
- For many of us, it is more rewarding to speak about our own ideas than to listen to others.

Listening accurately to an opposing position, however, gives us some clear advantages:

- We can learn what the opposition to our cause or issue believes, and we can then address our opponents more effectively on specific points.
- We can grow and adjust our position if new research or reasoning warrants the adjustment.
- When we are seen as secure enough in our position to listen to an opposing argument, our credibility increases.
- Our calm listening is often contagious; as we show our willingness to hear the other side fully, defenses are dropped and our opponents may listen to us as well. We have a better chance of explaining our viewpoint and not having it distorted by interruptions or polarized by angry rebuttals.
- In an atmosphere of reduced hostility, areas of agreement can be found. When areas of agreement are discovered, problems can be solved more creatively.

THE ART OF LISTENING WELL

Years ago, a southern California psychologist, Carl Rogers, created a listening exercise that has become a staple for counselors and teachers of communication. Rogers's technique is simple and very effective; if done correctly, both sides come out with **empathy**, that is a deeper understanding of the other's position.

Understanding does not necessarily mean agreement. We may know exactly what the other's position is and conclude that he is completely off base. The critical thinker is the one who draws conclusions based on an understanding of both her and her opponent's position, not solely on an emotional commitment to her original position.

The key element of Rogers's technique is paraphrasing (putting in your own words) the other person's thoughts so that you know what is truly being said before you respond with your own opinions. In normal dialogue, you won't be paraphrasing everything the other person says, but you should stop and paraphrase whenever you aren't sure about what he or she is saying. You can also use paraphrasing to cool down an emotional discussion. When people feel that they are truly being heard, there is no need for loud and strident dialogue.

Here is Rogers's listening exercise that is used to train people in basic paraphrasing skills:

1. Two people with opposing beliefs on an issue sit facing each other.
2. Person A begins with a brief statement about her opinion on an issue.
3. Person B paraphrases—puts person A's opinion in his own words. When person A agrees that person B has understood, then person B states his opinion.
4. Now person A has to paraphrase—restate in her own words what person B has said. When person B is satisfied that person A has understood him, person A can expand on her opinion.
5. This process is continued until both parties feel they have presented their cases and that they have been understood. It is helpful to allow each person a few minutes to summarize, as best he or she can, the complete position of the other person.
6. During the process, both parties attempt to be objective in their summaries of the other person's viewpoint and to avoid sarcasm, ridicule, or exaggeration of any points the other person makes.
7. It is also helpful to try to "read between the lines" and understand why the other person feels so strongly about his or her position. Often there is a significant personal experience that shaped the other person's viewpoint in a powerful way.

SKILL

Listen with empathy to an opposing viewpoint.

Example

Person A: I believe heroic medical interventions should not be made unless the doctors and nurses have permission of the patient or the patient's family members.

Person B: So you believe that extending life with technology should not be done unless a patient or his family wants his life extended?

Person A: That's right.

Person B: Well, it's my opinion that sometimes there isn't time for a discussion with the patient or the family members about the patient's chances for survival. The medical experts have to act or there is no decision to be made because the patient is dead!

Person A: So you think that using technology is totally up to the doctors?

Person B: (clarifying) I didn't mean that. I mean, if the patient is going to die if he's not hooked up to the machines, then he needs to be hooked up first and consulted later.

Person A: (trying to paraphrase more accurately) So you think in an emergency the doctors should be allowed to treat the patient in any way that will save his life and talk to him or his family members later.

Person B: That's right. You got it.

Person A: Well, I don't have a real problem with that. But I believe that if the patient doesn't want to be kept alive through technology, and if he or his family members tell the doctors that, then the doctors have to abide by his wishes and "pull the plug."

Person B: So, basically, you believe the patient should decide whether he will live or die—or, if he can't decide, then his family should decide for him.

Person A: (clarifying) That's not exactly it. He may live or die whether he's hooked up to life supports or not. But it's his choice—or his family's choice—whether he will be hooked up.

Person B: Okay, then it's the patient's choice, or secondly, his family's choice and not the doctor's choice to continue him on life supports.

Person A: Exactly.

Person B: I believe it is part of a doctor's job to assess a patient's chances for survival; the patient or the family can get too emotional and decide to let someone die rather than be uncomfortable; and meanwhile, the doctor may know there's a good chance for recovery. Also, doctors are trained to save life at all costs. If we train them to take the patient's advice, then they could let him die just so they could take off early to play golf.

Person A: That's a lot for me to paraphrase. You believe, if I have it right, that doctors are more objective and less emotional than patients and family members, and they have more of an expert opinion about chances for recovery. And also you think it's dangerous to let patients or family members decide to pull the plug because then doctors don't have to worry about whether the patient could have lived a full life or not.

Person B: You said it better than I did!

Person A: Well, what I really think is that doctors should give their expert opinion to the patient and the family members. If they then decide, for whatever reason, not to prolong life with technology, then the doctors would have to abide by their decision.

Person B: So you think that the doctor should be an adviser or counselor and give them all the information they need, but the family should have the final power to decide what will be done.

Person A: That's exactly right.

Person B: Well, that sounds fair, but I just believe it's better to go for life, whenever possible. There are many cases of people recovering from comas or serious strokes thanks to life-support systems. If their families had pulled the plug to spare them pain or expense, they would have lost a loved one. Give life a chance.

Person A: Well, my position is more simple. It's his body—or his parent's, wife's, or child's body. That gives him the right to decide what will or will not be done in a hospital. I agree it's important to get the doctor's opinion, but after that, his decision should be honored.

Person B: And I agree with you that it's his or her body, but I also think the doctors are more objective and knowledgeable, so they should be allowed to continue treatment if there's a chance for recovery. I can see why some of these cases have to be settled in court. That's not the ideal solution, but it's the best we've come up with so far.

QUESTIONS FOR DISCUSSION

1. The participants in this dialogue did not end by agreeing with much of each other's positions. How, then, is this form of communication useful?

2. Where did you spot inaccurate paraphrases of the other position? Why do you think these occurred?

3. Often, there is a strong emotional component to someone's position. Do you see hints of emotionalism in this dialogue? How does the paraphrasing minimize emotional outbursts or points of logical vulnerability? Under what circumstances should the emotional reactions of the participants also be brought to light?

laypeople = a person without knowledge in a particular subject

PRECAUTIONS ABOUT ACTIVE LISTENING

Active listening was first suggested as a technique to be used by professional therapists. Over the years, various workshops have been set up for the purposes of training laypeople to use active listening to improve their relationships. These workshops focus on the proper and improper use of the technique.

If you have never been formally trained in active listening, you may find it uncomfortable. However, practice and a basic knowledge of potential problems should enable you to use this very helpful communication tool successfully. Here is a summary of basic precautions in using active listening:

1. Avoid sarcasm and ridicule of the other person's statements; also don't add negative connotations to what he or she says.

2. Don't "parrot" the position of the other person; just paraphrase (put in your own words) the ideas you hear. *repeat mechanically*

3. If you find yourself getting upset, take some time out and assess what it is about this issue that makes it painful for you to be objective. There are

some issues we feel so strongly about that there is no room for discussion. These strong feelings are usually connected with a personal experience. For example, if your cousin was murdered, you may believe that the death penalty is justified, and any arguments against it make no impression when you consider the pain of your cousin and your close family. Your belief may be based on a value that you hold deeply; if you believe that abortion is the taking of innocent life, then statistics about overpopulation may not convince you to change your mind. (See Exercise 9.5 on p. 406.)

It is helpful, as a critical thinker, to know the areas in which you hold solid convictions. You can then acknowledge points on an opposing side but make it clear that those points are not strong enough for you to change your mind. The key is to understand both sides of an issue fully and to be open to new information; then you are responsible as a thinker when you, with good conscience, take a strong, even immovable, stand on an issue.

It is unrealistic to assume that you will have many opportunities for this kind of extended dialogue with someone who disagrees with you. The benefit of understanding the paraphrasing technique is that you can use it whenever it seems that something needs to be clarified in a discussion. Your use of this technique gives you credibility and the personal power that comes with a calm, rational approach to dialogue.

The person who stays cool and calm in a discussion seems secure in his or her position. The person who blows it by becoming overexcited and unfair to the opposition seems threatened—that is, logically vulnerable. Jumping up and down, name-calling, interrupting, and other forms of bullying serve only to make the person who uses these tactics seem foolish and unstable.

Your cool, clear mind—don't leave home without it!

LIFE APPLICATION

Use listening skills to uncover the viewpoints of those who believe differently from you on a particular issue. Try to uncover past experiences or present concerns that make them think as they do. Question and expand your own fair-mindedness by being aware of your own 'points of logical vulnerability' and by listening to others whose ideas are unlike your own.

CHAPTER EXERCISES

Exercise 9.1 *Purpose:* To understand why people rationalize rather than admit incongruities.

In a small group, take each of the examples of rationalization from pages 382–383 and discuss why someone might use that rationalization.

1. What need might he or she be trying to meet by rationalizing about that situation?

2. How is rationalization related to the attempt to preserve self-esteem?

3. How is rationalization harmful to the critical thinking and decision-making process?

Exercise 9.2   Purposes: To understand how feelings are connected to thoughts. To change reactions by rethinking a situation.

1. Think of some recent instances where you had a strong emotional reaction (anger, anxiety, guilt, sadness, embarrassment).

2. Identify the emotion and the thoughts or beliefs that created the emotion. What was your "self-talk" about the situation?

3. Create a different interpretation of the events—different self-talk. Would your emotions have changed with the new interpretation?

Example

I recently had surgery and my mom has been calling me every day to see if I need anything. I got irritated at her last week and told her to stop treating me like a little kid. My thoughts were that she doesn't trust me to take care of myself. I feel like my right to be treated as an adult was violated.

Looking back at this, I realize that she was just really concerned about my recovery and just wanted to be useful. That understanding made my irritation go away. In fact, I feel a little guilty now for being so rude to her when her motives were to help me be comfortable and get better.

Exercise 9.3   Purpose: To recognize areas of logical vulnerability.

Discover some of your points of logical vulnerability. Think about people whose opinions are not credible for you. Consider political or social issues (capital punishment, drug legalization, euthanasia, gun control, or AIDS research policies); or choose an issue about which you frequently argue with other people.

Can you think of any ways in which you might not have been objective in hearing evidence from others about this issue? Do you use denial or rationalization when confronted with your points of logical vulnerability? How could you respond differently?

Example

I don't like a congresswoman in my state. I heard her speak once and thought she was rude in the way she handled a question from the audience; also, she is against some of the legislation I consider important.

Once in a while, I'll hear her say something that makes sense, but I notice I discount whatever she says; if there's a negative way to look at her comments, I do. I guess I think she has some ulterior motive and I don't believe she has any positive contribution to make.

I don't like most of her positions and I'd never vote for her. But I could be more open and fair and admit that occasionally she does have a good idea and she might have real concern for the people in her district.

Exercise 9.4   Purpose: To practice using the semantic devices in order to make statements more accurate and rational.

1. Using the semantic devices (eliminating the all, indexing, citing specific behavior, and adding the *date* and the *etc.*), change the following irrational statements into logical statements. You may need to make up details.

    a. Women are terrible drivers. (Note the implied *all* before women.)
    b. Wealthy people are greedy and materialistic.
    c. Democrats are bleeding-heart liberals and can't be trusted.
    d. Republicans don't care about the poor and needy.
    e. People from Ivy League schools are elitists.
    f. People on welfare don't want to work.

    Can you add a statement that you've heard yourself (or a close friend) say?

2. Listen to yourself for a week and see if you tend to overgeneralize when confronted with your points of logical vulnerability. Try to stop yourself and to use the semantic devices to rephrase your opinions. What is the effect on your emotions and your conversations? You may note that if you try to get other people to be more specific and less prejudicial in their statements, you encounter some hostility. Why might that be? Write out several examples of instances in which you or someone else could have used the semantic devices to make more accurate statements.

Exercise 9.5   Purpose: To practice active listening.

1. In class, or at home, try using this listening technique when discussing an issue with someone who disagrees with you; for class, you can choose a social issue that usually creates opposing viewpoints, such as legalization of drugs, same-sex marriage, or whether spanking is an acceptable form of child discipline. Often, there are interesting controversial issues reported in daily papers, and you can choose one of those as your topic. For use at home, you might want to discuss a problem that needs to be solved, such as the division of labor or how to spend money. Be sure to tell the other person the active listening rules and get his or her commitment to abide by them or you may be in for a good fight. It may help to have a referee who is familiar with the technique and objective about the issue. Then report on your results by answering the following questions:

    a. Were you able to stay with the paraphrasing process? Why or why not?
    b. Did you and the other person attain greater understanding? If so, give some specific examples of what you learned about each other's positions.
    c. Was the relationship between you and the other person improved in any way?

2. Exchange a persuasive essay paper you have done (perhaps earlier in this course or in another class) with another student's essay; then do the following:

a. Write a paraphrase of the other's ideas, clearly focusing on thesis statements and evidence used to support the thesis.

b. Read the other student's paraphrase of your essay; comment on how well he or she understood and expressed your point of view. If there are misunderstandings in each other's viewpoints, try to discover why these occurred. If time permits, explain to the class any problems you encountered in trying to empathize with each other's ideas.

CHAPTER HIGHLIGHTS

1. Our thinking can become less egocentric and more clear and fair when we recognize our defense mechanisms and our areas of logical vulnerability and when we develop specific skills for understanding the viewpoints of others.

2. Rationalization is a defense mechanism in which we try to justify or make sense out of things that are not sensible or justifiable.

3. Denial is a defense mechanism that involves repressing or refusing to recognize threatening information.

4. Conformity can be an unconscious but powerful response to "social proof" and the human desire to belong to various groups.

5. Emotional reasoning can distort thinking; there are ways to overcome emotional reasoning.

6. Points of logical vulnerability are topics about which we have trouble being rational.

7. Thinkers can manage points of logical vulnerability through the use of semantic devices.

8. Active listening, when used properly, can help us clearly understand the viewpoints of others.

KEY TERMS

Ethnocentrism (sociocentrism) (p. 380)
Fair-mindedness (p. 380)
Egocentrism (p. 380)
Defense mechanism (p. 382)
Rationalization (p. 382)
Cognitive dissonance (p. 383)
Denial (p. 384)
Conformity (p. 389)
Groupthink (p. 389)
Emotional reasoning (p. 391)
Overgeneralizing (p. 393)

Mind reading (p. 393)
Filtering (p. 393)
Catastrophizing (p. 394)
Personalizing (p. 394)
Perfectionism (p. 394)
Points of logical vulnerability (p. 396)
General semanticists (p. 397)
Semantic devices (p. 397)
Indexing (p. 398)
Epathy (p. 400)
Active listening (p. 403)

CHAPTER CHECKUP

Sentence Completion

1. The tendency to view one's culture as central and superior is known as *ethnocentrism*

2. Respect, openness to hearing other viewpoints, and willingness to change characterize the trait of *fair-mindedness*

3. A defense mechanism that involves justifying or making sense of things that don't make sense is _____.

4. The tendency to view everything in relationship to oneself is called _____.

5. A defense mechanism in which we repress or refuse to recognize threatening or negative information is called _____.

6. A state of mind in which an idea and an action or two ideas clash is called _____.

7. The tendency to conform in group decision making results in what Janis calls _____.

8. Often, the way we feel is based on our _____ about a situation.

9. _____ occurs when negative details are magnified and positive details ignored.

10. When you imagine disastrous outcomes, you are _____.

Short Answer

11. Define points of logical vulnerability, using an example.

12. What are the semantic devices and how do they help us deal with points of logical vulnerability?

13. How is active listening used to create understanding of opposing viewpoints?

14. What are some ways we can overcome emotional reasoning?

ARTICLES FOR DISCUSSION

EXCERPTS FROM HOW DOCTORS THINK

Dr. Jerome Groopman

How we think affects us in both our personal and professional lives. Dr. Jerome Groopman has written a fascinating book—*How Doctor's Think*—about the common errors in thinking made by physicians, many of which are based on unrecognized emotions. Many of these errors are also found in other professions:

1. Pattern Recognition and Stereotyping. Groopman notes that there is plenty of time in a medical school classroom to consider various symptoms and hypotheses and then rule them out until the correct diagnosis emerges. In real life, particularly in emergency situations, doctors don't have the luxury of time and they rely on quick judgments.

> Physicians at the bedside do not collect a great deal of data and then leisurely generate hypotheses about possible diagnoses. Rather, physicians begin to think of diagnoses from the first moment they meet a patient. Even as they say hello they take the person's measure, registering his pallor or ruddiness, the tilt of his head, the movement of his eyes and mouth, the way he sits down or stands up, the timbre of his voice, the depth of his breathing. Their notions of what is wrong continue to evolve as they peer into the eyes, listen to the heart, press on the liver, inspect the initial set of x-rays. Research shows that most doctors quickly come up with two or three possible diagnoses from the outset of meeting a patient—a few talented ones can juggle four or five in their minds.

Groopman cites examples of well-trained physicians making "attribution errors"—snap judgments based on stereotypes—when they encounter a recognizable pattern. One such error, made during her medical training, is recounted by Dr. Karen Delgado:

> A young man was brought to the emergency ward of the hospital in the wee hours. The police had found him sleeping on the steps of a local art museum. He was unshaven, his clothes were dirty, and he was uncooperative, unwilling to rouse himself and respond with any clarity to the triage nurse's questions. Dr. Delgado was busy that night attending to other patients, so she "eyeballed" him and decided that he could stay on a gurney in the corridor, another homeless hippie who would be given breakfast in the morning and returned to the streets. Some hours later, she felt a nurse tugging at her sleeve. "I really want you to go back and examine that guy," the nurse said. Delgado was reluctant, but she had learned to respect an ER nurse who felt that something was really wrong with a patient. "His blood sugar was sky-high," Delgado told me. The young man was on the brink of a diabetic coma. He had fallen asleep near the art museum because he was weak and lethargic and unable to make it back to his apartment. It turned out that he was not a vagrant but a student, and his difficulties giving the police and the triage nurse information reflected the metabolic changes that typify out-of-control diabetes.

2. Availability. Availability is the tendency to focus on what seems to be the most reasonable explanation for a behavior or event and to ignore other real possibilities. For example, a pediatrician might see numerous cases of a stomach flu that is going around and miss a diagnosis of appendicitis in a child whose symptoms looked like everyone else's that day. Josephine Marcotty, writing in the *Minneapolis Star Tribune* on March 20, 2007, summarizes a story of the availability error from Groopman's book:

> The story of Rachel Stein and her adopted daughter is one of the detailed cases he uses to make his point. When she brought the infant home from Vietnam, the baby immediately crashed. Doctors at one of the best pediatric hospitals in the United States found her riddled with infections and concluded that she had a rare, inherited immune disorder called SCID.
>
> With prayer to give her confidence, and her own determination, the mother did her own research and began asking questions, including: "What could cause a baby to have so many infections other than AIDS or SCID?" Stein thought she could have a nutritional deficiency, but doctors said, no, she didn't fit the profile. They wanted to give her a dangerous bone marrow transplant for SCID.
>
> The day before the transplant, Stein insisted that they test her daughter's immune system again. She persisted in the face of the doctors' resistance to what they often view as a parent's "misconceived demands born of desperation." But she persuaded them that an enterprising researcher might be able to write a paper off the case.
>
> Her story was instead used at a conference at the hospital to teach doctors about how to do diagnoses—and how not to. The baby did not have SCID, nor did she undergo the bone marrow transplant that could have killed her. There was some unknown aspect to her diet in Vietnam that gave her a nutritional deficiency, just as her mother thought.
>
> "Rachel Stein...found a zebra," Groopman writes. But among doctors, "zebra hunters" are often viewed with disdain.

3. Confirmation Bias. Confirmation bias occurs when doctors selectively highlight evidence that supports what they expect to find and ignore information that contradicts their diagnosis. Groopman also cites researchers Tversky and Kahneman who call this phenomenon "anchoring."

> Anchoring is a shortcut in thinking where a person doesn't consider multiple possibilities but quickly and firmly latches on to a single one, sure that he has thrown his anchor down just where he needs to be. You look at your map but your mind plays tricks on you—confirmation bias—because you see only the landmarks you expect to see and neglect those that should tell you that in fact you're still at sea.

Groopman says that some doctors whose patients have seen a specialist tend to believe that the specialist has more expertise, and they look for evidence that confirms whatever diagnosis the specialist offers. He also cites other doctors who don't stop at the obvious, but ask themselves, "What else could this be?"

All excerpts from Jerome Groopman, *How Doctors Think* (Boston: Hougton-Mifflin Co., 2007), pp. 35, 55, 665.

QUESTIONS FOR DISCUSSION

1. Groopman notes that doctors sometimes misdiagnose by stereotyping patients as more healthy than they actually are. Professionals in other areas may also make attribution errors, stereotyping their clients or customers. Salespeople who work on commission may be attentive to well-dressed customers and ignore those who don't look as affluent; lenders may turn down borrowers who are self-employed, assuming that they are not good credit risks; jurors may assume that a quiet, sweet-looking woman wouldn't be "the type" to steal a watch. Teachers who have had two disruptive siblings in their class may assume that a third sibling will behave the same way. Can you think of other professional stereotypes that reflect the attribution error?

2. Other professionals also make the availability error. If there have been a string of gang-related murders in a certain neighborhood, detectives may miss the case of a husband murdering his wife and instead blame the crime on "the usual suspects." If a majority of students in a particular school are doing well or poorly, the credit or blame may be placed on the faculty. What availability errors are common in other professions?

3. What are some questions that patients could ask their doctors to help them avoid confirmation bias?

The following is an excerpt from Gerry Spence's book *How to Argue and Win Every Time*. Spence is a lawyer and television commentator; notice how he "reads between the lines" to understand the juror.

THE LOCK: THEY ARGUE AND I ARGUE BACK.
BUT I NEVER SEEM TO WIN. THE KEY:
LISTEN—JUST LISTEN, AND YOU'LL START TO WIN.

Gerry Spence

If I were required to choose the single essential skill from the many that make up the art of argument, it would be the ability to listen. I know lawyers who have never successfully cross-examined a witness, who have never understood where the judge was coming from, who can never ascertain what those around them are plainly saying to them. I know lawyers who can never understand the weaknesses of their opponent's case or the fears of the prosecutor; who, at last, can never understand the issues before them because they have never learned to listen. Listening is the ability to hear what people are saying, or *not saying* as distinguished from the words they enunciate.

Listening for what is not said: "How do you feel about a widow who is asking you for money for the death of her husband?" I once asked a prospective juror in a case in which I represented the widow.

"I don't know," the juror replied. "I don't know" did not mean that the juror didn't know. It meant he didn't feel comfortable telling me. If he felt all right about the money for justice, he would have said, "I feel fine about it."

"Do you have some feeling about this kind of a lawsuit?"

"Not really," the juror replied. "Not really" did not mean "not really." It meant probably. The juror did not want to get into a public argument with the likes of me. If he were at home with his wife he would have said something quite different. I followed with this question:

"If you were home and were talking about this case with your wife, is it possible you might say something like this to her: 'I don't think people should sue for their dead husbands. All the money in the world can't bring the man back. I think those kinds of lawsuits are wrong.'?"

"I don't talk about things like this with my wife," he replied. Now he was obviously refusing to answer the question at hand.

"If you and I were best friends and were talking about this case over a beer, what would you tell me?"

"I don't drink beer."

"How about coffee?" I gave him a big friendly smile to assure him I wasn't trying to push him around.

Suddenly the juror blurted it out: "My father was killed and my mother never got a cent." There it was! You could immediately feel all the pain—a boy without a father, a mother struggling to rear her family without a husband.

"It must have been pretty hard on your mother trying to raise a family by herself." (The words *It must have been* are magical words that say to the Other, "I understand how it was.")

"You bet." Now the juror and I were on the same side.

"And it must have been hard to grow up without a father."

He looked down at his hands.

"If you could have had the power as a boy to get help for your mother, would you have done so?"

"Sure. I did everything I could for her."

"Is it all right with you if I try to help Mrs. Richardson get justice in this case for herself and her children?"

"Yes," he said. And that was the end of it—the magical product of listening.

1. The juror in this case responded to Spence's early questions with "I don't know" and "Not really." How did Spence translate the meaning of these phrases?

2. How did Spence establish rapport with the juror?

3. Spence points out in his book that whenever pain or rage is expressed in words or silences, there is a need to be heard and understood. How did his understanding of the juror's pain enable him to establish both empathy and rapport?

The following article is about the dangers of "revisionist" history when unpleasant historical facts cause people to deny those facts. The author discusses the consequences of denying, rather than acknowledging and learning from the tragedies of the past.

IT HAPPENED

To Deny That the Holocaust Occurred Is to Set the Preconditions for Another One

Richard V. Pierard

The emergence of David Duke as a political figure has again drawn public attention to the contention that no Jewish Holocaust occurred in World War II. The ex-Klansman has said that Hitler and the Nazis did not systematically and successfully destroy most of Europe's Jews.

For years, Holocaust denial has been a stock-in-trade of shadowy creatures on the extreme Right. In recent times, several pseudo-scholars have come forward to argue against the "extermination legend" and "myth of the six million." Through an elaborate process of distortions, half-truths, and falsification of data, these "revisionists" seek to convince the gullible that Hitler did not order the annihilation of the Jews, but instead had this "alien minority" placed in labor camps where they could not subvert the war effort.

Harsh war-time conditions caused the epidemic diseases and malnutrition in the crowded camps; crematories were necessary to dispose of the remains of the few thousand who died. Cyanide gas was used for delousing and fumigation in order to check the spread of typhus. There were so few Jews left in Europe because most had emigrated to North America or Israel. Pictures of gas chambers and emaciated inmates are fabrications. And so the story goes.

In fact, Holocaust denial is the ultimate Big Lie. The whole process of destruction is so well-attested through eye-witness accounts, official documents, and contemporary press reports that no one in his or her right mind could deny that it happened.

So why is such a monstrous falsehood perpetrated? The answer is twofold. One reason is anti-Semitism—the ongoing hatred of Jews that animates extreme rightist groups in North America, Britain, France, Germany, and elsewhere. The other is the intention to deny Jews the right to a land of their own, where they may live peacefully within secure borders.

Is Holocaust denial merely a Jewish problem? No, it is also an American Christian problem. We must never forget that anti-Semitism has its roots in the theology and practice of the Christian church, from the writings of the church fathers, through the Inquisition, even in the comments of Martin Luther. Moreover, the U.S. government and people did little to help Jews in the years 1933 through 1945. Opinion polls in our "Christian nation" in 1942 found that people disliked Jews more than the German and Japanese enemies, while officials in Washington pooh-poohed the accounts of extermination programs as "atrocity stories."

Evangelicals may try to evade the issue by arguing that the Holocaust was a product of theological liberalism. But we cannot let ourselves off the hook so easily. Robert Ross excellently shows in *So It Was True* (1980) that while our magazines reported the grim details of the Nazi policies, our modest attempts to persuade the U.S. authorities to do something lacked moral passion.

Likewise, conservative free church Christians in Germany supported the Hitler regime just as fervently as most in the official church did. In 1984, the German Baptists even issued a formal statement confessing that they had been taken in by the "ideological seduction" of the time. They had not stood up for truth and righteousness.

The bottom line is that to deny the Holocaust is to set the preconditions for yet another one. It behooves evangelicals to stand up and utter a forthright no to the "revisionists" and their fellow travelers. The very credibility of our faith is at stake.

Richard V. Pierard, *Christianity Today,* March 9, 1992. Copyright © 1992. Reprinted by permission of the author.

QUESTIONS FOR DISCUSSION

1. What would cause a person or group of persons to deny the painful history of another group of people? Do ethnocentrism, egocentrism, and/or conformity and groupthink play a role in this denial?

2. What should be the guidelines for any form of "revisionist history"?

3. Why does the author say that "to deny the Holocaust is to set the preconditions for yet another one"?

4. What other historical persecutions have been denied or minimized and for what reasons?

A number of years ago, linguistic professor Deborah Tannen wrote the book *You Just Don't Understand* in which she discusses research that reveals differences between male and female conversational styles. Tannen has found some fascinating and informative differences in how men and women communicate.

The following excerpt is from a more recent bestseller entitled *For Women Only—What You Need to Know About the Inner Lives of Men*, based on the research commissioned by author Shaunti Feldhahn. Feldhahn was surprised by the answers to her national survey and what they reveal about the differences between men and women. Her comments reflect the generalizations that she drew from her findings. Feldhahn also discusses the implications of the research as they relate to improving dating and marital relationships. Since her survey on men and the resulting interest, Feldhahn and her husband Jeff commissioned another survey on women and have written a new book on their findings entitled *for men only*.

Author Note: The professional survey was designed with the guidance of Chuck Cowan of Analytic Focus (www.analyticfocus.com), the former chief of survey design at the U.S. Census Bureau. The survey was conducted by Decision Analyst (www.decisionanalyst.com) and was designed to deliver a random, representative, national sample of 400 men (the sample size suggested by Churck Cowan) who were heterosexual, lived within the United States, and were between the ages of 21 and 75.

FOR WOMEN ONLY—WHAT YOU NEED TO KNOW ABOUT THE INNER LIVES OF MEN

Shaunti Feldhahn

When I was a year or two out of college, I went on a retreat that profoundly impacted my understanding of men.

The theme of the retreat was "Relationships," which as you can imagine was of great interest to a group of single young adults.

For the very first session, the retreat speaker divided the room in half and placed the men on one side, women on the other.

"I'm going to ask you to choose between two bad things," he said. "If you had to choose, would you rather feel alone and unloved in the world OR would you rather feel inadequate and disrespected by everyone?"

I remember thinking. What kind of choice is that? Who would ever choose to feel unloved?

The speaker then turned to the men's side of the room. "Okay, men. Who here would rather feel alone and unloved?"

A sea of hands went up, and a giant gasp rippled across the women's side of the room.

He asked which men would rather feel disrespected, and we women watched in bemusement as only a few men lifted their hands.

Then it was our turn to answer and the men's turn to be shocked when most of the women indicated that they'd rather feel inadequate and disrespected than unloved.

What It Means

While it may be totally foreign to most of us, the male need for respect and affirmation—especially from his woman—is so hardwired and so critical that most men would rather feel unloved than disrespected or inadequate. Question 3 of the survey indicated that three out of four men would make that choice. When I originally tested the survey questions, I was perplexed that many men had a hard time answering the "unloved versus disrespected" question—because they appeared to equate the two. Chuck Cowan, the survey-design expert, warned me that might happen. *Why?* I wondered. *Those are two totally different things!* Then one of my readers tested my survey questions on ten men who didn't know me. When I got the surveys back, only one note was attached: "A lot of the guys fussed over Question 3. They did not feel the choices were different."

Finally, the lightbulb came one: *If a man feels disrespected, he is going to feel unloved.* And what that translates to is this: If you want to love your man in the way *he* needs to be loved, then you need to ensure that he feels your respect most of all.

The funny thing is—most of us do respect the man in our lives and often don't realize when our words or actions convey exactly the opposite! We may be totally perplexed when our man responds negatively in a conversation, helplessly wondering. *What did I say?* Combine this with the difficulty many men have articulating their feelings (i.e., why they are upset), and you've got a combustible—and frustrating—situation. . . . If a man can't articulate his feelings in the heat of the moment, he won't necessarily blurt out something helpful like "You're disrespecting me!" But rest assured, if he's angry at something you've said or done and you don't understand the cause, there is a good chance that he is feeling the pain or humiliataion of your disrespect.

If you want confirmation of this, consider the extremely telling response from the survey (see Question #14:)

Questions 14:

Even the best relationships sometimes have conflicts on day-to-day issues. In the middle of a conflict with my wife/significant other, I am more likely to be feeling...{Choose One Answer}

> Base = Respondents Who Answered Question **400**
> That my wife/significant other doesn't respect me right now. **81.5%**
> That my wife/significant other doesn't love me right now. **18.5%**
> Total **100%**

More than *80 percent* of men—four out of five—said that in a conflict they were likely to be feeling disrespected. Whereas we girls are far more likely to be wailing, "He doesn't love me!"

From *for women only*, by Shaunti Feldhahn, Multnomah Publishers, 2004, pages 21–25.

QUESTIONS FOR DISCUSSION

1. The author of the book *for women only* used a survey designed by a professional. What elements of the survey design give credibility to her findings? (See author's note at the beginning of the survey.)

2. What conclusions does Shaunti Feldhahn draw from the answers to Questions 3 and 14? What are the implications of these conclusions?

3. To what extent do the survey findings cited in this article match your experience of the difference between male and female communication styles?

4. For further results, read the full survey in the author's book or on her website. You may also want to look at the national survey of women that Feldhahn completed with her husband entitled "For Men Only."

The following story is about a father who finds himself irrationally upset one morning about his daughter's hairstyle. He realizes that her appearance has triggered a strong "point of logical vulnerability" in him, creating powerful and irrational responses. As you read, try to understand how one person's experience can negatively affect his or her perspective and communication with a loved one.

BREAKFAST AND TOUSLED CORNROWS

A Tale of Logical Vulnerability

John Dies

I sat staring at the back of her head for at least three hours. All right, maybe it was only twenty seconds, but it felt like three hours. What on earth is going on? In the front most of the braids seemed normal, but in some places the braids were so tight that the hair stood out at right angles before drooping to the shoulders. It looked a little like the action of a horse's tail, just before doing his business. In other areas the braids were loosely started, halfway down the gathered lock of hair. My nearly twelve year old daughter had set a new standard for cornrows, but it was a standard that I did not understand. It was a disturbing beginning for the day, particularly before breakfast.

"I like it," she said.

"Yes, well, I can see that you would. All you can see is the front. The front is fine, nicely spaced, even cornrows. It's the back I'm talking about," I explained. As if I even cared about the neat front rows. I just didn't like it. I was being tested, and I didn't like that either. I rustled about the kitchen gathering the various items to pack for her and her brother's school lunches.

"I looked at the back when I was doing it, it looks fine. I saw it in the mirror," she replied.

Yeah, right. My daughter is a brilliant girl, kind, funny, but not very objective when it comes to her own opinions. The word stubborn comes to mind. She wasn't budging an inch and the two dozen cornrows were staying firmly on her head. Understand, I like cornrows, I even like dreadlocks. But these things didn't even remotely pass as acceptable definitions.

"Listen, you're really pushing the limits here. I mean, I understand that you don't mind being different, but it seems to me that you have an unhealthy desire to be weird or something. I really think you should think this over before going to school like that."

I felt I had some pretty strong ground here. I was giving due respect, appealing to her logic, sharing my judgment on the merits. And if that didn't work then I guess I expected for her to come around to my point simply on the basis that I, as her father, was disturbed.

"Okay, I thought about it and I think it's fine," she offered, and that was the end of the conversation.

Hmm, this was not going well. It was almost as if she sensed that my arguments were unsound and therefore unworthy of further attention. Was this true? What was the basis of my dislike? Was it entirely based on the asymmetrical braids?

A few days earlier I had found a box that sort of fell out of the pile stacked in the garage. A carton of icons, each one loaded with an entire database of memories. Not a lot of written words, no notebooks of young angst, no diaries of adventures. Mostly objects. A fender mirror from my first vehicle, a half-eaten high school diploma, a paper placemat from a restaurant in West Yellowstone. Oddities with stories attached. My life in a box. And only one box at that. I could at least explain the half-eaten diploma. My dog ate it. He never touched my homework in three long years of high school, but as soon as I graduated, he ate my diploma.

Anyway, sorting through this collection I came upon an old photo of my ninth grade class. It was the typical photo where the entire class gathers on the front steps, and the photographer takes the shot hoping for a minimum of finger gestures, grimaces and general chaos. Somewhere on those steps was a younger and wiser version of myself. As I scanned those fresh faces I was surprised how familiar most of them were even after thirty-five years. Characters from the past, leaping fresh into my consciousness. It was a great time, a time of innocence, and years before any of these people made serious mistakes. It was, in some cases, the last year of the trouble free life of a child.

Laying my finger briefly on each face, I recalled what the future would bring. Here there was death in a traffic accident, speeding on a motorcycle, no helmet. Here there was madness, after a long series of drug addictions. And this fellow, a hopeless alcoholic. This young lady, drugs, welfare, four children before age twenty. More and more, drugs, jail, and death.

The whole class didn't fall into disaster. At least I don't think so. I'm not sure because I didn't know everybody. It just seemed that most of my friends had particularly hard lives. In fact, only two or three seemed to survive out of the two dozen that loosely hung together. I suppose I had thought about this before but this time I was struggling with the reasons. Was there something here, in this last innocent photo that gave a hint?

Suddenly it came to me. None of us fit in. All of us were somehow on the edge, not quite a part of the whole. Different in thought, different in deed. Our stumbling identities only defined by our own association with each other. Bright in some cases, talented in others, but uniformly weird in all instances.

And now my daughter seems bent upon being weird in her own right. I had this mental flash of how many could I save, if I could just go back in time and warn them. Would they listen to a caring stranger? If they wouldn't listen, could I force them? I couldn't do it for them, but this was my daughter, and I was not giving her up to the bleak future of nonconformity. At least not without a fight.

All of this seemed to solidify in the few minutes it took to make her school lunch. As I made the cheese sandwich, I pondered her future. As I bagged her tortilla chips I resolved to make a difference.

"Okay, that's it. No more cornrows. I tried to give you the freedom to make wise decisions and you refused, so now I'll step in and provide the rules. No more weirdness. You will not court weirdness nor seek to be different, or any of that stuff. You're too young and if you go on this way then what wild and crazy thing will you pull when you're eighteen? Later on, you can wear your hair however you want, but for right now, lose the braids."

Dead silence, shocked expressions. My son froze, his toast halfway to his mouth.

"Now?"

I could see in her eyes the deep hurt, even with the one word of acquiescence. She couldn't know what I was thinking, and didn't understand how I could react the way I was reacting. Her eyes just misted over and she prepared herself to walk whatever line I asked her to walk.

Now it was beginning to dawn on me that things hadn't gone quite the way I wanted. I knew I was struggling, but somehow the noose was just getting drawn tighter the more I twisted. I was almost swinging in the breeze due to my own efforts when my wife came in to the picture. Good, I'll explain what I did, she'll understand and together we will force, uh, together we will demand that, umm, together we will make it right.

"So, what do we do now?" I confided.

"Seems to me that *you* have done what you have pretty much on your own," she said quietly.

Whoops, definitely swinging in the breeze now, twisting slowly in the wind.

"Oh, sure. Now that's being supportive. I ask for help here and this is what I get," I said with some anger but more confusion.

"Its hard to be very supportive of someone who is wrong," she patiently explained.

Yeah, well, uh, huh. I knew it would come down to this. Skewered by the truth. It was the truth. My fear lead me to over-control. My love lead me to over-react. I can't stop my daughter from being different. I can't protect her from the unknown future. All I can do is love her and equip her with the tools of life. Part of those tools included discernment, confidence, faith in

God, compassion, service, and discipline. And ultimately I needed to trust in God as well.

So, I called her over to apologize and to try to explain my actions. I thanked her for being obedient and I hoped that she understood that even parents make mistakes, and when that happens I believe the parent should make it right and apologize. She listened, and nodded, and seemed saddened about my loss of friends. I told her that her hair was her business and that I was just scared. I still didn't like the asymmetrical arrangement. She smiled and said, "That's okay."

She seemed at that moment much wiser than I.

Reprinted by permission of John Diestler.

QUESTIONS FOR DISCUSSION

1. What was the "point of logical vulnerability," the subject about which this father had trouble being rational? Why was it a point of logical vulnerability for him?

2. When the author discovered how his emotions blinded his reasoning, how did he remedy his thinking and his behavior?

3. Has your concern for another person's welfare ever clouded your judgment and your communication with that person? Conversely, has someone's concerns for you ever clouded their judgment?

4. The author was concerned that his daughter's nonconformity would lead her into trouble. In what ways could her nonconformity be seen as a strength?

IDEAS FOR WRITING OR SPEAKING

1. The United States Declaration of Independence claims that "all men are created equal." How would a world in which all people were treated with equal respect and dignity work? Write or speak about what it would take to live in such a world and what that world would look like. If you don't believe that such a world could exist, write about the conditions that make it impossible.

2. Write or speak about a tragic event in human history. What lessons can we learn from this event? Are there actions that can be taken to prevent a reoccurrence of such an event?

3. Do an exploratory essay or speech on a current problem. List several of the solutions given for this problem and explore the pros and cons of each solution. Some problems you might explore are national health care, shelters for the homeless, teenage pregnancy, or illegal immigration. You might also want to choose a problem that has emerged on your campus. Use this format in preparing your essay or speech:

a. Clearly define the problem.

b. Establish criteria for solutions (e.g., consider time and money limits).

c. Come up with as many alternative solutions as possible. (If you are working in a group, brainstorm about possibilities.)

d. When possible alternatives are exhausted, evaluate each alternative against the criteria for solutions, showing an understanding of diverse viewpoints.

e. Choose the best alternative and explain why this alternative is the best.

4. Rent a copy of the classic (or remade) film *Twelve Angry Men.* This film depicts the various viewpoints and prejudices of a group of jurors who have to determine the guilt or innocence of a man accused of killing his father. Before viewing the tape, consider the following excerpt:

   The drive to help juries make the right decisions is drawing some ideas from human-behavior experts who have amassed a wealth of research on how jurors think. Decades ago, judges and lawyers assumed that jurors heard evidence piecemeal and began to analyze it in earnest only during deliberations. But extensive interviews of jurors in recent years have given rise to the theory that they construct evidence into mental "stories" that incorporate interpretations based on their personal experiences. "Jurors used to be viewed as passive objects," says Valerie Hans, a jury researcher at the University of Delaware. "Now we know they are very active in filling in missing evidence and making inferences." The studies are influencing some judges to give jurors more information about the cases they hear.[16]

   After viewing the film, discuss the problems of ethnocentrism and egocentrism that influence the decisions of different jurors and what arguments help them to be fair to the defendant.

5. Do an analysis of another film that deals with egocentrism or ethnocentrism, or with people's failures at understanding the perspectives of others. Some suggested titles include *Bend it Like Beckham, School Ties, To Kill a Mockingbird, The Great Santini, Philadelphia, Dead Poets Society, Schindler's List, Pride and Prejudice, Gandhi, As Good as It Gets, and In the Heat of the Night.* Explain how the problem of egocentrism, ethnocentrism, defensiveness, or lack of empathy is explored in the film. Then tell how the problem is resolved (or not resolved). Finally, state the applications of the film's theme to similar problems faced by people today. (See Films for Analysis and Discussion for more ideas.)

6. Choose an issue about which you feel strongly and argue for the position that is opposite to your own real beliefs. Construct a persuasive essay or

[16]Ted Gest with Constance Johnson, "The Justice System: Getting a Fair Trial," *U.S. News & World Report,* May 25, 1992, p. 38.

speech on this position, using one of the formats outlined in Chapter 10. Do thorough research on the stand you are defending, and be as convincing as you can.

In the conclusion of your essay or speech, explain whether this exercise caused you to be more or less convinced about your original position on this issue. What changes, if any, did you make in your perspective concerning this issue?

7. Create an essay or speech on an issue about which you have no strong feelings. Research both sides of the issue and become acquainted with the benefits and shortcomings of each.

In your discussion of this issue, articulate the conclusions of both sides and the reasons given for each conclusion. Note the strongest and weakest reasons for each side. Point out fallacious reasoning that is used to defend either position. In your conclusion, comment on whether you found either side to be more convincing and why.

FILMS FOR ANALYSIS AND DISCUSSION

Clint Eastwood's masterpiece *Letters from Iwo Jima* (2006, R) and his American counterpart *Flags of Our Fathers* (2006, R) are companion pieces that tell of the same event (the Battle of Iwo Jima in 1945) from two very different perspectives. It's a lesson in fair mindedness, approaching both films with an unwavering commitment to honesty. The scenes of war are harrowing from both perspectives, showing that the human side to tragedy is always the most compelling.

Similar Films and Classics

The Last Samurai (2004, R)

This is the story of Captain Nathan Algren, an American Civil War veteran who is hired to train the peasant conscripts for the first standing imperial army in Japan. Along the way, he learns deep respect for the traditional Japanese Samurai warriors. The film is a great example of the struggle between the beliefs and traditions of the past and the culture's emerging changes and the important values of both the old and the new.

Freaky Friday (2003, PG)

This film is a comic exploration of a generation gap between a mother and her daughter. Through magical circumstances, they are forced to live in one another's bodies until they resolve and respect their differences. Along the way, the daughter Anna discovers that her perceptions about her little brother and her mother's fiancé are also distorted, and her mother discovers that she needs to understand and respect her daughter's musical talents.

Pieces of April (2003, PG-13)

Pieces of April follows the adventures of April Burns as she tries to make a new start with her family by inviting them to travel from Pennsylvania to New York City for a Thanksgiving dinner. Because her oven doesn't work, she goes all over her apartment building for help and encounters differing perspectives on life and culture along the way. We also note her family's reluctance to give her another chance and to forgive her for past hurts.

Legally Blonde (2001, PG-13)

Legally Blonde follows the adventures of a southern California sorority girl named Elle Woods as she tries to fit into the privileged and academically demanding environment of Harvard Law School. It makes a strong statement against stereotyping people based on their background, and especially focuses on the ethnocentrism of people who identify with a particular socioeconomic class.

School Ties (1992, PG-13)

This film explores the tensions between class and religion that were especially powerful and apparent in the 1950s. A talented football player is recruited to help an exclusive prep school beat their rivals. He keeps both his poverty and his Jewish faith a secret until a series of events exposes both and his classmates' differing values are revealed.

The Doctor (1991, PG-13)

This film provides a great example of how a professional undergoes a transformation in his thinking because of a significant emotional event. When the doctor himself gets throat cancer, he experiences life from the viewpoint of a patient and is both enlightened and changed as a result.

Pretty Woman (1990, R)

Rich businessman Edward hires struggling prostitute Vivian to accompany him to society parties. As Vivian tries to fit in with the wealthy, she encounters both prejudice and acceptance along the way. Edward also questions his own beliefs as a result of Vivian's influence.

Stand and Deliver (1988, PG)

Stand and Deliver is based on the true story of high school math teacher Jaime Escalante and the unconventional methods he uses to turn gang members and students stereotyped as low achievers into some of the top calculus students in the country. It is a great illustration of what can happen when people are helped to move beyond limitations imposed by the negative expectations and environments of their past.

Guess Who's Coming to Dinner (1967)

This film explores race relations when a perfect young African American man—
a loving, handsome, brilliant doctor—and his family are introduced to a young
white woman's family to discuss the upcoming marriage between the couple.

Gentleman's Agreement (1947)

This classic film is about a journalist who pretends to be Jewish in order to
write an article about prejudice and anti-semitism in America. It explores both
the overt and subtle effects of racism and the effects on both the reporter and
his friends and family.

10

Persuasive Speaking

What's Your Point? How Do You Sharpen It?

A critical thinker can organize ideas and advocate for his or her beliefs.

This chapter will cover

- Techniques for handling the fear of public speaking
- The three elements of a persuasive message
- Methods of organizing persuasive speeches
- Collaborative problem solving

Most of this book has focused on evaluating the quality of arguments. As a critical thinker, you need to know what to look for when you read an article, watch a commentator or politician on television, or listen to a speech. Recognizing good content in the arguments of others will guide you as you make your own arguments, whether they are personal, social, or political. There are times to use your skills to argue for a specific belief or course of action. There are also times to work collaboratively with others to find acceptable solutions for problems.

Understanding the basic elements of public speaking that are covered in this chapter will help you be more clear and persuasive as you advocate for your ideas. When you present a formal argument, you are giving a persuasive speech with the goal of convincing your audience to accept certain viewpoints and take certain actions. Many of us have a picture of people who are convincing as having *charisma*, an intangible quality that attracts others to them and to their ideas. Some people seem to have this personal power and often we can't explain why.

However, beginning with Aristotle, we have explanations, verified by research, about what makes a clear and convincing argument, and those ideas have formed the recommendations in this book. If you use what you know about the content and organization of a good argument and add some basic tips on public speaking, you can successfully present your ideas to both groups and individuals.

This chapter will explain how to use the principles of argumentation to create formal arguments and solve problems.

BEING AN ADVOCATE OF IDEAS: COMMUNICATING PUBLICLY

> *Never doubt that a small group of thoughtful, committed citizens can change the world; it's the only thing that ever does.*
>
> Margaret Mead, *American Anthropologist* (1901–1978)
> Institute for Intercultural Studies

One of the best uses of your knowledge of critical thinking and the effective uses of argument is to be an advocate for ideas in which you believe. We can all learn the tools for public speaking and become better at organizing and presenting speeches.

We also need to have the motivation to speak out, the desire to move beyond personal interests and promote larger visions for the betterment of society. Tavis Smiley, former host of *BET Tonight with Tavis Smiley* and author of *Doing What's Right,* encourages people to get involved in the causes they endorse. He states that, "One person, fighting the good fight, can make a difference. And one person, joined by another, and another, quickly forms a coalition and, eventually, a movement. We *can* make a difference. Moreover, we *must*."[1]

---

[1]Tavis Smiley, *Doing What's Right* (New York: Doubleday, Random House, Inc., 2000), p. 38.

More of us might become involved in advocacy if we could get over the primary obstacle to effective public speaking, which is fear. Research published in *The Book of Lists* indicates that fear of public speaking is the most common fear of Americans, ranking above the fear of spiders, flying, and death. When we stand in front of a group, we expose our ideas, our egos, and our bodies to people who may or may not be sympathetic to our ideas. We may shake, quake, or decide not to show up when we are required to speak.

At one East Coast university, every graduate is required to take a basic public speaking class. When the administration discovered many students putting this class off until the last quarter of their senior year, or even not graduating because they refused to take the class, the speech department took action by initiating a special class for those who were terrified of public speaking. The class filled several sections every semester. So if you are experiencing anxiety about speaking and would rather skip this chapter and related assignments, take heart. You aren't alone in these feelings of fear. In fact, many famous people who have had to speak in public admit to having great fears and having to learn to overcome them; among them are Winston Churchill, James Earl Jones, Mark Twain, Dan Rather, Barbara Walters, Margaret Thatcher, Kim Basinger, Leonardo di Caprio, and Tom Brokaw.

It is possible to overcome public speaking fears to a great extent, and most students who take a course in public speaking report improvement in their feelings of confidence by the end of a semester. In addition, those who fear the most often prepare the best and therefore have well-researched and convincing arguments.

✳ THE BEST WAYS TO DEAL WITH SPEECH FEAR

All the great speakers were bad speakers at first.
> Ralph Waldo Emerson, "Power," *The Conduct of Life* (1860)

What would you advise someone who has to give a speech and is feeling terrified? You probably have some techniques you would use, such as breathing deeply to calm yourself or memorizing your opening line to get you started. This section covers the recommendations speech professionals give for dealing with speech fear.

The first way to gain confidence is to choose a topic you believe in. When you really care about your topic (which is most often the case when you take a stand on an issue), you can more easily concentrate on convincing your audience about your viewpoints, and that helps minimize your self-consciousness. Second, you need to prepare well; then you can be confident that what you are saying has value to your audience, is solid, and includes relevant information. Instead of procrastinating and avoiding your assignment, just get started. Use any resources that have been made available to you, such as a speech lab or librarians or tutors who will help you locate good, current information on your topic. Find evidence to support your stand on the issue and write a clear outline of your ideas. You can evaluate the evidence you find according to the principles discussed in Chapters 4 and 5, and this chapter will provide you with several organizational patterns for your ideas. Talk about the ideas in your speech with your friends and family, so that you feel really familiar and comfortable with the topic.

Finally, practice the speech so you know it well. Then, even if your mind goes blank temporarily, you can keep on going "on automatic." Some people like to practice in front of friends, and others like to practice alone—the best way to practice is the one that makes you the most comfortable. Use brief notes to help you with memory lapses; note cards function as mini security blankets. Number these cards (in case you drop them) and then refer to them only briefly as you speak. Also, get rest before you speak, and do whatever relaxation techniques work for you; for some people, deep breathing is very helpful. Exercising to release tension also works well. Turn any negative thoughts, such as "I can't do this" or "I'm going to fall apart," into positive thoughts, such as "I have something to say in this speech, and I have practiced it" or "I have something to share with the audience and I can do this."

When you stand up to speak, walk calmly to the podium and take a moment to pause, take a deep breath, and "collect" yourself. Sometimes it helps to memorize your first sentence so that you can get started comfortably. (However, don't memorize or read the speech; instead, just speak conversationally, as you would to a group of people you know well.) Use any fear that you feel inside as energy to help you project your voice; make your voice louder than normal—that will actually increase your confidence. When audience members can hear you clearly, they tend to listen better and give you more positive feedback.

As you speak, concentrate on your audience rather than on yourself; look around at all parts of the room. Some speakers feel more comfortable looking at their audiences' foreheads rather than their eyes; the audience members usually can't tell the difference. Look for friendly faces as you scan the room, and avoid people who look unhappy (unless everyone looks unhappy—then you might need to think about what you might have said to confuse or offend them). Realize that you have good information to give the audience and consider yourself someone who is there to help them understand new ideas and perspectives.

It is also helpful to use visual aids, such as a graph, a chart, an illustration, a list put on the overhead projector or the blackboard, or a PowerPoint presentation. Visual aids make your ideas clearer and more memorable for your audience; they also divert audience attention away from you, and that can make you more relaxed. In addition, visual aids often serve as a reminder to you of your points, so they can keep you on track during the presentation.

Finally, write out or memorize your concluding statement, so that you can end the speech with grace and confidence.

AUDIENCE ANALYSIS

One of the essential forms of preparation for a public speech is **audience analysis.** Knowing your audience gives you an added sense of preparation and familiarity that reduces your fears of the speaking situation. In addition, you can make the most of your limited time when you know some important facts about your listeners. These include both *demographic* and *situational* factors.

Demographic factors include age, gender, racial and ethnic group, religious affiliation, economic status, occupation, and education. By considering these aspects of the audience, a speaker can do better planning. For example, if the audience is made up of 16- to 18-year-old students, they may not be familiar with references to certain terms such as *record albums* or to some politicians and celebrities from the past. If most of the audience members are fine artists, they may not be as knowledgeable about applications of Internet technology as would an audience whose business involves the daily use of the Internet. To be sensitive to the make-up of a particular audience, the speaker can research these factors with the person who asked him or her to speak; a speaker may also have an opportunity to interview or poll a sample of audience members.

STOP AND THINK

How could each demographic factor be an important consideration to a persuasive speaker?

Even more important to a persuasive speaker are the situational factors of a given speech: What is the group's knowledge of the speaker's topic and its disposition toward the topic? If a speaker is discussing international trade agreement policies and discovers that the audience knows very little about these policies, then she needs to give more background information. If, on the other hand, this particular audience knows a great deal about the policies, the speaker can use her time more efficiently to press the audience to accept her position about trade agreements.

When you consider an audience's disposition toward a persuasive topic, you can classify the audience as believing, neutral, or hostile. A **believing audience** agrees with your position on an issue; it doesn't need to be convinced about the correctness of the actions you propose. To use your time most efficiently with this kind of audience, you should concentrate on getting it to act on any proposals you make. You want to move audience members from being passive believers to active participants in moving policies forward; you also want to reinforce and strengthen their reasons for agreeing with your position so that they may also advocate well.

A <u>neutral audience</u> either does not know enough or does not care enough about your topic to have taken a stand on it. With a neutral audience, you need to provide the information audience members need to understand the topic and its importance. For example, if you are speaking against a tax reform that is currently under consideration, you can show how the new tax structure being proposed will hurt them personally. Many people are moved primarily by realizing how an issue will directly affect their lives or the lives of their families and friends; show your neutral listeners how the position you support will help them maintain or improve their own interests.

A **hostile audience** is opposed to your ideas or policies. These audience members may not shout or become violent, but you know that they think you are wrong in the positions you take. Your goals for this kind of audience have to be much more modest than they would be for a believing audience. Often, the best thing you can do is present yourself and your positions in such a clear, calm, and reasonable way that the audience members can no longer negatively stereotype people who believe as you do. Focus your speech with a hostile audience on their reconsideration of some of their own ideas, rather than trying to move this kind of group to taking action on your ideas.

Hostile audiences often respond well to a persuasive speaking technique called **both-sides persuasion**. A speaker who uses both-sides persuasion will acknowledge the good points that cause the audience to believe as it does but will then demonstrate how even these good points are overshadowed by the strengths of the speaker's side of the issue. For example, if you favor dress codes in local public schools and your audience is against them because they violate personal freedom, you might say the following:

> It seems to go against all of our ideas of freedom of expression and individuality to restrict students to only a few items of clothing. How can they experiment with unique styles that make personal statements when they are forced into one general look? I agree that individuality is an important value and that the solution of dress codes is far from perfect. But I believe that these codes provide the best way we have found so far to safeguard another value, the value of life. Given the fact that teenagers are being killed because they are wearing what appear to be gang colors, and given the fact that several of our local youth have been killed over expensive shoes and jackets that the criminals wanted to steal, I believe that any measures taken to guard their safety when they are in the setting of public schools are worth pursuing.

Both-sides persuasion lets your audience know that you have considered their viewpoints and that you agree with some of their principles, but that you have come to a different conclusion about the issue. Most people will be more open to *your* ideas if they know that you understand and respect *their* ideas. Both-sides persuasion shows that while your solutions to a problem are different, your values and motives are very similar.

When you know the disposition of the majority of your audience members, you can also structure your speech with greater thoughtfulness. Hostile audiences are most likely to be persuaded when you lead off with your strongest points. If you save your most convincing points for later in the speech, you may lose them completely as they argue in their minds with the weaker points they have heard first. But if they hear a compelling reason to reconsider their position early on in your speech, then they may continue to listen with a more open mind. Believing audiences, on the other hand, respond well when you reserve your strongest points and end on a climactic note that creates unity and a desire to move forward to enact their beliefs. They like to be affirmed and inspired by an argument that builds from strong support to even stronger support in your final point.

THE THREE ELEMENTS OF A PERSUASIVE ARGUMENT: ETHOS, LOGOS, AND PATHOS

Aristotle (384–322 B.C.E.) studied with the great philosopher Plato and tutored young Alexander the Great. He wrote more than 400 books, including the *Rhetoric*, which is used to this day as a foundational work in the study of argumentation.

Aristotle said that rhetoric (argumentation) involves using all the available means of persuasion, which he defined as **ethos** (personal credibility), **logos** (logical organization and reasoning), and **pathos** (emotional appeal).

Ethos: Speaker Credibility

From his many observations of persuasive speeches given in the courts and in the marketplace, Aristotle concluded that ethos, the credibility, image, and reputation of a speaker, was one of the most important means of persuasion. Modern researchers have discovered that ethos involves three specific dimensions: expertise, trustworthiness, and dynamism.[2]

Much of your ethos, your credibility or reputation as a speaker, will come through the same methods that help you overcome speech fear. When you are well prepared to speak and have conviction about your topic, your audience will give you respect and attention. Speaker credibility can be achieved through specific effort and planning. Speakers are seen as credible when

- They can be clearly heard by the audience.
- They show that they have done their homework on a topic by using well-cited research to support their key points.
- They are easy to understand because they are well organized.
- They are easy to understand because they have rehearsed the speech before giving it.

[2]Charles U. Larson, *Persuasion*, 9th ed. (Belmont, CA: Wadsworth Publishing, 2001), pp. 205–208.

- They show respect for and understanding of the audience by using language and examples that can be understood (not too complex or too simplified) by the members of that particular audience.
- They reduce nervous, distracting mannerisms to a minimum (this can be done with practice).
- They dress appropriately for the speaking occasion.

When you enhance your credibility with these principles, believing audiences will be affirmed by your message, neutral audiences may be informed and even persuaded, and hostile audiences may be more open to your ideas.

Logos: Logical Organization and Credible Content

Logos, or logical appeals, are made through the use of good evidence of the kind we discussed in Chapters 4 and 5. Persuasive speakers cite statistics, relevant examples, analogies, controlled studies, and expert testimony to support their key ideas. They organize their points clearly, so that audiences can understand and follow their reasoning.

Several different organizational formats for persuasive speaking are highlighted in this chapter. Regardless of the format you choose, there are some essential ingredients to every organizational pattern that apply whether you have 2 minutes or 20 minutes to speak. To be a clearly organized speaker, use these principles, illustrated by Figure 10–1:

- Create an interesting introduction to capture the attention of the audience. Decide on your introduction after you structure the body of the speech, so that you know what it is you are introducing.
- Make your thesis statement (this is your conclusion about the issue) clear early in the speech, immediately following the introduction.
- Tell the audience how you plan to support your position; briefly list the key reasons (points) immediately after you give your thesis statement. This technique is called the *preview* of your speech; it helps you and your audience to stay focused.
- Explain each key point (reason). Figure 10–1 shows that each key point must be supported with evidence. The evidence must be cited (tell us where it comes from—the publication, author, and date). Use this structural outline to see which key points have enough verification and which need more supporting ideas. Note that each key point should also be strong enough to be a supporting pillar for the thesis statement.
- Use transitions between the key points for a smooth flow of ideas. Note that in Figure 10–1, the transitions flow between key points with a brief reference back to the thesis statement.
- Review your key points before making a concluding statement. The repetition of your ideas—first previewed in the introduction, then explained

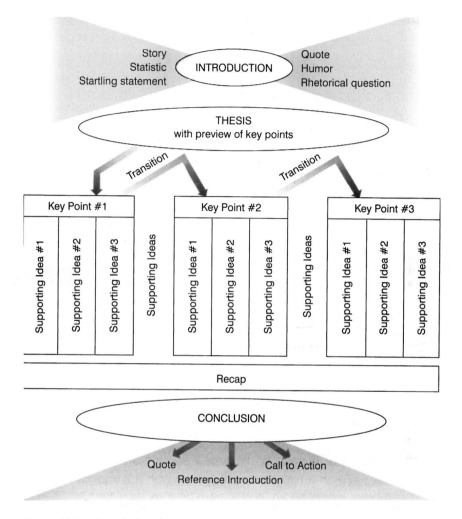

Figure 10.1   Speech Flowchart

in the body, and finally summarized in the conclusion—helps reinforce them in the mind of your audience.

As we have discussed, it is often effective to address and calmly refute the arguments for the opposing side of your speech. Do this both-sides persuasion early on, in the body of the speech, if your audience is neutral or hostile to your position. On the other hand, if your audience is supportive of your position, concentrate instead on moving it to action.

Several organizational structures are acceptable for the persuasive speech. Three of the most common will be highlighted in this chapter.

━ *Statement of Reasons Pattern.*   The first method follows Figure 10–1 and is simply a statement of your thesis (your conclusion about the issue) followed by key points that are the reasons (support) for the thesis statement. This speech is structured as follows:

*1. **Introduction: Statement of Reasons Format.***   In the introduction, you get the audience's attention and lead into your topic through the use of examples, quotations, statistics, or relevant anecdotes. In the last sentence of your introduction, you state your thesis (the conclusion or stand on your issue) and then preview (tell about) the key points that will be supporting your thesis. Essentially, your preview gives your audience an overview of the reasons you have come to your conclusion about the issue.

*2. **Body of the Speech.***   While the introduction serves to make a strong statement of your thesis, thereby letting the audience know where you stand on the issue, the body of the speech answers and elaborates on the question "Why do you believe what you believe about the issue?" The key points are all distinct reasons for drawing your conclusion. Cover each point, being sure to support each point (reason) with cited evidence.

*3. **Conclusion.***   The conclusion of your speech—which in this case means the ending of the speech, not your conclusion about the issue—should include a review of the key points that support your opinion. End the speech with a call to belief or action, telling the audience what you think it should believe or do as a result of the information you have presented.

The advantage of this method of presentation is that it is clear and simple; you are, in effect, saying, "I believe (*conclusion*) this way about the issue because of these reasons, and you should too!"

━ *Problem-Solution Format.*   A second method of structuring persuasive speeches has been outlined in the *Northern California Forensics Association Handbook*. This method also follows a problem-solution format:

*1. **Introduction.***   As in any speech, the introduction to a persuasive speech must put the audience at ease with the topic of the speech, must clearly state the purpose of the speech, and must give some direction about the course of the speech.

*2. **Harms.***   The harms section of the speech should answer the question, "How are we hurt by this problem?" Financial losses, personal injuries, and deaths caused by the problem are often detailed in the harms portion.

*3. **Inherency.***   The inherency section should answer the question, "Why does the problem exist?" The reasons for the existence of any problem can be categorized as either attitudinal inherency or structural inherency. Attitudinal inherency occurs when the sentiments of the public create a barrier to the solution of the issue or when those sentiments help to perpetuate the cause of difficulty. Structural inherency is a physical barrier that must be overcome in order to solve the problem. Such a barrier could be a law, the lack of trained personnel, or an inefficient system.

4. Significance. The notion of significance addresses the question, "What is the scope of the problem?" Significance is often described by details of the geographic range, quantitative preponderance, or qualitative weight of the problem. More often than not, the significance issue is handled within both the harms and inherency sections.

5. Solvency. This final section is arguably the most important part of the persuasive speech. It answers the question, "What can be done to remedy the problem?" It is important to address two issues within the solvency section. First, be sure to tell your audience how they can help specifically. Second, attempt to give an example of how your solution has worked in the past.

6. Conclusion. The conclusion of the persuasive speech should accomplish two goals. It should initially view how the advocated solution steps will affect the problem and it should make one last appeal to the audience.[3]

Sample Persuasive Speech Outline Using the Problem-Solution Format

ORGAN DONATION AND TRANSPLANTS

Susan Bain

Specific purpose for this speech: To persuade the audience to become organ donors.

Central idea: We need to take steps to address the shortage of available organs for transplanting because many people are dying needlessly.

Introduction

   I. **Attention Material**

   A. Imagine catching a cold or flu—it's not a big deal unless you become like half of all heart transplant patients who were normal and healthy until what was a minor infection attacked their heart. Then, imagine being told that you need an organ to survive, and then discovering that there is a critical shortage of organ donors. You will be placed on a waiting list, but you only have a 50 percent chance of becoming a recipient of a donated organ.

   B. This scenario is not uncommon. Many diseases can destroy organs or other necessary body parts. Currently there are 90,000 people on dialysis who could benefit from a new kidney. Every year approximately 15,000 people die who could have been saved by a new heart. Add thousands more who are told that they will need a new organ to survive.

   C. My own mother and a dear friend were recipients of organ donations. My cousin died while waiting for a liver donation.

[3]Joe Corcoran, *Northern California Forensics Association Handbook* (Northern California Forensics Association, 1988).

II. **Thesis (Conclusion):** Because of the shortage of available organs, many people will die; we need to make more organs available for transplanting.

III. **Preview of Main Points:** Today I will discuss how organ donations are desperately needed to help patients and their families. Then I will dispel some of the myths that make people hesitate to become organ donors. Finally, I will encourage and instruct you on how you can become an organ donor.

Body

I. **There is a great need for organ donations.**

A. People can be kept on organ transplant waiting lists for many years and, as a result, many die.

1. According to the United Network of Organ Sharing, there are currently 68,530 patients on an organ transplant waiting list.

2. Sadly, half of those awaiting organ transplants die because of the shortage of donated organs.

3. Every 90 minutes, the time it takes for the average American to commute to and from work, someone dies waiting for an organ transplant.

B. Transplantation of organs is no longer considered experimental but is an accepted form of treatment for certain end-stage diseases.

1. According to *The Encyclopedia of Health,* the transplanting of organs is now done with increasing success. For example, transplantation of the cornea has been done for many years and now there is a better than 90 percent chance of vision restoration in cases of blindness due to corneal disease.

C. Without an organ donation, the last three years of my mother's life could have been spent being hooked up to a kidney dialysis machine.

1. Because of the gift of a live kidney from her sister, my mother's last three years of life were spent traveling and spending time with her grandchildren, instead of worrying about being close to a dialysis machine.

D. Organ donation can be a source of comfort for a grieving family.

1. You may recall the story of Nicholas Greene, a young boy from California, who was killed by highway robbers while on vacation with his family in Italy. His family agreed to donate his organs, which went to seven Italians waiting for transplants. Within the first few days after his death, the number of people signing donation cards in Italy quadrupled. This is now known worldwide as the "Nicholas Effect," according to Reg Greene, the boy's father. He states that, "Few potential donors realize what a mighty gift they have in their hands. By one action they can save other families from the devastation they themselves face. Sometimes I wonder how there could be any other choice." (the Nicholas Effect)

(Transition) Now that we have looked at the benefits of organ donation, and the devastation many people face from the lack of available organs, let's look at what causes people to resist the thought of becoming a donor.

II. **There are several prevalent myths that often keep people from becoming organ donors.**

   A. One of the myths about organ donation states that if I am in an accident and the hospital knows I want to be a donor, they will not try as hard to save my life.

   1. According to Arthur Caplan, author of *The Ethics of Organ Transplanting,* the medical team treating you is separate from the transplant team. The organ procurement organization is not notified until all life-saving efforts have failed and death has been determined.

   B. Another common myth states that my body will be mutilated.

   1. Donated organs are removed surgically in a routine operation, similar to gallbladder or appendix removal.

   C. Some people say that my religion does not support organ donation.

   1. Most organized religions support donation, typically considering it a generous act that is the individual's choice.

   D. Some people are afraid to donate because they believe their family would have to pay for donating their organs.

   1. This concern is also unfounded. A donor's family is not charged for donation.

   E. People may believe that their loved one would not want his or her organs donated or that they should only donate if asked by their loved one's doctor.

   1. Families may not be aware of the potential donor's wishes, and according to *The Book of Medical Ethics,* many doctors hesitate to ask a grieving family about donating their loved one's organs.

(Transition) Now that we have looked at some of the reasons why people may reject the idea of donating organs, let's look at the ways we can resolve the shortage of organ donors.

III. **The solution to the scarcity of organ donations is to increase the number of donors.**

   A. According to Mark Dowie, author of *The Bold New World of Organ Transplanting,* "As successful organ replacements increasingly occur, more people become aware of the various diseases and disorders that can be treated and cured by transplantation; therefore, more people will want to become donors."

   B. You can personally help solve this problem by signing a donor card.

   1. You can help save lives by becoming a donor now. You can also tell others that thousands die needlessly each year due to the lack of organ and tissue donors.

   C. It is important that you share your decision with your family today.

   1. At the time of your death your family may be asked about donation. Sharing your decision now will help them carry out your wishes later.

Conclusion

I. **Review of Key Points**

   A. Today I spoke with you about the critical need for organ donors. I shared with you some of the benefits of becoming an organ donor and dispelled some common myths about organ donation. I encouraged you to become an organ donor by signing an organ donation card.

II. **Clincher**

   A. Finally, I want to say that if you do decide to become a donor, please sign the consent form and most importantly, remember to share your wishes with your family.

   B. Your decision to be a donor is an honorable act and can improve the lives of others.

   C. Your gift of organ donation could very well be a source of lasting consolation to your family.

Bibliography

The Ethics of Organ Transplanting: The Current Debate, Arthur Caplan, 1998, pp. 41–43.
The Encyclopedia of Health, Dale C. Garell, M.D. General Editor, Jeffrey Finn and Eliot Marshall, 1990, pp. 67–69, 95–97.
United Network of Organ Sharing, www.organdonor.com.
Biomedical Ethics, Opposing Viewpoints, David L. Bender, executive editor, Brenda Staler, managing editor, pp. 70, 73–74.
We Have a Donor: The Bold New World of Organ Transplanting, Mark Dowie, 1998, pp. 133–135.
The Nicholas Greene Effect: A Boy's Gift to the World, Reg Greene, 1999, pp. 181–183.

Reprinted by permission of Susan Bain.

Monroe's Motivated Sequence.   A third organizational method is called **Monroe's Motivated Sequence.**[4] Monroe's steps are especially effective when a speaker wants to motivate the audience to take action. Monroe's sequence involves the following five steps:

1. *Attention:* Get the audience's interest and attention; you can do this with provocative questions, statistics, or a relevant anecdote. End your attention step with your thesis statement (main idea) and a preview of your key ideas. This step is similar to the "introduction" step of the first method.

2. *Need:* The body of your speech begins with this step. Here you show your audience that a serious problem must be addressed. Discuss the extent and scope of the problem and how we are hurt by the problem.

3. *Satisfaction:* At this point, you present a solution to the problem that was introduced in the need step.

---

[4]Allan H. Monroe, *Principles and Types of Speech Communication,* 11th ed. (Glenview, IL: Scott, Foresman, 1990), pp. 180–203.

4. *Visualization:* This last part of the body of your speech is used to help listeners form a picture of what it would be like if your solution were in place. If there are aspects of the solution that would be of personal benefit to audience members, visualize those benefits in this step.
5. *Action:* This step is considered the conclusion of the speech. Here you summarize your ideas and request specific action from the audience members.

Following is an example of an outline that uses Monroe's Motivated Sequence:

CONSIDER FAIR TRADE COFFEE

Kris Anne Bordalo Nuguid

I. Attention

A. **Attention Getter/Introduction.** Imagine drinking the blood, sweat, and tears of laborers around the world. That is probably a very unpleasant image for you. However, you might as well be doing this if you drink coffee produced by unfair business practices.

1. (Statistics) According to Margot Roosevelt in her article for *Time Magazine* in March of 2004, coffee is second only to oil as the most traded product in the world. Ernesto Illy, writing in the March 2002 issue of *Scientific American* observed that about 400 billion cups of coffee are consumed every year, and most of it is grown and harvested by small farming families in developing countries. For many of these families, the coffee crop is their only source of income.

2. (Testimony) Cathy Cockrell of the Public Affairs office at UC Berkeley calculated that there are about 80 million people *worldwide* whose lives are directly affected by the coffee trade.

B. **Thesis (conclusion).** According to Peter Fritsch of the *Wall Street Journal*, "the collapse of world coffee prices is contributing to societal meltdowns affecting an estimated 125 million people." As the largest importers of coffee, U.S citizens must take responsibility for the consequences of our actions: we can do so by purchasing coffee obtained through the practice of equity, respect, and cooperation with poor farmers, producers, and workers, known as "fair trade."

C. **Preview Statement.** Today I will discuss the devastation unjust coffee practices bring to people around the world. Then, I will present some solutions on how we can fix this current crisis, describe the positive changes that will take place if my solutions were implemented, and finally, provide tips on how you can do your part in improving the quality of the lives of impoverished coffee farm workers.

II. **Need**

A. Folgers, Kraft, Maxwell, Phillip Morris, and Sara Lee Corporation. Do these companies sound familiar? In 2002, Peter Fritsch of the *Associated Press* stated that these major corporations buy coffee beans that were obtained at low costs from poor farming families. The low costs allow the corporations to generate fortunes by distributing the coffee beans around the globe. Unfortunately, such fortunes have not reached the homes of those who have slaved to harvest this ever-popular product: the farmers.

  1. Poor farming families are the main harvesters of coffee, but because they cannot process the coffee beans, they have to sell the beans to "coyotes," or traders, who often take advantage of them by purchasing the beans at excessively low prices.

    a. In 2005, *Global Exchange*, an international human rights organization, revealed that the farmers are paid between 30–50 cents per pound of beans.

  2. Do you know how much consumers pay for coffee? Maxwell House coffee sells for $16.69 for 39 ounces. The median income of American families in 2005, according to the Census Bureau, was $46,236.00, which makes coffee an affordable item. But the average yearly income of farming families is only $500–$1000.

  3. With their minimal incomes, these families cannot even afford the fruits of their labor. Furthermore, the practice of the larger corporations driving down the prices of coffee beans often results in the already struggling smaller farmers losing their businesses.

    a. In 2005, Merling Ramos, the Director of PRODECOOP Fair Trade co-operative in Nicaragua, stated that unfair trading practices subject small farming families to a life of destitution and hardship.

    b. In 2005, Nestor Osorio, head of the International Coffee Organization in London, stated, "The low bean prices fueling corporate profits are . . . forcing desperate peasants into everything from crime and illicit crops to illegal migration."

B. As you can see, the social and economic implications of these extortive practices are great—but these aren't the only aspects of people's lives that are affected. The welfare of workers and the educational opportunities for their children are also impacted by their exploitation.

  1. Small farmers aren't the only producers of coffee beans: large coffee plantations also exist, which directly grow, harvest, and process coffee beans: conditions aren't much better for the workers on such plantations.

  2. On many of these coffee plantations, human rights are being violated. In 2005, *Global Exchange* reported that, "coffee pickers [in Guatemala] have to pick a 100-pound quota" in order to earn their

less than $3 wage. Because of this quota, many coffee-farm workers bring their children to pick beans with them.

    a. In a 2004 *Time* article, Josafat Hernandez, the co-president of a fair trade coffee farm, observed that in Mexico City farms, "children as young as 5 pick coffee, baskets strapped to their waists."

  3. The income that these small farmers can earn makes the difference between survival and death; as a result, the children often devote their time to working: this leaves little or no time for education or play.

    a. In 2005, *Global Exchange* reported that a study of coffee plantations in Guatemala revealed that only 13% of coffee workers have completed their primary education. The limited education that children of coffee farming families attain leaves them with fewer opportunities to improve their economic standing, and traps their families in a cycle of poverty.

III. Satisfaction

  A. (Main Point) Fair Trade is a practical solution to the "coffee crisis."

    1. In 2007, *Equal Exchange Incorporated*, the leading provider of Fair Trade coffee in the U.S., explained that Fair Trade coffee receives certification that ensures consumers who buy the product that the coffee being purchased was produced under fair conditions for the farmers.

    2. Just this year, *PTs Coffee Roasting Company,* a Fair Trade partner, assured consumers that Fair Trade coffee farmers are guaranteed a minimum "fair trade price" of $1.26/lb for their coffee beans. This practice would guarantee that poor farmers would earn a living wage regardless of the fluctuations in the coffee market. Thus, these farmers would gain greater economic stability. With fair trade prices and policies, small-scale farmers avoid dealing with conniving "coyotes": thus, they are able to realize a higher profit for their labor.

IV. Visualization

  A. (Main Point) The development of fair trade practices between developing countries and their wealthier counterparts such as the U.S. and Europe would improve the living conditions of millions of laborers around the world.

    1. Fair Trade policies guarantee that farming operations and other worker's groups receive a fair price for their products. The Fair Trade price means that farmers can feed their families and that their children can go to school.

    2. A portion of revenues generated from Fair Trade are also contributed to local projects in education, health, and environmental protection for developing areas. In 2007, *Equal Exchange* representatives stated, "A coffee processing plant in El Salvador, community stores in Columbia, the training of doctors in Mexico, reforestation programs in Costa

Rica, [and] new schools in Peru," are all examples of gifts that Fair Trade co-ops have endowed on their communities (What).

Transition. By choosing to drink Fair Trade coffee, you will make life better for the small farm workers and their families hundreds of miles away.

V. Action

A. Food for Thought. The only things to lose now are a few more cents at the coffee pump. I ask you: "Is the cost of cheap coffee worth the human lives that are being destroyed?"

B. I hope that I have convinced you that Fair Trade coffee is the way to go. So what can you do about it?

  1. Put pressure on the large corporations that sell coffee. Some people don't take action because they don't think their letters and speeches can make a difference. OXFAM (Oxford Committee for Famine Relief) America begs to differ.

    a. In an article that appeared on the OXFAM America Web page, writer Kelley Damore reporte that, "In September 2003, Procter & Gamble (P&G), the largest seller of coffee in the US, announced it would introduce Fair Trade Certified™ coffee products" (Damore).

  2. Why the sudden change? Apparently, Procter & Gamble was influenced by coffee drinkers, human rights activists, and members of the House of Representatives and the Senate, all urging it to become Fair Trade Certified.

  3. A *BBC* News Report from October, 2005, revealed that Nestle followed Procter & Gamble's lead, launching its first Fair Trade coffee line: it too was persuaded by the consumer's demands. So do not hesitate to write to government officials or the corporations themselves, and voice your opinion.

C. **Review.** We have seen the hardship that unjust coffee practices bring to farmers, workers, and their children in impoverished areas of the world. We've discussed how fair trade practices can help eradicate poverty and bring about a better standard of living for laborers. Finally, we've seen that more large corporations will be willing to incorporate fair trade when consumers press for such changes.

D. **Clincher.** We can all do our part in improving the quality of the lives of impoverished coffee farm workers

As cultural anthropologist Margaret Mead put it, "Never doubt that a small group of thoughtful, committed citizens can change the world. Indeed, it is the only thing that ever has."

Bibliography

1. "Coffee Workers in Guatemala; A Survey of Working and Living Conditions on Coffee Farms COVERCO." Commission for the Verification of Codes of Conduct (COVERCO).

Feb 2000. 27 Mar 2007 <http://www. usleap.org/Coffee/sbcovercorpt/sbcovercorpt.html>

2. Damore, Kelley. "Coffee Talk." 2006. *Oxfam America*. 27 Mar 2007 <http://www.oxfamamerica.org/newsandpublications/ news_updates/ archive2004/ art6877.html>

3. DeNavas-Walt, et al. "Income, Poverty, and Health Insurance Coverage in the United States: 2006." *Current Population Reports*. Census Bureau, 2006. *SIRS Knowledge Source*. SIRS Government_Reporter. Contra Costa College Library. 27 Mar 2007 <http://0-www.sirs.com.alice.dvc.edu:80>

4. "Frequently Asked Questions About Fair Trade Coffee." *Global Exchange*. 01 April 2005. 27 March 2007 <http://www. globalexchange.org/campaigns/fairtrade/coffee/coffeeFAQ.html>

5. Fritsch, Peter.: *The Wall Street Journal*.–"Coffee-bean oversupply deepens Latin America's woes." *Organic Consumers Association*. 08 Jul 2002. 27 Mar 2007 <http://www.organicconsumers. org/ starbucks/coffee-beans. cfm>

6. "Nestle launches fair trade coffee." *BBC News*. 07 Oct 2005. 27 Mar 2007. <http://news.bbc. co. uk/1/ hi/business/4318882. stm>

7. Raburn, Ilana. "The Central American Coffee Crisis: Why Producers Are Failing to Make a Profit From 'Top Quality' Coffee." *The Globalist Foundation*. 23 Dec 2006. 27 Mar 2007 <http://www. global21online. org/cambridge/i1003. html>

8. Roosevelt, Margot. "The Coffee Clash." *Time*, 01 Mar 2004. 25 Nov 2006 <http://www.time. com/time/insidebiz/article/0,9171,1101040308-596156-1,00. html>

9. "What Is Fair Trade Coffee?" *Equal Exchange, Inc*. 2007. 27 Mar 2007. <http://www.equalexchange. com/what-is-fair-trade-coffee->

10. Illy, Ernesto. "The Complexity of Coffee." *Scientific American, Inc*. 2002. 28 March 2007 <http://www. illyusa.com/pr/coffee. pdf>

11. "Life in the USA: Coffee." *Elliot Essman*. 2007. 28 March 2007 <http://www.lifeintheusa. com/food/ coffee. htm>

12. "About Coffee." *PTs Coffee Roasting Co*. 2007. 28 March 2007 <http://www.ptscoffee. com/aboutcoffee/aboutcoffee.php? tid=39>

13. Cockrell, Cathy. "Caffeine with a conscience." The Regents of the University of California. 12 Sept 2001. 28 March 2007 <http://www. berkeley.edu/news/berkeleyan/2001/09/12_coffe.html>

Reprinted by permission of Kris Anne Bordalo Nuguid.

As we have seen, there are several good methods of organizing your speeches. When you choose one that fits your content, your audience is able to clearly follow your logic, and your credibility is increased.

Pathos: Emotional Appeal

Both positive and negative emotions can influence our thoughts and actions. As critical thinkers, we should be aware of a speaker who uses *only* emotional appeals as reasons for a conclusion. As speakers, we should appeal to our listener's emotions only when we believe it is appropriate and relevant to the issue we are discussing.

Most of the big issues we confront as a society, and many smaller ones, involve deep-seated feelings. Consider the reasons why people are for or against capital punishment, abortion, euthanasia, and a host of environmental issues. If a group is protesting the creation and sale of fur coats, the members of this group most likely feel deeply for the animals that are used to make the coats.

On the other hand, those who have spent a lifetime learning to make the coats or who have a family depending on the sale of the coats feel equally strongly about their livelihoods. Whatever your position on this issue, you can imagine the personal feelings that accompany advocacy on both sides.

Emotional appeal is important in making issues real for audience members. Hearing statistics about thousands of victims of drunk drivers does not move us as much as hearing the personal story of one victim and his or her family.

Responsible and effective speakers will use emotional appeal to show the human impact of an attitude or a policy that needs to be changed. Let's say a speaker wants to persuade his or her audience that homeless individuals who are schizophrenic need to be hospitalized and given treatment. The speaker can and should use logos in the form of statistics, giving the estimated number of homeless who are schizophrenic and the medical needs that they have. However, the factor that will convince the audience to listen, the factor that will highlight the importance of this issue, is likely to come in the form of an emotional appeal. A few case histories of homeless schizophrenics and examples of the problems they face will do much to make an audience receptive to this problem and its possible solution.

Are emotional appeals ethical? Yes, if they are

1. True and accurate
2. Accompanied by solid reasoning
3. Based on healthy emotions

The third category, healthy emotions, needs to be evaluated by the speaker. Psychologist Abraham Maslow has suggested that all human beings have the same basic needs, which form the basis of human motivation.[5] When we as speakers or writers want to bring our audience to action, we can appeal to these needs.

The needs are listed in a hierarchy (see Figure 10–2). The lower level needs must be satisfied before people become concerned with higher level needs. We can ethically address *these* needs, using examples that stir the emotions of audience members:

1. Physical needs. These include the needs that guarantee our survival as people and as a species, such as food, air, water, rest, and the ability to reproduce.

> *Example of use in a speech:* Although you can discuss facts about scarcities of food and water in a speech, you also can use emotional appeals by asking your audience members to imagine a world in which their children would not have enough food or water to survive. Since we all have the same needs, you can then ask them to empathize with people in other nations who are without adequate supplies of food or water. The speech on fair trade coffee appealed to the need of coffee workers to make a sustainable living wage. Truthful fear appeals, such as

---

[5]A. H. Maslow, *Toward a Psychology of Being* (New York: Van Nostrand Reinhold, 1968).

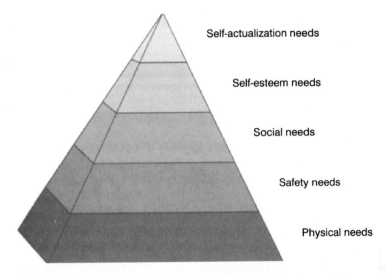

Figure 10.2   Maslow's Hierarchy of Needs (From *Motivation and Personality,* 3rd ed. by A. H. Maslow, R. D. Frager, J. Fadiman. Copyright ©
1997. Adapted by permission of Pearson Education, Inc., Upper Saddle
River, NJ.)

those warning of the dangers of smoking, obesity, or promiscuous sex,
are used by speakers to persuade audiences to change harmful
behaviors.

2. Safety needs. Safety needs involve the desire to be protected from
harm to our persons and to have adequate levels of comfort, such as decent
housing, safe products, and prevention and treatment of sickness.

> *Examples of use in a speech:* Speakers can legitimately use emotional
> appeals, such as graphic examples of accidents that have occurred at a
> dangerous intersection when they are advocating for a needed
> stoplight. They can tell about children who died or were disabled from
> faulty toys that should be recalled. They can describe the fear of those
> who live near "crack houses" to emphasize the need for more effective
> neighborhood law enforcement. Speakers who urge others to prepare
> for earthquakes or hurricanes appeal to their audiences' need for safety.

3. Social needs. These needs involve our desires to form alliances with
others, to be included in group interactions, and to have close friends who
love and respect us.

> *Examples of use in a speech:* Speakers can give examples of children with
> AIDS who have not been included in their peer groups as part of a
> speech on their need for acceptance in the community. Speakers

promoting a social cause sometimes appeal to audience members' social needs by offering some form of group identification to them; for example, many fund-raisers offer T-shirts to contributing audience members.

4. *Self-esteem needs.* These needs concern our desire to feel like worth-while, contributing members of society, whose lives have meaning and purpose.

Examples of use in a speech: Speakers can appeal to our altruism in helping others in need, which in turn gives us a feeling of making an important contribution. They also can honor professionals who are worthy of more respect than they are generally given, such as homemakers, preschool teachers and mechanics. Seminar leaders often motivate audience members by promising to give them skills that will help them become more effective workers.

5. *Self-actualization needs.* When their basic needs are met, people are motivated to develop various potentials, to expand their horizons by trying new things, or to become better at familiar skills. Included in the need for per-sonal development is gaining a greater understanding of spiritual matters.

Examples of use in a speech: Speakers can appeal to audience members' desires to become more well rounded by using examples of people who have taken on new professions or challenges late in life. They can describe the thrill of an outdoor adventure when encouraging audience members to buy a vacation package. They can also appeal to the desire to leave a lasting legacy by contributing personally or financially to the welfare of others. (See Exercises 10.1 and 10.2 on p. 452)

REMINDER

Use emotional appeals as a means of involving and motivating your audience.

PROBLEM SOLVING AND COLLABORATIVE DECISION MAKING

As we have discussed, there are times when it is necessary to advocate strongly for our own ideas and desired actions and against other ideas or actions. This is especially true when only one outcome is possible, as in the following examples:

You are campaigning for a candidate who you believe is the best one for the job.
You want to receive a promotion at work.

Despite her protests, your training tells you that your relative is experiencing
a stroke and you need to rush her to a hospital.
A group to which you belong wants to create a new policy that you believe
is wrong.
You are a coach and want your players to execute a specific play.
Someone wants you to copy your test answers, and you don't want to let
that person cheat.

All of these situations call for a win-lose approach. If your goals are met,
someone else's goals are not met. One candidate will win, and one will lose.
If there is only one promotion to be had, only one person will receive it. Your
relative will either get the help she needs or suffer medical consequences.
There are legitimate reasons to advocate strongly for a "win" in these types of
situations.

In many other circumstances, your skill as a thinker, listener, and advocate is best used to facilitate a solution to a problem that incorporates your
own goals with the goals and ideas of others. The problem-solving method we
will discuss in this chapter has been used to create "win-win" strategies for
complex dilemmas in which it is preferable and possible to accommodate more
than one individual's wishes and objectives.

Prerequisites to Problem Solving

Just as courses of study have educational prerequisites (e.g., the need to be
competent in Algebra I before taking Algebra II/Trigonometry), there are cognitive and character prerequisites to problem solving. The steps toward coming to a joint solution are not difficult; most obstacles are created by participants
who are unable or unwilling to work collaboratively with others. Following
are the optimal characteristics of problem solvers:

1. ***Optimism.*** Optimism can be seen simply as a belief that a solution to the
problem may be difficult but is possible. An optimistic attitude creates an
expectation of a positive resolution for the present dilemma. Optimists
don't feel helpless and overwhelmed when facing problems. They realize that conflict is an everyday occurrence, but that most problems can
be managed; they don't catastrophize and dwell on the worst possible
outcomes.

2. ***Respect.*** People with respect for others are able to see how someone else
might perceive a situation differently than they do; they also realize that
others have individual needs and goals and they see these differences as
legitimate.

3. ***Goodwill.*** When people approach problem solving with goodwill, they
have a desire for the best results for both themselves and the other people involved. Problem solving works best when everyone involved has
goodwill and is working for a lasting and satisfying solution for all parties.

THE PROBLEM-SOLVING METHOD

The problem-solving method involves several steps. Each step is important and should be followed in sequence. Prior to meeting, establish a time and place that is suitable for everyone involved. If the problem involves more than two individuals, it is ideal to get a space with a flipchart or blackboard or another means of projecting ideas in a way that everyone can see. If the problem is about a close relationship, it's good to have a private setting with enough time for meaningful interaction.

   1. Distinguish needs from solutions. Before meeting, each person should think about the unmet needs that are involved in the problem; it is important to distinguish needs from solutions, particularly if people are strongly dissatisfied with some aspect of the current situation. Note the difference between needs—that can be met in any number of ways—and solutions—that set up a win-lose scenario.

Needs	Solutions (masked as needs)
"I need a quiet workspace."	"I need Wesley's office."
"I need to get away."	"I need to stay at a four-star hotel with a spa."
"I'm overwhelmed with my workload."	"I need a personal assistant."
"Our office needs better coordination."	"We need to complain to the president about our boss."
"Our store needs to attract business."	"We need an espresso bar outside."
"Our students aren't testing well."	"We need better computers."
"We aren't able to pay our bills."	"We need to work longer hours."
"Our staff needs to take fewer sick days"	"We need a pool and fitness center to keep us healthy."

There is an extremely important distinction between understanding and expressing true *needs* and using the word *need* to express a solution. The solution you offer may end up being useful, but if you start with solutions, you are led off track into a discussion and perhaps argument about a specific end result instead of understanding the real needs that lead you to desire that particular end. The needs listed earlier can be met in various ways, but any solution should include a consideration of available resources and the needs of others. A need for a quiet workspace would be understood by everyone of goodwill, but the desire to have someone else's office would not be seen as reasonable. The need to get away can be met in any number of ways that are more affordable than a four-star hotel. Students might profit from new computers, but the computers will probably not solve the problem of low test scores. All stores need to attract business, but an espresso bar may lead to spending money that doesn't address the real need of getting people into the store. If people aren't paying their bills, they may need to cut back on luxury items rather than creating more stress with longer working hours.

2. Describe the needs of everyone involved in the problem or its resolution. When the needs of individuals or the organization are clearly stated, solutions that address those needs can be found. At this point, the prerequisites of optimism, respect, and goodwill are very important. We need to view other people's comments with the same validity as our own. We may not agree with or even understand their viewpoints, but a mutual resolution will take them into account.

It is often, though not always, helpful to write all of the needs out so that they can be clearly seen. For example, a supervisor might write down the conflicting, but valid needs of his staff who all share a small office space. Suzana needs a quiet place to do accounting, while Alex needs to be making phone calls to clients, and the supervisor wants everyone who comes into the office to be greeted warmly and immediately. All of the needs are valid but can sometimes conflict; solutions need to address everyone's issues in order for the office to run well.

3. Brainstorm solutions. At this point, we realize the conflicting needs and want to be as creative as possible in coming up with viable outcomes that meet most if not all of the needs of the parties concerned. **Brainstorming** is a specific technique that has been used for many years to find imaginative results to problems. The advertising industry uses brainstorming to come up with innovative and successful product campaigns, and many businesses and industries also rely on brainstorming to maximize the resourcefulness of their employees.

Brainstorming can be broken down into four steps:

1. Look at and consider all of the various needs.
2. Quickly come up with as many ideas as possible that might meet most or all of the needs.
3. As ideas are voiced, have someone make a list that everyone can see.
4. Avoid any evaluations, positive or negative, during the brainstorming process. Don't say "Oh, that would never work," or "That's the best idea."

When brainstorming is done quickly without evaluation, it is thought to access the creative powers of the right side of the brain. Conversely, the left side of the brain is used for evaluating and linear thinking. If evaluations are made during a productive brainstorming session, the flow of ideas may cease as the group is moved from the spontaneous and free-flowing creativity of the right brain to a more studied consideration of the pros and cons of each idea. The necessary process of evaluation will be done in the next step, but it is important to first take time to think "outside the box" where original and innovative approaches may well be found.

4. *Evaluate the proposed solutions.* At this point, everyone can discuss which solutions may work and which may not. This is also the time to see if some of the proposed solutions can be combined to create the best outcomes. As in the other steps, the prerequisites of respect, goodwill, and optimism should be evident. There's no need to say "spending more money is a terrible idea" when you can say, "That would solve the problem, but we don't have the budget for that right now." Discuss each idea with courtesy, and see if some of the ideas can be combined.

5. *Choose the best solution.* Pick the solution that is most viable to everyone concerned. If someone remains disgruntled, try to find out the needs that he feels would not be met by the solution and if anything can be done to address his concerns. When people feel heard, respected, and considered, they are often willing to try a solution that seems best to the majority.

6. *Follow up on the solution.* The only way to see if a solution will work is to try it out. It may work well, it may need to be tweaked, or it may not work at all. If it doesn't work, don't give up or blame other people. Instead, try to see why the solution didn't meet the needs that were expressed and what could be done to make it better. There is usually great benefit in going through the problem-solving process, even when perfect solutions are not found.

When the solutions do work well, groups and organizations gain confidence in their abilities to be creative, productive, and healthy. The optimism that is generated from successful problem solving creates a positive climate in which everyone involved can safely try new things and come up with promising new approaches to problems.

Example

Let's say that the Kim, supervisor in the previous example, sat down with Suzana and Alex at a time and place convenient for all of them. The needs were written for all to see:

Suzana: A quiet place to do accounting without the distraction of conversations around me.
Alex: The ability to talk to clients by phone while Suzana is working.
Kim: Someone to greet our customers immediately and to make them feel comfortable.

After writing all their needs, the small group decided to brainstorm and came up with the following possible solutions:

Earphones or iPod for Suzana
Rent a new office space with a separate room for accounting
Alex returns calls after greeting clients
Kim greets clients or does calling
Hire a receptionist
Hire an accountant and let Suzana be the receptionist

Kim does accounting
Have Kim's teenage daughter do reception sometimes

After brainstorming, the group went on to evaluating and combining the proposed solutions. Suzana said that earphones didn't block the noise and the music was distracting also, so they crossed out the first idea. Kim decided to look into office space that was configured differently in another building. Alex said that he could let the message machine take calls and he could return them later, but even then, new clients might walk in, so that suggestion was deleted. Kim could do the calling, but she needs to visit clients away from the office, and even if she took the calls, that would still disturb Suzana. They all agreed that there was no money for a full-time receptionist or accountant.

After eliminating the solutions that were unworkable, the group found several that were promising. Kim said that she could pick up some of the accounting when she was in the office, since the calls don't distract her and she has to go over the books eventually anyway. That would allow Suzana to do the reception. Kim's teenage daughter was happy about the idea of helping out in exchange for a small hourly fee, since it was her first job. She was able to commit to four afternoons a week.

Kim looked for and found a new office space with a small side office for accounting that would be the same rent as they were paying for the larger office without the separate space. The only problem was that it wouldn't be available for three months. Suzana then asked if she could do reception in the morning and the accounting from home on the days that Kim's daughter came in. Kim agreed. Alex was able to continue calling clients as he had always done.

The solutions chosen by the group were implemented and worked well with one exception. Suzana didn't finish all of the accounting on the four days that Kim's daughter came in because she needed some of the office equipment. She decided to come in after hours one evening a week to finish and—since she had done her required hours by Friday at noon—to take off early on Fridays.

When people are able to be flexible and creative and come up with workable solutions, satisfaction at work and in other relationships increase. Perfect outcomes can't always be found, but great improvements can be made if some time and effort are directed toward problem solving. (See Exercise 10.3, p. 452.)

LIFE APPLICATION

Be a thoughtful advocate for important issues and in your relationships. Use the skills of organizing and presenting your ideas to make a difference in local, national, and international issues that concern you. When delivering speeches, speak loud enough to be heard and practice using eye contact that includes all of the members of your audience.

With your coworkers, friends, and family, speak up about your needs and goals and show consideration and empathy for theirs, using the collaborative problem solving skills whenever appropriate. Voice your opinions and draw out the concerns of others, particularly those who may not easily express their own viewpoints. Use your active listening skills to include everyone so that a group decision is made by consensus rather than coercion.

CHAPTER EXERCISES

Exercise 10.1   Purpose: To incorporate the knowledge of pathos into the writing of a speech.

Take each of Maslow's needs and write your own examples of how they could be incorporated into a speech as an emotional appeal.

Exercise 10.2   Purpose: To recognize the use of pathos in a speech.

Write or tell about a speech you heard that included an effective appeal to emotion. You might use the following format:

1. Explain the issue and the conclusion of the speaker.
2. Discuss the audience's predisposition to the speech and the speaker.
3. Explain how the speaker specifically used the appeal to emotion. Was it a story, an example, or a personal testimony?
4. Talk about the placement of the appeal to emotion. Did it come in the introduction, body, or conclusion of the speech, or was it referenced throughout the speech?
5. Summarize your reasons for finding this appeal effective. Then comment on whether you believe the appeal was ethical.

Exercise 10.3   Purpose: To practice collaborative problem solving.

Practice the problem-solving strategies at home, at work, or at school. Some possible problems to solve would be division of responsibilities, preparation and presentation of a group project, coming up with a marketing strategy, deciding the details of a family vacation, or planning an event such as a reunion or conference. Ask the people involved to help you gain skill in problem solving by meeting and going through the steps of the method. Report your results to the class or instructor.

Example

My best friend was tired from work and school and wanted me to go away with her this weekend to a place her family owns about three hours from here. There is a lot to do up there and it's relaxing, but I wanted to stay home and write an essay, finish my other homework, and change the oil in my car. We followed the steps:

1. We defined our needs, not as the solutions of "getting away" or "staying home" but as her need to relax and have a change of scenery and my need to get some work done.
2. We described the needs—she wants to hike and sit at the lake, just to have a minivacation. I have a lot of tasks that have to be done, but I'd also like to spend some time with her.

3. We brainstormed and came up with some ideas:

> We stay home and go next weekend when I'm more available.
> I change the car oil next week.
> I get my work done before we go.
> We go from Saturday to Sunday instead of leaving on Friday.
> We go to a lake closer to home.
> We hike closer to home.
> I do my work on the road and some of the time we are there.

4. We then evaluated and combined the solutions. I had to change the oil before we took the car anywhere, so that wasn't possible to put off. She really wants to be away, so hiking or going to a lake closer to home or going next week didn't work for her. I could get my work done early, but that would be rushing it.

   After looking at our list, we decided that she would take my car and get the oil changed. I would try to get some work done before we left and bring the rest. She would drive while I did some homework, and I would get up earlier on Saturday and do my homework while she went to the lake. Then we could go for a hike and relax later.

5. We went with the solution, and it worked well for the most part. We had a great time, and I got most of my work done.

6. The main difficulty was that I couldn't really work in the car and I slept in Saturday, so I had to finish work when we got home on Sunday night. We decided to plan some weekends ahead of time so we can enjoy them more.

CHAPTER HIGHLIGHTS

1. A critical thinker considers the best ways to organize and present ideas in order to be a strong advocate for an issue.

2. The best ways to deal with speech fear are to choose an issue of interest to you, prepare thoroughly, and practice.

3. Good persuasive speakers analyze their audiences before preparing their speeches. Audiences may be characterized as believing, neutral, or hostile.

4. Ethos, the credibility of the speaker, is an important element of persuasion. Ethos is enhanced by the careful preparation of the speaker and the manner in which he or she presents the speech.

5. Logos, the content and organization of the speech, is crucial to a persuasive message. Several organizational structures can be used to enhance the clarity and persuasiveness of a speech.

6. Pathos, emotional appeal, is powerful in its ability to persuade and should be used ethically.

7. Collaborative problem solving can be used to find a solution that is satisfactory to everyone affected by a problem.

Audience analysis (p. 429)   Ethos (p. 431)
Believing audience (p. 429)   Pathos (p. 431)
Neutral audience (p. 429)   Logos (p. 431)
Hostile audience (p. 430)   Monroe's Motivated Sequence (p. 438)
Both-sides persuasion (p. 430)   Brainstorming (p. 449)

CHAPTER CHECKUP

Matching

A. Logos
B. Pathos
C. Ethos

1. The use of emotional appeal to support conclusions.
2. Logical organization and credible content used to support conclusions.
3. The credibility or reputation of a speaker.

Sentence Completion

4. The statement of key ideas that immediately follows the thesis statement is called the _____.
5. Organizing a persuasive speech with your strongest points first is a good strategy in dealing with a _____ audience.
6. Each key point must be supported with _____.
7. A speaker's position on an issue is often called his or her _____ _____.

Short Answer

8. What are effective ways to handle speech fear?
9. Why should speakers review their key ideas at the end of a speech?
10. What are some ways to add interest to introductions and conclusions?
11. What are the six steps of the collaborative problem-solving method?
12. Why is brainstorming a useful technique for generating ideas?

ARTICLES FOR DISCUSSION

The following article is about a woman who achieved some fame as a writer and then was terrified when she received requests for speaking engagements. She forced herself to confront her fears and found, to her great surprise, that she even grew to enjoy public speaking. The author admits that she is still anxious when approaching public speaking, but she is determined not to allow her fears to quiet her voice.

SPEAK FOR YOURSELF

Susan Faludi

I am at the boiling point! If I do not find some day the use of my tongue … I shall die of an intellectual repression, a woman's rights convulsion.

Elizabeth Cady Stanton, in a letter to Susan B. Anthony

"Oh, and then you'll be giving that speech at the Smithsonian Tuesday on the status of American women," my publisher's publicist reminded me as she rattled off the list of "appearances" for the week.

"What?" I choked out. "I thought that was at least another month away."

But the speech was distant only in my wishful consciousness, which pushed all such events into a mythical future when I would no longer lunge for smelling salts at the mention of public speaking.

For the author of what was widely termed an "angry" and "forceful" book, I exhibit a timorous verbal demeanor that belies my barracuda blurbs.

My fingers may belt out my views when I'm stationed before the computer, but stick a microphone in front of me and I'm a Victorian lady with the vapors.

Like many female writers with strong convictions but weak stomachs for direct confrontation, I write so forcefully precisely because I speak so tentatively.

One form of self-expression has overcompensated for the weakness of the other, as a blind person develops a hypersensitive ear.

"Isn't it wonderful that so many people want to hear what you have to say about women's rights?" the publicist prodded. I grimaced. "About as wonderful as walking down the street with no clothes on."

Yes, I wanted people to hear what I had to say. Yes, I wanted to warn women of the backlash to our modest gains. But couldn't they just read what I wrote? Couldn't I just speak softly and carry a big book?

It has taken me a while to realize that my publicist is right. It's not the same—for my audience or me.

Public speech can be a horror for the shy person, but it can also be the ultimate act of liberation. For me, it became the moment where the public and the personal truly met.

For many years, I believed the imbalance between my incensed writing and my atrophied vocal cords suited me just fine.

After a few abysmal auditions for school plays—my one role was Nana the dog in *Peter Pan,* not a speaking role—I retired my acting aspirations and retreated to the school newspaper, a forum where I could bluster at injustices large and small without public embarrassment.

My friend Barbara and I co-edited the high school paper (titled, interestingly, *The Voice*), fearlessly castigating all scoundrels from our closet-size office. But we kept our eyes glued to the floor during class discussion.

Partly this was shyness, a genderless condition. But it was a condition reinforced by daily gendered reminders—we saw what happened to the girls who argued in class. The boys called them "bitches" and they sat home Saturday nights.

Popular girls raised their voices only at pep squad.

Whereas both sexes fear public speaking (pollsters tell us it's the public's greatest fear, rivaling even death), women—particularly women challenging the status quo—seem to be more afraid and with good reason.

We do have more at stake. Men risk loss of face, women a loss of femininity.

Men are chagrined if they blunder at the podium; women face humiliation either way. If we come across as commanding, our womanhood is called into question. If we reveal emotion, we are too hormonally driven to be taken seriously.

I had my own taste of this double standard while making the rounds of radio and television talk shows for a book tour. When I disputed a point with a man, male listeners would often phone in to say they found my behavior "offensive" or even "unattractive."

And then there were my own internalized "feminine" voices: Don't interrupt, be agreeable, keep the volume down.

"We're going to have to record that again," a weary radio producer said, rewinding the tape for the fifth time. "Your words are angry, but it's not coming through in your voice."

In replacing lacerating speech with a literary scalpel, I had adopted a well-worn female strategy, used most famously by Victorian female reformers protesting slavery and women's lowly status.

"I want to be doing something with the pen, since no other means of action in politics are in a woman's power," Harriet Martineau, the British journalist, wrote in 1832.

But although their literature makes compelling reading, the suffrage movement didn't get under way until women took a public stand from the platform of the Seneca Falls Women's Rights Convention.

And while Betty Friedan's 1963 *The Feminine Mystique* raised the consciousness of millions of women, the contemporary women's movement began to affect social policy only when Friedan and other feminists started addressing the public.

Public speech is a more powerful stimulus because it is more dangerous for the speaker. An almost physical act, it demands projecting one's voice, hurling it against the public ear.

Writing, on the other hand, occurs at one remove. The writer asserts herself from behind the veil of the printed page.

The dreaded evening of the Smithsonian speech finally arrived. I stood knock-kneed and green-gilled before 300 people. Was it too late to plead a severe case of laryngitis? I am Woman, hear me whisper.

I cleared my throat and, to my shock, a hush fell over the room. People were listening—with an intensity that strangely emboldened me.

It was as if their attentive silence allowed me to make contact with my own muffled self. I began to speak. A stinging point induced a ripple of agreement. I told a joke and they laughed.

My voice got surer, my delivery rising. A charge passed between me and the audience, uniting and igniting us both.

That internal "boiling point" that Elizabeth Cady Stanton described was no longer under "intellectual repression." And its heat, I discovered, could set many kettles to whistling.

Afterward it struck me that in some essential way I hadn't really proved myself a feminist until now.

Until you translate personal words on a page into public connections with other people, you aren't really part of a political movement.

I hadn't declared my independence until I was willing to declare it out loud. I knew public speaking was important to reform public life—but I hadn't realized the transformative effect it could have on the speaker herself.

Women need to be heard not just to change the world, but to change themselves.

I can't say that this epiphany has made me any less anxious when approaching the lectern. But it has made me more determined to speak in spite of the jitters—and more hopeful that other women will do the same.

Toward that end I'd like to make a modest proposal for the next stage of the women's movement. A new method of consciousness-raising: Feminist Toastmasters.

QUESTIONS FOR DISCUSSION

1. Comment on the following statement by the author of this article: "Public speech can be a horror for the shy person, but it can also be the ultimate act of liberation." How can public speaking, even when we dread it, be liberating?

2. The author attributes some of her hesitancy to speak out to her experience as a female. To what extent, if any, do you believe that women today still feel these same hesitancies?

3. The author states, "Until you translate personal words on a page into public connections with other people, you aren't really part of a political movement." In what ways do you believe that speaking is essential for those involved with political, social, and religious movements?

This next article gives an eloquent explanation of what is genuinely persuasive. The writer acknowledges that reasonable people may disagree about issues and that the best way to get the ear of an opponent is to show some understanding of his or her viewpoint.

CHANGING A MAN'S MIND

Thomas Aquinas, who knew more about education and persuasion than almost anybody who ever lived, once said that when you want to convert someone to your view, you go over to where he is standing, take him by the hand (mentally speaking), and guide him to where you want him to go. You don't stand across the room and shout at him. You don't call him a dummy. You don't order him to come over to where you are. You start where he is, and work from that position. That's the only way to get him to budge.

We have lost sight of this elementary psychological fact. The world is full of passionate advocates, screaming their own prejudices, and excoriating their opponents.

This does three things: (a) it makes the people who agree with you feel better, (b) it makes the people who disagree with you stiffen their resistance, and (c) it makes the people on the fence uneasy and skeptical that you are speaking the whole truth.

I have never known a single passionate and partisan argument to win over a person who disagreed with it, or even to persuade a person who was neutral on the subject. The chief reason being that all passionate and partisan arguments overstate their case and understate their opponents' case.

When you think that someone is wrong, and you disagree with him, the first task is to determine in what way he is right. This is not as paradoxical as it sounds: no view can be entirely wrong, and everybody has a little piece of truth by the tail. This is the piece we start with; we work from there, and concede as much as we honestly can.

Lord Acton said that we have no right to oppose a position until we can state that position in a way that fully satisfies those who hold it; until, indeed, we can make out a better case for it than the proponent himself can. (Most of us, of course, distort or lampoon the opposite position, and then proceed to demolish this straw man.)

And all this is much more than an academic exercise. The arts of argument and persuasion are so little known and practiced that disputants have no recourse to anything but violence. If people can't agree on how to disagree, there is no hope of reconciliation or compromise. And the art of argument is learning how to disagree productively.

We begin to fight when words fail us. And words fail us when we use the wrong ones to the wrong people for the wrong reasons.

It is far easier to be passionate in defense of what one believes than to comprehend why somebody believes something different. But, ultimately, only this comprehension (which is not agreement) can replace violence with dialog instead of the deafening monologues that lead to war.

Anonymous, given as a conference handout at the Seventh Annual and Fifth International Conference on Critical Thinking and Educational Reform.

1. Comment on the following statement from this essay: "I have never known a single passionate and partisan argument to win over a person who disagreed with it, or even to persuade a person who was neutral on the subject. The chief reason being that all passionate and partisan arguments overstate their case and understate their opponents' case." Have you found that people who argue passionately overstate their own case and understate their opponent's case? Can you think of examples of this overstatement and understatement?

2. Can someone be persuasive and passionate and still be fair to the other side of the argument? If so, how? If not, why not?

3. Think of an issue that concerns you deeply. Can you see the "piece of truth" held by the other side? How could you use that truth to persuade your opponent to consider the value of your position?

One of the most eloquent speeches in American history was President Abraham Lincoln's Gettysburg Address. The Battle of Gettysburg was fought July 1 to July 3, 1863. At the end of those few days, more than 51,000 Americans were classified as wounded, missing, or dead. (To put this one battle in perspective, there were 4,435 deaths in the Revolutionary War and 47,378 in the Vietnam War.) After the battle, the governor of Pennsylvania, Andrew Curtin, commissioned the creation of a cemetery on 17 acres of the battlefield. The cemetery was dedicated four months later, on November 19, 1863. The main speaker for the dedication was Edward Everett, one of the nation's most famous orators. President Lincoln was also invited to speak "as Chief Executive of the nation, formally [to] set apart these grounds to their sacred use by a few appropriate remarks." At the ceremony, Everett spoke for more than two hours; Lincoln spoke for only a few minutes. In those few minutes, Lincoln reflected upon the ideals of liberty and equality that accompanied the birth of the nation, the valor and commitment of soldiers who died for those ideals, and the challenge of those who were left living to continue in safeguarding those ideals. In his address, Lincoln also transformed the war from a war for union to a war for both union and freedom.

As you read his words, consider the audience of mourners that Lincoln was addressing at the cemetery, and also the audience of the larger nation who would be reading the address in the newspapers.

THE GETTYSBURG ADDRESS

Abraham Lincoln

Fourscore and seven years ago our fathers brought forth on this continent a new nation, conceived in liberty and dedicated to the proposition that all men are created equal. Now we are engaged in a great civil war, testing whether that nation or any nation so conceived and so dedicated can long endure. We are met on a great battlefield of that war. We have come to dedicate a portion of that field as a final resting-place for those who here gave their lives that that nation might live. It is altogether fitting and proper that we should do this. But in a larger sense, we cannot dedicate, we cannot consecrate, we cannot hallow this ground. The brave men, living and dead who struggled here have consecrated it far above our poor power to add or detract. The world will little note nor long remember what we say here, but it can never forget what they did here. It is for us the living rather to be dedicated here to the unfinished work which they who fought here have thus far so nobly advanced. It is rather for us to be here dedicated to the great task remaining before us—that from these honored dead we take increased devotion to that cause for which they gave the last full measure of devotion—that we here highly resolve that these dead shall not have died in vain, that this nation under God shall have a new birth of freedom, and that government of the people, by the people, for the people shall not perish from the earth.

QUESTIONS FOR DISCUSSION

1. The keynote speaker for the dedication of the cemetery at Gettysburg spoke for two hours, and Lincoln spoke for two minutes. Lincoln said, "The world will little note nor long remember what we say here," but his words have been remembered and quoted by millions. What elements of Lincoln's address made it so memorable?

2. Lincoln, like many other speakers before and since, had a burden to give comfort to his particular audience. How were his words designed to comfort those grieving their loved ones who died in battle?

3. As the leader of the nation, how did President Lincoln place this devastating battle in a historical context? Why do you think he started with a reference to the vision of our forefathers?

4. How did the president use the conclusion of his brief address to give hope and direction to his audience?

Dr. Martin Luther King used ethos, logos, and pathos in the following speech, which is considered a classic modern American address. He spoke at a time when segregation was still the law in many states. Although he was directly addressing the crowd gathered in Washington, D.C., he was also aware of the larger audience, many of whom were hostile, that was reached through print and electronic media. No one could have foretold the dramatic and historic effect that this speech would have for decades to come.

I HAVE A DREAM

Dr. Martin Luther King

I am happy to join with you today in what will go down in history as the greatest demonstration for freedom in the history of our nation.

Five score years ago, a great American, in whose symbolic shadow we stand today, signed the Emancipation Proclamation. This momentous decree came as a great beacon light of hope to millions of Negro slaves, who had been seared in the flames of withering injustice. It came as a joyous daybreak to end the long night of their captivity.

But one hundred years later, the Negro is still not free. One hundred years later, the life of the Negro is still sadly crippled by the manacles of segregation and the chains of discrimination. One hundred years later, the Negro lives on a lonely island of poverty in the midst of a vast ocean of material prosperity. One hundred years later, the Negro is still languished in the corners of American society and finds himself an exile in his own land. So we have come here today to dramatize a shameful condition.

In a sense we've come to our nation's Capital to cash a check. When the architects of our republic wrote the magnificent words of the Constitution and the Declaration of Independence, they were signing a promissory note to which every American was to fall heir. This note was a promise that all men—yes, black men as well as white men—would be guaranteed the unalienable rights of life, liberty, and the pursuit of happiness.

It is obvious today that America has defaulted on this promissory note insofar as her citizens of color are concerned. Instead of honoring this sacred obligation, America has given the Negro people a bad check; a check which has come back marked "insufficient funds." But we refuse to believe that the bank of justice is bankrupt. We refuse to believe that there are insufficient funds in the great vaults of opportunity of this nation. So we've come to cash this check—a check that will give us upon demand the riches of freedom and the security of justice. We have also come to this hallowed spot to remind America of the fierce urgency of now. This is no time to engage in the luxury of cooling off or to take the tranquilizing drug of gradualism. Now is the time to make real the promises of Democracy. Now is the time to rise from the dark and desolate valley of segregation to the sunlight of racial justice. Now is the time to lift our nation from the quicksands of racial injustice to the solid rock of brotherhood. Now is the time to make justice a reality for all of God's children.

It would be fatal for the nation to overlook the urgency of the moment. This sweltering summer of the Negro's legitimate discontent will not pass until there is an invigorating autumn of freedom and equality. Nineteen sixty-three is not an end, but a beginning. Those who hope that the Negro needed to blow off steam and will now be content will have a rude awakening if the nation returns to business as usual. There will be neither rest nor tranquility in America until the Negro is granted his citizenship rights. The whirlwinds of revolt will continue to shake the foundations of our nation until the bright day of justice emerges.

But there is something that I must say to my people who stand on the warm threshold which leads into the palace of justice. In the process of gaining our rightful place we must not be guilty of wrongful deeds. Let us not seek to satisfy our thirst for freedom by drinking from the cup of bitterness and hatred.

We must forever conduct our struggle on the high plane of dignity and discipline. We must not allow our creative protest to degenerate into physical violence. Again and again we must rise to the majestic heights of meeting physical force with soul force. The marvelous new militancy which has engulfed the Negro community must not lead us to distrust of all white people, for many of our white brothers, as evidenced by their presence here today, have come to realize that their destiny is tied up with our destiny. And they have come to realize that their freedom is inextricably bound to our freedom. We cannot walk alone.

And as we walk, we must make the pledge that we shall always march ahead. We cannot turn back. There are those who ask the devotees of civil rights, "When will you be satisfied?" We can never be satisfied as long as the Negro is the victim of the unspeakable horrors of police brutality. We can never be satisfied as long as our bodies, heavy with the fatigue of travel, cannot gain lodging in the motels of the highways and the hotels of the cities. We cannot be satisfied as long as the Negro's basic mobility is from a smaller ghetto to a larger one. We can never be satisfied as long as our children are stripped of their selfhood and robbed of their dignity by signs stating "For Whites Only." We cannot be satisfied as long as a Negro in Mississippi cannot vote and a Negro in New York believes he has nothing for which to vote. No, no, we are not satisfied, and we will not be satisfied until justice rolls down like waters and righteousness like a mighty stream.

I am not unmindful that some of you have come here out of great trials and tribulations. Some of you have come fresh from narrow jail cells. Some of you have come from areas where your quest for freedom left you battered by the storms of persecution and staggered by the winds of police brutality. You have been the veterans of creative suffering. Continue to work with the faith that unearned suffering is redemptive.

Go back to Mississippi, go back to Alabama, go back to South Carolina, go back to Georgia, go back to Louisiana, go back to the slums and ghettos of our northern cities knowing that somehow this situation can and will be changed. Let us not wallow in the valley of despair.

I say to you today, my friends, so even though we face the difficulties of today and tomorrow, I still have a dream. It is a dream deeply rooted in the American dream.

I have a dream that one day this nation will rise up and live out the true meaning of its creed: "We hold these truths to be self-evident; that all men are created equal."

I have a dream that one day on the red hills of Georgia the sons of former slaves and the sons of former slaveowners will be able to sit down together at the table of brotherhood.

I have a dream that my four little children will one day live in a nation where they will not be judged by the color of their skin but by the content of their character; I have a dream today.

I have a dream that one day down in Alabama, with its vicious racists, with its governor having his lips dripping with the words of interposition and nullification, one day right there in Alabama little black boys and black girls will be able to join hands with little white boys and white girls as sisters and brothers; I have a dream today.

I have a dream that one day every valley shall be exalted, every hill and mountain shall be made low, and rough places will be made plane and crooked places will be made straight, and the glory of the Lord shall be revealed, and all flesh shall see it together.

This is our hope. This is the faith that I go back to the South with. With this faith we will be able to hew out of the mountain of despair a stone of hope. With this faith we will be able to transform the jangling discords of our nation into a beautiful symphony of brotherhood. With this faith we will be able to work together, to pray together, to struggle together, to go to jail together, to stand up for freedom together, knowing that we will be free one day.

This will be the day—this will be the day when all of God's children will be able to sing with new meaning "My country 'tis of thee, sweet land of liberty, of thee I sing. Land where my fathers died, land of the pilgrim's pride, from every mountainside, let freedom ring." And if America is to be a great nation, this must become true.

So let freedom ring from the prodigious hilltops of New Hampshire. Let freedom ring from the mighty mountains of New York. Let freedom ring from the heightening Alleghenies of Pennsylvania!

Let freedom ring from the snowcapped Rockies of Colorado!

Let freedom ring from the curvaceous slopes of California!

But not only that; let freedom ring from Stone Mountain of Georgia!

Let freedom ring from Lookout Mountain of Tennessee!

Let freedom ring from every hill and mole hill of Mississippi. From every mountainside let freedom ring.

And when this happens, when we allow freedom to ring—when we let it ring from every village and every hamlet, from every state and every city—we will be able to speed up that day when all of God's children, black men and white men, Jews and Gentiles, Protestants and Catholics, will be able to join hands and sing in the words of the old Negro spiritual, "Free at last! Free at last! Thank God Almighty, we are free at last!"

QUESTIONS FOR DISCUSSION

1. How did Dr. King use the principles given in the essay "Changing a Man's Mind" to persuade his listeners?

2. How did Dr. King use ethos, logos, and pathos in this speech?

3. What aesthetic elements were used to create a unified, eloquent whole?

1. Dr. Martin Luther King's speech seemed to set the criteria for reaching the "promised land." Write a speech or an essay about what needs to be done in order for us to build the kind of society that was modeled in the "I Have a Dream" speech.

2. Putting it all together: To practice the elements of public speaking discussed in this chapter, create a persuasive speech using one of the three methods of organization. Consider methods of increasing personal credibility that are covered in the ethos section. Include emotional appeals and solid research. Use the following suggestions to guide your preparation. Do a structural outline, like the one illustrated in Figure 10–1 as you complete the following steps:

   a. Choose an issue that concerns you. You can try to persuade your audience about a factual issue (caffeine is/is not bad for your heart), an issue of value (it is/is not wrong for couples to live together before marriage), or a policy issue (ruling by instant replay rather than by the calls of referees and umpires should/should not be mandatory in all televised sporting events).

   b. Take a stand (conclusion) on your issue and support your stand with at least three reasons.

   c. Give evidence to support your reasons; use evidence in the form of statistics, studies, authoritative testimony, and examples. You may also interview an expert about your issue. Be sure to give the source and the date when you cite your evidence in the speech. Strive to keep your evidence current and turn in an outline and a bibliography on the day of your speech.

   d. Think about evidence that opponents to your position might offer. Within the body of your speech, handle opposing viewpoints with both-sides persuasion; acknowledge the good reasoning of an opposing viewpoint, but explain why it is not as sound as your own.

   e. Add emotional appeal through anecdotes, examples, or personal testimony.

   f. Begin the speech with a story, statistic, or quote that gets the audience's attention and explains the importance of your issue.

   g. Close by repeating the issue, your conclusion, and your reasons. End with a strong quote, a reference to the introductory story, or a reminder to audience members of how they should believe or act now that they have this information.

   h. Begin planning your speech as soon as it is assigned to you so that you have time to find evidence, get organized, and practice before the due date. Rehearse the speech so that you feel comfortable looking at the audience, and make your delivery conversational. Practice handling questions with friends or family members before you give the speech.

3. Find an issue of the journal *Vital Speeches* in your college or community library, or do a search for speeches online. Choose a speech that interests you and analyze it, using the following questions as a guide:

    a. What were the interests and concerns of the audience the speaker was addressing? Was the audience supportive of, neutral to, or hostile to the speaker's position? How well did the speaker adapt to his or her audience?

    b. What were the issue and conclusion of the speaker?

    c. How did the speaker use ethos, logos, and pathos to be persuasive? In what areas could the speaker have improved the speech?

    d. Were the reasons given to support the conclusion backed up by solid evidence? Were these the best reasons given?

    e. Did the speaker address the opposing viewpoints in any way? Did the speaker refute the important points of the opposition in a fair and appropriate manner?

    f. Were there any fallacies in the reasoning of the speaker? Were the studies and experts cited clear and convincing?

    g. Were there aesthetic factors that helped the speech to be tightly woven and eloquent? Did the speaker use language elements, such as repetition or beautiful prose, to make his or her points? Did the speaker use the conclusion to refer back to attention-getting points made in the introduction?

    h. What is your overall impression of this speech?

4. Listen to a persuasive speech or sermon or watch one on television (if you get C-SPAN, you might be able to listen to a speech presented before Congress, the National Press Club, or another organization). Then analyze the speech, using the following suggestions:

    a. What were the speaker's issue, conclusion, and reasons?

    b. Was the audience for this speaker supportive of, neutral to, or hostile to his or her ideas?

    c. To what extent did the speaker use ethos to establish credibility, logos to support his or her conclusion, and pathos to appeal to the audience's emotions?

    d. How did the speaker introduce and conclude the speech? Were there clear transitions throughout the speech? Give specific examples of these.

    e. Were you persuaded in any way by this speech? Explain why or why not.

   f. If you were hired as a consultant to this speaker, what advice would
   you give to improve his or her speaking?

FILMS FOR ANALYSIS AND DISCUSSION

Both *In Good Company* and *Thank You For Smoking* are fine examples of persuasive speaking and communicating ideas, even if the ideas these films present
are meant to be humorous. The characters in these films, Carter Duryea and
Nick Naylor respectively, are both masters of the spoken word and know the
effects of credibility and emotional appeal.

   There have been many examples of argumentation in films. Below are a
few movie titles with reference to specific speeches. For more ideas, check out
the excellent selections of movie speeches and the video and audio clips given
by American Rhetoric on their website: http://www.americanrhetoric.com/
moviespeeches.htm.

Friday Night Lights (2004, PG-13)

Note the speeches given by Coach Gaines, particularly on "Being Perfect."

Miracle (2004, PG)

Note Coach Brooks' several speeches, including his pep talk to the team before
the Soviet Game.

Gods and Generals (2003, PG)

Note Colonel Joshua Chamberlain's Abolition Speech.

We Were Soldiers (2002, R)

Note the several speeches of Lt. Col. Hal Moore, especially "I Will Leave No
One Behind."

Brian's Song (2001, G)

Note Gale Sayers addressing the team on Brian Piccolo's cancer.

The Contender (2000, R)

Note President Jackson Evans address to Congress on Vice-Presidential nominee Senator Hanson.

The Family Man (2000, PG-13)

Note the interpersonal argumentation in Jack's plea to Kate: "I Choose Us."

Crimson Tide (1995, R)

Note Captain Ramsey's address to the crew of the USS Alabama.

The Shawshank Redemption (1994, R)

Note the address of Ellis Boyd to his parole board.

Quiz Show (1994, PG-13)

Note Charles Van Doren's testimony before the House Committee on Interstate and Foreign Commerce.

Malcolm X (1992, PG-13)

Note several addresses by Malcolm, including his Harlem Address and his Harvard University Address.

Lean on Me (1989, PG-13)

Note Principal Clark's addresses to his staff, his students, and their parents.

Gandhi (1982, PG)

Note Gandhi's advocacy of the policy of nonviolence, his address to the Indian National Congress, and his address to British authorities, "It Is Time You Left."

Chariots of Fire (1981, PG)

Note several addresses by Eric Liddell, particularly his speech at the Scotland vs. Ireland races.

Norma Rae (1979, PG)

Note Reuben Warshovsky's address to the plant workers.

Jesus of Nazareth (1977, NR)

Note the Beatitudes (Sermon on the Mount).

A Man for All Seasons (1966, G)

Note Thomas More's Address to the Court.

Judgment at Nuremberg (1961, PG)

Note Judge Hayward's speech on the Decision of the Court.

All the King's Men (1949, NR)

Note Willie Stark's speeches as he campaigns for governor and addresses the people.

It's a Wonderful Life (1946, PG)

Note George Bailey's address to the Bailey Building and Loan Board.

The Pride of the Yankees (1942, PG)

Note Lou Gehrig's Farewell Address to Baseball.

Mr. Smith Goes to Washington (1939, PG)

Note Senator Smith's several speeches, especially his speeches that continue and then end the filibuster.

Glossary

Active listening—Paraphrasing the thoughts of the speaker with the aim of empathic understanding of his or her viewpoint.

Ad hominem: Attacking the person—A Latin term meaning "to the man" or attacking the person. Ad hominem occurs when a person is attacked on a personal quality that is irrelevant to the issue under discussion.

Ad populum—A fallacy that consists of a false appeal to the authority of "everyone." This fallacy is based on the assumption that a course of action should be taken or an idea should be supported because "everyone" is doing it or believes it.

Ambiguity—Having two or more possible meanings. Ambiguity in language occurs when the meaning of words is unclear or uncertain; such ambiguity can lead to confusion and misunderstanding.

Analogy—Explanation of one idea, object, process, or policy by comparing it to another similar idea, object, process, or policy. Analogies are used to strengthen inductive arguments.

Appeal to pity—A logical fallacy that occurs when someone argues that others should follow a course of action or hold a certain belief for no other reason than that they should feel compassion for the irrelevant claims of the speaker.

Appeal to tradition—A fallacy that occurs when a belief or action is supported on the ground that it conforms to traditional ideas or practices.

Argument—A conclusion about an issue that is supported by reasons.

Argument by elimination—A valid syllogism that seeks to logically rule out various possibilities until only a single possibility remains.

Assumption—A belief, usually taken for granted, that is based on the experience, observations, or desires of an individual or group.

Audience analysis—A careful consideration of the demographic and situational factors of an audience in preparation for a speech to that audience.

Backing—Evidence used to support a warrant.

Begging the question—A fallacy that occurs when a speaker or writer assumes what needs to be proven.

Believing audience—An audience that agrees with the conclusion and reasoning of the speaker.

Biased—A sample that does not reflect a random, representative population. A biased sample does not provide adequate evidence to support a conclusion.

Blind studies—Studies in which subjects are not told whether they belong to the control group or the experimental group.

Both-sides persuasion—A technique in which the speaker acknowledges one or more of the best arguments of the opposition without specifically agreeing with those arguments.

Brainstorming—A process of soliciting many and diverse ideas in quick succession—and without immediate evaluation—in order to find imaginative solutions to problems.

Catastrophizing—A form of emotional reasoning in which one imagines and anticipates disastrous outcomes or future problems.

Categorical statement—A statement in which members of one class are said to be included in another class. This statement may be used as the major premise of a syllogism.

Causal generalizations—Generalizations based on causal factors; that is, they state that a particular factor is responsible for a specific effect. These generalizations are used to strengthen inductive arguments.

Causation—A connection between two events in which it is established that one event caused the other.

Certainty—The certainty of the conclusion in a deductive argument is established when the argument contains true premises (reasons) that are stated in the correct form; when the argument has formal validity and true premises, then the conclusion must also be true.

Chain argument—A form of argument that builds and depends upon a series of conditions being met.

Characteristic of interest—The specific question that a researcher seeks to answer concerning a given population.

Claim—A statement or conclusion about an issue that is either true or false. The advocate for a claim will seek to prove the truth of the claim through evidence.

Cogent argument—An inductive argument based on strong, credible evidence.

Cognitive dissonance—A state of mental discomfort that occurs whenever two ideas (or cognitions) are out of sync.

Conclusion—A position taken about an issue, also called a claim or an opinion; in deductive reasoning, the inference drawn from the major and minor premises; in research, the meaning and significance of the data as interpreted by the researcher.

Conditional syllogram—In deductive reasoning, a major premise that states that if the condition cited in the first part of a statement is true, the claim cited in the second part of the statement will follow.

Conformity—The tendency to follow others, usually to gain acceptance or avoid conflict; the practice of using the beliefs and actions of others as a primary guide to personal thoughts and actions.

Connotation—All the images—positive, negative, or neutral—that are associated with any given denotation by an individual or a group. The connotations of words include their emotional meanings. Both concrete and abstract words have connotations that are different for different individuals.

Control—The process of weeding out extraneous factors that could affect the outcome of a study between two groups of subjects in which one group is exposed to a variable and the other is not.

Control group—A group of subjects from the sample who are not exposed to a variable created by the researcher.

Controlled studies—Research involving specific methods for comparing groups of subjects, in which one group is exposed to a variable (or suspected causal factor) and the other is not. Controlled studies should be designed so that they can be duplicated (and verified or disproven) by other researchers.

Correlation—A relationship or connection between two objects or events. Noting a correlation is sometimes the first step in exploring causation.

Credibility—The *ethos* or believability of a speaker; the reliability of an expert or a study.

Critical thinker—Someone who uses specific criteria to evaluate reasoning, form positions, and make decisions.

Data—The observations made and information collected by the researcher as he or she completes a study.

Deductive argument—An argument that follows formal patterns of reasoning and is aimed at establishing the certainty of a conclusion through presenting true premises in valid form.

Deductive reasoning—The process of inferring a conclusion by putting forth true premises in a valid format.

Defense mechanisms—Techniques aimed at self-protection through the avoidance of unpleasant realities.

Denial—A state of mind that blocks critical thinking by the repression of or refusal to recognize any negative or threatening information.

Denotation—The specific object or action that a word points to, refers to, or indicates.

Double-blind studies—Studies in which neither the experimenter nor the subjects know which is the control group and which is the experimental group.

Doublespeak—Language used to lie or mislead while pretending to tell the truth. Doublespeak includes the use of *euphemism, jargon, gobbledygook,* and *weasel words.*

Egalitarianism—A belief system in which behavior is considered to be ethical when equal opportunities and consequences apply to all people.

Egocentrism—The individual version of ethnocentrism, the tendency to view everything else in relationship to oneself; one's desires, values, beliefs, and actions seem to be self-evidently correct or superior to those of others.

Either-or fallacy—Polarizing a situation by presenting only two alternatives, at two extremes of the spectrum of possibilities; also called *false dilemma.*

Emotional reasoning—The process of using one's feelings as definitive proof of an accurate analysis of a situation.

Empathy—The ability to understand another person's thoughts and emotions concerning an issue. Empathy does not necessarily imply agreement.

Enthymeme—A syllogism with a key part or parts implied rather than directly stated.

Equivocation—A logical fallacy in which the same word is used with two different meanings.

Ethics—Standards of conduct reflecting what is considered to be right or wrong behavior.

Ethnocentrism (sociocentrism)—The tendency to view one's own race or culture as central, based on the deep-seated belief that one's own group is superior to all others.

Ethos—One's credibility or reputation as a speaker; ethos is one of three persuasive elements of public speaking, along with *logos* and *pathos*.

Euphemism—The use of a less direct but softer or more acceptable term to describe an event, person, or object.

Experimental group—A group of subjects from the sample who are exposed to a variable created by the researcher.

Expert—An individual who has education, significant experience, or both in a given area. The testimony of experts is used to support conclusions in arguments.

Eye tracking—Using photographic technology to record exactly where a person is looking as he or she is interacting with some kind of visual display in order to create ads and Web sites that attract a target audience.

Fair-mindedness—A trait of a critical thinker involving respect for others, willingness to hear and understand different viewpoints on an issue, and an openness to change when new information or insight warrants change.

Fairness doctrine—A former U.S. policy by which broadcasters must allow equal air time for all sides of an issue.

Fallacies—Errors in reasoning. Fallacies can be seen as (1) reasons that seem logical but don't necessarily support the conclusion or (2) statements that distract listeners from the real issue.

False cause or Post Hoc Ergo Propter Hoc—A fallacy that occurs when there is no real proof that one event caused another event; there is only

evidence that one event came after another event.

False dilemma (either-or fallacy)—An error in reasoning that occurs when one polarizes a situation by presenting only two alternatives, at two extremes of the spectrum of possibilities.

Faulty analogy—Comparison of one situation or idea to another that disregards significant differences that make the comparison invalid.

Filtering—The process of distorting reality by focusing on all the negative details of a situation and filtering out all the positive.

Framing—The deliberate or unconscious use of camera shots to influence audiences; also, the use of a number of techniques by journalists and broadcasters to create a particular impression of reality.

Fuzzy words—Weasel words that create an impression without specifically defining a concrete meaning for the words or phrases used.

General semanticists—Individuals who study the effects of words on human perception.

Gestalt principle—A principle that states that our minds strive toward congruence and completion of information. If a message strikes us as incomplete, we will fill in the missing details ourselves.

Gobbledygook—Vague or inflated language used to confuse and overwhelm those who hear it.

Groupthink—The tendency for group members to rigidly conform to and reinforce a collective opinion or judgment about an issue.

Hasty conclusion—A fallacy in which a generalization is drawn from a small and thus inadequate sample of information.

Higher principles test—An ethical test by which one determines if the principle on which one is basing an action is consistent with a higher or more general principle that one accepts.

Hostile audience—An audience that is opposed to the conclusion and reasoning of the speaker.

Hypothesis—A speculation about what will be discovered from a research study.

Hypothetical syllogism—*See* Conditional syllogism.

Ideal value—A value considered to be right and good.

Immediate cause—A causal factor that immediately precedes the effect.

Independent variable—The special treatment received by the experimental group in a controlled study.

Indexing—A process by which one takes general labels (women, Catholics, Asians, Americans) and gives them a reference to actual people. Indexing is used to prevent stereotyping.

Induction—The process of drawing generalizations from known facts or research to give strength and support to conclusions.

Inductive reasoning—The process of finding truth by making observations; inferring general laws and truths from specific instances.

Issue—The question or subject under discussion.

Jargon—Specialized language sometimes used to exclude or impress people who don't understand the terminology.

Lead—The introductory sentence of a story that is meant to give a reader the essence or general meaning of the story.

Libertarianism—A system in which behavior is considered ethical when it allows for one's individual freedom and does not restrict the freedom of others.

Logos—Logical organization and credible content in a speech; logos is one of three persuasive elements of public speaking, along with *ethos* and *pathos*.

Look Who's Talking—A fallacy that is committed when someone denies a claim because they believe the speaker who is making the claim is hypocritical.

Margin of error—A statistical range qualifying the limits of a survey's conclusion; the margin of error decreases as the random, representative sample of the population increases.

Method of agreement—A theory of causation postulating that the cause of an effect is found by noting that *x* is the only factor always present when *y* (the problem or the good effect) occurs; therefore, *x* causes *y*.

Method of difference—A theory of causation postulating that the cause of an effect is found by noting that the only difference between the event or effect (called *y*) happening or not happening is whether one element—*x*—is present.

Mind reading—Assuming that what would be true for you in any given circumstance is true for the other person; making assumptions about the thoughts, feelings, or motives of another and taking the assumptions as true without further proof or discussion.

Modus Ponens—A valid conditional/hypothetical syllogism in which the antecedent is affirmed.

Modus Tollens—A valid conditional/hypothetical syllogism in which the consequent is denied.

Monroe's Motivated Sequence—A five-step method of organizing speeches; the steps include attention, need, satisfaction, visualization, and action.

Morals—Principles that distinguish right from wrong behavior; *see also* Ethics.

Multiple causes—A combination of causes that are presumed to lead to a specific effect.

Necessary condition—A condition (state of affairs, thing, process, etc.) that must be present if a particular effect is present. Equivalently, if the necessary condition is absent, then the effect cannot occur.

Neuromarketing—Using technology to determine consumers' internal, subconscious reactions to products and brand names in order to plan effective marketing strategies.

Neutral audience—An audience that does not have a strong opinion on the speaker's conclusion about an issue.

New cases test—A test for ethical decision making that asks whether a decision is consistent with decisions that would be made in similar, harder cases.

Opinion leaders—People who are well informed, often through the media, about specific information and issues.

Overgeneralizing—Coming to a general conclusion on the basis of a single incident or a few incidents.

Pathos—The use of emotional appeal to support conclusions; pathos is one of three persuasive elements of public speaking, along with *ethos* and *logos*.

Perfectionism—A form of emotional reasoning based on a desire and belief that one should be without flaws; good qualities, good work, or the good parts of a situation are minimized and focus is placed on how others or oneself have not measured up.

Personalizing—A form of emotional reasoning in which a person relates everything that happens to him- or herself, assuming that general statements or actions are personally directed. Personalizing also involves the belief that one's characteristics or actions are continually being compared, favorably or unfavorably, against the characteristics or actions of other people.

Placebo—A sugar pill or other benign treatment given to a control group while another group is given the treatment the researcher wishes to explore.

Points of logical vulnerability—Topics about which a person has difficulty being rational or objective.

Post hoc—*See* False cause.

Premise—In deductive reasoning, a proposition, either major or minor, from which a conclusion is derived.

Premise of contention—The premise of a deductive argument that is under dispute.

Prima facie values—See Univeral ethical norms.

Product placement—The practice of integrating or embedding products in films, television programs, and other media in order to reach consumers.

Projection of meaning—The process of assuming that what another person means is what we would mean if we had used the same words or if we had acted in the same way.

Protocol—The design of a controlled research study.

Question—The characteristic of interest concerning a targeted population.

Randomness—A condition that allows every member of a target population to have an equal chance of being chosen as part of the sample.

Rationalization—A defense mechanism that underlies many others; it involves justifying or making sense of things that don't make sense and explaining things away that should be brought under examination.

Real value—A value considered to be right and good and that is acted upon in one's life.

Reality assumptions—Assumptions about what is true and factual that are sometimes stated and sometimes implied; these assumptions are often taken for granted.

Reasoning by analogy—Comparing one idea or plan to another for the purpose of supporting a conclusion. When we reason by analogy, we assume that since an idea, process, or event is similar in one way to another idea, process, or event that it is also similar in another significant way.

Reasons—Statements given to support conclusions.

Red herring—A fallacy in which reasons offered to support conclusions lead the listener away from the issue under consideration.

Reification—A process by which words become more powerful and real than objective reality.

Religious values—An ethical system based on the principles of loving God and loving one's neighbor.

Representative—A quality of a research sample in which the sample has the same significant characteristics in the same proportion as the target population.

Representer—A term used synonymously with the word *reporter* to indicate that reporters make strategic choices that frame news stories.

Role exchange test—A test for ethical decision making that involves empathizing with the people affected by an action that is being considered.

Romancing the product—A technique used by advertisers in which consumers are asked to associate a product with something bigger, better, or more interesting.

Sample—Members of the target population who are studied by a researcher.

Self-fulfilling prophecy—A process whereby an expectation becomes a reality.

Semantic devices—Tools created by general semanticists that help people make their words more accurately reflective of reality.

Semantic differential—A tool that allows semanticists to assess the cultural connotations of a word.

Semanticists—Scholars who study the meaning of words.

Sensationalism—A method used to attract viewers by presenting more exciting stories over less exciting but perhaps more newsworthy ones; the most bizarre, visually interesting, or *sensational* elements of these stories are featured.

Slippery slope—A fallacy that occurs when serious consequences of a potential action or policy are predicted and not substantiated by evidence.

Sociocentrism—*See* Ethnocentrism.

Social proof—The idea that if the majority thinks or does something, it must be correct.

Sound argument—A valid deductive argument whose premises are true.

Sound bite—An excerpt from a speech or report that is presented as summarizing but may actually distort the sentiments of the speaker or writer.

Spin—The use of language, particularly in politics and public relations, to create a biased, positive connotation for ideas, events, or policies that one favors and a biased negative impression about ideas, events, or policies that one dislikes.

Statistical evidence—Data collected by polling and research studies that can be used to make statistical generalizations.

Statistical generalizations—Inferences drawn from statistical evidence that are used to give strength to inductive arguments.

Statistically significant—The result of an experiment that will occur again in similar circumstances.

Statistics—Data, usually numerical, collected and classified by polling and research.

Stereotyping—Classifying people, places, or things solely on common traits while ignoring individual differences that make these comparisons invalid.

Straw man—A fallacy in which an opponent's argument is distorted or exaggerated and then more easily attacked.

Subjects—People or animals studied to get information about a target population.

Subliminal persuasion—Information meant to affect people on an unconscious level, some of which can be detected with training and some of which cannot be detected with the conscious mind, regardless of training. The existence and effectiveness of this latter form of subliminal persuasion remains under dispute.

Sufficient condition—A condition (state of affairs, thing, process, etc.) that automatically leads to the production of another event. If the condition is present, then the effect will definitely occur. The sufficient condition creates or causes the effect.

Suggestion—The presentation of ideas or images in such a way as to reveal certain ideas or qualities and to conceal others.

Syllogism—A deductive argument usually consisting of two premises and a conclusion.

Target population—The group about which a researcher wishes to generalize.

Technical causation—A method of determining causation by examining differences between causes and effects.

Theory of cognitive dissonance—A theory that states that the need for congruence (consonance, harmony) is not only a human need but a drive, just as powerful as our drives for food and water. We are motivated by this drive and so we try to either understand or rationalize incongruence between beliefs and actions.

Two Wrongs Make a Right—A fallacy that is used to excuse bad behavior on the grounds of other bad behavior; the fallacy occurs when someone rationalizes that one person or one group's action is justified because some other person or group's action is just as bad or worse.

Two-step flow—The phenomenon of consulting friends or acquaintances who have expertise in a given area before making decisions. The friends, called opinion leaders, first (step 1) get their information from the media and then (step 2) pass this information on to others.

Universal consequences test—A test for ethical decision making that focuses on the general consequences of an action under consideration.

Universal ethical norms—Ethical principles that are considered to be self-evident to rational individuals of every culture.

Utilitarianism—A system in which behavior is considered ethical when it promotes the greatest general happiness and minimizes unhappiness.

Vagueness—A problem that arises with the use of nonspecific or abstract words. A word or phrase is vague when its meaning is unclear.

Valid argument—An argument structured in a correct deductive format; an argument structured in such a way that if its premises are true, then its conclusion must be true.

Value assumptions—Beliefs about what is good and important that form the basis of an individual's opinion on issues.

Value conflicts—Disagreements about the priority different values should have in decision making.

Value prioritization—The process of choosing the most important values in an issue.

Values—Beliefs, ideas, or things that are considered worthy and held in high regard.

Warrants—Unstated, but necessary links between reasons and claims; the assumptions made by the speaker or writer that connect claims and reasons.

Weasel word—A word used to evade or retreat from a direct or forthright statement or position.

Index